Environmental Protection Act 1990

Second Edition

AUSTRALIA
The Law Book Company
Brisbane : Sydney : Melbourne : Perth

CANADA
Carswell
Ottawa : Toronto : Calgary : Montreal : Vancouver

Agents:
Steimatzky's Agency Ltd., Tel Aviv;
N. M. Tripathi (Private) Ltd., Bombay;
Eastern Law House (Private) Ltd., Calcutta;
M.P.P. House, Bangalore;
Universal Book Traders, Delhi;
Aditya Books, Delhi;
MacMillan Shuppan KK, Tokyo;
Pakistan Law House, Karachi

Environmental Protection Act 1990

Second Edition

with annotations by

Stephen Tromans
M.A., Solicitor, Partner and Head of Environmental Law Department, Simmons & Simmons

LONDON
SWEET & MAXWELL
1993

Published in 1993 by
Sweet & Maxwell Limited of
South Quay Plaza,
183 Marsh Wall, London
Typeset by MFK Typesetting Ltd.,
Hitchin, Herts
Printed and bound in Great Britain by
Butler & Tanner Ltd, Frome and London

First Edition 1991
  Reprinted 1991
  Reprinted 1992
Second Edition 1993
  Reprinted 1995

A CIP catalogue record for this book is available from The British Library

ISBN 0–421–50780–2

All rights reserved.
U.K. statutory material in this publication is acknowledged as Crown copyright.
No part of this publication may be reproduced or transmitted in any form or by any means, or stored in any retrieval system of any nature, without prior written permission, except for permitted fair dealing under the Copyright, Designs and Patents Act 1988, or in accordance with the terms of a licence issued by the Copyright Licensing Agency in respect of photocopying and/or reprographic reproduction. Application for permission for other use of copyright material including permission to reproduce extracts in other published works shall be made to the publishers. Full acknowledgment of author, publisher and source must be given.

© *Sweet & Maxwell 1993*

CONTENTS

Environmental Protection Act 1990 (Second Edition)

References are to page numbers

Table of Cases	ix
Table of Statutes	xv
Table of Statutory Instruments	xxvii
Table of European Legislation and Treaties	xxxi

Part I:	Integrated Pollution Control and Air Pollution Control By Local Authorities	43–8
Part II:	Waste on Land.	43–110
Part III:	Statutory Nuisances and Clean Air	43–206
Part IV:	Litter Etc.	43–227
Part V:	Amendment to the Radioactive Substances Act 1960 [Repealed by the Radioactive Substances Act 1993]	43–248
Part VI:	Genetically Modified Organisms	43–249
Part VII:	Nature Conservation in Great Britain and Countryside Matters in Wales	43–278
Part VIII:	Miscellaneous	43–288
Part IX:	General	43–311
Schedules		43–318
Appendices		43–365
Index		[1]

PREFACE

I understand that it is unprecedented for Sweet & Maxwell to publish a Second Edition of a Current Law Statute Annotated Reprint: that demand has been sufficient for them to do so in this case is a reflection of the immense interest which the Environmental Protection Act 1990 has generated, not only within the legal profession but in the wider worlds of industry and commerce. Not all of that attention has been favourable, and the post-enactment life of the Environmental Protection Act has not been an entirely happy one.

Some provisions of the Act have indeed encountered potentially terminal problems, most notably section 143, dealing with the proposed registers of land subject to contaminative uses. Pending the outcome of the review now being undertaken by the Department of Environment into contaminated land liability issues, it is uncertain whether that section will ever be implemented in its present form. The future of some of the provisions in Part II of the Act, dealing with waste on land, also looks increasingly uncertain, implementation now having been deferred twice, the second time on the expressed grounds of potential incompatibility with European Community requirements. The current Government initiative to achieve deregulation of industry may also call into question the rationale for other provisions introduced by the Act, though it is to be hoped that the Government will not lose sight of the dangers, problems and practices which created the impetus for those reforms in the first place—as evidenced by the many Parliamentary, Royal Commission and other reports and departmental consultation papers which preceded the Bill.

There have been other important developments on the world, European and domestic stages since November 1990. Notable amongst these is the announcement of the Government's intention to create a unified environmental protection agency—an initiative which has subsequently languished for want of Parliamentary time, having achieved if nothing else the generation of a considerable amount of inter-departmental heat. European Community and international commitments continue to constitute both a complicating factor and a sometimes welcome impetus for continued developments.

When the First Edition of this book was being prepared, the various regulations and guidelines were still in the early stages of their introduction. Most of the regulations are now in place, and this is reflected in the updated Appendices to this edition. It is of course impossible to include all of these materials and my choice as to what to include has therefore inevitably been arbitrary and subjective. One major omission is the implementing regulations and guidance in relation to the waste management licensing system, for the simple reason that these have not yet been made. Various drafts have been issued for consultation, but given the uncertainty as to the introduction of the waste management licensing system it seemed preferable to avoid the potential confusion which might result from including draft material. Also the amendments to the Radioactive Substances Act 1960 referred to in Part V of the 1990 Act have now been consolidated in the Radioactive Substances Act 1993.

As with the preface to the First Edition, I should like to take the opportunity to thank those who have assisted with the Second. Most notably, I would extend my gratitude to Dr Albert Mumma, the Environmental Law Department Research Officer of Simmons & Simmons, who has done sterling service in collating subsequent material and updating the annotations as part of his work as an assistant editor of the Encyclopedia of Environmental Law, due to be published shortly by Sweet & Maxwell. My thanks also go to Sweet & Maxwell for their initiative in producing what I

PREFACE

hope will be a welcome Second Edition of the book, and for their practical help on editorial matters.

STEPHEN TROMANS
Simmons & Simmons
14 Dominion Street
London EC2M 2RJ

June 24, 1993

TABLE OF CASES

References are to section and Schedule number

Where a section number appears followed by (N), this refers to the notes for that particular section or subsection.
e.g. s.33(N) refers to the General Note following s.33
s.33(5N) refers to the notes for subs. (5) of s.33

Abernethie v. Kleiman (A.M. & J.) [1970] 1 Q.B. 10; [1969] 2 W.L.R. 1364; 113 S.J. 307; [1969] 2 All E.R. 790; 20 P. & C.R. 561, C.A.	s.79N
Adsett v. K. and L. Steelfounders and Engineers [1953] 1 W.L.R. 773; 97 S.J. 419; [1953] 2 All E.R. 320; 51 L.G.R. 418, C.A.; affirming [1953] 1 W.L.R. 137; 97 S.J. 49; [1953] 1 All E.R. 97n; 51 L.G.R. 99	s.7N
Alphacell v. Woodward [1972] A.C. 824; [1972] 2 W.L.R. 1320; 116 S.J. 431; [1972] 2 All E.R. 475; 70 L.G.R. 455; [1972] Crim.L.R. 41, H.L.; affirming [1972] 1 Q.B. 127; [1971] 3 W.L.R. 445; 115 S.J. 464; [1971] 2 All E.R. 910; 69 L.G.R. 561, D.C.	s.33N
American Cynamid Co. v. Ethicon [1975] A.C. 396; [1975] 2 W.L.R. 316; 119 S.J. 136; [1975] 1 All E.R. 504; [1975] F.S.R. 101; [1975] R.P.C. 513, H.L.; reversing [1974] F.S.R. 312, C.A.	s.81N
Armour v. Skeen [1977] I.R.L.R. 310; 1977 J.C. 15; 1977 S.L.T. 71, High Ct. of Judiciary	s.157N
Ashcroft v. Cambro Waste Products [1981] 1 W.L.R. 1349; (1981) 125 S.J. 288; [1981] 3 All E.R. 699; [1981] 79 L.G.R. 612; [1982] J.P.L. 176, D.C.	s.33N
Atkinson v. Bettison [1955] 1 W.L.R. 1127; 99 S.J. 761; [1955] 3 All E.R. 340, C.A.	s.10N
Att.-Gen. (Gambia) v. N'Jie [1961] A.C. 617; [1961] 2 W.L.R. 845; 105 S.J. 421; [1961] 2 All E.R. 504, P.C.	s.82N
Att.-Gen's Reference (No. 2 of 1988) [1990] 1 Q.B. 77; [1989] 3 W.L.R. 397; (1989) 153 J.P. 574; (1989) 133 S.J. 978; (1989) 89 Cr.App.R. 314; (1989) 153 J.P.N. 577; (1989) 153 L.G.Rev. 787; [1990] L.S.Gaz, January 31, 67, C.A.	s.35N, Pt. IIN
Austin Rover Group v. H.M. Inspector of Factories; *sub nom.* Maiter v Austin Rover Group [1990] 1 A.C. 619; [1989] 3 W.L.R. 520; [1989] 2 All E.R. 1087; (1989) 133 S.J. 1661, [1989] IRLR 404; [1990] I.C.R. 133; [1990] C.O.D. 35, H.L.; affirming [1988] Crim.L.R. 752, D.C.	s.33N
Aviation & Shipping Co. v. Murray [1961] 1 W.L.R. 974; 105 S.J. 441; [1961] 2 All E.R. 805; [1961] 1 Lloyd's Rep. 513; 39 T.C. 595; 40 A.T.C. 143; *sub nom.* Murray v.. Aviation and Shipping Co. [1961] T.R. 133, C.A.; reversing [1961] 1 W.L.R. 129; 105 S.J. 88; [1961] 1 All E.R. 126; [1960] T.R. 269; 53 R. & I.T. 799; 39 A.T.C. 281	s.79N
Bacup Corporation v. Smith (1890) 44 Ch. D. 395	s.80N
Balabel v. Air India [1988] Ch. 317; [1988] 2 W.L.R. 1036; (1988) 132 S.J. 699; [1988] 2 All E.R. 246; (1988) 138 New L.J. 85, C.A.	s.17N
Berridge Incinerators v. Nottinghamshire County Court (Unreported, Nottingham Crown Ct., June 12, 1992)	s.33N, s.59N
Berridge Incinerators v. Nottinghamshire County Council (Unreported, High Ct. 1987)	s.36N, s.75N
Betts v. Penge Urban District Council [1942] 2 K.B. 154, D.C.	s.79N
Birchall v. Wirral Urban District Council (1953) 117 J.P. 384; *sub nom.* Wirral Urban District Council v. Birchall 51 L.G.R. 486, C.A.	s.82N
Birmingham District Council v. McMahon (1987) 151 J.P. 709; (1987) 19 H.L.R. 452; (1988) 86 L.G.R. 63; (1987) 151 L.G. Rev. 690; (1987) 151 J.P.N. 622; (1987) 84 L.S. Gaz 690	s.82N
Bishop Auckland Local Board v. Bishop Auckland Iron and Steel Co. (1882) 10 Q.B.D. 138	s.79N
Blackburn Corporation v. Micklethwaite (1886) 54 L.T. 539	s.80N
Blue v. Pear Assurance Co. [1940] 3 W.W.R. 13	s.33N

TABLE OF CASES

Cardiff Rating Authority v. Guest Keen Baldwin's Iron and Steel Co. [1949] 1 K.B. 385; [1949] L.J.R. 713; 65 T.L.R. 159; 113 J.P. 78; 93 S.J. 117; [1949] 1 All E.R. 27; 47 L.G.R. 159; 42 R. & I.T. 2; C.A.; affirming 64 T.L.R. 314; [1948] 1 All E.R. 830 .... s.80N
Charles Neil Ashcroft v. Michael McErlain (Unreported, Divisional Court, January 30, 1985) s.75N
City Equitable Fire Insurance Co., Re [1925] Ch. 407 .... s.157N
Clark v. Epsom Rural District Council [1929] 1 Ch. 287 .... s.79N
Clayton v. Sale Urban District Council [1926] 1 K.B. 415 .... s.80N
Colpron v. Canadian National Rly. Co. [1934] S.C.R. 189 .... s.118N
Coltness Iron Co. v. Sharp [1938] A.C. 90 .... s.7N
Cooke v. Adatia (1989) J.P. 129; [1989] C.O.D. 327; (1989) 153 L.G. Rev. 189, D.C. s.80N
Coventry City Council v. Cartwright [1975] 1 W.L.R. 845; 119 S.J. 235; [1975] 2 All E.R. 99; 73 L.G.R. 218, D.C. s.79N
—— v. Doyle [1987] 1 W.L.R. 1325; [1981] 2 All E.R. 184; [1987] J.P.L. 666, D.C. s.80N
Crompton (Alfred) Amusement Machines v. Customs and Excise Commissioners (No. 2) [1974] A.C. 405; [1973] 3 W.L.R. 268; 117 S.J. 602; [1973] 2 All E.R. 1169; H.L.; affirming on different grounds [1972] 2 Q.B. 102; [1972] 2 W.L.R. 835; 116 S.J. 198; [1972] 2 All E.R. 353, C.A.; reversing (1971) 115 S.J. 587; *The Times*, July 16, 1971 .... s.69N
Customs & Excise Commissioners v. Fisher (Lord) [1981] 2 All E.R. 147; [1981] S.T.C. 238 .... s.79N

Dean v. Hiesler [1942] 2 All E.R. 340 .... s.157N
Debtor, A (No. 490 of 1935), Re [1936] Ch. 237 .... s.79N
Devon County Council v. Gateway Foodmarkets (1990) 154 J.P. 557; [1990] C.O.D. 324; [1990] 154 J.P.N. 422; *Daily Telegraph*, March 22, 1990, D.C. s.99N
Durham County Council v. Peter Connors Industrial Services (Unreported, Divisional Court, May 19, 1992) s.33N

Ebor Land & Development Co. v. Benfield (1969) 213 E.G. 759; (1969) 68 L.G.R. 237, D.C. s.80N
Eduards v. National Coal Board (1949) 1 K.B. 704 .... s.7N
Epping Forest District Council v. Essex Rendering [1983] 1 W.L.R. 158; (1983) 147 J.P. 101; (1983) 127 S.J. 84; [1983] 1 All E.R. 359; (1983) 81 L.G.R. 252; (1983) New L.J. 106, H.L. s.84N

Ferro-Alloys and Metals Smelter, Glossop [1990] 1 LMELR 175 .... Pt. IN

Gardiner v. Sevenoaks Rural District Council [1950] W.N. 260; 66 T.L.R. (Pt. 1) 1091; 114 J.P. 352; 94 S.J. 385; [1950] 2 All E.R. 84; 48 L.G.R. 360, D.C. .. s.79N
Gillingham Borough Council v. Medway (Chatham) Dock Co. [1992] 3 W.L.R. 449; [1992] 3 All E.R. 923; (1991) 63 P. & C.R. 205; [1992] 1 PLR 113; [1992] J.P.L. 458; [1991] EGCS 101; [1991] NPC 97; *The Independent*, September 20, 1991; *The Times*, October 10, 1991 .... s.80N
Gordon v. Kirkcaldy District Council 1990 S.L.T. 644; 1990 S.C.L.R. 104, Ct. of Session; reversing 1989 S.L.T. 507; 1989 S.C.L.R. 90 .... s.75N
Granada Theatres v. Freehold Investment (Leytonstone) [1959] Ch. 592; [1959] 1 W.L.R. 570; 103 S.J. 392; [1959] 2 All E.R. 176, C.A.; varying [1958] 1 W.L.R. 845; 102 S.J. 563; [1958] 2 All E.R. 551 .... s.80N
Grant v. Anderson & Co [1892] 1 Q.B. 108, C.A. s.36N
Griffin, Re, ex p. Board of Trade (1890) 60 L.J.Q.B. 235 .... s.79N

Hall v. Manchester Corporation (1915) 84 L.J. Ch. 732 .... s.82N
Hammersmith London Borough Council v. Magnum Automated Forecourts [1978] 1 W.L.R 50; [1977] 1 All E.R. 401; (1977) 76 L.G.R. 159; 121 S.J. 529; [1978] J.P.L. 106, C.A. s.81N
Holland (Lady) v. Kensington Vestry (1867) L.R. 2 C.P. 565 .... s.80N
Hillil Property & Investment Co. v. Naraine Pharmacy (1979) 123 S.J. 437; (1979) 39 P. & C.R. 67; [1979] 252 E.G. 1013, C.A. s.1N
Hirschler v. Birch (1987) 151 J.P. 396; [1987] R.T.R. 13; [1988] TLR 120; (1987) 151 J.P.N. 287 .... s.157N

Table of Cases

Hodgetts v. Chiltern District Council [1983] A.C. 120; [1983] 2 W.L.R. 577; (1983) 147 J.P. 372; [1983] 1 All E.R. 1057; (1983) 45 P. & C.R. 402; [1983] J.P.L. 377, H.L. s.23N
Horner v. Franklin [1905] 1 K.B. 479 .... s.81N
Huckerby v. Elliot (1969) 113 S.J. 1001; [1970] All E.R. 189, D.C. s.157N
Hughes, Re [1943] 2 All E.R. 26 .... s.157N

Johnsons News of London v. Ealing London Borough Council [1990] C.O.D. 135; (1990) 154 J.P. 33; (1989) 153 J.P.N. 756; (1989) 130 New L.J. 1104 ... s.81N
Johnstone Fear & Kingham v. Commonwealth (1943) 67 C.L.R. 314 .... s.86N

Kensington London Borough Council v. Allen [1926] 1 K.B. 576 .... s.80N
Kent County Council v. Queensborough Rolling Mill Co. 89 L.G.R. 306; (1990) 154 J.P. 530; [1990] Crim. L.R. 813; (1990) 154 J.P.N. 442, D.C. s.75N

Lambeth London Borough Council v. Stubbs [1980] J.P.L. 517; (1980) 78 L.G.R. 650; [1980] 255 E.G. 789, D.C. s.80N
Lancashire County Council v. Dodd, Dodd and Drydale (Unreported, Preston Cty. Ct., February 19, 1992) s.33N
Leanse v. Lord Egerton [1943] 1 K.B. 323 .... s.80N
Leigh Land Reclamation v. Walsall Metropolitan Borough Council [1991] J.P.L. 867; [1991] C.O.D. 152; (1991) 155 J.P. 547; [1991] Crim.L.R. 298; [1991] 155 L.G.Rev. 507; (1991) 155 J.P.N. 332; *The Independent*, November 2, 1990, D.C. s.29N, s.33N
Lewis v. Graham (1888) 22 Q.B.D. 1, C.A. s.6N
Lloyds Bank v. Guardian Assurance and Trollope & Colls (1987) 35 Build. L.R. 34, C.A. s.81N
Long v. Brooke [1980] Crim. L.R. 109, Bradford Crown Ct. s.75N

McLeod v. Buchanan [1940] 2 All E.R. 179 .... s.33N
Mayor and Commonalty of the City of London v. Bovis Construction [1989] J.P.L. 263 .... s.81N
Midland Bank v. Conway Corporation [1965] 1 W.L.R. 1165; 129 J.P. 466; 109 S.J. 494; [1965] 2 All E.R. 972, 63 L.G.R. 346, D.C. s.80N
Milford v. Hughes (1846) 16 M. & W. 174 .... s.34N
Millard v. Wastall [1898] 1 Q.B. 342 .... s.80N
Miller-Mead v. Minister of Housing and Local Government [1963] 2 Q.B. 196; [1963] 2 W.L.R. 225; 127 J.P. 122; 106 S.J. 1052; [1963] 1 All E.R. 459; 14 P. & C.R. 266; 61 L.G.R. 152, C.A.; reversing in part [1962] 2 Q.B. 555; [1962] 3 W.L.R. 654; 126 J.P. 457; 106 S.J. 492; [1962] 3 All E.R. 99, 13 P. & C.R. 425; 60 L.G.R. 340, D.C. s.13N
Mills & Rochleys v. Leicester City Council [1946] 1 All E.R. 424 .... s.80N
Monro v. Lord Burghclere [1918] 1 K.B. 291 .... s.81N
Monk v. Arnold [1902] 1 K.B. 761 .... s.81N
Morgan v. Liverpool Corporation [1927] 2 K.B. 131, C.A. s.82N

Nash v. Hollinshead [1901] 1 K.B. 700, C.A. s.75N
National Coal Board v. Neath Borough Council [1976] 2 All E.R. 478, D.C. . s.79N
Northern Ireland Trailers v. Preston Corporation [1972] 1 W.L.R. 203; (1971) 116 S.J. 100; *sub nom.* Northern Ireland Trailers v. County Borough of Preston [1972] 1 All E.R. 260, D.C. s.80N, s.82N
Nottingham City District Council v. Newton; Nottingham Friendship Housing Association v. Newton [1974] 1 W.L.R. 923; 113 S.J. 462 *sub nom.* Nottingham Corporation v. Newton; Nottingham Friendship Housing Association v. Newton [1974] 2 All E.R. 760; 72 L.G.R. 535, D.C. s.80N, s.82N
Nurse v. Morganite Crucible [1989] A.C. 692; [1989] 2 W.L.R. 82; [1989] I.C.R. 15; (1989) 153 J.P. 398; (1989) 133 S.J. 81; (1989) 1 All E.R. 113; [1989] IRLR 88; [1989] C.O.D. 265; [1989] L.S. Gaz., February 1, 41, H.L.; reversing [1988] Crim.L.R. 691; [1989] C.O.D. 194, C.A. s.1N

Palser v. Grinling; Property Holding Co. v. Mischeff [1948] A.C. 291; [1948] L.J.R. 600; 64 T.L.R. 2; [1948] 1 All E.R. 1; *sub nom.* Property Holding Co. v. Mischeff; Palser v. Grinling 92 S.J. 53, H.L.; affirming [1946] K.B. 631 .... s.10N
Pardoe v. Pardoe (1900) 82 L.T. 547 .... s.86N

Table of Cases

Parry v. News Group Newspapers (1990) New L.J. 1719; *The Times*, November 22, 1990, C.A. s.17N
Pasmore v. Oswaldtwistle Urban District Council [1898] A.C. 387 .... s.79N
Pollway Nominees v. Havering London Borough Council 88 L.G.R. 192; (1989) 21 H.L.R. 462; *The Independent*, May 5, 1989, D.C. s.79N
Poplar Board of Works v. Love (1874) 29 L.T. 915 .... s.80N
Price v. Cromack [1975] 1 W.L.R. 988; 119 S.J. 458; [1975] 2 All E.R. 113, D.C. ... s.33N

R. v. Birmingham Justices, *ex p.* Guppy (1988) 152 J.P. 159; (1988) 86 L.G.R. 264; (1988) 152 L.G. Rev. 713, D.C. s.80N
R. v. Boal (Francis) [1992] 1 Q.B. 591; [1992] 2 W.L.R. 890; [1992] 3 All E.R. 177; (1992) 136 S.J. (LB) 100; (1992) 156 J.P. 617; [1992] I.C.R. 495; [1992] IRLR 420; (1992) 95 Cr.App.R. 272; [1992] BCLC 872; (1992) 156 L.G.Rev. 763 .... s.157N
R. v. Breeze [1973] 1 W.L.R. 994; [1973] 2 All E.R. 1141; [1973] Crim.L.R. 458; *sub nom.* Architects' Registration Council v. Breeze, 117 S.J. 284; 57 Cr.App.R. 654, C.A. s.79N
R. v. Epping (Waltham Abbey) Justices, *ex p.* Burlinson [1948] 1 K.B. 79; [1948] L.J.R. 298; 63 T.L.R. 628; 112 J.P. 3; 92 S.J. 27; [1947] 2 All E.R. 537; 46 L.G.R. 6 .... s.82N
R. v. Fenny Stratford Justices, *ex p.* Watney Mann (Midlands) [1976] 1 W.L.R. 1101; 120 S.J. 201; [1976] 2 All E.R. 888, D.C. s.80N, s.82N
R. v. Holborn Licensing Justices, *ex p.* Stratford Catering Co. (1927) 136 L.T. 278 .... s.74N
R. v. Inner London Crown Court, *ex p.* Bentham [1989] 1 W.L.R. 408; (1989) 21 H.L.R. 171; (1989) 133 S.J. 785; [1989] C.O.D. 293; [1989] Crim.L.R. 450; (1989) 153 L.G.Rev. 372; (1989) 153 J.P. 262, D.C. s.82N
R. v. Kensington and Chelsea (Royal) London Borough Council, *ex p.* Birdwood (1976) 74 L.G.R. 424, D.C. s.79N
R. v. Metropolitan Stipendiary Magistrate, *ex p.* London Waste Regulation Authority; Berkshire County Council v. Scott, *The Times*, January 14, 1993 .... s.29N, s.59N
R. v. Newham East Justices, *ex p.* Hunt; R. v. Oxted Justices, *ex p.* Franklin [1976] 1 W.L.R. 420; 120 S.J. 131; [1976] 1 All E.R. 839; [1976] L.G.R. 305, D.C. s.82N
R. v. Rotherham Metropolitan Borough Council, *ex p.* Rankin [1990] 1 PLR 93; [1990] J.P.L. 503; [1990] C.O.D. 212 .... s.75N
Riverstone Meat Co. Pty. v Lancashire Shipping Co. [1961] A.C. 807; [1961] 2 W.L.R. 269; 105 S.J. 148; [1961] 1 All E.R. 495; *sub nom.* Riverstone Meat Co. Pty. v. Lancashire Shipping Co. (The Muncaster Castle) [1961] 1 Lloyd's Rep. 57; H.L.; reversing [1960] 1 Q.B. 536; [1960] 2 W.L.R. 86; 104 S.J. 50; [1960] 1 All E.R. 193; [1959] 2 Lloyd's Rep. 553, C.A.; reversing [1959] 1 Q.B. 74; [1958] 3 W.L.R. 482; 102 S.J. 656; [1958] 3 All E.R. 261; [1958] 2 Lloyd's Rep. 255 .... s.33N, s.118N
Rolls v. Miller (1894) 27 Ch. D. 71 .... s.79N
Russel v. London Borough of Southwark (Unreported, November 1985) s.80N

Saddleworth Urban District Council v. Aggregate and Sand (1970) 114 S.J. 931; 69 L.G.R. 103, D.C. s.80N
St. Helen's Corporation v. Kirkham (1885) 16 Q.B.D. 403 .... s.80N
Salford City Council v. McNally [1976] A.C. 379; [1975] 3 W.L.R. 87; 119 S.J. 475; [1975] 2 All E.R. 860; 73 L.G.R. 408, H.L.; affirming [1975] 1 W.L.R. 365; (1974) 119 S.J. 151; [1975] 1 All E.R. 597; (1974) 73 L.G.R. 151, D.C. s.79N; s.80N; s.82N
Sandwell Metropolitan Borough Council v. Bujok [1990] 1 W.L.R. 1350; [1990] 3 All E.R. 385; (1990) 134 S.J. 1300; (1991) 23 H.L.R. 48; 89 L.G.R. 77; (1991) L.G. Rev. 228; (1991) 3 Admin. L.R. 426; (1991) 155 J. P.N. 554, H.L.; affirming (1990) 22 H.L.R. 87; (1990) 154 J.P. 608; 88 L.G.R. 521; [1990] C.O.D. 206; (1990) 154 L.G. Rev. 611; (1990) 154 J.P.N. 528, D.C. s.82N
Sedleigh-Denfield v. O'Callaghan [1940] A.C. 880 .... s.80N
Shave v. Rosner [1954] 2 Q.B. 113; [1954] 2 W.L.R. 1057; 118 J.P. 364; 98 S.J. 355; [1954] 2 All E.R. 280; 52 L.G.R. 337, D.C. s.33N
Sheffield City Council v. A.D.H. Demolition (1984) 82 L.G.R. 177; (1984) J.P.L. 658, D.C. s.1N

TABLE OF CASES

Skinner v. Jack Breach [1927] 2 K.B. 220	s.79N
Smith v. Anderson (1880) 15 Ch. D. 247, C.A.	s.6N
South Wales Aluminium Co. v. Neath Assessment Committee [1943] 2 All E.R. 587	s.80N
Southern Water Authority v. Pegrum (1989) 153 J.P. 581; [1989] Crim.L.R. 442; (1989) 153 L.G.Rev. 672; (1989) 153 J.P.N. 578, D.C.	s.33N
Southwark London Borough Council v. Ince (1989) 21 H.L.R. 504; [1989] C.O.D. 549; (1989) 153 J.P. 597; (1989) 153 L.G.Rev. 831, D.C.	s.79N
Strathclyde Regional Council v. Tudhope [1983] J.P.L. 536, High Ct. of Justiciary	s.80N
Tower Hamlets London Borough Council v. Manzoni and Walder (1984) 148 J.P. 123; [1984] J.P.L. 436	s.79N
Town Investments v. Department of the Environment (1976) 120 S.J. 435; [1976] 3 All E.R. 479; sub nom. Town Investments v. Department of the Environment; London County Freehold and Leasehold Properties v. Same; HEPC (Mayfair Properties) v. Same (1976) 1 W.L.R. 1126, C.A.	s.79N
Vessoso and Zanetti (C-206/88, 207/88) [1990] 2 LMELR	s.75N
Vibroplant v. Holland (Inspector of Taxes) (1982) 126 S.J. 82; [1982] 1 All E.R. 792; [1981] T.R. 485; (1984) T.C. 658; [1982] S.T.C. 164, C.A.; affirming (1980) 124 S.J. 561; (1981) 1 All E.R. 526; [1980] T.R. 313; [1980] S.T.C. 671	s.1N
Walford v. Hackney Board of Works (1894) 43 W.R. 110	s.80N
Wandsworth Corporation v. Baines [1906] 1 K.B. 470	s.46N
Warner v. Lambeth London Borough Council (1984) 15 H.L.R. 42, D.C.	s.82N
Waste Incineration Services v. Dudley Metropolitan Borough Council [1992] 1 Envir.L.R. 29	s.33N
Watney Combe Reid & Co. v. Westminster (City) London Borough Council (1970) 214 E.G. 1631; (1970) 68 L.G.R. 639, C.A.	s.81N
Wellingborough Borough Council v. Gordon [1991] J.P.L. 874; [1991] C.O.D. 154; (1991) 155 J.P. 494; (1991) 155 J.P.N. 314; (1991) 155 L.G.Rev. 408; The Times, November 9, 1990, D.C.	s.80N
West Mersea Urban District Council v. Fraser [1950] 2 K.B. 119; 66 T.L.R. (Pt. 1) 891; 114 J.P. 282; 94 S.J. 271; [1950] 1 All E.R. 990; 48 L.G.R. 418, D.C.	s.79N
Whatling v. Rees (1914) 84 L.J.K.B. 1122	s.80N
Williams Will Trusts, Re; Chartered Bank of India, Australia and China v. Williams [1953] Ch. 138; [1953] 2 W.L.R. 418; 97 S.J. 133; [1953] 1 All E.R. 536	s.79N
Wilson v. West Sussex County Council [1963] 2 Q.B. 764; [1963] 2 W.L.R. 669; 127 J.P. 243; 107 S.J. 114; [1963] 1 All E.R. 751; 14 P. & C.R. 301; 61 L.G.R. 287; [1963] R.V.R. 278; C.A.; affirming (1962) 13 P. & C. R. 310, Lands Tribunal	s.1N, s.29N
Wivenhoe Port v. Colchester Borough Council [1985] J.P.L. 396, C.A.; affirming [1985] J.P.L. 175	s.79N, s.80N, s.82N
Wood v. London County Council [1948] 2 K.B. 232, C.A.	s.75N
Wycombe District Council v. Jeffways and Pilot Coaches (1983) 81 L.G.R. 662, C.A.	s.81N
Wyre Forest District Council v. Secretary of State for the Environment and Allen's Caravans (Estates) [1990] 2 A.C. 357; [1990] 2 W.L.R. 517; [1990] 1 All E.R. 780; (1990) 60 P. & C.R. 195; [1990] 2 PLR 95, H.L.; reversing [1989] 1 PLR 79; [1989] J.P.L. 362 (1989) P. & C.R. 132, C.A.	s.75N
Zanetti & Others (C-359/88)	s.75N

TABLE OF STATUTES

References are to section and Schedule number

Where a section number appears followed by (N), this refers to the notes for that particular section or subsection.
e.g. s.33(N) refers to the General Note following s.33
s.33(5N) refers to the notes for subs. (5) of s.33

1875	Explosives Act (38 & 39 Vict., c.17) .... s.75(2)(*b*)		1944	Education Act (7 & 8 Geo. 6, c.31)—
	s.3	s.75N		s.100(1)(*b*) ....s.98(2)(*c*)
	s.104	s.75N	1945	Law Reform (Contributory) Negligence) Act (8 & 9 Geo. 6, c.28) .... s.73(8), s.73(9)(*b*)
1883	Explosive Substances Act (46 & 47 Vict., c.3) .... s.142(7)			
1897	Public Health (Scotland) Act (60 & 61 Vict., c.38) ... Pt. IIN		1947	Crown Proceedings Act (10 & 11 Geo. 6, c.44)—
	s.16	s.83(2)		s.38(3) .... s.159(5)
	s.22	s.74N		Agriculture Act (10 & 11 Geo. 6, c.48) .... s.75(7)(*c*), s.75N, s.152(5)
	s.32 .... s.84(2)(*a*)(*b*), s.84(4)(*b*),	s.84N		
	(1) .... s.84(1)(*b*),	s.84N		s.109(3) s.75N
	(3)	s.84N	1948	Agriculture (Scotland) Act (11 & 12 Geo. 6, c.45)—
1906	Alkali etc. Works Regulation Act (6 Edw. 7, c.14) ..... s.7N, s.8N, s.162N, Pt. IN			s.75(7)(*c*), ... s.75N, s.152(5)
	Pt. I .... s.79(10)		1949	National Parks and Access to the Countryside Act (12, 13 & 14 Geo. 6, c.97) .... s.130(2)(*a*)
	Dogs Act (6 Edw. 7, c.32)—			
	s.4	s.150N		s.1 .... s.130(1), s.130N
1925	Theatrical Employers Registration Act (15 & 16 Geo. 5, c.50)	s.75N		s.15 .... s.132(1)(*b*)
				Pt. IV s.139N
1936	Public Health Act (26 Geo. 5 & Edw. 8, c.49) . s.80N, Pt IIN		1951	Rivers (Prevention of Pollution (Scotland) Act (14 & 15 Geo. 6, c.64) ... s.1(8)(*a*), s.30(6)
	s.74	s.45N		
	s.77	s.45N		
	s.91(1)(*a*)	s.79N	1952	Visiting Forces Act (15 & 16 Geo. 6, c.64) .... s.79(2)(*b*)
	s.92(1)	s.79N		
	(*e*)	s.79N	1954	Mines and Quarries Act (2 & 3 Eliz. 2, c.70)—
	(*f*)	s.79N		
	(2) .... Pt. IIN			s.151 .... s.79N
	s.93 .... s.80N, Pt IIN		1956	Clean Air Act (4 & 5 Eliz. 2, c.52) .... s.79(7), s.162N, Pt. IN, Pt. IIIN
	(1)(*c*)	s.79N		
	s.94	s.82N		
	(1) .... Pt. IIN			s.3 .... s.85N
	(2) .... Pt. IIN			s.7 .... s.85N
	(5)	s.79N		s.16 .... s.80N
	s.95(1) .... s.74N, Pt. IIN			s.18(2) s.85N
	(2) .... Pt. IIN			s.19(3) s.85N
	s.96	s.81N		s.20(4) s.85N
	s.98	s.81N		s.22(1) s.85N
	s.99 .... s.82N, Pt. IIIN			s.34(2) .... s.79(7)
	s.100 .... s.81N, Pt. IIIN		Hotel Proprietors Act (4 & 5 Eliz. 2, c.62)—	
	s.107 ...... s.84(1)(*a*), s.84(2)(*a*), s.84(4)(*a*), s.84(5), s.84N			
	s.108	s.84N		s.1(3) s.75N
	(2) .... s.84(2)(*b*),	s.84N	1960	Radioactive Substances Act (8 & 9 Eliz. 2, c.34) ... s.28(2), s.78, s.78N, s.142(7), s.156(2)(*d*), s.156(4)(*b*), s.156N, s.164(4), Pt. IN
	s.109	s.79N		
	s.110(1)	s.79N		
	s.141	s.79N		
	s.259	s.79N		
	s.268	s.79N		
	s.343(1)	s.79N		s.19(1) s.78N
	Pt. I	s.84(5)		(2) s.78N

xv

TABLE OF STATUTES

1960 Caravan Sites and Control of
Development Act (8 & 9
Eliz. 2, c.34)—
s.29(1) .... s.75(5)(*b*), s.75N
1961 Factories Act (9 &10 Eliz. 2,
c.34) .... s.75(6)(*a*)
s.175 .... s.75N
1962 Pipe-lines Act (10 & 11 Eliz.
2, c.58) .... s.45(10)(*b*)
1964 Continental Shelf Act (c.29)—
s.1(7) .... s.127(2), s.146(7)
Sched. 2 .... s.146(8)
para. 3(3) .... s.146(8)
1968 Countryside Act (c.41) ... Pt. VIIN
s.15(2) s.132N
Sewerage (Scotland) Act
(c.47) .... s.1(11)(*c*)
s.2 .... s.45(10)
s.3 .... s.45(10)
s.4 .... s.45(10)
s.41 .... s.45(10)
Clean Air Act (c.62) s.1N,
s.79(x), s.162N,
Pt. IN, Pt IIIN
s.2 .... s.7(12), s.85N
s.3 .... s.85N
s.4 .... s.85N
s.5 .... s.85N
s.7 .... s.85
s.7A s.85
Medicines Act (c.67)—
Pt. II .... s.142(7)
Pt. III .... s.142(7)
Pt. VIII .... s.142(7)
Transport Act (c.73)—
s.69 .... s.33N, s.162N
s.110 .... s.155
1969 Public Health (Recurring
Nuisances) Act (c.25) .. s.80N,
Pt. IIIN
s.1 .... Pt. IIIN
s.2 .... Pt. IIIN
s.3(1) .... Pt. IIIN
1971 Fire Precautions Act (c.40) . s.157N
Prevention of Oil Pollution
Act (c.60) .... s.148(1)
s.2(2A) .... s.148(2), s.148N
s.19A .... s.148(2)(*b*)
s.19(4A) .... s.148(2)(*a*)
s.20 .... s.148(2)(*b*)
1972 Superannuation Act (c.11)—
s.1 .... s.154
Sched. 1 .... s.154
Town and Country Planning
(Scotland) Act (c.52) .. s.36(2)
s.90 .... s.36(2)(*b*)
(7) s.36N
European Communities Act
(c.68) .... Pt. VIN
s.2 .... s.7(12)
(2) .... s.67(4)
Local Government Act (c.70)
s.101 .... s.90(5)
s.222 .... s.81N
s.233 .... s.80N
Sched. 14,
para. 11 .... s.84N

1972 Local Government Act—
cont.
Sched. 17,
para. 1 .... s.88(10)
para. 3 .... s.88(10)
para. 5 .... s.88(10)
1973 Northern Ireland Constitution Act (c.36)—
s.3 .... s.153(5)
(1)(*a*) .... s.3(8)
Sched. 3 .... s.3(8), s.153(5)
Nature Conservancy Council
Act (c.54) .. s.131(1), Pt. VIIN
Powers of Criminal Courts
Act (c.62)—
s.35 .... s.82N
Local Government (Scotland) Act (c.65)—
s.95 .... s.88(10)
s.172 .... s.36(6)(*a*)(*iii*),
s.39(8)(*a*)(*ii*), s.54(4)(*b*)(*iii*)
s.192 .... s.80N
s.235(1) .... s.98N, s.98(4)
1974 Health and Safety at Work
etc. Act (c.37) .... Pt. VIN
s.5 ...... s.79(10), s.162N, Pt. IN
Pt. I .... s.7(1)(*c*), s.7(12), Pt. IN
Control of Pollution Act
(c.40) s.35N, s.36N,
s.37N, s.38N, s.39N,
s.40, s.41N, s.162N
s.2 .... s.50N, s.77(1)
s.3 .... s.33N, s.74N, s.77(1)
(1)(*a*) s.33N
(3) s.33N
(4) s.33N
(*a*) s.33N
s.4 .... s.77(1)
s.5 . s.34(3)(*b*), s.61(3)(*a*), s.77(1)
(2) s.36N
(3) s.35N, s.36N
(6) s.74N
s.6 .... s.35N, s.77(1)
(1) s.33N
(2) .... s.35N, Pt. IIN
(3) s.33N
s.7 .... s.77(1)
s.8 .... s.77(1)
s.9 .... s.77(1)
s.10 .... s.35N, s.77(1)
s.11 .... s.54N, s.77(3), s.77N
s.12 .... s.45N
s.14(4) .... s.77(6)(*b*), s.77(8)
s.16 .... s.33N
(4) s.74N
s.17 .... s.62N
s.18(2) s.74N
s.22(1) s.89N
(2) s.89N
(3) s.75N
s.30 .... s.75N
s.31(1) s.74N
(7)(*a*) .... s.145(2)
s.31A(2)(*c*)(*i*) .... s.145(2)
s.32(1) s.74N
(7)(*a*) .... s.145(2)
s.34(5) s.74N
s.58 .... s.79N, s.80N

xvi

Table of Statutes

1974 Control of Pollution Act—*cont.*
  s.58(5) s.79N
  (6) s.80N
  (7) s.81N
  (8) s.81N
  s.59 .... s.79N, s.82N
  s.60 .... s.80(9)(*a*), s.80N, s.81(6)
  s.61 ... s.80(9)(*a*), s.80N, s.81(6), s.81N
  s.65 .... s.80(9)(*a*), s.80N
  s.66 .... s.80(9)(*b*), s.80N
  s.67 .... s.80(9)(*c*), s.80N
  s.71 .... s.79(9)(*d*), s.79N
  s.72 .... s.79N
  s.77(2) s.37N
  s.78 .... s.74N
  s.92(6) s.74N
  s.93(3) s.74N
  s.100 .. s.140N, s.162(5), s.164(2)
   (1)(*b*) s.140N
  Sched. 2 .... s.77(3)(*a*)
  Pt. I ... s.54(16), s.77(1), Pt. IIN
  Pt. II .... s.1(6), s.7(12), s.54(11)
  Pt. III .... s.7(12), Pt. IIIN
  Pt. IV .... s.7(12)
  Rehabilitation of Offenders Act (c.53)— s.74N
1976 Fatal Accidents Act (c.30) s.73(9)(*a*)
  Licensing (Scotland) Act (c.66)—
  s.139(1) s.75N
1978 Refuse Disposal (Amenity) Act (c.3)—
  s.2 .... s.74N
  Interpretation Act (c.30)—
  s.7 .... s.160(4), s.160(5)
1979 Merchant Shipping Act (c.39)—
  s.20(1) .... s.148(2)
  (3) .... s.148(2)
  (4) .... s.148(2)
1980 Education (Scotland) Act (c.44)—
  s.77(5) .... s.98(3)(*d*)
  s.135(1) .... s.98(3)(*f*)(*g*)
  Limitation Act (c.58) .... s.73(9)(*c*)
  Highways Act (c.66) . s.89N, s.98(5)
  s.10(1) s.98N
  s.16 .... s.98N
  s.19 .... s.98N
  s.239(1) s.98N
  s.328 .... s.98N
1981 Animal Health Act (c.22)—
  s.13 .... s.151(1)
  s.50(1) .... s.151(2)
  s.60(1) .... s.151(3)
  Wildlife and Countryside Act (c.69) ... s.133(2)(*a*), Pt. VIIN
  s.28(1) .... s.36(7), s.54(4)(*e*)
  s.29 .... s.132N
  s.38 .... s.134N
1982 Civic Government (Scotland) Act (c.45)—
  s.124 .... s.162(3)
1983 Litter Act (c.35)—
  s.1 .... s.87N
  s.2 .... s.87N

1984 Public Health (Control of Disease) Act (c.22)—
  s.2 .... s.4(12), s.79(8)
  Road Traffic Regulation Act (c.27) s.89N
  s.14(1) .... s.89(6)(*b*)
  (3) .... s.89(6)(*b*)
  s.64(1) .... s.89(14)
  Roads (Scotland) Act (c.54) .... s.98(5), s.149(11)(*ii*)
1985 Companies Act (c.6) .... s.30(5)(*b*)
  s.303 .... s.32N
  s.736 .... s.32N
  Food and Environment Protection Act (c.48)—
  s.5 .... s.146(2)
  (*a*) .... s.146(2)(*a*)
  (*b*) s.146N
  (*c*)(*i*) s.146N
  s.6 .... s.146(3)
  s.9(1) .... s.74N, s.146(6)(*a*)
  (5) .... s.146(3)
  s.11 .... s.146(5)
  (2)(*b*) .... s.146(5)(*a*)
  (3)(*a*) .... s.146(5)(*b*)
  s.14 .... s.147
  s.21 .... s.146(6)
  (2) .... s.146(6)(*a*)
  s.24(1) .... s.146(7)
  Pt. II ... s.146(1), s.146N, s.147, s.147N
  Pt. III .... s.142(7)
  Local Government Act (c.51)—
  s.10 .... s.30(4)
1986 Airports Act (c.31)—
  Pt. V .... s.98(6)(*c*)
1988 Income and Corporation Taxes Act (c.1)—
  s.508 .... s.75N
  Local Government Act (c.9)—
  Pt. I .... s.97(1)(*b*), s.97N
  Education Reform Act (c.40)—
  s.131 ...... s.98(2)(*a*), s.98(3)(*a*)
  s.132 .... s.98(2)(*d*)
  s.218 .... s.98(2)(*c*)(*ii*)
  City of Westminster Act ... s.88N
1989 Control of Pollution (Amendment) Act (c.141) .... s.34(4)(*c*), s.16N, Pt. IIN
  s.1 .... s.74N
  (3) .... s.34(3)(*e*)
  s.2 .... s.34(3)(*d*)
  s.3(5) s.74N
  (6) s.74N
  s.5 .... s.74N
  s.6 .... s.33N
  (9) s.74N
  s.7(3) s.74N
  Water Act (c.15)—
  s.107 .... s.74N
  (6) .... s.145(1)
  s.108 .... Pt. IN
  s.117(1)(*f*) .... s.20(9)
  s.118(4) s.74N

TABLE OF STATUTES

1989 Water Act—*cont.*
    s.175(1) s.74N
    Pt. III .... Pt.IN
        Ch. I .... s.6N, s.28(3)
    Dangerous Dogs Act (c.30) . s.149N
    Self-Governing Schools etc. (Scotland) Act (c.39)—
        s.1(3) .... s.98(3)(*h*)
        s.65(1) .... s.98(3)(*c*)(*ii*)
        s.68(1) .... s.98(3)(*e*)
        s.80(1) .... s.98(3)(*c*)(*i*)
    Local Government and Housing Act (c.42)—
        s.68 .... s.32(11), s.32N
            (1) s.32N
            (6) s.32N
        s.70 .... s.32N
        s.73 .... s.32(11), s.32N
        Pt. V .... s.32(9), s.32N

1990 Town and Country Planning Act (c.8) ...... s.36(2), s.50N, Pt. IIN, Pt. VIIN
    s.191 .... s.36N
        (7) s.36N
    s.192 .... s.36(2)(*b*)
    s.288 .... s.15N
    Planning (Hazardous Substances) Act (c.10) s.144N
    Food Safety Act (c.16) ..... s.142(7)
    Environmental Protection Act (c.43)—
        s.1 .... Intro, **s.1**, Pt. IN
            (2) s.2N, s.3N, s.4N, s.7N
            (3) ... s.3N, s.4N, s.7N, s.14N, s.17N
            (4) s.7N, s.18N, s.27N
            (5) s.2N, s.3N, s.4N, s.6N, s.7N, s.8N, s.9N, s.10N, s.11N, s.12N, s.13N, s.14N, s.16N, s.17N, s.20N, s.28N, s.29N
            (6) s.4N
            (7) s.6N, s.7N, s.8N, s.9N, s.10N, s.11N, s.12N, s.13N, s.14N,s.15N,s.17N,s.19N, s.20N, s.21N, s.22N, s.24N, s.28N
            (8) s.6N, s.7N, s.8N, s.9N, s.10N, s.11N, s.12N, s.13N, s.14N, s.15N, s.17N, s.19N, s.20N, s.21N, s.22N, s.24N, s.28N
            (9) ... s.2N, s.8N, s.9N, s.10N, s.11N, s.12N, s.13N, s.14N, s.15N, s.20N, s.22N, s.23N, s.28N
            (10) ... s.2N, s.3N, s.4N, s.7N, s.10N, s.11N, s.28N
            (11)(*c*) .... Pt. IN
            (13) ... s.2N, s.3N, s.4N, s.7N, s.10N, s.11N, s.18N, s.28N
        s.2 .... Intro, **s.2**, Pt. IN
            (1) .... s.1(5), s.6(1)
        s.3 ...... Intro, **s.3**, s.6N, s.7(12), s.7N, Pt. IN
            (1) .... Pt. IN

1990 Environmental Protection Act—*cont.*
    s.3(2) .... Pt. IN
        (4) .... Pt. IN
        (5) .. s.7(2)(*d*), s.164(4), Pt. IN
        (6) .... s.164(4)
        (7) .... s.164(4)
        (8) .... s.164(4)
    s.4 ...... Intro, s.1(7)(8)(*b*), **s.4**, Pt. IN
        (2) .... s.5(1), Pt. IN
        (3) .... Pt. IN
        (4) .... s.16(1), Pt. IN
        (11) .... Pt. IN
        (12)(*e*) s.7
    s.5 .... Intro, **s.5**, Pt. IN
        (1) .... s.4(2)
        (2) .... s.7(9)
    s.6 .... Intro, s.1(9), s.IN, s.2(1), **s.6**, s.7N, s.9(3), s.10N, s.84(1)(*a*)(*ii*), s.84(1)(*b*)(*ii*), Pt. IN
        (1) .... s.23(1)(*a*), Pt. IN
        (4) s.9N
    s.7 ...... Intro, s.6(3), **s.7**, s.10N, s.11(8)(*a*), s.23(1)(*i*)(*f*), s.25(2)(*a*), Pt. IN
        (1) .... Pt. IN
            (*a*) .... Pt. IN
            (*c*) .... Pt. IN
        (2) .... s.5(2)(*b*), s.6N
        (3) .... Pt. IN
        (4) ...... s.6N, s.25(1), Pt. IN
        (6) s.25N
        (7) s.6N
        (10) .... Pt. IN
        (11) .... Pt. IN
        (12)(*e*) s.7
    s.8 .... Intro, **s.8**, s.10(4)(*b*), s.11(8)(*a*), Pt. IN
        (2) .... Pt. IN
            (*a*) .... s.6(2)
        (9) .... Pt. IN
        (11) .... Pt. IN
    s.9 .... Intro, **s.9**, Pt. IN
        (2) .... s.23(1)(*b*)
    s.10 .... Intro, **s.10**, Pt. IN
        (5) s.20N
        (6) .... Pt. IN
        (7) .... s.11N, Pt. IN
        (8) s.11N
    s.11 .... Intro, s.10(6)(*b*), s.10(7), s.10(8), **s.11**, s.15(1)(*c*), Pt. IN
        (4)(*b*) s.11N, s.20N
    s.12 .... Intro, s.9N, **s.12**, s.15(1)(*d*), Pt. IN
        (*e*) s.7N
        (5) s.7N
    s.13 ..... Intro, s.9N, **s.13**, s.14N, Pt. IN
        (3) .... Pt.IN
    s.14 ..... Intro, s.9N, **s.14**, Pt.IN
        (4) .... Intro

Table of Statutes

1990 Environmental Protection
Act—cont.
- s.15 .... Intro, s.11N, **s.15**, s.20(1)(e), s.20N, Pt. IN
  - (1)(c) s.11N
  - (2) s.14N
  - (3) .... s.22(6)
  - (5) .... s.22(6)
  - (7) s.13N
  - (10) .... Intro, s.22(6)
- s.16 .... Intro, s.4(2), **s.16**, Pt. IN
  - (8) s.17N, s.23N
- s.17 .... Intro, s.16(7), **s.17**, s.23(1)(d), s.27N, s.140(3)(c), Pt. IN
  - (3) .... s.23(1)(e)
  - (4) .... Pt.IN
  - (8) s.18N
  - (9) .... Pt. IN
  - (10) s.69N
- s.18 ... Intro, s.16(7), **s.18**, Pt. IN
- s.19 .... Intro, **s.19**, Pt. IN
  - (2) .... s.20N, s.22(2)(c), s.23(1)(g)
- s.20 ..... Intro, s.6N, **s.20**, s.20N, s.22(6), Pt. IN
  - (1) .... Pt. IN
  - (6) .... Pt. IN
- s.21 .... Intro, s.20(1)(i), s.20(6) **s.21**, Pt. IN
- s.22 .. Intro, s.20(1)(i), s.20(5)(6), s.20N, **s.22**, s.66N, Pt. IN
- s.23 ... Intro, s.17(3)(h)(iii), **s.23**, s.26(3), Pt. IN
  - (1) ... s.9N, s.17N, s.20(1)(f), s.20N, s.74N
  - (a) s.25(1), s.26(1), s.27(1)
  - (c) .... s.13N, s.14N, s.24, s.27(1)
  - (g) s.19N
  - (h) s.19N
  - (i) s.19N
  - (l) s.26N
  - (5) .... Pt. IN
- s.24 .... Intro, **s.24**, Pt. IN
- s.25 .... Intro, **s.25N**, Pt. IN
- s.26 . Intro, s.23(1)(l), **s.26**, Pt. IN
  - (9) s.77N
- s.27 .... Intro, **s.27**, Pt. IN
  - (2) .... Pt. IN
- s.28 .... Intro, s.7(9), **s.28**, Pt. IN
  - (1) .... s.29N, Pt. IN, Pt. IIN
  - (2) .... Pt. IN
  - (3) s.5N
    - (a) .... Pt. IN
    - (b) .... Pt. IN
  - (4) .... Pt. IN
- s.29 .... Intro, **s.29**, s.33N, s.34N, s.35N
  - (3) s.33N, s.36N, s.37N, s.38N, s.39N, s.42N, s.43N, s.50N, s.54N, s.61N, s.69N, s.70N
  - (4) s.64N

1990 Environmental Protection
Act—cont.
  - (5) s.33N, s.36N, s.37N, s.38N, s.39N, s.42N, s.43N, s.54N, s.59N, s.62N, s.69N, s.70N
  - (6) s.30N, s.32N, s.33N, s.34N, s.35N, s.39N, s.50N, s.51N, s.52N, s.53N, s.55N, s.57N, s.58N, s.59N, s.60N, s.62N, s.63N, s.64N, s.69N, s.73N
  - (7) s.33N
  - (9) s.33N, s.35N, s.54N
  - (11) s.70N
- s.30 ... Intro, **s.30**, s.32N, Pt. IIN
  - (1) .... s.31(1), s.141N
  - (2) .... s.77(5)
  - (3) s.141N
  - (5) ..... s.32N, s.48N, s.49N, s.50N, s.51N, s.55N, s.60N, s.77N, Pt. IIN
  - (7) .... s.54N, Pt. IIN
- s.31 .... Intro, **s.31**, Pt. IIN
- s.32 ...... Intro, s.30(5)(a), **s.32**, s.32N, s.77(1), Pt. IIN
  - (2) .... Pt. IIN
  - (9) s.63N
- s.33 .. s.29N, **s.33**, s.34N, s.54(1), s.59N, s.74N, Pt. IIN
  - (1) .... s.34(3)(c), s.59(1), s.73(6), s.77(1)
  - (c) .... Intro, s.33N
  - (2) .... Intro
  - (3) ..... Intro, s.33N, Pt. IN, Pt. IIN
  - (4) .... Intro, s.33N
  - (c) .... Pt. IN, Pt IIN
  - (6) ..... Intro, s.33N, s.42(5)
  - (7) .... Intro, s.73(7)
  - (8) .... Intro
  - (9) .... Intro, s.33N
- s.34 .... Intro, **s.34**, Pt. IN
  - (1)(c)(ii) s.34N
  - (2) s.75N
  - (5) .... Intro
  - (6) s.74N
  - (7) .... Intro, Pt. IIN
  - (8) .... Intro
  - (9) .... Intro
  - (11) .... Intro
- s.35 ..... s.34(3)(b), **s.35**, Pt. IIN
  - (1) .... Pt. IIN
  - (3) .... Pt.IIN
  - (6) .... s.37(2)(g)
  - (7) .... Pt. IIN
  - (8) .... Pt. IIN
  - (11) .... Pt. IIN
  - (12) s.36N, s.37N, s.38N, s.39N, s.40N, s.41N, s.42N, s.43N, s.44N, s.50N, s.61N, s.64N, s.66N, s.67N, s.77N
- s.36 .... **s.36**, s.74N

xix

Table of Statutes

1990 Environmental Protection Act—*cont.*

s.36(2)	Pt. IIN
(*a*)	s.36N
(3)	s.35N, Pt. IIN
(4)	s.37(5)
(5)	s.37(5), Pt. IIN
(6)	s.37(5), Pt. IIN
(7)	s.37(5)
(8)	s.37(5)
(9)	s.64(3)
(10)	s.37(5), s.39(11)
s.37	**s.37**, s.43(6), s.64(1)(*c*)(*d*), Pt. IIN
(3)	Pt. IIN
s.38	s.35(11), **s.38**, s.43(1)(*e*), s.43(6), s.64(1)(*e*), s.74N, Pt. IIN
(2)	Pt. IIN
(5)	s.41(8), s.42(7)
(7)	Pt. IIN
(8)	s.42(7)
(9)	s.42(7)
(10)	s.42(7), Pt. IIN
(11)	s.42(7), Pt. IIN
s.39	s.35(9)(11), **s.39**, s.61N, s.61(9), Pt. IIN
(3)	Pt. IIN
(7)	Pt. IIN
(8)	Pt. IIN
(9)	s.64(1)(*g*)
s.40	s.35(1), **s.40**, Pt. IIN
(6)	s.40N
s.41	s.36N, s.39(3), s.40(3), **s.41**, Pt. IIN
s.42	**s.42**, s.43(1)(*e*), s.43(6), s.61N, s.64(1)(*j*), s.67(2)(*b*), Pt. IIN
(5)	s.64(1)(*h*)
(*a*)	s.38N
(*b*)	s.38N
(6)(*c*)	s.38N
(8)	Pt. IIN
s.43	**s.43**, s.64(1)(*f*), Pt. IIN
(1)(*a*)	s.37N
(*c*)	s.37N
(*d*)	s.38N
(*e*)	s.38N
(*f*)	s.39N
(*g*)	s.40N
(2)	s.66(6)
(4)	s.38N
(5)	s.38N
(6)	s.38N
(8)	s.66(6)
s.44	**s.44**, s.74N, Pt. IIN
s.45	Intro, **s.45**, s.48(1), s.52(1)(2)(3)(4), s.53(1)(2) Intro
(*a*)	s.46(1)
(2)	Intro, s.63(4)
(3)	Intro
(4)	Intro
(5)	Intro

1990 Environmental Protection Act—*cont.*

s.45(5)(*a*)	Intro, s.53(4)
(6)	Intro, s.53(4)
(7)	Intro
(8)	Intro
(9)	Intro, s.55N
(10)	Intro
(11)	Intro
(12)	Intro, s.53N
s.46	Intro, **s.46**, s.60(1)(*c*), Pt. IIN
(2)	Pt. IIN
(7)	s.73N
s.47	Intro, s.60(1)(*c*), Pt. IIN
(1)	s.63(4)
(6)	s.74N
(7)	s.73N
s.48	**s.48**, Pt. IIN
(1)	Intro, s.45(9)
(2)	Intro, s.52(1), Pt. IIN
(3)	Intro
(4)	Intro
(5)	Intro
(6)	Intro, s.49(3)(*e*)
(8)	Intro
(9)	Intro
s.49	Intro, s.48N, **s.49**, Pt. IIN
(4)	Pt. IIN
(7)	Pt. IIN
s.50	Intro, **s.50**, s.67(2)(*c*), s.77(4), Pt. IIN
(4)	Pt. IIN
(9)	Pt. IIN
(11)	Pt.IIN
s.51	Intro, **s.51**
(1)	s.55(2)(*a*), s.55(2)(*d*), s.77(6)(*a*), s.77(7), s.77(9)
(*a*)	Pt. IIN
(*b*)	Pt.IIN
(4)(*a*)	Pt. IIN
(*c*)	s.32N
(*d*)	s.32N
(5)(*b*)	s.32N
(*c*)	s.32N
s.52	**s.52**
(1)	Intro, Pt. IIN
(3)	Intro
(4)	Intro
(5)	Intro
(6)	Intro
(7)	Intro
(8)	Intro
(9)	Intro
(10)	Intro
(11)	Intro
s.53	Intro, s.49(3)(*e*), **s.53**, Pt. IIN
s.54	s.33(1), s.54, s.64(1)(*l*), s.67(2)(*b*), Pt. IIN
s.55	Intro, **s.55**, Pt. IIN
s.56	Intro, **s.56**, Pt. IIN
s.57	**s.57**

TABLE OF STATUTES

1990 Environmental Protection Act—*cont.*
- s.57(1) .... Pt. IIN
- (2) .... Pt. IIN
- (5) s.74N
- s.58 .... **s.58**
- s.59 .... **s.59**, Pt IIN
- (2) s.73N
- (5) .... s.74N, Pt. IIN
- s.60 .... Intro, **s.60**
- s.61 .. **s.61**, s.64(1)(*j*), s.67(2)(*b*), Pt. IIN
- (8) s.39N
- (9) s.39N
- (11) .... Pt. IIN
- s.62 ...... s.34N, **s.62**, s.67(2)(*b*), s.75(9), s.75N, Pt. IIN
- (*e*) .... s.164(4)
- (*g*) .... Pt. IIN
- s.63 .... **s.63**
- (2) . s.61(3)(*c*), s.73(6), s.73N, s.74N, Pt. IIN
- s.64 .... **s.64**, s.65(1), s.65N, s.66(1), Pt. IIN
- (1) .... s.62(2)(*f*)
- s.65 .... s.64(1), **s.65**, Pt. IIN
- s.66 ...... s.64(1), s.64(2), **s.66**, Pt. IIN
- (5) .... Pt. IIN
- s.67 .... Pt. IIN
- s.68 .... Intro, **s.68**
- (1) .... Pt. IIN
- (2) .... Pt. IIN
- (3) s.70N
- (5) s.69N
- s.69 .... Intro, s.68(4), **s.69**
- (3) .... s.141(5)(*d*)
- (9) .... s.74N, Pt. IIN
- s.70 .... Intro, s.68(4), **s.70**
- (4) .... s.74N, Pt. IIN
- s.71 .... Intro
- (1) .... Pt. IIN
- (2) .... s.66(2)(*c*)
- (3) .... s.74N, Pt. IIN
- s.72 .... Intro, **s.72**, s.161(1)
- (1) .... Pt. IIN
- (4) .... Pt. IIN
- s.73 .... **s.73**
- (1) .... Intro
- (2) .... Intro
- (3) .... Intro
- (4) .... Intro
- (5) .... Intro
- (6) .... Pt. IIN
- s.74 .... s.35N, s.36N, s.38N, s.40N, Pt. IIN
- (3) s.74N
- (6) s.38N
- s.75 .. Intro, s.29N, s.34N, s.64N, **s.75**, s.78N, s.96(3), Pt. IIN
- (2) s.29N, s.30N, s.32N, s.33, s.35N, s.39N, s.45N, s.47N, s.48N, s.49N, s.50N, s.51N, s.52N, s.53N, s.55N, s.56N, s.59N, s.60N, s.62N, s.63N, s.67N, s.73N, s.141N

1990 Environmental Protection Act—*cont.*
- s.75(3) s.141N
- (4) ..... s.29N, s.33N, s.34N, s.35N, s.49N, s.50N, s.51N, s.53N, s.54N, s.57N, s.58N, s.59N, s.61N, s.62N, s.63N, s.69N, s.77N, Pt. IIN
- (5) ..... s.33N, s.34N, s.45N, s.46N, s.48N, s.49N, s.51N, s.61N, s.61(3)(*c*), Pt. IIN
- (6) ..... s.45N, s.47N, s.51N, s.61(3)(*c*), s.61N, Pt. IIN
- (7) ..... s.45N, s.47N, s.48N, s.49N, s.51N, s.61N, s.61(3)(*c*), Pt. IIN
- (*c*) .... s.63(1)(*a*), s.75N
- (8) .... s.61(3)(*c*)
- (9) s.33N, s.38N, s.62N, s.63N
- s.76 .... **s.76**
- s.77 . Intro, s.51(7), **s.77**, s.162(2)
- (2) s.38N, s.40N, s.41N
- (4) s.50N
- s.78 .... Intro, Pt. IIN
- s.79 ... Intro, **s.79**, s.80N, s.83(1), s.164(2)
- (1) .... s.80(8)(*a*), s.80(8)(*b*), s.80(8)(*c*), s.80(9), s.80N, s.81(6), s.81N, s.82(7)(*a*), s.82(10)(*a*), s.82(10)(*b*), s.82(10)(*c*), s.82N
- (*e*) .... Pt. IIN
- (6) s.81N, s.82N, s.84N
- (7) s.80N
- (9) s.80N, s.82N
- (1) .... Pt. IN, Pt. IIN
- s.80 ...... Intro, s.79(1)(*h*), **s.80**, s.81(1), s.81(2), s.81N, s.83(1), s.164(2)
- (1) .... Pt. IIIN
- (3) .... Pt. IIIN
- (4) ... s.74N, s.81(3), s.81(5), Pt. IIIN
- (7) s.79N
- (9) s.79N
- s.81 ... Intro, **s.81**, s.82N, s.83(1), s.164(2)
- (3) .... Pt. IIIN
- (4) .... Pt.IIIN
- (5) .... s.24N, Pt. IIIN
- s.82 . Intro, s.82, s.83(1), s.164(2), Pt. IIIN
- s.83 .... Intro, **s.83**, s.164(2)
- s.84 .... Intro, **s.84**, s.164(2), Pt. IIIN
- s.85 .... Intro, **s.85**, s.164(2), Pt. IIIN
- s.86 .... **s.86**
- (1) .... Intro, Pt. IVN
- (2) ..... s.87N, s.89N, s.90N, s.92N, s.93N, s.95N, s.96N, Pt. IVN
- (3) ...... Intro, s.89N, s.90N, s.91N, s.92N, s.93N, s.95N, s.96N
- (4) ...... Intro, s.89N, s.91N, s.94N, Pt. IVN

Table of Statutes

1990 Environmental Protection Act—*cont.*
- s.86(5) ...... Intro, s.87N, s.89N, s.91N, s.92N, Pt. IVN
- (6) ..... s.87N, s.89N, s.91N, Pt. IVN
- (7) ..... s.87N, s.91N, s.92N, Pt. IVN
- (8) .... Intro, Pt. IVN
- (9) ...... Intro, s.87N, s.89N, s.91N, s.93N
- (10) ..... Intro, s.87N, s.89N, s.93N
- (11) .... Intro, Pt. IVN
- (12) ..... Intro, s.87N, s.89N, s.91N, s.92N
- (13) .... Intro
- (14) .... Intro, Pt. IVN
- (15) .... Intro
- s.87 ...... **s.87**, s.88(1), Pt. IVN
  - (1) .... Intro
  - (2) .... Intro
  - (3)(*a–e*) .... Intro
  - (*f*) .... Intro
  - (4) .... Intro
  - (5) .... Intro
  - (6) .... Intro
  - (7) .... Intro
- s.88 .... **s.88**, Pt. IVN
  - (1) .... Intro
  - (2) .... Intro
  - (3) .... Intro
  - (4) .... Intro
  - (5) .... Intro, Pt. IVN
  - (7) .... Intro, Pt. IVN
  - (8) .... Intro
  - (9)(*a*) .... Intro
  - (*b*) .... Intro, Pt. IVN
  - (*c*) .... Intro
  - (*d*) .... Intro
  - (*e*) .... Intro
  - (10) .... Intro
- s.89 .... s.75N, **s.89**, s.97(1), Pt. IVN
  - (1) .... s.89N, s.91(4)(7)(10), s.92(5), s.96(1)(*a*)
    - (*a*) ... Intro, s.86N, s.97(3)
    - (*b*) .... Intro, s.86N
    - (*c*) .... Intro, s.97(3)
    - (*d*) .... Intro
    - (*e*) .... Intro
    - (*f*) .... Intro, s.97(3)
    - (*g*) .... Intro, s.86N
  - (2) ...... Intro, s.75N, s.89N, s.91(4), s.91(7), s.91(10)
    - (*a*) .... s.97(3)
  - (3) .... Intro
  - (4) .... Intro, Pt. IVN
  - (5) .... Intro
  - (6) .... Intro, s.91(8)
  - (7) ... Intro, s.91(11), s.92(8), Pt. IVN
  - (8) .... Intro, Pt. IVN
  - (9) .... Intro, Pt. IVN

1990 Environmental Protection Act—*cont.*
- s.89(10) .... Intro
- (11) .... Intro, Pt. IVN
- (12) .... Intro, Pt. IVN
- (13) .... Intro, Pt. IVN
- (14) .... Intro
- s.90 .... **s.90**, Pt. IVN
  - (1) .... Intro, Pt. IVN
  - (2) .... Intro, Pt. IVN
  - (3) .... Intro, s.95(1)(*a*)
  - (4) .... Intro
  - (5) .... Intro
  - (6) .... Intro
  - (7) .... Intro, Pt. IVN
- s.91 .... **s.91**
  - (1)(*a*)–(*g*) .... Intro
  - (*g*) s.86N
  - (2) .... Intro
  - (3) .... Intro
  - (4) .... Intro
  - (5) .... Intro
  - (6) .... Intro
  - (7) .... Intro
  - (8) .... Intro
  - (9) .... Intro
  - (10) .... Intro
  - (11) .... Intro
  - (12) .... Intro
  - (13) .... Intro
- s.92 .... **s.92**, Pt. IVN
  - (1)(*a*) .... Intro, s.80N
  - (*b*) .... Intro
  - (*c*) .... Intro, s.80N
  - (*d*) .... Intro, s.80N
  - (2) .... Intro
  - (3) .... Intro
  - (4) .... Intro
  - (5) .... Intro
  - (6) .... Intro
  - (7) .... Intro
  - (8) .... Intro
  - (9) ... Intro, s.75N, s.96(1)(*b*)
  - (10) .... Intro
- s.93 .... Intro, s.75N, s.82N, **s.93**, s.96(1)(*c*)
  - (1) .... s.95(1)(*b*)
  - (4) s.94N
- s.94 .... s.93(1), s.93(4), **s.94**
  - (1) .... Intro, Pt. IVN
  - (*a*) .... s.93(2)
  - (2) ... Intro, s.93(3), Pt. IVN
  - (3) .... Intro, s.93(3)
  - (4) .... Intro, s.93(3)
  - (5) .... Intro
  - (6) .... Intro
  - (7) .... Intro, s.95(2)
  - (8) .... Intro
  - (9) .... Intro
- s.95 .... Intro, **s.95**
- s.96 .... **s.96**
  - (1) .... Intro
  - (2) .... Intro, Pt. IVN
  - (3) .... Intro, Pt. IVN

TABLE OF STATUTES

1990 Environmental Protection Act—*cont.*
s.96(5) s.93N
s.97 .... Intro, **s.97**, s.164(2), Pt. IVN
s.98 .... **s.98**
(1) .... Intro
(2) ...... Intro, s.86N, s.87N, s.89N, s.91N, s.92N
(3) ...... Intro, s.86N, s.87N, s.89N, s.91N, s.92N
(4) ...... Intro, s.92N, s.93N
(5) ...... Intro, s.86N, s.87N, s.89N, s.91N
(6) ...... Intro, s.87N, s.89N, s.91N, s.92N
s.99 .... Intro, **s.99**, s.164(2), Pt. IVN
s.100 .... Intro
s.101 .... Intro
s.102 .... Intro
s.103 .... Intro
s.104 .... Intro
s.105 .... Intro, s.164(4)
s.106 ..... **s.106**, s.107N, s.108N, s.109N, s.110N, s.111N, s.115N, s.116N, s.117N, s.118N, Pt. VIN
(1) .... Pt. VIN
(4) .... Intro
(5) .... Intro
s.107 ..... **s.107**, s.109N, s.110N, s.111N, s.112N, s.115N, s.116N, s.117N, Pt. VIN
(3) s.108N, s.123N
(6) s.121N
(8) .... Intro
(10) s.108N
(11) s.108N
s.108 .. **s.108**, s.109(5)(*a*), s.109N, s.118(1)(*m*), s.122(1)(*a*), Pt. VIN
(1) .... s.118(1)(*a*)
(*a*) .... Pt. VIN
(*b*) .... Intro
(3) .... s.118(1)(*b*)
(*b*) .... Intro
(5) .... Intro, s.118(1)(*e*)
(7) .... Intro
(8) .. s.111(1)(*b*), s.122(1)(*b*)
(*b*) .... s.111(2)(*b*)
(9) .... Intro
s.109 .... **s.109**, Pt. VIN
(2) .... s.118(1)(*d*)
(3)(*a*) .... s.118(1)(*d*)
(*b*) .... s.118(1)(*d*)
(*c*) .... s.118(1)(*d*), s.119(1)(*b*)
(4) .... s.118(1)(*d*)
(*c*) .... s.119(1)(*b*)
s.110 .... **s.110**, s.125(2), s.125N, Pt. VIN
s.111 ..... s.109N, **s.111**, s.112N, s.118(1)(*m*), s.118(1)(*n*), s.124(1)(*a*), s.125N, s.127, Pt. VIN

1990 Environmental Protection Act—*cont.*
s.111(1) .... Intro, s.118(1)(*c*)
(*a*) .... s.108(2)
(2) .... Intro, s.108(4), s.118(1)(*c*)
(4) .... Intro
(5) .... Intro
(6A) .... s.111N, s.118(1)(*e*)
(7) .... Intro
(11) .... Intro
s.112 .. s.111N, **s.112**, s.124(1)(*a*), s.125N, Pt. VIN
(3) .... s.123(7)(*e*)
(4) .... s.123(7)(*e*)
(*c*) .... s.119(1)(*a*)
(5) .... s.123(7)(*e*)
(7) .... s.123(7)(*e*)
s.113 .... Intro, s.111(4), s.111N, **s.113**, s.124(1)(*a*), Pt. VIN
s.114 ..... **s.114**, s.125N, Pt. VIN
(1) .... Intro, s.125(2)
(2) .... Intro
(3) .... Intro
(4) .... s.125(2)
(5) . s.115N, s.117N, s.118N, s.125N
s.115 . s.114(3), **s.115**, s.118(1)(*g*), s.125(2), s.125N, Pt. VIN
(3) .... s.118(1)(*h*)
(4) .... Intro
s.116 .... **s.116**, s.118(1)(*k*), s.125(2), s.125N, Pt. VIN
s.117 .... s.114(3), **s.117**, s.118(1)(*i*), s.118(1)(*j*), s.125(2), s.125N, Pt. VIN
s.118 ...... s.115(3)(*f*)(*iii*), **s.118**, Pt. VIN
(1) .... s.114(8)
(*a*) .... s.120(1), s.121(1)
(*b*) .... s.120(1), s.121(1)
(*c*) .... s.119(1)(*a*), s.120(1), s.121(1)
(*d*) .... s.119(1)(*b*), s.120(1), s.121(1)
s.118(1)(*e*) ..... s.118N, s.120(1), s.121(1)
(*f*) .... s.120(1), s.121(1)
(10) .... s.125(2), s.125N
s.119 .... **s.119**, Pt. VIN
s.120 .... Pt. VIN, **s.120**
s.121 .... **s.121**, s.125(2), Pt. VIN
s.122 .... **s.122**, s.123(1), s.123N, Pt. VIN
(1) .... Intro
(*a*) .... s.123(7)
(*d*) .... s.123(7)
(*e*) .... s.123(7)
(4) .... Intro
s.123 . s.122(1)(*n*), **s.123**, Pt. VIN
(7) .... Intro
(9) .... Intro
s.124 ... Intro, s.122(1)(*d*), **s.124**, Pt. VIN

1990 Environmental Protection Act—*cont*.

s.125	Intro, s.114(5), **s.125**, Pt. VIN
s.126	Intro, **s.126**
s.127	s.113N, **s.127**
(1)	s.107N, s.108N, s.109N, s.110N, s.111N, s.112N, s.115N, s.116N, s.117N, s.118N, s.119N, s.122N
(2)	s.164(4)
s.128	Intro, **s.128**, Pt. VIN
s.129	**s.129**
s.130	Intro, **s.130**, s.136(1), Pt. VIN
(4)	s.137(3)(*a*), s.161(4)
s.131	**s.131**, Pt. VIIN
(3)	s.36(8), s.54(4)(*e*)(*ii*), s.135(4), s.137(1), s.137(2), s.137N, s.138(1), s.161(4)
(6)	s.132N, s.133N, s.134N
s.132	Intro, s.131(1), s.131N, **s.132**, s.133(3), Pt. VIIN
(1)	s.133N
(*a*)	s.131(4)
s.133	s.131(1), s.131N, **s.133**, Pt. VIIN
(2)	s.132(3)(*b*)
(*a*)	s.131(5)
(3)	s.132(1)(*e*), s.132(3)(*b*), s.133N
s.134	s.131(1), s.132(1)(*d*), s.132(1)(*e*), s.132(2)(*a*), **s.134**
s.135	**s.135**, s.136N, s.138(*b*)(*ii*), Pt. VIIN
s.136	**s.136**
s.137	**s.137**, Pt. VIIN
s.138	**s.138**, Pt. VIIN
(2)	s.161(4)
s.139	**s.139**
s.140	Intro, **s.140**, s.156(2)(*d*), s.156(3)(*a*), s.158, s.162(5), s.164(2), s.164(4), Pt. VIIIN
(5)	s.142(3), s.142N
s.141	Intro, **s.141**, s.156(2)(*d*), s.156(4)(*a*), s.158, s.164(2), s.164(4), Pt. VIIIN
s.142	Intro, **s.142**, s.156(2)(*d*), s.156(4)(*a*), s.158, s.164(2), s.164(4), Pt. VIIIN
s.143	**s.143**, Pt. VIIIN
(1)	Intro
(5)	Intro
(6)	Intro, Pt. IIN
s.144	Intro, **s.144**, Pt. VIIIN
s.145	Intro, **s.145**, s.164(2), Pt. VIIIN
s.146	Intro, **s.146**, s.164(2)(4), Pt. VIIIN
s.147	Intro, **s.147**, s.164(4), Pt. VIIIN
s.148	Intro, **s.148**, s.148N, s.164(2), s.164(4), Pt. VIIIN

1990 Environmental Protection Act—*cont*.

s.149	Intro, **s.149**, s.149N, s.150(2), s.164(*b*)(7), Pt. VIIIN
s.150	Intro, s.149N, **s.150**, Pt. VIIIN
s.151	Intro, s.149N, **s.157**, Pt. VIIIN
s.152	Intro, **s.152**, Pt. VIIN
s.153	Intro, **s.153**, s.164(2)(4)
s.154	Intro, **s.154**, s.164(2)
s.155	Intro, **s.155**, s.164(2)
s.156	Intro, **s.156**, s.164(4), Pt. IVN
s.157	Intro, s.164(2)
s.158	Intro, s.164(4)
s.159	Intro, **s.159**
(2)	s.92N
s.160	Intro, s.149(11)(*ii*), **s.160**, s.164(2)
s.161	Intro, s.164(2)
s.162	Intro, s.33N, **s.162**
(1)	Intro, s.164(2)
(2)	Intro, s.164(2), Pt. VIIN
(3)	Intro
s.163	Intro, **s.163**, s.164(2)
s.164	**s.164**
(2)	Intro, s.140N, s.142N, s.145N, s.146N, s.148N, s.153N, s.155N, s.157N, s.161N, s.162N, s.163N, Pt. IIIN
(3)	s.62N, s.77(1), s.143N, s.144N, s.149N, s.159N, s.161(4), Pt. IN
(4)	s.140N, s.141N, s.142N, s.143N, s.144N, s.145N, s.146N, s.147N, s.148N, s.150N, s.153N, s.154N, s.155N, s.157N, s.158N, s.159N, s.160N, s.161N, s.162N, s.163N, Pt. IVN
Sched. 1	s.6(8), s.75N, **Sched. 1**
para. 1(3)	s.20N
para. 2	s.20N
para. 5(1)	s.6N
para. 6	s.20N
para. 7	s.20N
Pt. I	s.6(2), s.6N
Pt. II	s.10(1), s.10N, s.11(8)(*a*)
para. 7	s.11N
Sched. 2	s.32(2)(*b*), s.32(4)(*b*), s.32(11), s.32N, s.77(1), s.77(6)(*a*)(*i*), **Sched. 2**
para. 6(7)	s.32N
(8)	s.32N
para. 7	s.32N
para. 8(4)	s.32N
(5)	s.32N
para. 9	s.32N
(1)	s.32N
para. 10	s.32N
para. 13	s.32N

Table of Statutes

1990 Environmental Protection
Act—cont.
Sched. 2—cont.
para. 14 .... s.32N
para. 19(1)(b) .... Pt. IIN
para. 23 .... s.32N
Pt. I .... s.32(6), Pt. IIN
Pt. II ...... s.32(6), s.51(1)(b),
s.77(6)(b), Pt. IIN
Sched. 3 ... s.75N, s.87(7), s.81N,
Sched. 3
para. 4 .... s.79N, s.161(1)
Sched. 4 .. s.75N, s.99(1), s.99(6),
s.99N, **Sched. 4**
Sched. 5 .... **Sched. 5**
para. 7 .... s.164(2)
para. 13 .... s.164(2)
para. 14 .... s.164(2)
para. 15 .... s.164(2)
Sched. 6 ...... s.128(5), **Sched. 6**
Sched. 7 .... s.128(5), s.128N,
Sched. 7
Sched. 8 .... s.130(4), s.130N,
Pt. VIIN, **Sched. 8**
para. 1(2) s.130N
Sched. 9 .... s.132(1)(a), s.132N,
Sched. 9
para. 11(9) s.132N
Sched. 10 .... **Sched. 10**
para. 14(3) s.137N
para. 14(4) s.137N
para. 15 .... s.137N
para. 16 .... s.137N
para. 17(1) s.137N
Pt. I .... s.135(5), s.135N
Pt. II .... s.136(3)
Pt. III .... s.137(4), s.137N
Sched. 11 .... s.139, s.162(2),
Sched. 11
para. 5 .... s.139N
Sched. 12 .... s.140(5), **Sched. 12**
Sched. 13 .... s.144, **Sched. 13**
Sched. 14 ...... s.148(1), s.148N,
Sched. 14
para. 2 .... s.148N
para. 3 .... s.148N
Sched. 15 ..... s.162(1), s.164(5),
Sched. 15
para. 3 .... s.150N
para. 10 .... s.33N
para. 23 .... s.89N

1990 Environmental Protection
Act—cont.
Sched. 15—cont.
para. 28 .... Pt. IN
para. 29 .... s.20N
Sched. 16 ..... s.162(2), s.164(5),
Sched. 16
Pt. I ... s.1N, s.7N, s.15N, s.19N,
s.20N, s.25N, s.26N, s.66N,
s.147N, s.156(2)(a), s.158,
Pt. IN
Pt. II ..... s.6N, s.28(1), s.30N,
s.50N, s.63N, s.68N,
s.140(3)(a)(i), s.141(6),
s.144N,
s.156(2)(a), s.158, s.159(7),
Pt. IN, Pt. IIN
Pt. III .. Pt. IN, Pt. IIN, Pt. IIIN
Pt. IV .... s.158, s.159(7)
Pt. V .... s.164(4)
Pt. VI s.126N, s.127N,
s.156(2)(c), s.158, s.164(4)
Pt. VIII .... Pt. IIN, Pt. VIIN
1991 Planning and Compensation
Act (c.34) ...... s.50N, Pt. IIN
s.10 .... s.36N
s.42 .... s.36N
Water Industry Act
(c.56) .... s.1(11)(c)
s.118 .... Pt. IN
Pt. IV, Ch. III .... s.162N, Pt. IN
Water Resources Act
(c.57) .... s.22N, Pt. IIN
s.85 .... s.74N
(3)(b) s.1N
s.88(1)(b) .... Pt. IN
s.104(1)(a) s.1N
(d) s.1N
(4) s.1N
s.190 .... s.20N
s.202(4) s.74N
s.206 .... s.74N
Pt. III ...... s.1(6), s.1N, s.162N,
Pt. IN
Water Consolidation (Consequential Provisions) Act
(c.60)—
s.2 .... s.1N, s.7N
Sched. 1 .... s.1N, s.7N
1993 Radioactive Substances Act
(c.12) s.78N

TABLE OF STATUTORY INSTRUMENTS

References are to section and Schedule numbers

Where a section number appears followed by (N), this refers to the notes for that particular section or subsection.
e.g. s.33(N) refers to the General Note following s.33
s.33(5N) refers to the notes for subs. (5) of s.33

1975	Council of Noise (Appeals) Regulations (S.I. 1975 No. 2116)	s.81N
1980	Control of Pollution (Special Waste) Regulations (S.I. 1980 No. 1709) ..	s.33N, s.62N, s.74N, Pt. IIN
	reg. 14	s.33N
1981	Control of Noise (Code of Practice on Noise from Ice-Cream Van Chimes etc.) Order (S.I. 1981 No. 1828)	s.79N
	Control of Noise (Code of Practice on Noise from Audible Intruder Alarms) Order (S.I. 1981 No. 1829)	s.79N
	Control of Noise (Code of Practice on Noise from Model Aircraft) Order (S.I. 1981 No. 1830) ...	s.79N
1982	Control of Noise (Code of Practice for Construction Sites) (Scotland) Order (S.I. 1982 No. 601(S81))	s.79N
	Notification of New Substances Regulations (S.I. 1982 No. 1496)	s.142N
1983	Health and Safety (Emissions in the Atmosphere) Regulations (S.I. 1983 No. 943)	Pt. IN
	Merchant Shipping (Prevention of Oil Pollution) Order (S.I. 1983 No. 1106)	s.148N
	Control of Noise (Appeals) (Scotland) Regulations (S.I. 1983 No. 1455) ...	s.81N
1984	Control of Noise (Codes of Practice for Construction and Open Sites) Order (S.I. 1984 No. 1992)	s.79N
1985	Waste Regulation and Disposal (Authorities) Order (S.I. 1985 No. 1884) ...	s.30(4)
1987	Control of Pollution (Landed Ships' Waste) Regulations (S.I. 1987 No. 402)	s.62N
1987	Control of Noise (Code of Practice for Construction and Open Sites) Order (S.I. 1987 No. 1730)	s.79N
1988	Collection and Disposal of Waste Regulations (S.I. 1988 No. 819)	s.45N
	Town and Country Planning (Assessment of Environmental Effects) Regulations (S.I. 1988 No. 1199)	Pt. IIN
	Transfrontier Shipment of Hazardous Waste Regulations (S.I. 1988 No. 1562)	s.62N, s.74N
	Control of Pollution (Special Waste) (Amendment) Regulations (S.I. 1988 No. 1790)	s.62N
1989	Control of Pollution (Landed Ships' Waste) (Amendment) Regulations (S.I. 1989 No. 65)	s.62N
	Trade Effluent (Prescribed Processes and Substances) Regulations (S.I. 1989 No. 1156) ...	Pt. IN
	Sludge (Use in Agriculture) Regulations (S.I. 1989 No. 1263)	s.75N
1990	Sludge (Use in Agriculture) (Amendment) Regulations (S.I. 1990 No. 880)	s.75N
	Environmental Protection Act 1990 (Commencement No. 1) Order (S.I. 1990 No. 2226 (C.57))	Intro, Pt. VIIN
	Environmental Protection Act 1990 (Commencement No. 2) Order (S.I. 1990 No. 2243 (C.59))	Intro, Pt. IVN
	Statutory Nuisance (Appeals) Regulations (S.I. 1990 No. 2276)	s.81N, App. 6
	reg. 2(2)(g)	s.80N
	(h)	s.80N
	(i)	s.80N

TABLE OF STATUTORY INSTRUMENTS

1990 Statutory Nuisance (Appeals) (Amendment) Regulations (S.I. 1990 No. 2483) s.81N
Environmental Protection Act 1990 (Commencement No. 3) Order (S.I. 1990 No. 2565) .. Intro, s.162N
Environmental Protection Act 1990 (Commencement No. 4) Order (S.I. 1990 No. 2635 (C.74)) . Intro, s.159N, s.162N

1991 Environmental Protection Act 1990 (Commencement No. 5) Order (S.I. 1991 No. 96 (C.3)) .... Intro, s.162N, Pt. IVN
Litter (Fixed Penalty Notices) Order (S.I. 1991 No. 111) s.88N
Highway Litter Clearance and Cleaning (Transfer of Duties) Order (S.I. 1991 No. 337) s.86N
Environmental Protection (Prescribed Processes and Substances) Regulations (S.I. 1991 No. 472) ..... s.2N, Pt. IN, **App. 1**
Sched. 1,
  s.1.1 .... Pt. IN
  s.1.3 .... Pt. IN
  s.1.4 .... Pt. IN
  s.3.1 .... Pt. IN
  s.3.2 .... Pt. IN
  s.3.3 .... Pt. IN
  s.3.5 .... Pt. IN
  s.3.6 .... Pt. IN
  s.5.1 .... Pt. IN, s.29N
  s.5.2 .... Pt. IN
Sched. 3,
  Pt. I .... Pt. IN
  Pt. II .... Pt. IN
Sched. 5 .... Pt. IN
Environmental Protection (Applications, Appeals and Registers) Regulations (S.I. 1991 No. 507) ...... s.6N, s.11N, s.15N, s.20N, Pt. IN, **App. 2**
reg. 2(1) s.6N
    (2) s.6N
reg. 4 .... s.6N
    (1) s.6N, s.20N
reg. 5 .... s.6N
reg. 6 .... s.6N
reg. 7 .... s.21N
reg. 10 .... s.15N
reg. 11 .... s.15N
reg. 12 .... s.15N
reg. 13 .... s.15N
reg. 15(1) s.20N
reg. 17 .... s.20N

1991 Environmental Protection (Authorisation of Processes) (Determination of Periods) Order (S.I. 1991 No. 513) s.6N
Litter (Designated Educational Institutions) Order (S.I. 1991 No. 561) s.86N
Financial Protection for Environmental Purposes Order (S.I. 1991 No. 682) s.153N
Environmental Protection Act 1990 (Commencement No. 6 and Appointed Day) Order (S.I. 1991 No. 685) .... Intro, s.130N, s.131N, s.162N, Pt. VIIN
Environmental Protection (Amendment of Regulations) Regulations (S.I. 1991 No. 836) s.2N
Litter (Animal Droppings) Order (S.I. 1991 No. 961) s.86N
Environmental Protection Act 1990 (Commencement No. 7) Order (S.I. 1991 No. 1042 (C.27)) . Intro, s.156N, s.158N, s.162N, Pt. IVN
Litter (Statutory Undertakers) (Designation and Relevant Land) Order (S.I. 1991 No. 1043) .... s.86N, Pt. IVN
Financial Assistance (U.K. 2000 Scotland) (Scotland) Order (S.I. 1991 No. 1179) s.153N
Environmental Protection Act 1990 (Commencement No. 8) Order (S.I. 1991 No. 1319 (C.36)) . Intro, s.29N, s.30N, s.31N, s.32N, s.50N, s.51N, s.60N, s.68N, s.70N, s.72N, s.147N, s.162N
Street Litter Control Notices Order (S.I. 1991 No. 1324) .... Pt. IVN
Litter Control Areas Order (S.I. 1991 No. 1325) .... s.90N, Pt. IVN
Advisory Committee on Hazardous Substances Order (S.I. 1991 No. 1487) s.140N
Advisory Committee on Hazardous Substances (Terms of Office) Regulations (S.I. 1991 No. 1488) s.140N

Table of Statutory Instruments

1991 Environmental Protection Act 1990 (Commencement No. 9) Order (S.I. 1991 No. 1577 (C.42)) . Intro, s.49N, s.152N
Crop Residues (Restrictions on Burning) (No. 2) Regulations (S.I. 1991 No. 1590) s.152N
Environmental Protection Act 1990 (Commencement No. 4) Order (S.I. 1991 No. 2635) .... Pt. IN
Environmental Protection Act 1990 (Commencement No. 10) Order (S.I. 1991 No. 2829) ... Intro, s.33N, s.34N, s.52N, s.69N, s.70N, s.162N
Environmental Protection (Duty of Care) Regulations (S.I. 1991 No. 2839) .... s.34N, **App. 4**
   reg. 2(1) s.34N
   (2) s.34N
   reg. 3 .... s.34N
   reg. 4 .... s.34N
Nature Conservancy Council (Dissolution) Order (S.I. 1991 No. 2923) . Pt. VIIN

1992 Environmental Protection (Controls on Injurious Substances) Regulations (S.I. 1992 No. 31) s.140N
Environmental Protection Act 1990 (Commencement No. 11) Order (S.I. 1992 No. 266 (C.5)) .... Intro, s.45N, s.46N, s.47N, s.48N, s.52N, s.53N, s.55N, s.56N, s.73N, s.149N, s.150N, s.162N
Environmental Protection (Stray Dogs) Regulations (S.I. 1992 No. 288) s.149N
Litter (Statutory Undertakers) (Designation and Relevant Land) (Amendment) Order (S.I. 1992 No. 406) .... Pt. IVN
Environmental Protection (Waste Recycling Payments) Regulations (S.I. 1992 No. 462) .. s.52N, Pt. IIN
   reg. 2(2) s.52N
   (3) s.52N
   (5) s.52N
Controlled Waste Regulations (S.I. 1992 No. 588) .... s.75N, Pt. IIN
   reg. 2(2) s.34N, s.75N

1992 Controlled Waste Regulations (S.I. 1992 No. 588)—*cont.*
   reg. 3 .... s.75N
   (1) s.33N
   (2) s.34N
   reg. 4 .... s.45N
   reg. 5(1) s.75N
   (2) s.34N
   reg. 6 .... s.75N
   reg. 7(1) s.75N
   (2) s.34N, s.75N
   Sched. 2 .... s.45N
Environmental Protection (Prescribed Processes and Substances) (Amendment) Regulations (S.I. 1992 No. 614) .... s.5N, Pt. IN
   reg. 4 .... Pt. IN
   Sched. 2 .... Pt. IN
   Sched. 3 .... Pt. IN
   Sched. 4 .... Pt. IN
   Sched. 5 .... Pt. IN
   Sched. 6 .... Pt. IN
Environmental Protection (Controls on Injurious Substances) (No. 2) Regulations (S.I. 1992 No. 1583) s.140N
Environmental Protection Act 1990 (Modification of s.112) Regulations (S.I. 1992 No. 2617) ... s.112N
Genetically Modified Organisms (Contained Use) Regulations (S.I. 1992 No. 3217) .... Pt. VIN, **App. 8**
Environmental Information Regulations (S.I. 1992 No. 3240) s.20N
Genetically Modified Organisms (Deliberate Release) Regulations (S.I. 1992 No. 3280) .... s.112N, Pt. VIN, **App. 9**
   reg. 13 .... s.111N
   (2) s.118N
Environmental Protection (Determination of Enforcing Authority etc.) (Scotland) Regulations (S.I. 1992 No. 530) s.5N

1993 Environmental Protection (Controls on Injurious Substances) Regulations (S.I. 1993 No. 1) s.140N
Genetically Modified Organisms (Contained Use) Regulations (S.I. 1993 No. 15) .... Pt. VIN

Table of Statutory Instruments

1993 Environmental Protection Act 1990 (Commencement No. 13) Order (S.I. 1993 No. 274) s.35N, s.36N, s.38N, s.39N, s.40N, s.41N, s.42N, s.43N, s.54N, s.63N, s.64N, s.65N, s.66N, s.74N, s.162N

1993 Environmental Protection (Waste Recycling Payments) (Amendment) Regulations (S.I. 1993 No. 445) s.52N

Financial Assistance for Environmental Purposes Order (S.I. 1993 No. 1062) s.153N

TABLE OF EUROPEAN LEGISLATION AND TREATIES

References are to section and Schedule number

Where a section number appears followed by (N), this refers to the notes for that particular section or subsection.
e.g. s.33(N) refers to the General Note following s.33
s.33(5N) refers to the notes for subs. (5) of s.33

1967	Dir. 67/548/EEC (O.J. L196/1)	s.142N
1975	Dir. 75/439/EEC (O.J. L194/23) June 16, 1975	Pt. IIN
	Dir. 75/442/EEC (O.J. L194/39) July 25, 1975	s.75N, Pt. IIN
1976	Dir. 76/403/EEC (O.J. L198/41) April 6, 1976	Pt. IIN
	Dir. 76/464/EEC (O.J. L129/32) May 4, 1976	Pt. IN
	Art. 2	Pt. IN
	Art. 3	Pt. IN
	Art. 5	Pt. IN
	(3)	Pt. IN
	(4)	Pt. IN
	Art. 6	Pt. IN
	(1)	Pt. IN
	(2)	Pt. IN
	(3)	Pt. IN
	Art. 7(2)	Pt. IN
1978	Dir. 78/319/EEC (O.J. L84/43) March 31, 1978	s.62N, s.75N, Pt. IIN
	Dir. 78/176/EEC (O.J. L54/19) February 20, 1976	Pt. IIN
1979	Dir. 79/831/EEC (O.J. L259/10) October 15, 1979	s.142N
1980	Dir. 80/68/EEC (O.J. L20/26) January 26, 1980	s.1N, s.35N, s.37N, Pt. 11N
1984	Dir. 84/360/EEC (O.J. L188/20) July 16, 1984	Pt. IN
	Art. 2(3)	Pt. IN
	Art. 3	Pt. IN
	(2)	Pt. IN
	Art. 8	Pt. IN
	Art. 12	Pt. IN
	Art. 13	Pt. IN
1984	Dir. 84/631/EEC (O.J. L326/31) December 6, 1984	s.62N, Pt. IIN
1985	Dir. 85/469/EEC (O.J. L272) October 12, 1985	s.62N
1986	Dir. 86/278/EEC (O.J. L181/6) June 12, 1986	Pt. IIN
	Dir. 86/280/EEC (O.J. L181/16) June 12, 1986	s.10N, Pt. IN
	Art. 3(4)	Pt. IN
1987	Dir. 87/112/EEC (O.J. L48/31) February 17, 1987	s.62N
1988	Dir. 88/609/EEC (O.J. L336/1)	Pt. IN
	Art. 1	Pt. IN
	Art. 3	Pt. IN
	(1)	Pt. IN
	Art. 10	Pt. IN
	Art. 13	Pt. IN
	Art. 16	Pt. IN
1989	Dir. 89/369	Pt. IN
1990	Dir. 90/219/EEC (O.J. L117/1) May 8, 1990	Pt. VIN
	Dir. 90/220/EEC (O.J. L117/15) May 8, 1990	Pt. VIN
	Dir. 90/313/EEC (O.J. L158/56) June 23, 1990	s.20N
	Dir. 90/202/EEC (O.J. L105/27)	Pt. VIN
1991	Dir. 91/156/EEC (O.J. 78/32)	s.33N, s.34N, s.75N, Pt. IIN
	Dir. 91/157	Pt. IIN
	Dir. 91/689	Pt. IIN
	Dir. 91/869	s.62N

ENVIRONMENTAL PROTECTION ACT 1990

(1990 c. 43)

ARRANGEMENT OF SECTIONS

PART I

INTEGRATED POLLUTION CONTROL AND AIR POLLUTION CONTROL BY LOCAL AUTHORITIES

Preliminary

SECT.
1. Preliminary.
2. Prescribed processes and prescribed substances.
3. Emission etc. limits and quality objectives.
4. Discharge and scope of functions.
5. Further provisions as to discharge and scope of functions: Scotland.

Authorisations

6. Authorisations: general provisions.
7. Conditions of authorisations.
8. Fees and charges for authorisations.
9. Transfer of authorisations.
10. Variation of authorisations by enforcing authority.
11. Variation of conditions etc.: applications by holders of authorisations.
12. Revocation of authorisation.

Enforcement

13. Enforcement notices.
14. Prohibition notices.
15. Appeals as respects authorisations and against variation, enforcement and prohibition notices.
16. Appointment of chief inspector and other inspectors.
17. Powers of inspectors and others.
18. Power to deal with cause of imminent danger of serious harm.
19. Obtaining of information from persons and authorities.

Publicity

20. Public registers of information.
21. Exclusion from registers of information affecting national security.
22. Exclusion from registers of certain confidential information.

Provisions as to offences

23. Offences.
24. Enforcement by High Court.
25. Onus of proof as regards techniques and evidence.
26. Power of court to order cause of offence to be remedied.
27. Power of chief inspector to remedy harm.

Authorisations and other statutory controls

28. Authorisations and other statutory controls.

PART II

WASTE ON LAND

Preliminary

29. Preliminary.
30. Authorities for purposes of this Part.
31. Power to create regional authorities for purposes of waste regulation.
32. Transition to waste disposal companies etc.

Prohibition on unauthorised or harmful depositing, treatment or disposal of waste

33. Prohibition on unauthorised or harmful deposit, treatment or disposal etc. of waste.

Environmental Protection Act 1990

Duty of care etc. as respects waste

34. Duty of care etc. as respects waste.

Waste management licences

35. Waste management licences: general.
36. Grant of licences.
37. Variation of licences.
38. Revocation and suspension of licences.
39. Surrender of licences.
40. Transfer of licences.
41. Fees and charges for licences.
42. Supervision of licensed activities.
43. Appeals to Secretary of State from decisions with respect to licences.
44. Offences of making false statements.

Collection, disposal or treatment of controlled waste

45. Collection of controlled waste.
46. Receptacles for household waste.
47. Receptacles for commercial or industrial waste.
48. Duties of waste collection authorities as respects disposal of waste collected.
49. Waste recycling plans by collection authorities.
50. Waste disposal plans of waste regulation authorities.
51. Functions of waste disposal authorities.
52. Payments of recycling and disposal etc. of waste.
53. Duties of authorities as respects disposal of waste collected: Scotland.
54. Special provisions for land occupied by disposal authorities: Scotland.
55. Powers for recycling waste.
56. Powers for recycling waste: Scotland.
57. Power of Secretary of State to require waste to be accepted, treated, disposed of or delivered.
58. Power of Secretary of State to require waste to be accepted, treated, disposed of or delivered: Scotland.
59. Powers to require removal of waste unlawfully deposited.
60. Interference with waste sites and receptacles for waste.
61. Duty of waste regulation authorities as respects closed landfills.

Special waste and non-controlled waste

62. Special provision with respect to certain dangerous or intractable waste.
63. Waste other than controlled waste.

Publicity

64. Public registers.
65. Exclusion from registers of information affecting national security.
66. Exclusion from registers of certain confidential information.
67. Annual reports.

Supervision and enforcement

68. Functions of Secretary of State and appointment etc. of inspectors.
69. Powers of entry etc. of inspectors.
70. Power to deal with cause of imminent danger of serious pollution etc.
71. Obtaining of information from persons and authorities.
72. Default powers of Secretary of State.

Supplemental

73. Appeals and other provisions relating to legal proceedings and civil liability.
74. Meaning of "fit and proper person".
75. Meaning of "waste" and household, commercial and industrial waste and special waste.
76. Application of this Part to Isles of Scilly.
77. Transition from Control of Pollution Act 1974 to this Part.
78. This Part and radioactive substances.

PART III

STATUTORY NUISANCES AND CLEAN AIR

Statutory nuisances: England and Wales

79. Statutory nuisances and inspections therefor.

80. Summary proceedings for statutory nuisances.
81. Supplementary provisions.
82. Summary proceedings by persons aggrieved by statutory nuisances.

Statutory nuisances: Scotland

83. Statutory nuisances: Scotland.

Termination of existing controls over offensive trades and businesses

84. Termination of Public Health Act controls over offensive trades etc.

Application to gases of certain Clean Air Act provisions

85. Application to gases of certain Clean Air Act provisions.

PART IV

LITTER ETC.

Provisions relating to litter

86. Preliminary.
87. Offence of leaving litter.
88. Fixed penalty notices for leaving litter.
89. Duty to keep land and highways clear of litter etc.
90. Litter control areas.
91. Summary proceedings by persons aggrieved by litter.
92. Summary proceedings by litter authorities.
93. Street litter control notices.
94. Street litter: supplementary provisions.
95. Public registers.
96. Application of Part II.
97. Transitional provision relating to section 89.
98. Definitions.

Abandoned trolleys

99. Powers in relation to abandoned shopping and luggage trolleys.

PART V

AMENDMENT OF THE RADIOACTIVE SUBSTANCES ACT 1960

100.–105. [*Repealed*].

PART VI

GENETICALLY MODIFIED ORGANISMS

Preliminary

106. Purpose of Part VI and meaning of "genetically modified organisms" and related expressions.
107. Meaning of "damage to the environment," "control" and related expressions in Part VI.

General controls

108. Risk assessment and notification requirements.
109. General duties relating to importation, acquisition, keeping, release or marketing of organisms.
110. Prohibition notices.

Consents

111. Consents required by certain persons.
112. Consents: limitations and conditions.
113. Fees and charges.

Inspectors

114. Appointment etc. of inspectors.

115. Rights of entry and inspection.

Enforcement powers and offences

116. Obtaining of information from persons.
117. Power to deal with cause of imminent danger of damage to the environment.
118. Offences.
119. Onus of proof as regards techniques and evidence.
120. Power of court to order cause of offence to be remedied.
121. Power of Secretary of State to remedy harm.

Publicity

122. Public register of information.
123. Exclusion from register of certain information.

Supplementary

124. Advisory committee for purposes of Part VI.
125. Delegation of enforcement functions.
126. Exercise of certain functions jointly by Secretary of State and Minister of Agriculture, Fisheries and Food.
127. Definitions.

PART VII

NATURE CONSERVATION IN GREAT BRITAIN AND COUNTRYSIDE MATTERS IN WALES

New Councils for England, Scotland and Wales

128. Creation and constitution of new Councils.
129. Grants by Secretary of State to new Councils.

Countryside matters

130. Countryside functions of Welsh Council.

Nature conservation in Great Britain

131. Nature conservation functions: preliminary.
132. General functions of the Councils.
133. Special functions of Councils.
134. Grants and loans by the Councils.

Transfer of property, rights and liabilities to new Councils

135. Schemes for the transfer of property etc. of the Nature Conservancy Council.
136. Transfer to Welsh Council of certain property etc. of Countryside Commission.

Employment by new Councils of staff of existing bodies

137. Offers of employment to employees of Nature Conservancy Council and certain employees of Countryside Commission.

Dissolution of Nature Conservancy Council

138. Winding up and dissolution of Nature Conservancy Council.

Transitional provisions and savings

139. Transitional provisions and savings.

PART VIII

MISCELLANEOUS

Other controls on substances, articles or waste

140. Power to prohibit or restrict the importation, use, supply or storage of injurious substances or articles.
141. Power to prohibit or restrict the importation or exportation of waste.

142. Powers to obtain information about potentially harmful substances.
143. Public registers of land which may be contaminated.
144. Amendments of hazardous substances legislation.
145. Penalties for offences of polluting controlled waters etc.

Pollution at sea

146. Deposits of substances and articles in the sea, etc.
147. Public registers relating to deposits in the sea and incineration at sea.
148. Oil pollution from ships.

Control of dogs

149. Seizure of stray dogs.
150. Delivery of stray dogs to police or local authority officer.
151. Enforcement of orders about collars and tags for dogs.

Straw and stubble burning

152. Burning of straw and stubble etc.

Environmental expenditure

153. Financial assistance for environmental purposes.
154. The Groundwork Foundation: superannuation.
155. Remuneration of chairman of Inland Waterways Amenity Advisory Council.

PART IX

GENERAL

156. Power to give effect to Community and other international obligations etc.
157. Offences by bodies corporate.
158. Offences under Parts I, II, IV, VI, etc. due to fault of others.
159. Application to Crown.
160. Service of notices.
161. Regulations, orders and directions.
162. Consequential and minor amendments and repeals.
163. Financial provisions.
164. Short title, commencement and extent.

SCHEDULES:
  Schedule 1—Authorisations for Processes: Supplementary Provisions.
  Schedule 2—Waste Disposal Authorities and Companies.
  Schedule 3—Statutory Nuisances: Supplementary Provisions.
  Schedule 4—Abandoned Shopping and Luggage Trolleys.
  Schedule 5—[*Repealed*].
  Schedule 6—The Nature Conservancy Councils for England and Scotland and the Countryside Council for Wales: Constitution.
  Schedule 7—The Joint Nature Conservation Committee.
  Schedule 8—Amendment of Enactments relating to Countryside Matters.
  Schedule 9—Amendment of Enactments conferring Nature Conservancy Functions.
  Schedule 10—Transfer Schemes and Staff of Existing Councils.
  Schedule 11—Transitional Provisions and Savings for Part VII.
  Schedule 12—Injurious or Hazardous Substances: Advisory Committee.
  Schedule 13—Amendments of Hazardous Substances Legislation.
  Schedule 14—Amendments of the Prevention of Oil Pollution Act 1971.
  Schedule 15—Consequential and Minor Amendments of Enactments.
  Schedule 16—Repeals.

Commencement and territorial extent
  Details of commencement dates and territorial extent are given in the General Note of each Part of the Act in relation to that Part.

Environmental Protection Act 1990

The following are details of sections in force:

Section	Date of Commencement	S.I.
1	01.01.1991	1990 No. 2635
2	01.01.1991	1990 No. 2635
3	19.12.1990	1990 No. 2635
4–28	01.01.1991	1990 No. 2635
29–32	31.05.1991	1991 No. 1319
33(1)(c)	01.04.1992	1991 No. 2829
33(2)	01.04.1992	1991 No. 2829
33(3) and (4)	13.12.1991	1991 No. 2829
33(6)–(9) (partially)	01.04.1992	1991 No. 2829
34(5), (7), (8), (9) and (11)	13.12.1991	1991 No. 2829
34	01.04.1992	1991 No. 2829
45 (partially)	14.02.1992	1992 No. 266
45(1), (3)–(12)	01.04.1992	1992 No. 266
45(2) (Scotland)	01.04.1992	1992 No. 266
46	01.04.1992	1992 No. 266
47	01.04.1992	1992 No. 266
48(1)–(6), (8) and (9)	01.04.1992	1992 No. 266
49	01.08.1991	1991 No. 1577
50–51	31.05.1991	1991 No. 1319
52(1), (3)–(7), (9)–(11)	01.04.1992	1992 No. 266
52(8) (partially)	13.12.1991	1991 No. 2829
53	01.04.1992	1992 No. 266
55	01.04.1992	1992 No. 266
56	01.04.1992	1992 No. 266
60 (partially)	31.05.1991	1991 No. 1319
68	31.05.1991	1991 No. 1319
69–70	01.04.1992	1991 No. 2829
71, 72, 75 and 77	31.05.1991	1991 No. 1319
73(1)–(5)	01.04.1992	1992 No. 266
78	13.12.1991	1991 No. 2829
79–85	01.01.1991	s.164(2)
86(1), (4), (5) and (13)	01.04.1991 (Scotland only)	1991 No. 1042
86(1), (4), (5), (9) and (13)	13.02.1991 (England & Wales only)	1991 No. 96
86(2), (6), (7), (8), (11), (14) and (15)	14.01.1991	1991 No. 96
86(3) and (10)	01.04.1991	1991 No. 1042
86(12)	01.06.1991	1991 No. 1042
87(1), (2), (3)(a–e), (4), (5) and (6)	01.04.1991 (Scotland only)	1991 No. 1042
87(1), (2), (3)(a–e), (4), (5) and (6)	13.02.1991 (England & Wales only)	1991 No. 96
87(3)(f)	01.06.1991	1991 No. 1042
87(7)	01.04.1991	1991 No. 1042
88(1), (2), (3) and (4)	13.02.1991 (England & Wales only)	1991 No. 96
88(1), (2), (3) and (4)	01.04.1991 (Scotland only)	1991 No. 1042
88(5), (7) and (9)(b))	14.01.1991	1991 No. 96
88(6), (8), (9)(a), (c)–(e) and (10)	13.02.1991 (England & Wales only)	1991 No. 96
88(6), (8), (9)(a), (c), (d) and (10)	01.04.1991 (Scotland only)	1991 No. 1042
89(1)(a)–(f)	01.04.1991	1991 No. 1042
89(1)(g)	01.06.1991	1991 No. 1042
89(2), (3), (5), (6), (10) and (14)	01.04.1991	1991 No. 1042
89(4)	14.01.1991	1991 No. 96

Section	Date of Commencement	S.I.
89(7), (8), (9), (11), (12) and (13)	13.11.1990	1990 No. 2243
90(1), (2) and (7)	14.01.1991	1991 No. 96
90(3), (4), (5) and (6)	01.06.1991	1991 No. 1042
91(1)(a)–(f), (2)–(13)	01.04.1991	1991 No. 1042
91(1)(g)	01.06.1991	1991 No. 1042
92(1)(a)–(c), (2)–(10)	01.04.1991	1991 No. 1042
92(1)(d)	01.06.1991	1991 No. 1042
93	01.04.1991	1991 No. 1042
94(1) and (2)	14.01.1991	1991 No. 96
94(3)–(9)	01.04.1991	1991 No. 1042
95	01.04.1991	1991 No. 1042
96(1)	01.04.1991	1991 No. 1042
96(2) and (3)	14.01.1991	1991 No. 96
97	01.01.1991	s.164(2)
98(1), (5) and (6)	01.04.1991 (Scotland only)	1991 No. 1042
98(3) and (4)	01.04.1991	1991 No. 1042
98(1), (2), (5) and (6)	13.02.1991 (England & Wales only)	1991 No. 96
99	01.01.1991	s.164(2)
100–104	01.01.1991	1990 No. 2635
105 (partially)	01.01.1991	1990 No. 2635
105 (partially)	01.01.1991	s.164(2)
105 (partially)	07.12.1990	1990 No. 2565
106(4) and (5)	01.04.1991	1991 No. 1042
107(8)	01.04.1991	1991 No. 1042
108(1)(b), (3)(b), (5), (7) and (9)	01.04.1991	1991 No. 1042
111(1), (2), (4), (5), (7) and (11)	01.04.1991	1991 No. 1042
113	01.04.1991	1991 No. 1042
114(1), (2) and (3)	01.04.1991	1991 No. 1042
115(4)	01.04.1991	1991 No. 1042
122(1) (partially)	01.04.1991	1991 No. 1042
122(4)	01.04.1991	1991 No. 1042
123(7 and 9)	01.04.1991	1991 No. 1042
124–126	01.04.1991	1991 No. 1042
128–139 (save for the amendments made by sections 128, 130 and 132)	05.11.1990	1990 No. 2226
Amendments made by 128, 130 and 132	01.04.1991	1991 No. 685
140–142	01.01.1991	s.164(2)
143(1), (5) and (6)	14.02.1992	1992 No. 266
144 (partially)	01.01.1992	1991 No. 2829
145 and 146	01.01.1991	s.164(2)
147	31.05.1991	1991 No. 1319
148	01.01.1991	s.164(2)
149 (partially)	14.02.1992	1992 No. 266
149	01.04.1992	1992 No. 266
150 (partially)	14.02.1992	1992 No. 266
150	01.04.1992	1992 No. 266
151 (partially)	14.02.1992	1992 No. 266
151	01.04.1992	1992 No. 266
152	10.07.1991	1991 No. 1577
153–155 and 157	01.01.1991	s.164(2)
156 and 158	01.04.1991	1991 No. 1042

Section	Date of Commencement	S.I.
159	01.01.1991	1990 No. 2635
160 and 161	01.01.1991	s.164(2)
162 (partially)	14.01.1991	1991 No. 96
162 (partially)	01.01.1991	s.164(2)
162(1) (partially)	31.05.1991	1991 No. 1319
162(1) (partially)	01.04.1992	1991 No. 2829
162(1) (partially)	01.04.1992	1992 No. 266
162(2) (partially)	01.01.1991	1990 No. 2635
162(2) (partially)	31.05.1991	1991 No. 1319
162(2) (partially)	01.04.1991	1991 No. 685
162(1) and (2) (partially)	01.04.1991	1991 No. 1042
162(2) (partially)	01.01.1992	1991 No. 2829
162(2) (partially)	01.04.1992	1991 No. 2829
162(2) (partially)	01.04.1992	1992 No. 266
162(3)	01.04.1992	1992 No. 266
163	01.01.1991	s.164(2)

The Government's plans for implementation of the Act were given in DoE News Release No. 665 (November 28, 1990). A timetable was given in two parts: Pt. A sets the target dates for each subject area, whilst Pt. B gives the target dates in chronological order. These original target dates were subsequently varied in a number of respects.

PART I

INTEGRATED POLLUTION CONTROL AND AIR POLLUTION CONTROL BY LOCAL AUTHORITIES

GENERAL NOTE

The purpose of Pt. I of the Act is described in the Preamble as "to make provision for the improved control of pollution arising from certain industrial and other processes." The provisions of Pt. I establish two separate systems of control: integrated pollution control (IPC) and local authority air pollution control (LAAPC).

The two systems share a number of features, for example: the prescription of processes and substances for control; authorisations, which may be subject to conditions; enforcement powers; publicity provisions; and offences. However, in England and Wales IPC will be administered by Her Majesty's Inspectorate of Pollution (HMIP) under its Chief Inspector and in Scotland by Her Majesty's Industrial Pollutions Inspectorate (HMIPI), whereas LAAPC will be exercised by the "local authorities" as defined in the Act (s.4(11)). Further, IPC is to be exercisable "for the purpose of preventing or minimising pollution of the environment due to the release of substances into any environmental medium" (s.4(2)); LAAPC, by contrast, "shall be exercisable for the purpose of preventing or minimising pollution of the environment due to the release of substances into the air (but not into any other environmental medium)" (s.4(3)).

Background

The background to the proposals can be traced through a number of consultation papers:
 (a) *Integrated Pollution Control* (DoE/Welsh Office, July 1988), reaffirming acceptance of the position of the RCEP that wastes should be disposed of according to the Best Practicable Environmental Option and proposing "that a system of integrated pollution control (IPC) should be introduced for certain types of industrial processes that discharge significant quantities of harmful wastes." Such processes would be scheduled by the Secretary of State and HMIP would examine, and where appropriate authorise, the process technology and methods of operation to be adopted, and the levels of discharge into all three environmental media in the context of the environment as a whole. Such control should recognise two basic concepts:
  (i) that pollutants have effects in media other than those into which they have been released; and
  (ii) that reducing opportunities to dispose of a waste to one medium often increases the need to dispose of the waste (or its modified components) into one of the other

media. The proposed system was also intended to accord with the UK's E.C. and international obligations.

(b) *Inputs of Dangerous Substances to Water: Proposals for a Unified System of Control* (DoE/Welsh Office, July 1988) setting out the Government's proposals for tightening control over the input of the most dangerous substances to water. The paper proposed the use, for the first time, of technology-based emission standards, based on "best available technology not entailing excessive cost," applied to discharges to water of those substances identified as representing the greatest threat because of their toxicity, persistence and capacity for bio-accumulation. The paper identifies some 26 such substances ("the Red List") and makes the case for seeking to combine the environmental quality objectives (EQO) and uniform emission standards (UES) approaches. As with the IPC proposals, the suggestion was to introduce a system of "scheduling" of industrial processes discharging significant amounts of "Red List" substances, and the progressive application of technology-based emission standards to those processes. Possible models for the relationship between HMIP and the NRA were also discussed.

(c) *Trade Effluent Discharges to Sewers* (DoE/Welsh Office, April 1988) envisaged that the privatised sewerage utility companies would in future be responsible for granting consents in respect of discharges of most substances to sewers. However, dischargers of "Red List" substances would require authorisation from HMIP in addition to consent from the utility company. Two possible models for operating such a system were put forward.

(d) *Air Pollution Control in Great Britain: Review and Proposals* (DoE/Scottish Development Department/Welsh Office, December 1986) proposed retention of the principle of "best practicable means" but allowing its use to be adapted to take account of existing and prospective E.C. legislation. The proposal was to establish a common system of control, giving local authorities powers of prior approval over certain processes, with a system of consents setting out "the main elements of the bpm agreement by the control authorities." A "middle tier" of industrial processes was identified, where existing controls were seen to be inadequate or inconsistent with emerging E.C. legislation: these included the small ferrous-metal industries, plants manufacturing asbestos-based products or producing bulk glass and ceramics, hospital incinerators and "plants disposing of non-toxic and non-dangerous waste by incineration." "*Post facto*" control by nuisance powers was not regarded as suitable for such works; nor could planning conditions "enforce the ongoing good housekeeping and operational systems that are essential to proper control." Increasing account would need to be taken of E.C. and other air quality standards and emission limits.

(e) *Air Pollution Control in Great Britain: Follow-up to Consultation Paper of December 1986* (DoE/Scottish Development Department/Welsh Office, December 1988) summarised the responses to the 1986 Consultation Paper and indicated one major change in thinking on the part of the Government. This change was to combine the bpm and consent-based approaches, by setting conditions for certain aspects of a plant's control, while retaining the general bpm duty in respect of all residual matters.

(f) *Air Pollution Control in Great Britain: Works Proposed to be Scheduled for Prior Authorisation* (DoE/Scottish Development/Welsh Office, December 1988) sought comments on proposals for the precise definition of the processes to be scheduled for national and local control. A change of format in the designation of processes was proposed, having regard not only to the type of process (as previously) "but also to the end-product, in terms both of the commodity produced and the nature of the pollution." The intention was to make the new Schedule easier to use, and also to align it more closely in content with the provisions of E.C. Directive 84/360/EEC on the combating of air pollution from industrial plants (see later). That Directive requires that certain categories of plant be authorised before commencing operation and also subsequently if subject to significant modification. It also provides for the gradual improvement of existing plant to current standards, taking into account certain factors including "the desirability of not entailing excessive costs for the plant . . . having regard in particular to the economic situation of undertakings belonging to the category in question."

The main strands of Pt. I of the Act may therefore be discerned: an integrated approach to pollution of all three media; concentration on the most difficult or potentially problematic processes and substances; control by prior approval; specific conditions combined with a residual duty; the use of best available technology (later techniques) not entailing excessive cost; and the need to comply with E.C. requirements, specifically Directive 84/360.

Prescribed processes and prescribed substances

Processes may be prescribed for control by regulations, as may substances the release of which is subject to control (s.2). The Department of Environment prescribed two lists of processes, the "A list" being those subject to central control (IPC) and the "B list" being those subject to LAAPC. The lists were discussed in the consultative papers referred to above and issued for consultation in the context of the specific legislation in April 1990. Draft regulations under the Act were issued for consultation on November 5, 1990 and made on March 12, 1991 (the Environmental Protection (Prescribed Processes and Substances) Regulations 1991 (S.I. 1991 No. 472)). These have now been amended (by the Environmental Protection (Prescribed Processes and Substances) (Amendment) Regulations 1992, S.I. 1992 No. 614) and are reproduced as Appendix 1. In March 1993 the Government issued a Consultation Paper proposing a number of amendments to the 1991 regulations. This followed a review of the practical issues which have come to light in the course of implementing the regulations. It is likely that the amendments will be consolidated into replacement regulations. As well as prescribing the processes for central or local control, the regulations contain provision as to exceptions (reg. 4), rules for the interpretation of the prescriptive descriptions (Sched. 2), the date from which authorisation is required for the various processes (Sched. 3), and prescribed substances for release into the air, water and land (Scheds. 4–6). Sched. 1 to the regulations divides processes into six main industry sectors as follows:

Chapter 1:   Fuel Production Processes, Combustion Processes (including power generation) and Associated Processes
Chapter 2:   Metal Production and Processing
Chapter 3:   Mineral Industries
Chapter 4:   The Chemical Industry
Chapter 5:   Waste Disposal and Recycling
Chapter 6:   Other Industries.

Each Chapter is subdivided into main categories of process. For example, Chapter 3 (Mineral Industries) is divided into the following:

3.1   Cement and lime manufacture and associated processes
3.2   Processes involving asbestos
3.3   Other mineral fibres
3.4   Other mineral processes
3.5   Glass manufacture and production
3.6   Ceramic production.

Each sub-category is further divided into detailed descriptions of actual processes or operations falling within two sections. Pt. A (IPC) or Pt. B (LAAPC). For example, category 3.1 (cement and lime manufacture) is divided into the following:

Part A   (a)   making cement clinker;
         (b)   grinding cement clinker;
         (c)   various named processes associated with (a) and (b);
         (d)   heating of calcium carbonate or calcium magnesium carbonate for the purpose of making lime;
         (e)   the slaking of lime when related to a process in (d).

Part B   (a)   storing cement in bulk prior to further transportation in bulk;
         (b)   various processes involving blending, loading and bagging of cement, the batching of ready mixed concrete and the manufacture of concrete blocks and cement products;
         (c)   the slaking of lime for the purpose of making calcium hydroxide.

Quite clearly, disputes may arise as to the category or categories into which a particular plant falls. Sched. 2 to the 1991 regulations gives nine rules of interpretation, and indeed some of the sections of Sched. 1 themselves make specific provision to resolve such questions. Of particular importance are rr. 3 and 4 of Sched. 2.

Rule 3
This states that where processes falling within two or more descriptions set out in the same section of Sched. 1 under the heading "Pt. A" or the heading "Pt. B" are carried on by the same person at the same location those processes are to be treated as a single process falling within the description within which the principal process so carried on falls.

Rule 4
This states that where a process falls within two or more descriptions, the process shall be regarded as falling only within the description which fits it most aptly, but (a) if the possible descriptions include both Pt. A and Pt. B processes, no regard shall be had to Pt. B; and (b)

special rules apply for determining the category of process to be applied in the case of Chapter 4 (the chemical industry).

Regulation 4 of the regulations contains excepting provisions which in particular provide that a process shall not be taken to fall within Sched. 1 if it *cannot* result:
  (a) in the release to air of prescribed substances (or there is no likelihood that it will result in such releases except in a quantity "so trivial that it cannot result in any harm");
  (b) in the release into water of prescribed substances except in a concentration which is greater than the "background concentration" as defined in reg. 4(7); and
  (c) in the release into land of any prescribed substance.

The Government's original criteria for processes to be scheduled for IPC control are set out at para. 27 of the Consultation Paper of July 1988, *Integrated Pollution Control*. They are: (a) processes in Air Pollution Control List "A" (see above); (b) processes discharging "Red List" substances to water and sewers in significant quantities (see above); and (c) processes generating large amounts of special wastes (see Pt. II of the Act). The long term aim is to evolve a single coherent set of criteria related to potential for harm of the substances discharged, judged on the basis of toxicity, persistence, difficulty of control and potential for cross-media transfers.

The substances prescribed in Scheds. 4–6 to the regulations largely follow the previous proposals in the case of air and water. The substances proposed to be prescribed for air are those set out in the 1984 Air Framework Directive 84/360/EEC (see below) with the addition of a few others. For water, the proposed prescribed substances follow the "Red List" (see above). In the case of substances prescribed for release to land, the expectation was that criteria based on special waste generally would be adopted. However, the list adopted is in the event much narrower than the list of special wastes and appears to be based on substances which are likely to be particularly hazardous if disposed of directly to landfill (see ENDS report 190, November 1990, pp. 31–32).

It will be seen that the new systems involve a considerable number of processes and substances coming for the first time under prior control, though some will already have been controlled by HMIP or HMIPI for air quality purposes under s.5 of the Health and Safety at Work, etc. Act 1974 and the Health and Safety (Emissions in the Atmosphere) Regulations 1983 (S.I. 1983 No. 943).

It has been estimated that the new systems will bring some 5,000 individual plants under central control and some 27,000 under local control (12,000 industrial processes and 15,000 small waste oil burning appliances).

Functions of the Secretary of State

Apart from prescribing the processes and substances to be controlled, the Secretary of State has considerable powers in relation to the IPC and LAAPC systems. His functions include:
  (1) establishing standards, objectives or requirements (s.3(1));
  (2) making regulations to establish quantitative and qualitative standard limits on substances which may be released (s.3(2));
  (3) prescribing standard requirements for the measurement or analysis of prescribed substances, or their release;
  (4) prescribing standards or requirements as to any aspect of a prescribed process (s.3(2));
  (5) establishing quality objectives or standards for any environmental medium in relation to substances to be released into that medium (s.3(4));
  (6) making plans to establish limits for the total amount of substances to be released into the environment in the UK or any area of the UK, for allocating quotas as to the release of substances to persons carrying on processes where such limits are prescribed, and using such limits so as to reduce pollution progressively and to achieve progressive improvements in quality objectives and standards (s.3(5));
  (7) directing that functions being exercised by local authorities should be exercised instead by HMIP (s.4(4));
  (8) making regulations determining the allocation of functions between HMIPI and river purification authorities in Scotland, and consultation procedures (s.5);
  (9) giving directions specifying conditions which are or are not to be included in authorisations (s.7(3));
  (10) issuing guidance as to the techniques and environmental options that are appropriate for any description of prescribed process (s.7(11));
  (11) making with the approval of the Treasury, schemes as to fees payable for applications for authorisations and variations, and charges in respect of the subsistence of authorisations (s.8(2));
  (12) in England and Wales, making payments to the National Rivers Authority of such

Environmental Protection Act 1990

amounts as appears to be required to meet the estimated relevant expenditure of that authority attributable to authorisations (s.8(9));
(13) In Scotland, determining the amounts to be paid by HMIPI to the river purification authority in default of agreement between the inspectorate and the authority (s.8(11));
(14) giving directions as to the exercise of variation powers, and what constitutes a "substantial change" in a prescribed process for the purpose of those powers (ss.10(6) and (7));
(15) giving directions as to the exercise of revocation powers (s.12(5));
(16) giving directions as to the exercise of enforcement powers (s.13(3));
(17) giving directions as to the exercise of powers relating to prohibition notices (s.14(4));
(18) determining appeals or directing determination by an appointed person (s.15);
(19) making regulations as to appeals (s.15(10));
(20) in relation to IPC processes, appointment of inspectors and of the Chief Inspectors for England and Wales and for Scotland (s.16);
(21) making regulations as to procedures for sampling by inspectors (s.17(4));
(22) authorisation of other persons to exercise certain powers of inspectors (s.17(9));
(23) requiring information from enforcing authorities and any other persons (s.19);
(24) making regulations as to public registers of information to be maintained by the enforcing authorities (s.20(1));
(25) giving directions as to the removal of information from registers (s.20(6));
(26) determining whether the inclusion of information in a register would be contrary to national security and giving directions accordingly (s.21);
(27) determining appeals on whether information is commercially confidential so as not to require inclusion on the register, making regulations as to such appeals, and giving directions as to commercially confidential information which nonetheless should be included within the register on grounds of public interest (s.22);
(28) authorisation of inspectors to prosecute in magistrates' courts (s.23(5));
(29) approval as to exercise of powers by HMIP, HMIPI and river purification boards to remedy harm caused by offences (s.27(2)).

Authorisations, conditions and BATNEEC

Subject to transitional provisions made by regulations, authorisation is required to carry on a prescribed process after the date prescribed in the regulations (s.6(1)). The authorisation must contain such specific conditions as the enforcing authority considers appropriate for achieving certain stated objectives (s.7(1)(a)) and may contain such other conditions as appear to the enforcing authority to be appropriate (s.7(1)(c)). All authorisations will also be subject to a general condition as to the use of best available techniques not entailing excessive cost to minimise pollution (s.7(4)). These provisions are considered more fully in the relevant annotations, but the importance of the phrase "best available techniques not entailing excessive cost" (BATNEEC) should be noted. This phrase clearly requires more than simply the use of certain technology or equipment: it includes also adequate personnel and premises (s.7(10)). The Government published guidance on April 26, 1990 (DoE News Release No. 271) as to the interpretation of BATNEEC. It is clear from this guidance that the concept should in practice offer the measure of flexibility necessary to take account of local conditions and circumstances, both of the process and of the environment. As regards the issue of "excessive cost," a different approach will be adopted as between existing processes and new processes. In particular, the Guidance makes clear that BATNEEC is not the sole determinant of an application, but is "one feature of a complex of objectives." Thus, for example, regardless of BATNEEC, no release can be tolerated which would constitute a recognised health hazard, short or long term. Similarly, in reducing the emissions to the lowest practicable amount, account needs to be taken of local conditions and circumstances both of the process and of the environment, the current state of knowledge, and the financial implications in relation to capital cost. Explicit reference is made to the Air Framework Directive 84/360/EEC, which the system is to some extent intended to implement.

Guidance on the meaning of BATNEEC has been more recently set out again in the DoE's *Integrated Pollution Control: A Practical Guide* (1993, HMSO) reproduced as Appendix 3.

IPC and LAAPC Guidance

Published guidance is issued to inspectors and local authorities as to the application of IPC and LAAPC for the various classes of process: this includes reference to BATNEEC. The first step towards the provision of IPC guidance was the issue of five industry guidance notes by HMIP. These cover the main industry sectors as follows:
  1. Fuel and Power Industry Sector
  2. Metal Industry Sector

3. Mineral Industry Sector
4. Chemical Industry Sector
5. Waste Disposal Industry Sector

All five notes follow a common format of: (a) an introductory section; (b) details of the scheduled processes within the sector; (c) a list of relevant E.C. Directives and other international guidance and obligations; (d) further details of processes with reasons for scheduling, likely prescribed substances and major substances requiring control, and levels of release regarded as achievable with appropriate techniques under normal conditions; (e) details of available abatement technologies and techniques; and (f) emission sampling and monitoring.

The intention is that, based upon this general guidance for industry sectors, detailed process guidance notes for over 200 individual processes will be produced containing information about the characteristics of the process, why it is being prescribed and the particular features to which assessment, authorisation and subsequent enforcement have to have regard. The guidance also deals with the upgrading of existing processes and is introduced well in advance of such existing processes coming under control (see details as to implementation, below).

Chief Inspector's Guidance to Inspectors

The Chief Inspector of HMIP has already issued a series of Guidance Notes to HMIP inspectors: the Notes are intended both to provide guidance to inspectors in their functions relating to IPC authorisations, and for use by applicants and other interested parties as to the criteria against which inspectors will judge the acceptability of applications or variations and the types of conditions to be imposed.

The guidance takes two forms. Each main industry sector has a General Guidance Note: In addition, the intention is to issue Process Guidance Notes specific to each prescribed process. The relevance of the Process Guidance Notes is considered in the annotations to s.7 of the EPA 1990.

Each of the Process Guidance Notes follows a similar format, namely:
(a) An introduction, including a full description of the process.
(b) Standard general provisions on applications, authorisations and consultees.
(c) A section on release levels. This section applies the Standards in the Notes to new plant from the prescribed date. For existing plant, minimum standards are given for immediate application (based on existing or former statutory requirements such as the Alkali and Works Regulation Act 1906, the Clean Air Acts 1956 and 1968 and the statutory nuisance provisions of EPA 1990, Pt. III). A deadline is also given by which existing plant is to be upgraded to achieve the standards of the Note: earlier upgrading would be achieved where possible, for example were alterations are made to the plant. Only in "exceptional circumstances" should the deadline be extended, and as part of the first application for authorisation the applicant should provide the inspector with a detailed programme for upgrading or closing the plant.
(d) A section on releases into air, giving the technical reference conditions for concentrations of substances in emissions to air and stating detailed requirements for specific emissions (such as smoke, sulphur dioxides and oxides of nitrogen). The section also deals with monitoring; most figures are given for non-continuous monitoring, and for continuous monitors, the emission limit values are complied with if 95 per cent. of the half-hourly average readings for each rolling 24-hour period do not exceed the emission limit values, and the peak value does not exceed three times the limit value.
(e) A section on releases into water. Typically this states the relationship with environmental quality objectives set for controlled waters. It also states that limits may be expressed either as absolute maxima or as percentiles requiring a number of measurements over a defined period; percentile limits, where appropriate, will normally be additional to absolute limits for which compliance may be tested by a single spot sample. The total load of a pollutant discharged in a given time period should be controlled and monitored where appropriate.
(f) A section on releases into land where applicable, bearing in mind that the disposal of controlled waste off site and the consignment of special waste are the subject of separate legislation and should not be covered by the authorisation.
(g) A section dealing with what constitutes a "substantial change", to be read in conjunction with s.10(7) of the EPA 1990 and with the DoE publication: *Integrated Pollution Control—A Practical Guide* (see Appendix 3). Examples are given of substantial changes, contrasted with examples of changes that are not substantial but which will require a variation of the authorisation conditions.
(h) Annex 1, giving basic information on the nature of the prescribed processes covered by the Note currently employed in England and Wales. In some cases the description will be relatively simple, giving the characteristics of the process and noting the environmental

problems which may arise: an example is Process Guidance Note IPR 1/7 on *Combustion of Solid Fuel Manufactured from or Comprised of Poultry Litter in Appliances with a Net Rated Thermal Input of 3 MW or more*. In other cases the description may be complex, for example IPR 1/10 on *Carbonisation and Associated Processes: Smokeless Fuel, Activated Carbon and Carbon Black Manufacture*: this covers four main separate types of manufacturing operations, in some cases with separate types of process applied within each main category.

(i) Annex 2, listing the prescribed substances for release to air, water and land. Those listed are the substances most likely to be present in releases and of principle concern; the Notes point out that it is for the applicant to identify all releases of prescribed substances.

(j) Annex 3, giving the required techniques for pollution abatement: these deal with materials handling generally, and with releases to the three environmental media.

(k) Annex 4 on compliance monitoring: the term including sampling, analysis and testing as well as periodic and continuous monitoring. Again, releases to the three media are dealt with separately, and there are sections on quality assurance and general monitoring requirements. For example, preference should be given, where available, to analytical methods published by the British Standards Institute and related committees, *e.g.* The Standing Committee of Analysts.

(l) Annex 5 on "additional requirements", a number of which are standard form (for example, requiring use of properly qualified staff, the provision of process and waste flow diagrams and commissioning or other trials, and requiring a generally high standard of housekeeping. In some cases, more specific requirements will be added to this section, for example relating to water cooling towers or storage tanks.

Table of Process Guidance Notes

The following table lists Chief Inspector's Process Guidance Notes issued so far, with details of the main features, such as date for upgrading existing plant, prescribed substances, etc. The table is intended as a checklist and brief guide only and readers should refer to the Guidance Note themselves where appropriate (the relevant ISBN number is given in each case for convenience).

IPC PROCESS GUIDANCE NOTES

Process Guidance Note	Main Features
IPR1/1: Combustion Processes—Large Boilers and Furnaces 50 MW(th) and Over 1991 ISBN 0-11-752439-5	*Process:* Burning any fuel for the primary purpose of producing energy in a boiler or furnace with a net rated thermal input of 50 MW or more in any two or more boilers or furnaces with an aggregate net rated thermal input of 50 MW or more if they are so installed that waste gases may be emitted through a common stack (aggregate plants).
	Statutory reference: Prescribed Processes and Substances Regulations 1991, Schedule 1, section 1.3.
	Latest date for upgrading existing plant: Programmes for improvement to be achieved by April 1, 1995 or next review of authorisation whichever is earlier. All processes to achieve levels for new plant by April 1, 2001 at the latest.
	The Secretary of State intends to direct HMIP to impose conditions requiring retrofitting and use of Flue Gas Desulphurisation in respect of 8 GW of existing coal-fired station capacity; to be installed by December 1998 at the latest. Further FGD retrofits may be necessary to secure compliance with the UK's *Programme and National Plan for Reducing Emissions of SO_2 and NO_x from Existing Large Combustion Plants* (December 20, 1990) between 1998 and 2003; HMIP will be discussing with the operators a timetable for upgrading each remaining plant.
	Air
	Prescribed substances:
	— oxides of sulphur and other sulphur compounds

— oxides of nitrogen and other nitrogen compounds
— oxides of carbon
— organic compounds and partial oxidation products
— metals, metalloids and their compounds
— particulate matter
— halogens and their compounds.

Note:

Particulate matter:
1. Emissions should be free from visible smoke.
2. For new plant and plant in existence after July 1, 1987 the following requirements for particulate matter apply

Fuel	Calendar monthly not to exceed: (mg/m³)	No more than 3 per cent of all 48 hr averages to exceed in a calendar year: (mg/m³)	The average over 2 hrs continuous operation not to exceed: (mg/m³)
Solid fuel			
50–500 MW(th)	100	110	90
500 MW(th) or more	50	55	90
Liquid fuel	50	55	90
Gas fuel			
Methane, vaporised LPG, refinery gas, natural gas and other gas fuel	5	6	
Blast Furnace Gas	10	11	
Coke over and other steel industry gases	50	50	

3. For individual boilers and furnaces of 50 MW(th) and over burning solid fuel and all other plants in existence before July 1, 1987, emissions of particulate matter not to exceed 140 mg/m³ as an average over any 2 hours continuous operation. For individual boilers and furnaces burning solid fuel less than 50 MW(th) which form part of an aggregate plant less than 100 MW(th), the concentration of particulate matter not to exceed 300 mg/m³ as average over any 2 hours continuous operation.
4. For all plants, concentration of particulate matter from non-combustion sources not to exceed 50 mg/m³.

Sulphur dioxide:
5. For new plants and plants in existence after July 1, 1987 (with the exception of those burning solid indigenous fuel (see next note) the following requirements apply:

Fuel	Calendar monthly average would not exceed: (mg/m³)	No more than 3 per cent of all 48 hr averages to exceed in a calendar year: (mg/m³)
Solid fuel		
50–100 MW(th)	2000	2200
100–500 MW(th)	2000–4 MW(th)–100)	2200–4.4(MW(th)–100)
> 500 MW(th)	400	400
Liquid fuel		
50–300 MW(th)	1700	1870

300–500 MW(th)	1700–6.5(MW(th)–300)	1870–7.15(MW(th)–300)
> 500 MW(th)	400	440

Gas fuel

Liquified Gas	5	6
Low calorific value gases from refinery residues, coke over gas, blast furnace gas	800	880
All other gas fuel	35	38

5. For all new plants and plants in existence after July 1, 1987 which burn indigenous solid fuel and, owing to the nature of which, are unable to meet the requirements for solid fuel at note 4 above without using excessively expensive techniques, the following levels apply;

Sulphur dioxide (g/m^3)

Individual boilers/furnaces of 500100 MW(th)	2250 (calendar monthly average)
Individual boilers/furnaces less than 50 MW(th) forming part of aggregate plant less than 100 MW(th)	3000 (calendar monthly average)
For boilers or furnaces of 100 MW(th) or greater, the equivalent proportion of SO_2 removed compared with that contained in the fuel should exceed:	100 MW(th)–166 MW(th)–40% at 500 MW(th) and above–90% [Linear extrapolition from 166–500 MW(th) calculated from 40 + 0.15 (MW(th)–166)%]

6. For plants in existence before July 1, 1987, total annual emissions of SO_2 will have to be reduced to meet the National Plan (see above).

Nitrogen oxides:

7. For new plants and plants in existence after July 1, 1987:

	Calendar monthly average not to exceed: (mg/m^3)	No more than 5 per cent of all 48 hr averages should exceed in a calendar year: (mg/m^3)
Solid Fuel	650	715
Liquid Fuel	450	495
Gas Fuel	350	385

7. For existing plants before July 1, 1987 the total annual emissions of NO_x may have to be reduced to meet the requirements of the National Plan (see above). Low nitrogen oxide emitting burners to be fitted at first major outage, subject to any case to the contrary by the operator; where fitted the aim should be to reduce concentrations of NO_x by the maximum possible; achieving 650 mg/m^3 at all times.

Ammonia:

8. Where the ammonia or similar compounds are injected into the gas stream, concentration of ammonia in emissions to air should be kept to the lowest practicable value.

Water

Prescribed substances:

— cadmium and its compounds
— mercury and its compounds

Land

Prescribed substances:

— organic solvents
— halogens and their covalent compounds
— polychlorinated dibenzofuran and any congener
— polychlorinated dibenzo-p-dioxin and any congener
— alkali metals and alkaline earth metals and their respective oxides.

Examples of Substantial Change:

— conversion from oil firing to oil emulsion firing
— installation of flue gas desulphurisation plant, wet or dry
— increasing the amount of limestone feed to be fluidised bed combustor.

Examples of changes requiring variation:

— refurbishment or enlargement of an electrical precipitator
— installation of low nitrogen oxide burners
— increase of chimney height, final gas temperature or efflux velocity.

IPR 1/2: Combustion Processes—Gas Turbines
1992 ISBN 0-11-752569-3

Process: gas turbines with net rated thermal input of 50 mw or more.

Statutory reference: Prescribed Processes and Substances Regulations 1991 Schedule 1, Section 1.3.

Last date for upgrading existing processes: April 1, 1997.

Air

Prescribed substances:

— oxides of sulphur and other sulphur compounds
— oxides of nitrogen and other nitrogen compounds
— oxides of carbon
— organic compounds and partial oxidation products.

Note:

1. Emission to be free from visible smoke
2. Sulphur emissions controlled by sulphur content of fuel
3. Oxides of nitrogen in final emissions not to exceed 165 mg/m^3 for liquid fuel oils, 125 mg/m^3 for natural or petroleum derived gas, 125–165 mg/m^3 or lower if practicable for other fuels or for combinations of fuels.

Water

Prescribed substances:
None identified

Land

Prescribed substances:
None identified

Examples of substantial change:

— conversion from gas firing to oil firing
— use of oil beyond periods necessary to meet any interruptible gas contract
— significant increase in number of operational hours per calendar year.

Environmental Protection Act 1990

Example of change requiring variation:
— installation of low nitrogen oxide combustion
— installation of steam or water injection
— increase of chimney length final gas temperature, or efflux velocity.

IPR 1/3: Combination Processes in Compression Ignition Engines 50 mw(th) and over
1992 ISBN 0-11-757270-7

Process: CI engines of net rated thermal input pf 50 mw or more.

Statutory reference: Prescribed Processes and Substances Regulations, Schedule 1, Section 1.3.

Last date for upgrading existing processes: October 1, 1999.

Air

Prescribed substances:

— oxides of sulphur and other sulphur compounds
— oxides of nitrogen and other nitrogen compounds
— oxides of carbon
— organic compounds and partial oxidation products
— particulate matter.

Note:
1. Emissions to be free from visible smoke.
2. Levels for calendar monthly emissions of oxides of nitrogen given for existing engines and for new engines, now and from October 1, 1999/1996 respectively, based on burning residual fuel, distillate fuel and gas fuel. Figures range from 1800 mg/m^3 for existing engine burning residual or distillate fuel now to 250 mg/^{3} for new engines burning gas fuel from October 1, 1996. Figures for new engines from October 1, 1996 based on use of Selective Catalytic Reduction (SCR) or similar techniques.
3. Calendar monthly average emissions of hydrocarbons from any engine (expressed as carbon) not to exceed 150 mg/m^3 for residual or distillate fuel and 200 mg/m^3 for gas fuel.
4. Calendar monthly average emissions of carbon monoxide not to exceed 450 mg/m^3 for engines with thermal input of 6 mw or less; if input greater than 6 mw not to exceed 150 mg/m^3 for residual or distillate fuel or 450 mg/m^3 for gas fuel.
5. Sulphur content of fuel not to exceed given levels.
6. All emissions to be free of offensive odour outside processes boundary.

Water

Prescribed substances:

— cadmium and its compounds
— mercury and its compounds

Land

Prescribed substances:

— alkaline earth metal oxides

Examples of substantial change:

— changes in process operating parameters, *e.g.* temperature, pressure, rate of throughput
— changes in process equipment likely to change accepted operating conditions.

Examples of change requiring variation:

— increase of chimney height, final gas temperature or of efflux velocity
— installation or replacement of abatement techniques.

IPR 1/4: Combustion Processes—Waste and Recovered Oil Burners 3 mw (th) and Over
1992 ISBN 0-11-752571-5

Process: Burning of waste and/or recovered oil primarily for purpose of producing energy in an appliances with net rated thermal input of 3 mw or more.

Statutory reference: Prescribed Processes and Substances Regulations 1991, Schedule 1, Section 1.3.

Last date for upgrading existing processes: April 1, 1996.

Air

Prescribed substances:

— oxides of sulphur and other sulphur compounds
— oxides of nitrogen and other nitrogen compounds
— oxides of carbon
— organic compounds and partial oxidation products
— metals, metalloids and their compounds
— particulate matter
— halogens and their compounds

Note:

1. Emission to be free from visible smoke.
2. Emissions of particulate matter not to exceed 100 mg/m^3 from plant of up to 50 mw input, for plant over that input, such emissions not to exceed 50 mg/m^3 as calendar monthly average (not more than 3 per cent of all 48 hour averages to exceed 55 mg/m^3 per calendar year and average over 2 hours continuous operation not to exceed 90 mg/m^3).
3. Emissions of cadmium not to exceed 0.5 mg/m^3; nickel 1 mg/m^3; chromium, copper and vanadium 1.5 mg/m^3; lead 5 mg/m^3).
4. Emissions of acid gases not to exceed following limits:
   chlorine—100 mg/m^3
   fluorine—5 mg/m^3
   sulphur dioxide—2250 mg/m^3
   oxides of nitrogen—650 mg/m^3.
5. Concentration of PCBs in waste and recovered oil used as fuel not to exceed 10 ppm.
6. All emissions to be free of offensive odour at the site boundary.

Water

Prescribed substances:

— cadmium and its compounds
— mercury and its compounds

Land

Prescribed substances:

— organic solvents
— halogens and solvent compounds
— polychlorinated dibenzo-p-dioxin and any congener
— alkaline earth metal oxides.

Examples of substantial changes:

— conversion from oil to oil emulsion or waste oil firing
— installation of fuel gas desulphurisation plant.

Examples of change requiring variation:

— installation of low nitrogen oxide burners.
— increase of chimney height, final gas temperature or efflux velocity.

IPR 1/5: Combustion Processes—Combustion of Solid Fuel Manufactured from Municipal Waste in Appliances with Net Rate Thermal Input of 3 mw or more.
1992 ISBN 0-11-752572-3

Process: Burning of solid fuel made from municipal waste primarily for the purpose of producing energy in an appliance with a net rated thermal input of 3 mw or more.

Statutory reference: Prescribed Processes and Substances Regulations 1991, Schedule 1, Section 1.3.

Last date for upgrading existing processes: April 1, 1996.

Air

Prescribed substances:

— oxides of sulphur and other sulphur compounds
— oxides of nitrogen and other nitrogen compounds
— oxides of carbon
— organic compounds and partial oxidation products
— metals, metalloids and their compounds
— particulate matter
— halogens and their compounds

Note:

1. For new plant and plant which came into existence after April 1, 1991 releases not to exceed

Pollutant	mg/m^3
Total particulate matter	30
Hydrogen chloride	50
Hydrogen fluoride	2
Sulphur dioxide	300
Carbon monoxide	100
Organic compounds (total carbon)	20
The sum of lead, chromium, copper and manganese	5
The sum of nickel and arsenic	1
The sum of cadmium and mercury	0.2

2. New plants are subject to Directive 89/369/EEC on the prevention of air pollution from new municipal waste plants; derogation under article 10 is available in some circumstances, but prior written consent of Secretary of State must be obtained and emission values must remain as close as practicable to those given above and in no event exceed a separate table given at para 4.3.4.
3. Emission of PCDDs and PCDFs to be reduced as far as possible by progressive techniques and not to exceed a Toxic Equivalent Value of $1 \, mg/m^3$; the aim should be to achieve a TEQ value of $0.1 \, mg/m^3$.
4. All emissions to aim to be colourless, free from persistent mist or fume and from droplets and free of offensive odour outside the process plant boundary.
5. All emissions to be free from visible smoke and not to exceed equivalent of Ringelman Shade 1 (BS 2742: 1969)
6. Particulate matter in emissions to air from non combustion processes not to exceed $50 \, mg/m^3$.

Water

Prescribed substances:

— cadmium and its compounds
— mercury and its compounds.

Land

Prescribed substances:

— organic solvents
— halogens and their solvent compounds
— polychlorinated dibenzofuran and any congener

— polychlorinated dibenzo-p-dioxin and any congener
— alkaline earth metal oxides.

Examples of substantial change:
— change in authorised operating conditions in respect of type or quantity of fuel; temperature, pressure on other operating parameters; or equipment used.

Examples of change requiring variation:
— refurbishing or enlargement of an electrical precipitator, leading to reduction of emission of particulate matter
— increase of chimney height, final gas temperature or efflux velocity.

IRP 1/6: Combustion Processes—Combustion of Fuel Manufactured or Comprised of Tyres, Tyre Rubber or Similar Rubber Waste in Appliances with a Net Rated Thermal Input of 3 mw or More.
1992 ISBN 0-11-7525731

Process: Burning of solid fuel made from or comprised of tyres, tyre rubber or similar rubber waste primarily for the purpose of producing energy, in an appliance with a net rated thermal input of 3 mw or more, otherwise than as a process related to a Part B process.

Statutory reference: Prescribed Processes and Substances Regulations 1991, Schedule 1, Section 1.3.

Last date for upgrading existing processes: April 1, 1996.

Air

Prescribed substances:
— oxides of sulphur and other sulphur compounds
— oxides of nitrogen and other nitrogen compounds
— oxides of carbon
— organic compounds and partial oxidation products
— metals, metalloids and their compounds
— particulate matter
— halogens and their compounds

Note:
1. Emissions to air should not exceed the following levels:

Pollutant	1 tonnes/hr (mg/m^3)	1–3 tonnes/hr (mg/m^3)	3 tonnes/hr (mg/m^3)
Total particulate matter	100	100	30
Hydrogen chloride	250	250	50
Sulphur dioxide	—	300	300
Carbon monoxide	100	100	100
Volatile organic compounds (expressed as carbon)	20	20	20
Sum of lead, chromium (expressed as carbon)	—	5	5
Sum of nickel and arsenic	—	1	1
Cadmium	0.2	0.2	0.2
Mercury	—	0.2	0.2

NB: 1 tonne/hr is approximately equal to 10 mw thermal input

2. All emissions to be colourless and free from persistent mist or fume and from droplets; to be free from offensive odour outside the process plant boundary.
3. Emissions under normal operation free from visible smoke and not to exceed equivalent of Ringelman Shade 1 (BS 2742: 1969)
4. Concentration of particulate matter in emissions from non-combustion processes not to exceed 50 mg/m^3.

Water
Prescribed substances:
— cadmium and its compounds
— mercury and its compounds
— hexachlorobenzene
— hexachlorobutadiene
— polychlorinated biphenyls

Land
Prescribed substances:
— organic solvents
— halogens and their solvent compounds
— alkaline earth metal oxides

Examples of substantial change:
— change in authorised operating conditions as to type or quantity of fuel; temperature, pressure or other operating parameters; or equipment used.

Examples of changes requiring variation:
— refurbishing or enlargement of an electrical precipitator, leading to a reduction of particulate emissions
— increase of chimney height, final gas temperature or efflux velocity.

IPR 1/7: Combustion Processes—Combustion of Solid Fuel Manufactured from or Comprised of Poultry Litter in Appliance with a Net Rated Thermal Input of 3 mw or more
1992 ISBN 0-11-752574 X

Process: Burning of solid fuel made from or comprised of poultry litter primarily for the purpose of producing energy in an appliance with a net rated thermal input of 3 mw or more, other than as a process related to a Part B process.

Statutory reference: Prescribed Processes and Substances Regulations 1991, Schedule 11, Section 1.3

Last date for upgrading existing processes: April 1, 1996.

Air
Prescribed substances
— oxides of sulphur and other sulphur compounds
— oxides of nitrogen and other nitrogen compounds
— oxides of carbon
— organic compounds and partial oxidation products
— metals, metalloids and their compounds
— halogens and their compounds

Note:
1. Emissions not to exceed:

Pollutant	mg/m^3
Total particulate matter	100
Hydrogen chloride	250
Sulphur dioxide	300
Carbon monoxide	500
Volatile organic compounds (total carbon)	20
Oxides of nitrogen (No. 2 equivalent)	600

2. The aim, after further development work, should be to reduce carbon monoxide emissions to 250 mg/m^3 and oxides of nitrogen to 435 mg/m^3. A level for carbon monoxide may not need to be set "if other methods are used to secure efficient and effective combustion".
3. All emissions to air to be colourless, free from persistent mist or fume and from droplets. Emissions to be free from offensive odour outside the process plant boundary.

4. Emissions under normal operation to be free from visible smoke and not to exceed equivalent of Ringelman Shade 1 (BS 2742: 1969).
5. Particulate matter in emissions to air from non-combustion processes not to exceed 50 mg/m^3.

Water

Prescribed substances:

— cadmium and its compounds
— mercury and its compounds

Land

Prescribed substances:

— alkaline earth metal oxides

Examples of substantial change:

— change in authorised operating conditions in respect of type or quantity of fuel; temperature, presume or other operating parameters; or equipment used.

Examples of change requiring variation:

— refurbishment or enlarging of an electrical precipitator, leading to a reduction of the emission of particulate matter
— increase of chimney height, final gas temperature, or efflux velocity.

IPR 1/8: Combustion Processes—Combustion of Solid Fuel Manufactured from or Comprised of Wood Waste or Straw in Appliances with a Net Rated Thermal Input of 3 mw or more
1992 ISBN 0-11-752575-8

Process: Burning of solid fuel manufactured from or comprised of wood waste or straw primarily for the purpose of producing energy, in an appliance with a net rated thermal input of 3 mw or more, other than as a process related to a Part B process. "Straw" is taken to include any dry plant residues gathered from crops such as oil seed rape, as well as the stalks of cereal crops.

Statutory reference: Prescribed Processes and Substances Regulations 1991, Schedule 1, Section 1.3.

Last date for upgrading existing processes: April 1, 1996.

Air

Prescribed substances:

— oxides of nitrogen and other nitrogen compounds
— oxides of carbon
— organic compounds and partial oxidation products
— particulate matter
— halogens and their compounds.

Note:

1. Emissions not to exceed:

Pollutant	mg/m^3
Total particulate matter	100
Carbon monoxide	500
Volatile organic compounds (total carbon)	20

2. If the process burns treated or coated wood waste, also:

Pollutant	mg/m^3
Formaldehyde	5
Hydrogen chloride	100
Hydrogen cyanide	5

3. All emissions to be colourless, free from persistent mist or fumes and from droplets. All emissions to be free from offensive odour outside process plant boundary.
4. Emissions under normal operations to be free from visible smoke and not to exceed equivalent of Ringelman Shade 1 (BS 2742: 1969).
5. Concentration of particulate matter in emissions from non-combustion processes not to exceed 50 mg/m^3.

Water
Prescribed substances:
— pentachlorophenol and its components.

Land
Prescribed substances:
— halogens and their covalent compounds
— pentachlorophenol and its compounds
— alkaline earth metal oxides
— pesticides.

Examples of substantial change:
— change in authorised operating conditions as to type of fuel used; temperature, pressure or other operating parameters; or equipment used.

Examples of changes requiring variation:
— refurbishment or enlargement of an electrical precipitator, leading to a reduction in emission of particulate matter
— increase of chimney height, final gas temperature or efflux velocity.

IPR 1/9: Carbonisation and Associated Processes—Coke Manufacture
1992 ISBN 0-11-752576-6

Process: The manufacture of coke by the high temperature carbonisation of coal and the processing of by-products.

Statutory reference: Prescribed Processes and Substances Regulations 1991, Schedule 1, Section 1.2.

Note:
1. The manufacture of petroleum coke is covered in IPR 1/15
2. The manufacture of smokeless fuel, activated carbon and carbon black is covered in IPR 1/10.

Final date for upgrading existing processes: April 1, 1998.

Air
Prescribed substances:
— oxides of sulphur and other sulphur compounds
— oxides of nitrogen and other nitrogen compounds
— oxides of carbon
— organic compounds and partial oxidation products
— metals, metalloids and their compounds
— particulate matter
— halogens and their compounds.

Note:
1. For all plant, emissions of particulate matter from contained sources in normal operation should be free from visible smoke.
2. For all new plant and plant which came into existence on or after April 1, 1991, particulate matter in emissions from contained sources should not exceed

50 mg/m³ as an average over any 2 hours continuous operation.
3. For all existing plant before April 1, 1991, particulate matter in emissions from contained sources should not exceed 140 mg/m³ as an average over any 2 hours continuous operation.
4. For all plant the concentration of particulate matter in emissions vented to air from materials handling should not exceed 50 mg/m³.
5. For all new plant in normal operations there should be no emissions of particulate matter from non-contained sources.
6. For existing plant emissions of particulate matter to the air from non-contained sources should be minimised. Door Leakage Control Factor (DLCF) and Tops Leakage Control Factor (TLCF) should be evaluated and should not be less than 98 per cent.
7. For new plant the concentration of sulphur dioxide in emissions from the battery chimney should not exceed 800 mg/m³ as a calendar monthly average; for existing plant the concentration should not exceed the previous standard required.
8. For all new plant the calendar monthly average concentration of oxides of nitrogen should not exceed 350 mg/m³; for ammonia incineration plant, the concentration should not exceed 140 mg/m³. The emissions should be substantially colourless.
9. For existing plant, total emissions of oxides of nitrogen may have to be reduced; programmes will be set by the inspector in consultation with industry and the operator.
10. For new and existing plant the concentration of ammonia from all contained sources should not exceed 30 mg/m³.
11. For new and existing plant the concentrations of benzene from contained sources should not exceed 5 mg/m³.
12. For new and existing plant the concentration of hydrogen sulphide from contained sources should not exceed 5 mg/m³.
13. For new and existing plant the concentration of tar fume (measured as organic matter extractable by solvent) from contained sources not to exceed 5 mg/m³.
14. For new and existing plant emissions to air are to be essentially free from offensive odour as perceived at the site boundary.

Water

Prescribed substances

— cadmium and its compounds
— mercury and its compounds

Land

Prescribed substances

— organic solvents
— halogens and their covalent compounds
— polychlorinated dibenzofuran and any congener
— polychlorinated dibenzo-p-dioxin and any congener
— alkaline earth metal oxides

Examples of substantial change

— installation of more ovens
— change of gas desulphurisation from dry to wet, or installation of new plant

- installation of plant to incinerate ammonia gas/liquor or for flaring of excess undesulphurised gas
- installation of coke-side arrestment

Examples of change requiring variation
- installation of new oven doors with more reliable sealing
- adoption of sequential charging with installation of new charging cars
- installation of abatement or incineration equipment or vents from by-product storage and handling facilities
- increase in chimney height, final gas temperature, or efflux velocity
- refurbishment or enlargement of arrestment plant
- increase in size of coal gas purification plant not associated with a significant increase in amount of by-product for treatment in existing plant
- introduction of heat recovery in ammonia incineration plant.

IPR 1/10: Carbonisation and Associated Processes—Smokeless Fuel, Activated Carbon and Carbon Black Manufacture
1992 ISBN 0-11-752577-4

Process: Manufacture of smokeless fuel, activated carbon and carbon black.

Statutory reference: Prescribed Processes and Substances Regulations 1991, Schedule 1, Section 1.2.

Latest date for upgrading existing processes: April 1, 1998.

Air

Prescribed substances:
- oxides of sulphur and other sulphur compounds
- oxides of nitrogen and other nitrogen compounds
- oxides of carbon
- organic compounds and partial oxidation products
- metals, metalloids and their compounds
- particulate matter
- halogens and their compounds.

Note:

Smokeless fuel and activated carbon manufacture
1. For new plant, emissions of particular matter should not exceed 50 mg/m^3 as an average over 2 hours continuous operation; for existing plant the figure is 140 mg/m^3.
2. Emissions to air should be free from visible smoke at all times.

Carbon Black manufacture
3. For new plant, emissions of particulate matter should not exceed 20 mg/m^3; for existing plant the figure is 40 mg/m^3.
4. For all plant the concentration of particulate matter on emissions to air should be minimised.
5. Emissions to air should be free from visible smoke at all times.

Smokeless fuel and activated carbon manufacture
6. For new plant, emissions of sulphur dioxide not to exceed 800 mg/m^3 as monthly average; for existing plant not to exceed previous requirements.

Carbon Black manufacture
7. For new plant, sulphur dioxide not to exceed 2300 mg/m^3 as monthly average; for existing plant not to exceed previous requirements.

Smokeless fuel and activated carbon manufacture

8. For new plant, oxides of nitrogen not to exceed $350\,mg/m^3$; for ammonia incineration plant the figure is $140\,mg/m^3$ (both figures as monthly averages). The emissions shall be colourless. For existing plant, the total emissions of oxides of nitrogen may have to be reduced: programmes for such reduction will be set.

Carbon Black manufacture

9. For all new plant, oxides of nitrogen should not exceed $500\,mg/m^3$ (monthly average). The emissions should be colourless. For existing plant, total emissions of oxides of nitrogen may have to be reduced; programmes for such reductions will be set.

Smokeless fuel manufacture

10. For all plant the concentration of tar fume from contained sources (measured as organic matter extractable by solvent) not to exceed $5\,mg/m^3$.

All plant

11. Ammonia concentrations not to exceed $30\,mg/m^3$.
12. Benzene concentrations not to exceed $5\,mg/m^3$.
13. Hydrogen sulphide concentrations not to exceed $5\,mg/m^3$.
14. Emissions to air to be essentially free of offensive odour as perceived at site boundary.

Water

Prescribed substances:

— cadmium and its compounds
— mercury and its compounds.

Land

Prescribed substances:

— oxidising agents
— organic solvents
— halogens and their covalent compounds
— polychlorinated dibenzofuran and any congener
— polychlorinated dibenzo-p-dioxin and any congener
— alkaline earth metal oxides.

Examples of substantial change

— change of process of desulphurisation from dry to wet or installation of new plant
— installation of plant to incinerate ammonia gas/liquor or for flaring excess undesulphurised coal gas
— installation of additional carbonisation plant, or increase of throughput of existing plant
— alteration in technology resulting in change of raw materials of the process or plant and resulting in an increase in releases.

Examples of changes requiring variation

— installation of abatement or incineration equipment on vents from by-product storage and handling facilities leading to a reduction in emissions of odorous gases to air
— increase in chimney height, final gas temperature, or efflux velocity
— refurbishment or enlargement of arrestment plant
— increase in size of coal gas purification plant
— introduction of heat recovery in ammonia incineration plant.

IPR 1/11: Gasification Processes—Gasification of Solid and Liquid Feedstocks
1992 ISBN 0-11-752578-2

Process: The gasification of solid and liquid feedstocks where the primary objective of the process is complete gasification of carbonaceous materials to produce a gaseous product for conversion to substitute natural gas (SNG) or for direct use as a fuel. "Process" comprises the whole process including the treating, handling and storage of any materials used in, and products and wastes produced by the process.

Statutory reference: Prescribed Processes and Substances Regulations 1991, Schedule 1, Section 1.1.

Latest date for upgrading existing plant: There are at present no commercially operated gasification units either in use or planned in the United Kingdom.

Air

Prescribed substances:

— oxides of sulphur and other sulphur compounds
— oxides of nitrogen and other nitrogen compounds
— organic compounds and partial oxidation products
— metals, metalloids and their compounds
— particulate matter
— halogens and their compounds.

Note:

The concentration of the specified substances in releases to air should not exceed the figures below—

	mg/m^3
Sulphur dioxide (expressed as a 30 day rolling average)	2250
Sulphur recovery plants to be greater than 98 per cent efficient in mass of sulphur recovered	
Oxides of nitrogen (expressed as nitrogen dioxide)	650
Particulate matter	50
Hydrogen sulphide	1
Volatile organic compounds (excluding particular matter and the aim is to prevent releases expressed as total carbon)	
Organic sulphur compounds (expressed as total sulphur)	1

Water

Prescribed substances:

— cadmium and its compounds
— mercury and its compounds.

Land

Prescribed substances:

— organic solvents
— halogens and their covalent compounds
— polychlorinated dibenzofuran and any congener
— polychlorinated dibenzo-p-dioxin and any congener
— alkaline earth metal oxides.

IPR 1/12: Gasification Processes—Refining of Natural Gas
1992 ISBN 0-11-752579-0

Process: Refining of natural gas.

Statutory reference: Prescribed Processes and Substances Regulations 1991, Schedule 1, Section 1.1.

Latest date for upgrading existing plant: April 1, 1998.

Air

Prescribed substances:

— oxides of sulphur or other sulphur compounds

— oxides of nitrogen and other nitrogen compounds
— oxides of carbon
— organic compounds and hydrocarbons, including partial oxidation products.
— halogens and their compounds
— particulate matter.

Note:

The concentration of the specified substances in releases to air should not exceed the following figures:

	mg/m^3
Sulphur dioxide calendar monthly should not exceed:	
Fuel Type	
Liquid	1700
Vaporised LPG	5
Other gaseous fuel	35

As an alternative, for small sulphur recovery plants a mass emission limit may be set by the Inspector.

Where the size of plant permits, sulphur recovery should be greater than 98 per cent efficient in mass of sulphur recovered.

	mg/m^3
— oxides of nitrogen (expressed as nitrogen dioxide)	350
— Particulate matter	50
— Volatile organic compounds; the aim is to prevent releases (excluding particulate matter, and expressed as total carbon)	
— hydrogen sulphide	5

Water

Prescribed substances:

— mercury and its compounds
— cadmium and its compounds.

Land

Prescribed substances:

— organic solvents
— halogens and their covalent compounds
— alkaline earth metal oxides.

IPR 1/13: Gasification Processes—The Refining of Natural Gas at Liquified Natural Gas Sites
1992 ISBN 0-11-752530-4

Process: The refining of natural gas at liquified natural gas storage sites.

Statutory reference: Prescribed Processes and Substances Regulations 1991, Schedule 1, Section 1.1.

Latest date for upgrading existing plant: April 1, 1998.

Air

Prescribed substances:

— oxides of sulphur and other sulphur compounds
— oxides of carbon
— organic compounds and hydrocarbons
— halogens and their compounds.

Note:

1. The concentration of hydrogen sulphide in emissions to air should not exceed 5 mg/m^3.
2. The concentration of organic sulphur compounds in emissions to air should not exceed 1 mg/m^3 measured as sulphur.
3. The aim should be to prevent releases of volatile organic compounds (VOCs).

43 *Environmental Protection Act* 1990

4. The concentration of pollutants in emissions to air from combustion processes should meet the requirements in Guidance Note IPR 1/1 for gas fixed plant.

Water
Prescribed substances:
In normal operation there should be no prescribed substances released.

Land
Prescribed substances:
In normal operations there should be no prescribed substances released.

IPR 1/14: Gasification Processes—The Odorising of Natural Gas or Liquified Petroleum Gas
1991 ISBN 0-11-752581-2

Process: The refining of natural gas or liquified petroleum gas (LPG).

Statutory reference: Prescribed Processes Regulations 1991 Schedule 1, Section 1.1.

Latest date for upgrading existing plant: April 1, 1998.

Air
Prescribed substances:
— oxides of sulphur and other sulphur compounds
— oxides of carbon
— organic mercaptans and sulphide compounds.

Note:
1. In normal operations there should be no emissions to air of odorant.
2. During deliveries of odorant and prior to major maintenance there may be small omissions of sulphur dioxide from the odorant blanket gas flare incinerator.

Water
Prescribed substances:
None identified.

Land
Prescribed substances:
None identified.

IPR 1/15: Petroleum Processes—Crude Oil Refineries Liquified Petroleum Gas
1992 ISBN 0-11-752582-0

Process: Crude oil refineries and others which have the function of producing hydrocarbon based products such as liquified petroleum gases, petrol, diesel, aviation fuel, heating oils, lubricating oils and greases, bitumen and petroleum coke by the application of physical, physiochemical and chemical processing methods. These methods involve the removal of non-hydrocarbon substances, as sulphur, which may be useful by-products in themselves. Crude oil handling and storage facilities are also included.

Crude oils are made up of hydrocarbons of all chemical types, *e.g.* aliphatic, aromatic, saturated, unsaturated compounds and have wide boiling ranges.

Statutory reference: Prescribed Processes and Substances Regulations 1991, Schedule 1, Section 1.4.

Latest date for upgrading existing plant: April 1, 1998.

In addition, plants falling within the definition of "existing plants" in Article 2.10 of the Large Combustion Plants Directive (LCPD) (88/609/EEC) will need to comply with the UK's Programme and National Plan for reducing omissions of sulphur dioxide and oxides of nitrogen from existing large combustion plants (December 20, 1990, DoE) to achieve the overall reductions of emissions required by the LPCD. It is expected that for combustion plant on refineries, the normal process of applying BATNEEC when plant is upgraded or replaced will achieve the overall emission reductions required of the sector between now and 2003.

Air

Prescribed substances:

— oxides of sulphur and other sulphur compounds
— oxides of nitrogen and other nitrogen compounds
— oxides of carbon
— organic compounds and partial oxidation products
— metals, metalloids and their compounds
— particulate matter
— halogens and their compounds.

Note:

1. For non-combustion sources the concentration of specified substances in releases to air should not exceed the figures given below.

Prescribed Substance	mg/m^3
Hydrogen sulphide	5
Hydrogen fluoride	5
Volatile organic compounds	The aim is to prevent releases
Particulate matter (processing units)	100
Particulate matter (materials handling)	50

All emissions to air should be colourless, free from persistent mist or fume and free from droplets.

2. For combustion sources the levels in the Guidance Note for boilers and furnaces (IPR 1/1) gas turbines (IPR 1/.2) and compression engines (IPR 1/3) should be followed.

Water

Prescribed substances:

— cadmium and its compounds
— mercury and its compounds.

Land

Prescribed substances:

— organic solvents
— halogens and their covalent compounds
— organo-metallic compounds
— polychlorinated dibenzofuran and any congener
— polychlorinated dibenzo-p-dioxin and any congener
— alkaline earth metal oxides.

Examples of substantial change:

— the addition of any self-standing unit operation;
— the use of a higher activity catalyst permitting a higher throughput leading to an increase in releases to all media;
— an increase in the sulphur content of the crude feed with a resultant increase in releases requiring additional abatement requirement;

— a major (25%) debottlenecking of a unit requiring, for example, a larger furance and/or increased process water and/or an increased usage of catalyst leading to an increase in releases.

IPR 1/16: Petroleum Processes—On-shore Oil Production
1992 ISBN 0-11-752583-9

Process: On shore oil facilities whose basic purpose is to produce a sweet stabilised crude oil for export off-site.

Statutory reference: Prescribed Processes and Substances Regulations 1991, Schedule 1, Section 1.4.

Latest date for upgrading existing plant: April 1, 1996.

Air
Prescribed substances:
— oxides of sulphur and other sulphur compounds
— oxides of nitrogen and other nitrogen compounds
— oxides of carbon
— organic compounds and hydrocarbons, including partial oxidation products
— particular matter.

Note:
Particulate matter
1. For all plant, emissions should be free from viable smoke. Emissions of acid shoots should be prevented at all times including start-up from cold.
2. For all new plant and plant which came into existence on or after April 1, 1991 the following requirements apply:

Fuel type	Calendar monthly average should not exceed: mg/m^3
Liquid	50
Gaseous	5

For plant in existence before April 1, 1991, any emissions of particulate matter should not exceed any previous standard required.

Sulphur Dioxide
3. For all new plant which came into existence on or after April 1, 1991 the following requirements apply:

Fuel type	Calendar monthly average should not exceed: mg/m^3
Liquid	400
Gaseous	350

For all plant in existence before April 1, 1991 the omissions of oxides of nitrogen should not exceed the previous standard required.

4. *Hydrogen Sulphide*
For all new plant and plant which came into existence on or after April 1, 1991, emissions of hydrogen sulphide should not exceed 5 mg/m^3.

5. *Offensive Odour*
All emissions should be free from offensive odour as perceived outside the process boundary.

Water
Prescribed substances:
— cadmium and its compounds
— mercury and its compounds.

Land

Prescribed substances:

— organic solvents
— alkaline earth metal oxides.

Examples of substantial change:

— any operation where conditions change from sweet to spur on a permanent basis.

Examples of changes requiring variation:
— refurbishment or enlargement of arrestment plant leading to a reduction in release to any medium.
— increase of chimney height or of a final gas temperature or of efflux velocity.

IPR 1/17: Combustion Processes—Reheat and Heat Treatment Furnaces 50 MW(th) and Over
1992 ISBN 0-11-752584-7

Process: Reheat and heat treatment furnaces with a net rated external input of 50 megawatts or more or any of two or more furnaces with an aggregate net rated thermal input of 50 megawatts or more if they are so installed that waste gases may be emitted through a common stack.

Statutory reference: Prescribed Processes and Substances Regulations 1991, Schedule 1, Section 1.3.

Latest date for upgrading existing plant: April 1, 1996.

Air

Prescribed substances:

— oxides of sulphur and other sulphur compounds
— oxides of nitrogen and other nitrogen compounds
— oxides of carbon
— organic compounds and partial oxidation products
— metals, metalloids and their compounds
— particular matter.

Note:

1. *Particulate matter*

For all plant emissions should be free from visible smoke.

For all new plant and plant which came into existence on or after April 1, 1991 the following requirements apply:

Calendar monthly average should not exceed:	No more than 3 per cent. of all 48 hrs average should exceed in a calendar year	The average over 2 hrs—continuous operation should not exceed:
50 mg/m^3	55 mg/m^3	90 mg/m^3

For existing plant the emissions of particulate matter should not exceed 140 mg/m^3 as an average over any 2 hours continuous operation.

2. *Sulphur dioxide*

For all new plant and plant which come into existence on or after April 1, 1991 the calendar monthly averages should not exceed:

	mg/m^3
Liquid fuel	1700
Natural gas or other gas not given below	35
Liquified gas	5
Coke oven gas, blast furnace gas and other gases from the steel industry	250

43–33

For all plant in existence before April 1, 1991 the calendar monthly average should not exceed:

	mg/m^3
Liquid fuel	1700
Natural gas or other gas not given below	35
Liquified gas	5
Coke over gas, blast furnace gas and other gases from the steel industry	800

3. *Oxides of Nitrogen*

For all new plant and plant which came into existence on or after April 1, 1991 the calendar monthly averages should not exceed:

Air preheat °C	mg/m^3
Nil	650
400	900
600	1800
1000	3000

Water
Prescribed substances:
— cadmium and its compounds
— mercury and its compounds.

Land
Prescribed substances:
— polychlorinated dibenzofuran and any congener
— polychlorinated dibenzo-prodioxin and any congener.

Examples of substantial change:
— conversion from oil to oil emulsion as waste oil firing.
— installation of flue gas desulphurisation plant, either wet or dry.

Examples of changing requiring variation:
— the installation of low nitrogen oxide burners on existing plants
— an increase of chimney height, of final gas temperature or of efflux velocity
— installation or replacement of abatement techniques.

IPR 5/1: Waste Disposal and Recycling—Merchant & Inhouse Chemical Waste Incineration
1992 ISBN 0-11-752653-3

Process: Chemical waste incineration.

Statutory reference: Prescribed Processes and Substances Regulations 1991, Schedule 1, Section 5.1.

Last date for updating existing processes: December 1, 1996.

Air
Prescribed substances:
— particulate matters
— metals, metalloids and their compounds
— oxides of sulphur and other sulphur compounds
— oxides of nitrogen and other nitrogen compounds
— halogens and their compounds
— organic compounds and partial oxidation products
— oxides of carbon.

Note: For new plant the following limits apply to releases from contained sources

	mg/m^3
— volatile organic compounds expressed as total organic carbon	20
— total particulate matter	20
— hydrogen chloride	10
— hydrogen fluoride	2

— sulphur dioxide 50
— oxides of nitrogen (expressed as nitrogen dioxide) 350
— dioxins 1
— cadmium and thallium taken together 0.1
— mercury 0.1
— antimony, arsenic, chromium, cobalt, copper, lead, manganese, nickel, tin and vanadium taken together 1.0
— carbon monoxide: 50 mg/m^3 of combustion gas determined as a daily average value; 100 mg/m^3 determined as an hourly average value; 150 mg/m^3 of at least 95 per cent of all measurements determined as 10 minute average values taken in any 24 hour period.
— PCDDS and PCDFs should be reduced as far as possible by progressive technique, the aim being to achieve a guide TEQ of 0.1 mg/m^3

Emissions should not give rise to an offensive smell noticeable outside the premises and should be free from visible smoke.

Water

Prescribed substances:

— mercury and its compounds
— cadmium and its compounds
— PCBs
— other substances dependent on the waste being incinerated.

Note:

The flow weighted monthly average concentration in a final effluent should not exceed 50 mg/1 for cadmium and 20 mg/1 for mercury.

Land

Prescribed substances:

— organic solvents
— halogen covalent compounds
— organic metallic compounds
— PCDDs
— PCDFs
— PCBs
— PCTs
— PCNs
— Alkaline earth metal oxides

Examples of Substantial Change:

— an increase in rate on overall throughput beyond 5 per cent of the design capacity or the authorisation conditions;
— changes in the process operating parameters, *e.g.* temperature, pressure, type of feed to the incinerator; and
— changes in process equipment likely to change the accepted operating conditions.

Examples of change requiring variation:

— an increase of chimney height, or a final gas temperature or of efflux velocity (under a limiting value) on an existing plant and without an increase in the emission;
— upgrading of the combustion chamber
— the installation or replacement of abatement technology.

IPR 5/2: Waste Disposal and Recycling—Chemical Waste Incineration
1992 ISBN 0-11-752652-5

Process: Chemical waste incinerators on premises where there is plant designed to incinerate such waste at a rate of 1 tonne or more per hour.

Statutory reference: Prescribed Processes and Substances Regulations 1991, Schedule 1, Section 5.1.

Last date for upgrading existing processes: December 1, 1996.

Air

Prescribed substances:
— particulate matter
— metals, metalloids and their compounds
— oxides of sulphur and other sulphur compounds
— oxides of carbon
— Halogens and their compounds
— organic compounds and partial oxidation products.

Note: For new plant the following limits apply to releases from contained sources:

	mg/m^3
— total particulate matter	30
— volatile organic compounds (excluding particulate matter) expressed as carbon	20
— hydrogen chloride	30
— hydrogen fluoride	2
— sulphur dioxide	300
— oxides of nitrogen (expressed as nitrogen dioxide)	350
— dioxins	$1mg/m^3$
— cadmium	0.1
— mercury	0.1
— arsenic, chromium, copper, lead, manganese, nickel, and tin taken together	1.0

— carbon monoxide—$50\,mg/m^3$ of combustion gas determined as a daily average value; $100\,mg/m^3$ at least 95 per cent of all measurements determined as 10 minute average values taken in any 24 hour period.
— The emission of PCDDs and PCDFs should be reduced as far as possible by progressive techniques, the aim being a TEQ value of $0.1\,ng^3$
— Emissions from the process should not give rise to an offensive small noticeable outside the premises and should be free from visible smoke.

Water

Prescribed substances:
— mercury and its compounds
— cadmium and its compounds.

The flow weighted average monthly concentration in a final effluent not to exceed $50\,mg/l$ for cadmium and $20\,mg/l$ for mercury.

Land

Prescribed substances:
— organic metallic compounds
— PCDDs
— PCBs
— Alkaline earth metal oxides.

Examples of Substantial Change:
— an increase in part or overall throughput beyond 5 per cent of the design capacity or the authorisation conditions;

— changes in the process operating parameters, *e.g.* temperature, pressure; and
— changes in process equipment likely to change the accepted operating conditions.

Changes requiring variation:
— an increasing of chimney height, or of final gas temperature or of efflux velocity (under a limiting value) on an existing plant and without an increase in the emission;
— upgrading of the combustion chamber; and
— the installation or replacement of abatement technology.

IPR 5/3: Waste Disposal and Recycling—Municipal Waste Incineration
1992 ISBN 0-11-752649-5

Process: Municipal waste incinerators with a capacity of 1 tonne or more per hour.

Statutory Reference:
Prescribed Processes Regulations 1991, Schedule 1, Section 5.1.

Last date for upgrading existing processes: December 1, 1996.

Air

Prescribed substances:
— particulate matter
— metals, metalloids and their compounds
— oxide of sulphur and other sulphur compounds
— oxides of nitrogen and other nitrogen compounds
— oxides of carbon
— halogens and their compounds
— organic compounds and partial oxidation products.

For all new plant limits apply to releases from contained sources.

	mg/m^3
— total particulate matter	30
— volatile organic compounds (excluding particulate matter) expressed as carbon	20
— sulphur dioxide	300
— oxides of nitrogen (expressed as nitrogen dioxide)	350
— hydrogen chloride	30
— hydrogen fluoride	2
— dioxins	$1\,ng/m^3$
— arsenic, chromium, copper, lead, manganese, nickel, and tin taken together	1.0
— cadmium	0.1
— mercury	0.1
— carbon monoxide.	

By December 1, 1988 existing plant with a capacity of at least 6 tonnes per hour must comply with the following combustion conditions: the gases, resulting from the combustion of the waste must be raised to at least 850°C for at least two seconds in the presence of at least 6°C oxygen. Other plant must comply by December 1, 1995.

Carbon Monoxide:
The concentration should not exceed $100\,mg/m^3$ of combustion gas determined as an hourly average value; 150 mg/m of at least 95 per cent of all measurements determined as 10 minute average values taken in any 24 hour period.

Dioxins:

PCCDs and PCDFs should be reduced as far as possible by progressive techniques, the aim being to achieve a guide TEQ value of 0.1 ng/m^3.

Odours and Smoke:

The process should not give rise to an offensive smell noticeable outside the premises where the process is carried on and should be free from visible smoke.

Water

Prescribed substances:

— substances listed in Schedule 5 to the Prescribed Processes and Substances Regulations 1991 Emission limits specified for:

ng/l	*Spot Sample* Sample	*Monthly* ng/l
— dieldrin	100	50
— Gamma-hexachlorocylohexane	100	100
— polychlorinated biphenyls	100	50
— trifluralin	50	50
— hexachlorobenzene	400	300
— hexachlobutadiene	50	50
— trichlorobenzene	50	50
— dichlorvos	50	50
— fenitrothion	100	100
— simazine	400	300
— atrazine	400	300
— pentachlorophenol and its compounds	500	300
— tributyltin compounds	200	100
— triphenyltin compounds	200	100
— total cadmium	60,000	50,000
— total mercury	15,000	20,000

Land

Prescribed substances:

PCDDs
PCDFs
PCBs
Alkaline and earth metal oxides.

Examples of substantial change:

— an increase in rate on overall throughput beyond 5 per cent of the design capacity or the authorisation conditions;
— changes in the process operating parameters, *e.g.* temperature, pressure, type of waste fed to the incinerator; and
— changes in the process equipment likely to change the accepted operating conditions.

Examples of change requiring variation:

— an increase in chimney height, or of final gas temperature or of efflux velocity (under a limiting value) on an existing plant and without an increase in the emission;
— upgrading of the combustion chamber; and
— the installation on replacement of abatement technology.

IPR 5/4: Waste Disposal or Recycling—Animal Carcass Incineration
1992 ISBN 0-11-752654-1

Process: Incineration of animal carcasses on plant designed to incinerate such waste of a rate of 1 tonne or more per hour.

Statutory reference: Prescribed Processes and Substances Regulations 1991, Schedule 1, Section 5.1.

Last date for upgrading existing processes: December 1, 1996.

Air

Prescribed substances:

— particulate matter
— oxides of sulphur and other sulphur compounds
— oxides of nitrogen and other nitrogen compounds
— oxides of carbon
— halogens and their compounds
— organic compounds and partial oxidation products.

Emission limits on new plants specified for:

	mg/m^3
— total particulate matters	100
— hydrogen chloride	30
— sulphur dioxide	300
— dioxins	1 ng/m^3
— carbon monoxide	

Carbon Monoxide:

The concentration not to exceed 100 mg/m^3 of combustion gas determined as an hourly average value; 150 mg/^3 at least 95 per cent of all measurements determined as 10 minute average values taken in any 24 hour period.

Dioxins:

Emission of PCDDs and PCDFs to be reduced as far as possible by progressive techniques, the aim being to achieve a TEQ value of 0.1 ng/m^3.

Note:

The process should not give rise to an offensive smell noticeable outside the premises and should be free from visible smoke.

Water

Prescribed substances:

— None identified.

The flow weighted monthly average concentration in a final effluent not to exceed 50 mg/1 for cadmium or 20 mg/1 for mercury.

Land

Prescribed substances:

None specified.

Examples of substantial change:

— an increase in rate of overall throughput beyond 5 per cent of the design capacity or the authorisation conditions;
— changes in process operating parameters, *e.g.* temperature, pressure, type of materials fed to the incinerator;
— changes in process equipment likely to change the accepted operating conditions.

Changes requiring variation:
— an increase of chimney height, or of final gas temperature or of efflux velocity (under a limiting value) on an existing plant, without an increase in the emission;
— upgrading the combustion chamber;
— installation or replacement of abatement technology.

IPR 5/5: Waste Disposal & Recycling—The Burning Out of Metal Containers
1992 ISBN 0-11-752651-7

Process: The cleaning for reuse of metal containers used for the transport or storage of a chemical by burning out their residual content.

Statutory reference: Prescribed Processes and Substances Regulations 1991, Schedule 1, Section 5.1.

Last date for upgrading existing processes: December 1, 1996.

Air

Prescribed substances:
— particulate matter
— metals, metalloids and their compounds
— oxides of sulphur and other sulphur compounds
— oxides of nitrogen and other nitrogen compounds
— oxides of carbon
— organic compounds and partial oxidation products
— halogens and their compounds
— Emission limits specified for:

	mg/m^3
Total particulate matter	30
Hydrogen chloride	30
Sulphur dioxide	800
Dioxins	$1\,ng/m^3$
Antimony, arsenic, cadmium, chromium, cobalt, copper, lead, manganese, nickel, thallium, tin and vanadium taken together	$4\,mg/m^3$

Carbon monoxide—$100\,mg/m^3$ of combustion gas determined as hourly average value; and $150\,mg/m^3$ at least 95 per cent of all measurements determined as 10 minute average values taken in any 24 hour period.

Dioxins:
The emission of PCDDs and PCDFs to be reduced as far as possible, the aim being to achieve a guide TEQ value of $0.1\,ng/^3$.

Note: The process should not give rise to an offensive smell outside the premises where the process is carried on and should be free from visible smoke.

Water

Prescribed substances:
— mercury and its compounds
— cadmium and its compounds

The flow weighted monthly average concentration in a final effluent not to exceed $50\,mg/l$ for cadmium or $20\,mg/l$ for mercury.

Land

Prescribed substances:
— organic solvents
— alkaline earth metal oxides.

Examples of substantial change
— an increase in rate or overall throughput beyond 5 per cent of the design capacity or the authorisation conditions;

— changes in the operating parameters, *e.g.* temperature, pressure, rate of production or feedstock; and
— changes in the process equipment

Examples of change requiring variation:
— an increase in height of discharge, or of final gas temperature or of efflux velocity (within a limiting value) on an existing plant and without an accompanying increase in the emission; and
— the installation or replacement of abatement technology.

IPR 5/6: Waste Disposal & Recycling—Making Solid Fuel From Waste
1992 ISBN 0-11-752647-9

Process: Production of fuel from waste by any process involving the use of heat, other than the making of charcoal.

Statutory Reference: Prescribed Processes and Substances Regulations 1991, Schedule 1, Section 5.3.

Last date for upgrading existing processes: December 1, 1996.

Air

Prescribed substances:
— particulate matter.

For new plant limits apply to releases from contained sources.

	mg/m^3
— total particulate matter	50
— arsenic, chromium, copper, lead, manganese, nickel, and tin taken together	1.0
— cadmium	0.1
— mercury	0.1

Note: Emissions should not give rise to an offensive smell noticeable outside the premises where the process is carried on.

Water

Prescribed substances:

— mercury and its compounds
— cadmium and its compounds

The flow weighted monthly average concentration in a final effluent not to exceed 50 mg/l for cadmium or 30 mg/l for mercury.

Land

Prescribed substances:
None specified.

Examples of substantial change:
— an increase in rate or overall throughput beyond 5 per cent of the design capacity or the authorisation conditions;
— change in the process operating parameter, *e.g.* temperature, pressure, type of foodstock; and
— changes in process equipment likely to change the accepted operating conditions.

Examples of change requiring variation:
— an increase in the height of discharge of an existing plant and without an accompanying increase in the emission; and
— the installation or replacement of abatement technology.

IPR 5/7: Waste Disposal and Recycling—Cleaning and Regeneration of Carbon
1992 ISBN 0-11-752655-X

Process: Cleaning or regeneration of carbon.

Statutory reference: Prescribed Processes and Substances Regulations 1991, Schedule 1, Section 5.2.

Last date for upgrading existing processes: December 1, 1996.

Air

Prescribed substances:
— particulate matters
— metals, metalloids and their compounds
— oxides of sulphur and sulphur compounds
— oxides of nitrogen and nitrogen compounds
— oxides of carbon
— halogens and their compounds
— organic compounds and partial oxidation products.

	mg/m^3
— total particulate matter	20
— hydrogen sulphide	30
— sulphur dioxide	300
— oxides of nitrogen (expressed as nitrogen dioxide)	650
— carbon monoxide	50
— volatile organic compounds (excluding particulate matter) expressed as carbon	20

— dioxins—PCDDs and PCDFs should be reduced as far as possible, the aim being to achieve a guide TEQ value of $0.1 \, ng/^3$.

Note:
Emissions from the process should not give rise to an offensive smell noticeable outside the premises and should be free from visible smoke.

Water

Prescribed substances:
The flow weighted monthly average concentration in a final effluent not to exceed 50 mg/1 for cadmium or 20 mg/1 for mercury.

Land

Prescribed substances:
None specified.

Examples of substantial change:
— an increase in rate or overall throughput beyond 5 per cent of the design capacity or the authorisation conditions;
— changes in the operating parameters, *e.g.* feedstock; and
— changes in the process equipment likely to affect the releases to any media.

IPR 5/8: Waste Disposal and Recycling—Recovery of Organic Solvents by Distillation
1992 ISBN 0-11-752645-2

Process: Recovery of organic solvents by distillation.

Statutory reference: Prescribed Processes and Substances Regulations 1991, Schedule 1, Section 5.2.

Last date for upgrading existing processes: December 1, 1996.

Air

Prescribed Processes:
— oxides of sulphur and other sulphur compounds
— oxides of nitrogen and other nitrogen compounds

- oxides of carbon
- halogens and their compounds
- organic compounds and partial oxidation products.

For new plant limits apply to releases from contained sources:

	mg/m^3
— volatile organic compounds (excluding particulate matter) expressed as carbon	50
— ammonia	10
— amines	5
— hydrogen sulphide	1
— volatile organic sulphur compounds	1

Note:

Emissions should not give rise to an offensive smell outside the premises where the process is carried on.

Water

Prescribed substances:

- PCBs
- 1,2 Dichloroethane
- Hexachlorobenzene
- Hexachlorobutadiene
- Trichlorobenzene

The flow weighted monthly average concentration in a final effluent should not exceed 50 mg/1 for mercury.

Land

Prescribed substances:

- organic solvents
- halogens and their covalent compounds
- organic-metallic compounds
- PCDDs
- PCDFs
- PCBs
- PCTs
- PCNs
- alkaline earth metal oxides.

Examples of substantial change:

- an increase in rate or overall throughput beyond 5 per cent of the design capacity or the authorisation conditions;
- changes in the operating parameters, *e.g.* temperature, pressure, rate of production or feedstock; and
- changes in the process equipment.

Examples of changes requiring variation:

- an increase in the height of discharge, or of final gas temperature or of efflux velocity (within a limiting value) an accompanying increase in the emission; and
- the installation or replacement of abatement technology.

IPR 5/9: Waste Disposal and Recycling—Regeneration of Ion Exchange Resins
1992 ISBN 0-11-752650-9

Process: The regeneration of ion exchange resins.

Statutory reference: Prescribed Processes and Substances Regulations 1991, Schedule 1, Section 5.2.

Last date for upgrading existing processes: December 1, 1996.

Air

Prescribed substances:
— carbon dioxide.

Water

Prescribed substances:
The flow weighted monthly average concentration in a final effluent should not exceed 50 mg/l for cadmium or 20 mg/l for mercury.

Land

Prescribed substances:
None specified.

Examples of substantial change:
— an increase in rate or overall throughput beyond 5 per cent of the design capacity or the authorisation conditions;
— change in the operating parameters, *e.g.* rate of production or contaminants in the waste resins; and
— changes in the process equipment.

Examples of change requiring variation:
— the installation or replacement of abatement technology.

IPR 5/10: Waste Disposal and Recycling—Recovery of Oil by Distillation
1992 ISBN 0-11-752648-7

Process: The recovery of oil by a process involving distillation.

Statutory reference: Prescribed Processes and Substances Regulations 1991, Schedule 1, Section 5.2.

Last date for upgrading existing processes: December 1, 1996.

Air

Prescribed processes:
— particulate matter
— metals, metalloids and their compounds
— oxides of sulphur and other sulphur compounds
— oxides of nitrogen and other nitrogen compounds
— oxides of carbon
— halogen and their compounds
— organic compounds and partial oxidation products.

Emission limits specified for:

	mg/m^3
— volatile organic compounds (excluding particulate matter) expressed as carbon	
— ammonia	50
— amines	10
— hydrogen sulphide	5
— volatile organic sulphur compounds	1

Note: Emissions should not give rise to an offensive smell outside the premises.

Water

Prescribed substances:

— cadmium and its compounds
— PCBs
— 1,2 Dichloroethane
— Hexachlorobenzene
— Hexachlorobutadiene
— Trichlorobenzene.

The flow weighted monthly average concentration in a final affluent should not exceed 50 mg/1 for cadmium or 20 mg/1 for mercury.

Land

Prescribed substances:

— organic solvents
— halogens and their covalent compounds
— organic metallic compounds
— PCDDs
— PCBs
— PCTs
— PCNs
— alkaline earth metal oxides.

Examples of substantial change:

— an increase in rate or overall throughput beyond 5 per cent of the design capacity or the authorisation conditions
— changes in the operating parameters, *e.g.* temperature, pressure, or feedstock; and
— changes in the process equipment.

Examples of change requiring variation:

— an increase in height of discharge, on an existing plant and without an accompanying increase in the emission; and
— the installation on replacement of abatement technology.

IPR 5/11: Waste Disposal and Recycling: Sewage Sludge Incineration
1992 ISBN 0-11-752646-0

Process: The incineration of sewage sludge.

Statutory reference: Prescribed Processes and Substances Regulations 1991, Schedule 1, Section 5.1.

Last date for upgrading existing processes: December 1, 1996.

Air

Prescribed substances:

— particulate matter
— metals, metalloids and their compounds
— oxides of sulphur and other sulphur compounds
— oxides of nitrogen and other nitrogen compounds
— halogens and their compounds
— organic compounds and partial oxidation products
— oxides of carbon

For new plants the following limits apply to releases from contained sources:

	mg/m^3
— total particulate matter	20
— hydrogen chloride	30
— hydrogen fluoride	2
— sulphur dioxide	300
— oxides of nitrogen (expressed as nitrogen dioxide)	650
— volatile organic compounds (excluding particulate matter) expressed as carbon	20
— dioxins	$1 \, ng/m^3$
— arsenic, chromium, copper, lead, manganese, nickel and tin taken together	1.0

— cadmium	0.1
— mercury	0.1

— carbon monoxide—50 mg/m^3 of combustion gas determined as a daily average value; 100 mg/m^3 of at least 95 per cent of all measurements determined as 10 minute average values taken in any 24 hour period.

Note:

Emissions from the process should not give rise to an offensive smell outside the premises and should be free from visible smoke.

Water

Prescribed substances:

— mercury and its compounds
— cadmium and its compounds
— PCBs.

Average concentration in a final effluent should not exceed 50 mg/l for cadmium or 20 mg/l for mercury.

Land

Prescribed substances:

— halogens and their covalent compounds
— organo-metallic compounds
— PCDDs
— PCDFs
— PCBs
— alkaline earth metal oxides
— other heavy metals.

Examples of substantial change:

— an increase in rate of overall throughput beyond 5 per cent of the design capacity or the authorisation conditions;
— changes in the process operating parameters, *e.g.* temperature, pressure, type of raw materials fed to the incinerator; and
— changes in the process equipment likely to change the accepted operating conditions.

Examples of change requiring variation:

— an increase in chimney height, or final gas temperature or of efflux velocity (under a limiting value) on an existing plant and without an increase in the emission;
— upgrading of the combustion chamber
— the installation or replacement of abatement technology.

IPR 3/1: Cement Manufacture and Associated Processes
1992 ISBN 0-11-752681-9

Process: The manufacture of cement and associated processes.

Statutory reference: Prescribed Processes and Substances Registrations 1991, Schedule 1, Section 3.1.

Latest date for upgrading existing processes: April 1, 1997.

Air

Prescribed substances:

— particulate matter
— oxides of sulphur and other sulphur compounds
— oxides of nitrogen and other nitrogen compounds
— oxides of carbon

Note:

1. For new plant and existing plant where indicated releases should not exceed:

Particulate matter	mg/m^3
Kilns (existing kilns have until April 1, 1998)	− 50
Clinker coolers	− 100
Milling & grinding	− 50
All other contained sources	− 50
Oxides of sulphur (expressed as sulphur dioxide)	− 750
Oxides of nitrogen (expressed as nitrogen dioxide) wet process	− 1800
Semi-dry/semi-wet process	− 1500
Dry process	− 1200

Water

Prescribed substances:

None specified.

Land

Prescribed substances:

Alkaline earth metal oxides.

Examples of substantial change:

— an increase in rate of or overall throughput beyond 5 per cent of the design capacity or the authorisation conditions;
— replacement of a kiln, cement mill or clinker cooler;
— addition of another preheater string;
— change of process such as wet to semi-wet or dry.

Examples of change requiring variation:

— the installation or replacement of abatement technology without an increase in releases
— an increase of chimney height, or significant change in exhaust gas temperature or efflux velocity;
— conversion of grinding systems from open to closed circuit;
— replacement of separators in closed-circuit grinding systems;
— installation or replacement of cement bag packer;
— extension of materials storage capacity.

IPR 3/2: Lime Manufacture and Associated Process
1992 ISBN 0-11-752682-7

Process: The manufacture of lime and associated process.

Statutory reference: Prescribed Processes and Substances Regulations, Schedule 1, Section 3.1.

Latest date for upgrading existing processes: April 1, 1997.

Air

Prescribed Process:

— particulate matter
— oxides of sulphur and other sulphur compounds
— oxides of nitrogen and other nitrogen compounds
— oxides of carbon.

Note:

For all new plant and existing plant where indicated emissions should not exceed:

Particulate matter	mg/m^3
Limestone preparation	− 100
Kiln (for existing kilns the relevant date is April 1, 1998)	− 50
Milling and grinding	− 50
Lime slaking	− 100

All other contained sources — 50
Oxides of sulphur (expressed as sulphur dioxide) — 750
Oxides of nitrogen (expressed as nitrogen dioxide) — 1800

Water

Prescribed substances:
None.

Land

Prescribed substances:
Alkaline earth metal oxides

Examples of substantial change:
— an increase in rate of, an overall throughput beyond 5 per cent of the design capacity or the authorisation conditions;
— replacement or major modification of a kiln;
— changes in process equipment likely to change the accepted operating conditions.

Examples of change requiring variation:
— the refurbishment or enlargement of an electrostatic precipitator, leading to a reduction of the emission of particular matter;
— an increase of chimney height, or significant change in exhaust gas temperature or efflux velocity;
— the installation or replacement of abatement technology without an increase in releases;
— extension of materials storage capacity.

IPR 3/3: Processes Involving Asbestos
1992 ISBN 0-11-752683-5

Process: Processes involving asbestos.

Statutory references: Prescribed Processes and Substances Regulations, Schedule 1, Section 3.2.

Latest date for regrading existing processes: April 1, 1993 for railway vehicle incineration processes and April 1, 1997 for all other processes.

Air

Prescribed substances:
— particulate matter
— asbestos
— organic compounds (*e.g.* formaldehyde)
— oxides of sulphur
— oxides of nitrogen
— halogens and their compounds

Note:

For all new plant except railway vehicle incineration plant, emissions should not exceed:

Asbestos

Fibre concentration	1 fibre/cm^3
or mass concentration	0.1 mg/m^3

	(mg/m^3)
particular matter	30
formaldehyde	5
ammonia	30
amines	5
volatile organic compounds (expressed as carbon)	50

For new railway incineration plants emissions should not exceed:

Asbestos fibre concentration	0.1 fibre/m^3
	(mg/m^3)
— carbon monoxide	100
— hydrogen chloride	30
— particulate matter (other than asbestos)	30
— vinyl chloride monomer	1
— hydrogen cyanide	1
— sulphur dioxide	300
— dioxins	1 ng/m^3 TEQ

For existing plant emissions should not exceed:

Asbestos

Fibre concentration	2 fibres/cm^3
or mass concentration	0.1 mg/m^3
crocidolite/amosite fibre concentration	0.8 fibres/cm^3
particulate matter	50 mg/m^3

Water

Prescribed substances:
None identified.

Land

Prescribed substances:
None identified.

Examples of substantial change:
— an increase in rate of, or overall throughout beyond 5 per cent of the design capacity or the authorisation conditions;
— changes in the process operating parameters;
— changes in process equipment likely to change the accepted operating conditions.

Examples of change requiring variation:
— an increase in vent height, or in final gas temperature or of efflux velocity (under a limiting value) on an existing plant and without an increase in the emission.
— the installation or replacement of abatement technology without an increase in releases.

IPR 3/4: Glass Fibre & Non-Asbestos Mineral Fibres
1992 ISBN 0-11-752684-3

Process: The manufacture of glass and any fibre from any mineral.

Statutory reference: Prescribed Processes and Substances Regulations, Schedule 1, Section 3.3.

Latest date for upgrading existing processes: April 1, 1997.

Air

Prescribed substances:

— oxides of sulphur and other sulphur compounds
— oxides of carbon
— halogens and their compounds
— organic compounds and partial oxidation products
— particulate matter
— glass fibres and mineral fibres.

Note:

Emissions should not exceed:

(a) *Melting processes:*

	The mass emission should not exceed	The concentration should not exceed
Particulate matter (total)	.5 kg/hr	50 mg/m^3
Sulphur oxides (expressed as sulphur dioxide)		
— gas fired	5 kg/hr	750 mg/m^3
— oil fired	5 kg/hr	1750 mg/m^3
Nitrogen oxides (expressed as nitrogen dioxide)	5 kg/hr	1500 mg/m^3
Fluorides (expressed as hydrogen fluoride)	50 g/hr	5 mg/m^3
— where the raw materials contain significant quantities of fluorides	50 g/hr	20 mg/m^3
Chlorides (expressed as hydrogen chloride)	300 g/hr	50 mg/m^3
Hydrogen sulphide		5 mg/m^3

(b) *Downstream processes:*

	mg/m^3
— Total particulate matter (including fibres)	50
— Glass fibre or mineral fibre	20
— Total volatile organic compounds (including phenol, formaldehyde and amines and measured as carbon)	50
— Phenol excluding derivatives	10
— Formalehyde	5
— Ammonia	30
— Amines	5

Water

Prescribed substances:
None.

Land

Prescribed substances:
Organic solvents.
Alkaline earth metal oxides.

Examples of substantial change;
— an increase in rate of, or overall throughput beyond 5 per cent of the design capacity or the authorisation conditions;
— any significant changes in the process operating parameters;
— any changes in process equipment likely to change the accepted operating conditions;
— installation of abatement plant which will increase any disposal of prescribed substances to land.

Examples of change requiring variation:
— an increase of vent height, or of final gas temperature or of efflux velocity (under a limiting value) on an existing plant and without an increase in the emission.
— the installation or replacement of abatement technology without an increase in releases.

IPR 3/5: Glass Manufacture and Production Glass Frit and Enamel Frit
1992 ISBN 0-11-752685-1

Process: The manufacture of glass frit or enamel frit and its use in any process where that process is related to its manufacture.

Statutory reference: Prescribed Processes and Substances Regulations, Schedule 1, Section 3.5.

Latest date for upgrading existing processes: April 1, 1998.

Air

Prescribed substances:
— oxides of sulphur and other sulphur compounds
— oxides of nitrogen and other nitrogen compounds
— oxides of carbon
— organic compounds and partial oxidation products
— metals, metalloids and other compounds
— particulate matter
— halogens and their compounds
— phosphorus and its compounds.

Note: Particulate matter
New and existing plant should not exceed:

Emission Rate	Emission Limit (mg/m^3)
Greater than 0.5 kg/h	50
0.5 kg/h or less	100

Oxide of Sulphur

	Emission Limit (mg/m^3)
— gas fired	750
— oil fired	1750
Oxides of Nitrogen	— 2700 mg/m^3
Fluorides	— 5 mg/m^3 (where the emission rate exceeds 50 g/h)

Metals

Metal	The mass emission should not exceed g/hour	The concentration should not exceed mg/m^3
Lead	25	5
Cadmium	1	0.2
Total lead and cadmium	25	5
Total arsenic, nickel, selenium, antimony and copper	5	1
Total manganese, vanadium and tin	25	5

Water

Prescribed substances:
Cadmium and its compounds.

Land

Prescribed substances:
Alkaline earth metal oxides.

Examples of substantial change:
— a change in frit formulation or in the range of formulations such as the first use, or an increased use of fluorides, nitrates or lead compounds;
— an increase in the rate of or overall throughput beyond 5 per cent of the design capacity or the authorised conditions;
— conversion from gas to oil firing, on the grounds of increased oxides of sulphur;

— use of oil beyond the periods necessary to meet the demands of any interruptible gas contract; and
— conversion to oxygen enriched air, on the grounds of increased oxides of nitrogen.

Examples of change requiring variation:
— a change in frit formulation which would result in the reduction of emissions of more toxic compounds
— an increase in chimney height, or of final gas temperature or of efflux velocity (under a limiting value) on an existing plant and without an increase in the emission; and
— the installation or replacement of abatement technology without an increase in releases.

IPR 3/6: Ceramic Processes
1992 ISBN 0-11-752686-X

Process: Ceramic processes which come under Part A.

Statutory reference: Prescribed Processes and Substances Regulations, Schedule 1, Section 3.6.

Latest date for upgrading existing plant: April 1, 1998.

Air
Prescribed substances:
— oxides of sulphur and other sulphur compounds
— oxides of nitrogen and other nitrogen compounds
— oxides of carbon
— halogens and their compounds
— organic compounds and partial oxidation products
— particulate matter

Note:
Emission limits should not exceed:

Existing plant	mg/m^3
— particulate matter	100
— oxides of sulphur (expressed as sulphur dioxide)	2000
— Total fluorides (expressed as hydrogen fluoride)	25
— Total chlorides (expressed as hydrogen chloride)	5
New Plant	mg/m^3
— particulate matter	50
— oxides of sulphur (expressed as sulphur dioxide)	1500
— carbon monoxide	200
— Total fluorides (expressed as hydrogen fluoride)	10
Total chlorides (expressed as hydrogen chloride)	30

Water
Prescribed substances:
None.

Land
Prescribed substances:
Halogen compounds

Examples of substantial change:
— an increase in rate of or overall throughput beyond 5 per cent of the design capacity of the authorisation conditions;
— a kiln rebuilt from ground level
— any significant changes in the process operating parameters; and
— any changes in process equipment likely to change the accepted operating conditions;

Examples of change requiring variation:
— an increase in chimney height or of final gas temperature or of efflux velocity (under a limiting value) on an existing plant and without an increase in the emission
— the installation or replacement of abatement technology without an increase in releases
— a process change which results in the reduction of releases from the process.

SECRETARY OF STATE'S GUIDANCE ON PROCESSES PRESCRIBED FOR LOCAL AUTHORITY AIR POLLUTION CONTROL

GENERAL NOTE

For LAAPC processes, the procedure is that draft guidance is being discussed at joint industry/local authority working parties and approved subsequently by the HMIP/local liaison committee. Drafts are then issued generally for consultation.

The Secretary of State has now issued Guidance Notes on "Pt. B" processes prescribed for control by local authorities under Pt. I of EPA 1990. These notes fall into three categories.

1. *General Guidance*

Five General Guidance Notes have been issued, as follows:

GG1 (91)—Introduction to Part I of the Act: This note contains a brief introduction to the relevant provisions of the Act and provides a certain amount of guidance on issues such as the meaning of BATNEEC, the meaning of "substantial change" and handling commercially confidential information.

GG2 (91)—Authorisations: This contains guidance on the content of authorisations and on the drafting of appropriate conditions; some 72 specimen conditions are given as an Appendix.

GG3 (91)—Applications and Registers: This provides guidance on the content of applications, the procedural requirements for handling applications, and on the public registers. A suggested form of application is given.

GG4 (91)—Interpretation of Terms Used in Process Guidance Notes: This Note provides interpretation of some of the terms commonly used in Process Notes (see below) for example: "colourless"; "offensive odour"; and "continuous monitoring."

GG5 (91)—Appeals: This contains guidance on the appeals procedures set out in the Environmental Protection (Applications, Appeals and Registers) Regulations 1991 No. 507 (set out as Appendix 2).

2. *Process Guidance*

A series of Guidance Notes relating to specific processes and containing guidance on the techniques appropriate for air pollution control. Guidance is given for both new and existing processes, together with information about any directions, limits, requirements, quality objectives or quality standards in force at the date of publication. These notes are significantly less complex than those for processes prescribed for IPC with less detailed omission levels given and with a certain amount of common material, for example on "general operations."

3. *Upgrading Guidance*

One Upgrading Guidance Note has been issued by the Secretary of State to local authorities: *UG–1 (May 1992)—Revisions/Additions to Existing Process and General Guidance Notes*. Upgrading Guidance Notes revise and add to the advice that was given in previous Guidance Notes. It is intended that such notes will be published as the need arises.

An important distinction should be noted between the status of the General and Process specific notes. Section 7(11) of the EPA 1990 provides that it shall be the duty of enforcing authorities to have regard to any guidance issued to them by the Secretary of State as to techniques appropriate to any description of process. The Process Guidance Notes constitute such guidance, and additionally the Notes state that the Secretary of State will treat the guidance as one of the material considerations when determining any appeals made against a local authority decision. By contrast, General Notes 1–3 and 5 state expressly that they do not constitute guidance to local authorities under s.7(11); nor should they be taken as an authoritative interpretation of the primary or secondary legislation. GG4 on *Interpretation of Terms* is silent as to its status under s.7(11). Though presumably, as it seeks to interpret terms used in the Process Guidance Notes, it should constitute statutory guidance as do those notes.

The Process Guidance Notes are listed below, and any features of particular interest are summarised briefly.

PROCESS GUIDANCE NOTES

Many process guidance notes contain requirements as to:
(a) emissions free from persistent mist and fume and free from droplets;
(b) emissions free from offensive odour outside the process boundary, as perceived by the local authority inspector;
(c) emissions free from visible smoke in normal operation;
(d) proper materials handling;
(e) chimney height and efflux velocity.

Any notable additional requirements are summarised below, together with the latest date (save in exceptional circumstances) for upgrading existing plant.

LAAPC PROCESS GUIDANCE NOTES

PG 1/1 (91) Waste oil burners, less than 0.4 MW net rated thermal input February 1991 ISBN 0-11-753407-7	Upgrading existing processes: October 1, 1994
PG 1/2 (91) Waste oil or recovered oil burners, less than 3 MW net rated thermal input February 1991 ISBN 0-11-752405-0	Upgrading existing processes: October 11, 1996 Specific emission limits for cadmium, nickel, chromium, copper, vanadium lead, chloride, fluoride and total particulate matter, where combustion of waste oil forms part of another Part B process and net rated thermal input of appliance is 3 MW or more.
PG 1/3 (91) Boilers and furnaces, 20–50 MW net rated thermal input February 1991 ISBN 0-11-752384-4	Upgrading existing processes: October 1, 1997 1. Emission levels for sulphur dioxide, oxides of nitrogen and total particulate matter for solid and liquid fuel firing and for natural gas firing. 2. Specific provision for dark smoke emissions for existing processes.
PG 1/4 (91) Gas turbines, 20–50 MW net rated thermal input February 1991 ISBN 0-11-752392-5	Upgrading existing processes: October 1, 1994, October 1, 1996 or October 1, 1998 depending on type of fuel and number of operating hours p.a. Specific limits for nitrogen oxides.
PG 1/5 (91) Compression ignition engines, 20–50 MW net rated thermal input February 1991 ISBN 0-11-752389-5	Upgrading existing processes: October 1, 1999 (progressive interim emission limits given). Specific limits for nitrogen oxides, particulate matter, non-methane hydrocarbons and carbon monoxide.
PG 1/6 (91) Tyre and rubber combustion processes between 0.4 and 3 MW net rated thermal input February 1991 ISBN 0-11-752404-2	Upgrading existing processes: October 1, 1995 Specific emission limits for total particulate matter, carbon monoxide, sulphur dioxide, particulate matter, organic compounds, and total heavy metals.
PG 1/7 (91) Straw combustion processes between 0.4 and 3 MW net rated thermal input February 1991 ISBN 0-11-752401-8	Upgrading existing processes: October 1, 1995 Specific emission limits for total particulate matter (combustion and handling) and organic compounds.
PG 1/8 (91) Wood combustion processes between 0.4 and 3 MW net rated thermal input February 1991 ISBN 0-11-752406-9	Upgrading existing processes: October 1, 1995 1. Specific emission limits for total particulate matter (combustion and handling) and organic compounds. 2. Where treated or laminated wood is burned, limits on carbon monoxide, formaldehyde, hydrogen chloride and hydrogen cyanide may apply.

PG 1/9 (91) Poultry litter combustion processes between 0.4 and 3 MW net rated thermal input February 1991 ISBN 0-11-752399-2	Upgrading existing processes: October 1, 1995 Specific emission limits for total particulate matter, carbon monoxide, sulphur dioxide, hydrogen chloride, nitrogen oxides, particulate matter, ammonia and organic compounds.
PG 1/10 (92) February 1992 Waste derived fuel burning processes less than 3 MW net rated thermal input ISBN 0-11-752594-4	Upgrading of existing processes: December 1, 1994 Specified emission limits for: particulate matter (excluding handling of raw materials and products); hydrogen chloride, carbon monoxide; sulphur dioxide; organic compounds; total of lead and cadmium and their compounds; particulate matter (from handling of raw materials and residues).
PG 2/1 (91) Furnaces for the extraction of non-ferrous metal from scrap February 1991 ISBN 0-11-752398-4	Upgrading existing processes: April 1, 1994 Specific emission limits for chloride, total particulate matter, total cadmium, lead and their compounds.
PG 2/2 (91) Hot dip galvanising processes July 1991 ISBN 0-11-752479-4	Upgrading existing processes: October 1, 1996 Specific emission concentration limits for total particulate matter, chlorides, lead and its compounds, VOCs and ammonia.
PG 2/3 (91) Electrical and rotary furnaces July 1991 ISBN 0-11-752476-X	Upgrading existing processes: April 1, 1997
PG 2/4 (91) Iron, steel and non-ferrous metal foundry processes July 1991 ISBN 0-11-752478-6	Upgrading existing processes: April 1, 1997 Specific emission limits for total particulate matter, copper, lead, cadmium, amines and amides, VOCs, hydrogen sulphide and ammonia.
PG 2/5 (91) Hot and cold blast cupolas July 1991 ISBN 0-11-752474-3	Upgrading existing processes: April 1, 1997 Specific emission limits for total particulate matter.
PG 2/6 (91) Aluminium and aluminium alloy processes July 1991 ISBN 0-11-752467-0	Upgrading existing processes: April 1, 1997 Specific emission limits for total particulate matter, copper, inorganic chloride, fluoride and VOCs.
PG 2/7 (91) Zinc and zinc alloy processes July 1991 ISBN 0-11-752460-3	Upgrading existing processes: April 1, 1997 Specific emission limits for particulate matter, inorganic chloride, lead and cadmium.
PG 2/8 (91) Copper and copper alloy processes July 1991 ISBN 0-11-752473-5	Upgrading existing processes: April 1, 1997 Specific emission limits for total particulate matter, copper, lead, nickel, tin and fluoride.
PG 2/9 (91) Metal decontamination processes July 1991 ISBN 0-11-752481-6	Upgrading existing processes: October 1, 1994 Specific emission limits for total particulate matter, chlorides and organic compounds.

Environmental Protection Act 1990

PG 3/1 (91) Blending, packing, loading and use of bulk cement February 1991 ISBN 0-11-752385-2	Upgrading existing processes: April 1, 1996 Specific emission limits for total particulate matter, nitrogen oxides, sulphur oxides, fluoride and chloride.
PG 3/2 (91) February 1991 Manufacture of heavy clay goods and refractory goods ISBN 0-11-752386-0	Upgrading existing processes: September 30, 1997 Specified emission limits for total particulate matter, nitrogen oxide, sulphur oxides (expressed as sulphur dioxide), fluoride (expressed as hydrogen fluoride), chloride (expressed as hydrogen chloride).
PG 3/3 (91) February 1991 Glass (excluding lead glass) manufacturing processes ISBN 0-11-752394-1	Upgrading existing processes: October 1, 2001 1. Specific emission limits for sulphur oxides, nitrogen oxides, fluoride, chloride, and total particulate matter. 2. Levels vary depending on nature of glass.
PG 3/4 (91) February 1991 Lead glass manufacturing processes ISBN 0-11-752393-3	Upgrading existing processes: October 1, 2001 Specific emission limits for sulphur oxides, nitrogen oxides, fluoride, chloride, and total particulate matter.
PG 3/5 (91) July 1991 Coal, coke and coal product processes ISBN 0-11-752469-7	Upgrading existing processes: October 1, 1996 Specific emission limits for total particulate matter.
PG 3/6 (91) February 1991 Processes for the polishing or etching of glass or glass products using hydrofluoric acid ISBN 0-11-752395-X	Upgrading existing processes: October 1, 1995 Specific emission limits for fluoride, total particulate matter and ammonia.
PG 3/7 (91) July 1991 Exfoliation of vermiculite and expansion of perlite ISBN 0-11-752459-X	Upgrading existing processes: April 1, 1998 Specific emission limits for total particulate matter.
PG 3/8 (91) July 1991 Quarry processes including roadstone plants, and the size reduction of bricks, tiles and concrete ISBN 0-11-752463-8	Upgrading existing processes: There are three different dates depending on the emissions in question. 1. processes relating to loading of road vehicles, and internal road transport of processed materials likely to generate dust: April 1, 1993 in England and Wales and August 31, 1993 in Scotland; 2. roadstone coating plant as regards particulate matter April 1, 1997; 3. otherwise the date for the remaining processes is April 1, 1997. There are specific emission limits for particulate matter.
PG 3/9 (91) July 1991 Sand drying and cooling ISBN 0-11-752474-7	Upgrading existing processes: April 1, 1996 Specific emission limits for total particulate matter.

PG 3/10 (91) July 1991 China and ball clay ISBN 0-11-752470-0	Upgrading existing processes: April 1, 1991 Specific emission limits for particulate matter and fluoride.
PG 3/11 (91) July 1991 Spray drying of ceramic materials ISBN 0-11-752468-9	Upgrading existing processes: March 31, 1992 Specific emission limits for particulate matter.
PG 3/12 (91) July 1991 Plaster processes ISBN 0-11-752458-1	Upgrading existing processes: varies depending on the emissions in question: 1. in relation to particulate matter where a standard of 230 mg/m^3 has been set under previous legislation, within 20 years from the commencement of commissioning of the assessment plant; 2. in relation to the loading of dusty materials to or from lorries, April 1, 1993 in England and Wales and September 1, 1993 in Scotland; 3. in all other cases April 1, 1995. Specific emission limits for particulate matter.
PG 3/13 (91) July 1991 Asbestos processes ISBN 0-11-752482-4	Upgrading of existing processes: January 1, 1995 Specific emission limits for asbestos and particulate matter.
PG 3/14 (91) July 1991 Lime slaking processes ISBN 0-11-752480-8	Upgrading of existing processes: April 1, 1995 Specific emission limits for total particulate matter.
PG 5/1 (91) February 1991 Clinical waste incineration processes under 1 tonne an hour ISBN 0-11-752388-7	Upgrading of existing processes: October 1, 1995 Specific emission limits for chloride, total particulate matter, carbon monoxide, sulphur dioxide, organic compounds excluding particulate matter, heavy metals and their compounds (total of cadmium, mercury, arsenic, lead, chromium, nickel, copper and manganese) expressed as metal.
PG 5/2 (91) February 1991 Crematoria ISBN 0-11-752390-9	Upgrading of existing processes: April 1, 1998 Specific emission limits for chloride expressed as hydrogen chloride, total particulate matter from cremation, carbon monoxide, organic compounds (excluding particulate matter) expressed as total carbon, and particulate matter from cremated remains treatment plant.
PG 5/3 (91) February 1991 Animal carcase incineration processes under 1 tonne an hour ISBN 0-11-752383-6	Upgrading of existing processes: October 1, 1995 Specific emission limits for total particulate matter, chloride, carbon monoxide, sulphur dioxide, organic compounds excluding particulate matter.

PG 5/4 (91) February 1991 General waste incineration processes under 1 tonne an hour ISBN 0-11-752397-6	Upgrading of existing processes: October 1, 1995 Specific emission limits for carbon monoxide, organic compounds, expressed as total carbon (excluding particulate matter), total particulate matter, heavy metals (total of cadmium, mercury, arsenic, lead, chromium, nickel, copper and manganese and their compounds), chloride, expressed as hydrogen chloride and sulphur dioxide.
PG 5/5 (1991) February 1991 Sewage sludge incineration processes under 1 tonne an hour ISBN 0-11-752641-1	Specific emission limits for organic compounds expressed as total carbon (excluding particulate matter) total particulate matter, carbon monoxide, heavy metals (total of cadmium, antimony, mercury, arsenic, lead, chromium, nickel, copper, manganese vanadium and cobalt and their compounds, chloride, fluoride, sulphur dioxide.
PG 6/1 (91) July 1991 Animal by-product rendering ISBN 0-11-752461-1	Upgrading of existing processes: April 1, 1997 Specific emission limits for total particulate matter, ammonia, chlorides, amines and amides, hydrogen sulphide, sulphides and mercaptans.
PG 6/2 (91) February 1991 Manufacture of timber and wood based products ISBN 0-11-752403-4	Upgrading of existing processes: October 1, 1996 Specific emission limits for total particulate matter.
PG 6/3 (91) February 1991 Chemical treatment of timber and wood based products ISBN 0-11-752402-6	Upgrading of existing processes: October 1, 1996 Specified emission limits for volatile organic compounds (excluding particulate matter) expressed as carbon, and total particulate matter.
PG 6/4 (91) February 1991 Processes for the manufacture of particleboard and fibreboard ISBN 0-11-752387-9	Upgrading of existing processes: October 1, 1996 Specified emission limits for particulate matter, volatile organic compounds (excluding particulate matter) and formaldehyde.
PG 6/5 (91) February 1991 Maggot breeding processes ISBN 0-11-752396-8	Upgrading of existing processes: April 1, 1993 in England and Wales and February 1, 1994 in Scotland. Specified emission limits for ammonia, amines and amides, and organic and inorganic sulphides including mercaptans and hydrogen sulphide (as total sulphur).
PG 6/6 (91) February 1991 Fur breeding processes ISBN 0-11-752391-7	Upgrading of existing processes: April 1, 1994 Specified emission limits for ammonia, organic, and inorganic sulphides including mercaptans and hydrogen sulphide (as total sulphur).
PG 6/7 (91) July 1991 Printing and coating of metal packaging ISBN 0-11-752462-X	Upgrading of existing processes: April 1, 1997 Specified emission limits for total particulate matter, volatile organic compounds (expressed as total carbon excluding particulate matter) other than from mixing vessels, volatile organic compounds (expressed as total carbon excluding particulate matter) from mixing vessels where the total emission of volatile organic compounds from that vessel exceeds 1 kg in any 8 hour period, carbon monoxide from incinerators) measured as nitrogen dioxide, isocyanates.

PG 6/8 (91)
July 1991
Textile and fabric coating and finishing processes
ISBN 0-11-752466-2

Upgrading existing processes: October 1, 1997

Specified emission limits for volatile organic compounds (as total carbon excluding particulate matter), total particulate matter (including emissions from material handling), carbon monoxide (from incinerators) isocyanates, formaldehyde, and nitrogen oxides from incinerators (measured as nitrogen dioxide).

PG 6/9 (91)
July 1991
Manufacture of coating powder
ISBN 0-11-752471-9

Upgrading of existing processes: October 1, 1995

Specified emission limits for total particulate matter.

PG 6/10 (92)
July 1992
Coating manufacturing process
ISBN 0-11-752595-2

Upgrading of existing processes: April 1, 1999

Specified emission limits for volatile organic compounds (as total carbon excluding particulate matter) where mass emission of volatile organic compounds from any individual emission source exceeds 1 kg in any 8 hour period, total particulate matter, carbon monoxide (from incinerators), nitrogen oxides from incinerators (as nitrogen dioxide).

PG 6/11 (92)
February 1992
Manufacture of printing ink
ISBN 0-11-752596-0

Upgrading of existing processes: October 1, 1997

Specified emission limits for: volatile organic compounds from the production of solvent-based inks (expressed as total carbon excluding particulate matter); extract from Change Pan processes in defined circumstances; emissions from semi-automatic and automatic pan washing machines; from manual washing of small pans; particulate matter; carbon monoxide (from incinerators); and nitrogen oxides, expressed as nitrogen oxide (from incinerators).

PG 6/12 (91)
July 1991
Production of natural sausage casings, tripe, chitterlings and other boiled green offal products
ISBN 0-11-752465-4

Upgrading of existing processes: April 1, 1996

Specific emission limits on visible smoke.

PG 6/13 (91)
July 1991
Coil coating processes
ISBN 0-11-752472-7

Upgrading of existing processes: October 1, 1996

Specified emission limits for volatile organic compounds (as total carbon excluding particulate matter), total particulate matter (including emissions from material handling), nitrogen oxides from incinerators (measured as nitrogen dioxide) carbon monoxide (from incinerators) fluoride (expressed as hydrogen fluoride, and isocyanates.

PG 6/14 (91)
Film coating processes
July 1991
ISBN 0-11-752477-8

Upgrading of existing processes: April 1, 1997

Specified emission limits for volatile organic compounds (as total carbon excluding particulate matter), total particulate matter (including emissions from material handling), nitrogen oxides from incinerators (measured as nitrogen dioxide) carbon monoxide (from incinerators) fluoride (expressed as hydrogen fluoride, and isocyanates.

PG 6/15 (91) July 1991 Coating in drum manufacturing and reconditioning processes ISBN 0-11-752475-1	Upgrading of existing processes: April 1, 1997 Specified emission limits for volatile organic compounds (expressed as total carbon excluding particulate matter) other than from mixing vessels, carbon monoxide (from incinerators), nitrogen oxides from incinerators (measured as nitrogen dioxide) isocyanates, total particulate matter, volatile organic compounds (expressed as total carbon excluding particulate matter) from mixing vessels where the mass emission of volatile organic compounds exceeds 1 kg in any 8 hour period.
PG 6/16 (92) February 1992 Printworks ISBN 0-11-752597-9	Upgrading existing processes: December 1, 1996 Special emission limits for: total particulate matter; volatile organic compounds (as total carbon content excluding particulate matter); carbon monoxide; and nitrogen oxides expressed as nitrogen dioxide.
PG 6/17 (92) February 1992 Printing of flexible packaging ISBN 0-11-752598-7	Upgrading of existing processes: December 1, 1998 except for printing process lines using aromatic solvents for which the date is December 1, 1995. Specified emission limits for volatile organic compounds (as total carbon excluding particulate matter); carbon monoxide (from incinerators); nitrogen oxides (from incinerators).
PG 6/18 (92) February 1992 Paper coating processes ISBN 0-11-752599-5	Upgrading of existing processes: April 1, 1997 Specified emission limits for: volatile organic compounds (as total carbon excluding particulate matter); total particulate matter (including emissions from material handling); isocyanates; nitrogen oxides from incinerators (as nitrogen dioxide); carbon monoxide from incinerators.
PG 6/19 (92) February 1992 Fish meal and fish oil processes ISBN 0-11-752600-2	Upgrading of existing processes: October 1, 1999 Specified emission limits for total particulate matter; ammonia; amines and amides; hydrogen sulphide; sulphides and mercaptan.
PG 6/20 (92) February 1992 Paint application in vehicle manufacturing ISBN 0-11-752601-0	Specified emission limits for volatile organic compounds from oven and spray booth VOC arrestment plant (as total carbon excluding particulate matter); particulate matter (spray booth emissions); particulate matter (other sources); total acidity (expressed as SO_3 equivalent); carbon monoxide (from incinerators); nitrogen oxides, from incinerators (expressed as nitrogen dioxide); isocyanates, excluding particulate matter; volatile organic compounds from paint mixing vessels and circulation systems (as total carbon excluding particulate matter) where the mass emission of volatile organic compounds from any individual emission source exceeds 1 kg in any 8-hour period.
PG 6/21 (92) February 1992 Hide and skin processes ISBN 0-11-752602-9	Upgrading of existing processes: October 1, 1995 Specified emission limits for ammonia; hydrogen sulphide, sulphides and mercaptans (expressed as sulphur); total particulate matter; and volatile organic compounds (expressed as total carbon excluding particulate matter).

PG 6/22 (92) February 1992 Leather finishing processes ISBN 0-11-752603-7	Upgrading of existing processes: April 1, 1996 Specified emission limits for total particulate matter from automated spray machines; volatile organic compounds from arrestment equipment; carbon monoxide (from incinerators); nitrogen oxides measured as nitrogen dioxides (from incinerators).
PG 6/23 (92) February 1992 Coating of metal and plastic ISBN 0-11-752604-5	Upgrading of existing processes: April 1, 1998 Specified emission limits for total particulate matter; volatile organic compounds (expressed as total carbon excluding particulate matter) other than from coating mixing vessels, organic solvent cleaning or degreasing operations or chemical stripping operations; carbon monoxide (from incinerators); nitrogen oxides measured as nitrogen dioxide (from incinerators); isocyanates; volatile organic compounds (expressed as total carbon excluding particulate matter) from coating mixing vessels, organic solvent cleaning or degreasing operations or chemical stripping operations where (a) the individual source gives rise to mass emission of non-chlorinated volatile organic compounds which exceeds 1 kg in any 3 hour period, (b) the individual source gives rise to a mass emission of chlorinated volatile organic compounds which exceeds 1 per cent. of the total solvent holding capacity of the equipment in any 8 hour period.
PG 6/24 (92) February 1992 Pet food manufacturing processes ISBN 0-11-752605-3	Upgrading of existing processes: October 1, 1996 Specified emission limits for total particulate matter.
PG 6/25 (92) February 1992 Vegetable oil extraction and fat and oil refining processes ISBN 0-11-752606-1	Upgrading of existing processes: April 1, 1996 Specified emission limits for total particulate matter; hexane from solvent extraction operations; organic solvents from solvent fractionation processes and any other fat or oil refining processes involving the use of organic solvents, and from degumming carried out as part of fat or oil refining.
PG 6/26 (82) February 1992 Animal feed compounding processes ISBN 0-11-752607-X	Upgrading of existing processes: April 1, 1996 Specified emission limits for total particulate matter.
PG 6/27 (92) February 1992 Vegetable matter drying processes ISBN 0-11-752608-8	Upgrading of existing processes: October 1, 1998 in respect of emissions from dryers and product coolers; otherwise October 1, 1996. Specified emission limits for total particulate matter; nitrogen oxides; and sulphur dioxide.
PG 6/28 (92) February 1992 Rubber processes ISBN 0-11-752609-6	Upgrading of existing processes: April 1, 1999 for certain specified processes (specified by Clause 22); otherwise April 1, 1996. Specified emission limits for: total particulate matter from the storage, handling or mixing of carbon black; total particulate matter other than from the storage, handling or mixing of carbon black; isocyanates excluding particulate matter; volatile organic compounds (as total carbon excluding participate matter); carbon monoxide (from incinerators); nitrogen oxides, measured as nitrogen dioxide (from incinerators).

PG 6/29 (92) February 1992 Di-isocyanate processes ISBN 0-11-752610-X	Upgrading of existing processes: October 1, 1997 Specified emission limits for de-isocyanates; and total particulate matter (including handling processes).
PG 6/30 (92) February 1992 Production of compost for mushrooms ISBN 0-11-752611-8	Upgrading of existing processes: April 1, 1994.
PG 6/31 (92) February 1992 Powder coating processes, including sheradising ISBN 0-11-752612-6	Upgrading of existing processes: October 1, 1995 Specified emission limits for total particulate matter and hydrogen chloride.
PG 6/32 (92) February 1992 Adhesive coating processes ISBN 0-11-752613-4	Upgrading of existing processes: April 1, 1999 for processes specified in Clause 21; otherwise April 1, 1996. Specified emission limits for: volatile organic compounds (expressed as total carbon excluding particulate matter) from coating mixing vessels, organic solvent cleaning or degreasing operations or chemical stripping operations and from other sources; total particulate matter; isocyanates; nitrogen oxides from incinerators (as nitrogen dioxide); and carbon monoxide from incinerators.
PG 6/33 (92) February 1992 Wood coating processes ISBN 0-11-752614-2	Upgrading of existing processes: April 1, 1999 Specified emission limits for total particulate matter; volatile organic compounds (expressed as total carbon excluding particulate matter) other than from dip tanks or cleaning operations; carbon monoxide (from incinerators); volatile organic compounds (expressed as total carbon excluding particulate matter) from individual dip tanks or cleaning operations where the mass emission of volatile organic compounds from an individual source exceeds 1 kg in any 8 hour period; nitrogen oxides expressed as nitrogen dioxide (from incinerators); isocyanates.
PG 6/34 (92) February 1992 Respraying of road vehicles ISBN 0-11-752615-0	Upgrading of existing processes: October 11, 1994 except for: 1. requirements relating to the organic solvent contents of the coatings as applied for which the date is April 1, 1995. 2. the use of improved transfer efficiency paint application equipment for passenger car top coats for which the date is April 1, 1998. 3. the concentration of total particulate matter in the final discharge to air from the spray booth at $10\,\text{mg/m}^3$ for which the date is April 1, 1998. Specified emission limit for: organic solvents; volatile organic compounds, expressed as total carbon; total particulate matter.
PG 6/35 (92) February 1992 Metal and other thermal spraying processes ISBN 0-11-752616-9	Upgrading of existing processes: October 1, 1996 Specified emission limits for total particulate matter, chromium, nickel, copper, cobalt, lead.

PG 6/36 (92) February 1992 Tobacco processing ISBN 0-11-752617-7	Upgrading of existing processes: October 1, 1996 Specified emission limits for particulate matter.
PG 6/37 (92) February 1992 Knackers yards ISBN 0-11-752618-5	
PG 6/38 (92) February 1992 Blood processing ISBN 0-11-752619-3	Upgrading of existing processes: April 1, 1997 Specified emission limits for ammonia, amines and amides, and total of hydrogen sulphide, sulphides and mercaptans (expressed as sulphur).
PG 6/39 (92) February 1992 Primal by-product dealers ISBN 0-11-752620-7	Upgrading of existing processes: October 1, 1995 Specified emission limits for ammonia; total of hydrogen sulphide, sulphides and mercaptans (expressed as sulphur).

Fees and charges

Fees and charges are payable to the enforcing authority in accordance with a scheme made by the Secretary of State, with the approval of the Treasury (s.8(1), (2)). In framing the scheme the Secretary of State must, so far as practicable, secure that fees and charges payable are sufficient to cover the expenditure incurred by the enforcing authorities (and the NRA, so far as relevant) in exercising their regulatory functions.

Initial suggestions as to possible charging regimes were floated in the DoE/Welsh Office consultation paper, *Cost Recovery Charging for Integrated Pollution Control* (April 1989). The Government's considered proposals for a charging scheme for IPC in the light of responses that Consultation paper were set out in a statement on January 30, 1990 (DoE News Release 50). This "simple and practical" scheme would comprise an initial charge for each application, and then an annual charge. The system is to be based on the number of components for a process and will thus relate to the scale of operations of the relevant business: "Smaller and simpler installations will involve fewer components and will pay smaller charges." It was suggested in the statement that a steel works will typically involve 20 or more components, whereas a metal plating works may only involve one component. It is important to note that such "components" are for charging purposes only, not technical control, and there is no implication that a process will necessarily be assessed, or IPC authorisations granted, in the same terms.

These proposals were outlined in more detail by HMIP in its Paper, *Pollution Regulation: Cost Recovery Charges*, issued on July 24, 1990. This Paper contains proposals for IPC and LAAPC and also charges for regulations under the Radioactive Substances Act 1960. Ss.1 and 2 deal with IPC and LAAPC. It is proposed that charges should be related to the relevant administrative workload, under which the size and complexity of a process will be determined by the number of defined "components" it contains. The components are defined solely for charging, and not technical, purposes. Charges are to operate on the basis of "flat-rate per-component fees." By way of example, in the case of iron and steel processes, it is proposed that handling and storage would constitute one component, and each treatment undertaken outside the main furnace (*e.g.* alloying, decarbonising, degassing) would constitute a further component. For ceramic processes, each separate kiln and ancillary operation would be a component. The charge will be the relevant flat rate, multiplied by the total number of components for 1991/92 fees and charges were (per component):—

IPC   New processes transferring to IPC: £1,800
           Installations with existing approvals transferring to IPC: £1,200
           Substantial changes to processes: £600
           Annual charge: £400 plus charges to reflect NRA costs.

LAAPC   Initial Application fee: £800 (£200)
              Annual charge: £500 (£100)

(Figures for waste oil burners in brackets).

It was decided that HMIP underestimated the cost of processing applications and monitoring authorisations in the 1991/92 year. Therefore, the IPC fees for 1992/93 are substantially higher.

As well as raising the fees generally HMIP have also had to impose a further charge in order to recoup its excess costs. This claw-back charge will be added to the annual fee for those processes authorised in 1991/92. It is envisaged that this claw-back charge will be imposed for two years only.

Local authority air pollution control charges have also been increased, but not by such a significant margin. Only the application and annual charges for small waste oil burners have remained unchanged.

A table setting out the fees for both IPC and LAAPC is set out below.

	IPC Charge per Component £	LAAPC Charge £
Application	3,650.00	900.00
Application where plant already controlled by HMIP	2,450.00	580.00
Substantial variation	1,200.00	580.00
Annual	1,500.00	550.00
Claw-back	610.00	—
Claw-back where already controlled by HMIP	410.00	—
Small waste burners application and annual	—	100.00

It will be appreciated that these relate only to recovery of the costs of administering the scheme. More radical proposals for charges related to the effect on the receiving environment have been under consideration by the Government, and remain a possibility to be considered for the future. Annex A, para. A13 of the Government's September 1990 White Paper, *This Common Inheritance* (Cm. 1200) points out that:

"Charges for discharges set to recover administrative costs only are likely to be low in relation to the wider costs imposed on society by that pollution or abstraction. [These] might therefore be worth considering for the longer term."

Similarly, para. A19 of the White Paper states:

"The Government is considering, with HMIP and NRA, whether a greater degree of incentive charging could in the longer term be incorporated in their charging schemes and will be commissioning studies into the possibilities. Incentive charging would require legislation."

Enforcement

HMIP and local authorities have a wide range of enforcement powers at their disposal under Part I. These are:
1. Variation of authorisation: s.10.
2. Revocation of authorisations: s.12.
3. Enforcement notices: s.13.
4. Prohibition notices: s.14.
5. Powers of entry, examination and investigation: s.17.
6. Powers of seizure: s.18.
7. Powers to require information: s.19.
8. Power to take High Court proceedings to secure compliance with enforcement or prohibition notices: s.24.
9. Power to take steps to remedy harm and recover the cost of such steps from the offender: s.27.

Additionally, where a person is convicted of carrying on a prescribed process without authorisation or of breach of authorisation conditions or of enforcement or prohibition notice, the court may order the offender to take steps to remedy matters which appear to the court to be within his power to remedy (s.26).

Information

Part I of the Act, like other parts, contains provision for the maintenance of comprehensive public registers of applications, authorisations, notices, appeals, convictions and information obtained pursuant to conditions of authorisations (s.20). The important implications of the availability of such information have already been mentioned in the General Note to the Act. Only two exemptions to public registration apply: information affecting national security (s.21) and certain confidential information (s.22). An indication of the Government's thinking behind the provisions may be found in the Consultation Paper, *Integrated Pollution Control and Local Authority Air Pollution Controls: Public Access to Information* (August 1989).

Implementation of E.C. and international requirements
The importance of certain E.C. directives in relation to Pt. I of the Act has already been mentioned. Section 3 of the Act provides the means by which those requirements may be translated into binding limits, quotas, objectives or standards under domestic law. At the present time the following Directives are of most immediate general relevance.
   (a) *Directive 84/360/EEC on the combating of air pollution from industrial plants* (O.J. L188/20, July 16, 1984). This Directive lists in Annex I various categories of industrial plant and provides (Art. 3) that Member States must take the necessary measures to ensure that the operation of such plants requires prior authorisation by competent authorities, the necessity to meet any relevant requirements being taken into account at the design stage. Authorisation is also required (Art. 3(2)) for "substantial alterations" to such plants. Article 4 requires that an authorisation should only be issued upon the competent authority being satisfied that: (a) all appropriate preventive measures against air pollution have been taken, including the use of best available technology, provided that the application of such measures does not entail excessive cost; (b) the use of the plant will not cause significant air pollution, particularly from the emission of substances listed in Annex II (including sulphur dioxide, oxides of nitrogen, hydrocarbons, heavy metals, chlorine, asbestos and fluorine, and their respective compounds); (c) no applicable emission limit values will be exceeded; and (d) all applicable air quality limit values will be taken into account. By Article 8 the Council is given power, acting unanimously on a proposal from the Commission, to fix emission limit values. By Art. 12, Member States must follow developments "as regards the best available technology and the environmental situation" and in the light of this must, if necessary, impose appropriate conditions on the basis of those developments and the desirability of avoiding excessive costs, having regard to "the economic situation of the plants belonging to the category concerned." Article 13 requires policies to be implemented for the "gradual adaptation" of existing plants to the best available technology, taking into account in particular the plant's technical characteristics; its rate of utilisation and length of its remaining life; the nature and volume of polluting emissions from it; and the desirability of not entailing excessive costs for the plant concerned, having regard in particular to the economic situation of undertakings belonging to the category in question. "Existing plant" means a plant in operation before July 1, 1987 or built or authorised before that date (Art. 2(3)). The implementation date for the Directive is June 30, 1987.
   (b) *Directive 88/609/EEC on the limitation of emissions of certain pollutants into the air from large combustion plants* (O.J. L336/1, December 12, 1988). By Art. 1 the Directive applies to combustion plants the rated thermal input of which is 50 MW or more, irrespective of the type of fuel used, be it solid, liquid or gaseous. Article 3 requires Member States, no later than July 1, 1990, to draw up appropriate programmes for the progressive reduction of total annual emissions from existing plants (*i.e.* those for which the original construction licence was granted before July 1, 1987). Such programmes are to be drawn up and implemented with the aim of complying with (at least) the emission ceilings and percentage reductions for sulphur dioxide and oxides of nitrogen in Annexes I and II. These reduction targets are to be reviewed by the Commission in 1994 (Art. 3(4)). By Art. 4, Member States must take appropriate measures to ensure that all licences for the construction or operation of new plant contain conditions relating to compliance with the emission limit values fixed in Annexes III to VII in respect of sulphur dioxide, oxides of nitrogen and dust. By Art. 10, waste gases from combustion plants must be discharged "in controlled fashion by means of a stack" and the competent authorities shall in particular ensure that the stack height is calculated in such a way as to safeguard health and the environment. By Art. 13, Member States must take the necessary measures to ensure monitoring of emissions in accordance with Annex IX: the methods and equipment used must correspond to "the best industrial measurement technology." The programmes drawn up in accordance with Art. 3(1) must be notified to the Commission not later than December 31, 1990 (Art. 16) and the relevant laws and provisions necessary to comply with the Directive must be in force no later than June 30, 1990.
   (c) *Directive 76/464/EEC on pollution caused by dangerous substances discharged into the aquatic environment of the Community* (O.J. L129/32, May 4, 1976). This Directive applies to inland territorial, coastal and ground waters and by Art. 2 requires Member States to take the appropriate steps: (a) to eliminate pollution of such waters by dangerous substances in the families and groups of substances in List I of the Annex; and

(b) to reduce pollution of such waters by the dangerous substances in the families and groups of List II of the Annex. The Annex contains the two lists. List I ("the Black List") contains substances, families and groups selected mainly on the basis of their toxicity, persistence or bio-accumulation, with the exception of those that are biologically harmless or are "rapidly converted" into substances that are biologically harmless. List II ("the Grey List") is composed of two main classes of substance, namely: (a) substances within List I for which the limit values have not yet been determined under the Directive; and (b) certain listed substances and categories of substance, and which, in the case of both (a) and (b), have a deleterious effect on the aquatic environment which can, however, "be confined to a given area and which depend on the characteristics and location of the water into which they are discharged." All discharges "liable to contain" List I substances require prior authorisation laying down emission standards; where necessary to implement the Directive, emission standards must also be set for discharges to sewer (Art. 3). These emission standards must, by Art. 5, determine the permissible maximum concentration of the substances in question and the maximum permissible quantity over time. Articles 5(3) and (4) state unequivocally that authorisation for the discharge shall be refused where it appears that the discharge is unable to comply with such standards and that if the standards are not in fact complied with, appropriate steps must be taken to ensure that the discharge is prohibited. Under Art. 6 the Council, on a proposal from the Commission, shall lay down limit values for the various substances, which domestic emission standards must not exceed. Where appropriate, by Art. 6(1), limit values applicable to industrial effluents shall be established "according to sector and type of product."

Discharges liable to contain List II substances also require prior authorisation, with emission standards laid down (Art. 7(2)). Advice as to implementation of the Directive is contained in DoE Circ. 7/89 (W.O. 16/89): *Water and the Environment*. This points out that particular substances are, in the terms of the Directive, not confirmed as warranting List I methods of control until a "daughter" directive setting the limit values has been agreed, and that progress to agreeing such directives has been slow. It also points out that by Art. 6(3) the relevant limit values do not apply where a member state can prove to the Commission that quality objectives established by the Council under Art. 6(2) "are being met and continuously maintained throughout the area which might be affected by the discharges." The Government intends to make use of this provision "wherever possible" (para. 10). Where there are cases where exceptionally the appropriate quality objective cannot initially be met, "competent authorities may need to apply the limit value approach until such time as the quality objectives can be achieved" (para. 14). In relation to discharges to sewer, the Circular interprets the Directive as requiring that all discharges of List I substances to sewer must be controlled by authorisation, with specific emission standards, where these are likely to lead to or contribute towards any appreciable effect in the ultimate receiving waters (para. 16). Paragraphs 17 and 18 explain how the quality objective and limit value approaches apply to such discharges.

(d) *Directive 86/280/EEC on limit values and quality objectives for discharges of certain dangerous substances included in List I of the Annex to Directive 76/464/EEC* (O.J. L181/16, June 12, 1986). This Directive lays down limit values and quality objectives for specified families or groups of substances (carbon tetrachloride, DDT and pentachlorophenol) in respect of discharges from industrial plant handling those substances. By Art. 3(4), Member States may grant authorisations for "new plants" only if those plants apply "the standards corresponding to the best technical means available when that is necessary for the elimination of pollution in accordance with Art. 2 of Directive 76/464/EEC or for the prevention of distortions of competition." "New plants" means: (a) plant becoming operational later than 12 months after notification of the Directive; and (b) existing industrial plant, whose capacity for handling the relevant substances is "substantially increased" after that date. This is interpreted by the UK government as an overall increase of 20 per cent. or more in handling capacity for that substance (Circ. 7/89, para. 22).

It can be seen that many of the provisions of Pt. I of the Act are framed with a view to complying with the requirements of these and other Directives, and that those provisions will need to be read in the light of applicable E.C. law.

Increasingly, it may also be necessary to utilise Pt. I to implement wider international obligations under Conventions relating to, for example, the emission of greenhouse gases and ozone-depleting substances and the protection of marine ecosystems. The work of UNEP and the UN Conference on Environment and Development in Rio de Janeiro in 1992 is important, since one of the achievements of the Conference was to secure agreement to a convention on climate change. Other important areas of international co-operation are the 1985 Vienna Convention and 1987 Montreal Protocol on consumption and production of chlorofluorocarbons, the 1979 Geneva Convention on Long Range Transboundary Air Pollution and the 1988 Sofia No_x Protocol made thereunder, and the three North Sea Conferences.

Relationship with other areas of control

As a new area of statutory control, IPC and LAAPC will inevitably raise issues of duplication or overlap with other areas of control. Examples are matters of health and safety at work, statutory nuisances, water pollution and waste disposal.

(a) *Health and Safety at Work:* No condition may be imposed on an IPC or LAAPC authorisation for the purpose only of securing the health of persons at work (within the meaning of Pt. I of the Health and Safety at Work etc. Act 1974 (s.7(1)).

(b) *Deposit of controlled waste:* No condition may be attached to an authorisation so as to regulate the final disposal by deposit in or on land of controlled waste, nor shall any condition apply to such a disposal (s.28(1)). However, where a prescribed process does involve the final disposal of controlled waste by deposit in or on land, that fact must be notified by the enforcing authority to the relevant waste regulation authority (s.28(1)).

Under s.33(3), the Secretary of State may make regulations excluding the deposit, treatment, keeping or disposal of controlled waste from control under Pt. II of the Act. In exercising this power, the Secretary of State is to have regard to the expediency of excluding cases for which adequate controls are provided otherwise than by s.33 (s.33(4)(c)). Thus, forms of waste disposal activity other than landfill, *e.g.* incineration, may be brought within Pt. I of the Act.

(c) *Radioactive substances:* Where activities comprised within a prescribed process are regulated both by authorisation under Pt. I and by registration or authorisation under the Radioactive Substances Act 1960, then if different obligations are imposed as respects the same matter by the relevant conditions, those conditions imposed under Pt. I are not binding (s.28(2)). Thus, the supremacy of the Radioactive Substances Act conditions is secured.

(d) *Water pollution:* Where the activities comprising a process prescribed for IPC include the release of any substances into controlled waters for the purposes of Pt. III of the Water Resources Act 1991, control remains with HMIP. Sched. 15, para. 29, amends the Water Act 1989, s.108, now s.88(1)(b) of the Water Resources Act 1991, to provide that no offence is committed where a discharge is made under and in accordance with an IPC authorisation. However:

(i) HMIP shall not grant an authorisation if the NRA certifies that in its opinion the release will result in or contribute to a failure to achieve any water quality objective in force under Pt. III of the Water Act 1989 (s.28(3)(a));

(ii) any authorisation granted must include such conditions as appear to the NRA to be appropriate for the purposes of Pt. I of the 1990 Act and which are notified in writing to HMIP (s.28(3)(b)); and

(iii) HMIP shall exercise its statutory powers of variation so as to vary the conditions of an authorisation as required by notice in writing given by the NRA (s.28(4)). This last obligation appears to apply also to processes scheduled for local control so far as they involve the release of any substances into controlled waters.

(e) *Trade effluent:* Under Chapter III of Pt. IV of the Water Industry Act 1991, the Secretary of State is enabled to exercise ultimate control over the discharge of certain types of trade effluent to sewers. The Trade Effluent (Prescribed Processes and Substances) Regulations 1989 (S.I. 1989 No. 1156) prescribe the relevant substances and processes. Sched. 15, para. 28 of the Environmental Protection Act amends the Water Act 1989 by providing that Sched. 9 (now Chapter III of Pt. IV of the Water Industry Act 1991) (which confers the relevant controls on the Secretary of State) shall not apply in relation to trade effluent produced or to be produced in a process prescribed for central (IPC) control under Pt. I of the Environmental Protection Act. The definition of release into water as including releases to sewers (s.1(11)(c)) enables HMIP to control discharges to sewers from prescribed processes by means of conditions. However, the sewer and its contents are to be disregarded in determining whether there is pollution of the environment. Thus, plant subject to IPC which discharge trade effluent to sewers will be subject to IPC conditions in relation to that discharge. They will also require consent from the sewerage undertaker under s.118 of the Water Industry Act 1991, which may include conditions as to volume, composition, temperature and other matters, as well as setting the charge to be paid.

(f) *Statutory nuisances:* In the case of statutory nuisances consisting of smoke emitted from premises, dust, steam, smell or other effluvia arising on industrial, trade or business premises, or any accumulation or deposit, a local authority may not issue summary proceedings under Pt. III of the Act without the consent of the Secretary of State, if proceedings in respect thereof might be instituted under Pt. I of the Act (s.79(10)). Given the breadth of the definitions of "pollution of the environment" and "harm" contained in s.1 of the Act, control under Pt. I can clearly embrace matters of public health and, indeed, activities causing offence to man's olfactory or other senses.

(g) *Planning control:* There is no explicit linkage between planning control and the provisions of Pt. I of the Act. Unlike a waste management licence under Pt. II, there is no requirement that planning permission be in force before authorisation is granted under Pt. I. Clearly there is a danger that conditions attached to planning permissions or terms contained in planning agreements could conflict with the conditions of the Pt. I authorisation. The traditional approach of the Secretary of State to planning conditions is that they will be unnecessary so far as they duplicate other, more specific, areas of control, and *ultra vires* in so far as they conflict with other such controls. However, there have been cases where planning conditions have been upheld, notwithstanding a degree of overlap with industrial air pollution controls, on the basis that they provide better protection than the more specifically-based controls: see, *e.g.* the *Ferro-Alloys and Metals Smelter, Glossop* decision noted at [1990] 1 LMELR 175.

Implementation of Part I
Part I of the Act comes into force on such day or days as the Secretary of State may by order appoint: s.164(3). Section 3 (Emission, etc. limits and quality objectives) came into force on December 19, 1990. Sections 1, 2 and 4–28 came into force on January 1, 1990. See the Environmental Protection Act 1990 (Commencement No. 4) Order 1991 (S.I. 1991 No. 2635).

The original proposals for implementation were announced by the Minister of State for the Environment on April 26, 1990 (DoE News Release No. 271). The intention was to introduce the IPC system in England and Wales on January 2, 1991, from which date all new processes, and all existing processes to be substantially altered, would be required to apply for authorisation. Existing processes would be brought within the system by a sectoral phased programme. The first sector, combustion processes (including plant covered by the E.C. Large Combustion Plants Directive), would have been within the system from January 2, 1991.

That timetable was subsequently revised, as the Minister of State announced on July 24, 1990 (DoE News Release No. 441). The initial date for implementing IPC was postponed to April 1, 1991 for new prescribed processes, processes undergoing a substantial change and large combustion plant. Other prescribed processes are to be phased in over four years from April 1, 1992. DoE News Release No. 455 (August 9, 1990) contained a timetable for implementing IPC, relating to the issue of final guidance and the date by which IPC authorisation is to be required.

	Issue Final Guidance	IPC Authorisation Required
Interim Guidance for Industries		
— Fuel and Power industry		
— Metal industry		
— Mineral industry	2.1.91	1.4.91
— Chemical industry		
— Waste Disposal industry		

Guidance on individual processes
Schedule
Reference Process

Fuel and Power Industry
1.3	Combustion (>50MWth Boilers and Furnaces)	2.1.91	1.4.91
1.1	Gasification		
1.2	Carbonization	1.10.91	1.4.92
1.3	Combustion (remainder)		
1.4	Petroleum		

Waste Disposal Industry
5.1	Incineration		
5.2	Chemical recovery	1.6.92	1.12.92
5.3	Chemical waste treatment		
5.4	Waste derived fuel		

Mineral Industry
3.1	Cement		
3.2	Asbestos		
3.3	Fibre	1.9.92	1.3.93
3.5	Glass		
3.6	Ceramic		

	Chemical Industry		
4.1	Petrochemical		
4.2	Organic	1.12.92	1.6.93
4.7	Chemical pesticide		
4.8	Pharmaceutical		
4.3	Acid manufacturing		
4.4	Halogen	1.4.93	1.10.93
4.6	Chemical fertiliser		
4.9	Bulk chemical storage	1.9.93	1.3.94
4.5	Inorganic chemical		
	Metal Industry		
2.1	Iron and Steel	1.5.94	1.11.94
2.3	Smelting		
2.2	Non-ferrous	1.8.94	1.2.95
	Other Industry		
6.1	Paper manufacturing		
6.2	Di-isocyanate		
6.3	Tar and Bitumen		
6.4	Uranium	1.5.95	1.11.95
6.5	Coating		
6.6	Coating manufacturing		
6.7	Timber		
6.8	Animal and plant treatment		
	Full implementation		1.4.96

A more detailed timetable is now provided by the Environmental Protection (Prescribed Processes and Substances) Regulations 1991 (S.I. 1991 No. 472), as amended (see Appendix 1). Sched. 3, Pt. I of the regulations requires new IPC processes to obtain authorisations as from April 1, 1991. Existing processes, *e.g.* those being carried on at some time in the 12 months immediately preceding April 1, 1991, must obtain authorisation if a "substantial change" in the process is made after that date. If no such substantial change is made, existing processes must in any event apply for authorisation within a three-month "window" defined in a table to Sched. 3: *e.g.* waste disposal and recycling processes between December 1, 1992 and February 28, 1993 and the "other industries" category between November 1, 1995 and January 31, 1996. Part II of Sched. 3 divides LAAPC processes into three groups, giving prescribed dates of, respectively, April 1, 1991, October 1, 1991 and April 1, 1992 for new processes. For "existing" processes, a further six months is given after those dates within which application for authorisation must be made. If a "substantial change" is due, then the date at which the change is made is the prescribed date.

Obviously, in practice implementation will be dependent upon the speed with which the requisite advice to HMIP and guidance to local authorities is formulated, and other practical factors such as the availability of resources to HMIP.

Preliminary

Preliminary

1.—(1) The following provisions have effect for the interpretation of this Part.

(2) The "environment" consists of all, or any, of the following media, namely, the air, water and land; and the medium of air includes the air within buildings and the air within other natural or man-made structures above or below ground.

(3) "Pollution of the environment" means pollution of the environment due to the release (into any environmental medium) from any process of substances which are capable of causing harm to man or any other living organisms supported by the environment.

(4) "Harm" means harm to the health of living organisms or other interference with the ecological systems of which they form part and, in the case of man, includes offence caused to any of his senses or harm to his property; and "harmless" has a corresponding meaning.

(5) "Process" means any activities carried on in Great Britain, whether on premises or by means of mobile plant, which are capable of causing pollution

of the environment and "prescribed process" means a process prescribed under section 2(1) below.

(6) For the purposes of subsection (5) above—

"activities" means industrial or commercial activities or activities of any other nature whatsoever (including, with or without other activities, the keeping of a substance);

"Great Britain" includes so much of the adjacent territorial sea as is, or is treated as, relevant territorial waters for the purposes of [Part III of the Water Resources Act 1991] or, as respects Scotland, Part II of the Control of Pollution Act 1974; and

"mobile plant" means plant which is designed to move or to be moved whether on roads or otherwise.

(7) The "enforcing authority," in relation to England and Wales, is the chief inspector or the local authority by whom, under section 4 below, the functions conferred or imposed by this Part otherwise than on the Secretary of State are for the time being exercisable in relation respectively to releases of substances into the environment or into the air; and "local enforcing authority" means any such local authority.

(8) The "enforcing authority," in relation to Scotland, is—

(a) in relation to releases of substances into the environment, the chief inspector or the river purification authority (which in this Part means a river purification authority within the meaning of the Rivers (Prevention of Pollution) (Scotland) Act 1951),

(b) in relation to releases of substances into the air, the local authority,

by whom, under section 4 below, the functions conferred or imposed by this Part otherwise than on the Secretary of State are for the time being exercisable; and "local enforcing authority" means any such local authority.

(9) "Authorisation" means an authorisation for a process (whether on premises or by means of mobile plant) granted under section 6 below; and a reference to the conditions of an authorisation is a reference to the conditions subject to which at any time the authorisation has effect.

(10) A substance is "released" into any environmental medium whenever it is released directly into that medium whether it is released into it within or outside Great Britain and "release" includes—

(a) in relation to air, any emission of the substance into the air;
(b) in relation to water, any entry (including any discharge) of the substance into water,
(c) in relation to land, any deposit, keeping or disposal of the substance in or on land;

and for this purpose "water" and "land" shall be construed in accordance with subsections (11) and (12) below.

(11) For the purpose of determining into what medium a substance is released—

(a) any release into—
  (i) the sea or the surface of the seabed,
  (ii) any river, watercourse, lake, loch or pond (whether natural or artificial or above or below ground) or reservoir or the surface of the riverbed or of other land supporting such waters, or
  (iii) ground waters,
 is a release into water;
(b) any release into—
  (i) land covered by water falling outside paragraph (a) above or the water covering such land; or
  (ii) the land beneath the surface of the seabed or of other land supporting waters falling within paragraph (a)(ii) above,
 is a release into land; and
(c) any release into a sewer (within the meaning of [Water Industry Act 1991] or, in relation to Scotland, of the Sewerage (Scotland) Act 1968) shall be treated as a release into water;

but a sewer and its contents shall be disregarded in determining whether there is pollution of the environment at any time.

(12) In subsection (11) above "ground waters" means any waters contained in underground strata, or in—
  (a) a well, borehole or similar work sunk into underground strata, including any adit or passage constructed in connection with the well, borehole or work for facilitating the collection of water in the well, borehole or work; or
  (b) any excavation into underground strata where the level of water in the excavation depends wholly or mainly on water entering it from the strata.

(13) "Substance" shall be treated as including electricity or heat and "prescribed substance" has the meaning given by section 2(7) below.

AMENDMENTS
The words in square brackets in subss. (6) and (11)(c) were substituted by the Water Consolidation (Consequential Provisions) Act 1991, s.2 and Sched. 1.

GENERAL NOTE
This section contains a series of definitions which are of central importance to the systems of control instituted by Part I.

Subs. (2)
The environment. It should be noted that the definition includes the medium of air within buildings and other structures above or below ground.

Subs. (3)
Pollution of the environment. The term "pollution" is not directly defined, but one well-known definition runs as follows:
  "The introduction by man into the environment of substances or energy liable to cause hazards to human health, harm to living resources and ecological systems, damage to structures or amenity, or interference with legitimate use of the environment." M.W. Holdgate, *A Perspective on Environmental Pollution* (Cambridge, 1979).

It is the likelihood of undesirable effects that distinguishes pollution from contamination, in the sense of the introduction of alien substances into the environment: see RCEP Tenth Report Cm. 9149, paras. 1.9–1.13.

However, subs. (3) refers to the release of substances *capable* of causing harm as defined: pollution as the term is used in the subsection does not require proof of *actual* harm but simply the potential to cause harm.

Subs. (4)
Harm. This subsection extends considerably the definition of "pollution of the environment" by reference to the health of all living organisms, the ecological systems supporting them, offence to any human senses and harm to property.

Subs. (5)
Process. The term is given a wide meaning to include any activities capable of causing pollution of the environment. Such activities may either be carried out on premises or by means of mobile plant. In other statutory contexts the term "process" has been held to involve some degree of continuity and repetition of acts, albeit not of long duration: see *Nurse* v. *Morganite Crucible* [1989] 2 A.C. 692 (H.L.); *Vibroplant* v. *Holland (Inspector of Taxes)* (1982) 126 S.J. 82 (C.A.). The definition in subs. (5), however, does not appear to be qualified in that way. The burning of rubbish on a demolition site has been held to fall within the Clean Air Act 1968 as being "in connection with an industrial or trade process," namely demolition: *Sheffield City Council* v. *A.D.H. Demolition* (1984) 82 L.G.R. 177.

Subs. (6)
Activities. The term is given an extremely wide interpretation to cover activities of any nature and also to cover the passive keeping of substances. This avoids any doubt as to whether pure storage, whether of materials or of waste, could constitute an "activity": see *Hillil Property & Investment Co.* v. *Naraine Pharmacy* (1979) 123 S.J. 437.

Great Britain. The relevant "territorial waters" for the purposes of Pt. III of the Water Resources Act 1991 are "waters which extend seaward and for three miles from the baselines from which the breadth of the territorial sea adjacent to England and Wales is measured: Water Resources Act 1991, s.104(1)(a). It is possible for the Secretary of State to extend this jurisdiction to other areas of territorial sea up to the general 12 mile territorial limit by order made under s.104(4) of the Water Resources Act. The Water Resources Act expressly deals with the situation of trade or sewage effluent which is discharged from land in England and Wales through a pipe, into the sea outside the relevant seaward limits (s.85(3)(b)). Such a provision is not necessary for the purposes of Pt. I of the Environmental Protection Act, for the reason that territoriality is only relevant for the purposes of the location of the process (subs. (5)), and not for the concept of pollution (subss. (3) and (10)).

Mobile plant. The crucial test is whether the plant is "designed" to move or be moved. The word "designed" is ambiguous and in the context of Town and Country Planning legislation has been said to mean "intended" rather than technically designed: *Wilson* v. *West Sussex County Council* [1963] 2 Q.B. 764, 780, 783.

Subs. (10)
Release. As mentioned above, Part I is concerned with releases into the environment both within and outside Great Britain.

Subs. (11)
Medium of release. This subsection contains important rules for the purpose of determining whether a substance is released into water or into land. It also establishes that release into a sewer can be controlled as a release into water, though on determining whether there is pollution of the environment any effect on the sewer and its contents is to be disregarded. However, the definition of "sewer" in this sense would not extend to sewage treatment works, so it would seem that the effect on such works and the effluent they treat could be considered.

Subs. (12)
Ground waters. The definition of ground waters here is the same as that of the Water Resources Act 1991, s.104(1)(d). It may be contrasted with that contained in the E.C. Groundwaters Directive (80/68/EEC) which reads as follows:
"All water which is below the surface of the ground in the saturation zone and in direct contact with the ground or subsoil."
See also DoE Circ. 20/90 (W.O. 34/90), para. 6.

Subs. (13)
Substance. "Substance," as well as including electricity or heat as expressly stated, would include natural or artificial substances, whether in solid or liquid form or in the form of a gas or vapour.

Prescribed processes and prescribed substances

2.—(1) The Secretary of State may, by regulations, prescribe any description of process as a process for the carrying on of which after a prescribed date an authorisation is required under section 6 below.

(2) Regulations under subsection (1) above may frame the description of a process by reference to any characteristics of the process or the area or other circumstances in which the process is carried on or the description of person carrying it on.

(3) Regulations under subsection (1) above may prescribe or provide for the determination under the regulations of different dates for different descriptions of persons and may include such transitional provisions as the Secretary of State considers necessary or expedient as respects the making of applications for authorisations and suspending the application of section 6(1) below until the determination of applications made within the period allowed by the regulations.

(4) Regulations under subsection (1) above shall, as respects each description of process, designate it as one for central control or one for local control.

(5) The Secretary of State may, by regulations, prescribe any description of substance as a substance the release of which into the environment is subject to control under sections 6 and 7 below.

(6) Regulations under subsection (5) above may—

(a) prescribe separately, for each environmental medium, the substances the release of which into that medium is to be subject to control; and
(b) provide that a description of substance is only prescribed, for any environmental medium, so far as it is released into that medium in such amounts over such periods, in such concentrations or in such other circumstances as may be specified in the regulations;

and in relation to a substance of a description which is prescribed for releases into the air, the regulations may designate the substance as one for central control or one for local control.

(7) In this Part "prescribed substance" means any substance of a description prescribed in regulations under subsection (5) above or, in the case of a substance of a description prescribed only for releases in circumstances specified under subsection (6)(b) above, means any substance of that description which is released in those circumstances.

DEFINITIONS
"authorisation": s.1(9).
"environment": s.1(2).
"environmental medium": s.1(2).
"prescribed process": s.1(5).
"process": s.1(5).
"release": s.1(10).
"substance": s.1(13).

GENERAL NOTE
This section deals with the prescription of processes and substances for (a) central or (b) local control. (See also the General Note to Pt. I). In relation to processes wide discretion is given as to how the description of the process is framed, to provide different prescribed dates for different descriptions of operator, and to make transitional provisions (subss. (2) and (3)).

In relation to substances, prescription may relate to a specific environmental medium and may incorporate thresholds as to quantities over time, concentrations, or indeed, other circumstances (subs. (6)). "Prescribed substance" is then construed by reference to such thresholds.

In the case of prescribed processes, designation as to central or local control will determine whether control is exercised by HMIP over releases to all media, or by local authorities over releases to the air (subs. (4)). In relation to a substance prescribed for releases into the air, the substance may be designated as one for either central or local control. Where the substance is prescribed in relation to releases to all media, or to the media of water or land, the inference is that the designation must be for central control. It would appear theoretically possible, though it might be technically undesirable, for the same substance to be prescribed for central control if released into water or land, but for local control if released into the air.

Further details on prescription, proposals for prescribed processes and substances, and for the prescribed dates are given in the General Note to Pt. I.

The Environmental Protection (Prescribed Processes and Substances) Regulations 1991 (S.I. 1991 No. 472) as amended by S.I. 1991 No. 836 and S.I. 1992 No. 614 were made under these powers. (See Appendix 1).

Emission etc. limits and quality objectives

3.—(1) The Secretary of State may make regulations under subsection (2) or (4) below establishing standards, objectives or requirements in relation to particular prescribed processes or particular substances.

(2) Regulations under this subsection may—
(a) in relation to releases of any substance from prescribed processes into any environmental medium, prescribe standard limits for—
   (i) the concentration, the amount or the amount in any period of that substance which may be so released; and
   (ii) any other characteristic of that substance in any circumstances in which it may be so released;
(b) prescribe standard requirements for the measurement or analysis of, or of releases of, substances for which limits have been set under paragraph (a) above; and

(c) in relation to any prescribed process, prescribe standards or requirements as to any aspect of the process.

(3) Regulations under subsection (2) above may make different provision in relation to different cases, including different provision in relation to different processes, descriptions of person, localities or other circumstances.

(4) Regulations under this subsection may establish for any environmental medium (in all areas or in specified areas) quality objectives or quality standards in relation to any substances which may be released into that or any other medium from any process.

(5) The Secretary of State may make plans for—
(a) establishing limits for the total amount, or the total amount in any period, of any substance which may be released into the environment in, or in any area within, the United Kingdom;
(b) allocating quotas as respects the release of substances to persons carrying on processes in respect of which any such limit is established;
(c) establishing limits of the descriptions specified in subsection (2)(a) above so as progressively to reduce pollution of the environment;
(d) the progressive improvement in the quality objectives and quality standards established by regulations under subsection (4) above;

and the Secretary of State may, from time to time, revise any plan so made.

(6) Regulations or plans under this section may be made for any purposes of this Part or for other purposes.

(7) The Secretary of State shall give notice in the London, Edinburgh and Belfast Gazettes of the making and the revision of any plan under subsection (5) above and shall make the documents containing the plan, or the plan as so revised, available for inspection by members of the public at the places specified in the notice.

(8) Subject to any Order made after the passing of this Act by virtue of subsection (1)(a) of section 3 of the Northern Ireland Constitution Act 1973, the making and revision of plans under subsection (5) above shall not be a transferred matter for the purposes of that Act but shall for the purposes of subsection (2) of that section be treated as specified in Schedule 3 to that Act.

DEFINITIONS
"environment": s.1(2).
"environmental medium": s.1(2).
"pollution of the environment": s.1(3).
"prescribed processes": s.1(5).
"processes": s.1(5).
"releases": s.1(10).
"substances": s.1(13).

GENERAL NOTE
The general purpose of this provision is to allow the Secretary of State power to achieve uniformity of approach and to further national strategies for pollution abatement. At the same time, considerable discretion as to making different provision for different cases is given by subs. (3).

In practice the use of such powers will be driven by obligations under European Community law (for example in the case of emission limits, quality objectives and quality standards) or obligations to the wider international community (for example, limits on the total amounts of substances released within the UK and plans for the progressive reduction of pollution). See further General Note to Pt. I, under the heading *Implementation of E.C. and International Requirements*.

Subs. (5)
Plans. On September 18, 1990 the Government issued a consultation paper and draft national plan on the implementation of the Large Combustion Plants Directive for reductions of emissions of sulphur dioxide and oxides of nitrogen from existing large plants within the UK. The plan was ultimately made as a statutory plan under s.3 on December 20, 1990. The plan sets

yearly targets for SO_2 and NO_x emissions from 1990–2003 and 1990–1998 respectively, for three separate sectors: power stations; refineries; and "other industry."

Discharge and scope of functions

4.—(1) This section determines the authority by whom the functions conferred or imposed by this Part otherwise than on the Secretary of State are exercisable and the purposes for which they are exercisable.

(2) Those functions, in their application to prescribed processes designated for central control, shall be functions of the chief inspector appointed for England and Wales by the Secretary of State under section 16 below and, in relation to Scotland, of the chief inspector so appointed for Scotland or of the river purification authority, as determined under regulations made under section 5(1) below, and shall be exercisable for the purpose of preventing or minimising pollution of the environment due to the release of substances into any environmental medium.

(3) Subject to subsection (4) below, those functions, in their application to prescribed processes designated for local control, shall be functions of—
  (a) in the case of a prescribed process carried on (or to be carried on) by means of mobile plant, the local authority in whose area the person carrying on the process has his principal place of business; and
  (b) in any other cases, the local authority in whose area the prescribed processes are (or are to be) carried on;
and the functions applicable to such processes shall be exercisable for the purpose of preventing or minimising pollution of the environment due to the release of substances into the air (but not into any other environmental medium).

(4) The Secretary of State may, as respects the functions under this Part being exercised by a local authority specified in the direction, direct that those functions shall be exercised instead by the chief inspector while the direction remains in force or during a period specified in the direction.

(5) A transfer of functions under subsection (4) above to the chief inspector does not make them exercisable by him for the purpose of preventing or minimising pollution of the environment due to releases of substances into any other environmental medium than the air.

(6) A direction under subsection (4) above may transfer those functions as exercisable in relation to all or any description of prescribed processes carried on by all or any description of persons (a "general direction") or in relation to a prescribed process carried on by a specified person (a "specific direction").

(7) A direction under subsection (4) above may include such saving and transitional provisions as the Secretary of State considers necessary or expedient.

(8) The Secretary of State, on giving or withdrawing a direction under subsection (4) above, shall—
  (a) in the case of a general direction—
    (i) forthwith serve notice of it on the chief inspector and on the local enforcing authorities affected by the direction; and
    (ii) cause notice of it to be published as soon as practicable in the London Gazette or, as the case may be, in the Edinburgh Gazette and in at least one newspaper circulating in the area of each authority affected by the direction;
  (b) in the case of a specific direction—
    (i) forthwith serve notice of it on the chief inspector, the local enforcing authority and the person carrying on or appearing to the Secretary of State to be carrying on the process affected, and
    (ii) cause notice of it to be published as soon as practicable in the London Gazette or, as the case may be, in the Edinburgh

Gazette and in at least one newspaper circulating in the authority's area;
and any such notice shall specify the date at which the direction is to take (or took) effect and (where appropriate) its duration.

(9) It shall be the duty of the chief inspector or, in Scotland, of the chief inspector and river purification authorities to follow developments in technology and techniques for preventing or reducing pollution of the environment due to releases of substances from prescribed processes; and the local enforcing authorities shall follow such of those developments as concern releases into the air of substances from prescribed processes designated for local control.

(10) It shall be the duty of the chief inspector, river purification authorities and the local enforcing authorities to give effect to any directions given to them under any provision of this Part.

(11) In this Part "local authority" means, subject to subsection (12) below—
  (a) in Greater London, a London borough council, the Common Council of the City of London, the Sub-Treasurer of the Inner Temple and the Under Treasurer of the Middle Temple;
  (b) outside Greater London, a district council and the Council of the Isles of Scilly; and
  (c) in Scotland, an islands or district council.

(12) Where, by an order under section 2 of the Public Health (Control of Disease) Act 1984, a port health authority has been constituted for any port health district, the port health authority shall have by virtue of this subsection, as respects its district, the functions conferred or imposed by this Part and no such order shall be made assigning those functions; and "local authority" and "area" shall be construed accordingly.

DEFINITIONS
"environment": s.1(2).
"mobile plant": s.1(6).
"pollution of the environment": s.1(3).
"prescribed processes": s.1(5).
"process": s.1(5).
"release": s.1(10).
"substances": s.1(13).

GENERAL NOTE
This section explains the distinction between centrally and locally controlled processes. The functions conferred or imposed by Pt. I of the Act fall to the chief inspector of pollution in the case of centrally controlled processes, or in some cases the river purification authority in Scotland. The functions relating to locally controlled processes fall to the relevant local authority at district level (see subs. (11)).

The functions are to be exercised for the purpose of preventing or minimising pollution of the environment due to the release of substances into any medium in the case of centrally-controlled processes (subs. (2)). For locally-controlled processes, the functions are exercisable for preventing or minimising pollution of the environment due to the release of substances into the air. It should be noted that the functions are not limited to reducing or preventing pollution of the air: they could be used in relation to pollution of soil or water caused by substances originally released into the air.

Subs. (4)
Transfer of functions. It is possible for the Secretary of State to transfer functions from local authorities to the chief inspector by means of a general or specific direction given under subss. (4) and (6). Such a transfer does not, however, widen control beyond the release of substances to the air (subs. (5)).

Subs. (9)
Developments in technology and techniques. Both the chief inspector and local authorities are under a statutory duty to follow developments in pollution abatement technology and tech-

niques in relation to the relevant processes. This duty is important in relation to the concept of use of best available techniques not entailing excessive cost.

Further provision as to discharge and scope of functions: Scotland

5.—(1) For the purposes of section 4(2) above in its application to Scotland, the Secretary of State shall make regulations prescribing—
   (a) the method and arrangements for determining whether the functions referred to in that subsection shall be functions of the chief inspector or of a river purification authority;
   (b) if the functions are determined under paragraph (a) above to be functions of a river purification authority, the river purification authority by whom they are to be exercised.

(2) The Secretary of State may make regulations prescribing—
   (a) the circumstances and manner in which consultation shall be carried out between—
      (i) whichever of the chief inspector or river purification authority is determined under regulations made under subsection (1) above to be the enforcing authority, and
      (ii) the other (the "consulted authority"),
   before granting, varying, transferring or revoking an authorisation or serving an enforcement or prohibition notice;
   (b) the circumstances in which the consulted authority may require the enforcing authority to include, in an authorisation, conditions which the consulted authority reasonably believe will achieve the objectives specified in section 7(2) below.

(3) Regulations under this section may contain such incidental, supplemental and consequential provision as the Secretary of State considers appropriate.

(4) This section applies to Scotland only.

GENERAL NOTE

This section allows the Secretary of State to allocate centrally controlled functions in Scotland between the chief inspector and river purification authorities.

The Environmental Protection (Determination of Enforcing Authority etc.) (Scotland) Regulations 1992 (S.I. 1992 No. 530) have been made under these powers prescribing those cases when HMIPI is the enforcing authority in Scotland and where the relevant river purification authority will be the enforcing authority. In England and Wales HMIP is always the enforcing authority although s.28(3) gives the NRA a veto power over authorisations that would lead to a breach of water quality objectives.

Authorisations

Authorisations: general provisions

6.—(1) No person shall carry on a prescribed process after the date prescribed or determined for that description of process by or under regulations under section 2(1) above (but subject to any transitional provision made by the regulations) except under an authorisation granted by the enforcing authority and in accordance with the conditions to which it is subject.

(2) An application for an authorisation shall be made to the enforcing authority in accordance with Part I of Schedule 1 to this Act and shall be accompanied by the fee prescribed under section 8(2)(a) below.

(3) Where an application is duly made to the enforcing authority, the authority shall either grant the authorisation subject to the conditions required or authorised to be imposed by section 7 below or refuse the application.

(4) An application shall not be granted unless the enforcing authority considers that the applicant will be able to carry on the process so as to comply with the conditions which would be included in the authorisation.

(5) The Secretary of State may, if he thinks fit in relation to any application for an authorisation, give to the enforcing authority directions as to whether or not the authority should grant the authorisation.

(6) The enforcing authority shall, as respects each authorisation in respect of which it has functions under this Part, from time to time but not less frequently than once in every period of four years, carry out a review of the conditions of the authorisation.

(7) The Secretary of State may, by regulations, substitute for the period for the time being specified in subsection (6) above such other period as he thinks fit.

(8) Schedule 1 to this Act (supplementary provisions) shall have effect in relation to authorisations.

DEFINITIONS
"enforcing authority": s.1(7) and (8).
"prescribed process": s.1(5).
"process": s.1(5).

GENERAL NOTE
The effect of this section is that a prescribed process may only be lawfully carried on after the relevant prescribed date (see General Note to Pt. I) if an authorisation has been granted and if the process is carried on in accordance with the conditions to which the authorisation is subject.

Carry on. Questions may arise as to what constitutes the "carrying on" of a process. Cases on the expression "carry on business" suggests that: (a) a repetition or series of acts is required (*Smith* v. *Anderson* (1880) 15 Ch.D. 247, 277, 278 (C.A., *per* Brett L.J.)); and (b) the person carrying on the process must have control and direction with regard to it (*Lewis* v. *Graham* (1888) 22 Q.B.D. 1, 5 (C.A., *per* Fry L.J.)).

Subs. (2)
Applications for authorisation. By Pt. I of Sched. 1 to the Act the form of application, the information it must contain, and the advertisement required, may be prescribed by regulations. The application itself will be subject to the publicity provisions of s.20, by which prescribed particulars of the application will be contained in the public register.

Subs. (4)
Ability of applicant. Whilst Pt. I does not contain any provisions equivalent in sophistication to the concept of "fit and proper person" contained in Pt. II in relation to waste management licensing, it is clear from this subsection that the enforcing authority must have regard to characteristics of the applicant in so far as they are relevant to the applicant's ability to comply with the proposed conditions.

Subs. (6)
Review of authorisations. The conditions of an authorisation must be reviewed from time to time and at least once every four years. No doubt the frequency of review will be affected by the use made by the Secretary of State of his powers under s.3, and by requirements of European Community law.

Supplementary provisions. Schedule 1 contains supplementary provisions as to the grant and variation of authorisations. These provisions deal with:
  (a) form of applications;
  (b) advertisement of applications;
  (c) requests for further information;
  (d) consultation;
  (e) representations by other persons;
  (f) transmission of applications to the Secretary of State for determination;
  (g) public inquiries or hearings in transmitted cases;
  (h) directions to enforcing authorities by the Secretary of State;
  (i) period for determination and deemed refusal (four months);
  (j) procedure for variation of authorisations, both by the enforcing authority and on application by the person carrying on the process.

Regulations on applications. Regulations dealing with, *inter alia*, applications were made on March 6, 1991 and came into force on April 1, 1991 in England and Wales and on April 1, 1992 in Scotland (Environmental Protection (Applications, Appeals and Registers) Regulations 1991 (S.I. 1991 No. 507)). For the text of the Regulations, see Appendix 2. These provide that

applications for authorisation shall be made in writing on a form provided by the enforcing authority (reg. 2(1)) and shall contain the following information (reg. 2(1)):
  (a) the name and address of the applicant and, if the applicant is a registered company, its registered number and registered office;
  (b) in a case where the prescribed process will be carried on by means of mobile plant, the name of the local authority in whose area the applicant has his principal place of business and, in any other case, the name of any local authority in whose area the prescribed process will be carried on;
  (c) in a case where the prescribed process will not be carried on by means of mobile plant, the address of the premises where the prescribed process will be carried on, a map or plan showing the location of those premises and, if only part of those premises will be used for carrying on the process, a plan or other means of identifying that part;
  (d) a description of the prescribed process;
  (e) a list of prescribed substances (and any other substances which might cause harm if released into any environmental medium) used in connection with or resulting from the prescribed process;
  (f) a description of the techniques to be used for preventing the release into any environmental medium of such substances, for reducing the release of such substances to a minimum and for rendering harmless any such substances which are released;
  (g) details of any proposed release of such a substance into any environmental medium and an assessment of the environmental consequences;
  (h) proposals for monitoring any release of such substances, the environmental consequences of any such release and the use of techniques mentioned in sub-para. (f) above;
  (i) the matters on which the applicant relies to establish that the objectives mentioned in section 7(2) of the Act (including the objective referred to in s.7(7) of the Act) will be achieved and that he will be able to comply with the condition implied by s.7(4) of the Act;
  (j) any additional information which he wishes the enforcing authority to take into account in considering his application.

In relation to LAAPC processes, by reg. 2(2), the reference to release of substances relates only to releases to air, and no reference is made to a form to be provided by the enforcing authority.

Consultations and advertisement. The regulations on applications, appeals and registers (above) provide for the following persons to be consulted on applications (reg. 4(1)):
  (a) the Health and Safety Executive, in all cases;
  (b) the Minister of Agriculture, Fisheries and Food, in the case of all prescribed processes designated for central control which will be carried on in England;
  (c) the Secretary of State for Wales, in the case of all prescribed processes designated for central control which will be carried on in Wales;
  (d) the Secretary of State for Scotland, in the case of all prescribed processes designated for central control which will be carried on in Scotland;
  (e) the National Rivers Authority, in the case of all prescribed processes designated for central control which will be carried on in England and Wales and which may result in the release of any substance into waters which are controlled waters for the purposes of Chapter I of Part III of the Water Act 1989;
  (f) the sewerage undertaker or, in relation to Scotland, the regional or islands council, in the case of all prescribed processes designated for central control which may involve the release of any substance into a sewer vested in the undertaker or the council;
  (g) the Nature Conservancy Council for England, the Nature Conservancy Council for Scotland or the Countryside Council for Wales—
    (i) in the case of all prescribed processes designated for central control which may involve a release of any substance;
    (ii) in the case of all prescribed processes designated for local control which may involve a release of any substance into the air,
    which may affect a site of special scientific interest within the Council's area;
  (h) the harbour authority, in the case of all prescribed processes designated for central control which may involve a release of any substance into a harbour managed by the harbour authority.

Regulation 5 deals with the required advertisement procedures. By reg. 6, neither reg. 4 nor 5 applies to waste oil burners with a net rated thermal input of less than 0.4 MW.

Period for consideration of applications. The general period given for consideration and determination of applications is four months (Sched. 1, para. 5(1)). This period has been extended to 18 months for existing processes involving the use of waste oil as fuel in appliances having a thermal input of less than 0.4 MW and to 12 months in the case of all other Part B existing processes: Environmental Protection (Authorisation of Processes) (Determination of Periods) Order 1991 (S.I. 1991 No. 513).

Conditions of authorisation

7.—(1) There shall be included in an authorisation—
(a) subject to paragraph (b) below such specific conditions as the enforcing authority considers appropriate, when taken with the general condition implied by subsection (4) below, for achieving the objectives specified in subsection (2) below;
(b) such conditions as are specified in directions given by the Secretary of State under subsection (3) below; and
(c) such other conditions (if any) as appear to the enforcing authority to be appropriate;

but no conditions shall be imposed for the purpose only of securing the health of persons at work (within the meaning of Part I of the Health and Safety at Work etc. Act 1974).

(2) Those objectives are—
(a) ensuring that, in carrying on a prescribed process, the best available techniques not entailing excessive cost will be used—
 (i) for preventing the release of substances prescribed for any environmental medium into that medium or, where that is not practicable by such means, for reducing the release of such substances to a minimum and for rendering harmless any such substances which are so released; and
 (ii) for rendering harmless any other substances which might cause harm if released into any environmental medium;
(b) compliance with any directions by the Secretary of State given for the implementation of any obligations of the United Kingdom under the Community Treaties or international law relating to environmental protection;
(c) compliance with any limits or requirements and achievement of any quality standards or quality objectives prescribed by the Secretary of State under any of the relevant enactments;
(d) compliance with any requirements applicable to the grant of authorisations specified by or under a plan made by the Secretary of State under section 3(5) above.

(3) Except as respects the general condition implied by subsection (4) below, the Secretary of State may give directions to the enforcing authorities as to the conditions which are, or are not, to be included in all authorisations, in authorisations of any specified description or in any particular authorisation.

(4) Subject to subsections (5) and (6) below, there is implied in every authorisation a general condition that, in carrying on the process to which the authorisation applies, the person carrying it on must use the best available techniques not entailing excessive cost—
(a) for preventing the release of substances prescribed for any environmental medium into that medium or, where that is not practicable by such means, for reducing the release of such substances to a minimum and for rendering harmless any such substances which are so released; and
(b) for rendering harmless any other substances which might cause harm if released into any environmental medium.

(5) In the application of subsections (1) to (4) above to authorisations granted by a local enforcing authority references to the release of substances into any environmental medium are to be read as references to the release of substances into the air.

(6) The obligation implied by virtue of subsection (4) above shall not apply in relation to any aspect of the process in question which is regulated by a condition imposed under subsection (1) above.

(7) The objectives referred to in subsection (2) above shall, where the process—

(a) is one designated for central control; and
(b) is likely to involve the release of substances into more than one environmental medium;

include the objective of ensuring that the best available techniques not entailing excessive cost will be used for minimising the pollution which may be caused to the environment taken as a whole by the releases having regard to the best practicable environmental option available as respects the substances which may be released.

(8) An authorisation for carrying on a prescribed process may, without prejudice to the generality of subsection (1) above, include conditions—
   (a) imposing limits on the amount or composition of any substance produced by or utilised in the process in any period; and
   (b) requiring advance notification of any proposed change in the manner of carrying on the process.

(9) This section has effect subject to section 28 below and, in relation to Scotland, to any regulations made under section 5(2) above.

(10) References to the best available techniques not entailing excessive cost, in relation to a process, include (in addition to references to any technical means and technology) references to the number, qualifications, training and supervision of persons employed in the process and the design, construction, lay-out and maintenance of the buildings in which it is carried on.

(11) It shall be the duty of enforcing authorities to have regard to any guidance issued to them by the Secretary of State for the purposes of the application of subsections (2) and (7) above as to the techniques and environmental options that are appropriate for any description of prescribed process.

(12) In subsection (2) above "the relevant enactments" are any enactments or instruments contained in or made for the time being under—
   (a) section 2 of the Clean Air Act 1968;
   (b) section 2 of the European Communities Act 1972;
   (c) Part I of the Health and Safety at Work etc. Act 1974;
   (d) Parts II, III or IV of the Control of Pollution Act 1974;
   (e) [the Water Resources Act 1991]; and
   (f) section 3 of this Act.

DEFINITIONS
   "enforcing authority": s.1(7) and (8).
   "environment": s.1(2).
   "environmental medium": s.1(2).
   "harm": s.1(4).
   "harmless": s.1(4).
   "pollution of the environment": s.1(3).
   "prescribed process": s.1(5).
   "process": s.1(5).
   "release": s.1(10).
   "substances": s.1(13).

AMENDMENTS
   The words in square brackets in subs. (12)(e) were substituted by the Water Consolidation (Consequential Provisions) Act 1991, s.2 and Sched. 1.

GENERAL NOTE
   This section is of central importance to Pt. I of the Act, dealing with the conditions to be imposed on authorisations, and introducing the key concepts of best available techniques not entailing excessive cost (BATNEEC) and best practicable environmental option (BPEO). Each authorisation incorporates a general implied condition (subs. (4)) and in addition may contain specific express conditions (subs. (1)) falling into one of three categories:
      (a) conditions considered appropriate by the enforcing authority for achieving objectives stated in subs. (2);
      (b) conditions specified by direction of the Secretary of State (subs. (3)); and

(c) such other conditions, if any, as appear to the enforcing authority to be appropriate.

The validity of all conditions (and perhaps particularly those in category (c)) will no doubt be subject to general principles of administrative law and *ultra vires*. For example, a condition imposed by a local enforcing authority which purported to control emissions to media other than air would appear to be *ultra vires*. It may be possible to draw analogies from the general principles evolved by the courts in relation to conditions attached to planning permissions.

Some guidance as to the attitude of the Secretary of State to conditions is to be found in general guidance note *GG2: Authorisations*. In relation to air pollution, control GG2 suggests tests based on clarity, relevance and workability. It is possible for the Secretary of State, under subs. (3), to give directions as to the conditions which are not to be included in authorisations as well as those that are. This power could be used to prevent an authority from including unjustified or irrelevant conditions: see Standing Committee H, Seventh Sitting, February 1, 1990, col. 227.

All specific conditions are subject to the statutory principle in subs. (1) that they shall not be imposed for the purpose *only* of securing the health of persons at work; however, it would be possible to have a valid condition which secures that purpose along with that of preventing or minimising pollution. In relation to the objectives contained in subs. (2) the linkage with s.3, by which the Secretary of State may prescribe limits requirements, standards, objectives and plans, should be noted.

BATNEEC. The concept of BATNEEC runs throughout s.6. Subsection (10) makes it clear that the term is not restricted to the application of technology, but also takes in matters of staffing, training, building layout and maintenance. As to the Government's guidance as to the meaning of BATNEEC, see the General Note to Part I.

Both in relation to specific conditions and the general implied condition, BATNEEC is to be used for two purposes, namely:
(1) preventing the release of substances prescribed for any environmental medium into that medium (or in the case of LAAPC preventing the release of substances prescribed for air into the air) or, where that is not practicable by the application of BATNEEC, reducing release to a minimum and rendering any releases harmless; and
(2) rendering harmless any other (non-prescribed) substances that might cause harm if released into any environmental medium (or, in the case of LAAPC, into the air).

The dichotomy created by the Alkali etc. Works Regulation Act 1906 (and earlier legislation) between: (a) preventing release where practicable; and (b) rendering releases harmless where prevention is not practicable is thereby preserved in the case of prescribed substances. The first step would therefore appear to be to identify those techniques which do not entail excessive cost for preventing the release of such substances and then to ask whether it is practicable to prevent release by those means. Traditional judicial interpretations of the term "practicable" have brought in questions of cost and risk: see, *e.g. Adsett* v. *K. and L. Steelfounders and Engineers* [1953] 1 W.L.R. 773; *Edwards* v. *National Coal Board* [1949] 1 K.B. 704; *Coltness Iron Co.* v. *Sharp* [1938] A.C. 90. This has also been the view expressed by HMIP in its Note on *Best Practicable Means: general principles and practice* (BPM 1/88, January 1988) paras. 10–16. It is therefore not entirely clear how BATNEEC relates to practicability in this sense: in particular if a technique which could prevent release has been identified as one not entailing excessive cost, is it still possible to argue that it is not practicable to prevent release by that technique?

With non-prescribed substances, the position is clearer. It should be asked whether the substance might cause harm if released, and if so BATNEEC is to be used to render it harmless, but not necessarily to prevent its release.

Subs. (7)

BPEO. Where a process is subject to central control and is likely to involve the release of substances into more than one environmental medium, the concept of BPEO comes into play. BATNEEC is to be used to minimise pollution caused to the environment as a whole (not just the receiving medium) having regard to the best practicable environmental option available as respects the substances that may be released. The complex process envisaged by the subsection therefore appears to be:
(1) identification of the substances that may be released;
(2) deciding what is the best practicable environmental option in relation to such substance or substances (or possibly combinations of substances);
(3) "having regard" to the BPEO so identified, identifying the BATNEEC which will minimise the pollution which may be caused to the environment as a whole, focusing here on the carrying on of the process rather than simply on the substances.

It appears therefore on the wording of the subsection that the crucial concept is still BATNEEC: the objective is to minimise pollution by the application of BATNEEC, having regard to BPEO.

Meaning of BPEO. BPEO is not defined in the Act but was considered at length by the Royal Commission on Environmental Pollution in their Eleventh Report of that name (Cm. 310). The RCEP's definition is given at para. 2.1 of the Report, as follows:

"A BPEO is the outcome of a systematic consultative and decision-making procedure which emphasises the protection and conservation of the environment across land, air and water. The BPEO procedure establishes, for a given set of objectives, the option that provides the most benefit or least damage to the environment as a whole, at acceptable cost, in the long term as well as in the short term."

The Report stresses:
(a) the width of options to be considered (para. 2.3);
(b) the evaluation of options for their environmental effects early in the decision-making process (para. 2.4);
(c) that "practicable" entails the option being in accordance with current technical knowledge and must not have disproportionate financial implications (para. 2.6);
(d) that local derogations to BPEO should not be admitted for social or political reasons (para. 2.7); and
(e) that it is doubtful whether there is ever an absolute best (para. 2.9).

Chapter 3 of the Report gives the RCEP's views on the procedure for arriving at BPEO, including the importance of maintaining a properly recorded "audit trail." The Report is generally an extremely full and careful examination of the concept, which defies concise summary.

Subs. (8)

Under this subsection, conditions may: (a) impose limits on the amount or composition of input and output substances in relation to a process; and (b) require advance notification of proposed changes in the manner of carrying on a process. The Government's thinking behind (a) is shown clearly by the following comments from Mr David Trippier in Committee:

"It is not our intention that enforcing authorities should in the normal course of events restrict the production capacity of a process, or the nature of the products that it produces, or set requirements as to inputs. Unless overriding considerations prevail, decisions on these matters are for industry itself. Enforcing authorities have no basis for getting involved, and no need to. But there will be some cases where such controls have to be exercised, if emissions are to be properly controlled. It might help if I give a couple of examples. If a certain piece of hardware is to be used to control emissions, it may be that there needs to be a limit on the throughput in the process, because that hardware is only effective up to certain levels of throughput. Higher throughput would require more sophisticated control technology. Therefore, it is important that limits can be set on the throughput. Conditions might be required in similar circumstances to regulate the type of feedstock. Such controls can be regarded as interim measures before more suitable emission control equipment is installed.

We also need to provide against cases where, for example, a combustion plant using high sulphur fuel causes significant air pollution. Enforcing authorities need to be able to limit the amount of such fuel that is used, or to specify less polluting fuel.

But I emphasise that that power is intended to be used infrequently, and only when necessary. Wherever possible, industry will have full flexibility to make its own decisions on inputs and throughputs within the parameters required by the necessary controls over releases." (H.C. Standing Committee H, Seventh Sitting, February 1, 1990, cols. 228–299.)

Subs. (11)

Guidance. The Secretary of State may achieve consistency as to BATNEEC for LAAPC and as to BATNEEC and BPEO for IPC by means of guidance as to techniques and environmental options relating to any description of prescribed process. The enforcing authorities are under a statutory duty to have regard to such guidance. Further detail as to guidance proposed and issued is given in the General Note to Pt. I, under the heading *Authorisations, Conditions and BATNEEC.*

Fees and charges for authorisations

8.—(1) There shall be charged by and paid to the enforcing authority such fees and charges as may be prescribed from time to time by a scheme under subsection (2) below (whether by being specified in or made calculable under the scheme).

(2) The Secretary of State may, with the approval of the Treasury, make, and from time to time revise, a scheme prescribing—
 (a) fees payable in respect of applications for authorisations;
 (b) fees payable by persons holding authorisations in respect of, or of applications for, the variation of authorisations; and
 (c) charges payable by such persons in respect of the subsistence of their authorisations.

(3) The Secretary of State shall, on making or revising a scheme under subsection (2) above, lay a copy of the scheme or of the alterations made in the scheme or, if he considers it more appropriate, the scheme as revised, before each House of Parliament.

(4) The Secretary of State may make separate schemes for fees and charges payable to the chief inspector or, as the case may be, river purification authority and fees and charges payable to local enforcing authorities under this Part.

(5) A scheme under subsection (2) above may, in particular—
 (a) make different provision for different cases, including different provision in relation to different persons, circumstances or localities;
 (b) allow for reduced fees or charges to be payable in respect of authorisations for a number of prescribed processes carried on by the same person;
 (c) provide for the times at which and the manner in which the payments required by the scheme are to be made; and
 (d) make such incidental, supplementary and transitional provision as appears to the Secretary of State to be appropriate.

(6) The Secretary of State, in framing a scheme under subsection (2) above, shall, so far as practicable, secure that the fees and charges payable under the scheme are sufficient, taking one financial year with another, to cover the relevant expenditure attributable to authorisations.

(7) The "relevant expenditure attributable to authorisations" is the expenditure incurred by the enforcing authorities in exercising their functions under this Part in relation to authorisations together with the expenditure incurred by the National Rivers Authority in exercising the authority's functions in relation to authorisations for processes which may involve the release of any substance into water.

(8) If it appears to the enforcing authority that the holder of an authorisation has failed to pay a charge due in consideration of the subsistence of the authorisation, it may, by notice in writing served on the holder, revoke the authorisation.

(9) The Secretary of State may make to the National Rivers Authority payments of such amounts as appear to him to be required to meet the estimated relevant expenditure of the authority attributable to authorisations.

(10) Subsections (7) and (9) above shall not apply to Scotland, but in relation to Scotland the "relevant expenditure attributable to authorisations" is the expenditure incurred by the enforcing authorities in exercising their functions under this Part or in relation to consultation carried out under regulations made under section 5(2) above.

(11) In Scotland, the chief inspector may make to a river purification authority and a river purification authority may make to the chief inspector payments of such amounts as are appropriate to meet their estimated relevant expenditure attributable to authorisations, such amounts to be determined by the Secretary of State if the chief inspector and the authority fail to agree on an appropriate amount of payment.

DEFINITIONS
 "authorisation": s.1(9).
 "enforcing authority": s.1(7) and (8).
 "prescribed processes": s.1(5).

GENERAL NOTE
This section gives wide power to the Secretary of State, with Treasury approval, to set a scheme of fees and charges for IPC and for LAAPC. Fees are payable on applications for authorisation and in respect of variation or applications for variation.

The essential concept is that of "relevant expenditure attributable to authorisations," defined in subs. (7) (subs. (10) for Scotland). This includes the relevant expenditure of the NRA, and the section contains provisions for payment to the NRA (or, in Scotland, to river purification authorities) of sums to meet their estimated relevant expenditure.

The sanction for non-payment of charges for subsistence of the authorisation is notice revoking the authorisation (subs. (8)). If the fee is not paid in respect of an application for authorisation or for variation, then the application is not duly made, and need not be considered by the enforcing authority (ss.6(2) and (3) and 11(9)).

Further information on proposals for the charging regime is given in the General Note to Pt. I under the heading *Fees and Charges*. The current charging schemes for England and Wales are set out in:

(i) *Fees and Charges for Integrated Pollution Control 1993–94*.
After a significant increase in fees for integrated pollution control for 1992/93, the increase for 1993/94 is at an average rate per component of 2.5 per cent.

The application fee for 1993/94 is £2,500 per component for processes which have previously been subject to air pollution control and £3,750 per component for processes coming under regulation by HMIP for the first time. The variation fee is £1,250 per component, and the annual subsistence charge is £1,540 per component.

(ii) *Fees and Charges for Local Authority Air Pollution Control 1993/94*.
The application fee for 1993/94 is £935, the annual subsistence charge fee is £600, and where a substantial change is made for the purpose of implementing a programme for upgrading an existing process the fee is £100. The application and subsistence fee for small waste oil burners is £100 and the application fee for processes registered under the Alkali etc. Works Act 1906 is £580.

The current charging schemes for Scotland are set out in the Integrated Pollution Control (Scotland) Fees and Charges Scheme 1993/94 and the Local Authority Air Pollution Control (Scotland) Fees and Charges Scheme 1993/94.

Transfer of authorisations

9.—(1) An authorisation for the carrying on of any prescribed process may be transferred by the holder to a person who proposes to carry on the process in the holder's place.

(2) Where an authorisation is transferred under this section, the person to whom it is transferred shall notify the enforcing authority in writing of that fact not later than the end of the period of 21 days beginning with the date of the transfer.

(3) An authorisation which is transferred under this section shall have effect on and after the date of the transfer as if it had been granted to that person under section 6 above, subject to the same conditions as were attached to it immediately before that date.

DEFINITIONS
"authorisation": s.1(9).
"enforcing authority": s.1(7) and (8).
"prescribed process": s.1(5).

GENERAL NOTE
This section deals with transfer of authorisations. It is open to the holder of an authorisation to transfer it to any person who proposes to carry out the process in the holder's place. This wording appears to imply that the transfer may only be made prospectively and not once control of the process itself has been transferred. There is no requirement that the transfer of the authorisation be effected in writing, though this may in practice be prudent. By subs. (3) the effect of the transfer is that the authorisation forthwith takes effect as if granted to the transferee, and subject to the same conditions as before.

There is no obligation to obtain the prior consent of the enforcing authority to a transfer, but simply for the transferee to notify the authority in writing of the fact of transfer not later than 21 days beginning with the date of the transfer. Failure to give such notice is an offence (s.23(1)(b)). The authority have no specific power to object to the transfer, despite the fact that on grant of an authorisation they must have regard to the capability of the applicant (see s.6(4) and notes thereto.) If the authority entertained serious doubts as to the ability or intentions of the transferee to carry on the process in accordance with the conditions, then it could serve an enforcement notice (s.13), or in an extreme case serve a prohibition notice (s.14) or revoke the authorisation (s.12).

Variation of authorisations by enforcing authority

10.—(1) The enforcing authority may at any time, subject to the requirements of section 7 above, and, in cases to which they apply, the requirements of Part II of Schedule 1 to this Act, vary an authorisation and shall do so if it appears to the authority at that time that that section requires conditions to be included which are different from the subsisting conditions.

(2) Where the enforcing authority has decided to vary an authorisation under subsection (1) above the authority shall notify the holder of the authorisation and serve a variation notice on him.

(3) In this Part a "variation notice" is a notice served by the enforcing authority on the holder of an authorisation—
  (a) specifying variations of the authorisation which the enforcing authority has decided to make; and
  (b) specifying the date or dates on which the variations are to take effect;
and, unless the notice is withdrawn, the variations specified in a variation notice shall take effect on the date or dates so specified.

(4) A variation notice served under subsection (2) above shall also—
  (a) require the holder of the authorisation, within such period as may be specified in the notice, to notify the authority what action (if any) he proposes to take to ensure that the process is carried on in accordance with the authorisation as varied by the notice; and
  (b) require the holder to pay the fee (if any) prescribed by a scheme under section 8 above within such period as may be specified in the notice.

(5) Where in the opinion of the enforcing authority any action to be take by the holder of an authorisation in consequence of a variation notice served under subsection (2) above will involve a substantial change in the manner in which the process is being carried on, the enforcing authority shall notify the holder of its opinion.

(6) The Secretary of State may, if he thinks fit in relation to authorisations of any description or particular authorisations, direct the enforcing authorities—
  (a) to exercise their powers under this section, or to do so in such circumstances as may be specified in the directions, in such manner as may be so specified; or
  (b) not to exercise those powers, or not to do so in such circumstances or such manner as may be so specified;
and the Secretary of State shall have the corresponding power of direction in respect of the powers of the enforcing authorities to vary authorisations under section 11 below.

(7) In this section and section 11 below a "substantial change," in relation to a prescribed process being carried on under an authorisation, means a substantial change in the substances released from the process or in the amount or any other characteristic of any substance so released; and the Secretary of State may give directions to the enforcing authorities as to what does or does not constitute a substantial change in relation to processes generally, any description of process or any particular process.

(8) In this section and section 11 below—
  "prescribed" means prescribed in regulations made by the Secretary of State;
  "vary," in relation to the subsisting conditions or other provisions of an authorisation, means adding to them or varying or rescinding any of them;
and "variation" shall be construed accordingly.

DEFINITIONS
"authorisation": s.1(9).
"enforcing authority": s.1(7) and (8).
"prescribed process": s.1(5).
"process": s.1(5).
"released": s.1(10).
"substances": s.1(13).

GENERAL NOTE
This section gives enforcing authorities power to vary authorisations. "Variation" can include the addition or rescission of conditions (subs. (8)). Subs. (1) gives authorities a general power of variation at any time, subject to the general objectives and provisions of s.7. It also places a duty on authorities to vary conditions if it appears that s.7 would require different conditions to be imposed from those subsisting. As mentioned in the notes to s.6, authorities are under a continuing duty to keep authorisations under review.

Part II of Sched. 1 contains provisions which apply where an enforcing authority is of the view that action to be taken in consequence of a variation will involve "a substantial change in the manner in which the process is being carried on". In such cases the authority is required to advertise the action, give notice of it to prescribed persons, and consider any representations received.

Variation is effected by means of a variation notice served on the holder of the authorisation. The variations take effect from the date or dates specified in the notice (subs. (3)). If the authority is of the opinion that any action to be taken in consequence of the variation notice will involve a substantial change in the manner in which the process is being carried on, this opinion is to be notified to the holder of the authorisation (subs. (5)). "Substantial change" in this context is defined in subs. (7) by reference to the amount or other characteristics of substances released from the process; the Secretary of State may additionally give directions as to what does or does not constitute such a change. "Substantial" has been said to mean "considerable, solid, or big"; it will be a question for the discretion of the judge of fact, applying as much precision as is attainable in the context of the subject-matter being considered (see *Palser* v. *Grinling, Property Holding Co.* v. *Mischeff* [1948] 1 All E.R. 1, 11, H.L., *per* Viscount Simon and also *Atkinson* v. *Bettison* [1955] 3 All E.R. 340, 342, C.A., *per* Denning L.J.; [1955] 1 W.L.R. 1127). In the context of E.C. Directive 86/280/EEC on limit values and quality objectives for discharges of dangerous substances to the aquatic environment, the Government interprets "substantial change" as meaning an overall increase in capacity of 20 per cent. or more (see Circ. 7/89, para. 2, referred to in the General Note to Pt. I).

Variation of conditions etc.: applications by holders of authorisations

11.—(1) A person carrying on a prescribed process under an authorisation who wishes to make a relevant change in the process may at any time—
   (a) notify the enforcing authority in the prescribed form of that fact, and
   (b) request the enforcing authority to make a determination, in relation to the proposed change, of the matters mentioned in subsection (2) below;
and a person making a request under paragraph (b) above shall furnish the enforcing authority with such information as may be prescribed or as the authority may by notice require.

(2) On receiving a request under subsection (1) above the enforcing authority shall determine—
   (a) whether the proposed change would involve a breach of any condition of the authorisation;
   (b) if it would not involve such a breach, whether the authority would be likely to vary the conditions of the authorisation as a result of the change;
   (c) if it would involve such a breach, whether the authority would consider varying the conditions of the authorisation so that the change may be made; and
   (d) whether the change would involve a substantial change in the manner in which the process is being carried on;
and the enforcing authority shall notify the holder of the authorisation of its determination of those matters.

(3) Where the enforcing authority has determined that the proposed change would not involve a substantial change, but has also determined under paragraph (b) or (c) of subsection (2) above that the change would lead to or require the variation of the conditions of the authorisation, then—
  (a) the enforcing authority shall (either on notifying its determination under that subsection or on a subsequent occasion) notify the holder of the authorisation of the variations which the authority is likely to consider making; and
  (b) the holder may apply in the prescribed form to the enforcing authority for the variation of the conditions of the authorisation so that he may make the proposed change.

(4) Where the enforcing authority has determined that a proposed change would involve a substantial change that would lead to or require the variation of the conditions of the authorisation, then—
  (a) the authority shall (either on notifying its determination under subsection (2) above or on a subsequent occasion) notify the holder of the authorisation of the variations which the authority is likely to consider making; and
  (b) the holder of the authorisation shall, if he wishes to proceed with the change, apply in the prescribed form to the enforcing authority for the variation of the conditions of the authorisation.

(5) The holder of an authorisation may at any time, unless he is carrying on a prescribed process under the authorisation and wishes to make a relevant change in the process, apply to the enforcing authority in the prescribed form for the variation of the conditions of the authorisation.

(6) A person carrying on a process under an authorisation who wishes to make a relevant change in the process may, where it appears to him that the change will require the variation of the conditions of the authorisation, apply to the enforcing authority in the prescribed form for the variation of the conditions of the authorisation specified in the application.

(7) A person who makes an application for the variation of the conditions of an authorisation shall furnish the authority with such information as may be prescribed or as the authority may by notice require.

(8) On an application for variation of the conditions of an authorisation under any provision of this section—
  (a) the enforcing authority may, having fulfilled the requirements of Part II of Schedule 1 to this Act in cases to which they apply, as it thinks fit either refuse the application or, subject to the requirements of section 7 above, vary the conditions or, in the case of an application under subsection (6) above, treat the application as a request for a determination under subsection (2) above; and
  (b) if the enforcing authority decides to vary the conditions, it shall serve a variation notice on the holder of the authorisation.

(9) Any application to the enforcing authority under this section shall be accompanied by the applicable fee (if any) prescribed by a scheme made under section 8 above.

(10) This section applies to any provision other than a condition which is contained in an authorisation as it applies to a condition with the modification that any reference to the breach of a condition shall be read as a reference to acting outside the scope of the authorisation.

(11) For the purposes of this section a relevant change in a prescribed process is a change in the manner of carrying on the process which is capable of altering the substances released from the process or of affecting the amount or any other characteristic of any substance so released.

DEFINITIONS
  "authorisation": s.1(9).
  "enforcing authority": s.1(7) and (8).
  "prescribed": s.10(8).
  "prescribed process": s.1(5).

"process": s.1(5).
"released": s.1(10).
"substances": s.1(13).
"substantial change": s.10(7).
"variation": s.10(8).
"vary": s.10(8).

GENERAL NOTE

This section provides a number of means by which conditions of an authorisation may be varied at the instigation of the holder of the authorisation. The section applies not only to variation of conditions but also limitations or other provisions contained in an authorisation (subs. (10)).

(1) The first method, where the holder of the authority wishes to make a "relevant change" in the process, is to notify the authority of that fact and to request the authority to make a determination on various matters (subs. (1)). The matters for determination are set out in subs. (2). The authority may determine that the change would not involve breach of any condition and would not lead the authority to vary the conditions—in that case the holder of the licence is presumably free to make the change, though it appears this would not preclude the authority from keeping the conditions under review and exercising its own powers of variation under s.10. Alternatively, the authority may determine that the change would not involve any breach but that the authority would be likely to vary the conditions as a result of the change; or that it would involve a breach but that the authority would consider varying the conditions to allow the change to be made. In either case the authority should notify the variations it would be likely to consider making, and the holder of the authorisation may then apply for the relevant variations (subs. (3)). If the applicant disagrees with the determination, there is no right of appeal under s.15. In such circumstances the options open to the applicant would appear to be to make the relevant change (in which case enforcement action might follow) or to make an application for variation and then to appeal if refused. A separate procedure applies where the authority determines under subs. (2)(d) that the change would involve a substantial change in the manner of the process (as defined in s.10(7)). See subs. (4) and Sched. 1, Pt. II. Here the holder of the authorisation, if he wishes to proceed with the change, must apply for variation (subs. (4)(b)).

(2) The second method applies to the holder of an authorisation who does not wish to make a relevant change in the process he is carrying on. Here the procedure is a straightforward application for variation under subs. (5). This procedure could therefore be used either: (a) where no prescribed process is actually being carried on; or (b) where the proposed change is not "relevant" as defined in subs. (11).

(3) The third method applies to the person carrying on a process and who wishes to make a relevant change. Where it appears to him that the change will require variation of the conditions, an application for variation may be made under subs. (6), thus bypassing the complex provisions involving determination by the authority under subss. (1) and (2) as described above.

It is perhaps easier to compare these alternative procedures diagrammatically: See pp. 43–90 to 43–91.

Regulations. Regulations have been made dealing with variation procedures: Environmental Protection (Applications, Appeals and Registers) Regulations 1991 (S.I. 1991 No. 507) (see Appendix 2). These deal with the information to be given on applying for a determination or variation.

Schedule 1, Part II, para. 7

Procedure for substantial changes. Where the authority has determined that a proposed change would be substantial and an application is subsequently made under s.11(4)(b) for variation, para. 7(1) of the Schedule applies requirements of consultation, advertisement and consideration of representations. These procedures appear not to apply where an application for variation is made which involves a substantial change, but has not been the subject of a previous determination to that effect. It is however, open to the authority to treat the application for variation as an application for a determination and proceed accordingly (subs. 8(a)).

Relevant change and *substantial change*. The differing effects of these expressions should be noted. A "relevant change" is one that triggers the procedures under subs. (1) (notification and request for determination) and (6) (application for variation). "Relevant change" is defined by subs. (11) as one which is capable of altering the substances released or their amount or other characteristics. A "substantial change" is one that triggers the procedure of subs. (4) and consequently the requirements of Sched. 1, para. 7 as to advertisement and consultation. A "substantial change" is defined by s.10(7) as one leading to a substantial change in the substances released or in their amounts or characteristics. Thus not all "relevant" changes will be "substantial," but all "substantial" changes will be "relevant."

43/11 *Environmental Protection Act* 1990

HOLDER OF AUTHORISATION (UNLESS CARRYING ON PROCESS AND WISHING TO MAKE A RELEVANT CHANGE)

Appeals
Appeal against refusal of a variation lies to the Secretary of State under s.15(1)(c).

Revocation of authorisation

12.—(1) The enforcing authority may at any time revoke an authorisation by notice in writing to the person holding the authorisation.

(2) Without prejudice to the generality of subsection (1) above, the enforcing authority may revoke an authorisation where it has reason to believe that a prescribed process for which the authorisation is in force has not been carried on or not for a period of 12 months.

(3) The revocation of an authorisation under this section shall have effect from the date specified in the notice; and the period between the date on which the notice is served and the date so specified shall not be less than 28 days.

(4) The enforcing authority may, before the date on which the revocation of an authorisation takes effect, withdraw the notice or vary the date specified in it.

(5) The Secretary of State may, if he thinks fit in relation to an authorisation, give to the enforcing authority directions as to whether the authority should revoke the authorisation under this section.

DEFINITIONS
"authorisation": s.1(9).
"enforcing authority": s.1(7) and (8).
"prescribed process": s.1(5).

GENERAL NOTE
In addition to the general power of revocation conferred by subs. (1), a specific power of revocation is given by subs. (2) where the relevant process has not been carried on for a period of 12 months (presumably ending with the date of the revocation notice, though the subsection does not say this). There is obviously a drafting slip in subs. (2): presumably what is intended is that the authorisation may be revoked if the process has not been carried on at all or has not been carried on for a period of 12 months. The question of whether a process is or is not being "carried on" is therefore important (see note to s.6).

Enforcement

Enforcement notices

13.—(1) If the enforcing authority is of the opinion that the person carrying on a prescribed process under an authorisation is contravening any condition of the authorisation, or is likely to contravene any such condition, the authority may serve on him a notice ("an enforcement notice").

(2) An enforcement notice shall—
(a) state that the authority is of the said opinion;
(b) specify the matters constituting the contravention or the matters making it likely that the contravention will arise, as the case may be;
(c) specify the steps that must be taken to remedy the contravention or to remedy the matters making it likely that the contravention will arise, as the case may be; and
(d) specify the period within which those steps must be taken.

(2) The Secretary of State may, if he thinks fit in relation to the carrying on by any person of a prescribed process, give to the enforcing authority directions as to whether the authority should exercise its powers under this section and as to the steps which are to be required to be taken under this section.

DEFINITIONS
"authorisation": s.1(9).
"enforcing authority": s.1(7) and (8).
"prescribed process": s.1(5).

GENERAL NOTE
Enforcement notices under this section may be served not only where a condition or conditions are being contravened, but also where contravention appears likely to take place.

Failure to comply with the notice is an offence under s.23(1)(c). The requirements as to the matters to be contained in an enforcement notice under subs. (2) are mandatory and it appears that any notice which on its face does not comply with those requirements will be a nullity and, as such, so much waste paper that can be ignored or challenged in proceedings: *Miller-Mead* v. *Minister of Housing and Local Government* [1963] 2 Q.B. 196, 226 (C.A., *per* Upjohn L.J.). In practice, it is perhaps unlikely that many notices will fail to comply with these requirements on their face: rather, the question is likely to be whether the notice is bad for failure to specify the required matters with sufficient accuracy and precision. The most widely accepted test as to these matters in the case of planning enforcement notices is whether the notice tells the recipient "fairly what he has done wrong and what he must do to remedy it": *Miller-Mead* v. *Minister of Housing and Local Government* [1963] 2 Q.B. 196, 232 (C.A., *per* Upjohn L.J.). There seems no reason why the same test should not be applied to notices under s.13.

It should be noted that on an appeal against an enforcement notice, the Secretary of State may by s.15(7) either quash or affirm the notice and, if affirming it, do so either in its original form or with such modifications as he thinks fit. Though it does not say so explicitly, this power may well allow the Secretary of State to correct defects in a notice, but it is questionable whether it will be possible to cure fundamental defects that make the notice a nullity. Reference to the considerable body of case-law on defective enforcement notices under the Town and Country Planning Acts may provide some degree of assistance as to the likely attitude of the courts on this question, and in general the courts have become increasingly reluctant to hold that notices cannot be served.

Prohibition notices

14.—(1) If the enforcing authority is of the opinion, as respects the carrying on of a prescribed process under an authorisation, that the continuing to carry it on, or the continuing to carry it on in a particular manner, involves an imminent risk of serious pollution of the environment the authority shall serve a notice (a "prohibition notice") on the person carrying on the process.

(2) A prohibition notice may be served whether or not the manner of carrying on the process in question contravenes a condition of the authorisation and may relate to any aspects of the process, whether regulated by the conditions of the authorisation or not.

(3) A prohibition notice shall—
(a) state the authority's opinion;
(b) specify the risk involved in the process;

(c) specify the steps that must be taken to remove it and the period within which they must be taken; and
(d) direct that the authorisation shall, until the notice is withdrawn, wholly or to the extent specified in the notice cease to have effect to authorise the carrying on of the process;

and where the direction applies to part only of the process it may impose conditions to be observed in carrying on the part which is authorised to be carried on.

(4) The Secretary of State may, if he thinks fit in relation to the carrying on by any person of a prescribed process, give to the enforcing authority directions as to—
(a) whether the authority should perform its duties under this section; and
(b) the matters to be specified in any prohibition notice in pursuance of subsection (3) above which the authority is directed to issue.

(5) The enforcing authority shall, as respects any prohibition notice it has issued to any person, by notice in writing served on that person, withdraw the notice when it is satisfied that the steps required by the notice have been taken.

DEFINITIONS
"authorisation": s.1(9).
"enforcing authority": s.1(7) and (8).
"pollution of the environment": s.1(3).
"prescribed process': s.1(5).
"process": s.1(5).

GENERAL NOTE

The power conferred by this section to serve a prohibition notice is not limited to cases where a condition is being contravened, and extends to any aspect of the process, whether regulated by a condition or not (subs. (2)). The issue is whether the process involves "an imminent risk of serious pollution of the environment." Under the definition in s.1(3) and (4) this would include harm to human health or property and offence to human senses, though it will no doubt be questionable whether offence to senses would be "serious" in the sense contemplated by the section. An example of the circumstances where a prohibition notice might be appropriate was given by Lord Reay in the following extract:

"Prohibition notices are slightly different. They are not designed primarily to be served when an operator is breaching or is likely to breach the conditions of an authorisation. They are designed to cover circumstances in which a process is being operated in a perfectly reasonable manner and within the conditions of the authorisation but where some event external to the process requires quick and decisive action. For example, an accident at one process could release substances which could react with those normally allowed to be released by a nearby process, so causing serious pollution. In those circumstances it would be right to close down temporarily the second process even though it was operating within its authorisation." (*Hansard*, H.L. Vol. 520, col. 897).

See also H.C. Standing Committee H, Eighth Sitting, February 6, 1990, cols. 249–250.

As with enforcement notices, breach of a prohibition notice is an offence (s.23(1)(c)) and an appeal against the notice lies to the Secretary of State (s.15(2)). There are mandatory requirements as to the matters to be included in a notice (subs. (3)) and the comments made in the note to s.13 as to the effect of non-compliance with those requirements would appear to apply equally.

Appeals as respects authorisations and against variation, enforcement and prohibition notices

15.—(1) The following persons, namely—
(a) a person who has been refused the grant of an authorisation under section 6 above;
(b) a person who is aggrieved by the conditions attached, under any provision of this Part, to his authorisation;
(c) a person who has been refused a variation of an authorisation on an application under section 11 above;

(d) a person whose authorisation has been revoked under section 12 above;

may appeal against the decision of the enforcing authority to the Secretary of State (except where the decision implements a direction of his).

(2) A person on whom a variation notice, an enforcement notice or a prohibition notice is served may appeal against the notice to the Secretary of State.

(3) Where an appeal under this section is made to the Secretary of State—
  (a) the Secretary of State may refer any matter involved in the appeal to a person appointed by him for the purpose; or
  (b) the Secretary of State may, instead of determining the appeal himself, direct that the appeal or any matter involved in it shall be determined by a person appointed by him for the purpose;

and a person appointed under paragraph (b) above for the purpose of an appeal shall have the same powers under subsection (5), (6) or (7) below as the Secretary of State.

(4) An appeal under this section shall, if and to the extent required by regulations under subsection (10) below, be advertised in such manner as may be prescribed by regulations under that subsection.

(5) If either party to the appeal so requests or the Secretary of State so decides, an appeal shall be or continue in the form of a hearing (which may, if the person hearing the appeal so decides, be held, or held to any extent, in private).

(6) On determining an appeal against a decision of an enforcing authority under subsection (1) above, the Secretary of State—
  (a) may affirm the decision;
  (b) where the decision was a refusal to grant an authorisation or a variation of an authorisation, may direct the enforcing authority to grant the authorisation or to vary the authorisation, as the case may be;
  (c) where the decision was as to the conditions attached to an authorisation, may quash all or any of the conditions of the authorisation;
  (d) where the decision was to revoke an authorisation, may quash the decision;

and where he exercises any of the powers in paragraphs (b), (c) or (d) above, he may give directions as to the conditions to be attached to the authorisation.

(7) On the determination of an appeal under subsection (2) above the Secretary of State may either quash or affirm the notice and, if he affirms it, may do so either in its original form or with such modifications as he may in the circumstances think fit.

(8) Where an appeal is brought under subsection (1) above against the revocation of an authorisation, the revocation shall not take effect pending the final determination or the withdrawal of the appeal.

(9) Where an appeal is brought under subsection (2) above against a notice, the bringing of the appeal shall not have the effect of suspending the operation of the notice.

(10) Provision may be made by the Secretary of State by regulations with respect to appeals under this section and in particular—
  (a) as to the period within which and the manner in which appeals are to be brought; and
  (b) as to the manner in which appeals are to be considered.

DEFINITIONS
  "authorisation": s.1(9).
  "enforcing authority": s.1(7) and (8).

GENERAL NOTE
  This section, together with the regulations to be made under it, governs all appeals under Part I of the Act. There is power for the Secretary of State either to determine the appeal himself or

to transfer jurisdiction to an inspector (subs. (3)). The two modes of appeal contemplated are written representations and a hearing, either in public or in private. Wide discretion is given as to the disposition of appeals, including substitution of new conditions and modification of notices.

Appeals regulations
Regulations dealing with appeals were made on March 6, 1991 and came into force on April 1, 1991 in England and Wales: Environmental Protection (Applications, Appeals and Registers) Regulations 1991 (S.I. 1991 No. 507). See Appendix 2. Regulation 9 provides for written notices of appeal and for the following documents to be included with any notice of appeal:
   (a) a statement of the grounds of appeal;
   (b) a copy of any relevant application;
   (c) a copy of any relevant authorisation;
   (d) a copy of any relevant correspondence between the appellant and the enforcing authority;
   (e) a copy of any decision or notice which is the subject-matter of the appeal;
   (f) a statement indicating whether the appellant wishes the appeal to be in the form of a hearing or to be disposed of on the basis of written representations.

Regulation 10 gives a two month time limit for the bringing of appeals. Regulations 11–13 provide for the procedure to be followed on appeals. There is no provision for the award of costs.

Effect of appeal
An appeal against revocation of an authorisation has the effect of suspending the revocation until final determination or withdrawal of the appeal (subs. (8)). An appeal against a variation, prohibition or enforcement notice, by contrast, does not have the effect of suspending the operation of the notice (subs. (9)).

Challenge to decisions
No express means or grounds for challenging a decision on appeal are provided by the Act (*cf.* Town and Country Planning Act 1990, s.288).

Guidance on appeals
Explanatory guidance on the regulations dealing with appeals has been issued by the Secretary of State (GG5/91).

Appointment of chief inspector and other inspectors

16.—(1) The Secretary of State may appoint as inspectors (under whatever title he may determine) such persons having suitable qualifications as he thinks necessary for carrying this Part into effect in relation to prescribed processes designated for central control or for the time being transferred under section 4(4) above to central control, and may terminate any appointment made under this subsection.

(2) The Secretary of State may make to or in respect of any person so appointed such payments by way of remuneration, allowances or otherwise as he may with the approval of the Treasury determine.

(3) In relation to England and Wales the Secretary of State shall constitute one of the inspectors appointed under subsection (1) above to be the chief inspector for England and Wales and in relation to Scotland the Secretary of State shall constitute one of the said inspectors to be the chief inspector for Scotland.

(4) The functions conferred or imposed by or under this Part on the chief inspector as the enforcing authority may, to any extent, be delegated by him to any other inspector appointed under subsection (1) above.

(5) A river purification authority may appoint as inspectors (under whatever title the authority may determine) such persons having suitable qualifications as the authority thinks necessary for carrying this Part into effect in relation to prescribed processes designated for central control and may terminate any appointment made under this subsection.

(6) Any local authority may appoint as inspectors (under whatever title the authority may determine) such persons having suitable qualifications as the authority think necessary for carrying this Part into effect in the

authority's area in relation to prescribed processes designated for local control (and not so transferred), and may terminate any appointment made under this subsection.

(7) An inspector shall not be liable in any civil or criminal proceedings for anything done in the purported performance of his functions under section 17 or 18 below if the court is satisfied that the act was done in good faith and that there were reasonable grounds for doing it.

(8) In the following provisions of this Part "inspector" means a person appointed as an inspector under subsection (1), (5) or (6) above.

DEFINITIONS
"prescribed processes": s.1(5).

GENERAL NOTE
This section provides for the appointment of inspectors by the Secretary of State, river purification authorities and local authorities, and the appointment of chief inspectors for England and Wales and for Scotland.

The relevant inspectorate in England and Wales is HM Inspectorate of Pollution and, in Scotland, HM Industrial Pollutions Inspectorate. Subs. (7) confers immunity from civil and criminal proceedings for anything done in good faith and on reasonable grounds in performance of an inspector's functions.

HMIPI
As to the activities and structure of HMIPI, reference may be made to the first report of HMIPI for 1987–1988 (HMSO, 1990).

Powers of inspectors and others

17.—(1) An inspector may, on production (if so required) of his authority, exercise any of the powers in subsection (3) below for the purposes of the discharge of the functions of the enforcing authority.

(2) Those powers, so far as exercisable in relation to premises, are exercisable in relation—
  (a) to premises on which a prescribed process is, or is believed (on reasonable grounds) to be, carried on; and
  (b) to premises on which a prescribed process has been carried on (whether or not the process was a prescribed process when it was carried on) the condition of which is believed (on reasonable grounds) to be such as to give rise to a risk of serious pollution of the environment.

(3) The powers of an inspector referred to above are—
  (a) at any reasonable time (or, in a situation in which in his opinion there is an immediate risk of serious pollution of the environment, at any time) to enter premises which he has reason to believe it is necessary for him to enter;
  (b) on entering any premises by virtue of paragraph (a) above to take with him—
    (i) any person duly authorised by the chief inspector, the river purification authority or, as the case may be, the local enforcing authority and, if the inspector has reasonable cause to apprehend any serious obstruction in the execution of his duty, a constable; and
    (ii) any equipment or materials required for any purpose for which the power of entry is being exercised;
  (c) to make such examination and investigation as may in any circumstances be necessary;
  (d) as regards any premises which he has power to enter, to direct that those premises or any part of them, or anything in them, shall be left undisturbed (whether generally or in particular respects) for so long

as is reasonably necessary for the purpose of any examination or investigation under paragraph (c) above;
(e) to take such measurements and photographs and make such recordings as he considers necessary for the purpose of any examination or investigation under paragraph (c) above;
(f) to take samples of any articles or substances found in or on any premises which he has power to enter, and of the air, water or land in, on, or in the vicinity of, the premises;
(g) in the case of any articles or substance found in or on any premises which he has power to enter, being an article or substance which appears to him to have caused or to be likely to cause pollution of the environment, to cause it to be dismantled or subjected to any process or test (but not so as to damage or destroy it unless this is necessary);
(h) in the case of any such article or substance as is mentioned in paragraph (g) above, to take possession of it and detain it for so long as is necessary for all or any of the following purposes, namely—
  (i) to examine it and do to it anything which he has power to do under that paragraph;
  (ii) to ensure that it is not tampered with before his examination of it is completed;
  (iii) to ensure that it is available for use as evidence in any proceedings for an offence under section 23 below or any other proceedings relating to a variation notice, an enforcement notice or a prohibition notice;
(i) to require any person whom he has reasonable cause to believe to be able to give any information relevant to any examination or investigation under paragraph (c) above to answer (in the absence of persons other than a person nominated to be present and any persons whom the inspector may allow to be present) such questions as the inspector thinks fit to ask and to sign a declaration of the truth of his answers;
(j) to require the production of, or where the information is recorded in computerised form, the furnishing of extracts from, any records which are required to be kept under this Part or it is necessary for him to see for the purposes of an examination or investigation under paragraph (c) above and to inspect and take copies of, or of any entry in, the records;
(k) to require any person to afford him such facilities and assistance with respect to any matters or things within that person's control or in relation to which that person has responsibilities as are necessary to enable the inspector to exercise any of the powers conferred on him by this section;
(l) any other power for the purpose mentioned in subsection (1) above which is conferred by regulations made by the Secretary of State;
and in so far as any of the powers specified above are applicable in relation to mobile plant an inspector shall have, in circumstances corresponding to those specified in subsection (2) above, powers corresponding to those powers.

(4) The Secretary of State may by regulations make provision as to the procedure to be followed in connection with the taking of, and the dealing with, samples under subsection (3)(f) above.

(5) Where an inspector proposes to exercise the power conferred by subsection (3)(g) above in the case of an article or substance found on any premises, he shall, if so requested by a person who at the time is present on and has responsibilities in relation to those premises, cause anything which is to be done by virtue of that power to be done in the presence of that person.

(6) Before exercising the power conferred by subsection (3)(g) above in the case of any article or substance, an inspector shall consult such persons as appear to him appropriate for the purpose of ascertaining what dangers, if

any, there may be in doing anything which he proposes to do under the power.

(7) Where under the power conferred by subsection (3)(h) above an inspector takes possession of any article or substance found on any premises, he shall leave there, either with a responsible person or, if that is impracticable, fixed in a conspicuous position, a notice giving particulars of that article or substance sufficient to identify it and stating that he has taken possession of it under that power; and before taking possession of any such substance under that power an inspector shall, if it is practical for him to do so, take a sample of it and give to a responsible person at the premises a portion of the sample marked in a manner sufficient to identify it.

(8) No answer given by a person in pursuance of a requirement imposed under subsection (3)(i) above shall be admissible in evidence in England and Wales against that person in any proceedings, or in Scotland against that person in any criminal proceedings.

(9) The powers conferred by subsection (3)(a), (b)(ii), (c), (e) and (f) above shall also be exercisable (subject to subsection (4) above) by any person authorised for the purpose in writing by the Secretary of State.

(10) Nothing in this section shall be taken to compel the production by any person of a document of which he would on grounds of legal professional privilege be entitled to withhold production on an order for discovery in an action in the High Court or, in relation to Scotland, on an order for the production of documents in an action in the Court of Session.

DEFINITIONS
"enforcing authority": s.1(7) and (8).
"inspector": s.16(8).
"pollution of the environment": s.1(3).
"prescribed process": s.1(5).

GENERAL NOTE
This section gives inspectors wide powers of entry, examination, investigation, sampling, testing, detention of substances and articles and requisitioning of information. The only express exemption from such powers relates to documents covered by legal professional privilege (subs. (10)). This exemption would cover communications between clients and legal professional advisors, whether independent or "in-house." It would not cover communications with other professional advisors, such as engineers or chemists. Attendance notes recording meetings or advice between legal advisors and clients would also be privileged (*Balabel* v. *Air India* [1988] Ch. 317 (C.A.)) but not notes simply recording meetings or conversations between opposing parties or their legal advisors (*Parry* v. *News Group Newspapers* [1990] New L.J. 1719 (C.A.)). Nor is legal professional privilege conferred simply by marking a document "without prejudice."

Failure to comply with requirements under the section, or intentional obstruction of an inspection in the course of those powers, is a criminal offence under s.23(1)(d)–(f). It should be noted that by subs. (2) the powers are exercisable not only in relation to premises on which a prescribed process is carried on, but also premises where a prescribed process (or a process which subsequently became a prescribed process) was carried out, whether the condition of those premises is such as to give rise to a risk of serious pollution of the environment or not.

Power to deal with cause of imminent danger of serious harm

18.—(1) Where, in the case of any article or substance found by him on any premises which he has power to enter, an inspector has reasonable cause to believe that, in the circumstances in which he finds it, the article or substance is a cause of imminent danger of serious harm he may seize it and cause it to be rendered harmless (whether by destruction or otherwise).

(2) Before there is rendered harmless under this section—
  (a) any article that forms part of a batch of similar articles; or
  (b) any substance,
the inspector shall, if it is practicable for him to do so, take a sample of it and give to a responsible person at the premises where the article or substance

was found by him a portion of the sample marked in a manner sufficient to identify it.

(3) As soon as may be after any article or substance has been seized and rendered harmless under this section, the inspector shall prepare and sign a written report giving particulars of the circumstances in which the article or substance was seized and so dealt with by him, and shall—
   (a) give a signed copy of the report to a responsible person at the premises where the article or substance was found by him; and
   (b) unless that person is the owner of the article or substance, also serve a signed copy of the report on the owner;
and if, where paragraph (b) above applies, the inspector cannot after reasonable inquiry ascertain the name or address of the owner, the copy may be served on him by giving it to the person to whom a copy was given under paragraph (a) above.

DEFINITIONS
   "harm": s.1(4).
   "inspector": s.17(8).
   "substance": s.1(13).

GENERAL NOTE
Power is given by this section to deal with substances or articles which are a likely cause of imminent danger of serious harm as defined in s.1. The power is to seize the article or substance and render it harmless.

Obtaining of information from persons and authorities

19.—(1) For the purposes of the discharge of his functions under this Part, the Secretary of State may, by notice in writing served on an enforcing authority, require the authority to furnish such information about the discharge of its functions as an enforcing authority under this Part as he may require.

(2) For the purposes of the discharge of their respective functions under this Part, the following, that is to say—
   (a) the Secretary of State,
   (b) a local enforcing authority,
   (c) the chief inspector, and
   (d) in relation to Scotland, a river purification authority,
may, by notice in writing served on any person, require that person to furnish to the authority such information which the authority reasonably considers that it needs as is specified in the notice, in such form and within such period following service of the notice as is so specified.

(3) For the purposes of this section the discharge by the Secretary of State of an obligation of the United Kingdom under the Community Treaties or any international agreement relating to environmental protection shall be treated as a function of his under this Part.

DEFINITIONS
   "enforcing authority": s.1(7) and (8).

GENERAL NOTE
This section gives power to the Secretary of State to obtain information from enforcing authorities in furtherance of his functions under Pt. I, including the discharge of any obligations of the UK under European Community or other treaty obligations relating to environmental protection.

Also, the Secretary of State and central and local enforcing authorities are empowered to require any person to furnish them with such information as they reasonably consider is needed in the discharge of their functions. Failure to comply with such a requirement is an offence (s.23(1)(g)), as is the giving of false or misleading information knowingly or recklessly (s.23(1)(h)(i)).

Publicity

Public registers of information

20.—(1) It shall be the duty of each enforcing authority, as respects prescribed processes for which it is the enforcing authority, to maintain, in accordance with regulations made by the Secretary of State, a register containing prescribed particulars of or relating to—
  (a) applications for authorisations made to that authority;
  (b) the authorisations which have been granted by that authority or in respect of which the authority has functions under this Part;
  (c) variation notices, enforcement notices and prohibition notices issued by that authority;
  (d) revocations of authorisations effected by that authority;
  (e) appeals under section 15 above;
  (f) convictions for such offences under section 23(1) below as may be prescribed;
  (g) information obtained or furnished in pursuance of the conditions of authorisations or under any provision of this Part;
  (h) directions given to the authority under any provision of this Part by the Secretary of State; and
  (i) such other matters relating to the carrying on of prescribed processes or any pollution of the environment caused thereby as may be prescribed;
but that duty is subject to sections 21 and 22 below.

(2) Subject to subsection (4) below, the register maintained by a local enforcing authority shall also contain prescribed particulars of such information contained in any register maintained by the chief inspector or river purification authority as relates to the carrying on in the area of the authority of prescribed processes in relation to which the chief inspector or river purification authority has functions under this Part; and the chief inspector or river purification authority shall furnish each authority with the particulars which are necessary to enable it to discharge its duty under this subsection.

(3) In Scotland, the register maintained by—
  (a) the chief inspector shall also contain prescribed particulars of such information contained in any register maintained by a river purification authority as relates to the carrying on in the area of the authority of prescribed processes in relation to which the authority has functions under this Part, and each authority shall furnish the chief inspector with the particulars which are necessary to enable him to discharge his duty under this section;
  (b) each river purification authority shall also contain prescribed particulars of such information contained in any register maintained by the chief inspector as relates to the carrying on in the area of the authority of prescribed processes in relation to which the chief inspector has functions under this Part, and the chief inspector shall furnish each authority with the particulars which are necessary to enable them to discharge their duty under this section.

(4) Subsection (2) above does not apply to port health authorities but each local enforcing authority whose area adjoins that of a port health authority shall include corresponding information in the register maintained by it; and the chief inspector shall furnish each such local enforcing authority with the particulars which are necessary to enable it to discharge its duty under this subsection.

(5) Where information of any description is excluded from any register by virtue of section 22 below, a statement shall be entered in the register indicating the existence of information of that description.

(6) The Secretary of State may give to enforcing authorities directions requiring the removal from any register of theirs of any specified information not prescribed for inclusion under subsection (1) or (2) above or which, by virtue of section 21 or 22 below, ought to have been excluded from the register.

(7) It shall be the duty of each enforcing authority—
  (a) to secure that the registers maintained by them under this section are available, at all reasonable times, for inspection by the public free of charge; and
  (b) to afford to members of the public facilities for obtaining copies of entries, on payment of reasonable charges.

(8) Registers under this section may be kept in any form.

(9) For the purpose of enabling the National Rivers Authority to discharge its duty under section 117(1)(f) of the Water Act 1989 to keep corresponding particulars in registers under that section, the chief inspector shall furnish the Authority with the particulars contained in any register maintained by him under this section.

(10) In this section "prescribed" means prescribed in regulations under this section.

DEFINITIONS
  "authorisation": s.1(9).
  "enforcing authority": s.1(7) and (8).
  "prescribed processes": s.1(5).

GENERAL NOTE
  As mentioned in the General Note to Part I of the Act, public access to information is an important aspect of environmental policy, and ss.20–22 deal with the public registers to be created. These provisions need to be read in conjunction with E.C. Directive 90/313/EEC of June 7, 1990 on the freedom of access to information on the environment (O.J. L158/56 June 23, 1990). Under this Directive, as from December 31, 1992, Member States are to ensure that public authorities are required to make available information relating to the environment to any natural or legal person at his request and without his having to prove an interest. It is questionable whether these obligations can be fully satisfied by a system of registers: see House of Lords Select Committee on the European Communities, 1st Report Session 1989–90 on *Freedom of Access to Information on the Environment* (H.L. Paper November 22, 1989) paras. 40–42 and 77–80. The Government issued a consultation paper in January 1992 setting out how Directive 90/313/EEC will be implemented in the UK and giving the public a right to information beyond that on registers (The Government's Proposals for the Implementation in the UK Law of the EC Directive on Freedom of Access to Information on the Environment, DoE, W.O.) Subsequently the Environmental Information Regulations 1992 (S.I. 1992 No. 3240) were made to implement the Directive with effect from December 31, 1992.

Contents of registers
  The matters to be covered in the registers are set out in subs. (1) and the relevant particulars to be included are prescribed in regulations. Of particular significance and sensitivity to holders of authorisations is likely to be information contained in authorisations about the relevant processes (sub-para. (a)), details of authorisations and conditions attached thereto (sub-para. (b)), convictions (sub-para. (f)) and information obtained or furnished in pursuance of conditions (sub-para. (g)). The list does not include data obtained by enforcing authorities under their general powers of sampling, but it seems likely that such information will be prescribed for inclusion under sub-para. (i) as relating to the carrying on of prescribed processes or pollution caused thereby—certainly the E.C. Directive 90/313 referred to above would require this. The Environmental Protection (Application, Appeals and Registers) Regulations 1991 (S.I. 1991 No. 507) state that the following matters should be contained within the registers (reg. 15(1)):
  "(a) a copy of any application for an authorisation made to the authority;
  (b) a copy of any information furnished in response to a notice to the appellant by the enforcing authority under para. 1(3) of Sched. 1;
  (c) all particulars of any representations made by any person registered to be consulted under paras. 2, 6 or 7 of Sched. 1 to the 1990 Act pursuant to reg. 4(1).
  (d) a copy of any authorisation granted by the authority;

(e) a copy of any variation notice, enforcement notice, or prohibition notice issued by the authority;
(f) a copy of any notice issued by the authority withdrawing a prohibition notice;
(g) a copy of any notification of the holder of an authorisation by the authority under s.10(5);
(h) a copy of any application for the variation of the conditions of an authorisation under s.11(4)(b);
(i) a copy of any revocation effected by the authority;
(j) a copy of any notice of appeal under s.15, any decision letter of the Secretary of State relating to such an appeal and any report by an inspector, or in Scotland, a reporter, accompanying any such decision letter;
(k) details of any conviction for any offence under s.23(1), including the name of the offender, the date of conviction, the penalty imposed and the name of the Court;
(l) any monitoring information relating to a prescribed process obtained by the authority as a result of its own monitoring or furnished to the authority in writing by virtue of a condition of the authorisation or s.19(2);
(m) in a case where any such monitoring information is omitted from the register by virtue of s.22, a statement by the authority, based on the monitoring information from time to time obtained by or furnished to them, indicating whether or not there has been compliance with any relevant condition of the authorisation;
(n) all particulars of any report published by an enforcing authority relating to an assessment of the environmental consequences of the carrying on of a prescribed process in the locality of premises where the prescribed process is carried on under an authorisation granted by the authority; and
(o) a copy of any direction given to the authority by the Secretary of State under any provision of Pt. I."

It is stated (reg. 17) that monitoring information need not be kept on the register for more than four years (but presumably may be if the authority chooses). Registers may be kept in any form, including electronically: subs. (8).

Who keeps the registers?

Registers are maintained by HMIP or HMIPI, local authorities, river purification authorities and port health authorities in relation to prescribed processes for which they are the enforcing authority. In addition, local authorities keep on their registers information from the register of HMIP relating to centrally controlled processes in their area, thereby making such information available locally (see subs. (2)). In Scotland under subs. (3) information is mutually duplicated on the registers kept by HMIPI and river purification authorities.

Subs. (9)

National Rivers Authority. Schedule 15, para. 29 to the Act amends s.190 of the Water Resources Act 1991 by requiring inclusion in registers kept under the 1991 Act of prescribed particulars of any matter about which particulars are required to be kept under s.20 of the 1990 Act. To enable the NRA to fulfil this duty HMIP must furnish the NRA with information from their register. Thus information as to aquatic discharges of prescribed processes can also be obtained from the NRA's registers.

Exclusion from registers of information affecting national security

21.—(1) No information shall be included in a register maintained under section 20 above if and so long as, in the opinion of the Secretary of State, the inclusion in the register of that information, or information of that description, would be contrary to the interests of national security.

(2) The Secretary of State may, for the purpose of securing the exclusion from registers of information to which subsection (1) above applies, give to enforcing authorities directions—

(a) specifying information, or descriptions of information, to be excluded from their registers; or
(b) specifying descriptions of information to be referred to the Secretary of State for his determination;

and no information referred to the Secretary of State in pursuance of paragraph (b) above shall be included in any such register until the Secretary of State determines that it should be so included.

(3) The enforcing authority shall notify the Secretary of State of any information it excludes from the register in pursuance of directions under subsection (2) above.

(4) A person may, as respects any information which appears to him to be information to which subsection (1) above may apply, give a notice to the Secretary of State specifying the information and indicating its apparent nature; and, if he does so—
  (a) he shall notify the enforcing authority that he has done so; and
  (b) no information so notified to the Secretary of State shall be included in any such register until the Secretary of State has determined that it should be so included.

DEFINITIONS
"enforcing authority": s.1(7) and (8).

GENERAL NOTE
The Secretary of State may give directions under subs. (2) as to the exclusion of information on grounds of national security. Such information is to be excluded from the register for so long as the Secretary of State is of the opinion that inclusion would be contrary to the interests of national security. Any person may notify to the Secretary of State their view that information should be excluded under the section, and such information may then not be included on the register until the Secretary of State determines otherwise (subs. (4)(b)).

For the procedures, see reg. 7 of the Environmental Protection (Applications, Appeals and Registers) Regulations 1991 (S.I. 1991 No. 507).

Exclusion from registers of certain confidential information

22.—(1) No information relating to the affairs of any individual or business shall be included in a register maintained under section 20 above, without the consent of that individual or the person for the time being carrying on that business, if and so long as the information—
  (a) is, in relation to him, commercially confidential; and
  (b) is not required to be included in the register in pursuance of directions under subsection (7) below;
but information is not commercially confidential for the purposes of this section unless it is determined under this section to be so by the enforcing authority or, on appeal, by the Secretary of State.

(2) Where information is furnished to an enforcing authority for the purpose of—
  (a) an application for an authorisation or for the variation of an authorisation;
  (b) complying with any condition of an authorisation; or
  (c) complying with a notice under section 19(2) above;
then, if the person furnishing it applies to the authority to have the information excluded from the register on the ground that it is commercially confidential (as regards himself or another person), the authority shall determine whether the information is or is not commercially confidential.

(3) A determination under subsection (2) above must be made within the period of 14 days beginning with the date of the application and if the enforcing authority fails to make a determination within that period it shall be treated as having determined that the information is commercially confidential.

(4) Where it appears to an enforcing authority that any information (other than information furnished in circumstances wthin subsection (2) above) which has been obtained by the authority under or by virtue of any provision of this Part might be commercially confidential, the authority shall—
  (a) give to the person to whom or whose business it relates notice that that information is required to be included in the register unless excluded under this section; and
  (b) give him a reasonable opportunity—

(i) of objecting to the inclusion of the information on the ground that it is commercially confidential; and

(ii) of making representations to the authority for the purpose of justifying any such objection;

and, if any representations are made, the enforcing authority shall, having taken the representations into account, determine whether the information is or is not commercially confidential.

(5) Where, under subsection (2) or (4) above, an authority determines that information is not commercially confidential—

(a) the information shall not be entered on the register until the end of the period of 21 days beginning with the date on which the determination is notified to the person concerned;

(b) that person may appeal to the Secretary of State against the decision;

and, where an appeal is brought in respect of any information, the information shall not be entered on the register pending the final determination or withdrawal of the appeal.

(6) Subsections (3), (5) and (10) of section 15 above shall apply in relation to appeals under subsection (5) above.

(7) The Secretary of State may give to the enforcing authorities directions as to specified information, or descriptions of information, which the public interest requires to be included in registers maintained under section 20 above notwithstanding that the information may be commercially confidential.

(8) Information excluded from a register shall be treated as ceasing to be commercially confidential for the purposes of this section at the expiry of the period of four years beginning with the date of the determination by virtue of which it was excluded; but the person who furnished it may apply to the authority for the information to remain excluded from the register on the ground that it is still commercially confidential and the auhority shall determine whether or not that is the case.

(9) Subsections (5) and (6) above shall apply in relation to a determination under subsection (8) above as they apply in relation to a determination under subsection (2) or (4) above.

(10) The Secretary of State may, by order, substitute for the period for the time being specified in subsection (3) above such other period as he considers appropriate.

(11) Information is, for the purposes of any determination under this section, commercially confidential, in relation to any individual or person, if its being contained in the register would prejudice to an unreasonable degree the commercial interests of that individual or person.

DEFINITIONS
"authorisation": s.1(9).
"enforcing authority": s.1(7) and (8).

GENERAL NOTE
The general principle of the section is that information which is commercially confidential shall not be included within a register without the consent of the person or business to whose affairs it relates: subs. (1). However, information is not commercially confidential in this sense merely upon the *ipse dixit* of the relevant person, but only if determined to be so by the enforcing authority or the Secretary of State. Commercial confidentially is defined in subs. (11) by reference to the prejudice caused to the relevant commercial interests, and whether that prejudice would be unreasonable. The Government has indicated that it will look on claims to commercial confidentially sceptically: in DoE News Release No. 56 (January 30, 1990) Mr David Trippier, Minister for the Environment, was quoted as saying that "cogent and specific evidence" would be required to substantiate such claims and that he was strengthened in that view by the fact that to date no application had been made for commercial confidentiality under the Water Resources Act 1991. Draft Guidance on commercial confidentiality was issued with that News Release and contains the following paragraph:

"If the Secretary of State receives an appeal against a decision by an enforcing authority not to withhold information from the IPC register, he will require cogent and specific evidence to substantiate the claim that disclosure would prejudice to an unreasonable degree some person's commercial interests. This would need to demonstrate that disclosure of information would negate or significantly diminish the commercial advantage that one operator has over another. This might for instance relate to preserving the secrecy of a new process technology, or of a particular raw material or catalyst, or of the capacity of the process, or some other specific feature which if known to competitors might diminish a legitimate commercial advantage. Arguments based on general claims, for instance, that disclosure might damage the reputation of the operator and hence his commercial competitiveness, are unlikely to be given weight. Where information is withheld from the register, the register will indicate that there has been an omission. The authority will periodically include a statement indicating whether the operator has complied with terms and conditions of the authorisation which are withheld from the register."

The issue of confidentially can arise in various ways. Where information is furnished to the enforcing authority for the purpose of an application for authorisation or variation, in pursuance of a condition, or pursuant to a statutory requisition, the person furnishing the information may apply on grounds of commercial confidentiality for exclusion of the information (subs. (2)). The argument as to confidentiality can relate to the commercial interests of the person furnishing the information, or to those of some other person.

Where information is obtained by an authority in other circumstances and it appears that it might be confidential, under subs. (4) the authority must notify the relevant person or business and give a reasonable opportunity of objecting to inclusion and making representations in support of such objection.

In either case the authority will determine whether or not the information is commercially confidential and in the event of an adverse determination, a 21 day period is given for an appeal to the Secretary of State. The information may not be entered on the register whilst the appeal is pending: subs. (5).

HMIP's Annual Report for 1991/92 indicates that 67 applications for exemption on grounds of commercial confidentiality were made. A number went to appeal. The Secretary of State released his decision on the Confidentiality Appeals by PowerGen (against inclusion of forecast schedules of emissions for 1991) and by National Power (against inclusion of data about the type and quality of fuel it planned to burn) on November 19, 1992. The appeal by PowerGen was dismissed (after a 12 day private hearing) on the basis of the "significance of the information to the processes of application and authorisation and the consequent importance of its being available to the public, and my conclusions on the likelihood and extent of prejudice". The disputed information is now on the public registers. The National Power appeal (conducted by way of written representation) was allowed on the basis that the Secretary of State was satisfied that "the information is not directly relevant to determination of the applications for authorisation themselves or to any of the conditions which are likely to be imposed in the authorisations, and is not necessary to enable the public to comment effectively on the applications".

Public interest

It is possible for the Secretary of State to override the confidentiality exemption on public interest grounds by a direction given under subs. (7).

Review of confidentiality

A determination of confidentiality lapses after a period of four years and application may be made by "the person who furnished it" (who may of course be different to the person later carrying on the prescribed process) for the information to remain excluded on the ground it is still commercially confidential (subs. (8)).

Provisions as to offences

Offences

23.—(1) It is an offence for a person—
 (a) to contravene section 6(1) above;
 (b) to fail to give the notice requred by section 9(2) above;
 (c) to fail to comply with or contravene any requirement or prohibition imposed by an enforcement notice or a prohibition notice;
 (d) without reasonable excuse, to fail to comply with any requirement imposed under section 17 above;
 (e) to prevent any other person from appearing before or from answering

any question to which an inspector may by virtue of section 17(3) require an answer;
(f) intentionally to obstruct an inspector in the exercise or performance of his powers or duties;
(g) to fail, without reasonable excuse, to comply with any requirement imposed by a notice under section 19(2) above;
(h) to make a statement which he knows to be false or misleading in a material particular, or recklessly to make a statement which is false or misleading in a material particular, where the statement is made—
   (i) in purported compliance with a requirement to furnish any information imposed by or under any provision of this Part; or
   (ii) for the purpose of obtaining the grant of an authorisation to himself or any other person or the variation of an authorisation;
(i) intentionally to make a false entry in any record required to be kept under section 7 above;
(j) with intent to deceive, to forge or use a document issued or authorised to be issued under section 7 above or required for any purpose thereunder or to make or have in his possession a document so closely resembling any such document as to be likely to deceive;
(k) falsely to pretend to be an inspector;
(l) to fail to comply with an order made by a court under section 26 below.

(2) A person guilty of an offence under paragraph (a), (c) or (l) of subsection (1) above shall be liable:
   (a) on summary conviction, to a fine not exceeding £20,000;
   (b) on conviction on indictment, to a fine or to imprisonment for a term not exceeding two years, or to both.

(3) A person guilty of an offence under paragraph (b), (g), (h), (i) or (j) of subsection (1) above shall be liable—
   (a) on summary conviction, to a fine not exceeding the statutory maximum;
   (b) on conviction on indictment, to a fine or to imprisonment for a term not exceeding two years, or to both.

(4) A person guilty of an offence under paragraph (d), (e), (f) or (k) of subsection (1) above shall be liable, on summary conviction, to a fine not exceeding the statutory maximum.

(5) In England and Wales an inspector, if authorised to do so by the Secretary of State, may, although not of counsel or a solicitor, prosecute before a magistrates' court proceedings for an offence under subsection (1) above.

DEFINITIONS
"authorisation": s.1(9).
"inspector": s.16(8).

GENERAL NOTE
This section creates the various offences under Pt. I and prescribes the various penalties. Subsection (5) allows inspectors, if authorised by the Secretary of State, to take prosecutions in magistrates' courts.

The main offence of carrying on a prescribed process except under an authorisation and in accordance with its conditions (subs. (1)(a)) is subject to a maximum fine of £20,000 on summary conviction and to an unlimited fine and imprisonment not exceeding two years on conviction on indictment (subs. (2)). The offence appears to be one of strict liability, and ignorance that a condition was being contravened would not provide a defence. Nor is there any defence of "reasonable excuse," such as applies to some of the other offences. It would appear that the subs. (1)(a) offence of carrying on a process without authorisation or without complying with conditions may take place "whether continuously or intermittently, over a period of time" (*Hodgetts* v. *Chiltern District Council* [1983] 2 A.C. 120, 128, *per* Lord Roskill). It can still, according to that case, constitute a single offence and it appears could be charged either "on and since" a specific date, or between two specified dates, without the charge being bad for duplicity. Each case will need careful consideration, however, especially where breach of conditions has been intermittent: in some cases it may be appropriate to frame the charge as relating to "divers days" between two specified dates, or in some cases as specimen charges related to single days.

Enforcement by High Court

24.—If the enforcing authority is of the opinion that proceedings for an offence under section 23(1)(c) above would afford an ineffectual remedy against a person who has failed to comply with the requirements of an enforcement notice or a prohibition notice, the authority may take proceedings in the High Court or, in Scotland, in any court of competent jurisdiction for the purpose of securing compliance with the notice.

DEFINITIONS
"enforcing authority": s.1(7) and (8).

GENERAL NOTE
This section gives an alternative remedy for non-compliance with an enforcement or prohibition notice where the enforcing authority believes that criminal proceedings would be an ineffectual remedy, for example where urgent action is required or where the criminal penalties available might not be an adequate deterrent. The authority may take High Court proceedings to secure compliance in such cases.

The authority would on general principles, and in any event, have the ability to take civil proceedings for an injunction in appropriate cases to secure compliance: see note to s.81(5) below.

Onus of proof as regards techniques and evidence

25.—(1) In any proceedings for an offence under section 23(1)(a) above consisting in a failure to comply with the general condition implied in every authorisation by section 7(4) above, it shall be for the accused to prove that there was no better available technique not entailing excessive cost than was in fact used to satisfy the condition.

(2) Where—
(a) an entry is required under section 7 above to be made in any record as to the observance of any condition of an authorisation; and
(b) the entry has not been made;
that fact shall be admissible as evidence that that condition has not been observed.

GENERAL NOTE
This section is of great importance in that it deals with the onus of proof as to certain matters in prosecutions under Pt. I. Where the alleged offence is failure to comply with the *general* condition as to the use of BATNEEC implied by s.7(4), the onus rests with the accused to show that there was no better available technique not entailing excessive cost than that actually employed (subs. (1)).

It is important to note that the presumption does not apply to *specific* conditions requiring the use of BATNEEC. This is significant when read in conjunction with s.7(6), which provides that the general condition does not apply in relation to any aspect of the process which is regulated by a specific condition. Thus the impact of subs. (1) may be less than appears at first sight.

Secondly, if an express condition requires records to be kept as to the observance of conditions, the absence of a relevant entry is admissible (though not conclusive) as evidence that the condition has not been observed (subs. (2)).

Power of court to order cause of offence to be remedied

26.—(1) Where a person is convicted of an offence under section 23(1)(a) or (c) above in respect of any matters which appear to the court to be matters which it is in his power to remedy, the court may, in addition to or instead of imposing any punishment, order him, within such time as may be fixed by the order, to take such steps as may be specified in the order for remedying those matters.

(2) The time fixed by an order under subsection (1) above may be extended or further extended by order of the court on an application made before the end of the time as originally fixed or as extended under this subsection, as the case may be.

(3) Where a person is ordered under subsection (1) above to remedy any matters, that person shall not be liable under section 23 above in respect of those matters in so far as they continue during the time fixed by the order or any further time allowed under subsection (2) above.

GENERAL NOTE

This section allows a court to order a person convicted of certain offences under Pt. I to take specified steps in respect of matters which appear to be within his power to remedy. The relevant offences are carrying on a prescribed process without authorisation or without complying with conditions, or contravention of an enforcement notice or prohibition notice. It is not clear whether such an order is limited to steps required to comply with the conditions or notice, or whether it can extend to more general remedial measures, perhaps for example in relation to contamination occurring after the date of the relevant notice. The strict test appears to be that the matters ordered to be remedied must be matters in respect of which the offender was convicted, not, as suggested by the marginal note, the cause of the offence.

Failure to comply with the order is an offence (s.23(1)(l)): presumably, in the case of an order made by the High Court, it may also be contempt. No offence is committed in respect of matters continuing during the time fixed by the order for the relevant remedial measures (subs. (3)).

Power of chief inspector to remedy harm

27.—(1) Where the commission of an offence under section 23(1)(a) or (c) above causes any harm which it is possible to remedy, the chief inspector or, in Scotland, a river purification authority may, subject to subsection (2) below—

(a) arrange for any reasonable steps to be taken towards remedying the harm; and

(b) recover the cost of taking those steps from any person convicted of that offence.

(2) The chief inspector or, as the case may be, the river purification authority shall not exercise their powers under this section except with the approval in writing of the Secretary of State and, where any of the steps are to be taken on or will affect land in the occupation of any person other than the person on whose land the prescribed process is being carried on, with the permission of that person.

DEFINITIONS

"harm": s.1(4).

GENERAL NOTE

This section gives an important general power to the chief inspector, or river purification authorities in Scotland, to remedy harm caused by the commission of certain offences and to recover the cost of any reasonable steps from the person or persons convicted. The relevant offences are, first, carrying on a prescribed process without an authorisation or in breach of conditions and, secondly, non-compliance with an enforcement or prohibition notice.

The power may be used in conjunction with the wide powers of entry contained in s.17, but if any of the steps are to be taken on or will affect land in the occupation of anyone other than the owner of the land on which the prescribed process is being carried on, then the permission of that person is necessary (subs. (2)).

It does not appear that the inspectorate must wait for a conviction before exercising the powers, though no cost can be recovered until conviction, and the written approval of the Secretary of State is necessary before taking any steps.

The power is only to remedy actual harm and does not cover anticipatory or preventive measures.

The power does not extend to local authorities in their enforcement role, though it seems that the chief inspector can exercise his powers under the section in respect of offences relating to both centrally and locally controlled processes.

Authorisation and other statutory controls

Authorisations and other statutory controls

28.—(1) No condition shall at any time be attached to an authorisation so as to regulate the final disposal by deposit in or on land of controlled waste (within the meaning of Part II), nor shall any condition apply to such a disposal; but the enforcing authority shall notify the authority which is the waste regulation authority under that Part for the area in which the process is to be carried on of the fact that the process involves the final disposal of controlled waste by deposit in or on land.

(2) Where any of the activities comprising a prescribed process are regulated both by an authorisation granted by the enforcing authority under this Part and by a registration or authorisation under the Radioactive Substances Act 1960, then, if different obligations are imposed as respects the same matter by a condition attached to the authorisation under this Part and a condition attached to the registration or authorisation under that Act, the condition imposed by the authorisation under this Part shall be treated as not binding the person carrying on the process.

(3) Where the activities comprising a prescribed process designated for central control include the release of any substances into water included in waters which are controlled waters for the purposes of Chapter I of Part III of the Water Act 1989, then—
  (a) the enforcing authority shall not grant an authorisation under this Part if the National Rivers Authority certifies to the enforcing authority its opinion that the release will result in or contribute to a failure to achieve any water quality objective in force under Part III of that Act; and
  (b) any authorisation that is granted shall, as respects such releases, include (with or without others appearing to the enforcing authority to be appropriate) such conditions as appear to the National Rivers Authority to be appropriate for the purposes of this Part as that Authority requires by notice in writing given to the enforcing authority;

but the enforcing authority may, if it appears to be appropriate to do so, make the authorisation subject to conditions more onerous than those (if any) notified to it under paragraph (b) above.

(4) Where the activities comprising a prescribed process carried on under an authorisation include the release of any substances into water as mentioned in subsection (3) above then, if at any time it appears to the National Rivers Authority appropriate for the purposes of this Part that the conditions of the authorisation should be varied, the enforcing authority shall exercise its powers under section 10 above so as to vary the conditions of the authorisation as required by the National Rivers Authority by notice in writing given to the enforcing authority.

DEFINITIONS
  "authorisation": s.1(9).
  "enforcing authority": s.1(7) and (8).
  "prescribed process": s.1(5).
  "process": s.1(5).
  "release": s.1(10).
  "substances": s.1(13).

GENERAL NOTE
  This section deals with the relationship between authorisations under Pt. I and other systems

of statutory control. See the General Note to Pt. I under the heading *Relationships with Other Areas of Control.*

PART II

WASTE ON LAND

GENERAL NOTE

Pt. II of the Act deals with the collection, recycling, deposit and other forms of disposal of waste. It replaces, with various amendments, the provisions of Pt. I of the Control of Pollution Act 1974. However, Pt. II is more than simply a re-enactment of previous law, and introduces significant innovations, which in some cases implement long-standing proposals for reform from the Royal Commission on Environmental Pollution and various Parliamentary and Departmental committees.

The reforms can perhaps be marshalled into two broad groups: (a) changes to the waste management licensing system; and (b) re-casting of the institutional local framework for waste regulation and disposal. Relevant background materials include:
(1) Report of The House of Lords Select Committee on Science and Technology, *Hazardous Waste Disposal* (Session 1980–81, 1st Report, July 1981).
(2) Reports 1–3 of the Hazardous Waste Inspectorate (June 1985, July 1986, June 1988).
(3) Report of a Review of the Control of Pollution (Special Waste) Regulations 1980 (April 1985).
(4) DoE Consultation Papers on Waste Disposal Law Amendment (September 15, 1986 and November 23, 1988) and Decisions following Consultation (June 29, 1988 and September 26, 1989).
(5) DoE Consultation Paper on the Role and Functions of Waste Disposal Authorities (January 24, 1989) and Decisions following Consultation (September 26, 1989).
(6) Report on the House of Lords Select Committee on Science and Technology, *Hazardous Waste Disposal* (Session 1988–89, Fourth Report, April 19, 1989).
(7) Government's Response to the Select Committee on Science and Technology, Fourth Report (Cm. 763, July 1989).
(8) Report of Commons Environment Committee, *Toxic Waste* (Session 1988–89, Second Report, February 1989).
(9) Government's Response to the House of Commons Environment Committee Second Report (Cm. 679, April 1989).
(10) Royal Commission on Environmental Pollution, Eleventh Report, *Managing Waste: The Duty of Care* (Cm. 9675, December 1985).
(11) Pollution Paper No. 24 (response to RCEP Eleventh Report, 1986).

The innovative features of Pt. II include:
(1) reorganisation of waste functions, including the separation of operational and regulatory functions within local authorities, and power to create regional authorities;
(2) the imposition of a duty of care upon persons importing, producing, carrying, keeping, treating or otherwise disposing of controlled waste;
(3) greater powers of discrimination in the grant of waste management licences, by reference to the concept of "fit and proper person";
(4) the holders of licences are no longer able to surrender them at will, but only if the authority accepts the surrender;
(5) greater emphasis is placed on waste recycling with greater powers, mandatory waste recycling plans and a system of credits for waste recycled by collection authorities;
(6) a duty is placed on authorities to monitor and remedy closed landfills in respect of matters such as leachate contamination and methane generation;
(7) more comprehensive provision is made for the provision of information on public registers.

EC and international law

As with many other Parts of the 1990 Act, it is important to view Pt. II against the backcloth of European Community strategies and directives on waste, a subject which has become an increasing preoccupation within the Community. EEC law and policy relating to waste includes the following:
(1) Directive 75/442/EEC on Waste (O.J. 1975 L194, p. 39, July 25, 1975).
(2) Directive 78/319/EEC on Toxic and Dangerous Wastes (O.J. 1978 L84, p. 43, March 31, 1978).

(3) Directive 86/278/EEC on the use of sewage sludge in agriculture (O.J. 1986 L181, p. 6, June 12, 1978).
(4) Directive 75/439/EEC on the disposal of waste oils (O.J. 1975 L194, p. 23, June 16, 1975).
(5) Directive 76/403 on disposal of PCBs and PCTs (O.J. 1976 L198, p. 41, April 6, 1976). Proposal for a Council Directive on the Disposal of PCBs and PCTs (O.J. 88/C319/06); Amended Proposal for a Council Directive on the Disposal of PCBs and PCTs (O.J. 91/C299/05).
(6) Directive 78/176/EEC on waste from the titanium dioxide industry (O.J. 1978 L54, p. 19, February 20, 1976).
(7) Directive 84/631/EEC on the transfrontier shipment of hazardous waste (O.J. 1984 L326, p. 31, December 6, 1984).
(8) Directive 80/68/EEC on the protection of groundwater against pollution by certain dangerous substances (O.J. 1980 L20, p. 26, January 26, 1980).
(9) Directive 91/156/EEC amending Directive 75/442/EEC on waste (O.J. 1991 L78, p, 32, March 26, 1991).
(10) Directive 91/689/EEC on hazardous waste (O.J. 1991 L377, p. 20, December 31, 1991).
(11) Directive 91/157/EEC on batteries and accumulators containing certain dangerous substances (O.J. 1991 L78, March 26, 1991).

Current EC proposals on waste incude:
(1) Proposal for a Directive on the landfill of waste submitted on April 23, 1991 COM (91) 102 (O.J. 1991 C190, p. 1, July 22, 1991).
(2) Amended proposal for a Directive on civil liability for damage caused by waste submitted on June 28, 1991 COM (91) 219 (O.J. 1991 C192, p. 6, July 23, 1991).
(3) Amended proposal for a Regulation on the supervision and control of shipments of waste within, into and out of the European Community submitted on March 23, 1992 COM (92) 121 (O.J. 1992 C115, p. 4, May 6, 1992).
(4) Proposal for a Directive on the incineration of hazardous waste submitted on March 23, 1992 COM (92) 9 (O.J. 1992 C130, p. 1, May 21, 1992).
(5) Draft proposal for a Directive on packaging and packaging waste COM (92) 278 final SYN 436 (O.J. C263/1).
(6) *Community Strategy for Waste Management* SEC (89) 934, September 18, 1989.

Reference is made to the various E.C. measures and proposals in the annotations to the relevant sections of Pt. II.

International law is also of growing importance in relation to waste policy; specifically the Basel Convention of 1989 on The Control of Transboundary Movements of Hazardous Wastes and their Disposal (Cm 984) which came into force on May 5, 1992 and has been signed by both the UK and E.C., though as yet ratified by neither.

Organisation of functions
Sections 30–32 deal with the reorganisation of waste regulation, collection and disposal functions. Three types of authority are constituted, namely: (1) waste regulation authorities; (2) waste disposal authorities; and (3) waste collection authorities. Their composition and functions are as follows:

(1) Waste regulation authorities
In England, county councils are the waste regulation authorities (WRAs) save for Greater London and the metropolitan areas, where the authority is either a statutorily constituted waste authority or the district council. District councils are the WRAs in Wales, and islands or district councils in Scotland. The main function of WRAs are:
  (a) waste management licensing (s.35);
  (b) supervision of the new duty of care as to waste (s.34);
  (c) inspecting land before accepting surrender of licences (s.39);
  (d) supervision of licensed activities (s.42);
  (e) investigation of the need for arrangements for dealing with controlled waste arising within their area and preparation of waste disposal plans (s.50);
  (f) powers to require removal of waste unlawfully deposited (s.59);
  (g) inspection of land for risks of pollution or harm to human health caused by gases or liquids arising from deposits of waste and action to avoid such pollution or harm (s.61);
  (h) maintenance of public registers (s.64); and
  (i) publication of annual reports (s.67).
Section 31 creates a reserve power for the Secretary of State to set up regional authorities to discharge any of the functions of the two or more WRAs involved. It is open to WRAs to enter

into such joint arrangements voluntarily, and the Secretary of State's power is intended for use where a regional approach would be advantageous but is not adopted voluntarily.

(2) Waste Disposal Authorities

Waste disposal authorities (WDAs) are the county councils in non-metropolitan areas; special arrangements at present apply in some metropolitan counties and in London, and in other metropolitan areas the district councils are the WDAs. In Wales the district councils are the WDAs and in Scotland the functions fall to islands or district councils.

The functions, powers and duties of WDAs under Pt. II are:
(a) formation of waste disposal companies and transfer of relevant parts of their undertakings to such companies (s.32);
(b) direction of waste collection authorities as to places to which collected waste is to be delivered (s.51(4)(a));
(c) arranging for the disposal of controlled waste collected in the area by waste collection authorities (s.51(1)(a));
(d) arrangement for the provision of places at which residents of the area may deposit household waste and for the disposal of waste so deposited (s.51(1)(b));
(e) arrangement for the provision of places where collected waste may be treated or kept prior to removal for treatment or disposal (*e.g.* transfer stations) (s.51(4)(b));
(f) making payments to waste collection authorities for savings in disposal costs in respect of waste retained for recycling (s.52(1)); and
(g) waste recycling (s.55).

Separate provisions apply to waste disposal authorities in Scotland in relation to a number of these matters (ss.53, 54 and 56).

In exercising these functions, the scheme of the Act is that regulatory and disposal functions shall be kept separate (s.30(7)). Operational disposal functions are not carried out by the disposal authorities themselves, but through "waste disposal contractors" defined as companies formed for the purpose of collection, keeping, treating or disposing of waste in the course of a business (s.30(5)). Such companies may either be private sector businesses or companies formed by waste disposal authorities. Section 32 and Sched. 2, Pt. I make provision for the transition of undertakings of waste disposal authorities to such local authority waste disposal companies (LAWDCs). The intention is that LAWDCs and private sector waste disposal companies will compete for business on equal terms, and Sched. 2, Pt. II contains detailed provisions as to contracts and putting such contracts to tender.

(3) Waste Collection Authorites

Waste collection functions fall to district councils in England and Wales, London boroughs, the Common Council of the City or the Temple authorities in Greater London, and islands or district councils in Scotland. The functions of such authorities are:
(a) to arrange for the collection of household waste in their area and to arrange for the collection of commercial or industrial waste on request (s.45);
(b) to arrange for the emptying of privies or cesspools in their areas (s.45);
(c) to determine the nature and source of receptacles in which household waste is to be placed for collection (s.46);
(d) to supply receptacles for commercial or industrial waste (s.47);
(e) to deliver for disposal waste collected to such places as the waste disposal authority directs (s.48);
(f) to carry out investigations as to appropriate arrangements for dealing with waste for the purpose of recycling and to prepare a statement of such arrangements (s.49); and
(g) to retain waste which the authority has decided to recycle and to make arrangements for recycling it (s.48).

Central control

Central Government control over the activities of waste regulation, disposal and collection authorities is provided by a variety of powers conferred on the Secretary of State to give directions on a wide range of matters, including:
(1) arrangements for transition to waste disposal companies (s.32(2));
(2) exercise of licensing functions, both specific directions and general guidance (s.35(7) and (8));
(3) disagreements as to licensing between waste regulation authorities and the NRA (s.36(5));
(4) modification and variation of licences (s.37(3));
(5) revocation and suspension of licences (s.38(7));
(6) supervision of licensed activities (s.42(8));

(7) content and preparation of waste recycling plans (s.49(4) and (7));
(8) content and preparation of waste disposal plans (s.50(9) and (11));
(9) acceptance of waste by holders of licences and delivery of waste by persons keeping control of it (s.57(1) and (2); and
(10) inspection and modification of closed landfills (s.61(11)).

Additionally, the Secretary of State makes the various regulations required under Pt. II (including those regulating special waste), issues the Code of Practice on the duty of care relating to waste (s.34(7)) and exercises the appellate functions in matters of licensing (s.43) and exclusion of information from registers (s.66(5)). Apart from this, the Secretary of State has the general role of keeping under review the discharge by waste authorities of their functions (s.68(1)), appointing inspectors for that purpose and other purposes (s.68(2)) and obtaining information from waste regulation authorities (s.71(1)).

If satisfied that a waste regulation authority has failed to exercise its functions, then the Secretary of State may make an order declaring the authority to be in default (s.72(1)) and may ultimately transfer all or any functions of the authority to himself (s.72(4)).

As mentioned above, the Secretary of State also has power to establish single regional authorities for waste regulation purposes (s.31).

Role of Environment Agency

The Government's proposed Environment Agency will include within its responsibilities the waste regulation functions of local authorities in England and Wales. Separate arrangements will apply to Scotland. Detailed proposals as to how waste incineration and the regulation of closed landfill sites under s.61 might be dealt with were issued for consultation on January 29, 1992. A consultation paper on the arrangements for waste disposal planning under the Agency and in the interim period before its creation was issued by the Department of Environment on August 17, 1992. Consideration is being given to how arrangements should work for waste disposal planning under the Agency, the regulation of closed landfill sites and the control of incinerators.

The Secretary of State also has power to issue guidance to local authorities on their functions in relation to licences (s.35(8)). The Secretary of State has produced 28 waste management papers giving guidance of a technical nature on waste management. The list is as follows:

LIST OF WASTE MANAGEMENT PAPERS (HMSO PUBLICATIONS)

Number *Title*

1 A review of Options; Second Edition; 1992. (ISBN 0117526444)
2 Waste Disposal Surveys; 1976. (ISBN 0117510033)
3 Guidelines for the Preparation of a Waste Disposal Plan; 1976. (ISBN 0117511242)
4 The Licensing of Waste Facilities; Second Edition 1988. (ISBN 0117521574)
5 The Relationship between Waste Disposal Authorities and Private Industry; 1976. (ISBN 0117509205)
6 Polychlorinated Biphenyl (PCB) Wastes—a Technical Memorandum on Reclamation, Treatment and Disposal; 1976. (ISBN 011751009)
7 Mineral Oil Wastes—a Technical Memorandum on Arisings, Treatment and Disposal; 1976. (ISBN 0117510602)
8 Heat Treatment Cyanide Wastes—a Technical Memorandum on Arisings, Treatment and Disposals; Second Edition; 1985. (ISBN 0117518131)
9 Halogenated Hydrocarbon Solvent Wastes from Cleaning Processes—a Technical Memorandum on Reclamation and Disposal; 1976. (ISBN 011751103X)
10 Local Authority Waste Disposal Statistics 1974/75; 1976. (ISBN 011751120X)
11 Metal Finishing Wastes—a Technical Memorandum on Arisings, Treatment and Disposal; 1976. (ISBN 0117511226)
12 Mercury Bearing Wastes—a Technical Memorandum on Storage, Handling, Treatment, Disposal and Recovery; 1977. (ISBN 0117511269)
13 Tarry and Distillation Wastes and other Chemical Based Wastes—a Technical Memorandum on Arisings, Treatment and Disposal; 1977. (ISBN 0117511277)
14 Solvent Wastes (excluding Halogenated Hydrocarbons)—a Technical Memorandum on Reclamation and Disposal; 1977. (ISBN 0117511285)
15 Halogenated Organic Wastes—a Technical Memorandum on Arisings, Treatment and Disposal; 1978. (ISBN 0117513709)
16 Wood Preserving Wastes—a Technical Memorandum on Arisings, Treatment and Disposal; 1980. (ISBN 0117514764)
17 Wastes from Tanning, Leather Dressing and Fellmongering—a Technical Memorandum on Recovery, Treatment and Disposal; 1978. (ISBN 0117513202)

18 Asbestos Waste—a Technical Memorandum on Arisings and Disposal; 1979. (ISBN 0117513849)
19 Wastes from the Manufacture of Pharmaceuticals, Toiletries and Cosmetics—a Technical Memorandum on Arisings, Treatment and Disposal; 1978. (ISBN 0117513180)
20 Arsenic Bearing Wastes—a Technical Memorandum on Recovery, Treatment and Disposal; 1980. (ISBN 0117514721)
21 Pesticide Wastes—a Technical Memorandum on Arisings and Disposal; 1980. (ISBN 0117514845)
22 Local Authority Waste Disposal Statistics 1974/75 to 1977/78; 1978. (ISBN 0117514535)
23 Special Wastes—a Technical Memorandum Providing Guidance on their Definition; 1981. (ISBN 0117515558)
24 Cadmium Bearing Wastes—a Technical Memorandum on Arisings, Treatment and Disposal; 1984. (ISBN 011751716X)
25 Clinical Wastes—a Technical Memorandum on Arisings, Treatment and Disposal; 1983. (ISBN 0117517194)
26 Landfilling Wastes—a Technical Memorandum for the Disposal of Wastes on Landfill Sites; 1986. (ISBN 0117518913)
27 Landfill Gas—a Technical Memorandum on the Monitoring and Control of Landfill Gas; Second Edition 1991. (ISBN 0117524883)
28 Recycling—a Memorandum providing Guidance to Local Authorities on recycling; 1991. (ISBN 011752445X)

The Duty of Care
Section 34 contains a new duty of care as to the keeping, control and transfer of waste. The case for such a duty was put cogently by the RCEP in their Eleventh Report, *Managing Waste: The Duty of Care* (Cm. 9675, December 1985). Paras. 3.4–3.7 of that Report state as follows:
"The first task is for society to identify where the responsibility lies for ensuring that wastes are properly handled and disposed of. In our judgment this must rest with the individual organisation who controls the wastes. The producer incurs a *duty of care* which is owed to society, and we would like to see this duty reflected in public attitudes and enshrined in legislation and codes of practice . . . we believe that the waste producer's or handler's legal obligations towards the environment need to be classified and strengthened, with particular reference to the requirement to satisfy himself, when passing on the waste to somebody else, that it will be correctly dealt with. . . . We believe that, within the framework of the duty of care, a waste producer may assign responsibility to a person who he had good reason to believe is competent to handle the waste safely . . ."
The broad thrust of these recommendations was accepted by the Government in Pollution Paper No. 24 (1986) and the Government agreed that "this duty of care should find its main expression in ensuring the integrity of the waste stream on its journey from producer to disposer and beyond this to its safe containment or disposal over time" (para. 5).
The duty covers all those responsible for the arising or importation of controlled waste and those who have control of such waste at whatever point in the chain from arising to final disposal.
The standard is based on reasonableness in the light of the measures applicable to the relevant person in their particular capacity. Reasonable steps are required: (a) to prevent any other person contravening the law as to unauthorised deposit, treatment or disposal of the waste; (b) to prevent escape of the waste; (c) to secure that the waste is transferred only to an authorised person; and (d) to secure that a sufficient written description of the waste accompanies it on transfer.
The duty does not, however, apply to occupiers of domestic property in respect of their own household wastes (s.34(2)). Central to the operation of s.34 is the Code of Practice issued by the Secretary of State; such a code is admissible and relevant evidence in any proceedings as to whether the duty of care has been fulfilled (s.34(10)). The Code of Practice was issued in December 1991.
In considering the duty of care, attention should also be directed to the proposals of the European Commission for strict civil liability for damage caused by waste. Amended proposals for a directive were submitted on June 28, 1991 COM (91) 219 (O.J. 1991 C192 p. 6, July 23, 1991). If adopted, such proposals when implemented would in many cases create a parallel liability on a producer or controller of waste, with no-fault civil liability as distinct from criminal liability based on a test of reasonableness. Furthermore, the draft directive proposes a system of joint and several liability on producers whose wastes are mixed or disposed of together, and cause damage. On the other hand, liability under s.34 would arise whether or not damage resulted from the breach, whereas under the directive either personal injury, property damage, or injury to the environment would be a prerequisite of liability.

The possible relationship between the duty of care and the Directive were considered in evidence before the House of Lords European Communities Committee, Sub-Committee F and in the Report of that Committee, *Paying for Pollution: Civil Liability for Damage caused by Waste* (House of Lords, Session 1989–90, 25th Report, H.L. paper 84–I).

Waste management licensing
A waste management licence authorises the treatment, keeping or disposal of any specified description of controlled waste in or on specified land, or the treatment or disposal of any specified description of controlled waste by means of mobile plant (s.35(1)). "Controlled waste" is defined in s.75(4) to mean household, commercial and industrial waste; these categories are themselves defined in s.75(5)–(7), and the Controlled Waste Regulations 1992 (S.I. 1992 No. 588). The licence shall be granted on such terms and subject to such conditions as the authority thinks appropriate (s.35(3)) and continues in force until revoked or surrendered (s.35(11)).

Where planning permission is required for the use of land authorised by the licence, the licence may not be issued unless either: (a) such permission is in force; or (b) an established use certificate or certificate of lawful use or development is in force (s.36(2)). Subject to this requirement and to the obligations to refer the proposal to the National Rivers Authority and the Health and Safety Executive, the waste regulation authority may not reject an application unless either: (a) they are not satisfied that the applicant is a "fit and proper person"; or (b) they are satisfied that rejection is necessary for the prevention of harm to the environment, harm to human health, or serious detriment to the amenities of the locality (s.36(3)). This last ground of refusal does not apply where planning permission is in force in relation to the proposed use, presumably on the basis that in such a case, issues of amenity will have been addressed at the planning application or appeal stage. These grounds of refusal are different from the equivalent provisions under the Control of Pollution Act 1974, Pt. I. The question whether the applicant is "fit and proper" is completely new, and brings in considerations of technical competence, financial standing and the absence of relevant convictions (s.74). The previous consideration of pollution of water is widened to cover pollution of the environment generally, defined broadly by reference to the capability of causing harm to man or other living organisms (s.39(3)).

Pt. II contains provisions as to variation of licences (s.37), revocation and suspension of licences (s.38) and surrender and transfer of licences (ss.39 and 40 respectively). Under s.39 it is no longer possible to surrender a licence at will, but only if the authority accepts the surrender— this process involves inspection of the land, consultations with the NRA and the issue of a "certificate of completion" if the authority is satisfied that the condition of the land is unlikely to cause pollution of the environment or harm to human health. The acceptance of a surrender has important implications in relation to the provisions contained later in Pt. II as to the inspection of closed sites and necessary remedial work (s.61). Fees are payable for licence applications and charges are payable for the subsistence of licences, in each case in accordance with a scheme made by the Secretary of State (s.41). Appeal to the Secretary of State lies against the various decisions of waste regulation authorities under the licensing system (s.43).

Under s.62 the Secretary of State may make provision by regulations for the treatment, keeping, or disposal of controlled waste that may be difficult or dangerous: such waste is known as "special waste." Detailed control is at present exercised over such waste by the Control of Pollution (Special Waste) Regulations 1980 (S.I. 1980 No. 1709). This involves a system of documentation of the waste and of pre-notification to the relevant waste authorities of disposal of the waste. The Government is considering proposals for the reform of the Special Waste Regulations and a consultation document on *Special Waste and the Control of its Disposal* was issued in February 1990. Options under consideration include the requirement of contracts for disposal of the waste between the holder and the assignee or the ultimate disposer, such contracts to be "consistent with current best practice in the management and disposal of waste." The Consultation Paper is discussed further in the notes to s.62.

The deposit, treatment or disposal of controlled waste is an offence except under and in accordance with a waste management licence (s.33). Other offences include: the deposit of waste other than controlled waste in certain circumstances (s.63(2)); the making of false statements in relation to licence applications (s.44); breach of the regulations on special waste (authority to create an offence by delegated legislation being given by s.62(2)(g)); failure to comply with requirements to deal with pollution when a licence is suspended (s.38(10) and (11)); obstruction of inspectors (ss.69(9) and 70(4)); failure to comply with requirements to furnish information (s.71(3)); and failure to comply with a requirement to remove unauthorised waste deposited on land (s.59(5)). Also, damage caused by waste unlawfully deposited on land may give rise to civil liability under s.73(6).

Control of Pollution (Amendment) Act 1989
Pt. II of the Act will need to be read in conjunction with the Control of Pollution (Amendment) Act 1989, to come into force on a day to be appointed. The 1989 Act creates a scheme for

the registration of carriers of controlled waste with related offences and powers. As such, the 1989 Act is an important component of the statutory framework for controlling and regulating waste, in conjunction with the 1990 Act. In particular, registration of carriers is a vital precondition to the statutory duty of care on waste producers (see above).

Waste recycling

Current policy both at domestic level and within the European Community is beginning to give greater priority to waste recycling and reclamation, and this is reflected in the terms of Pt. II of the Act. The Government's views and policies on recycling are conveniently summarised at paras. 14.14–14.40 of the September 1990 White Paper, *This Common Inheritance* (Cm. 1200). The Government has set the target of recycling 50 per cent. of *recyclable* household waste by the year 2000 (approximately 25 per cent. of all household waste): para. 14.23.

Under s.46(2) a waste collection authority may require household waste to be placed in separate receptacles or compartments according to whether the waste is to be recycled or not. Waste collection and disposal authorities may make arrangements for the recycling of waste under express powers in s.55 (s.56 for Scotland). In respect of waste which the collection authority decides to recycle, the usual requirement of delivery to such place as the disposal authority directs does not apply (s.48(2)) and there is provision for the disposal authority to make payments to the collection authority in respect of net savings in disposal costs (s.52(1)). Provision for determination of net savings of expenditure is made by the Environmental Protection (Waste Recycling Payments) Regulations 1992 (S.I. 1992 No. 462) and the system is explained in Circ. 4/92 (W.O. 10/92).

Waste collection authorities are under a duty to carry out investigations as to the appropriate arrangements to facilitate recycling and to prepare waste recycling plans as to such arrangements (s.49). In preparing their waste disposal plans, waste regulation authorities are under a duty to have regard to the desirability, where reasonably practicable, of giving priority to recycling waste (s.50(4)). Finally, in determining the contents of waste disposal contracts they enter into with contractors, and in the tendering process for such contracts, waste disposal authorities must have regard to the desirability of including terms designed to maximise the recycling of waste (Sched. 2, para. 19(1)(b)).

Closed landfills

Considerable public concern has been expressed as to the problems caused by the methanogenic properties of landfilled domestic and other wastes: see for example the Report of the Non Statutory Inquiry of Gerrard Ryan, Q.C. on behalf of Derbyshire County Council into the explosion at Loscoe in 1986, and Waste Management Paper No. 27 on *The Control of Landfill Gas* (see note to s.61). Similarly, the accumulation of leachate, which may escape from the site and pollute ground or surface waters, is a cause for concern: see, for example, RCEP Eleventh Report (Cm. 9675) paras. 7.5–7.12.

An attempt is made to address these issues for the future by the new and more stringent provisions on surrender of site licences (see above). In relation to sites no longer in operation, new duties and powers are provided by s.61 under which waste regulation authorities must inspect their area to detect whether deposits of controlled waste on the land have led or are leading to noxious gases or liquids being concentrated or accumulated, and emitted or discharged so as to cause possible pollution of the environment or harm to human health. Substantial powers of entry are given, and if land is found to be in such a condition it must be kept under review until the authority are satisfied that no such pollution or harm will be caused. It is the duty of the authority to do works or take steps (whether on the land affected or on adjacent land) as necessary to avoid such pollution or harm. The cost of such measures may be recovered, in whole or in part, from the person for the time being the owner of the land, except where the surrender of the relevant waste management licence has already been accepted by the authority under s.39. Since the matters on which the authority has to be satisfied before accepting the surrender are precisely those of the condition of the land and the risk of pollution or harm to health, it seems that this exception will rarely arise in practice.

Public information

As with Pt. I and indeed the rest of the Act, Pt. II contains comprehensive provisions for the disclosure of information on public registers (s.64). The relevant information relates predominantly to the exercise of licensing powers, and there are provisions as to the exclusion of information on grounds of national security (s.65) and commercial confidentiality (s.66). Also, each waste regulation authority must publish an annual report on the discharge of its regulatory functions (s.67). The provisions for local registers of potentially contaminated sites in Pt. VIII of the Act (s.143) may also be of relevance, since the deposit of waste seems likely to be a "contaminative use" within the meaning of s.143(6). However the future of these registers seems uncertain now.

Relationship of waste licensing with other powers
Waste management licensing may to some extent be duplicated by other statutory controls. The relevant principles are as follows:
(a) *Integrated Pollution Control.* Conditions attached to IPC authorisations may not be framed so as to regulate the final disposal of controlled waste by deposit in or on land: other forms of disposal may be so regulated (s.28(1)). Where a prescribed process involves such final disposal by deposit in or on land, HMIP must notify the waste regulation authority for the area in which the process is carried on (s.28(1)). The Secretary of State may, by regulations, exclude the deposit, keeping treatment or disposal of waste from licensing requirements and from the offence of treating, keeping or disposing in a manner likely to cause pollution of the environment or harm to human health (s.33(3)). In exercising that power, the adequacy of other statutory controls (for example, IPC) is relevant (s.33(4)(c)).
The draft Waste Management Licensing Regulations, published for consultation in August 1992, make provision for excluding from the requirement for a waste management licence, the treatment, keeping or disposal of waste in accordance with an IPC authorisation, save in relation to the final deposit of controlled waste by deposit in or on land; a similar exemption is proposed for waste management in connection with the carrying on of a process prescribed for IPC where the prescribed date has not yet arrived (again subject to the qualification as to final disposal by deposit on land).
(b) *Statutory nuisances.* The provisions of Pt. III of the Act on statutory nuisances could apply to accumulations of controlled waste (s.79(1)(e)) or to smell or other effluvia from such waste (s.79(1)(d)). The relationship of waste licensing powers and control over statutory nuisances was considered by the Court of Appeal in *Att.-Gen.'s Reference (No. 2 of 1988)* [1989] 3 W.L.R. 397. It was held in that case that:
 (i) the primary purpose of waste disposal licensing powers under Pt. I of COPA 1974 was to avoid water pollution, serious detriment to the amenities of the locality and harm to public health; therefore the power to impose conditions under s.6(2) of COPA 1974 was not wide enough to allow a condition prohibiting public nuisances of all kinds, whether or not they had one of those three effects; and
 (ii) if such condition were valid, there would be no need to trace a nuisance back to a particular failure of management or operation in order to establish a breach.
It is questionable how far proposition (a) remains correct under Pt. II of the Act, where protection of water from pollution has been broadened to protection of the environment generally, and where "harm" to the environment receives a very broad statutory definition to include human senses.
(c) *Water pollution.* A waste site or installation that involves the discharge of effluent into controlled waters (for example a leachate treatment plant), or which results in polluting matter entering such waters, will require consent from the NRA under the Water Resources Act 1991. The NRA must be consulted before a waste management licence is issued and if the NRA requests that the licence is not issued or disagrees with the waste regulation authority as to the conditions, the licence may not be issued except in accordance with a decision of the Secretary of State, to whom either party may refer the matter (s.36(5)). Similar provisions apply in Scotland in relation to river purification authorities (s.36(6)). The same principles apply to proposals for modification of licences (s.37(5)). Any proposal to accept surrender of a licence must also be referred to the NRA (s.39(7)) and the river purification authority in Scotland (s.39(8)).
The draft Waste Management Licensing Regulations, published for consultation in August 1992, exclude from the need for a waste management licence the treatment, keeping or disposal of waste carried on in accordance with a discharge consent under the Water Resources Act 1991 or the Control of Pollution Act 1974.
(d) *Radioactive Substances.* By s.78, nothing in Pt. II of the Act applies to radioactive waste, but regulations may apply some or all of the provisions of Pt. II, with or without modification, for the purpose of dealing with such waste.
(e) *Town and Country Planning.* The prerequisite of either planning permission or an established use certificate or certificate of lawful use or development before a waste management licence can be granted has already been referred to (see above and the notes to s.36(2) *infra*). Another question which can arise is the relationship between planning and waste management licence conditions.
Guidance on this issue is provided by PPG *Planning and Pollution Control*, Annexes 4 and 5 and in Waste Management Paper No. 4, *Licensing of Waste Facilities* paras. 1.11–1.13. It should be noted that many types of waste facility may require environmental assessment under the

Town and Country Planning (Assessment of Environmental Effects) Regulations 1988 (S.I. 1988 No. 1199) prior to the grant of planning permission.

The Planning and Compensation Act 1991 amended the Town and Country Planning Act 1990 so as to require (s.38(2)) local planning authorities to prepare either a waste local plan or waste policies contained in their minerals local plan: in formulating such policies the local planning authority must have regard to any waste disposal plan for its area prepared under s.50 of EPA 1990 (Development Plan Regulations 1991, reg. 9(2)). The waste disposal plan will consider the types and quantities of waste arising in the area, the availability of disposal facilities and the need for further provisions, while the waste local plan addresses the land use implications of waste policies, such as suitable locations and the criteria likely to apply (PPG 12 para. 3.14).

(f) *Health and Safety at work.* The draft Waste Management Regulations provide (reg. 15) that no condition may be imposed in a waste management licence for the purpose only of securing the health of persons at work.

Territorial extent

Only s.62(2)(e) (keeping of records as to special waste) applies to Northern Ireland and only in relation to imports of waste (s.164(4)).

Commencement

The provisions of Pt. II of EPA 1990 on waste management are gradually being implemented. Sections 29–32 on waste regulation authorities, the Secretary of State's power to create regional waste regulation authorities, and waste disposal companies came into force on May 31, 1991. Section 34 on the Duty of Care came into force on April 1, 1992 along with the offence of treating, keeping, or disposing of controlled waste, in a manner likely to cause pollution of the environment or harm to human health (s.33(1)(c)). Sections 45–48 on the collection, disposal and treatment of controlled waste came into force on April 1, 1992. Section 49 on waste recycling plans came into force on August 1, 1991. Sections 50 and 51 on waste disposal plans and the functions of waste disposal authorities respectively came into force on May 31, 1991. Section 52 on payments for recycling and disposal of waste and s.55 on powers for recycling waste came into force on April 1, 1992. Section 75 on the definition of waste, including household, commercial and industrial waste and special waste come into force on May 31, 1991. See further, the Table in the General Introduction for the full list of Commencement Orders and dates. The provisions relating to waste management licensing were expected to come into force on April 1, 1993, but this date was postponed indefinitely (DoE News Release dated April 29, 1993).

Preliminary

Preliminary

29.—(1) The following provisions have effect for the interpretation of this Part.

(2) The "environment" consists of all, or any, of the following media, namely land, water and the air.

(3) "Pollution of the environment" means pollution of the environment due to the release or escape (into any environmental medium) from—
  (a) the land on which controlled waste is treated,
  (b) the land on which controlled waste is kept,
  (c) the land in or on which controlled waste is deposited,
  (d) fixed plant by means of which controlled waste is treated, kept or disposed of,
of substances or articles constituting or resulting from the waste and capable (by reason of the quantity or concentrations involved) of causing harm to man or any other living organisms supported by the environment.

(4) Subsection (3) above applies in relation to mobile plant by means of which controlled waste is treated or disposed of as it applies to plant on land by means of which controlled waste is treated or disposed of.

(5) For the purposes of subsections (3) and (4) above "harm" means harm to the health of living organisms or other interference with the ecological systems of which they form part and in the case of man includes offence to

any of his senses or harm to his property; and "harmless" has a corresponding meaning.

(6) The "disposal" of waste includes its disposal by way of deposit in or on land and, subject to subsection (7) below, waste is "treated" when it is subjected to any process, including making it re-usable or reclaiming substances from it and "recycle" (and cognate expressions) shall be construed accordingly.

(7) Regulations made by the Secretary of State may prescribe activities as activities which constitute the treatment of waste for the purposes of this Part or any provision of this Part prescribed in the regulations.

(8) "Land" includes land covered by waters where the land is above the low water mark of ordinary spring tides and references to land on which controlled waste is treated, kept or deposited are references to the surface of the land (including any structure set into the surface).

(9) "Mobile plant" means, subject to subsection (10) below, plant which is designed to move or be moved whether on roads or other land.

(10) Regulations made by the Secretary of State may prescribe descriptions of plant which are to be treated as being, or as not being, mobile plant for the purposes of this Part.

(11) "Substance" means any natural or artificial substance, whether in solid or liquid form on in the form of a gas or vapour.

DEFINITIONS
"controlled waste": s.75(4).
"waste": s.75(2).

COMMENCEMENT
May 31, 1991 (S.I. 1991 No. 1319).

GENERAL NOTE

Subss. (3) and (4)
Pollution of the Environment. This is an important definition in the light of the powers and duties contained later in Pt. II. The essential features are:
  (a) land, fixed plant or mobile plant on or by means of which controlled waste is treated, kept, deposited or disposed of;
  (b) the release or escape from such land or plant into any environmental medium of substances or articles constituting or resulting from the waste;
  (c) those substances or articles must be capable of causing harm to man or other living organisms supported by the environment;
  (d) "harm" in this sense is defined widely by subs. (5) to include harm to health, interference with ecological systems, offence to human senses and harm to property; and
  (e) the escape or release must result in "pollution of the environment," being all or any of the media of land, water or air.

Subs. (6)
Disposal. The definition makes it clear that "disposal" is a wider term than "deposit" and that disposal includes deposit in or on land as a means of disposal. It does not, however, appear to follow that every deposit of waste on land will constitute disposal: if the waste is not deposited as a means of disposing of it the act will simply be a deposit and not a disposal. As to the meaning of "deposit," see notes to s.33.

Some statutory provisions make reference to "final disposal" (for example s.28(1) of EPA and Sched. 1, para. 2(2) of the draft Waste Management Licensing Regulations. It therefore seems to be contemplated that there may be temporary, or interim, disposal of waste as opposed to final disposal.

The Queen's Bench Divisional Court decision in *R.* v. *Metropolitan Stipendiary Magistrate, ex p. London Waste Regulation Authority*; *Berkshire County Council* v. *Scott, The Times*, January 14, 1993, held that the decision in *Leigh Land Reclamation* v. *Walsall Metropolitan Borough Council* [1991] J.P.L. 867 was wrongly decided and the *Leigh* case should no longer be followed on this point. The Court concluded that "deposit" as used in s.3(1) of the Control of

Pollution Act 1974 was not to be applied to final deposits or disposals only. The defendants in the case had been operating a waste transfer station which was not licensed under the Act.

Subss. (6) and (7)
Treatment. Treatment is defined to mean the subjection of waste to any process. "Process" has been judicially defined in other contexts: see notes to s.1(5). It is expressly stated that making waste re-usable or reclaiming substances from it constitutes treatment, so that waste recycling activities such as solvent or scrap metal recovery could be included. In practice, the definition of what constitutes "waste" will also be important here, and reference should be made to the definition in s.75 in that respect. Schedule 1 to the draft Waste Management Licensing Regulations creates various exemptions from the need for a waste management licence, a number of which relate to processes in connection with recovery, recycling or re-use. These exemptions further the Government's policy to envisage re-use and recycling and to exempt such activities so far as is consistent with environmental protection.

Subs. (8)
Land. See notes to s.33 under the heading "Deposit."

Subss. (9) and (10)
Mobile Plant: The draft Waste Management Licensing Regulations, reg. 14, provides that an incinerator which is an exempt incinerator for the purposes of Sched. 1, s.5.1 to the Environmental Protection (Prescribed Processes and Substances) Regulations 1991 (S.I. 1991 No. 472) (*i.e.* an incinerator designed to incinerate waste, including animal remains, at a rate of not more than 50 kg per hour, other than one employed to incinerate clinical waste, sewage storage, sewage screenings or municipal waste) and which is designed to be moved on roads or other land shall be treated as mobile plant. Regulation 14 expressly provides that no other plant shall be treated as such. Paragraph 1.6 of Annex 1 to the draft Circular on *Waste Management Licensing* states that this was the only type of licensable mobile plant available for the disposal of controlled waste at the stage of making the Regulations. Any other forms of such plant will either need to be expressly provided for or will require a site licence for each location at which they operate.

Whether plant is "designed" to move or be moved on roads will be a question of fact, and is a different question from whether it is movable. "Designed" may mean either intended or alternatively designed in structural or engineering terms: see *Wilson* v. *West Sussex County Council* [1963] 2 Q.B. 764.

Authorities for purposes of this Part

30.—(1) For the purposes of this Part the following authorities are, subject to section 31 below, waste regulation authorities, namely—
  (a) for any non-metropolitan county in England, the county council;
  (b) for Greater London, the authority constituted as the London Waste Regulation Authority;
  (c) for the metropolitan county of Greater Manchester, the authority constituted as the Greater Manchester Waste Disposal Authority;
  (d) for the metropolitan county of Merseyside, the authority constituted as the Merseyside Waste Disposal Authority;
  (e) for any district in any other metropolitan county in England, the council of the district;
  (f) for any district in Wales, the council of the district;
  (g) in Scotland, an islands or district council;
and the authorities mentioned in paragraph (c) and (d) above shall for the purposes of their functions as waste regulation authorities be known as the Greater Manchester Waste Regulation Authority and the Merseyside Waste Regulation Authority respectively.

(2) For the purposes of this Part the following authorities are waste disposal authorities, namely—
  (a) for any non-metropolitan county in England, the county council;
  (b) in Greater London, the following—
    (i) for the area of a London waste disposal authority, the

authority constituted as the waste disposal authority for that area;
  (ii) for the City of London, the Common Council;
  (iii) for any other London borough, the council of the borough;
(c) in the metropolitan county of Greater Manchester, the following—
  (i) for the metropolitan district of Wigan, the district council;
  (ii) for all other areas in the county, the authority constituted as the Greater Manchester Waste Disposal Authority;
(d) for the metropolitan county of Merseyside, the authority constituted as the Merseyside Waste Disposal Authority;
(e) for any district in any other metropolitan county in England, the council of the district;
(f) for any district in Wales, the council of the district;
(g) in Scotland, an islands or district council.

(3) For the purposes of this Part the following authorities are waste collection authorities—
(a) for any district in England and Wales not within Greater London, the council of the district;
(b) in Greater London, the following—
  (i) for any London borough, the council of the borough;
  (ii) for the City of London, the Common Council;
  (iii) for the Temples, the Sub-Treasurer of the Inner Temple and the Under Treasurer of the Middle Temple respectively;
(c) in Scotland, an islands or district council.

(4) In this section references to particular authorities having been constituted as waste disposal or regulation authorities are references to their having been so constituted by the Waste Regulation and Disposal (Authorities) Order 1985 made by the Secretary of State under section 10 of the Local Government Act 1985 and the reference to London waste disposal authorities is a reference to the authorities named in Parts I, II, III, IV and V of Schedule 1 to that Order and this section has effect subject to any order made under the said section 10 establishing authorities to discharge any functions to which that section applies.

(5) In this Part "waste disposal contractor" means a person who in the course of a business collects, keeps, treats or disposes of waste, being either—
(a) a company formed for all or any of those purposes by a waste disposal authority whether in pursuance of section 32 below or otherwise; or
(b) either a company formed for all or any of those purposes by other persons or a partnership or an individual;
and "company" has the same meaning as in the Companies Act 1985 and "formed," in relation to a company formed by other persons, includes the alteration of the objects of the company.

(6) In this Part, in its application to Scotland, "river purification authority" means a river purification authority within the meaning of the River (Prevention of Pollution) (Scotland) Act 1951.

(7) It shall be the duty of each authority which is both a waste regulation authority and a waste disposal authority—
(a) to make administrative arrangements for keeping its functions as a waste regulation authority separate from its functions as a waste disposal authority; and
(b) to submit details of the arrangements which it has made to the Secretary of State.

(8) The Secretary of State may give to an authority to which subsection (7) above applies directions as to the arrangements which it is to make for the purpose of keeping its functions as a waste regulation authority separate from its functions as a waste disposal authority; and it shall be the duty of the authority to give effect to the directions.

DEFINITIONS
"disposes": s.29(6).
"treats": s.29(6).
"waste": s.75(2).

COMMENCEMENT
May 31, 1991 (S.I. 1991 No. 1319).

GENERAL NOTE

Waste Authorities
This section makes provision for the various waste authorities, namely:
(a) waste regulation authorities;
(b) waste disposal authorities; and
(c) waste collection authorities.
Their respective notes and functions are summarised at the General Note to Pt. II of the Act.

Subs. (5)
Waste Disposal Contractor. Waste disposal functions are to be discharged through waste disposal contractors as defined in subs. (5). Such a contractor may either be a private business operating through the medium of sole trader, partnership, or limited company or alternatively may be a company formed by the waste disposal authority (see also s.32 below). In either case, the contractor must be a person who collects, keeps, treats or disposes of waste "in the course of a business." The expression implies at least a degree of continuity of activity. "Business" has been said to be a wider term than "trade" and while naturally it will usually be carried on with a view to profit, this is not always an essential prerequisite (see *Stroud's Judicial Dictionary* (5th ed., 1986), Vol. I, pp. 323 *et seq.*). Clearly it is contemplated that the local authority companies will be run on a commercial profit-making basis.

Subss. (7) and (8)
Separation of regulation and disposal functions. One of the main objects of Pt. II of the Act is the separation of waste regulation and waste disposal functions, and the general duty to make administrative arrangements for that purpose reflects this.
Details of the administration arrangements regarding the separation of functions of the waste regulation authority from those of the waste disposal authority are provided in DoE Circ. 10/91 (W.O. 27/91) dated May 31, 1991 entitled "Separation of Local Authority Waste Regulation and Waste Disposal Functions". The Circular does not apply to Scotland.

Power to create regional authorities for purposes of waste regulation

31.—(1) If it appears to the Secretary of State in the case of any two or more of the authorities mentioned in section 30(1) above that those authorities (in this section referred to as "relevant authorities") could with advantage make joint arrangements for the discharge of all or any of their functions as waste regulation authorities, he may by order establish a single authority (a "regional authority") to discharge such of those functions as may be specified in the order for the area comprising the areas of those authorities.

(2) A regional authority shall exercise the functions specified in the order establishing it on and after a day specified in the order and, so far as the exercise of those functions (if not withdrawn) and any subsequently-conferred functions is concerned, shall (in place of the relevant authorities) be the waste regulation authority for the purposes of this Part.

(3) The members of a regional authority shall be appointed by the relevant authorities in accordance with the order establishing it and no person shall be such a member unless he is a member of one of the relevant authorities.

(4) The Secretary of State may by order made with respect to any regional authority—
(a) confer or impose on it further functions;
(b) withdraw from it any functions previously conferred or imposed; or
(c) dissolve it;

and functions may be so conferred or imposed or withdrawn as respects the whole or any part of the authority's area.

(5) An order under this section may contain such supplementary and transitional provisions as the Secretary of State thinks necessary or expedient, including provision for the transfer of property, staff, rights and liabilities.

COMMENCEMENT
March 31, 1991 (S.I. 1991 No. 1319).

GENERAL NOTE
This section gives the Secretary of State power to establish regional authorities to discharge some or all of the functions of waste regulation authorities forming part of the regional grouping. The criterion to be considered by the Secretary of State is simply whether the authorities in question could with advantage make joint arrangements for the discharge of all or any of their functions (subs. (1)). Membership of a regional authority will be composed of representatives of the relevant regulation authorities.

The case for regional waste authorities was made most strongly by the Report of the House of Commons Environment Committee, *Toxic Waste* (Session 1988–89, Second Report, February 1989) paras. 140–153. The suggestion was at first rejected by the Government (see Cm. 679, para. 2.27), but on July 11, 1990 the Government announced that agreement had been reached on new regional arrangements with the Local Authority Associations (DoE News Release No. 417). These arrangements would lead to the setting-up of a joint waste committee for each region to develop a common approach to licensing and enforcement and to formulate regional strategies. The detailed proposals of the Associations as to the make up and terms of reference of the Committee are awaited. At the same time, the Government warned that should such voluntary arrangements fail to achieve the desired objectives of consistency, self-sufficiency and appropriate strategies, "then the pressures for central Government intervention would be difficult to resist." The Government therefore decided to take the reserve power to create statutory regional authorities which now form s.31, saying, "We do not want to use these powers but if we must we will." See also *Hansard*, H.C. Vol. 178, cols. 780–782. These provisions will be rendered unnecessary once the Environment Protection Agency is set up since waste regulation will be one of the functions of the Agency. Similarly the changes brought about under the EPA and by the proposed Agency led the Government to announce (Press Release No. 206, March 6, 1992, DoE) the abolition of statutory joint waste disposal authorities which were set up under the Local Government Act 1985. The authorities have been directed to divest themselves of their waste disposal operations and set up separate waste disposal companies or privatise their disposal operations. The divestment is expected to be complete by April 1993.

Transition to waste disposal companies etc.

32.—(1) In this section "existing disposal authority" means any authority (including any joint authority) constituted as a waste disposal authority for any area before the day appointed for this section to come into force.

(2) The Secretary of State shall, subject to subsection (3) below, give directions to existing disposal authorities or, in the case of joint authorities, to the constituent authorities requiring them, before specified dates, to—
  (a) form or participate in forming waste disposal companies; and
  (b) transfer to the companies so formed, by and in accordance with a scheme made in accordance with Schedule 2 to this Act, the relevant part of their undertakings;
and a waste disposal authority shall accordingly have power to form, and hold securities in, any company so established.

(3) Subject to subsection (4) below, the Secretary of State shall not give any direction under subsection (2) above to an existing disposal authority, or to the constituent authorities of an existing disposal authority, as respects which or each of which he is satisfied that the authority—
  (a) has formed or participated in forming a waste disposal company and transferred to it the relevant part of its undertaking;
  (b) has, in pursuance of arrangements made with other persons, ceased to carry on itself the relevant part of its undertaking;

(c) has made arrangements with other persons to cease to carry on itself the relevant part of its undertaking; or
(d) has, in pursuance of arrangements made with other persons, ceased to provide places at which and plant and equipment by means of which controlled waste can be disposed of or deposited for the purposes of disposal.

(4) Subsection (3) above does not apply in a case falling within paragraph (a) unless it appears to the Secretary of State that—
  (a) the form of the company and the undertaking transferred are satisfactory; and
  (b) the requirements of subsections (8) and (9) below are fulfilled;
and "satisfactory" means satisfactory by reference to the corresponding arrangements to which he would give his approval for the purposes of a transfer scheme under Schedule 2 to this Act.

(5) Where the Secretary of State is precluded from giving a direction under subsection (2) above to any authority by reason of his being satisfied as to the arrangements mentioned in subsection (3)(c) above, then, if those arrangements are not implemented within what appears to him to be a reasonable time, he may exercse his power to give directions under subsection (2) above as respects that authority.

(6) Part I of Schedule 2 to this Act has effect for the purposes of this section and Part II for regulating the functions of waste disposal authorities and the activities of waste disposal contractors.

(7) Subject to subsection (8) below, the activities of a company which a waste disposal authority has formed or participated in forming (whether in pursuance of subsection (2)(a) above or otherwise) may include activities which are beyond the powers of the authority to carry on itself, but, in the case of a company formed otherwise than in pursuance of subsection (2)(a) above, only if the Secretary of State has determined under subsection (4)(a) above that the form of the company and the undertaking transferred to it are satisfactory.

(8) A waste disposal authority shall, for so long as it controls a company which it has formed or participated in forming (whether in pursuance of subsection (2)(a) above or otherwise), so exercise its control as to secure that the company does not engage in activities other than the following activities or any activities incidental or conducive to, or calcuated to facilitate, them, that is to say, the disposal, keeping or treatment of waste and the collection of waste.

(9) Subject to subsection (10) below, a waste disposal authority shall, for so long as it controls a company which it has formed or participated in forming (whether in pursuance of subsection (2)(a) above or otherwise), so exercise its control as to secure that, for the purposes of Part V of the Local Government and Housing Act 1989, the company is an arm's length company.

(10) Subsection (9) above shall not apply in the case of a company which a waste disposal authority has formed or participated in forming in pursuance of subsection (2)(a) above until after the vesting date for that company.

(11) In this section and Schedule 2 to this Act—
  "control" (and cognate expressions) is to be construed in accordance with section 68 or, as the case requires, section 73 of the Local Government and Housing Act 1989;
  "the relevant part" of the undertaking of an existing disposal authority is that part which relates to the disposal, keeping or treatment or the collection of waste;
and in this section "securities" and "vesting date" have the same meaning as in Schedule 2.

(12) This section shall not apply to Scotland.

DEFINITIONS
"disposal": s.29(6).
"treatment": s.29(6).
"waste": s.75(2).

COMMENCEMENT
May 31, 1991 (S.I. 1991 No. 1319).

GENERAL NOTE
Together with Sched. 2, this complex section provides the framework for the transition of waste disposal functions from disposal authorities to disposal contractors (see s.30 above). The Secretary of State is under a duty by subs. (2) to direct disposal authorities in existence on the appointed day to form waste disposal companies (LAWDCs) and to transfer the relevant part of their undertakings to such companies (the relevant part being that relating to the collection, disposal or treatment of waste: subs. (11)).

Disposal authorities may avoid being given such a direction by making their own arrangements to form waste disposal companies, transferring the relevant part of their undertaking and ceasing to carry on such parts themselves or making arrangements to do so (subs. (3)). However, authorities making such arrangements may still be subject to a direction if the Secretary of State is not satisfied that the arrangements are satisfactory, or if they are not implemented within what appears to be a reasonable time (subss. (4) and (5)).

The new arrangements are explained in DoE Circ. 8/91 *Competition for Local Authority Waste Disposal Contracts and New Arrangements for Disposal Operations* (W.O. 24/91). Notices of intention to direct the formation of LAWDCs were issued by the Secretary of State in May/June 1991, following which timetables were given to authorities to put in place the necessary arrangements. The first transfer schemes were approved by the Secretary of State during the Summer of 1992.

Formation of LAWDCs
Guidance as to the formation of LAWDCs and their constitution and management is given at paras. 26–34 and Annex C of Circ. 8/91. The main restrictions relating to LAWDCs concern the objects of the company and "arm's length" requirements.

Objects of Company. A "private sector" waste disposal contracting company may have any objects, so long as its business is defined in s.30(5). A waste contracting company formed by a waste disposal authority may have objects and engage in activities beyond the authority's own powers (subs. (7)), but so long as the authority controls the company it must exercise its control so as to secure that the company does not engage in activities other than the collection, disposal, keeping or treatment of waste, and ancillary activities (subs. (8)). The company may seek such business from any source.

Subs. (9)
Arm's length requirements. Part V of the Local Government and Housing Act 1989 deals with companies in which local authorities have interests. Section 68(1) of the 1989 Act defines a company "under the control of a local authority" as being one which by virtue of s.736 of the Companies Act 1985 is a subsidiary of the local authority if the authority have power to control a majority of votes at a general meeting, or power to appoint or remove a majority of the board of directors, or if the company is under the control of an intermediate company which is itself under the control of the authority. Notwithstanding that a company is under the control of an authority in that sense, by s.68(6) of the 1989 Act it is still an "arm's length company" for the purposes of Pt. V:

"In relation to any financial year if, at a time before the beginning of that year, the authority resolved that the company should be an arm's length company and, at all times from the passing of that resolution up to the end of the financial year in question the following conditions have applied while the company has been under the control of the local authority:
(a) that each of the directors of the company was appointed for a fixed term of at least two years;
(b) that, subject to subs. (7) below, no director of the company has been removed by resolution under s.303 of the Companies Act 1985;
(c) that not more than one-fifth of the directors of the company have been members or officers of the authority;
(d) that the company has not occupied (as tenant or otherwise) any land in which the authority have an interest other than for the best consideration reasonably obtainable;
(e) that the company has entered into an agreement with the authority that the company will use its best endeavours to produce a specified positive return on its assets;

(f) that except for the purpose of enabling the company to acquire fixed assets or to provide it with working capital, the authority have not lent money to the company or guaranteed any sum borrowed by it or subscribed for any securities in the company;

(g) that the authority have not made any grant to the company the amount of which is in any way related to the financial results of the company in any period."

The importance of being an "arm's length company" lies in the controls exercised by the Government over companies established by local authorities. The general philosophy is that local authority controlled companies or local authority influenced companies are extensions of local authorities, should observe the same principles of conduct as local authorities, and should be subject to the same statutory controls as local authorities. By s.70 of the 1989 Act, the Secretary of State may regulate the activities of such companies by orders, but different provision may be made in such orders for companies which are arm's length companies.

Control: The four ways in which a company may, by s.68 of the 1989 Act, be regarded as under the control of a local authority are referred to in the previous paragraph. Detailed provisions deal with what is meant by power to control a majority of votes at a general meeting, the right to appoint or remove a majority of the board of directors, and the circumstances in which a person's shareholding in the company is under the control of a local authority. Section 73 of the 1989 Act applies in cases where authorities act jointly to constitute or control a company, so that the company is not under the control of any one authority but is under the control of the authorities acting as one.

Transfer of undertaking

Waste disposal authorities are not required, in all cases, to set up LAWDCs. They may choose to make alternative arrangements for waste disposal to be carried out by the private sector (Circ. 8/91, para. 17). However, in either case the authority will need to divest itself of its waste disposal undertaking.

The disposal authority may continue to own the freehold of waste sites, but the leasehold interest would have to be vested in the LAWDC (or in a private contractor in the absence of a LAWDC) for the life of the site (see s.51(4)(d) and (5)(c)). The disposal authority must transfer all plant and equipment used for treatment, recycling or disposing of waste, but may own plant or equipment used for waste disposal contractors for enabling them to keep collected waste prior to its removal for disposal, or to treat such waste in connection with its keeping, or to facilitate its transportation, *e.g.* transfer station facilities such as balers and compactors (see s.51(4)(c) and (5)(b)). In any event, any transfer scheme will be subject to the approval of the Secretary of State, who will wish to ensure that the new companies will be financially viable.

The transfer scheme must also be supported by assurances from the directors of the LAWDC that the scheme does not withhold any staff, property or rights from the company which it would need to perform the disposal contracts it has won.

Transfer scheme

It is not necessary for assets to be transferred to a LAWDC by way of a transfer scheme under Sched. 2, though there are advantages in doing so, particularly in relation to capital allowances (Sched. 2, para. 9), the benefit of deemed planning permission (Sched. 2, para. 10) and the transfer of rights under otherwise unassignable agreements (Sched. 2, paras. 13 and 14).

The procedure for preparation submission and approval of transfer schemes is set out at Sched. 2, paras. 6–8 and at Annex D of Circ. 4/92. The effect of the scheme, when approved by the Secretary of State is to transfer to the company the assets, rights and liabilities specified in the scheme (Sched. 2, para. 6(7)). As a consequence of that vesting, the company issues to the authority such securities as are specified in the scheme (Sched. 2, para. 6(8)); these are treated as issued fully paid and as if paid up by virtue of payment to the company of their normal value in cash (Sched. 2, para. 9(1)).

The scheme will identify the property, rights and liabilities to be transferred (Sched. 2, para. 7), so that in general no separate conveyance or assignment will be necessary. However, the Scheme may make supplemental, necessary and consequential provisions, and the authority and company are under the duty to enter into such other written agreements as may be necessary to afford mutual rights and safeguards (Sched. 2, para. 8(4) and (5)). These may, for example, deal with indemnities for environmental impairment or other damage resulting from waste disposal operations prior to or after vesting, operational leases of sites, and provisions to allow the authority to participate in "windfall" profits which may accrue from future disposals of assets.

The DoE requires each transfer scheme to be supported by written assurances from the directors of the LAWDC and the authority, in the form, or substantially the form, set out at Annex E of Circ. 4/92.

Any provision fettering the right to transfer securities of a waste disposal contractor (not just a LAWDC) is void, so long as it relates to securities of a waste disposal contractor controlled by a waste disposal authority or to which the authority has transferred the relevant part of its undertaking (Sched. 2, para. 23).

Waste Disposal Contracts

Schedule 2, Pt. II deals with the terms of waste disposal contracts and the procedure for putting such contracts out to tender. Those provisions are explained and amplified at Annex A of Circ. 4/92.

The key principle is the avoidance of undue discrimination between "local authority" and "private sector" companies (para. 18). This is qualified by para. 19 which requires waste disposal authorities to have regard to the desirability of including in any contract terms designed to minimise pollution of the environment or harm to human health and to maximise the recycling of waste. Acceptance or refusal of tenders may be justified on such grounds, presumably even if the result is discrimination between classes of waste contractor. The procedural requirements for putting waste contracts to tender are set out in detail at para. 20, and by para. 21 the fact of whether a waste disposal contract is or is not controlled by the authority is to be disregarded. Once entered into, a waste disposal contract may not be varied so as to result in undue discrimination between classes of waste contractors (para. 22).

Reference is made at Circ. 4/92, Annex A, paras. A17–18 to the relevant existing and proposed E.C. requirements on competitive tendering, in particular the services directive proposal (COM (90) 372) on which further advice is to be issued.

Practical considerations

Disposal authorities have therefore been faced with a choice between the options of setting up a LAWDC or withdrawing completely from operational activities and disposing of assets by sale or lease to the private sector. If the first option is selected, the authority will need to decide how the LAWDC is to be controlled and whether it is to continue to be wholly owned by the authority. Which option proves to be appropriate will depend on the particular circumstances of the authority, the extent of private sector competition, and how viable a LAWDC is perceived to be. If a LAWDC is formed, there may be advantages in the disposal authority not retaining control. One advantage is the ability to diversify activities (s.32(8); see above). Another possible advantage is that where the authority's voting rights in the LAWDC are less than 20 per cent. the capital borrowings of the LAWDC will not count against credit approvals with respect to the credit arrangements and capital expenditure of the authority under Pt. IV of the Local Government and Housing Act 1989 (see s.69 of the 1989 Act). The Government's view on this issue was stated as follows by Baroness Blatch:

> "I do not intend to go over the same grounds at great length today. Suffice it to say that a major part of any government's economic policy must be to control public expenditure. Current local authority waste disposal operations are already subject to the capital finance regime, so these controls on local authorities are not new. LAWDCs will be set up as arm's length companies controlled by local authorities. It is only right and proper therefore that while LAWDCs continue to be controlled or influenced by local authorities they should be subject to the local authority capital finance rules. This general point was made, and accepted, during the passage of the Local Government and Housing Bill; and, again, because these companies are, to some extent, underwritten by the local authorities.
>
> It should also be remembered that if an authority chooses to relinquish control or influence of its LAWDC, the capital finance rules no longer apply. In this way, significant new private investment can be brought into waste disposal to meet the new higher standards which public sector regulators will concentrate on enforcing." (*Hansard*, H.L. Vol. 522, col. 308).

The risk attending loss of control is whether the authority is thereby exposed to the possibility of exploitation in the future, whether by the LAWDC or the private sector.

Scotland

Section 32 and Sched. 2 do not apply to Scotland, where authorities will continue to exercise both regulatory and disposal functions.

Prohibition on unauthorised or harmful depositing, treatment or disposal of waste

Prohibition on unauthorised or harmful deposit, treatment or disposal etc. of waste

33.—(1) Subject to subsection (2) and (3) below and, in relation to Scotland, to section 54 below, a person shall not—

(a) deposit controlled waste, or knowingly cause or knowingly permit controlled waste to be deposited in or on any land unless a waste management licence authorising the deposit is in force and the deposit is in accordance with the licence;
(b) treat, keep or dispose of contolled waste, or knowingly cause or knowingly permit controlled waste to be treated, kept or disposed of—
  (i) in or on any land, or
  (ii) by means of any mobile plant,
except under and in accordance with a waste management licence;
(c) treat, keep or dispose of controlled waste in a manner likely to cause pollution of the environment or harm to human health.

(2) Subsection (1) above does not apply in relation to household waste from a domestic property which is treated, kept or disposed of within the curtilage of the dwelling by or with the permission of the occupier of the dwelling.

(3) Subsection (1)(a), (b) or (c) above do not apply in cases prescribed in regulations made by the Secretary of State and the regulations may make different exceptions for different areas.

(4) The Secretary of State, in exercising his power under subsection (3) above, shall have regard in particular to the expediency of excluding from the controls imposed by waste management licences—
(a) any deposits which are small enough or of such a temporary nature that they may be so excluded;
(b) any means of treatment or disposal which are innocuous enough to be so excluded;
(c) cases for which adequate controls are provided by another enactment than this section.

(5) Where controlled waste is carried in and deposited from a motor vehicle, the person who controls or is in a position to control the use of the vehicle shall, for the purposes of subsection (1)(a) above, be treated as knowingly causing the waste to be deposited whether or not he gave any instructions for this to be done.

(6) A person who contravenes subsection (1) above or any condition of a waste management licence commits an offence.

(7) It shall be a defence for a person charged with an offence under this section to prove—
(a) that he took all reasonable precautions and exercised all due diligence to avoid the commission of the offence; or
(b) that he acted under instructions from his employer and neither knew nor had reason to suppose that the acts done by him constituted a contravention of subsection (1) above; or
(c) that the acts alleged to constitute the contravention were done in an emergency in order to avoid danger to the public and that, as soon as reasonably practicable after they were done, particulars of them were furnished to the waste regulation authority in whose area the treatment or disposal of the waste took place.

(8) Except in a case falling within subsection (9) below, a person who commits an offence under this section shall be liable—
(a) on summary conviction, to imprisonment for a term not exceeding six months or a fine not exceeding £20,000 or both; and
(b) on conviction on indictment, to imprisonment for a term not exceeding two years or a fine or both.

(9) A person who commits an offence under this section in relation to special waste shall be liable—
(a) on summary conviction, to imprisonment for a term not exceeding six months or a fine not exceeding £20,000 or both;
(b) on conviction on indictment, to imprisonment for a term not exceeding five years or a fine or both.

DEFINITIONS
"controlled waste": s.75(2) and (4).
"disposal": s.29(6).
"harm": s.29(5).
"household waste": s.75(5).
"mobile plant": s.29(9).
"pollution of the environment": s.29(3).
"special waste": s.75(9).
"treat": s.29(6).
"waste": s.75(2) and (4).

COMMENCEMENT
Subsections (3) and (4): December 12, 1991 (S.I. 1991 No. 2829). Subsection (1)(c): April 1, 1992 (S.I. 1991 No. 2829). Subsections (2) and (6)(a) so far as relating to subs. (1)(c): April 1, 1992 (S.I. 1991 No. 2829). Remainder: not yet in force.

GENERAL NOTE

Causing and knowingly permitting
The section forms the foundation of the waste licensing system by prohibiting the deposit, treatment, keeping or disposal of controlled waste in or on land, or by means of mobile plant, except under and in accordance with a waste management licence. It is an offence not only to carry out such activities, but also to "knowingly cause or knowingly permit" them. The different wording implies distinct offences, "permit" being a "looser and vaguer" term than "cause": see *McLeod* v. *Buchanan* [1940] 2 All E.R. 179, 187 (H.L., *per* Lord Wright).

The term "cause" should be approached in its everyday common sense, and does not imply intention or negligence: *Alphacell* v. *Woodward* [1972] A.C. 824. To "cause" a deposit or other act does, however, involve some positive participation on the defendant's part and where the defendant's role is entirely passive, a charge of "knowingly permitting" will be the more appropriate course: see *Price* v. *Cromack* [1975] 1 W.L.R. 988. Such a charge might, for example, be appropriate in the case of a waste producer who consigns waste to a contractor knowing that the latter intends to dispose of the waste unlawfully. Consequences following from some active operation involving the use, production or storage of material can be said to be caused by the person carrying out that operation, and the question of causation is to be decided in a commonsense way: *Southern Water Authority* v. *Pegrum and Pegrum* (1989) 153 J.P. 581. As to the distinction between causing and permitting, see also *Shave* v. *Rosner* [1954] 2 Q.B. 113. Unlike some provisions, "cause" is prefaced by "knowingly," so something more than a simple causal link is required.

The word "knowingly" has been construed as referring to knowledge of the deposit or other act involving the waste, and not to knowledge that such deposit is outside or is not in accordance with the terms of the licence: *Ashcroft* v. *Cambro Waste Products* [1981] 1 W.L.R. 1349. In the same case it was said that the prosecution simply has to prove that waste has been knowingly permitted to be deposited on land and it is then for the defence to establish that the deposit was in accordance with terms and conditions of a licence.

Changes from Control of Pollution Act 1974
Section 33 makes a number of changes from the equivalent section of COPA, s.3. In particular, the offences under COPA were confined to:
  (a) the deposit of controlled waste on land; and
  (b) the use of plant or equipment for the purpose of disposing of controlled waste or dealing with it in a prescribed manner.

The power to make regulations under s.6(1) of COPA as to conditions to be disregarded for certain offences, but contravention of which would be an offence *per se* (s.6(3)), was never exercised.

The main changes brought about by the EPA are as follows:
  (a) widening of offences to include treatment, keeping and disposal of controlled waste (subs. (1)(b));
  (b) treatment, keeping or disposal of controlled waste in a manner likely to cause pollution of the environment or harm to human health is itself an offence (subs. (1)(c)); and
  (c) contravention of a condition of a waste management licence is itself an offence (subs. (6)).

Meaning of "deposit"
As to the relationship of "disposal" to "deposit," see notes to s.29. Unlike "disposal," "deposit" is not defined.

The DoE has generally expressed the view that "deposit" includes both permanent and temporary deposit, *i.e.* final deposit in landfill or temporary deposit on land or in prohibition on unauthorised or harmful deposit, treatment or disposal etc. of waste containers pending final disposal, treatment or recovery elsewhere: See Circ. 13/88 (Welsh Office 19/88), Annex 1 para. 2.10. On the other hand, Regulation 14 of the Control of Pollution (Special Waste) Regulations 1980 (S.I. 1980 No. 1709) appears to envisage "deposit" as meaning the final resting place of waste. In *Leigh Land Reclamation* v. *Walsall Metropolitan Borough Council, The Times*, November 2, 1990, the Divisional Court, considering the word "deposit" in the context of COPA, took the view that it is a colourable word and in the context of COPA is concerned, primarily at least, with the manner in which the waste is disposed of:

> "Its provisions and the conditions in the licence, are directed towards the mode of final disposal and not to the intermediate processes. For the purposes of this Act, waste is, in my view, to be regarded as deposited when it is dumped on the site with no realisitic prospect of further examination or inspection to reject goods of which deposit is not allowed under the licence" (Bingham L.J.)

However, a different view appears to have been reached in *Lancashire County Council* v. *Dodd, Dodd and Dugdale* (written judgment of Preston Crown Court, February 19, 1992; summarised at *IWM Journal*, May 1992). The case did not concern a licensed site as did the *Leigh* case, but rather the tipping of waste onto unlicensed land. It was held that the *Leigh* case was to be distinguished on its facts and that in the absence of any statutory definition the word "deposit" was to be given its ordinary and natural meaning, which the court was satisfied included both a temporary and permanent disposal or setting down. Similarly in another Crown Court decision, *Berridge Incinerators* v. *Nottinghamshire County Council* (Nottingham Crown Court, June 12, 1992) the term "deposit" was equated with the activity simply of bringing waste onto land and putting it down there (a case on a notice requiring the removal of unlawfully deposited waste under s.16 of COPA). See also the *L.W.R.A.* and *Berkshire* cases referred to at the note to s.29(6) which suggest the *Leigh* decision is incorrect.

Treatment. This term is defined: see notes to s.29(6) and (7).

Keeping. The term is not defined but draft DoE Circ. on the Waste Management Licensing Regulations, Annex 1, para. 1.5, suggests that it covers situations where waste is retained in the lands of the holder, whether it can be said to be deposited or not. Whilst it is clearly a wider term than disposed of or deposit, it would seem to import retention of waste with at least some degree of continuity. For example, one could query whether an isolated incident where waste remained on premises for a short period by an oversight would constitute "keeping": compare *Blue* v. *Pear Assurance Co.* [1940] 3 W.W.R. 13, 19, 20 (a Canadian case on the "keeping" of gasoline). Storage of waste on the producer's premises pending disposal would constitute keeping, but may fall within one of a number of exemptions from the requirement of a licence provided by the Waste Management Licensing Regulations 1993 (see below).

Other offences

As well as the offences referred to above, the section creates two other offences. The first is that of treating, keeping or disposing of controlled waste "in a manner likely to cause pollution of the environment or harm to human health" (s.33(1)(c)). The width of these words has already been noted. The fact that a waste management licence is in force and that all conditions are being complied with would not preclude a prosecution for this offence.

The second offence is that of contravening any condition of a licence (s.33(6)). This has the effect, long urged from various quarters, of making breach of any condition *per se* an offence, whether or not the breach involves the disposal, keeping, treatment, etc. of waste and whether or not the condition relates to such matters. As was pointed out by the RCEP Eleventh Report (Cm. 9675, para. 840) relatively few conditions of licences relate to the actual deposit of waste and most relate to the proper management of the site as a whole, covering matters such as fencing, monitoring and record-keeping. This problem emerged for judicial consideration in *Leigh Land Reclamation* v. *Walsall Metropolitan Borough Council, The Times*, November 2, 1990. The Divisional Court held that under s.3(1)(a) of COPA, deposits made properly and in accordance with licence conditions could not be said to constitute an offence simply because there was some improper deposit previously or because, for example, there was no signboard on the site as required by a condition. This, in the view of the Court, would strain the language of the statute "beyond the limits acceptable in a criminal statute and ... a statute creating potentially serious indictable offence."

The position under s.33 is different. Even if actual deposit of waste on a site has ceased, permanently or temporarily, it would still be possible to prosecute for inactivity, for example failure to fulfil a restoration, landscaping or fencing condition. Similarly, the task of waste regulation authorities bringing prosecutions will be made easier in that they will simply have to identify breach of a licence condition by the holder and not prove an attendant deposit, disposal or other act by the licence-holder or knowingly permitted by him.

Special waste
Under s.3(3) of COPA, separate offences carrying substantially enhanced penalties were created where the waste in question was of a kind which was "poisonous, noxious or polluting" and where its presence on land was likely to give rise to an "environmental hazard." This language has now been replaced by a distinction between controlled waste and special waste in that the maximum term of imprisonment on conviction on indictment is greater in the case of an offence in relation to special waste (s.33(9)). It may be noted that maximum penalties on summary conviction are substantially increased from those in COPA (subss. (8) and (9)). Breach of the Control of Pollution (Special Waste) Regulations 1980 (S.I. 1980 No. 1709) will constitute a separate offence in its own right.

Deposit from motor vehicles
Special provision is made by subs. (5) for the case where waste is carried in and deposited from a motor vehicle. The person controlling the use of the vehicle or who is in a position to do so is treated as knowingly causing the waste to be deposited, whether or not any instructions were given to that effect. This provision is no doubt intended to make it easier to bring prosecutions in the case of fly-tipping, where the exact circumstances, beyond the fact of tipping and the identity of the vehicle, may be obscure. Powers also exist in s.6 of the Control of Pollution (Amendment) Act 1989 to seize and dispose of vehicles used for illegal waste disposal.

Relationship with goods vehicle licensing
Fly-tipping or other offences involving waste can now lead to loss of the goods vehicle operator's licence under the Transport Act 1968, s.69 (see Sched. 15, para. 10 and notes to s.162).

Exceptions: household waste
By subs. (2) the requirement of a licence does not apply to household waste from a domestic property which is treated, kept or disposed of within the curtilage of the dwelling by or with the permission of the occupier. However, by Regulation 3(1) of the Controlled Waste Regulations 1992 (S.I. 1992 No. 588) waste of the following descriptions shall not be treated as household waste for that purpose:
  (a) any mineral or synthetic oil or grease;
  (b) asbestos; and
  (c) clinical waste.

Exceptions: prescribed categories
By subss. (3) and (4) the Secretary of State may create exceptions to the requirements of s.33(1)(a), (b) and (c). The exceptions are provided by Regulation 2 of and Sched. 1 to the draft Waste Management Licensing Regulations. As the draft Circ. Annex 2, para. 1, points out, whilst the starting point in creating the exemptions was to preserve the position under the COPA, significant changes have been made. These arise from the increased scope of licensing under s.33 (see above), the need to implement E.C. requirements and from the Government's policies of encouraging recycling. In particular, the requirements of Directive 91/156/EEC have meant that the exceptions are more heavily qualified than before and that in some cases registration is required by the person wishing to claim the benefit of an exemption.

Defences
Subs. (7) provides three defences:
  (a) The defendant took all reasonable precautions and exercised all due diligence to avoid commission of the offence. As to the term "reasonable" in this context, *cf. Austin Rover Group* v. *H.M. Inspector of Factories* [1989] 3 W.L.R. 520, 527 (H.L.), *per* Lord Goff of Chieveley. As to due diligence, see the statement of Willmer L.J. in *Riverstone Meat Co.* v. *Lancashire Shipping Co.* [1960] 1 All E.R. 193, 219, equating it to an obligation to exercise reasonable care. COPA, s.3(4) contained the defence, not repeated in EPA, that the defendant took care to inform himself as to whether the deposit was lawful. That defence was held not to be available in the case of *Durham County Council* v. *Peter Connors Industrial Services* (Divisional Court, May 19, 1992) where a skip was provided for the use of the waste producer with no information being provided on specific consignments. It is also arguable that the requirements of the s.34 duty of care are relevant, by analogy, to this defence.
  (b) The defendant acted under instructions from his employer and neither knew nor had reason to suppose his acts were in contravention of the section. The defence of having taken care to inform himself, from persons in a position to provide the information, as to whether the deposit was unlawful (s.3(4)(a) of COPA) is no longer available;

(c) The acts were done in an emergency to avoid danger to the public and particulars were furnished to the waste regulation authority as soon as reasonably practicable thereafter. Obviously as a matter of practice, except in cases of extreme emergencies such as road accidents, it will be prudent to obtain the advice and permission of a waste disposal officer in advance of taking any action in reliance on this provision. On the issue of emergency, see *Waste Incineration Services Ltd.* v. *Dudley Metropolitan Borough Council* [1992] 1 Envir. L.R. 29.

Duty of care etc. as respects waste

Duty of care etc. as respects waste

34.—(1) Subject to subsection (2) below, it shall be the duty of any person who imports, produces, carries, keeps, treats or disposes of controlled waste or, as a broker, has control of such waste, to take all such measures applicable to him in that capacity as are reasonable in the circumstances—
 (a) to prevent any contravention by any other person of section 33 above;
 (b) to prevent the escape of the waste from his control or that of any other person; and
 (c) on the transfer of the waste, to secure—
  (i) that the transfer is only to an authorised person or to a person for authorised transport purposes; and
  (ii) that there is transferred such a written description of the waste as will enable other persons to avoid a contravention of that section and to comply with the duty under this subsection as respects the escape of waste.

(2) The duty imposed by subsection (1) above does not apply to an occupier of domestic property as respects the household waste produced on the property.

(3) The following are authorised persons for the purpose of subsection (1)(c) above—
 (a) any authority which is a waste collection authority for the purposes of this Part;
 (b) any person who is the holder of a waste management licence under section 35 below or of a disposal licence under section 5 of the Control of Pollution Act 1974;
 (c) any person to whom section 33(1) above does not apply by virtue of regulations under subsection (3) of that section;
 (d) any person registered as a carrier of controlled waste under section 2 of the Control of Pollution (Amendment) Act 1989;
 (e) any person who is not required to be so registered by virtue of regulations under section 1(3) of that Act; and
 (f) a waste disposal authority in Scotland.

(4) The following are authorised transport purposes for the purposes of subsection (1)(c) above—
 (a) the transport of controlled waste within the same premises between different places in those premises;
 (b) the transport to a place in Great Britain of controlled waste which has been brought from a country or territory outside Great Britain not having been landed in Great Britain until it arrives at that place; and
 (c) the transport by air or sea of controlled waste from a place in Great Britain to a place outside Great Britain;
and "transport" has the same meaning in this subsection as in the Control of Pollution (Amendment) Act 1989.

(5) The Secretary of State may, by regulations, make provision imposing requirements on any person who is subject to the duty imposed by subsection (1) above as respects the making and retention of documents and the furnishing of documents or copies of documents.

(6) Any person who fails to comply with the duty imposed by subsection (1) above or with any requirement imposed under subsection (5) above shall be liable—
  (a) on summary conviction, to a fine not exceeding the statutory maximum; and
  (b) on conviction on indictment, to a fine.

(7) The Secretary of State shall, after consultation with such persons or bodies as appear to him representative of the interests concerned, prepare and issue a code of practice for the purpose of providing to persons practical guidance on how to discharge the duty imposed on them by subsection (1) above.

(8) The Secretary of State may from time to time revise a code of practice issued under subsection (7) above by revoking, amending or adding to the provisions of the code.

(9) The code of practice prepared in pursuance of subsection (7) above shall be laid before both Houses of Parliament.

(10) A code of practice issued under subsection (7) above shall be admissible in evidence and if any provision of such a code appears to the court to be relevant to any question arising in the proceedings it shall be taken into account in determining that question.

(11) Different codes of practice may be prepared and issued under subsection (7) above for different areas.

DEFINITIONS
  "controlled waste": s.75(4).
  "disposes": s.29(6).
  "household waste": s.75(5).
  "treats": s.29(6).

COMMENCEMENT
  Subsections (5), (7), (8), (9) and (11): December 13, 1991 (S.I. 1991 No. 2829). Remainder: April 1, 1992 (S.I. 1991 No. 2829).

GENERAL NOTE
  This new provision can be seen as flowing from various calls for enhanced responsibility on the part of persons producing or having control of waste (see the General Note to Pt. II).
  Under s.34 it is no longer possible for the producer of waste to rid himself of responsibility for it simply by consigning the waste to an agent or contractor. However, the section does not create complete "cradle to grave" responsibility for waste as urged by some sources.
  Responsibility is primarily focused on the control of waste prior to transfer and the steps and precautions to be taken on transfer. However, it is also possible for a person to commit a breach of the duty of care after having transferred the waste, for example by failing to take reasonable steps to detect and prevent breaches by the transferee.
  The provisions are explained in DoE Circ. 19/91 (W.O. 63/91 and Scottish Office 25/91).

Scope of duty
  The duty applies to any person who imports, produces, carries, keeps, treats or disposes of controlled waste. As to the meaning of "waste" and "controlled waste" see notes to s.75. As to the meaning of "keeps," "treats" and "disposes," see notes to ss.29 and 33.
  The view of the Departments is that the starting point for identifying the producer is to decide how the material became waste. The producer may be the person taking the action which causes the material to become waste or who takes the decision that it is waste; Circ. 19/91, para. 16. In the context of works of construction or demolition, the view of the Departments is that the person undertaking the works will be the producer, not the person who let the contract or commissioned the works: however, a client or contractor may be regarded as a broker (see further, Circ. 19/91, para. 17).

Brokers
  The duty applies to a person who, as a broker has control of the waste.
  Brokers have been said to be, "Those that contrive, make, and conclude bargains and contracts between merchants and tradesmen for which they have a fee or reward": *Milford* v. *Hughes* (1846) 16 M. & W. 174, 177, *per* Alderson B. Waste brokerage can clearly take a wide

variety of contractual forms, but the broker will only be liable under the duty of care to the extent that he has control of what happens to the waste.

The Departments regard transfers where a broker is involved as being tripartite in nature: Circ. 19/91, para. 19 and Code of Practice, Annex B, para. B.13.

Article 12 of the E.C. Framework Directive on Waste (91/156/EEC) requires that undertakings which arrange for the disposal or recovery of waste on behalf of others (dealers or brokers) where not subject to authorisation, shall be registered. The Government has issued a Consultation Paper (August 1992) on a draft scheme for registration of brokers.

Exemptions

Subsection (2) exempts from the duty of care the occupier of domestic property as regards the household waste produced on that property. As to the meaning of "household waste" see notes to s.75. Waste from construction work on domestic premises is household waste for this purpose (Controlled Waste Regulations 1992 (S.I. 1992 No. 588), reg. 2(2), and see Circ. 14/92, para. 1.19). Where a contractor carries out works of construction or demolition, the waste will constitute household rather than commercial or industrial waste (see the Controlled Waste Regulations 1992, regs. 2(2) and 5(2)), but the occupier of the property will not usually be the producer (see above). The contractor will thus not benefit from the exemption; nor will a householder who disposes of waste from his neighbour's property or from his workplace (see Code of Practice, Annex A, para. A.7).

A temporary exemption applies to scrap metal, which by regs. 3(2) and 7(2) of the Controlled Waste Regulations 1992 is not to be treated as household, industrial or commercial waste for the purposes of s.34 at any time before April 1, 1993. For guidance on this issue, see Circ. 14/92, Annex 5, paras. 5.7–5.9.

Nature of duty

The duty is to take all measures applicable to the relevant person in their actual capacity and in the circumstances to prevent or secure the four matters at paras. (a)–(c) of subs. (1). The first two of these apply at all times; the third and fourth specifically on the transfer of the waste. "Transfer in this sense appears to indicate physical transfer, rather than transfer to the title in the waste. DoE Circ. 19/19, para. 8 suggests that holders' obligations are not confined to the transfer in which they hand waste on to another party; the are also under obligations to take reasonable steps with regard to any transfers in which they receive waste.

Subss. (7)–(11)

Code of Practice. Of central importance to the duty of care is the Code of Practice issued by the Secretary of State for the purpose of providing practical guidance on how persons subject to the duty may discharge it. Whilst not conclusive, the Code will be admissible and relevant in proceedings. The current Code of Practice was issued by the Department of Environment, Scottish Office and Welsh Office in December 1991. It contains step by step advice on following the duty, a summary checklist of the main steps and annexes on the relevant law, responsibilities on various parties, record-keeping requirements and other legal controls.

Subs. (5)

Documentation. Regulations have been made as to the making and retention of documents: the Environmental Protection (Duty of Care) Regulations 1991 (S.I. 1991 No. 2839). These require the transferee of controlled waste (as defined in the Regulations), at the same time as the written description of waste required by s.34(1)(c)(ii) is transferred, to ensure that a transfer note is completed and signed (reg. 2(1)). The transfer note must contain the information specified at reg. 2(2) and the Table to the Regulations. Both parties must keep the written description and transfer note for a period of two years from the transfer (reg. 3) and furnish the authority with a copy on demand (reg. 4).

Circular 19/91, paras. 18–25, explains these requirements. In particular, para. 21 suggests that it would be reasonable for a single transfer note to cover multiple consignments of waste transferred at the same time or over a period (not exceeding a year) provided that all the relevant details as to the waste and the parties remain the same throughout.

Written contracts. Neither s.34 nor the draft Code of Practice expressly requires contracts to be entered into between producers or other holders of waste and those to whom the waste is transferred. However, it is difficult to see how either party could effectively discharge the duty of care without a contract properly describing the waste and its destination and without being consistent in other respects with the duty of care.

Special waste. Special provisions apply to the more difficult and intractable wastes: see note to s.62. Such wastes remain subject to the duty of care in addition to the more specific controls of the Special Waste Regulations.

Waste Management Licences

Waste management licences: general

35.—(1) A waste management licence is a licence granted by a waste regulation authority authorising the treatment, keeping or disposal of any specified description of controlled waste or in or on specified land or the treatment or disposal of any specified description of controlled waste by means of specified mobile plant.

(2) A licence shall be granted to the following person, that is to say—

(a) in the case of a licence relating to the treatment, keeping or disposal of waste in or on land, to the person who is in occupation of the land; and

(b) in the case of a licence relating to the treatment or disposal of waste by means of mobile plant, to the person who operates the plant.

(3) A licence shall be granted on such terms and subject to such conditions as appear to the waste regulation authority to be appropriate and the conditions may relate—

(a) to the activities which the licence authorises, and

(b) to the precautions to be taken and works to be carried out in connection with or in consequence of those activities;

and accordingly requirements may be imposed in the licence which are to be complied with before the activities which the licence authorises have begun or after the activities which the licence authorises have ceased.

(4) Conditions may require the holder of a licence to carry out works or do other things notwithstanding that he is not entitled to carry out the works or do the thing and any person whose consent would be required shall grant, or join in granting, the holder of the licence such rights in relation to the land as will enable the holder of the licence to comply with any requirements imposed on him by the licence.

(5) Conditions may relate, where waste other than controlled waste is to be treated, kept or disposed of, to the treatment, keeping or disposal of that other waste.

(6) The Secretary of State may, by regulations, make provision as to the conditions which are, or are not, to be included in a licence; and regulations under this subsection may make different provision for different circumstances.

(7) The Secretary of State may, as respects any licence for which an application is made to a waste regulation authority, give to the authority directions as to the terms and conditions which are, or are not, to be included in the licence; and it shall be the duty of the authority to give effect to the directions.

(8) It shall be the duty of waste regulation authorities to have regard to any guidance issued to them by the Secretary of State with respect to the discharge of their functions in relation to licences.

(9) A licence may not be surrendered by the holder except in accordance with section 39 below.

(10) A licence is not transferable by the holder but the waste regulation authority may transfer it to another person under section 40 below.

(11) A licence shall continue in force until it is revoked entirely by the waste regulation authority under section 38 below or it is surrendered or its surrender is accepted under section 39 below.

(12) In this Part "licence" means a waste management licence and "site licence" and "mobile plant licence" mean, respectively, a licence authorising the treatment, keeping or disposal of waste in or on land and a licence authorising the treatment or disposal of waste by means of mobile plant.

DEFINITIONS
"controlled waste": s.75(2) and (4).
"disposal": s.29(6).
"mobile plant": s.29(9).
"treatment": s.29(6).
"waste": s.75(2) and (4).

COMMENCEMENT
Subsection (6): February 18, 1993 (S.I. 1993 No. 274). Remainder: no date has been set for commencement.

GENERAL NOTE
The term "waste management licence" replaces "waste disposal licence" as used in COPA. This change in terminology reflects the greater range of activities now embraced by licensing (see s.29). There are two types of waste management licence: those related to activity on land ("site licences") and those related to treatment or disposal carried out by mobile plant ("mobile plant licences").

The provisions on waste management licence are amplified by the draft Waste Management Licensing Regulations, and are explained in the accompanying draft Circular and in draft Waste Management Paper No. 4, *The Licensing of Waste Facilities* (revised 1992).

Licence conditions
The licence will specify the land or mobile plant and the description of controlled waste covered by the licence: additionally it may be granted "on such terms and subject to such conditions as appear to the authority to be appropriate" (subs. (3)). These conditions may relate not only to the authorised activities but also consequential or connected precautions or works. The relationship between licence conditions and planning conditions is discussed in the General Note to Pt. II.

Though the discretion to impose conditions is ostensibly very wide, such conditions must comply with ordinary principles of administrative law, that is to say they must be related to the underlying purpose of the legislation. For example, in the case of *Att.-Gen.'s Reference (No. 2 of 1988)* [1989] 3 W.L.R. 397, it was held that a condition prohibiting the creation of public nuisances of all kinds could not be lawfully imposed under s.6(2) of COPA. (See further General Note to Pt. II). The view that the licensing provisions of COPA were primarily intended to ensure that waste disposal takes place without risk of water pollution or danger to human health was also frequently expressed by the Secretary of State in appeals against conditions under s.10 of COPA.

The wording of the 1990 Act is different from that used in COPA, which at s.5(3) referred to "pollution of water or danger to public health" as grounds for rejecting a disposal licence application. The equivalent s.36(3) in the 1990 Act refers to (a) "pollution of the environment"; (b) "harm to human health" (which will include offence to senses and harm to property); and (c) (where planning permission is not in force) "serious detriment to the amenities of the locality." It appears therefore that the purposes for which licence conditions may be imposed are widened correspondingly.

It is also to be noted that s.6(2) of the 1974 Act contained a list of specific matters to which conditions might relate, without prejudice to the general words of the section. These were: (a) the duration of the licence; (b) supervision by the holder of activities to which the licence relates; (c) kinds and quantities of waste, methods of dealing with waste, and recording of information; (d) precautions to be taken on the site; (e) steps to facilitate compliance with any relevant planning conditions; (f) hours; and (g) works to be carried out before licensed activities commence or while they are continuing.

No doubt, although s.35 contains no such specific list, those matters will fall within the general words of the section and will continue to form the subject-matter of conditions in appropriate cases.

By the draft Waste Management Licensing Regulations, reg. 16, licences which authorise the regeneration or keeping of waste oils must contain conditions to the effect specified in that regulation.

Similarly, in appropriate cases, conditions must be imposed to safeguard groundwater against List I and List II substances under Directive 80/68/EEC (draft Waste Management Licensing Regulations, reg. 17).

No condition may be imposed solely for the purpose of securing the health of persons at work: draft Waste Management Licensing Regulations, reg. 15.

Departmental guidance on conditions

In appeals under s.10 of COPA the Secretary of State has also frequently stated his view that, whilst high standards with regard to waste handling and disposal are a desirable objective, conditions should be reasonable in that: (a) they should reflect the nature and scale of operations on, and the circumstances of, the particular site; (b) they should afford adequate protection to local amenities from operations on the site; and (c) they should not impose an unreasonable burden on the operator. Draft Waste Management Paper No. 4 on *The Licensing of Waste Facilities* contains further guidance on licence conditions and in particular their relationship to the Working Plan prepared by the operator, describing the site and how it is to be operated. Appendix B gives a checklist of conditions to be considered.

Authorities must have regard to this, and to any other, departmental guidance (subs. (8)).

Subs. (4)

Effect on third parties. This subsection merits specific mention because of its uncertain potential effect on third parties. As originally drafted, the clause simply read: "Conditions may require the holder of a licence to carry out works or do other such things notwithstanding that he is not entitled to carry out the works or do the thing." This was similar to the wording which appeared in s.6(2) of COPA, save that the earlier wording used the term "entitled as of right." In Committee stage in the Commons, Mr Malcolm Bruce MP introduced an amendment (No. 407), inserting the words "and the owner of the land shall grant to the licence-holder any necessary rights to carry out such works or do such things," the object of which was, in the words of Mr Bruce as follows:

"To clarify the arrangements of the management of sites so that an operator of a site who does not own the site but is a licensee can still do the work and that any contractual obligations he may have with the owner of the site will not prevent him from doing so. If a site has been closed, but continues to be a responsibility, there could be contractual obligations between the owner and the licensee that interfere with this duty of care. I am seeking clarification and pressing the point that a licensee should not be prevented by the owner from carrying out the necessary work." (Standing Committee H, Thirteenth sitting, February 13, 1990, cols. 462–3.)

The amendment was opposed by the Government and was withdrawn, Mr Heathcoat-Amory putting the Government position as follows:

"Under the Bill the regulatory authority can impose conditions that the landowner might seem powerless to implement, possibly because he does not own the adjoining land. This possibility demonstrates the strength and depth of our provisions because it is up to the licensee in such conditions to negotiate with the neighbouring landowner. If it proves impossible for him to return to the waste regulation authority to ask for the conditions to be modified or, in extremis, the licence may have to be surrendered. Giving a private person automatic rights to go on to land that is not his and carry out work that is perhaps to its detriment without any kind of notice, appeal or limitation does not solve the problem. I therefore reject the Draconian powers implicit in amendment No. 407. The conditions in the Bill are important, but it is up to the licensee to satisfy those conditions by negotiation or purchase of the land in question." (*ibid.*, col. 463).

However, the Government subsequently brought forward the present wording of the sub-subsection as Amendment No. 70 on Third Reading, without comment (see *Hansard*, H.C. Vol. 17, col. 1153). This wording appears to go even further than that proposed by Mr Bruce. On the plain wording of the subsection it appears that if a condition is imposed requiring the licence-holder to carry out works or do other things which he is not entitled to do without the consent of another person, then that person is under a duty to grant the licence-holder such rights "in relation to the land" as will enable the licence-holder to comply with the requirements imposed on him by the licence. It is not clear whether the words "in relation to the land" refer to the land specified in the licence on which the waste is kept, treated or deposited, or the land on which the works or acts required by the condition are to be carried out. Nor is there any mechanism for enforcing that duty or for compensation or assessment of consideration. An alternative interpretation, that the subsection simply allows the authority to make such consent a condition precedent of the licensed activities, seems more workable but could not be achieved without considerable violence to the actual words.

The draft Circular on Waste Management Licensing Regulations, para. 1.18 suggests that the more far reaching interpretation is correct, and that it is not desirable to rely on this power more often than is strictly necessary.

Subs. (5)
Waste other than controlled waste. This provision is useful where a site receives a mixture of controlled waste and waste which is not controlled; the non-controlled waste may be subject to licence conditions.

Subs. (6)
Provision as to conditions to be included. See the reference to waste oils and groundwater protection, above.

Bonds and financial provision
Though it has not been settled by the courts, it has been conceded in proceedings by the Secretary of State for the Environment that it is within the powers of s.6 of COPA (and no doubt therefore within the powers of the 1990 Act) to impose conditions requiring the licence-holder to: (a) enter into a financial bond before depositing waste at the site; and (b) take out a third party and public liability insurance policy.

It is now frequent practice to require financial assurance by way of bonds, deposit accounts or other provision by the prospective operator: and see the notes to s.74 on "fit and proper person."

Grant of licences

36.—(1) An application for a licence shall be made—
 (a) in the case of an application for a site licence, to the waste regulation authority in whose area the land is situated; and
 (b) in the case of an application for a mobile plant licence, to the waste regulation authority in whose area the operator of the plant has his principal place of business;
and shall be made in the form prescribed by the Secretary of State in regulations and accompanied by the prescribed fee payable under section 41 below.

(2) A licence shall not be issued for a use of land for which planning permission is required in pursuance of the Town and Country Planning Act 1990 or the Town and Country Planning (Scotland) Act 1972 unless—
 (a) such planning permission is in force in relation to that use of the land, or
 (b) an established use certificate is in force under section 192 of the said Act of 1990 or section 90 of the said Act of 1972 in relation to that use of the land.

(3) Subject to subsection (2) above and subsection (4) below, a waste regulation authority to which an application for a licence has been duly made shall not reject the application if it is satisfied that the applicant is a fit and proper person unless it is satisfied that its rejection is necessary for the purpose of preventing—
 (a) pollution of the environment;
 (b) harm to human health; or
 (c) serious detriment to the amenities of the locality;
but paragraph (c) above is inapplicable where planning permission is in force in relation to the use to which the land will be put under the licence.

(4) Where the waste regulation authority proposes to issue a licence, the authority must, before it does so,—
 (a) refer the proposal to the National Rivers Authority and the Health and Safety Executive; and
 (b) consider any representations about the proposal which the Authority or the Executive makes to it during the allowed period.

(5) If, following the referral of a proposal to the National Rivers Authority under subsection (4)(a) above, the Authority requests that the licence be not issued or disagrees about the condition of the proposed

licence either of them may refer the matter to the Secretary of State and the licence shall not be issued except in accordance with his decision.

(6) Subsection (4) above shall not apply to Scotland, but in Scotland where a waste regulation authority (other than an islands council) proposes to issue a licence, the authority must, before it does so,—
  (a) refer the proposal to—
    (i) the river purification authority whose area includes any of the relevant land;
    (ii) the Health and Safety Executive;
    (iii) where the waste regulation authority is not also a district planning authority within the meaning of section 172 of the Local Government (Scotland) Act 1973, the general planning authority within the meaning of that section whose area includes any of the relevant land; and
  (b) consider any representations about the proposal which the river purification authority, the Executive or the general planning authority makes to it during the allowed period,
and if the river purification authority requests that the licence be not issued or disagrees with the waste regulation authority about the conditions of the proposed licence either of them may refer the matter to the Secretary of State and the licence shall not be issued except in accordance with his decision.

(7) Where any part of the land to be used is land which has been notified under section 28(1) of the Wildlife and Countryside Act 1981 (protection for certain areas) and the waste regulation authority proposes to issue a licence, the authority must, before it does so—
  (a) refer the proposal to the appropriate nature conservation body; and
  (b) consider any representations about the proposal which the body makes to it during the allowed period;
and in this section any reference to the appropriate nature conservation body is a reference to the Nature Conservancy Council for England, the Nature Conservancy Council for Scotland or the Countryside Council for Wales, according as the land is situated in England, Scotland or Wales.

(8) Until the date appointed under section 131(3) below any reference in subsection (7) above to the appropriate nature conservation body is a reference to the Nature Conservancy Council.

(9) If within the period of four months beginning with the date on which a waste regulation authority received an application for the grant of a licence, of within such longer period as the authority and the applicant may at any time agree in writing, the authority has neither granted the licence in consequence of the application nor given notice to the applicant that the authority has rejected the application, the authority shall be deemed to have rejected the application.

(10) The period allowed to the National Rivers Authority, the Health and Safety Executive, the appropriate nature conservancy body, a river purification authority or general planning authority for the making of representations under subsection (4), (6) or (7) above about a proposal is the period of 21 days beginning with that on which the proposal is received by the authority or such longer period as the waste regulation authority and the Authority, the Executive, the body, the river purification authority or the general planning authority, as the case may be, agree in writing.

DEFINITIONS
  "fit and proper person": s.74.
  "harm": s.29(5).
  "licence": s.35(12).
  "mobile plant licence": s.35(12).
  "pollution of the environment": s.29(3).
  "site licence": s.35(12).

COMMENCEMENT

Subsection (1): February 18, 1993 (S.I. 1993 No. 274). Remainder: no date has been set for commencement.

GENERAL NOTE

This section, which deals with applications for, and the grant of, waste management licences, contains a number of modifications of the equivalent section in COPA. By far the most important of these is the introduction of the concept of "fit and proper person," a much recommended reform giving the licensing authority power to have regard to the personal character, experience, record and capability of the applicant. The phrase is amplified in s.74 and further reference should be made to that section and the notes thereto.

Subs. (1)

Prescribed form and fee. As to the prescribed form, the draft Waste Management Licensing Regulations, reg. 3, simply provides that the application is to be in writing. It is therefore a matter for each authority to devise its own forms having regard to the advice in Waste Management Paper No. 4 as to the information desirable (Circ. 1/92, Annex 1, para. 1.27).

As to fees, see the note to s.41.

Subs. (1)(b)

Principal place of business. It may be a difficult question as to where the principal place of business of a company is located: see *Grant* v. *Anderson & Co.* [1892] 1 Q.B. 108 (C.A.). Presumably where a company carrying on waste management activities in this country is domiciled overseas, the intention must be for the principal place of business in Great Britain to be the relevant one.

Subs. (2)

Planning status of land. If planning permission is required for the use to be made of the land under a site licence, then the licence shall not be issued unless either such permission is in force or an established use certificate is in force. Planning permission will not be needed for uses of land commenced prior to July 1, 1948 or for those for which permission has been granted by a special or general development order. Nor will planning permission be required for the use of Crown land where the Crown is the occupier. Also, by s. 191(7) of the Town and Country Planning Act 1990 (as substituted by s.10 of the Planning and Compensation Act 1991) a certificate of lawful use or development under s.191 of the 1990 Act shall have effect for the purpose of s.36(2)(a) as if it were a grant of planning permission. (For Scotland, see s.90(7) of the Town and Country Planning (Scotland) Act 1972 as substituted by s.42 of the Planning and Compensation Act 1991.)

It should be noted that subs. (2) is framed in terms of uses of land. Land may not require planning permission to be used for waste disposal for one or other of the reasons given above. Nonetheless, the proposed activities may involve operational development which does require planning permission. This was the situation in *Berridge Incinerators* v. *Nottinghamshire County Council* (High Court, 1987, unreported but cited at para. 2.7 of DoE Circ. 13/88, Judge P.J. Crawford Q.C.). In that case the Deputy Judge held that the issue of the use of land had to be considered separately from that of development on the land by the installation of plant or equipment. On that basis he found that planning permission was not required for the use of land but was required in respect of the plant or equipment, and on that basis the applicants would not satisfy the conditions precedent to the grant of a licence. However, whereas the Deputy Judge's reasoning was based on the wording of s.5(2) of COPA in referring to "a use of land, *plant or equipment* for which planning permission is required", subs. (2) of the 1990 Act omits the italicised words.

Subs. (3)

Grounds for refusal. This subsection effectively restricts the grounds on which a waste regulation authority may reject a licence application which has been duly made and where the conditions precedent as to planning permission in subs. (2) have been complied with. The equivalent provision in COPA (s.5(3)) was held in *Berridge Incinerators* v. *Nottinghamshire County Council* not to apply in a case where planning permission for the use was not required and where consequently no permission was in force: this problematic result is obviated by the new wording.

The significance of the introduction of the requirement that the authority be satisfied that the applicant is a "fit and proper person" has been already mentioned: and see notes to s.74.

The only other grounds on which the authority may lawfully reject an application are that rejection is necessary for the purpose of preventing: (a) pollution of the environment; or (b) harm to human health. The width of meaning given to these expressions by the legislation means that effectively the grounds for refusal are widened considerably beyond those in COPA. Further, where no planning permission is in force in relation to the proposed use, "serious detriment to the amenities of the locality" forms a further reason for rejection, presumably on the basis that there will have been no planning application stage where such matters could have been considered.

If the evils referred to in the subsection can be effectively prevented by the imposition of conditions, then it will not be, in the words of the subsection, "necessary" to reject the application.

Subss. (4)–(8)
Reference to other regulatory authorities. These subsections contain procedures whereby licence proposals are to be referred to the relevant authorities, and any representations made by such authorities within 21 days or such longer period as may be agreed in writing (subs. (10)) are to be considered. In the case of the NRA, the authority may request that the licence not be issued, or may disagree as to the conditions to be attached, in which case that matter may be referred to the Secretary of State and the licence may not be issued except in accordance with his decision (subs. (5)). In the case of consultations with the Health and Safety Executive (subs. (4)) or the relevant nature conservation body where any part of the site is notified as a SSSI (subs. (7)) the obligation is simply to consider any representations made within the allowed period.

Subs. (9)
Deemed rejection. This subsection provides a means by which an applicant may appeal to the Secretary of State if the waste regulation authority fails to issue a decision within four months or such longer period as may be agreed in writing.

Variation of licences

37.—(1) While a licence issued by a waste regulation authority is in force, the authority may, subject to regulations under section 35(6) above and to subsection (3) below,—
  (a) on its own initiative, modify the conditions of the licence to any extent which, in the opinion of the authority, is desirable and is unlikely to require unreasonable expense on the part of the holder; and
  (b) on the application of the licence holder accompanied by the prescribed fee payable under section 41 below, modify the conditions of his licence to the extent requested in the application.

(2) While a licence issued by a waste regulation authority is in force, the authority shall, except where it revokes the licence entirely under section 38 below, modify the conditions of the licence—
  (a) to the extent which in the opinion of the authority is required for the purpose of ensuring that the activities authorised by the licence do not cause pollution of the environment or harm to human health or become seriously detrimental to the amenities of the locality affected by the activities; and
  (b) to the extent required by any regulations in force under section 35(6) above.

(3) The Secretary of State may, as respects any licence issued by a waste regulation authority, give to the authority directions as to the modifications which are to be made in the conditions of the licence under subsections (1)(a) or (2)(a) above; and it shall be the duty of the authority to give effect to the directions.

(4) Any modification of a licence under this section shall be effected by notice served on the holder of the licence and the notice shall state the time at which the modification is to take effect.

(5) Section 36(4), (5), (6), (7), (8) and (10) above shall with the necessary modifications apply to a proposal by a waste regulation authority to modify a

licence under subsection (1) or (2)(a) above as they apply to a proposal to issue a licence, except that—
(a) the authority may postpone the reference so far as the authority considers that by reason of an emergency it is appropriate to do so; and
(b) the authority need not consider any representations as respects a modification which, in the opinion of the waste regulation authority, will not affect any authority mentioned in the subsections so applied.

(6) If within the period of two months beginning with the date on which a waste regulation authority received an application by the holder of a licence for a modification of it, or within such longer period as the authority and the applicant may at any time agree in writing, the authority has neither granted a modification of the licence in consequence of the application nor given notice to the applicant that the authority has rejected the application, the authority shall be deemed to have rejected the application.

DEFINITIONS
"harm": s.29(5).
"licence": s.35(12).
"pollution of the environment": s.29(3).

COMMENCEMENT
Subsection (3): February 18, 1993 (S.I. 1993 No. 274). Remainder: no date has been set for commencement.

GENERAL NOTE
This section provides the power by which licences may be varied so as to modify the conditions, either: (a) on the initiative of the waste regulation authority (where the modification, in the opinion of the authority, is desirable and is unlikely to require unreasonable expense on the part of the holder); or (b) on the application of the licence-holder.

Subs. (2)
This imposes a duty upon waste regulation authorities to modify licence conditions in certain circumstances. The provisions as to consultation with other regulatory authorities which apply on the grant of licences also apply to variations, with slight changes (subs. (5)). Appeal lies against modifications under s.43(1)(c) and against rejection of an application for modification under s.43(1)(a).

Subs. (6)
Deemed refusal. Failure by a waste regulation authority to issue a decision on an application for modification within two months constitutes deemed rejection, against which the applicant may appeal under s.43(1)(a). This should obviate the practical difficulties caused by the absence of any such provision in COPA.

Existing licences
The provisions as to variation of licences apply to subsisting licences issued under COPA (s.77(2)).

Guidance as to review of conditions
The need to review licence conditions in the light of regs. 15–17 of the draft Waste Management Licensing Regulations (see notes to s.35) is emphasised by the accompanying Circ. 92, Annex 1, para. 1.32.

Protection of groundwater
Circular 20/90 (W.O. 34/90) suggests (para. 3) that waste regulation authorities should review the disposal licences for landfill site involving the disposal of wastes containing substances within List I of the Groundwater Directive 80/68/EEC. Where the NRA advises that discharges are liable to affect groundwater adversely and that such water is not permanently unusable, the disposal licence should be reviewed. This may require the prohibition of the deposit of waste containing List I substances (para. 4). Para. 1.32 of Annex 1 to the draft Circular on Waste Management Licensing Regulations states that authorities should review

current licences in the light of reg. 17 of the draft Waste Management Licensing Regulations (protection of groundwater) as to which see notes to s.35.

Revocation and suspension of licences

38.—(1) Where a licence granted by a waste regulation authority is in force and it appears to the authority—
  (a) that the holder of the licence has ceased to be a fit and proper person by reason of his having been convicted of a relevant offence; or
  (b) that the continuation of the activities authorised by the licence would cause pollution of the environment or harm to human health or would be seriously detrimental to the amenities of the locality affected; and
  (c) that the pollution, harm or detriment cannot be avoided by modifying the conditions of the licence;
the authority may exercise, as it thinks fit, either of the powers conferred by subsections (3) and (4) below.

(2) Where a licence granted by a waste regulation authority is in force and it appears to the authority that the holder of the licence has ceased to be a fit and proper person by reason of the management of the activities authorised by the licence having ceased to be in the hands of a technically competent person, the authority may exercise the power conferred by subsection (3) below.

(3) The authority may, under this subsection, revoke the licence so far as it authorises the carrying on of the activities specified in the licence or such of them as the authority specifies in revoking the licence.

(4) The authority may, under this subsection, revoke the licence entirely.

(5) A licence revoked under subsection (3) above shall cease to have effect to authorise the carrying on of the activities specified in the licence or, as the case may be, the activities specified by the authority in revoking the licence but shall not affect the requirements imposed by the licence which the authority, in revoking the licence, specify as requirements which are to continue to bind the licence holder.

(6) Where a licence granted by a waste regulation authority is in force and it appears to the authority—
  (a) that the holder of the licence has ceased to be a fit and proper person by reason of the management of the activities authorised by the licence having ceased to be in the hands of a technically competent person; or
  (b) that serious pollution of the environment or serious harm to human health has resulted from, or is about to be caused by, the activities to which the licence relates or the happening or threatened happening of an event affecting those activities; and
  (c) that the continuing to carry on those activities, or any of those activities, in the circumstances will continue or, as the case may be, cause serious pollution of the environment or serious harm to human health;
the authority may suspend the licence so far as it authorises the carrying on of the activities specified in the licence or such of them as the authority specifies in suspending the licence.

(7) The Secretary of State may, if he thinks fit in relation to a licence granted by a waste regulation authority, give to the authority directions as to whether and in what manner the authority should exercise its powers under this section; and it shall be the duty of the authority to give effect to the directions.

(8) A licence suspended under subsection (6) above shall, while the suspension has effect, be of no effect to authorise the carrying on of the activities specified in the licence or, as the case may be, the activities specified by the authority in suspending the licence.

(9) Where a licence is suspended under subsection (6) above, the authority, in suspending it or at any time while it is suspended, may require the holder of the licence to take such measures to deal with or avert the pollution or harm as the authority considers necessary.

(10) A person who, without reasonable excuse, fails to comply with any requirement imposed under subsection (9) above otherwise than in relation to special waste shall be liable—
   (a) on summary conviction, to a fine of an amount not exceeding the statutory maximum; and
   (b) on conviction on indictment, to imprisonment for a term not exceeding two years or a fine or both.

(11) A person who, without reasonable excuse, fails to comply with any requirement imposed under subsection (9) above in relation to special waste shall be liable—
   (a) on summary conviction, to imprisonment for a term not exceeding six months or a fine not exceeding the statutory maximum or both; and
   (b) on conviction on indictment, to imprisonment for a term not exceeding five years or a fine or both.

(12) Any revocation or suspension of a licence or requirement imposed during the suspension of a licence under this section shall be effected by notice served on the holder of the licence and the notice shall state the time at which the revocation or suspension or the requirement is to take effect and, in the case of suspension, the period at the end of which, or the event on the occurrence of which, the suspension is to cease.

DEFINITIONS
   "fit and proper person": s.74.
   "harm": s.29(5).
   "licence": s.35(12).
   "pollution of the environment": s.29(3).
   "relevant offence": s.74(6).
   "special waste": s.75(9).

COMMENCEMENT
   Subsection (7): February 18, 1993 (S.I. 1993 No. 274). Remainder: no date has been set for commencement.

GENERAL NOTE
   This section allows waste regulation authorities to revoke licences in whole or in part and to suspend the licence in relation to all or some of the licensed activities. By s.77(2) these provisions apply by subsisting licences granted under COPA.

Revocation of licences
   There are two main powers of revocation:
   (a) *Revocation of authorisation as to licensed activities*. Under subs. (3), the authority may revoke the licence so far as it authorises the licensed activities, or such of them as the authority specifies. The effect of such revocation is that the relevant activities are no longer authorised, but the authority may specify licence requirements which are to continue to bind the licence-holder (subs. (5)); and
   (b) *Total revocation*. Under subs. (4) the authority may revoke the licence entirely, in which case the licence ceases to have effect for all purpose.
The grounds for revocation appear in subss. (1) and (2):
   (a) that the holder of the licence has ceased to be a fit and proper person by reason of conviction for a relevant offence (see s.74 and notes thereto);
   (b) that the continuation of the licensed activities would cause pollution of the environment or harm to human health or that they would be seriously detrimental to the amenities of the locality, and that, in each case, the pollution, harm or detriment could not be avoided by modifying the licence conditions; and
   (c) that the holder of the licence has ceased to be a fit and proper person by reason of the management of the activities having ceased to be in the hands of a technically competent person (see s.74 and notes thereto).

Grounds (a) and (b) allow the authority to exercise either of the powers of revocation mentioned above, whereas ground (c) does not allow total revocation under subs. (4).

Appeal against revocation lies to the Secretary of State under s.43(1)(e), and whilst the appeal is pending the revocation is ineffective (s.43(4)) unless a statement is made that immediate revocation is necessary for preventing or minimising pollution of the environment or harm to human health (s.43(6)).

Further powers of revocation exist under s.42(5)(a) and (b) where licence conditions are not being complied with, following notice by the authority.

Suspension of licences

Subsection (6) allows an authority to suspend a licence so far as it authorises the licensed activities or such of them as the authority specifies.

There are two grounds of suspension:
(a) that the licence-holder has ceased to be a fit and proper person by reason of the licensed activities having ceased to be in the hands of a technically competent person (see s.74 and notes thereto); and
(b) that serious pollution of the environment or serious harm to human health has resulted from the licensed activities or is about to be caused by those activities (or in either case, some event affecting those activities) and that continuance of all or any of the licensed activities will lead to such serious pollution or harm.

The problems justifying suspension therefore have to be of a serious and continuing nature.

The effect of suspension is that the relevant activities are no longer authorised during the period of suspension (subs. (8)). Additionally, the authority can require the licence-holder to take necessary measures to deal with, or avert, the pollution or harm (subs. (9)). Failure to comply with such a requirement is an offence (subss. (10) and (11)).

Appeal against suspension lies to the Secretary of State under s.43(1)(d) and, unlike revocation, a pending appeal does not affect the validity of the suspension (s.43(5)). A further power of suspension exists where licence conditions are not complied with following notice by the authority (s.42(6)(c)).

Surrender of licences

39.—(1) A licence may be surrendered by its holder to the authority which granted it but, in the case of a site licence, only if the authority accepts the surrender.

(2) The following provisions apply to the surrender and acceptance of the surrender of a site licence.

(3) The holder of a site licence who desires to surrender it shall make an application for that purpose to the authority in such form, giving such information and accompanied by such evidence as the Secretary of State prescribes by regulations and accompanied by the prescribed fee payable under section 41 below.

(4) An authority which receives an application for the surrender of a site licence—
  (a) shall inspect the land to which the licence relates, and
  (b) may require the holder of the licence to furnish to it further information or further evidence.

(5) The authority shall determine whether it is likely or unlikely that the condition of the land, so far as that condition is the result of the use of the land for the treatment, keeping or disposal of waste (whether or not in pursuance of the licence), will cause pollution of the environment or harm to human health.

(6) If the authority is satisfied that the condition of the land is unlikely to cause the pollution or harm mentioned in subsection (5) above, the authority shall, subject to subsection (7) below, accept the surrender of the licence; but otherwise the authority shall refuse to accept it.

(7) Where the authority proposes to accept the surrender of a site licence, the authority must, before it does so,—
  (a) refer the proposal to the National Rivers Authority; and
  (b) consider any representations about the proposal which the Authority makes to it during the allowed period;

and if the Authority requests that the surrender of the licence be not accepted either of them may refer the matter to the Secretary of State and the surrender shall not be accepted except in accordance with his decision.

(8) Subsection (7) above shall not apply to Scotland, but in Scotland where the authority (not being an islands council) proposes to accept the surrender of a licence, the authority must, before it does so,—
  (a) refer the proposal to—
    (i) the river purification authority whose area includes any of the relevant land;
    (ii) where the waste regulation authority is not also a district planning authority within the meaning of section 172 of the Local Government (Scotland) Act 1973, the general planning authority within the meaning of that section whose area includes any of the relevant land; and
  (b) consider any representations about the proposal which the river purification authority or the general planning authority makes to it during the allowed period,

and if the river purification authority requests that the surrender of the licence be not accepted by the waste regulation authority either of them may refer the matter to the Secretary of State and the surrender shall not be accepted except in accordance with his decision.

(9) Where the surrender of a licence is accepted under this section the authority shall issue to the applicant, with the notice of its determination, a certificate (a "certificate of completion") stating that it is satisfied as mentioned in subsection (6) above and, on the issue of that certificate, the licence shall cease to have effect.

(10) If within the period of three months beginning with the date on which an authority receives an application to surrender a licence, or within such longer period as the authority and the applicant may at any time agree in writing, the authority has neither issued a certificate of completion nor given notice to the applicant that the authority has rejected the application, the authority shall be deemed to have rejected the application.

(11) Section 36(10) above applies for the interpretation of the "allowed period" in subsections (7) and (8) above.

DEFINITIONS
"disposal": s.29(6).
"harm": s.29(5).
"licence": s.35(12).
"pollution of the environment": s.29(3).
"site licence": s.35(12).
"treatment": s.29(6).
"waste": s.75(2).

COMMENCEMENT
Subsection (3): February 18, 1993 (S.I. 1993 No. 274). Remainder: no date has been set for commencement.

GENERAL NOTE
This section makes significant amendments to the provisions on surrender of licences contained in COPA under which it was possible for the licence-holder to cancel the licence unilaterally. Such surrender is still possible for licences for mobile plant, but for site licences acceptance of the surrender by the authority is necessary.

Whether such acceptance is forthcoming depends upon whether the condition of the land is likely or unlikely to cause pollution of the environment or harm to human health, as far as that condition is the result of waste being treated, kept or disposed of on the land (subss. (5) and (6)). The NRA or, in Scotland, the river purification authority, must be consulted and may request that surrender should not be accepted (subss. (7) and (8)). Detailed guidance as to the criteria for acceptance of surrender is provided under s.35(8) by the draft Waste Management Paper No. 26A, *Completion of Waste Management Site Licences* (HMSO, 1992).

In particular, the acceptance of surrender has important implications in relation to steps taken subsequently under s.61 to remedy landfill gas generation or similar problems: the right of an authority to recover the cost of taking such steps from the owner of the relevant land does not apply where surrender of a licence has been accepted under s.39 (s.61(8) and (9)).

There is a right of appeal against refusal to accept surrender of a licence (s.43(1)(f)) or against deemed refusal if no decision is given by the authority within three months of the application to surrender (s.39(10)).

Applications and information requirements
By the draft Waste Management Licensing Regulations, reg. 4, applications for surrender are to be made in writing and are to be accompanied by the evidence prescribed by Sched. 2: this includes in particular details of all significant engineering works of an anti-pollution and restoration nature, and geological, hydrological, hydrogeological and monitoring data.

Existing licences
The new provisions on surrender apply to subsisting licences granted under COPA (s.77(2)).

Transfer of licences

40.—(1) A licence may be transferred to another person in accordance with subsections (2) to (6) below and may be so transferred whether or not the licence is partly revoked or suspended under any provision of this Part.

(2) Where the holder of a licence desires that the licence be transferred to another person ("the proposed transferee") the licence holder and the proposed transferee shall jointly make an application to the waste regulation authority which granted the licence for a transfer of it.

(3) An application under subsection (2) above for the transfer of a licence shall be made in such form and shall include such information as the Secretary of State prescribes by regulations and shall be accompanied by the prescribed fee payable under section 41 below and the licence.

(4) If, on such an application, the authority is satisfied that the proposed transferee is a fit and proper person the authority shall effect a transfer of the licence to the proposed transferee.

(5) The authority shall effect a transfer of a licence under the foregoing provisions of this section by causing the licence to be endorsed with the name and other particulars of the proposed transferee as the holder of the licence from such date specified in the endorsement as may be agreed with the applicants.

(6) If within the period of two months beginning with the date on which the authority receives an application for the transfer of a licence, or within such longer period as the authority and the applicants may at any time agree in writing, the authority has neither effected a transfer of the licence nor given notice to the applicants that the authority has rejected the application, the authority shall be deemed to have rejected the application.

DEFINITIONS
"fit and proper person": s.74.
"licence": s.35(12).

COMMENCEMENT
Subsection (3): February 18, 1993 (S.I. 1993 No. 274). Remainder: no date has been set for commencement.

GENERAL NOTE
In order to transfer a licence, a joint application by the licence-holder and proposed transferee is necessary, and the authority may only effect the transfer on being satisfied that the proposed transferee is "a fit and proper person" (as to which, see s.74). By reg. 5 of the draft Waste Management Licensing Regulations, the application must be made in writing and be accompanied by the information prescribed at Sched. 3 as to the proposed transferee, any relevant convictions and the identity of the proposed technically competent person or persons.

There is a right of appeal against refusal to effect a transfer, or failure either to effect a transfer or to reject the application within two months (ss.40(6) and 43(1)(g)).

Existing licences
Subsisting licences granted under COPA may only be transferred under s.40 (s.77(2)).

Fees and charges for licences

41.—(1) There shall be charged by and paid to waste regulation authorities, in respect of applications for licences or relevant applications in respect of licences, and in respect of the holding of licences, such fees and charges as may be provided for from time to time by a scheme under subsection (2) below.

(2) The Secretary of State may, with the approval of the Treasury, make, and from time to time revise, a scheme prescribing—
   (a) fees payable in respect of applications for licences or relevant applications in respect of licences, and
   (b) charges payable in respect of the subsistence of licences,
to waste regulation authorities by persons making applications for or in respect of licences, or holding licences, as the case may be.

(3) The applications in respect of licences which are relevant for the purposes of this section are—
   (a) applications for the modification of the conditions of a licence;
   (b) applications to surrender a licence; and
   (c) applications for the transfer of a licence.

(4) The Secretary of State shall, on making or revising a scheme under subsection (2) above, lay a copy of the scheme or of the modifications made in the scheme before each House of Parliament.

(5) A waste regulation authority in England and Wales shall pay to the National Rivers Authority, and a waste regulation authority in Scotland shall pay to any river purification authority which it consults in relation to a licence, out of any fee or charge which—
   (a) is payable to the authority under a scheme under subsection (2) above; and
   (b) is of a description prescribed in such a scheme for the purposes of this subsection,
such amount as may be prescribed in the scheme in relation to fees or charges of that description.

(6) A scheme under subsection (2) above may in particular—
   (a) provide for different fees or charges to be payable according to the description of activities authorised by licences and the descriptions and amounts of controlled waste to which those activities relate;
   (b) provide for the times at which and manner in which payments of fees or charges are to be made; and
   (c) make such incidental, supplementary and transitional provision as appears to the Secretary of State to be appropriate;
and different schemes may be made and revised for different areas.

(7) If it appears to the waste regulation authority that the holder of a licence has failed to pay a charge due in consideration of the subsistence of the licence, the authority may, by notice in writing served on the holder, revoke the licence so far as it authorises the carrying on of the activities specified in the licence.

(8) Section 38(5) above applies for the purposes of subsection (7) above as it applies for the purposes of subsection (3) of that section.

DEFINITION
   "licences": s.35(12).

COMMENCEMENT
   Subsections (2), (4), (5): February 18, 1993 (S.I. 1993 No. 274). Remainder: no date has been set for commencement.

GENERAL NOTE

Provision may be made by a scheme for fees to be payable on applications for the grant, modification, surrender or transfer of licences, and for charges to be payable for the subsistence of licences. In relation to applications, non-payment of the correct fee will mean that the application is not "duly made" and so need not be considered by the authority. The sanction for non-payment of a charge for subsistence of the licence is that the authority may revoke it (subs. (7)). A prescribed part of the fee or charge received by the waste regulation authority is to be paid to the NRA (or river purification authority in Scotland) if the WRA consults them in relation to the relevant licence (subs. (5)).

Because under s.77(2) subsisting licences under COPA are treated as site licences under the 1990 Act, it seems that such licences may be made subject, under the scheme, to charges for continued subsistence.

The intention as to the charges for licences was expressed by the Earl of Arran on behalf of the Government as follows:

"The charges for licences are intended to meet the estimated costs of waste regulatory activity for authorities taken as a whole. We are committed to introducing a national scale of charges, so that differences between authorities in the amount of resources they devote to waste regulation—which has been the subject of intense criticism—do not exacerbate the difference in costs of disposal in the areas of the good and not so good authorities. This inevitably means that costs of individual authorities will not necessarily be matched exactly by the revenue from licensing. However, for those authorities not currently providing the required level of regulation, the extra income will provide the resources to allow them to do so. We will of course keep the level of charges under review and will consult local authorities and industry on the level at which they should be set.

Regarding the further costs mentioned by the noble Lord, Lord McIntosh, the costs of inspecting and monitoring will be covered in the licence fee; the costs of prosecution will not. If the prosecution is successful costs will be awarded to the authority by the court."
(*Hansard*, H.L. Vol. 522, col. 335.)

A draft charging scheme was issued for consultation in August 1992 covering both application fees and subsistence charges. It also deals with payments to be made to the NRA or water purification authorities under subs. (5). The scheme will operate by reference to various factors including the activity authorised by the licence, the description of waste and the amount of waste.

In December 1992 the Government issued a draft scheme in a further consultation paper entitled "Waste Management Licensing (Fees and Charges) Scheme 1992." This contained guidance on the determination of fees and charges and on the proposed provisions of the formal charging scheme. The Annexes set out levels of fees appropriate to various circumstances and the payments that need to be made to the NRA and river purification authorities.

Supervision of licensed activities

42.—(1) While a licence is in force it shall be the duty of the waste regulation authority which granted the licence to take the steps needed—
  (a) for the purpose of ensuring that the activities authorised by the licence do not cause pollution of the environment or harm to human health or become seriously detrimental to the amenities of the locality affected by the activities; and
  (b) for the purpose of ensuring that the conditions of the licence are complied with.

(2) Where, at any time during the subsistence of a licence, it appears to the waste regulation authority that pollution of water is likely to be caused by the activities to which the licence relates, it shall be the duty of the authority to consult the National Rivers Authority or, in Scotland, the river purification authority whose area includes any of the relevant land as to the discharge by the authority of the duty imposed on it by subsection (1) above.

(3) For the purpose of performing the duty imposed on it by subsection (1) above, any officer of the authority authorised in writing for the purpose by the authority may, if it appears to him that by reason of an emergency it is necessary to do so, carry out work on the land or in relation to plant or equipment on the land to which the licence relates or, as the case may be, in relation to the mobile plant to which the licence relates.

(4) Where a waste regulation authority incurs any expenditure by virtue of subsection (3) above, the authority may recover the amount of the expenditure from the holder of the licence or, if the licence has been surrendered, from the former holder of it, except where the holder or former holder of the licence shows that there was no emergency requiring any work or except such of the expenditure as he shows was unnecessary.

(5) Where it appears to a waste regulation authority that a condition of a licence granted by it is not being complied with, then, without prejudice to any proceedings under section 33(6) above, the authority may—
  (a) require the licence holder to comply with the condition within a specified time; and
  (b) if in the opinion of the authority the licence holder has not complied with the condition within that time, exercise any of the powers specified in subsection (6) below.

(6) The powers which become exercisable in the event mentioned in subsection (5)(b) above are the following—
  (a) to revoke the licence so far as it authorises the carrying on of the activities specified in the licence or such of them as the authority specifies in revoking the licence;
  (b) to revoke the licence entirely; and
  (c) to suspend the licence so far as it authorises the carrying on of the activities specified in the licence or, as the case may be, the activities specified by the authority in suspending the licence.

(7) Where a licence is revoked or suspended under subsection (6) above, subsections (5) or (8) and (9), (10) and (11) of section 38 above shall apply with the necessary modifications as they respectively apply to revocations or suspensions of licences under that section; and the power to make a requirement under subsection (5)(a) above shall be exercisable by notice served on the holder of the licence (and "specified" shall be construed accordingly).

(8) The Secretary of State may, if he thinks fit in relation to a licence granted by a waste regulation authority, give to the authority directions as to whether and in what manner the authority should exercise its powers under this section; and it shall be the duty of the authority to give effect to the directions.

DEFINITIONS
  "harm": s.29(5).
  "licence": s.35(12).
  "pollution of the environment": s.29(3).

COMMENCEMENT
Subsection (8): February 18, 1993 (S.I. 1993 No. 274). Remainder: no date has been set for commencement.

GENERAL NOTE
Under this section, waste regulation authorities are under a duty to take a supervisory rôle as to licences, to ensure that pollution, harm or detriment as mentioned in subs. (1)(a) do not occur, and to ensure that the conditions of the licence are complied with. Two main powers arise in the event of default:
  (1) to carry out necessary work in the event of an emergency and to recover the expenditure (s.42(3) and (4)). The reference to recovery of expenditure from a former holder of a surrendered licence means that expenditure can be recovered for work done prior to the surrender; it does not allow work to be carried out after the licence has been surrendered, as in that case there would be no licence "in force" (subs. (1)); and
  (2) in the case of non-compliance with conditions, to serve notice requiring compliance and, in the event of default, to revoke the licence (subss. (5) and (6)).

Draft Waste Management Paper 4, *The Licensing of Waste Facilities*, provides guidance as to this inspecting and monitoring function. Appendix C of that Paper suggests site inspection frequencies for various types of sites; para. 2.71 suggests that inspections should normally be unannounced, though it is reasonable to inform the operator that a visit is being made where a specific problem or modification to the licence is being considered.

In December 1992, the DoE (together with the Scottish and Welsh Offices) issued a second consultation paper on Waste Management Licensing. This paper included a draft Appendix D to Waste Management Paper No. 4 on the monitoring of landfills. A continued regime of monitoring is proposed throughout the licensed life of the site up until the point at which surrender of the licence is contemplated. Such a regime should provided a complete position of the pollution potential of the site over most of its licensed life. Appendix D seeks to balance best practice with regard to monitoring and the costs to site operators.

Appeals to Secretary of State from decisions with respect to licences

43.—(1) Where, except in pursuance of a direction given by the Secretary of State,—
  (a) an application for a licence or a modification of the conditions of a licence is rejected;
  (b) a licence is granted subject to conditions;
  (c) the conditions of a licence are modified;
  (d) a licence is suspended;
  (e) a licence is revoked under section 38 or 42 above;
  (f) an application to surrender a licence is rejected; or
  (g) an application for the transfer of a licence is rejected;
then, except in the case of an application for a transfer, the applicant for the licence or, as the case may be, the holder or former holder of it may appeal from the decision to the Secretary of State and, in the case of an application for a transfer, the proposed transferee may do so.

(2) Where an appeal is made to the Secretary of State—
  (a) the Secretary of State may refer any matter involved in the appeal to a person appointed by him for the purpose;
  (b) the Secretary of State may, instead of determining the appeal himself, direct that the appeal or any matter involved in it shall be determined by a person appointed by him for the purpose (who shall have the same powers as the Secretary of State);
  (c) if a party to the appeal so requests, or the Secretary of State so decides, the appeal shall be or continue in the form of a hearing (which may, if the person hearing the appeal so decides, be held or held to any extent in private).

(3) Where, on such an appeal, the Secretary of State or other person determining the appeal determines that the decision of the authority shall be altered it shall be the duty of the authority to give effect to the determination.

(4) While an appeal is pending in a case falling within subsection (1)(c) or (e) above, the decision in question shall, subject to subsection (6) below, be ineffective; and if the appeal is dismissed or withdrawn the decision shall become effective from the end of the day on which the appeal is dismissed or withdrawn.

(5) Where an appeal is made in a case falling within subsection (1)(d) above, the bringing of the appeal shall have no effect on the decision in question.

(6) Subsection (4) above shall not apply to a decision modifying the conditions of a licence under section 37 above or revoking a licence under section 38 or 42 above in the case of which the notice effecting the modification or revocation includes a statement that in the opinion of the authority it is necessary for the purpose of preventing or, where that is not practicable, minimising pollution of the environment or harm to human health that that subsection should not apply.

(7) Where the decision under appeal is one falling within subsection (6) above or is a decision to suspend a licence, if, on the application of the holder or former holder of the licence, the Secretary of State or other person

determining the appeal determines that the authority acted unreasonably in excluding the application of subsection (4) above or, as the case may be, in suspending the licence, then—
  (a) if the appeal is still pending at the end of the day on which the determination is made, subsection (4) above shall apply to the decision from the end of that day; and
  (b) the holder or former holder of the licence shall be entitled to recover compensation from the authority in respect of any loss suffered by him in consequence of the exclusion of the application of that subsection or the suspension of the licence;
and any dispute as to a person's entitlement to such compensation or as to the amount of it shall be determined by arbitration or in Scotland by a single arbiter appointed, in default of agreement between the parties concerned, by the Secretary of State on the application of any of the parties.

(8) Provision may be made by the Secretary of State by regulations with respect to appeals under this section and in particular—
  (a) as to the period within which and the manner in which appeals are to be brought; and
  (b) as to the manner in which appeals are to be considered.

DEFINITIONS
"harm": s.29(5).
"licence": s.35(12).
"pollution of the environment": s.29(3).

COMMENCEMENT
Subsection (8): February 18, 1993 (S.I. 1993 No. 274). Remainder: no date has been set for commencement.

GENERAL NOTE
This section provides rights of appeal in relation to licensing decisions. Appeal is to the Secretary of State who may transfer jurisdiction to an appointed person. The appeal is conducted in writing, unless either party requests a hearing, which may be either public or private at the discretion of the inspector (subs. (2)(c)).

Effect of appeal
Where a licence is modified or revoked, and an appeal is made, the modification or revocation is ineffective until the appeal is dismissed or withdrawn (subs. (4)). The position is different in the case of appeal against suspension of licences, where the bringing of an appeal has no effect on the suspension (subs. (5)).
If an authority is of the view that modification or revocation should have immediate effect notwithstanding any appeal, a statement may be inserted in the modification or revocation notice excluding subss. (4) and (6). However, this course carries the risk of the authority having to pay compensation in the event that the authority is found to have acted unreasonably by the Secretary of State or inspector (subs. (7)(b)). The same risk applies to a decision to suspend a licence.

Form and manner of appeals
See the draft Waste Management Licensing Regulations, regs. 9–12 as to appeals procedure. Notice of appeal must be given in writing before the expiry of a period of six months beginning with the date of the relevant decision or deemed rejection, or within such longer period as the Secretary of State may allow.

Offences of making false statements

44. A person who, in an application for a licence, for a modification of the conditions of a licence or for the surrender or transfer of a licence, makes any statement which he knows to be false in a material particular or recklessly makes any statement which is false in a material particular shall be liable—
  (a) on summary conviction, to a fine not exceeding the statutory maximum; and

(b) on conviction on indictment, to imprisonment for a term not exceeding two years or to a fine or both.

DEFINITIONS
"licences": s.35(12).

COMMENCEMENT
No date has been set.

GENERAL NOTE
This section creates the offences of making, in relation to the various licence applications, statements which are: (a) known to be false in a material particular; or (b) false in a material particular and recklessly made.

Material particular. This suggests that the statement must relate to matters which would have the tendency, or natural and probable result, of inducing the authority to act on the faith of it in such a way as might affect the outcome of the decision. It does not appear to be an ingredient of the offence that the authority should *actually* have relied on the statement or that it should *actually* have influenced the decision, if any. In the context of waste licensing this would no doubt involve matters relating to whether the applicant is fit and proper (for example, as to the absence of relevant convictions or as to financial resources) and, in the context of surrender of licences, the condition of the site.

Collection, disposal or treatment of controlled waste

Collection of controlled waste

45.—(1) It shall be the duty of each waste collection authority—
 (a) to arrange for the collection of household waste in its area except waste—
  (i) which is situated at a place which in the opinion of the authority is so isolated or inaccessible that the cost of collecting it would be unreasonably high, and
  (ii) as to which the authority is satisfied that adequate arrangements for its disposal have been or can reasonably be expected to be made by a person who controls the waste; and
 (b) if requested by the occupier of premises in its area to collect any commercial waste from the premises, to arrange for the collection of the waste.

(2) Each waste collection authority may, if requested by the occupier of premises in its area to collect any industrial waste from the premises, arrange for the collection of the waste; but a collection authority in England and Wales shall not exercise the power except with the consent of the waste disposal authority whose area includes the area of the waste collection authority.

(3) No charge shall be made for the collection of household waste except in cases prescribed in regulations made by the Secretary of State; and in any of those cases—
 (a) the duty to arrange for the collection of the waste shall not arise until a person who controls the waste requests the authority to collect it; and
 (b) the authority may recover a reasonable charge for the collection of the waste from the person who made the request.

(4) A person at whose request waste other than household waste is collected under this section shall be liable to pay a reasonable charge for the collection and disposal of the waste to the authority which arranged for its collection; and it shall be the duty of that authority to recover the charge unless in the case of a charge in respect of commercial waste the authority considers it inappropriate to do so.

(5) It shall be the duty of each waste collection authority—
 (a) to make such arrangements for the emptying, without charge, of

privies, serving one or more private dwellings in its area as the authority considers appropriate;
(b) if requested by the person who controls a cesspool serving only one or more private dwellings in its area to empty the cesspool, to remove such of the contents of the cesspool as the authority considers appropriate on payment, if the authority so requires, of a reasonable charge.

(6) A waste collection authority may, if requested by the person who controls any other privy or cesspool in its area to empty the privy or cesspool, empty the privy or, as the case may be, remove from the cesspool such of its contents as the authority consider appropriate on payment, if the authority so requires, of a reasonable charge.

(7) A waste collection authority may—
(a) construct, lay and maintain, within or outside its area, pipes and associated works for the purpose of collecting waste;
(b) contribute towards the cost incurred by another person in providing or maintaining pipes or associated works connecting with pipes provided by the authority under paragraph (a) above.

(8) A waste collection authority may contribute towards the cost incurred by another person in providing or maintaining plant or equipment intended to deal with commercial or industrial waste before it is collected under arrangements made by the authority under subsection (1)(b) or (2) above.

(9) Subject to section 48(1) below, anything collected under arrangements made by a waste collection authority under this section shall belong to the authority and may be dealt with accordingly.

(10) In relation to Scotland, sections 2, 3, 4 and 41 of the Sewerage (Scotland) Act 1968 (maintenance of public sewers etc.) shall apply in relation to pipes and associated works provided or to be provided under subsection (7)(a) above as those sections apply in relation to public sewers but as if—
(a) the said section 2 conferred a power and did not impose a duty on a local authority to do the things mentioned in that section;
(b) in the said section 4, the words from "but before any person" to the end were omitted,
and the Pipe-lines Act 1962 shall not apply to pipes and associated works provided or to be provided under the said subsection (7)(a).

(11) In the application of this section to Scotland, subsection (5)(b) and the references to a cesspool occurring in subsection (6) shall be omitted.

(12) In this section "privy" means a latrine which has a moveable receptacle and "cesspool" includes a settlement tank or other tank for the reception or disposal of foul matter from buildings.

DEFINITIONS
"commercial waste": s.75(7).
"household waste": s.75(5).
"industrial waste": s.75(6).
"waste": s.75(2).

COMMENCEMENT
Partially: February 14, 1992 (S.I. 1992 No. 266). Subsections (1) and (3)–(12): April 1, 1992 (S.I. 1992 No. 266). Subsection (2) (Scotland): April 1, 1992 (S.I. 1992 No. 266).

GENERAL NOTE
This section replaces s.12 of COPA which was implemented in England and Wales by the Collection and Disposal of Waste Regulations 1988 (S.I. 1988 No. 819), and which in turn replaced ss.74–77 of the Public Health Act 1936.

Subs. (3)
Collection of household waste. No charge may be made for collection except in prescribed

cases. The cases were prescribed by the Controlled Waste Regulations 1992 (S.I. 1992 No. 588), reg. 4 and Sched. 2; see also DoE Circ. 14/92, Annex 1, paras. 1.23–1.46.

Subs. (9)
Title to waste. It is expressly provided that waste or anything else collected by the waste collection authority under s.45 belongs to the authority, *not* to the employees or agents of the authority.

Receptacles for household waste

46.—(1) Where a waste collection authority has a duty by virtue of section 45(1)(a) above to arrange for the collection of household waste from any premises, the authority may, by notice served on him, require the occupier to place the waste for collection in receptacles of a kind and number specified.

(2) The kind and number of the receptacles required under subsection (1) above to be used shall be such only as are reasonable but, subject to that, separate receptacles or compartments of receptacles may be required to be used for waste which is to be recycled and waste which is not.

(3) In making requirements under subsection (1) above the authority may, as respects the provision of the receptacles—
  (a) determine that they be provided by the authority free of charge;
  (b) propose that they be provided, if the occupier agrees, by the authority on payment by him of such a single payment or such periodical payments as he agrees with the authority;
  (c) require the occupier to provide them if he does not enter into an agreement under paragraph (b) above within a specified period; or
  (d) require the occupier to provide them.

(4) In making requirements as respects receptacles under subsection (1) above, the authority may, by the notice under that subsection, make provision with respect to—
  (a) the size, construction and maintenance of the receptacles;
  (b) the placing of the receptacles for the purpose of facilitating the emptying of them, and access to the receptacles for that purpose;
  (c) the placing of the receptacles for that purpose on highways or, in Scotland, roads;
  (d) the substances or articles which may or may not be put into the receptacles or compartments of receptacles of any description and the precautions to be taken where particular substances or articles are put into them; and
  (e) the steps to be taken by occupiers of premises to facilitate the collection of waste from the receptacles.

(5) No requirement shall be made under subsection (1) above for receptacles to be placed on a highway or, as the case may be, road, unless—
  (a) the relevant highway authority or roads authority have given their consent to their being so placed; and
  (b) arrangements have been made as to the liability for any damage arising out of their being so placed.

(6) A person who fails, without reasonable excuse, to comply with any requirements imposed under subsection (1), (3)(c) or (d) or (4) above shall be liable on summary conviction to a fine not exceeding level 3 on the standard scale.

(7) Where an occupier is required under subsection (1) above to provide any receptacles he may, within the period allowed by subsection (8) below, appeal to a magistrates' court or, in Scotland, to the sheriff by way of summary application against any requirement imposed under subsection (1), subsection (3)(c) or (d) or (4) above on the ground that—
  (a) the requirement is unreasonable; or

(b) the receptacles in which household waste is placed for collection from the premises are adequate.

(8) The period allowed to the occupier of premises for appealing against such a requirement is the period of 21 days beginning—
  (a) in a case where a period was specified under subsection (3)(c) above, with the end of that period; and
  (b) where no period was specified, with the day on which the notice making the requirement was served on him.

(9) Where an appeal against a requirement is brought under subsection (7) above—
  (a) the requirement shall be of no effect pending the determination of the appeal;
  (b) the court shall either quash or modify the requirement or dismiss the appeal; and
  (c) no question as to whether the requirement is, in any respect, unreasonable shall be entertained in any proceedings for an offence under subsection (6) above.

(10) In this section—
  "receptacle" includes a holder for receptacles; and
  "specified" means specified in a notice under subsection (1) above.

DEFINITION
"household waste": s.75(5).

COMMENCEMENT
April 1, 1992 (S.I. 1992 No. 266).

GENERAL NOTE
This section gives waste collection authorities the power to specify collection arrangements for household waste and the nature of the receptacles to be used in collection. The three options available under subs. (3) are: (a) provision of receptacles by the authority free of charge; (b) provision by the authority on payment by the occupier; and (c) provision by the occupier. Where the occupier is required to provide receptacles, he may appeal under subs. (7) to a magistrates' court (or, in Scotland, the Sheriff) on the ground that either: (a) the requirement is unreasonable; or (b) the receptacles already used are adequate. If an appeal is made, the first argument cannot subsequently be raised as a defence in criminal proceedings for failure to comply with the requirements (subs. (9)(c)).

Subs. (5)
  Placing of receptacles on highways or roads. If a receptacle is placed on a highway or road otherwise than in accordance with arrangements made under this subsection, an unlawful obstruction will result: see *Wandsworth Corporation* v. *Baines* [1906] 1 K.B. 470.

Receptacles for commercial or industrial waste

47.—(1) A waste collection authority may, at the request of any person, supply him with receptacles for commercial or industrial waste which he has requested the authority to arrange to collect and shall make a reasonable charge for any receptacle supplied unless in the case of a receptacle for commercial waste the authority considers it appropriate not to make a charge.

(2) If it appears to a waste collection authority that there is likely to be situated, on any premises in its area, commercial waste or industrial waste of a kind which, if the waste is not stored in receptacles of a particular kind, is likely to cause a nuisance or to be detrimental to the amenities of the locality, the authority may, by notice served on him, require the occupier of the premises to provide at the premises receptacles for the storage of such waste of a kind and number specified.

(3) The kind and number of the receptacles required under subsection (2) above to be used shall be such only as are reasonable.

(4) In making requirements as respects receptacles under subsection (2) above, the authority may, by the notice under that subsection, make provision with respect to—
  (a) the size, construction and maintenance of the receptacles;
  (b) the placing of the receptacles for the purpose of facilitating the emptying of them, and access to the receptacles for that purpose;
  (c) the placing of the receptacles for that purpose on highways or, in Scotland, roads;
  (d) the substances or articles which may or may not be put into the receptacles and the precautions to be taken where particular substances or articles are put into them; and
  (e) the steps to be taken by occupiers of premises to facilitate the collection of waste from the receptacles.

(5) No requirement shall be made under subsection (2) above for receptacles to be placed on a highway or, as the case may be, road unless—
  (a) the relevant highway authority or roads authority have given their consent to their being so placed; and
  (b) arrangements have been made as to the liability for any damage arising out of their being so placed.

(6) A person who fails, without reasonable excuse, to comply with any requirements imposed under subsection (2) or (4) above shall be liable on summary conviction to a fine not exceeding level 3 on the standard scale.

(7) Where an occupier is required under subsection (2) above to provide any receptacles he may, within the period allowed by subsection (8) below, appeal to a magistrates' court or, in Scotland, to the sheriff by way of summary application against any requirement imposed under subsection (2) or (4) above on the ground that—
  (a) the requirement is unreasonable; or
  (b) the waste is not likely to cause a nuisance or be detrimental to the amenities of the locality.

(8) The period allowed to the occupier of premises for appealing against such a requirement is the period of 21 days beginning with the day on which the notice making the requirement was served on him.

(9) Where an appeal against a requirement is brought under subsection (7) above—
  (a) the requirement shall be of no effect pending the determination of the appeal;
  (b) the court shall either quash or modify the requirement or dismiss the appeal; and
  (c) no question as to whether the requirement is, in any respect, unreasonable shall be entertained in any proceedings for an offence under subsection (6) above.

(10) In this section—
  "receptacle" includes a holder for receptacles; and
  "specified" means specified in a notice under subsection (2) above.

DEFINITIONS
  "commercial waste": s.75(7).
  "industrial waste": s.75(6).
  "waste": s.75(2).

COMMENCEMENT
  April 1, 1992 (S.I. 1992 No. 266), except subs. (7) which is not yet in force.

Duties of waste collection authorities as respects disposal of waste collected

48.—(1) Subject to subsections (2) and (6) below, it shall be the duty of each waste collection authority to deliver for disposal all waste which is collected by the authority under section 45 above to such places as the waste disposal authority for its area directs.

(2) The duty imposed on a waste collection authority by subsection (1) above does not, except in cases falling within subsection (4) below, apply as respects household waste or commercial waste for which the authority decides to make arrangements for recycling the waste; and the authority shall have regard, in deciding what recycling arrangements to make, to its waste recycling plan under section 49 below.

(3) A waste collection authority which decides to make arrangements under subsection (2) above for recycling waste collected by it shall, as soon as reasonably practicable, by notice in writing, inform the waste disposal authority for the area which includes its area of the arrangements which it proposes to make.

(4) Where a waste disposal authority has made with a waste disposal contractor arrangements, as respects household waste or commercial waste in its area or any part of its area, for the contractor to recycle the waste, or any of it, the waste disposal authority may, by notice served on the waste collection authority, object to the waste collection authority having the waste recycled; and the objection may be made as respects all the waste, part only of the waste or specified descriptions of the waste.

(5) Where an objection is made under subsection (4) above, subsection (2) above shall not be available to the waste collection authority to the extent objected to.

(6) A waste collection authority may, subject to subsection (7) below, provide plant and equipment for the sorting and baling of waste retained by the authority under subsection (2) above.

(7) Subsection (6) above does not apply to an authority which is also a waste disposal authority; but, in such a case, the authority may make arrangements with a waste disposal contractor for the contractor to deal with the waste as mentioned in that subsection.

(8) A waste collection authority may permit another person to use facilities provided by the authority under subsection (6) above and may provide for the use of another person any such facilities as the authority has power to provide under that subsection; and—
  (a) subject to paragraph (b) below, it shall be the duty of the authority to make a reasonable charge in respect of the use by another person of the facilities, unless the authority considers it appropriate not to make a charge;
  (b) no charge shall be made under this subsection in respect of household waste; and
  (c) anything delivered to the authority by another person in the course of using the facilities shall belong to the authority and may be dealt with accordingly.

(9) This section shall not apply in Scotland.

DEFINITIONS
"commercial waste": s.75(7).
"household waste": s.75(5).
"waste": s.75(2).
"waste disposal contractor": s.30(5).

COMMENCEMENT
April 1, 1992 (S.I. 1992 No. 266).

GENERAL NOTE
The general duty on waste collection authorities by subs. (1) to deliver all waste collected to such places as the waste disposal authority directs for disposal is qualified by subs. (2) so as to allow collection authorities to retain household or commercial waste (but not industrial waste) for recyling. Collection authorities (but not disposal authorities) are given express powers

(subs. (6)) to provide plant or equipment for the sorting and baling of waste retained for recycling. Where there is a single collection and disposal authority therefore, as in some metropolitan areas and in Wales, the authority may need instead to make use of its powers as a disposal authority to make arrangements with a disposal contractor to carry out the sorting and baling. The section does not prevent, in the Government's view, disposal authorities from providing receptacles for the collection of waste for recycling, such as bottle banks: *Hansard*, H.L. Vol. 522, col. 1274.

Waste recycling plans by collection authorities

49.—(1) It shall be the duty of each waste collection authority, as respects household and commercial waste arising in its area—
 (a) to carry out an investigation with a view to deciding what arrangements are appropriate for dealing with the waste by separating, baling or otherwise packaging it for the purpose of recycling it;
 (b) to decide what arrangements are in the opinion of the authority needed for that purpose;
 (c) to prepare a statement ("the plan") of the arrangements made and proposed to be made by the authority and other persons for dealing with waste in those ways;
 (d) to carry out from time to time further investigations with a view to deciding what changes in the plan are needed; and
 (e) to make any modification of the plan which the authority thinks appropriate in consequence of any such further investigation.

(2) In considering any arrangements or modification for the purposes of subsection (1)(c) or (e) above it shall be the duty of the authority to have regard to the effect which the arrangements or modification would be likely to have on the amenities of any locality and the likely cost or saving to the authority attributable to the arrangements or modification.

(3) It shall be the duty of a waste collection authority to include in the plan information as to—
 (a) the kinds and quantities of controlled waste which the authority expects to collect during the period specified in the plan;
 (b) the kinds and quantities of controlled waste which the authority expects to purchase during that period;
 (c) the kinds and quantities of controlled waste which the authority expects to deal with in the ways specified in subsection (1)(a) above during that period;
 (d) the arrangements which the authority expects to make during that period with waste disposal contractors or, in Scotland, waste disposal authorities and waste disposal contractors for them to deal with waste in those ways;
 (e) the plant and equipment which the authority expects to provide under section 48(6) above or 53 below; and
 (f) the estimated costs or savings attributable to the methods of dealing with the waste in the ways provided for in the plan.

(4) It shall be the duty of a waste collection authority, before finally determining the content of the plan or a modification, to send a copy of it in draft to the Secretary of State for the purpose of enabling him to determine whether subsection (3) above has been complied with; and, if the Secretary of State gives any directions to the authority for securing compliance with that subsection, it shall be the duty imposed by this section specified in the direction; and it shall be the duty of the authority to comply with the direction.

(5) When a waste collection authority has determined the content of the plan or a modification it shall be the duty of the authority—
 (a) to take such steps as in the opinion of the authority will give adequate publicity in its area to the plan or modification; and
 (b) to send to the waste disposal authority and waste regulation authority

for the area which includes its area a copy of the plan or, as the case may be, particulars of the modification.

(6) It shall be the duty of each waste collection authority to keep a copy of the plan and particulars of any modifications to it available at all reasonable times at its principal offices for inspection by members of the public free of charge and to supply a copy of the plan and of the particulars of any modifications to it to any person who requests one, on payment by that person of such reasonable charge as the authority requires.

(7) The Secretary of State may give to any waste collection authority directions as to the time by which the authority is to perform any duty of the authority to comply with the direction.

DEFINITIONS
"commercial waste": s.75(7).
"controlled waste": s.75(4).
"household waste": s.75(5).
"waste": s.75(2).
"waste disposal contractors": s.30(5).

COMMENCEMENT
August 1, 1991 (S.I. 1991 No. 1577).

GENERAL NOTE
This section introduces new duties as to planning for waste recycling. Waste recycling plans do not require the approval of the Secretary of State before adoption, but under subs. (4) must be submitted in draft to the Secretary of State, who may give directions to ensure compliance with the statutory requirements as to the content of plans.

Waste disposal plans of waste regulation authorities

50.—(1) It shall be the duty of each waste regulation authority—
  (a) to carry out an investigation with a view to deciding what arrangements are needed for the purpose of treating or disposing of controlled waste which is situated in its area and controlled waste which is likely to be so situated so as to prevent or minimise pollution of the environment or harm to human health;
  (b) to decide what arrangements are in the opinion of the authority needed for that purpose and how it should discharge its functions in relation to licences;
  (c) to prepare a statement ("the plan") of the arrangements made and proposed to be made by waste disposal contractors, or, in Scotland, waste disposal authorities and waste disposal contractors, for the treatment or disposal of such waste;
  (d) to carry out from time to time further investigations with a view to deciding what changes in the plan are needed; and
  (e) to make any modification of the plan which the authority thinks appropriate in consequence of any such further investigation.

(2) In considering any arrangements or modification for the purposes of subsection (1)(c) or (e) above it shall be the duty of the authority to have regard both to the likely cost of the arrangements or modification and to their likely beneficial effects on the environment.

(3) It shall be the duty of the authority to include in the plan information as to—
  (a) the kinds and quantities of controlled waste which the authority expects to be situated in its area during the period specified in the plan;
  (b) the kinds and quantities of controlled waste which the authority expects to be brought into or taken for disposal out of its area during that period;
  (c) the kinds and quantities of controlled waste which the authority expects to be disposed of within its area during that period;

(d) the methods and the respective priorities for the methods by which in the opinion of the authority controlled waste in its area should be disposed of or treated during that period;
(e) the policy of the authority as respects the discharge of its functions in relation to licences and any relevant guidance issued by the Secretary of State;
(f) the sites and equipment which persons are providing and which during that period are expected to provide for disposing of controlled waste; and
(g) the estimated costs of the methods of disposal or treatment provided for in the plan;

but provision may be made by the Secretary of State by regulations for modifying the foregoing paragraphs and for requiring waste regulation authorities to take into account in preparing plans and any modifications of plans under this section such factors as may be prescribed in the regulations.

(4) In considering what information to include in the plan under subsection (3)(d) above, it shall be the duty of the authority to have regard to the desirability, where reasonably practicable, of giving priority to recycling waste.

(5) It shall be the duty of the authority—
(a) in preparing the plan and any modification of it, to consult—
   (i) the National Rivers Authority or, in Scotland, any river purification authority any part of whose area is included in the area of the waste regulation authority;
   (ii) the waste collection authorities whose areas are included in the area of the authority;
   (iii) in a case where the plan or modification is prepared by a waste regulation authority in Wales, the county council whose area includes that of the authority;
   (iv) in a case where the plan or modification is prepared by a Scottish waste regulation authority other than an islands council, the council of the region in which the area of the authority is included;
   (v) in a case where provisions of the plan or modification relate to the taking of waste for disposal or treatment into the area of another waste regulation authority, that other authority; and
   (vi) in any case, such persons as the authority considers it appropriate to consult from among persons who in the opinion of the authority are or are likely to be, or are representative of persons who are or are likely to be, engaged by way of trade or business in the disposal or treatment of controlled waste situated in the area of the authority; and
(b) before finally determining the content of the plan or modification, to take, subject to subsection (6) below, such steps as in the opinion of the authority will—
   (i) give adequate publicity in its area to the plan or modification; and
   (ii) provide members of the public with opportunities of making representations to the authority about it;
and to consider any representations made by the public and make any change in the plan or modification which the authority considers appropriate.

(6) No steps need to be taken under subsection (5)(b) above in respect of a modification which in the opinion of the waste regulation authority is such that no person will be prejudiced if those steps are not taken.

(7) Without prejudice to the duty of authorities under subsection (5) above, it shall be the duty of the authority, in preparing the plan and any modification of it, to consider, in consultation with the waste collection authorities in its area and any other persons,—

(a) what arrangements can reasonably be expected to be made for recycling waste; and
(b) what provisions should be included in the plan for that purpose.

(8) An authority shall not finally determine the content of the plan or modification in a case falling within subsection (5)(a)(v) above except with the consent of the other waste regulation authority or, if the other authority withholds its consent, with the consent of the Secretary of State.

(9) It shall be the duty of the authority, before finally determining the content of the plan or modification, to send a copy of it in draft to the Secretary of State for the purpose of enabling him to determine whether subsection (3) above has been complied with; and, if the Secretary of State gives any directions to the authority for securing compliance with that subsection, it shall be the duty of the authority to comply with the direction.

(10) When an authority has finally determined the content of the plan or a modification it shall be the duty of the authority—
(a) to take such steps as in the opinion of the authority will give adequate publicity in its area to the plan or modification; and
(b) to send to the Secretary of State a copy of the plan or, as the case may be, particulars of the modification.

(11) The Secretary of State may give to any waste regulation authority directions as to the time by which the authority is to perform any duty imposed by this section specified in the direction; and it shall be the duty of the authority to comply with the direction.

DEFINITIONS
"controlled waste": s.75(4).
"disposing of": s.29(6).
"harm": s.29(5).
"licences": s.35(12).
"pollution of the environment": s.29(3).
"treating": s.29(6).
"waste": s.75(2).
"waste disposal contractors": s.30(5).

COMMENCEMENT
May 31, 1991 (S.I. 1991 No. 1319).

GENERAL NOTE
This section replaces s.2 of COPA dealing with the preparation of waste disposal plans. However, s.50 reflects the fact that operational aspects of disposal now fall to waste contractors rather than the authorities. Plans must now include information as to the policy of the authority as respects the discharge of its waste licensing functions (subs. (3)(e)). Also, a new duty is imposed upon authorities to have regard to the desirability, where reasonably practicable, of giving priority to waste recycling (subs. (4) and see also subs. (7)).

The institutional changes in Pt. II of the Act mean that waste disposal plans will serve a somewhat different purpose from their precursors under COPA, s.2. These differences were expressed by Lord Reay for the Government as follows:

"The first point to make is that although the name, waste disposal plan, is unchanged, the content of these new waste disposal plans should be quite different from the plans that have been compiled up to now. Current waste disposal plans are compiled by waste disposal authorities. They tend to be operational documents detailing what the authority does at its own sites with household waste. That is not the intention of our new waste disposal plans.

In future waste disposal plans will be compiled by regulation authorities. They will identify the current and projected amounts of waste arising in the area. The plan will match those arisings to existing and planned disposal facilities and will identify future needs for new facilities. They will also set out the regulation authorities' policies for waste disposal and recycling. Disposal plans will focus on additional disposal facilities which will be needed in the future. In that way they will act as a guide to investment by waste disposal contractors, who will actually provide the necessary facilities." (*Hansard*, H.L. Vol. 522, cols. 357–8.)

As well as the previous duties of consulting other relevant authorities and providing the public with opportunities to make representations, authorities must now consult such persons as the authority considers appropriate from amongst persons engaged in disposal or treatment of controlled waste in the area by way of trade or business (subs. (5)(a)(vi)).

The plan does not require formal approval by the Secretary of State, but it must be sent to him in draft, and he may give directions in order to secure compliance with the statutory requirements (subs. (9)). On the appointed day, existing waste disposal plans prepared under COPA are treated as the waste disposal plan under s.50 until such time as the s.50 plan is prepared (see s.77(4)).

Directions as to time
Considerable criticism has been levelled at the delays on the part of some waste disposal authorities in producing waste disposal plans under s.2 of COPA. Subsection (11) allows the Secretary of State to give directions to authorities as to the time by which the duty to prepare a plan is to be performed.

Relationship with waste disposal development plans
Waste disposal plans will be read in conjunction with waste disposal development plans prepared under the Town and Country Planning Act 1990 as amended by the Planning and Compensation Act 1991. As to the relationship between the two types of plan, see the General Note to Pt. II.

Waste Disposal Planning under the Environment Protection Agency
In a Consultation Paper issued on August 17, 1992 (The Environment Agency: Waste Disposal Planning, DoE) the Government proposed interim arrangements dealing with waste disposal planning under the Environment Protection Agency.

The Plan is to draw up a National Statement of Waste Policies and Priorities. This would set out a strategy and general guidance on the pollution control aspects of waste disposal with the objective of co-ordinating waste disposal policy and planning across the country as a whole. The statement would be issued by the Secretary of State based upon information and advice produced by the Agency, which would draw its raw data from a periodic national survey. The Agency would also seek advice from the local planning authorities, to aid its assessment of future waste disposal requirements. The National Statement would look ahead at waste disposal needs over the next 10–15 years, probably updated on the basis of a full review every five years.

Complementing and supplementing the National Statement would be specific regional planning guidance on waste issued by the Secretary of State. In drawing up their structure plan or unitary plans, planning authorities would be required to have direct regard to the relevant regional guidance on waste and the National Statement. In drawing up their waste local plan or district wide plan, planning authorities would need to have direct regard to the structure plan and the National Statement.

The Consultation Paper proposes that Waste Regulation Authorities should be directed to draw up waste disposal plans under s.50 over the next few years as an interim measure before the Agency is set up.

Functions of waste disposal authorities

51.—(1) It shall be the duty of each waste disposal authority to arrange—
  (a) for the disposal of the controlled waste collected in its area by the waste collection authorities; and
  (b) for places to be provided at which persons resident in its area may deposit their household waste and for the disposal of waste so deposited;
in either case by means of arrangements made (in accordance with Part II of Schedule 2 to this Act) with waste disposal contractors, but by no other means.

(2) The arrangements made by a waste disposal authority under subsection (1)(b) above shall be such as to secure that—
  (a) each place is situated either within the area of the authority or so as to be reasonably accessible to persons resident in its area;
  (b) each place is available for the deposit of waste at all reasonable times (including at least one period on the Saturday or following day of each week except a week in which the Saturday is December 25 or January 1);

(c) each place is available for the deposit of waste free of charge by persons resident in the area;

but the arrangements may restrict the availability of specified places to specified descriptions of waste.

(3) A waste disposal authority may include in arrangements made under subsection (1)(b) above arrangements for the places provided for its area for the deposit of household waste free of charge by residents in its area to be available for the deposit of household or other controlled waste by other persons on such terms as to payment (if any) as the authority determines.

(4) For the purpose of discharging its duty under subsection (1)(a) above as respects controlled waste collected as mentioned in that paragraph a waste disposal authority—
   (a) shall give directions to the waste collection authorities within its area as to the persons to whom and places at which such waste is to be delivered;
   (b) may arrange for the provision, within or outside its area, by waste disposal contractors of places at which such waste may be treated or kept prior to its removal for treatment or disposal;
   (c) may make available to waste disposal contractors (and accordingly own) plant and equipment for the purpose of enabling them to keep such waste prior to its removal for disposal or to treat such waste in connection with so keeping it or for the purpose of facilitating its transportation;
   (d) may make available to waste disposal contractors (and accordingly hold) land for the purpose of enabling them to treat, keep or dispose of such waste in or on the land;
   (e) may contribute towards the cost incurred by persons who produce commercial or industrial waste in providing and maintaining plant or equipment intended to deal with such waste before it is collected; and
   (f) may contribute towards the cost incurred by persons who produce commercial or industrial waste in providing or maintaining pipes or associated works connecting with pipes provided by a waste collection authority within the area of the waste disposal authority.

(5) For the purpose of discharging its duties under subsection (1)(b) above as respects household waste deposited as mentioned in that paragraph a waste disposal authority—
   (a) may arrange for the provision, within or outside its area, by waste disposal contractors of places at which such waste may be treated or kept prior to its removal for treatment or disposal;
   (b) may make available to waste disposal contractors (and accordingly own) plant and equipment for the purpose of enabling them to keep such waste prior to its removal for disposal or to treat such waste in connection with so keeping it or for the purpose of facilitating its transportation; and
   (c) may make available to waste disposal contractors (and accordingly hold) land for the purpose of enabling them to treat, keep or dispose of such waste in or on the land.

(6) Where the arrangements made under subsection (1)(b) include such arrangements as are authorised by subsection (3) above, subsection (5) above applies as respects household or other controlled waste as it applies as respects household waste.

(7) Subsection (1) above is subject to section 77.

(8) This section shall not apply to Scotland.

DEFINITIONS
   "commercial waste": s.75(7).
   "controlled waste": s.75(4).
   "disposal": s.29(6).

"household waste": s.75(5).
"industrial waste": s.75(6).
"treatment": s.29(6).
"waste": s.75(2).
"waste disposal contractors": s.30(5).

COMMENCEMENT
May 31, 1991 (S.I. 1991 No. 1319).

GENERAL NOTE
This section imposes two main duties on waste disposal authorities: (a) to arrange for the disposal of controlled waste collected within their areas; and (b) to arrange for the provision of places at which residents may deposit their household waste free of charge.

Such duties may only be discharged through arrangements made with waste disposal contractors, but waste disposal authorities may hold land and own plant or equipment to be made available to waste disposal contractors in relation to those functions (subss. (4)(c) and (d) and (5)(b) and (c)). See also the note to s.32 and para. D7 of Annex D to Circ. 8/91, entitled "Competition for Local Authority Waste Disposal Contracts and New Arrangements for Disposal Operations."

Payments for recycling and disposal etc. of waste

52.—(1) Where, under section 48(2) above, a waste collection authority retains for recycling waste collected by it under section 45 above, the waste disposal authority for the area which includes the area of the waste collection authority shall make to that authority payments, in respect of the waste so retained, of such amounts representing its net saving of expenditure on the disposal of the waste as the authority determines.

(2) Where, by reason of the discharge by a waste disposal authority of its functions, waste arising in its area does not fall to be collected by a waste collection authority under section 45 above, the waste collection authority shall make to the waste disposal authority payments, in respect of the waste not falling to be so collected, of such amounts representing its net saving of expenditure on the collection of the waste as the authority determines.

(3) Where a person other than a waste collection authority, for the purpose of recycling it, collects waste arising in the area of a waste disposal authority which would fall to be collected under section 45 above, the waste disposal authority may make to that person payments, in respect of the waste so collected, of such amounts representing its net saving of expenditure on the disposal of the waste as the authority determines.

(4) Where a person other than a waste collection authority, for the purpose of recycling it, collects waste which would fall to be collected under section 45 above, the waste collection authority may make to that person payments, in respect of the waste so collected, of such amounts representing its net saving of expenditure on the collection of the waste as the authority determines.

(5) The Secretary of State may, by regulations, impose on waste disposal authorities a duty to make payments corresponding to the payments which are authorised by subsection (3) above to such persons in such circumstances and in respect of such descriptions or quantities of waste as are specified in the regulations.

(6) For the purposes of subsections (1), (3) and (5) above the net saving of expenditure of a waste disposal authority on the disposal of any waste retained or collected for recycling is the amount of the expenditure which the authority would, but for the retention or collection, have incurred in having it disposed of less any amount payable by the authority to any person in consequence of the retention or collection for recycling (instead of the disposal) of the waste.

(7) For the purposes of subsections (2) and (4) above the net saving of expenditure of a waste collection authority on the collection of any waste not

falling to be collected by it is the amount of the expenditure which the authority would, if it had had to collect the waste, have incurred in collecting it.

(8) The Secretary of State shall, by regulations, make provision for the determination of the net saving of expenditure for the purposes of subsections (1), (2), (3), (4) and (5) above.

(9) A waste disposal authority shall be entitled to receive from a waste collection authority such sums as are needed to reimburse the waste disposal authority the reasonable cost of making arrangements under section 51(1) above for the disposal of commercial and industrial waste collected in the area of the waste disposal authority.

(10) A waste disposal authority shall pay to a waste collection authority a reasonable contribution towards expenditure reasonably incurred by the waste collection authority in delivering waste, in pursuance of a direction under section 51(4)(a) above, to a place which is unreasonably far from the waste collection authority's area.

(11) Any question arising under subsection (9) or (10) above shall, in default of agreement between the two authorities in question, be determined by arbitration.

DEFINITIONS
"disposal": s.29(6).
"waste": s.75(2).

COMMENCEMENT
Subsections (1), (3)–(7), (9)–(11): April 1, 1992 (S.I. 1992 No. 266). Subsection (8) (partially): December 13, 1991 (S.I. 1991 No. 2829).

GENERAL NOTE
This section makes provision for various financial adjustments in relation to the collection, recycling and disposal of waste (sometimes loosely referred to as "waste recycling credits").

The most significant payments contemplated by the section relate to recycling and are as follows:
(1) waste disposal authorities must pay to waste collection authorities who retain waste for recycling a sum representing their "net saving of expenditure on the disposal of the waste" (subs. (1));
(2) where a waste disposal authority so discharges its functions that waste does not fall to be collected by the collection authority, the collection authority must pay to the disposal authority a sum representing "its net saving of expenditure on the collection of the waste" (subs. (2));
(3) where some other person collects waste for recycling which would otherwise fall to be collected, the waste disposal authority *may* make payments representing the net saving of expenditure on disposal and the collection authority *may* make payments representing the net saving of expenditure on collection (subss. (3) and (4)).

The reasoning behind the decision to make payments falling into category (3) above voluntary rather than compulsory, initially at least, was explained by Baroness Blatch as follows:

"We do not believe that there is yet a need for the Secretary of State to make use of this power. It follows that we do not think it timely to place a duty on disposal authorities to pay credits to third parties.

It may take some time for local authorities to identify all those third parties in their area who have a claim to receive recycling credits. When they have identified all those bodies undertaking recycling in their area, they may decide that it would not be desirable for credits to be paid in every case. There may be instances where economies of scale make it more appropriate for the waste collection authority to undertake recycling rather than it being done by voluntary bodies. There may be other cases where a number of different bodies are undertaking similar schemes in the same area. It would not necessarily be appropriate for an authority to be required to pay recycling credits to a number of competing schemes in the same area, particularly where some of the schemes yielded only small quantities of waste. Giving disposal authorities discretion to pay credits will allow them to make sensible judgments about the type of third party recycling scheme which should be encouraged in their area." (*Hansard*, H.L. Vol. 522, col. 363).

Net Saving of Expenditure
Provision as to the determination of net saving of expenditure for the purposes of subss. (1) and (3) is made by the Environmental Protection (Waste Recycling Payments) Regulations 1992 (S.I. 1992 No. 462) as amended by S.I. 1993 No. 445. Net saving is defined as an amount equal to half the expenditure which the authority would have incurred in disposing of the waste at a cost per tonne equal to its average cost per tonne at the relevant time of disposing of similar waste using its most expensive disposal method unless it is shown that its net saving of expenditure is a higher amount (reg. 2(2)).

Various factors are to be taken into account in determining the average cost of disposing of similar waste (reg. 2(3)). These are: market value of assets, including land; expenditure in operating sites or transfer stations; transport costs; site closure and post-closure expenditure; and any other expenditure. If it is impossible to determine the net saving because accurate information is not available or could only be obtained at disproportionate cost, net saving is to be determined by reference to the figures at the Schedule to the Regulations (reg. 2(5))— ranging from £16·93 per tonne for inner London Boroughs to £4·62 for shire counties with no transport costs.

Guidance
Circular 4/92 (W.O. 10/92) *Environmental Protection Act 1990*. The Environmental Protection (Waste Recycling Payments) Regulations 1992 provide guidance on the statutory provisions and regulations, including eligibility for credits, calculation of credit values, and arrangements to prevent error or fraud.

Duties of authorities as respects disposal of waste collected: Scotland

53.—(1) It shall be the duty of each waste disposal authority to arrange for the disposal of any waste collected by it, in its capacity as a waste collection authority, under section 45 above; and without prejudice to the authority's powers apart from the following provisions of this subsection, the powers exercisable by the authority for the purpose of performing that duty shall include power—
   (a) to provide, within or outside its area, places at which to deposit waste before the authority transfers it to a place or plant or equipment provided under the following paragraph; and
   (b) to provide, within or outside its area, places at which to dispose of or recycle the waste and plant or equipment for processing, recycling or otherwise disposing of it.

(2) Subsections (7) and (10) of section 45 above shall have effect in relation to a waste disposal authority as if the reference in paragraph (a) of the said subsection (7) to the collection of waste included the disposal of waste in pursuance of this section and the disposal of anything produced from waste belonging to the authority.

(3) A waste disposal authority may permit another person to use facilities provided by the authority under the preceding provisions of this section and may provide for the use of another person any such facilities as the authority has power to provide under those provisions, and—
   (a) subject to the following paragraph, it shall be the duty of the authority to make a reasonable charge in respect of the use by another person of the facilities unless the authority considers it appropriate not to make a charge;
   (b) no charge shall be made under this section in respect of household waste; and
   (c) anything delivered to the authority by another person in the course of using the facilities shall belong to the authority and may be dealt with accordingly.

(4) References to waste in subsection (1) above do not include matter removed from privies under section 45(5)(a) or (6) above, and it shall be the duty of a waste collection authority (other than an islands council) by which matter is so removed—
   (a) to deliver the matter, in accordance with any directions of the

regional council, at a place specified in the directions (which must be in or within a reasonable distance from the waste collection authority's area), to the regional council or another person so specified;
  (b) to give to the regional council from time to time a notice stating the quantity of the matter which the waste collection authority expects to deliver to or as directed by the regional council under the preceding paragraph during a period specified in the notice.
(5) Any question arising under paragraph (a) of the preceding subsection as to whether a place is within a reasonable distance from a waste collection authority's area shall, in default of agreement between the waste collection authority and the regional council in question, be determined by a single arbiter appointed, in default of agreement between the parties concerned, by the Secretary of State on the application of any of the parties; and anything delivered to a regional council under that subsection shall belong to the council and may be dealt with accordingly.
(6) This section applies to Scotland only.

DEFINITIONS
  "disposal": s.29(6).
  "household waste": s.75(4).
  "privies": s.45(12).
  "waste": s.75(2).

COMMENCEMENT
  April 1, 1992 (S.I. 1992 No. 266).

GENERAL NOTE
  This section applies only to Scotland and specifies the duties of waste disposal authorities with regard to disposal of waste collected by them in their capacity as waste collection authorities. Separate arrangements apply (subss. (4) and (5)) to matter removed from privies (but not cesspools).

Special provisions for land occupied by disposal authorities: Scotland

54.—(1) Nothing in subsection (1)(a) and (b) of section 33 above shall apply to—
  (a) the deposit of controlled waste in or on land in the area of a waste disposal authority which is occupied by the authority; or
  (b) the treating, keeping or disposing of controlled waste—
      (i) in or on land so occupied;
      (ii) by means of any mobile plant operated by the waste disposal authority,
if the requirements of subsection (3) below are satisfied.
(2) If any land occupied by a waste disposal authority is used by the authority as a site in or on which to deposit, treat, keep or dispose of or permit other persons to deposit, treat, keep or dispose of controlled waste or if the authority operates their mobile plant for the purpose aforesaid, it shall be the duty of the waste regulation authority to ensure that the land is used and the mobile plant operated in accordance with conditions which are—
  (a) calculated to prevent the use from causing pollution of the environment or harm to human health or serious detriment to the amenities of the locality in which the land is situated or the mobile plant may be operated; and
  (b) specified in a resolution passed by the waste regulation authority in accordance with the following provisions of this section.
(3) The requirements mentioned in subsection (1) above are, where the deposit is made, or the treating, keeping or disposing is carried out—
  (a) by the waste disposal authority that, as respects the land or as the case

may be the mobile plant, conditions have been specified by the waste regulation authority by virtue of subsection (2)(b) above and (in so far as current) are complied with;
  (b) by another person, that it is with the consent of the waste disposal authority and in accordance with any conditions to which the consent is subject.

(4) Where a waste disposal authority proposes that any land which the waste disposal authority occupies or intends to occupy should be used by that authority or that any mobile plant should be operated by the authority as mentioned in the preceding subsection, it shall be the duty of the waste regulation authority before it gives effect to the proposal—
  (a) to prepare a statement of the conditions which the waste regulation authority intends to specify in a resolution to be passed by that authority under paragraph (d) below;
  (b) to refer the proposal and the statement—
     (i) to the river purification authority whose area includes any of the land in question;
     (ii) to the Health and Safety Executive;
     (iii) where the waste regulation authority is not also a district planning authority (within the meaning of section 172 of the Local Government (Scotland) Act 1973), to the general planning authority (within the meaning of that section) whose area includes any of the land; and
     (iv) in the case of a proposal to operate mobile plant, to the river purification authority whose area includes the area of the water disposal authority;
  (c) to consider any representations about the proposal and statement which the river purification authority, the Health and Safety Executive or the general planning authority makes to it during the allowed period;
  (d) subject to subsection (7) of this section, to pass a resolution—
     (i) authorising the deposit, keeping, treatment or disposal of any specified description of controlled waste in or on specified land occupied or to be occupied by the waste disposal authority or the treatment or disposal of any specified description of controlled waste by means of specified mobile plant;
     (ii) specifying the conditions in accordance with which the land in question or the mobile plant is to be used by the waste disposal authority as mentioned in the preceding subsection.
  (e) where any part of the land to be used is land which has been notified under section 28(1) of the Wildlife and Countryside Act 1981, to—
     (i) refer the proposal and the statement to the appropriate nature conservation body, and
     (ii) consider any representations about the proposal and the statement which that body makes to it during the allowed period,
     and in this subsection and subsection (13) of this section any reference to the appropriate nature conservation body is a reference, until the date appointed under section 131(3) below, to the Nature Conservancy Council or, after that date, to the Nature Conservancy Council for Scotland.

(5) In subsection (4) above, paragraphs (a) to (c), and in paragraph (d) the words "subject to subsection (7) of this section," shall have effect only in a case where the proposal is made by a waste disposal authority other than an islands council.

(6) A separate resolution under subsection (4)(d) above shall be passed by the authority—
  (a) in respect of each item of mobile plant; and
  (b) in relation to each site.

(7) If a river purification authority to which a proposal is referred by a waste regulation authority under paragraph (b) of subsection (4) of this section requests the authority not to proceed with the resolution or disagrees with the authority as to the conditions to be specified in the resolution under paragraph (d) of that subsection, either of them may refer the matter to the Secretary of State and it shall be the duty of the authority not to pass a resolution under that paragraph except in accordance with his decision.

(8) A waste regulation authority by which a resolution has been passed under paragraph (d) of subsection (4) of this section or this subsection may vary or rescind the resolution by a subsequent resolution of the authority.

(9) Paragraphs (a) to (c) of subsection (4) and subsection (7) of this section shall with the necessary modifications apply to a proposal to pass a resolution under subsection (8) above and to such a resolution as they apply to such a proposal as is mentioned in those provisions and to a resolution under the said paragraph (d), except that—
  (a) those provisions shall not apply to a resolution, or to a proposal to pass a resolution, which only rescinds a previous resolution; and
  (b) the waste regulation authority may postpone the reference under the said subsection (4) so far as the authority considers that by reason of an emergency it is appropriate to do so; and
  (c) the waste regulation authority may disregard any other authority or the Health and Safety Executive for the purposes of the preceding provisions of this subsection in relation to a resolution which, in the opinion of the waste regulation authority, will not affect the other authority.

(10) If while a resolution is in force under the preceding provisions of this section it appears to the authority which passed the resolution—
  (a) that the continuation of activities to which the resolution relates would cause pollution of the environment or harm to human health or would be seriously detrimental to the amenities of the locality affected; and
  (b) that the pollution, harm or detriment cannot be avoided by modifying the conditions relating to the carrying on of the activities,
it shall be the duty of the waste disposal authority to discontinue the activities and of the waste regulation authority to rescind the resolution.

(11) If it appears to a river purification authority that activities to which a resolution under this section relates are causing or likely to cause pollution to controlled waters (within the meaning of Part II of the Control of Pollution Act 1974) in the area of the authority, the authority may, without prejudice to the provisions of the preceding subsection or the said Part II, request the Secretary of State to direct the waste regulation authority which passed the resolution to rescind it and the waste disposal authority to discontinue the activities; and it shall be the duty of a waste disposal authority and a waste regulation authority to comply with a direction given to it under this subsection.

(12) It shall be the duty of waste regulation authorities to have regard to any guidance issued to them by the Secretary of State with regard to the discharge of their functions under this section.

(13) The period allowed to the river purification authority, the Health and Safety Executive and the general planning authority for the making of representations under subsection (4)(c) above or to the appropriate nature conservation body for the making of representations under subsection (4)(e) above about a proposal is the period of 21 days beginning with that on which the proposal is received by that body or such longer period as the waste regulation authority and that body agree in writing.

(14) The Secretary of State may, by regulations, make provision as to conditions which are, or are not, to be included in a resolution; and regulations under this subsection may make different provision for different circumstances.

(15) The Secretary of State may as respects any resolution made or to be made by the authority give to the authority directions—
(a) as to the conditions which are or are not to be included in the resolution;
(b) as to the modifications which it would be appropriate to make in the conditions included in a resolution by virtue of subsection (7) above;
(c) as to the rescinding of the resolution;
and it shall be the duty of the authority to give effect to the directions.

(16) Any resolution of a waste disposal authority under Part I of the Control of Pollution Act 1974 effective immediately before the commencement of this section shall have effect as if it were a resolution of a waste regulation authority under this section.

(17) This section applies to Scotland only.

DEFINITIONS
"controlled waste": s.75(4).
"deposit": s.29(6).
"harm": s.29(5).
"mobile plant": s.29(9).
"pollution of the environment": s.29(3).
"treatment": s.29(6).

COMMENCEMENT
Subsection (14): February 18, 1993 (S.I. 1993 No. 274). Remainder: no date has been set for commencement.

GENERAL NOTE
This provision, modelled largely upon s.11 of COPA, deals with the situation in Scotland, where waste disposal authorities may continue to carry out operational activities. The basic scheme is that the requirements of a site or mobile plant licence do not apply to land occupied or plant operated by a disposal authority. Control is exercised by the duty on the waste regulation authority in subs. (2) to ensure that the activities conform with conditions specified in a resolution passed by the regulation authority and calculated to prevent pollution of the environment, harm to human health or serious detriment to the amenities of the locality. The resolution thus effectively takes the place of the site or mobile plant licence and is subject to equivalent consultation procedures (subs. (4)). Such resolutions can be varied or rescinded (subs. (8)) and in certain circumstances must be rescinded (subs. (10))—the circumstances being equivalent to those in which a licence is to be revoked.

Scottish authorities are obliged by s.30(7) to make administrative arrangements keeping their regulatory and disposal functions separate.

For guidance as to these procedures, see draft Circular on Waste Management Licensing Regulations Annex 1, paras. 1.73–1.90 and draft Waste Management Paper 4.

Powers for recycling waste

55.—(1) This section has effect for conferring on waste disposal authorities and waste collection authorities powers of recycling waste.
(2) A waste disposal authority may—
(a) make arrangements with waste disposal contractors for them to recycle waste as respects which the authority has duties under section 51(1) above or agrees with another person for its disposal or treatment;
(b) make arrangements with waste disposal contractors for them to use waste for the purpose of producing from it heat or electricity or both;
(c) buy or otherwise acquire waste with a view to its being recycled;
(d) use, sell or otherwise dispose of waste as respects which the authority has duties under section 51(1) above or anything produced from such waste.
(3) A waste collection authority may—
(a) buy or otherwise acquire waste with a view to recycling it;
(b) use, or dispose of by way of sale or otherwise to another person, waste belonging to the authority or anything produced from such waste.

(4) This section shall not apply to Scotland.

DEFINITIONS
"disposal": s.29(6).
"treatment": s.29(6).
"waste": s.75(2).
"waste disposal contractors": s.30(5).

COMMENCEMENT
April 1, 1992 (S.I. 1992 No. 266).

GENERAL NOTE
This section contains express powers connected with the recycling of waste. Both disposal and collection authorities are given powers, which are in some respects different. Disposal authorities are given power to use, sell or otherwise dispose of waste collected in their area (subs. (2)(d)). Collection authorities have, by subs. (3)(b), similar powers in respect of waste belonging to them (as to which, see s.45(9)).

Powers for recycling waste: Scotland

56.—(1) Without prejudice to the powers of waste disposal authorities apart from this section, a waste disposal authority may—
  (a) do such things as the authority considers appropriate for the purpose of—
    (i) enabling waste belonging to the authority, or belonging to another person who requests the authority to deal with it under this section, to be recycled; or
    (ii) enabling waste to be used for the purpose of producing from it heat or electricity or both;
  (b) buy or otherwise acquire waste with a view to its being recycled;
  (c) use, sell or otherwise dispose of waste belonging to the authority or anything produced from such waste.
(2) This section applies to Scotland only.

DEFINITION
"waste": s.75(2).

COMMENCEMENT
April 1, 1992 (S.I. 1992 No. 266).

GENERAL NOTE
This section provides specific powers to Scottish waste disposal authorities in relation to recycling of waste.

Power of Secretary of State to require waste to be accepted, treated, disposed of or delivered

57.—(1) The Secretary of State may, by notice in writing, direct the holder of any waste management licence to accept and keep, or accept and treat or dispose of, controlled waste at specified places on specified terms.
(2) The Secretary of State may, by notice in writing, direct any person who is keeping controlled waste on any land to deliver the waste to a specified person on specified terms with a view to its being treated or disposed of by that other person.
(3) A direction under this section may impose a requirement as respects waste of any specified kind or as respects any specified consignment of waste.
(4) A direction under subsection (2) above may require the person who is directed to deliver the waste to pay to the specified person his reasonable costs of treating or disposing of the waste.

(5) A person who fails, without reasonable excuse, to comply with a direction under this section shall be liable on summary conviction to a fine not exceeding level 5 on the standard scale.

(6) A person shall not be guilty of an offence under any other enactment prescribed by the Secretary of State by regulations made for the purposes of this subsection by reason only of anything necessarily done or omitted in order to comply with a direction under this section.

(7) The Secretary of State may, where the costs of the treatment or disposal of waste are not paid or not fully paid in pursuance of subsection (4) above to the person treating or disposing of the waste, pay the costs or the unpaid costs, as the case may be, to that person.

(8) In this section "specified" means specified in a direction under this section.

DEFINITIONS
"controlled waste": s.75(4).
"dispose of": s.29(6).
"treat": s.29(6).

COMMENCEMENT
Not yet in force.

GENERAL NOTE
This is a comprehensive power allowing the Secretary of State to give directions as to the disposition of any specified kind or consignment of controlled waste. The direction can apply to licence-holders requiring them to accept the waste, and to keepers of waste, requiring them to deliver it for treatment or disposal. Failure to comply with a direction is an offence.

The power is intended to be used only in exceptional circumstances, if at all, as a matter of last resort, where attempts to secure agreement between the relevant parties have failed and where the waste regulation authority has been consulted (*Hansard*, H.L. Vol. 520, col. 1511).

Power of Secretary of State to require waste to be accepted, treated, disposed of or delivered: Scotland

58. In relation to Scotland, the Secretary of State may give directions to a waste disposal authority to accept and keep, or accept and treat or dispose of, controlled waste at specified places on specified terms; and it shall be the duty of the authority to give effect to the directions.

DEFINITIONS
"controlled waste": s.75(4).
"dispose of": s.29(6).
"treat": s.29(6).

COMMENCEMENT
Not yet in force.

GENERAL NOTE
This section applies to Scotland in addition to s.57, allowing directions to accept waste to be given to waste disposal authorities.

Powers to require removal of waste unlawfully deposited

59.—(1) If any controlled waste is deposited in or on any land in the area of a waste regulation authority or waste collection authority in contravention of section 33(1) above, the authority may, by notice served on him, require the occupier to do either or both of the following, that is—
   (a) to remove the waste from the land within a specified period not less than a period of 21 days beginning with the service of the notice;
   (b) to take within such a period specified steps with a view to eliminating or reducing the consequences of the deposit of the waste.

(2) A person on whom any requirements are imposed under subsection (1) above may, within the period of 21 days mentioned in that subsection, appeal against the requirement to a magistrates' court or, in Scotland, to the sheriff by way of summary application.

(3) On any appeal under subsection (2) above the court shall quash the requirement if it is satisfied that—
   (a) the appellant neither deposited nor knowingly caused nor knowingly permitted the deposit of the waste; or
   (b) there is a material defect in the notice;
and in any other case shall either modify the requirement or dismiss the appeal.

(4) Where a person appeals against any requirement imposed under subsection (1) above, the requirement shall be of no effect pending the determination of the appeal; and where the court modifies the requirement or dismisses the appeal it may extend the period specified in the notice.

(5) If a person on whom a requirement imposed under subsection (1) above fails, without reasonable excuse, to comply with the requirement he shall be liable, on summary conviction, to a fine not exceeding level 5 on the standard scale and to a further fine of an amount equal to one-tenth of level 5 on the standard scale for each day on which the failure continues after conviction of the offence and before the authority has begun to exercise its powers under subsection (6) below.

(6) Where a person on whom a requirement has been imposed under subsection (1) above by an authority fails to comply with the requirement the authority may do what that person was required to do and may recover from him any expenses reasonably incurred by the authority in doing it.

(7) If it appears to a waste regulation authority or waste collection authority that waste has been deposited in or on any land in contravention of section 33(1) above and that—
   (a) in order to remove or prevent pollution of land, water or air or harm to human health it is necessary that the waste be forthwith removed or other steps taken to eliminate or reduce the consequences of the deposit or both; or
   (b) there is no occupier of the land; or
   (c) the occupier neither made nor knowingly permitted the deposit of the waste;
the authority may remove the waste from the land or take other steps to eliminate or reduce the consequences of the deposit or, as the case may require, to remove the waste and take those steps.

(8) Where an authority exercises any of the powers conferred on it by subsection (7) above it shall be entitled to recover the cost incurred by it in removing the waste or taking the steps or both and in disposing of the waste—
   (a) in a case falling within subsection (7)(a) above, from the occupier of the land unless he proves that he neither made nor knowingly caused nor knowingly permitted the deposit of the waste;
   (b) in any case, from any person who deposited or knowingly caused or knowingly permitted the deposit of any of the waste;
except such of the cost as the occupier or that person shows was incurred unnecessarily.

(9) Any waste removed by an authority under subsection (7) above shall belong to that authority and may be dealt with accordingly.

DEFINITIONS
   "controlled waste": s.75(4).
   "deposited": s.29(6).
   "harm": s.29(5).
   "waste": s.75(2).

COMMENCEMENT
Not yet in force.

GENERAL NOTE
This section gives waste regulation and collection authorities power to deal with controlled waste which has been fly-tipped, or otherwise unlawfully deposited, within their areas. The procedure involves service of notice on the occupier of the land, requiring removal of the waste and steps to eliminate or reduce the consequences of the deposit. In the event of non-compliance the authority may take the necessary steps itself and recover the reasonable costs of doing so from the recipient of the notice.

Subsection (3) in effect provides the defence of "innocent occupier," in that the notice will be quashed on appeal if the occupier neither deposited the waste nor knowingly caused or knowingly permitted the deposit (as to which, see notes to s.33).

Powers to act immediately in certain cases to remove the waste or reduce the consequences of its deposit are given by subs. (7). The circumstances are: (a) where immediate action is necessary to prevent pollution of land, water or air (cf. "pollution of the environment") or harm to human health; or (b) where there is no occupier of the relevant land; or (c) where the occupier is innocent in relation to the deposit.

Under subs. (8), reasonable costs so incurred may be recovered in case (a) from the occupier unless he or she can prove their innocence and, in any of the cases, from any person who deposited the waste or knowingly caused or knowingly permitted the deposit.

For a case on the corresponding provision in COPA 1974, see *Berridge Incinerators* v. *Nottinghamshire County Council* (Crown Court, Nottingham, June 12, 1992) where conviction for failure to comply with a notice was quashed on the grounds, *inter alia*, that the notice was unreasonable and unfair.

See also *R.* v. *Metropolitan Stipendiary Magistrate, ex p. London Waste Regulation Authority*; *Berkshire County Council* v. *Scott, The Times*, January 14, 1993, where the validity of a notice under s.16 of COPA was upheld notwithstanding an argument that the description of the waste to be removed was too vague.

Interference with waste sites and receptacles for waste

60.—(1) No person shall sort over or disturb—
(a) anything deposited at a place for the deposit of waste provided by a waste collection authority, by a waste disposal contractor under arrangements made with a waste disposal authority or by any other local authority or person or, in Scotland, by a waste disposal authority;
(b) anything deposited in a receptacle for waste, whether for public or private use, provided by a waste collection authority, by a waste disposal contractor under arrangements made with a waste disposal authority, by a parish or community council or by a holder of a waste management licence or, in Scotland, by a waste disposal authority or a roads authority; or
(c) the contents of any receptacle for waste which, in accordance with a requirement under section 46 or 47 above, is placed on any highway or, in Scotland, road or in any other place with a view to its being emptied;
unless he has the relevant consent or right to do so specified in subsection (2) below.

(2) The consent or right that is relevant for the purposes of subsection (1)(a), (b) or (c) above is—
(a) in the case of paragraph (a), the consent of the authority, contractor or other person who provides the place for the deposit of the waste;
(b) in the case of paragraph (b), the consent of the authority, contractor or other person who provides the receptacle for the deposit of the waste;
(c) in the case of paragraph (c), the right to the custody of the receptacle, the consent of the person having the right to the custody of the receptacle or the right conferred by the function by or under this Part of emptying such receptacles.

(3) A person who contravenes subsection (1) above shall be liable on summary conviction to a fine of an amount not exceeding level 3 on the standard scale.

DEFINITIONS
"deposited": s.29(6).
"waste": s.75(2).
"waste disposal contractor": s.30(5).

COMMENCEMENT
In part: May 31, 1991 (S.I. 1991 No. 1319), "in part" meaning in so far as it relates to anything deposited at a place for the deposit of waste, or in a receptacle for waste, provided by a waste disposal contractor under arrangements made with a waste disposal authority.

GENERAL NOTE
This section creates the summary offence of sorting over or disturbing waste at waste sites or in bins or other receptacles for waste. No offence is committed if the sorting or disturbance takes place with the consent of the relevant person, as specified in subs. (2).

Duty of waste regulation authorities as respects closed landfills

61.—(1) Except as respects land in relation to which a site licence is in force, it shall be the duty of every waste regulation authority to cause its area to be inspected from time to time to detect whether any land is in such a condition, by reason of the relevant matters affecting the land, that it may cause pollution of the environment or harm to human health.

(2) The matters affecting land relevant for the purposes of this section are the concentration or accumulation in, and emission or discharge from, the land of noxious liquids caused by deposits of controlled waste in the land.

(3) For the purpose of discharging the duty imposed by subsection (1) above on a waste regulation authority, the authority may enter and inspect any land—
  (a) in or on which controlled waste has been deposited at any time under the authority of a waste management licence or a disposal licence under section 5 of the Control of Pollution Act 1974; or
  (b) as respects which the authority has reason to believe that controlled waste has been deposited in the land at any time (whether before or after January 1, 1976); or
  (c) in which there are, or the authority has reason to believe there may be, concentrations or accumulations of noxious gases or noxious liquids.

In this subsection "controlled waste" means household, industrial or commercial waste as defined in section 75(5), (6) and (7) below (subject, if the regulations so provide, to regulations under section 63(1) or 75(8) below).

(4) Where it appears to a waste regulation authority that the condition of any land in its area is such as is specified in subsection (1) above it shall be the duty of the authority, from time to time during the period of its responsibility for the land, to enter and inspect the land for the purpose of keeping its condition under review.

(5) Where, at any time during the period of its responsibility for any land, it appears to a waste regulation authority that the condition of the land is, by reason of the relevant matters affecting the land, such that pollution of water is likely to be caused, it shall be the duty of the authority to consult the National Rivers Authority or, in Scotland, the river purification authority whose area includes the land in question as to the discharge by the authority of the duty imposed on it in relation to the land by subsection (7) below.

(6) The "period of responsibility" for any land for the purposes of subsections (4) and (5) above extends from the time at which the condition of the land first appears to the authority to be such as is referred to in that subsection until the authority is satisfied that no pollution of the environ-

ment or harm to human health will be caused by reason of the relevant matters affecting the land.

(7) Where, on an inspection by a waste regulation authority of any land under this section, it appears to the authority that the condition of the land is, by reason of the relevant matters affecting the land, such that pollution of the environment or harm to human health is likely to be caused it shall be the duty of the authority to do such works and take such other steps (whether on the land affected or on adjacent land) as appear to the authority to be reasonable to avoid such pollution or harm.

(8) Where an authority exercises in relation to waste on any land the duty imposed by subsection (7) above, the authority shall, except in a case falling within subsection (9) below, be entitled to recover the cost or part of the cost incurred in doing so from the person who is for the time being the owner of the land, except such of the cost as that person shows was incurred unreasonably.

(9) Subsection (8) above does not apply in a case where the authority accepted the surrender under section 39 above of the waste management licence which authorised the activities in the course of which the waste was deposited.

(10) In deciding whether to recover the cost and, if so, how much to recover of the cost which it is entitled to recover under subsection (8) above, the authority shall have regard to any hardship which the recovery may cause to the owner of the land.

(11) It shall be the duty of waste regulation authorities to have regard to any guidance issued to them by the Secretary of State as respects the discharge of their functions under this section.

DEFINITIONS
   "commercial waste": s.75(7).
   "controlled waste": s.75(4).
   "harm": s.29(5).
   "household waste": s.75(5).
   "industrial waste": s.75(6).
   "pollution of the environment": s.29(3).
   "site licence": s.35(12).

COMMENCEMENT
   No date has been set.

GENERAL NOTE
   This important new section attempts to address the increasingly recognised problem of waste deposited in land generating methane or other gases so as to endanger nearby persons or property, or causing serious pollution of groundwater resources by escaping leachate. The dangers of methane gas in particular have been highlighted by the explosion at Loscoe, Derbyshire in 1986 (see the non-statutory report to Derbyshire County Council of Gerard Ryan Q.C. of February 1988) and by the fatal explosion at Abbeystead Pumping Station (caused by natural methane rather than methane generated by waste): see *Ekkersley* v. *Binnie & Partners* (February 18, 1988, unreported, Court of Appeal).
   Advice on the problems has now been issued by HMIP in Waste Management Paper No. 27, *The Control of Landfill Gas* and in DoE Planning Circ. 17/89, *Landfill Sites: Development Control* (W.O. 38/89).

Duty of inspection
   Waste regulation authorities are placed under a duty (subs. (1)) to inspect land within their area, except land in relation to which a site licence is in force (such land should be inspected under the general provisions on supervision of licensed activities in s.42). The purpose of the inspection is to discover whether the land is in such a condition, because of "relevant matters" affecting it, that it may cause pollution of the environment or harm to human health.

Relevant matters
   The "relevant matters" (subs. (2)) refer to noxious gases or liquids caused by deposits of

controlled waste in the land concentrated or accumulated in the land and emitted or discharged from the land. Thus, the section would clearly cover gases produced by microbiological processes within the waste or chemical compounds arising from reactions within the waste.

Powers of entry
Subsection (3) gives wide powers of entry for the purposes of inspecting land. The land covered includes not only former landfill sites, or land on which waste has been deposited but also any land on which there are, or the authority has reason to believe there are, concentrations or accumulations of noxious gases or liquids (subs. (3)(c)). Thus, although the marginal note to the section refers to "closed landfills" the powers of inspection are in fact wider than this would suggest.

Continued surveillance
Land identified as potentially harmful must by subs. (4) be kept under review until the authority is satisfied that it no longer presents a threat of pollution or harm. This period is known as the "period of responsibility" of the authority. Where pollution of water seems likely the NRA or Scottish river purification authority must be consulted (subs. (5)).

Remedial measures
If it appears that pollution of the environment or harm to human health is likely to be caused by the condition of the land, so far as attributable to "relevant matters," the authority is under a duty by subs. (7) to take the necessary preventive measures. These measures may be taken either on the land affected or on adjacent land.

Cost recovery
The cost in whole or in part of such measures taken by the authority "in relation to waste on any land" may be recovered from the person "who is for the time being the owner of the land" (query: the owner of the land on which the waste was deposited or the owner of the land on which the works were undertaken, if different?). Costs may not be recovered in this way in a case where surrender of the site licence authorising deposit of the relevant waste has been accepted by the authority under s.39 (subs. (9)).

Recovery of costs may be total or partial, and hardship to the owner is a material consideration in deciding whether to recover the cost and, if so, how much (subs. (10)).

Special waste and non-controlled waste

Special provision with respect to certain dangerous or intractable waste

62.—(1) If the Secretary of State considers that controlled waste of any kind is or may be so dangerous or difficult to treat, keep or dispose of that special provision is required for dealing with it he shall make provision by regulations for the treatment, keeping or disposal of waste of that kind ("special waste").

(2) Without prejudice to the generality of subsection (1) above, the regulations may include provision—
   (a) for the giving of directions by waste regulation authorities with respect to matters connected with the treatment, keeping or disposal of special waste;
   (b) for securing that special waste is not, while awaiting treatment or disposal in pursuance of the regulations, kept at any one place in quantities greater that those which are prescribed and in circumstances which differ from those which are prescribed;
   (c) in connection with requirements imposed on consignors or consignees of special waste, imposing, in the event of non-compliance, requirements on any person carrying the consignment to re-deliver it as directed;
   (d) for requiring the occupier of premises on which special waste is situated to give notice of that fact and other prescribed information to a prescribed authority;
   (e) for the keeping of records by waste regulation authorities and by persons who import, export, produce, keep, treat or dispose of special waste or deliver it to another person for treatment or disposal, for

the inspection of the records and for the furnishing by such persons to waste regulation authorities of copies of or information derived from the records,
  (f) for the keeping in the register under section 64(1) below of copies of such of those records, or such information derived from those records, as may be prescribed;
  (g) providing that a contravention of the regulations shall be an offence and prescribing the maximum penalty for to offence, which shall not exceed, on summary conviction, a fine at level 5 on the standard scale and on conviction on indictment, imprisonment for a term of two years or a fine or both.
(3) Without prejudice to the generality of subsection (1) above, the regulations may include provision—
  (a) for the supervision by waste regulation authorities of activities authorised by virtue of the regulations and for the recovery of the costs incurred by them from the persons carrying on the activities;
  (b) as to the recovery of expenses or other charges for the treatment, keeping or disposal or the re-delivery of special waste in pursuance of the regulations;
  (c) as to appeals to the Secretary of State from decisions of waste regulation authorities under the regulations.
(4) In the application of this section to Northern Ireland "waste regulation authority" means a district council established under the Local Government Act (Northern Ireland) 1972.

DEFINITIONS
  "controlled waste": s.75(4).
  "dispose of": s.29(6).
  "special waste": s.75(9).
  "treat": s.29(6).
  "waste": s.75(2).

COMMENCEMENT
  Not yet in force. It will come into force on a date to be appointed (s.164(3)).

GENERAL NOTE
  The current regulations dealing with special waste are the Control of Pollution (Special Waste) Regulations 1980 (S.I. 1980 No. 1709) as amended by S.I. 1988 No. 1790. Amendments to these Regulations relating to ships' tank washings and garbage which are special waste were made by the Control of Pollution (Landed Ships' Waste) Regulations 1987 (S.I. 1987 No. 402) and the Control of Pollution (Landed Ships' Waste) (Amendment) Regulations 1989 (S.I. 1989 No. 65). These Regulations are the means by which the E.C. Directive 78/319/EEC on Toxic and Dangerous Waste (O.J. L84, March 31, 1978) is implemented.
  Separate controls attach to the transfrontier movement of toxic or hazardous wastes, both under Community law (Directives 84/631/EEC (O.J. L326 December 13, 1984), 85/469/EEC (O.J. L272, October 12, 1985), 86/279/EEC (O.J. L181 July 4, 1986) and 87/112/EEC (O.J. L48 February 17, 1987)) and under UK law by the Transfrontier Shipment of Hazardous Waste Regulations 1988 (S.I. 1988 No. 1562).
  Within the E.C. a new Directive on hazardous waste, including a new definition on such waste superseding that of Directive 78/319/EEC has been agreed (91/869/EEC). Additionally, the UK Government signed the Basel Convention on *The Control of Transboundary Movements of Hazardous Wastes and their Disposal* (Cm. 984) on October 6, 1985. The Convention is now in force, having been ratified by 20 signatories, but has not yet been ratified by the UK or the E.C. The European Commission favours acceptance by the Community of the OECD Decision/Recommendation on *The Control of Transfrontier Movements of Hazardous Wastes*, which entails rapid signature and ratification of the Basel Convention and further work on harmonising notification systems and procedures (see SEC(89)1531 Final, September 22, 1989).
  The Government is currently reviewing the Special Waste Regulations in the light of these developments, and a Consultation Paper, *Special Waste and the Control of its Disposal* was issued by the DoE and Welsh Office in February 1990.

The main changes apparent between s.62 and the equivalent section under COPA, s.17, is that the Regulations made under s.62 may provide for the keeping of information in public registers and may impose requirements upon carriers of special waste to redeliver it in the event of non-compliance with the relevant requirements.

Waste other than controlled waste

63.—(1) The Secretary of State may, after consultation with such bodies as he considers appropriate, make regulations providing that prescribed provisions of this Part shall have effect in a prescribed area—
  (a) as if references in those provisions to controlled waste or controlled waste of a kind specified in the regulations included references to such waste as is mentioned in section 75(7)(c) below which is of a kind so specified; and
  (b) with such modifications as may be prescribed;
and the regulations may make such modifications of other enactments as the Secretary of State considers appropriate.
  (2) A person who—
  (a) deposits any waste other than controlled waste, or
  (b) knowingly causes or knowingly permits the deposit of any waste other than controlled waste,
in a case where, if the waste were special waste and any waste management licence were not in force, he would be guilty of an offence under section 33 above shall, subject to subsection (3) below, be guilty of that offence and punishable accordingly.
  (3) No offence is committed by virtue of subsection (2) above if the act charged was done under and in accordance with any consent, licence, approval or authority granted under any enactment (excluding any planning permission under the enactments relating to town and country planning).
  (4) Section 45(2) and section 47(1) above shall apply to waste other than controlled waste as they apply to controlled waste.

DEFINITIONS
  "controlled waste": s.75(4).
  "deposits": s.29(6).
  "special waste": s.75(9).
  "waste": s.75(2).

COMMENCEMENT
  Subsection (1): February 18, 1993 (S.I. 1993 No. 274). Remainder: no date has been set for commencement.

GENERAL NOTE
  Subs. (1) allows the Secretary of State to make regulations applying prescribed provisions of Pt. II to mine and quarry wastes and agricultural waste within a prescribed area and subject to such modifications as may be prescribed.
  Subs. (2) creates an offence of depositing waste which is not controlled waste or knowingly causing or knowingly permitting such deposit. The more severe penalties of s.32 relating to special waste (s.32(9)) apply to such offences. It is a defence that the act was done under and in accordance with any statutory consent or other statutory approval, but planning permission is not sufficient authorisation for this purpose.

Publicity

Public registers

64.—(1) Subject to sections 65 and 66 below, it shall be the duty of each waste regulation authority to maintain a register containing prescribed particulars of or relating to—
  (a) current or recently current licences ("licences") granted by the authority;
  (b) current or recently current applications to the authority for licences;

(c) applications made to the authority under section 37 above for the modification of licences;
(d) notices issued by the authority under section 37 above effecting the modification of licences;
(e) notices issued by the authority under section 38 above effecting the revocation or suspension of licences or imposing requirements on the holders of licences;
(f) appeals under section 43 above relating to decisions of the authority;
(g) certificates of completion issued by the authority under section 39(9) above,
(h) notices issued by the authority imposing requirements on the holders of licences under section 42(5) above;
(i) convictions of the holders of licences granted by the authority for any offence under this Part (whether in relation to a licence so granted or not);
(j) the occasions on which the authority has discharged any function under section 42 or 61 above;
(k) directions given to the authority under any provision of this Part by the Secretary of State;
(l) in Scotland, resolutions made by the authority under section 54 above;
(m) such matters relating to the treatment, keeping or disposal of waste in the area of the authority or any pollution of the environment caused thereby as may be prescribed;

and any other document or information required to be kept in the register under any provision of this Act.

(2) Where information of any description is excluded from any register by virtue of section 66 below, a statement shall be entered in the register indicating the existence of information of that description.

(3) For the purposes of subsection (1) above licences are "recently" current for the period of 12 months after they cease to be in force and applications for licences are "recently" current if they relate to a licence which is current or recently current or, in the case of an application which is rejected, for the period of 12 months beginning with the date on which the waste regulation authority gives notice of rejection or, as the case may be, on which the application is deemed by section 36(9) above to have been rejected.

(4) It shall be the duty of each waste collection authority in England which is not a waste regulation authority to maintain a register containing prescribed particulars of such information contained in any register maintained under subsection (1) above as relates to the treatment, keeping or disposal of controlled waste in the area of the authority.

(5) Waste regulation authorities in England which are not waste collection authorities shall furnish any waste collection authorities in their areas with the particulars necessary to enable them to discharge their duty under subsection (4) above.

(6) Each waste regulation authority and waste collection authority shall secure that any register maintained under this section is open to inspection at its principal office by members of the public free of charge at all reasonable hours and shall afford to members of the public reasonable facilities for obtaining, on payment of reasonable charges, copies of entries in the register.

(7) Registers under this section may be kept in any form.

(8) In this section "prescribed" means prescribed in regulations by the Secretary of State.

DEFINITIONS
"controlled waste": s.75.

"disposal": s.29(4).
"licences": s.35(12).
"treatment": s.29(6).

COMMENCEMENT
Subsections (1), (4), (8): February 18, 1993 (S.I. 1993 No. 274). Remainder: no date has been set for commencement.

GENERAL NOTE
This section makes provision for the keeping of registers by waste regulation authorities relating to waste management licences and other matters. The obligation extends only to "current or recently current" licences and applications. A licence is "current" while in force and "recently current" for 12 months after it ceases to be in force (subs. (3)). Applications are current, so long as the licence granted remains in force or is recently current or, in cases of rejection of the application, for 12 months from rejection (subs. (3)). Broad discretion is given for the Secretary of State to prescribe further matters for inclusion in relation to treatment, keeping or disposal of waste or pollution thereby caused (subs. (1)(m)). Registers must also be kept at waste collection authority level, on the basis of particulars supplied by the waste regulation authority (subss. (4) and (5)).

REGULATIONS
By reg. 13 of the draft Waste Management Licensing Regulations the register must contain full particulars of specified matters including current and recently current licences and applications, including supporting information, statutory notices, notices of appeal, relevant convictions, reports and monitoring information, special waste consignment notes and other documentation and, in Scotland, s.54 resolutions.

Exclusion from registers of information affecting national security

65.—(1) No information shall be included in a register maintained under section 64 above (a "register") if and so long as, in the opinion of the Secretary of State, the inclusion in the register of that information, or information of that description, would be contrary to the interests of national security.

(2) The Secretary of State may, for the purpose of securing the exclusion from registers of information to which subsection (1) above applies, give to the authorities maintaining registers directions—
   (a) specifying information, or descriptions of information, to be excluded from their registers; or
   (b) specifying descriptions of information to be referred to the Secretary of State for his determination;
and no information referred to the Secretary of State in pursuance of paragraph (b) above shall be included in any such register until the Secretary of State determines that it should be so included.

(3) An authority maintaining a register shall notify the Secretary of State of any information it excludes from the register in pursuance of directions under subsection (2) above.

(4) A person may, as respects any information which appears to him to be information to which subsection (1) above may apply, give a notice to the Secretary of State specifying the information and indicating its apparent nature; and, if he does so—
   (a) he shall notify the authority concerned that he has done so; and
   (b) no information so notified to the Secretary of State shall be included in the register kept by that authority until the Secretary of State has determined that it should be so included.

COMMENCEMENT
Subsection (2): February 18, 1993 (S.I. 1993 No. 274). Remainder: no date has been set for commencement.

GENERAL NOTE
This section provides for information to be excluded from the registers kept under s.64 where inclusion of the information would be contrary to the interests of national security.

"Cogent and specific evidence" will be required to substantiate claims for exemption on this ground (see *Hansard*, H.L. Vol. 522, col. 380).

Exclusion from registers of certain confidential information

66.—(1) No information relating to the affairs of any individual or business shall be included in a register maintained under section 64 above (a "register"), without the consent of that individual or the person for the time being carrying on that business, if and so long as the information—
 (a) is, in relation to him, commercially confidential; and
 (b) is not required to be included in the register in pursuance of directions under subsection (7) below;
but information is not commercially confidential for the purposes of this section unless it is determined under this section to be so by the authority maintaining the register or, on appeal, by the Secretary of State.

(2) Where information is furnished to an authority maintaining a register for the purpose of—
 (a) an application for, or for the modification of a licence;
 (b) complying with any condition of a licence; or
 (c) complying with a notice under section 71(2) below;
then, if the person furnishing it applies to the authority to have the information excluded from the register on the ground that it is commercially confidential (as regards himself or another person), the authority shall determine whether the information is or is not commercially confidential.

(3) A determination under subsection (2) above must be made within the period of 14 days beginning with the date of the application and if the authority fails to make a determination within that period it shall be treated as having determined that the information is commercially confidential.

(4) Where it appears to an authority maintaining a register that any information (other than information furnished in circumstances within subsection (2) above) which has been obtained by the authority under or by virtue of any provision of this Part might be commercially confidential, the authority shall—
 (a) give to the person to whom or whose business it relates notice that that information is required to be included in the register unless excluded under this section; and
 (b) give him a reasonable opportunity—
  (i) of objecting to the inclusion of the information on the grounds that it is commercially confidential; and
  (ii) of making representations to the authority for the purpose of justifying any such objection;
and, if any representations are made, the authority shall, having taken the representations into account, determine whether the information is or is not commercially confidential.

(5) Where, under subsection (2) or (4) above, an authority determines that information is not commercially confidential—
 (a) the information shall not be entered in the register until the end of the period of 21 days beginning with the date on which the determination is notified to the person concerned;
 (b) that person may appeal to the Secretary of State against the decision;
and, where an appeal is brought in respect of any information, the information shall not be entered in the register pending the final determination or withdrawal of the appeal.

(6) Subsections (2) and (8) of section 43 above shall apply in relation to appeals under subsection (5) above.

(7) The Secretary of State may give to the authorities maintaining registers directions as to specified information, or descriptions of information, which the public interest requires to be included in the registers notwithstanding that the information may be commercially confidential.

(8) Information excluded from a register shall be treated as ceasing to be commercially confidential for the purposes of this section at the expiry of the period of four years beginning with the date of the determination by virtue of which it was excluded; but the person who furnished it may apply to the authority for the information to remain excluded from the register on the ground that it is still commercially confidential and the authority shall determine whether or not that is the case.

(9) Subsections (5) and (6) above shall apply in relation to a determination under subsection (8) above as they apply in relation to a determination under subsection (2) or (4) above.

(10) The Secretary of State may, by order, substitute for the period for the time being specified in subsection (3) above such other period as he considers appropriate.

(11) Information is, for the purposes of any determination under this section, commercially confidential, in relation to any individual or person, if its being contained in the register would prejudice to an unreasonable degree the commercial interests of that individual or person.

DEFINITIONS
"licence": s.35(12).

COMMENCEMENT
Subsection (2): February 18, 1993 (S.I. 1993 No. 274). Remainder: no date has been set for commencement.

GENERAL NOTE
This section provides for the exclusion from the public registers kept under s.64 of information which is commercially confidential (as defined in subs. (11)) to an individual or business without their consent. As with the equivalent provision under Pt. I of the Act, s.22, the issue of confidentiality may be raised either by the person furnishing the information (subs. (2)) or by the authority maintaining the register (subs. (4)).

Again, as with registers under Pt. I, confidential information may be included if the Secretary of State so directs on the grounds that the public interest requires it (subs. (7)). Confidentiality lapses after four years and a new application will be necessary for continued exclusion (subs. (8)).

Annual reports

67.—(1) Each waste regulation authority shall, for each financial year of the authority, prepare and publish a report on the discharge by the authority of its functions under this Part or under any relevant instrument.

(2) A report under subsection (1) above shall include information as respects—
  (a) the licences respectively applied for, granted, in force, modified, revoked, suspended, surrendered or transferred during the year and the appeals made against decisions taken in respect of them;
  (b) the exercise by the authority of its powers under sections 42, 54, 61 or 62 of this Act or any relevant instrument;
  (c) the implementation of the authority's plan under section 50 above, with particular reference to recycling waste;
  (d) the number and description of prosecutions brought under this Part; and
  (e) the cost incurred, and the sums received, by the authority in discharging its functions under this Part.

(3) Each waste regulation authority shall—
  (a) arrange for the report for any year under subsection (1) above to be

published not later than the end of the period of six months following the end of the year to which the report relates; and

(b) when it publishes it, send a copy of the report to the Secretary of State.

(4) In subsections (1) and (2) above "relevant instrument" means any instrument under section 2(2) of the European Communities Act 1972 under which waste regulation authorities have functions.

DEFINITIONS
"licences": s.35(12).
"waste": s.75(2).

COMMENCEMENT
No date has been set.

GENERAL NOTE
This provision for annual reports on waste regulation functions is new. The aim is to make regulation authorities more publicly accountable and by so doing to raise the standards of waste regulation. It should be noted that the definition of "relevant instrument" in subs. (4) means that the reports will provide a means of monitoring performance in relation to relevant E.C. Directives.

Supervision and enforcement

Functions of Secretary of State and appointment etc. of inspectors

68.—(1) The Secretary of State shall have the function of keeping under review the discharge by waste regulation authorities of their functions under this Part.

(2) The Secretary of State may appoint as inspectors (under whatever title he may determine) such persons having suitable qualifications as he thinks necessary for assisting him in discharging his functions under this Part, and may terminate any appointment made under this subsection.

(3) Any waste regulation authority having functions under this Part may appoint as inspectors (under whatever title the authority may determine) such persons having suitable qualifications as the authority thinks necessary for carrying this Part into effect in the authority's area, and may terminate any appointment made under this subsection.

(4) An inspector shall not be liable in any civil or criminal proceedings for anything done in the purported performance of his functions under section 69 or 70 below if the court is satisfied that the act was done in good faith and that there were reasonable grounds for doing it.

(5) In the following provisions of this Part "inspector" means a person appointed as an inspector under subsection (2) or (3) above.

COMMENCEMENT
May 31, 1991 (S.I. 1991 No. 1319).

GENERAL NOTE
This section gives the Secretary of State the function of reviewing the discharge by waste regulation authorities of their functions under Pt. II of the Act. Inspectors may be appointed for that purpose under subs. (2) and this role will be fulfilled by HMIP regional offices (see *Hansard*, H.L. Vol. 520, col. 1121). The monitoring activities of HMIP over the period 1991/92 are described in its Annual Report.

By subs. (3) waste regulation authorities may appoint their own inspectors, who along with the Secretary of State's inspectors enjoy considerable statutory powers of entry and investigation.

Powers of entry etc. of inspectors

69.—(1) An inspector may, on production (if required) of his authority,

exercise any of the powers specified in subsection (3) below for the purpose of—
- (a) discharging any functions conferred or imposed by or under this Part on the Secretary of State or, as the case may be, a waste regulation authority or on the inspector;
- (b) determining whether, and if so in what manner, such a function should be discharged; or
- (c) determining whether any provision of this Part or of an instrument under it is being complied with.

(2) Those powers are exercisable in relation to—
- (a) land in or on which, or vessels in or by means of which, controlled waste is being or has been deposited, treated or disposed of;
- (b) land in or on which, or vessels in or by means of which, controlled waste is (on reasonable grounds) believed to be being, or to have been, deposited, treated, kept or disposed of;
- (c) land which is or is (on reasonable grounds) believed to be affected by the deposit, treatment, keeping or disposal of controlled waste on other land;

and in this section "premises" means any such land or any such vessel.

(3) The powers of an inspector referred to above are—
- (a) at any reasonable time (or, in a situation in which in his opinion there is an immediate risk of serious pollution of the environment or serious harm to human health, at any time) to enter premises which he has reason to believe it is necessary for him to enter;
- (b) on entering any premises by virtue of paragraph (a) above to take with him—
    - (i) any person duly authorised by the Secretary of State or, as the case may be, the waste regulation authority and, if the inspector has reasonable cause to apprehend any serious obstruction in the execution of his duty, a constable; and
    - (ii) any equipment or materials required for any purpose for which the power of entry is being exercised;
- (c) to make such examination and investigation as may in any circumstances be necessary;
- (d) as regards any premises which he has power to enter, to direct that those premises or any part of them, or anything in them, shall be left undisturbed (whether generally or in particular respects) for so long as is reasonably necessary for the purpose of any examination or investigation under paragraph (c) above;
- (e) to take such measurements and photographs and make such recordings as he considers necessary for the purpose of any examination or investigation under paragraph (c) above;
- (f) to take samples of any articles or substances found on any premises which he has power to enter, and of the air, water or land in, on, or in the vicinity of, the premises:
- (g) in the case of any article or substance found in any premises which he has power to enter, being an article or substance which appears to him to have caused or to be likely to cause pollution of the environment or harm to human health, to cause it to be dismantled or subjected to any process or test (but not so as to damage or destroy it unless this is necessary);
- (h) in the case of any such article or substance as is mentioned in paragraph (g) above, to take possession of it and detain it for so long as is necessary for all or any of the following purposes, namely—
    - (i) to examine it and do to it anything which he has power to do under that paragraph;
    - (ii) to ensure that it is not tampered with before his examination of it is completed;

(iii) to ensure that it is available for use as evidence in any proceedings under this Part;
(i) to require any person whom he has reasonable cause to believe to be able to give any information relevant to any examination or investigation under paragraph (c) above to answer (in the absence of persons other than a person nominated to be present and any persons whom the inspector may allow to be present) such questions as the inspector thinks fit to ask and to sign a declaration of the truth of his answers;
(j) to require the production of, or where the information is recorded in computerised form, the furnishing of extracts from, any records which are required to be kept under this Part or it is necessary for him to see for the purposes of an examination or investigation under paragraph (c) above and to inspect, and takes copies of, or of any entry in, the records;
(k) to require any person to afford him such facilities and assistance with respect to any matters or things within that person's control or in relation to which that person has responsibilities as are necessary to enable the inspector to exercise any of the powers conferred on him by this section.

(4) The Secretary of State may by regulations make provision as to the procedure to be followed in connection with the taking of, and the dealing with, samples under subsection (3)(f) above.

(5) Where an inspector proposes to exercise the power conferred by subsection (3)(g) above in the case of an article or substance found on any premises, he shall, if so requested by a person who at the time is present on and has responsibilities in relation to those premises, cause anything which is to be done by virtue of that power in the presence of that person.

(6) Before exercising the power conferred by subsection (3)(g) above in the case of any article or substance, an inspector shall consult such persons as appear to him appropriate for the purpose of ascertaining what dangers, if any, there may be in doing anything which he proposes to do under the power.

(7) Where under the power conferred by subsection (3)(h) above an inspector takes possession of any article of substance found on any premises, he shall leave there, either with a responsible person or, if that is impracticable, fixed in a conspicuous position, a notice giving particulars of that article or substance sufficient to identify it and stating that he has taken possession of it under that power; and before taking possession of any such substance under that power an inspector shall, if it is practical for him to do so, take a sample of it and give to a responsible person at the premises a portion of the sample marked in a manner sufficient to identify it.

(8) No answer given by a person in pursuance of a requirement imposed under subsection (3)(i) above shall be admissible in evidence in England and Wales against that person in any proceedings or in Scotland against that person in any criminal proceedings.

(9) Any person who—
(a) fails, without reasonable excuse, to comply with any requirement imposed under this section;
(b) prevents any other person from appearing before or from answering any question to which an inspector may by virtue of subsection (3) above require an answer; or
(c) intentionally obstructs an inspector in the exercise or performance of his powers or duties;
shall be liable, on summary conviction, to a fine not exceeding level 5 on the standard scale.

(10) The powers conferred by subsection (3)(a), (c), (e) and (f) above shall also be exercisable by any person authorised for the purpose in writing by the Secretary of State.

(11) Nothing in this section shall be taken to compel the production by any person of a document of which he would on grounds of legal professional privilege be entitled to withhold production on an order for discovery in an action in the High Court or, in relation to Scotland, on an order for the production of documents in an action in the Court of Session.

DEFINITIONS
"controlled waste": s.75(4).
"disposed of": s.29(6).
"harm": s.29(5).
"inspector": s.68(5).
"pollution of the environment": s.29(3).
"treated": s.29(6).

COMMENCEMENT
April 1, 1992 (S.I. 1991 No. 2829).

GENERAL NOTE
The section gives wide powers to inspectors appointed by the Secretary of State and by waste regulation authorities. These include powers of entry to land or vessels on which controlled waste is, or is reasonably believed to be, deposited, treated or disposed of (subs. (2)(a) and (b)) and land believed to be affected by the deposit, treatment or disposal of waste carried out on other land (subs. (2)(c)).

Subs. (11)
Legal professional privilege. This potentially very important exemption covers confidential communications passing between a client and his legal adviser and made for the purposes of obtaining or giving legal advice. Salaried legal advisers to companies are in the same position as an independent legal advisor: *Crompton (Alfred) Amusement Machines* v. *Commissioners of Customs and Excise Commissioners (No. 2)* [1974] A.C. 405. The privilege does not extend to communications with non-legal professional advisers. See also note to s.17(10), above.

Power to deal with cause of imminent danger of serious pollution etc.

70.—(1) Where, in the case of any article or substance found by him on any premises which he has power to enter, an inspector has reasonable cause to believe that, in the circumstances in which he finds it, the article or substance is a cause of imminent danger of serious pollution of the environment or serious harm to human health, he may seize it and cause it to be rendered harmless (whether by destruction or otherwise).

(2) Before there is rendered harmless under this section—
  (a) any article that forms part of a batch of similar articles; or
  (b) any substance,
the inspector shall, if it is practicable for him to do so, take a sample of it and give to a responsible person at the premises where the article or substance was found by him a portion of the sample marked in a manner sufficient to identify it.

(3) As soon as may be after any article or substance has been seized and rendered harmless under this section, the inspector shall prepare and sign a written report giving particulars of the circumstances in which the article or substance was seized and so dealt with by him, and shall—
  (a) give a signed copy of the report to a responsible person at the premises where the article or substance was found by him; and
  (b) unless that person is the owner of the article or substance, also serve a signed copy of the report on the owner;
and if, where paragraph (b) above applies, the inspector cannot after reasonable inquiry ascertain the name or address of the owner, the copy may be served on him by giving it to the person to whom a copy was given under paragraph (a) above.

(4) Any person who intentionally obstructs an inspector in the exercise of his powers under this section shall be liable—

(a) on summary conviction, to a fine not exceeding the statutory maximum;
(b) on conviction on indictment, to a fine or to imprisonment for a term not exceeding two years, or to both.

DEFINITIONS
"harm": s.29(5).
"harmless": s.29(5).
"inspector": s.68(3).
"pollution of the environment": s.29(3).
"substance": s.29(11).

COMMENCEMENT
April 1, 1992 (S.I. 1991 No. 2829).

GENERAL NOTE
This section gives additional powers to seize and render harmless substances or articles which constitute a source of imminent danger of serious pollution of the environment or serious harm to human health.

Obtaining of information from persons and authorities

71.—(1) For the purpose of the discharge of his functions under this Part, the Secretary of State may, by notice in writing served on a waste regulation authority, require the authority to furnish such information about the discharge of its functions under this Part as he may require.

(2) For the purpose of the discharge of their respective functions under this Part—
(a) the Secretary of State, and
(b) a waste regulation authority,

may, by notice in writing served on him, require any person to furnish such information specified in the notice as the Secretary of State or the authority, as the case may be, reasonably considers he or it needs, in such form and within such period following service of the notice as is so specified.

(3) A person who—
(a) fails, without reasonable excuse, to comply with a requirement imposed under subsection (2) above; or
(b) in furnishing any information in compliance with such a requirement, makes any statement which he knows to be false or misleading in a material particular, or recklessly makes a statement which is false or misleading in a material particular;

shall be liable—
   (i) on summary conviction, to a fine not exceeding the statutory maximum;
   (ii) on conviction on indictment, to a fine or to imprisonment for a term not exceeding two years, or to both.

COMMENCEMENT
May 31, 1991 (S.I. 1991 No. 1319).

GENERAL NOTE
Subsection (1) gives the Secretary of State power to require waste regulation authorities to furnish information about the discharge of their functions.
Subsection (2) gives power to the Secretary of State and waste regulation authorities to require any person to furnish information that the Secretary of State or authority reasonably consider they need.
Subsection (3): The statutory maximum is currently £5,000.

Default powers of Secretary of State

72.—(1) If the Secretary of State is satisfied that a waste regulation authority has failed, in any respect, to discharge any function under this Part which it ought to have discharged, he may make an order declaring the authority to be in default.

(2) The failure to discharge any such function may be a failure in a class of case to which the function relates or a failure in a particular case.

(3) An order made under subsection (1) above which declares an authority to be in default may, for the purpose of remedying the default, direct the authority ("the defaulting authority") to perform any function specified in the order (whether in relation to a class of case or a particular case) and may specify the manner in which and the time or times within which the function is to be performed by the authority.

(4) If the defaulting authority fails to comply with any direction contained in such an order the Secretary of State may, instead of enforcing the order by mandamus, make an order transferring to himself any function of the authority specified in the order, whether in relation to all the classes of case to which the function relates or to such of those classes or, as the case may be, such particular case as is specified in the order.

(5) Where any function of a defaulting authority if transferred under subsection (4) above, the amount of any expenses which the Secretary of State certifies were incurred by him in performing the function shall on demand be paid to him by the defaulting authority.

(6) Any expenses required to be paid by a defaulting authority under subsection (5) above shall be defrayed by the authority in like manner, and shall be debited to the like account, as if the functions had not been transferred and the expenses had been incurred by the authority in performing them.

(7) The Secretary of State may by order vary or revoke any order previously made by him under this section.

(8) An order transferring any functions of a defaulting authority may provide for the transfer to the Secretary of State of such of the property, rights, liabilities and obligations of the authority as he considers appropriate; and where such an order is revoked the Secretary of State may, by the revoking order or a subsequent order, make such provisions as he considers appropriate with respect to the property, rights, liabilities and obligations held by him for the purposes of the transferred function.

(9) Any order under this section may include such incidental, supplemental and transitional provisions as the Secretary of State considers appropriate.

(10) This section shall not apply to Scotland.

COMMENCEMENT
May 31, 1991 (S.I. 1991 No. 1319).

GENERAL NOTE
This section provides the means by which the Secretary of State may secure that waste regulation authorities discharge their functions properly. The procedure is by way of default order (subs. (3)), with the further remedy of either: (a) enforcing the order by writ of mandamus; or (b) transferring the functions of the defaulting authority to the Secretary of State (subs. (4)).

Scotland
The section does not apply to Scotland (subs. (10)).

Supplemental

Appeals and other provisions relating to legal proceedings and civil liability

73.—(1) An appeal against any decision of a magistrates' court under this Part (other than a decision made in criminal proceedings) shall lie to the Crown Court at the instance of any party to the proceedings in which the decision was given if such an appeal does not lie to the Crown Court by virtue of any other enactment.

(2) In Scotland an appeal against any decision of the sheriff under this Part (other than a decision made in criminal proceedings) shall lie to the Court of Session at the instance of any party to the proceedings in which the decision was given if such an appeal does not lie to the Court of Session by virtue of any other enactment.

(3) Where a person appeals to the Crown Court or the Court of Session against a decision of a magistrates' court or the sheriff dismissing an appeal against any requirement imposed under this Part which was suspended pending determination of that appeal, the requirement shall again be suspended pending the determination of the appeal to the Crown Court or Court of Session.

(4) Where an appeal against a decision of any authority lies to a magistrates' court or to the sheriff by virtue of any provision of this Part, it shall be the duty of the authority to include in any document by which it notifies the decision to the person concerned a statement indicating that such an appeal lies and specifying the time within which it must be brought.

(5) Where on an appeal to any court against or arising out of a decision of any authority under this Part the court varies or reverses the decision it shall be the duty of the authority to act in accordance with the court's decision.

(6) Where any damage is caused by waste which has been deposited in or on land, any person who deposited it, or knowingly caused or knowingly permitted it to be deposited, in either case so as to commit an offence under section 33(1) or 63(2) above, is liable for the damage except where the damage—
 (a) was due wholly to the fault of the person who suffered it; or
 (b) was suffered by a person who voluntarily accepted the risk of the damage being caused;
but without prejudice to any liability arising otherwise than under this subsection.

(7) The matters which may be proved by way of defence under section 33(7) above may be proved also by way of defence to an action brought under subsection (6) above.

(8) In subsection (6) above—
 "damage" includes the death of, or injury to, any person (including any disease and any impairment of physical or mental condition); and
 "fault" has the same meaning as in the Law Reform (Contributory Negligence) Act 1945.

(9) For the purposes of the following enactments—
 (a) the Fatal Accidents Act 1976;
 (b) the Law Reform (Contributory Negligence) Act 1945; and
 (c) the Limitation Act 1980;
and for the purposes of any action of damages in Scotland arising out of the death of, or personal injury to, any person, any damage for which a person is liable under subsection (6) above shall be treated as due to his fault.

DEFINITIONS
 "deposited": s.29(6).
 "waste": s.75(2).

COMMENCEMENT
 Subsections (1)–(5): April 1, 1992 (S.I. 1992 No. 266). Remainder: not yet in force.

GENERAL NOTE
 Appeals from decisions of magistrates' and sheriff's courts. Subsections (1)–(5) deal with appeals from decisions of magistrates' and sheriff courts made under Pt. II of the Act other than

in criminal proceedings. Appeal lies to the Crown Court or, in Scotland, the Court of Session. The relevant decisions that may be appealed against in this way are : (1) provision of receptacles for collection of waste (s.46(7)); (2) provision of receptacles for collection of commercial or industrial waste (s.47(7)); and (3) requirements to remove waste deposited on land (s.59(2)).

Civil liability. Subsections (6)–(9) deal with civil liability for damage caused by waste deposited on land without a licence, in contravention of licence conditions, or in breach of s.63(2). "Damage," as well as damage to property, includes death or personal injury or impairment (subs. (8)). These provisions should be read in the light of emerging E.C. proposals for a Directive on *Strict Civil Liability for Damage Caused by Waste* which in some respects would go much further than subss. (6)–(9).

Meaning of "fit and proper person"

74.—(1) The following provisions apply for the purposes of the discharge by a waste regulation authority of any function under this Part which requires the authority to determine whether a person is or is not a fit and proper person to hold a waste management licence.

(2) Whether a person is or is not a fit and proper person to hold a licence is to be determined by reference to the carrying on by him of the activities which are or are to be authorised by the licence and the fulfilment of the requirements of the licence.

(3) Subject to subsection (4) below, a person shall be treated as not being a fit and proper person if it appears to the authority—
   (a) that he or another relevant person has been convicted of a relevant offence;
   (b) that the management of the activities which are or are to be authorised by the licence are not or will not be in the hands of a technically competent person; or
   (c) that the person who holds or is to hold the licence has not made and either has no intention of making or is in no position to make financial provision adequate to discharge the obligations arising from the licence.

(4) The authority may, if it considers it proper to do so in any particular case, treat a person as a fit and proper person notwithstanding that subsection (3)(a) above applies in his case.

(5) It shall be the duty of waste regulation authorities to have regard to any guidance issued to them by the Secretary of State with respect to the discharge of their functions of making the determinations to which this section applies.

(6) The Secretary of State may, by regulations, prescribe the offences that are relevant for the purposes of subsection (3)(a) above and the qualifications and experience required of a person for the purposes of subsection (3)(b) above.

(7) For the purposes of subsection (3)(a) above, another relevant person shall be treated, in relation to the licence holder or proposed licence holder, as the case may be, as having been convicted of a relevant offence if—
   (a) any person has been convicted of a relevant offence committed by him in the course of his employment by the holder or, as the case may be the proposed holder of the licence or in the course of the carrying on of any business by a partnership one of the members of which was the holder or, as the case may be, the proposed holder of the licence;
   (b) a body corporate has been convicted of a relevant offence committed when the holder or, as the case may be, the proposed holder of the licence was a director, manager, secretary or other similar officer of that body corporate; or
   (c) where the holder or, as the case may be, the proposed holder of the licence is a body corporate, a person who is a director, manager, secretary or other similar officer of that body corporate—

(i) has been convicted of a relevant offence; or
(ii) was a director, manager, secretary or other similar officer of another body corporate at a time when a relevant offence for which that other body corporate has been convicted was committed.

COMMENCEMENT
Subsection (6): February 18, 1993 (S.I. 1993 No. 274). Remainder: no date has been set for commencement.

GENERAL NOTE
This extremely important section expands on the meaning of "fit and proper person" for the purposes of s.36. Under s.36 a waste regulation authority "shall not reject the application [for a waste management licence] if it is satisfied that the applicant is a fit and proper person unless it is satisfied that its rejection is necessary for [one or other of a number of specified purposes]." It follows therefore that an authority may reject a licence application on the ground that it is not satisfied that the applicant is a fit and proper person. There are three circumstances where the applicant shall be treated as not being a fit and proper person (s.74(3)). These are: (a) the applicant or a "relevant person" has been convicted of a "relevant offence"; (b) the management of the licensed activities is not or will not be in the hands of a technically competent person; and (c) the applicant has not made and has not the intention or means of making adequate financial provision to discharge the obligations arising from the licence.

In addition to the grant of licences, the concept of "fit and proper person" is also relevant to s.38 on the revocation and suspension of licences (see s.38(1)(a), (2) and (6)(a) and notes thereto).

The concept can be traced back to various calls for greater discrimination in the grant of waste licences; see for example the Eleventh Report on the Royal Commission on Environmental Pollution, *Managing Waste: the Duty of Care* (Cm. 9675, December 1985) at para. 8.41. Similarly, in his address to the 92nd Annual Conference of the Institute of Wastes Management (June 12, 1990) Lord Gregson put the position prior to the Act as follows:

"At present any person irrespective of their competence, knowledge or training or their financial or personal profit can set themselves up as waste managers. This is an absurd and dangerous situation to be in."

The present provisions have evolved through various Government announcements and consultation papers including Pollution Paper No. 24 (July 1986), Consultation Paper on *Waste Disposal Law: Amendments* (September 1986) and Paper on *Decisions following Public Consultations* (June 1988).

General considerations
It is clear that consideration of whether an applicant or licence-holder is fit and proper is to be made in the context of the activities authorised or to be authorised by the licence, and the fulfilment of the requirements of the licence (subs. (2)). Subs. (3) gives three instances where a person is to be treated as not being fit and proper, subject to the discretion of the authority to treat him as being so in one case (subs. (4)). However, it is questionable whether these three instances are exhaustive of the cases which can justify concluding a person not to be fit and proper, and there may be other factors that are of relevance to whether it is proper to grant a licence to a specific applicant. In any event, it seems clear that the authority must apply its mind in each case to the particular circumstances and may not fetter its discretion by applying general rules in a hard-and-fast way: see *R.* v. *Holborn Licensing Justices,* ex p. *Stratford Catering Company* (1927) 136 L.T. 278.

The Secretary of State may issue guidance to waste regulation authorities in making the relevant determinations, and such guidance will be crucial to achieving national consistency. The guidance is contained in Chap. 3 of the draft Waste Management Paper No. 4, *Licensing of Waste Facilities*. In January 1993 the DoE issued a revised draft of Chap. 3 following the responses to an earlier consultation in August 1992.

Relevant offence
Conviction of a relevant offence means that the offender will not be a fit and proper person, unless the authority considers it proper to treat the offender as fit and proper under subs. (4), notwithstanding the conviction. The offences that are "relevant" for this purpose are prescribed in Regulations made under subs. (6). The relevant provision is made by the draft Waste

Management Licensing Regulations, reg. 6, which specifies not only offences relating to waste but also a number of other pollution offences, as follows:
  (a) Public Health (Scotland) Act 1897, s.22;
  (b) Public Health Act 1936, s.95(1);
  (c) Control of Pollution Act 1974, ss.3, 5(6), 16(4), 18(2), 31(1), 32(1), 34(5), 78, 92(6) or 93(3);
  (d) Refuse Disposal (Amenity) Act 1978, s.2;
  (e) Control of Pollution (Special Waste) Regulations 1980;
  (f) Food and Environmental Protection Act 1985, s.9(1);
  (g) Transfrontier Shipment of Hazardous Waste Regulations 1988;
  (h) Merchant Shipping (Prevention of Pollution by Garbage) Regulations 1988;
  (i) Control of Pollution (Amendment) Act 1989, ss.1, 5, 6(9) or 7(3);
  (j) Water Act 1989, ss.107, 118(4) or 175(1);
  (k) Environmental Protection Act 1990, ss.23(1), 33, 34(6), 44, 47(6), 57(5), 59(5), 63(2), 69(9), 70(4), 71(3) or 80(4);
  (l) Water Resources Act 1991, ss.85, 202(4) or 206.

It should be noted that relevant convictions are not limited to those relating to incidents at the site in question. Thus in the case of a company operating a number of sites, a conviction in respect of any of those sites would potentially affect the position of the company as a fit and proper person in relation to the other sites. It may be, therefore, that waste companies will tend increasingly to separate out operations at different sites between different companies. Whilst common directors of the companies could result in conviction of one company affecting the position of others (see below), control of shares in the companies, or the fact that they are part of the same group, would not appear to have that effect under the legislation.

As to the significance of such offences, see below.

Relevant person

Subsection (7) contains complex provisions as to the persons who are "relevant" in that their convictions are imputed to the applicant or licence-holder. Broadly, the categories are:
  (a) employees of the applicant or licence-holder where the offence was committed in the course of their employment (subs. (7)(a));
  (b) business partners of the applicant or licence-holder where the offence was committed in the course of the partnership business (subs. (7)(a));
  (c) companies, where the offence was committed at a time where the applicant or licence-holder was a director, manager, secretary or other similar officer (subs. (7)(b));
  (d) directors, managers, secretaries and other similar officers of the applicant company or licence-holding company who were convicted of a relevant offence at any time (subs. (7)(c)(i)); and
  (e) directors, managers, secretaries and other similar officers of the applicant company or licence-holding company, where they held one or other of those offices in another company at a time when an offence was committed for which the company was convicted (subs. (7)(c)(ii)).

Whilst similar to the categories of "relevant person" in s.3(5) of the Control of Pollution (Amendment) Act 1989 (relating to registration of waste carriers), there is one important difference. Section 3(6) of the 1989 Act provides that the authority shall have regard to the degree of complicity of the applicant or carrier in the offence, if the offence was committed by some other relevant person. No such provision appears in s.74, though it would still appear to be a relevant consideration.

Spent convictions

The Rehabilitation of Offenders Act 1974 would not be of assistance in the majority of likely situations, since it applies only to convictions of individuals, and not companies. However, para. 3.7 of the draft Waste Management Paper No. 4 suggests that where the person convicted of the offence is a company the authority should normally have regard to whether the conviction would have become spent if committed by an individual.

Disregard of conviction

Subsection (4) allows an authority to treat a person as fit and proper despite a conviction or convictions of him or of a relevant person. Draft paras. 3.3–3.8 provide guidance as to the factors which an authority should take into account in reaching that decision. Three factors are relevant:
  (a) Whether it was the applicant/licence-holder or another relevant person who was convicted (despite any express provision to that effect as in the Control of Pollution

(Amendment) Act 1989). Different considerations may apply as between individuals, companies and partnerships.
(b) The nature and gravity of the relevant offences—whether they involved controlled or special waste, whether they caused serious pollution, and the penalty imposed.
(c) The number of relevant offences.

Technical competence

By subs. (3)(b) a person will be treated as not being fit and proper if the management of the licensed activities is not or will not be "in the hands of a technically competent person." The Secretary of State may, by regulations, prescribe the requisite qualifications and experience necessary to attain technical competence.

The criteria for technical competence were considered by the Waste Management Industry Training and Advisory Board (WAMITAB), a company limited by guarantee and founded by the Institute of Wastes Management, the National Association of Waste Disposal Contractors and the Road Haulage Association; an agreed programme for developing the qualification was drawn up and an agreement commencing on October 1, 1990 was entered into between the DoE and WAMITAB (see *Hansard*, H.L. Vol. 522, col. 290).

This work largely formed the basis of the provisions contained in reg. 7 of the draft Waste Management Licensing Regulations.

Under this provision, a person is technically competent in relation to the types of facility listed at Table 1 to the regulation if they hold the certificate of technical competence appropriate to that type of facility awarded by WAMITAB. Types of facilities are categorised by reference to their general nature (*e.g.* landfill, treatment, transfer, civic amenity) and by reference to the type of waste dealt with. Three main types of certificate, with different levels, are referred to, *i.e.* managing landfill sites, managing treatment plants, and managing civic amenity sites.

Technical competence: transitional provisions

WAMITAB proposed "grandfather rights" for those with five years' or more relevant experience and introduction of the scheme on a voluntary basis with the aim of ensuring sufficient qualified managers in place to implement the scheme and relevant provisions by what was then the target date for implementation, April 1, 1992.

Regulation 8 of the draft Waste Management Licensing Regulations in fact provides for more limited transitional provisions. Regulation 8(1) allows facility managers to register with WAMITAB as an applicant for a certificate by April 1, 1993 and to be treated as technically competent until April 1, 1998 in relation to the type of facility for which they were manager at any time in the period April 1, 1992 to March 31, 1993. This provision has been overtaken by the fact that the regulations did not come into force on April 1, 1993 and new dates will need to be specified.

Regulation 8(2) makes limited provision for "grandfather rights" in that a person aged 55 or over on April 1, 1993, who in the previous 10 years has had at least five years' experience as the manager of a facility, will be treated as technically competent in relation to that type of facility until April 1, 2003.

Technical competence: guidance

Guidance as to technical competence is contained at paras. 3.9–3.42 of the draft Waste Management Paper No. 4, *The Licensing of Waste Facilities*.

This suggests that the technically competent manager (TCM) will be the person responsible for the proper management of the site and should normally be expected to be present on the site during the working day to control operations and make management decisions (paras. 3.11 and 3.17); absences and changes of personnel should be notified to the waste regulation authority. Paragraph 3.15 suggests that acceptance of a new TCM should be permitted without written WRA approval (*i.e.* negative approval rather than positive confirmation). For larger, more complex operations, or continuous operations, an operator should designate more than one TCM and the authority should accept a reasonable number of duplicating and deputising TCMs (para. 3.18). It is also suggested that the decisions taken by the TCM should not be capable of being overruled (for example on cost grounds) where this would compromise the competent management of the site (para. 3.19). Normally the authority should expect there to be at least one TCM per site allocated on a full-time basis (para. 3.21). The Working Plan should contain a list of the current TCMs (para. 3.23).

Sites outwith the WAMITAB Scheme

Some sites will not be covered by the WAMITAB scheme for certificates of technical competence, *e.g.* small sites and scrap metal sites. Here the waste regulation authority will need to make an individual assessment of the TCM's fitness based on formal qualifications and experience: this should not involve the authority in accepting a lower standard of operation (draft Waste Management Paper 4, paras. 3.27 and 3.30). The draft Waste Management Paper suggests some of the types of qualification that may be acceptable and provides specific guidance for sites of less than 50,000 cubic metres taking small amounts of waste and for scrap metal facilities (paras. 3.35–3.42).

Adequate financial provision
By subs. (3)(c) the authority must consider whether the applicant or licence holder has made, has the intention of making, and is in a position to make, "financial provision adequate to discharge the operations arising from the licence." Subs. (6) does not give power to make Regulations as to what constitutes adequate financial provision, but guidance is given under subs. (5) by way of the draft Waste Management Paper No. 4, paras. 3.43–3.71.

Unlike relevant offences and technical competence, adequate financial provision is not a matter which needs to be kept under review as a possible basis for revocation or suspension of a licence: however, in the circumstances of an individual licence it will usually be appropriate to include a condition specifying the maintenance of an appropriate form of financial cover (draft Waste Management Paper No. 4, para. 3.43).

The DoE's guidance is that assessment of financial capability needs to be closely related to the various stages of a licensed operation and to the terms of the licence, for which provision is to be made. An initial financial appraisal by way of general enquiries and audited accounts might well be appropriate especially for smaller operations without a proven track record (para. 3.46).

Financial provision: landfill operations
The DoE suggests that four major difficulties may arise in relation to landfill site operations (draft Waste Management Paper No. 4, para. 3.47):
(a) working risks to life, limb and property as may arise in any industrial operation;
(b) technical operational risks such as litter, odour, infestation and nuisance;
(c) short-term hazards relating to spillages, leaks or inappropriate mixing of wastes; and
(d) environmental hazards associated and escape of polluting leachate or migration of gas.
These risks need to be addressed through the four stages of:
(a) site acquisition and preparation;
(b) site operation;
(c) restoration and landscaping or aftercare; and
(d) post closure control and monitoring.

Guidance is provided by paras. 3.50–3.64 as to possible appropriate financial mechanisms for each of these stages, such as insurance, self insurance, guarantees, provision for contingent liabilities, charges on assets, bonds and escrow accounts.

The possibility remains open of a suitable mutual scheme being agreed to provide joint protection (for example, the scheme considered by the National Association of Waste Disposal Contractors). The guidance suggests that any such scheme would need to be clear and binding in order to ensure the build-up of sufficient reserves. The requirements of the proposed E.C. Directive on Landfill (COM (91) 102) as to financial guarantees for closure and aftercare (Art. 17) and a landfill aftercare fund or funds (Art. 18) are also relevant.

See also the Report of the DoE Working Group on *Financial Guarantees against Environmental Damage in the Waste Management Industry (1991)*.

Financial provision: other sites
Paragraphs 3.65–3.71 of the draft Waste Management Paper No. 4 contains guidance as to the issue of financial provision for non-landfill sites, incineration, waste treatment and transfer facilities. Relevant to these type of facilities is the fact that greater investment in plant and equipment will be required than for landfill. The authority will need to consider the type of equipment needed, though it should not be necessary to go into great detail: the best course is simply to require inspection of equipment before operations can begin (para. 3.69). Long term consequences of operation, such as soil contamination, need to be considered, together with the use of the mechanisms to provide for clean-up on the analogy with landfill site restoration (para. 3.71).

Meaning of "waste" and household, commercial and industrial waste and special waste

75.—(1) The following provisions apply for the interpretation of this Part.
(2) "Waste" includes—

(a) any substance which constitutes a scrap material or an effluent or other unwanted surplus substance arising from the application of any process; and
(b) any substance or article which requires to be disposed of as being broken, worn out, contaminated or otherwise spoiled;

but does not include a substance which is an explosive within the meaning of the Explosives Act 1875.

(3) Any thing which is discarded or otherwise dealt with as if it were waste shall be presumed to be waste unless the contrary is proved.

(4) "Controlled waste" means household, industrial and commercial waste or any such waste.

(5) Subject to subsection (8) below, "household waste" means waste from—
(a) domestic property, that is to say, a building or self-contained part of a building which is used wholly for the purposes of living accommodation;
(b) a caravan (as defined in section 29(1) of the Caravan Sites and Control of Development Act 1960) which usually and for the time being is situated on a caravan site (within the meaning of that Act);
(c) a residential home;
(d) premises forming part of a university or school or other educational establishment;
(e) premises forming part of a hospital or nursing home.

(6) Subject to subsection (8) below, "industrial waste" means waste from any of the following premises—
(a) any factory (within the meaning of the Factories Act 1961);
(b) any premises used for the purposes of, or in connection with, the provision to the public of transport services by land, water or air;
(c) any premises used for the purposes of, or in connection with, the supply to the public of gas, water or electricity or the provision of sewerage services; or
(d) any premises used for the purposes of, or in connection with, the provision to the public of postal or telecommunications services.

(7) Subject to subsection (8) below, "commercial waste" means waste from premises used wholly or mainly for the purposes of a trade or business or the purposes of sport, recreation or entertainment excluding—
(a) household waste;
(b) industrial waste;
(c) waste from any mine or quarry and waste from premises used for agriculture within the meaning of the Agriculture Act 1947 or, in Scotland, the Agriculture (Scotland) Act 1948; and
(d) waste of any other description prescribed by regulations made by the Secretary of State for the purposes of this paragraph.

(8) Regulations made by the Secretary of State may provide that waste of a description prescribed in the regulations shall be treated for the purposes of provisions of this Part prescribed in the regulations as being or not being household waste or industrial waste or commercial waste; but no regulations shall be made in respect of such waste as is mentioned in subsection (7)(c) above and references to waste in subsection (7) above and this subsection do not include sewage (including matter in or from a privy) except so far as the regulations provide otherwise.

(9) "Special waste" means controlled waste as respects which regulations are in force under section 62 above.

DEFINITIONS
"substance": s.29(11).

COMMENCEMENT
Not yet in force.

Subss. (2) and (3)
Definition of "waste". The term is given a wide definition, though as is pointed out by para. 12 of Circ. 14/92, *The Environmental Protection Act 1990—Parts II and IV; The Controlled Waste Regulations 1992* (Welsh Office 30/92, Scottish Office 24/92) it is not an exhaustive definition. It includes within the ordinary meaning of the word waste certain substances, materials and articles about which there might otherwise have been doubt. The starting point is therefore the ordinary and natural meaning of the term "waste", subject to the gloss provided by subs. (2) and the presumption of subs. (3) which applies to material discarded or otherwise dealt with as if it were waste.

In considering the meaning of "waste" within the context of s.30 of the Control of Pollution Act 1974 (framed in identical terms) the courts have taken the view that waste is defined by reference to the point of view of the person producing or discarding it. On that basis the fact that material may have a use or value to the person removing or receiving it will not of itself prevent the material being waste. The three judicial decisions to that effect are referred to at paras. 14–17 of Circ. 14/92: *Long* v. *Brooke* [1980] Crim.L.R. 109; *Berridge Incinerators* v. *Nottinghamshire County Council* (1987, unrep.); *Kent County Council* v. *Queensborough Rolling Mill Co. Ltd.* (1990) 154 J.P. 530. A similar approach has been adopted in relation to Town and Country Planning legislation: *R.* v. *Rotherham Metropolitan Borough Council*, ex p. *Rankin* [1990] 1 P.L.R. 93, citing also *Charles Neil Ashcroft* v. *Michael McErlain Ltd.* (Divisional Court, January 30, 1985).

Paragraph 17 of Circ. 14/92 suggests that waste authorities may find it helpful to consider a series of questions from the point of view of the person producing or discarding the material in question:
(a) Is it what would ordinarily be described as a waste?
(b) Is it a scrap metal?
(c) Is it an effluent or other unwanted surplus substance arising from the application of any process?
(d) Does it require to be disposed of as broken, worn out, contaminated or otherwise spoiled?
(e) Is it being discarded or otherwise dealt with as if it were waste?

If the answer to any of these questions is "yes," the Circular suggests, the material should be considered to be waste. Despite this guidance, application of the law to specific facts may present some difficult questions: in particular the distinction between a by-product and a waste, suggested by Deputy Judge P. J. Crawford Q.C. in the *Berridge* case, may be a difficult one in practice.

E.C. law
The early Directives on waste, 75/442/EEC (the waste framework directive) and 78/319/EEC (the hazardous waste directive), defined waste as meaning: "any substance or object which the holder disposes of or is required to dispose of pursuant to the provisions of the national law in force." Circular 4/92 (paras. 5–8 and Annex 7) refers to the decisions of the European Court of Justice in joined cases C–206/88 and C–207/88 (*Vessoso* and *Zanetti* [1990] 2 L.M.E.L.R. 133) and case C–359/88 (*Zanetti* and others). The decision in C–206/88 and C–207/88 was that these E.C. definitions of waste did not exclude substances or objects capable of economic re-utilisation; it was also held that the intention of the holder to exclude all economic re-utilisation by others is not a necessary component of the definition. The European Court held in case C–359/88 that national legislation which defines waste so as to exclude substances or objects capable of economic re-utilisation is not compatible with Directives 75/442 and 78/319.

Directive 91/156/EEC, amending 75/442 defines waste by reference to a list of categories Q1–Q16 at Annex I of the Directive; any substance or object in those categories which the holder discards or intends or is required to discard is within the definition. The "holder" is defined as the producer of the waste or the natural or legal person who is in possession of it. The categories of Annex I are as follows:

Q1   Production or consumption residues not otherwise specified
Q2   Off-specification products
Q3   Products whose date for appropriate use has expired
Q4   Materials spilled, lost or having undergone other mishap, including any materials, equipment, etc. contaminated as a result of the mishap
Q5   Materials contaminated or soiled as a result of planned actions (*e.g.* residues from cleaning operations, packing materials, containers, etc.)
Q6   Unusable parts (*e.g.* reject batteries, exhausted catalysts, etc.)
Q7   Substances which no longer perform satisfactorily (*e.g.* contaminated acids, contaminated solvents, exhausted tempering salts, etc.)

Q8   Residues of industrial processes (*e.g.* slags, still bottoms, etc.)
Q9   Residues from pollution abatement processes (*e.g.* scrabber sludges, baghouse dusts, spent filters, etc.)
Q10 Machining/finishing residues (*e.g.* lathe turnings, mill scales, etc.)
Q11 Residues from raw materials extraction and processing (*e.g.* mining residues, oil field slops, etc.)
Q12 Adulterated materials (*e.g.* oils contaminated with PCBs, etc.)
Q13 Any materials, substances or products whose use has been banned by law
Q14 Products for which the holder has no further use (*e.g.* agricultural, household, office, commercial and shop discards, etc.)
Q15 Contaminated materials, substances or products resulting from remedial action with respect to land
Q16 Any materials, substances or products which are not contained in the above categories.

Whilst category Q16 is clearly so extensive as to call into question the usefulness of the efforts to define categories Q1–Q15, the intention behind the categorisation is to provide a common terminology whilst avoiding the escape of materials from control by failure to fall within any particular category. Article 1(a) of the Directive requires the Commission, not later than April 1, 1993 to draw up a list of wastes within those categories; the list is to be periodically reviewed and, if necessary, revised. The requirements of the Directive have influenced the UK government in its approach to the definition of controlled waste (see below).

The E.C. categorisation scheme may be contrasted with that contained in the Basel Convention on the *Control of Transboundary Movements of Hazardous Wastes and Their Disposal* (1984) Annexes I and II.

Subs. (2)
Explosives. Substances which are explosives within the meaning of the Explosives Act 1875 are not included within the definition of waste. The term is defined by s.3 of the 1875 Act to mean:

"(1) Gunpowder, nitro-glycerine, dynamite, gun-cotton, blasting powders, fulminate of mercury or other metals, coloured fires, and every other substance, whether similar to those above mentioned or not, used or manufactured with a view to produce a practical effect by explosion or a pyrotechnic effect; and
(2) includes fog-signals, fireworks, fuses, rockets, percussion caps, detonators, cartridges, ammunition of all descriptions, and every adaptation or preparation of an explosive as above defined."

By s.104 of the 1875 Act, any substance appearing to be specially dangerous to life or property by reason either of its explosive properties or of any such properties in its manufacturing processes, may be declared to be an explosive by Order in Council.

However, Directive 91/156/EEC excludes from the scope of the Directive only "decommissioned explosives" (Art. 2.1(b)(v)) and where they are covered by other legislation.

Subs. (4)
Controlled waste. The three categories of controlled waste are defined in subss. (5)–(7) and by the Controlled Waste Regulations 1992 (S.I. 1992 No. 588) and the draft Waste Management Licensing Regulations 1993. The Controlled Waste Regulations are explained in Circ. 14/92 (Welsh Office 30/92; Scottish Office 24/92).

Subs. (5)
Household waste. The primary definition of household waste is contained in subs. (5) but in addition waste of the descriptions set out in Sched. 1 to the Controlled Waste Regulations 1992 is to be treated as household waste. These are waste from:
(a) a hereditament on premises exempted from local non-domestic voting;
(b) premises occupied by a charity and wholly or mainly used for charitable purposes;
(c) any land belonging to or used in connection with domestic property, a caravan or a residential home;
(d) a private garage which either has a floor area of $25m^2$ or less or is used wholly or mainly for the accommodation of a private motor vehicle;
(e) storage premises used wholly or mainly for the storage of articles of domestic use;
(f) moored vessel used wholly for the purposes of living accommodation;
(g) a camp site;
(h) a prison or other penal institution;

(i) a hall, or other premises used wholly or mainly for public meetings;
(j) a royal palace;
(k) arising from the discharge by a local authority of its duty under s.89(2) (duty to keep roads and highways clean).

Two categories of waste are treated as household waste for the purposes of the exemption from the duty of care under s.34(2) but for no other purpose: Controlled Waste Regulations 1992, reg. 2(2). These are:

(a) waste arising from works of construction or demolition, including preparatory works;
(b) septic tank sludge.

Domestic property. The building or the self-contained part of a building in question must be used wholly for the purposes of living accommodation; mixed use buildings would therefore be excluded in the absence of a self-contained domestic part.

Caravan. The terms "caravan" and "caravan site" are defined in the Caravan Sites and Control of Development Act 1960, s.29(1) as follows:

"any structure designed or adapted for human habitation which is capable of being moved from one place to another (whether by being towed, or by being transported on a motor vehicle or trailer) and any motor vehicle so designed or adapted, but does not include:
(a) any railway rolling-stock which is for the time being on rails forming part of a railway system, or
(b) any tent."

The express reference to caravans should avoid some of the difficulties encountered in *Gordon* v. *Kirkcaldy District Council* 1990 S.C.L.R. 104 (Court of Session) as to whether a caravan can be described as a dwelling-house. See also on the meaning of "caravan" *Wyre Forest District Council* v. *Secretary of State for the Environment* [1990] 2 W.L.R. 517 (H.L.).

By reg. 3 of the Controlled Waste Regulations 1992 certain types of waste are excluded from the definition of household waste so as not to fall within the exemption from waste management licensing for household waste from domestic property disposed of within the curtilage of the dwelling. These are:

(a) mineral or synthetic oil or grease;
(b) asbestos;
(c) clinical waste.

By reg. 3(2) scrap metal is not to be treated as household waste for the purposes of the s.34 duty of care at any time before the waste management licensing Provisions of Pt. II of the EPA 1990 come into effect.

Subs. (6)
Industrial waste

Waste from a factory. An extended definition of "factory" is provided by s.175 of the Factories Act 1961:

"(1) Subject to the provisions of this section, the expression 'factory' means any premises in which, or within the close or curtilage or precincts of which, persons are employed in manual labour in any process for or incidental to any of the following purposes, namely:
(a) the making of any article or of part of any article; or
(b) the altering, repairing, ornamenting, finishing, cleaning, or washing or the breaking up or demolition of any article; or
(c) the adapting for sale of any article; or
(d) the slaughtering of cattle, sheep, swine, goats, horses, asses or mules; or
(e) the confinement of such animals as aforesaid while awaiting slaughter at other premises, in a case where the place of confinement is available in connection with those other premises, is not maintained primarily for agricultural purposes within the meaning of the Agriculture Act 1947, or, as the case may be, the Agriculture (Scotland) Act 1948, and does not form part of premises used for the holding of a market in respect of such animals;

being premises in which, or within the close or curtilage or precincts of which, the work is carried on by way of trade or for purposes of gain and to or over which the employer of the persons employed therein has the right of access or control.

(2) The expression 'factory' also includes the following premises in which persons are employed in manual labour (whether or not they are factories by virtue of subs. (1) of this section), that is to say,—
(a) any yard or dry dock (including the precincts thereof) in which ships or vessels are constructed, reconstructed, repaired, refitted, finished or broken up;
(b) any premises in which the business of sorting any articles is carried on as a preliminary to the work carried on in any factory or incidentally to the purposes of any factory;
(c) any premises in which the business of washing or filling bottles or containers or packing articles is carried on incidentally to the purposes of any factory;

(d) any premises in which the business of hooking, plaiting, lapping, making-up or packing of yarn or cloth is carried on;
(e) any laundry carried on as ancillary to another business, or incidentally to the purposes of any public institution;
(f) except as provided in subs. (10) of this section, any premises in which the construction, reconstruction or repair of locomotives, vehicles or other plant for use for transport purposes is carried on as ancillary to a transport undertaking or other industrial or commercial undertaking;
(g) any premises in which printing by letterpress, lithography, photogravure, or other similar process, or bookbinding is carried on by way of trade or for purposes of gain or incidentally to another business so carried on;
(h) any premises in which the making, adaptation or repair of dresses, scenery or properties is carried on incidentally to the production, exhibition or presentation by way of trade or for purposes of gain of cinematograph films or theatrical performances, not being a stage or dressing-room of a theatre in which only occasional adaptations or repairs are made;
(j) any premises in which the business of making or mending nets is carried on incidentally to the fishing industry;
(k) any premises in which mechanical power is used in connection with the making or repair of articles of metal or wood incidentally to any business carried on by way of trade or for purposes of gain;
(l) any premises in which the production of cinematograph films is carried on by way of trade or for purposes of gain, so, however, that the employment at any such premises of theatrical performers within the meaning of the Theatrical Employers Registration Act 1925 and of attendants on such theatrical performers shall not be deemed to be employment in a factory;
(m) any premises in which articles are made or prepared incidentally to the carrying on of building operations or works of engineering construction, not being premises in which such operations or works are being carried on;
(n) any premises used for the storage of gas in a gasholder having a storage capacity of not less than [140 cubic metres].

(3) Any line or siding (not being part of a railway or tramway) which is used in connection with and for the purposes of a factory, shall be deemed to be part of the factory; and if any such line or siding is used in connection with more than one factory belonging to different occupiers, the line or siding shall be deemed to be a separate factory.

(4) A part of a factory may, with the approval in writing of the chief inspector, be taken to be a separate factory and two or more factories may, with the like approval, be taken to be a single factory.

(5) Any workplace in which, with the permission of or under agreement with the owner or occupier, two or more persons carry on any work which would constitute the workplace a factory if the persons working therein were in the employment of the owner or occupier, shall be deemed to be a factory for the purposes of this Act, and, in the case of any such workplace not being a tenement factory or part of a tenement factory, the provisions of this Act shall apply as if the owner or occupier of the workplace were the occupier of the factory and the persons working therein were persons employed in the factory.

(6) Where a place situate within the close, curtilage, or precincts forming a factory is solely used for some purpose other than the processes carried on in the factory, that place shall not be deemed to form part of the factory for the purposes of this Act, but shall, if otherwise it would be a factory, be deemed to be a separate factory.

(7) Premises shall not be excluded from the definition of a factory by reason only that they are open air premises.

(8) Where the Minister by regulations so directs as respects all or any purposes of this Act, different branches or departments of work carried on in the same factory shall be deemed to be different factories.

(9) Any premises belonging to or in the occupation of the Crown or any municipal or other public authority shall not be deemed not to be a factory, and building operations or works of engineering construction undertaken by or on behalf of the Crown or any such authority shall not be excluded from the operation of this Act, by reason only that the work carried on thereat is not carried on by way of trade or for purposes of gain.

(10) Premises used for the purpose of housing locomotives or vehicles where only cleaning, washing, running repairs or minor adjustments are carried out shall not be deemed to be a factory by reason only of para. (f) of subs. (2) of this section, unless they are premises used for the purposes of a railway undertaking where running repairs to locomotives are carried out."

The question will ultimately be one of fact and common sense: see *Wood* v. *L.C.C.* [1948] 2 K.B. 232 (C.A.); also *Nash* v. *Hollinshead* [1901] 1 K.B. 700 (C.A.). In any event the definition of household waste as including waste from a number of institutional premises avoids any doubt as to the status of such premises.

Waste to be treated as industrial waste. By reg. 5(1) of the Controlled Waste Regulations 1992, waste of the descriptions set out at Sched. 3 is to be treated as industrial waste. These are waste from:
(1) premises used for maintaining vehicles, vessels or aircraft, not being waste from a private garage which falls under domestic waste by virtue of Sched. 1;
(2) a laboratory;
(3) a workshop or similar premises not being a factory within the meaning of s.175 of the Factories Act 1961 because the people working there are not employees or because the work there is not carried on by way of trade or for purposes of gain, excluding premises at which the principal activities are computer operations or the copying of documents by photographic or lithographic means;
(4) premises occupied by a scientific research association approved by the Secretary of State under s.508 of the Income and Corporation Taxes Act 1988;
(5) dredging operations;
(6) tunnelling or any other excavation;
(7) sewage not falling within a description in reg. 7 which—
   (a) is treated, kept on disposed of in or on land, other than by means of a privy, cesspool or septic tank;
   (b) is treated, kept on disposal of by means of mobil plant; or
   (c) has been removed from a privy or cesspool.
(8) clinical waste other than—
   (a) clinical waste from a domestic property, caravan, residential home or from a moored vessel used wholly for the purposes of living accommodation;
   (b) waste collected under s.22(3) of the Control of Pollution Act 1974 (waste collected by a local authority under arrangement with any person who has an interest in or is the occupier of any relevant land);
   (c) waste collected under s.89 (local authority's duty to keep land and highways clear of litter); s.92(9) (waste collected by a local authority after a failure by any person to obey a litter abatement notice); or s.93 (power to serve street litter control notices).
(9) any aircraft vehicle or vessel which is not occupied for domestic purposes;
(10) waste which has previously formed part of any aircraft vehicle, or vessel and which is not household waste;
(11) waste, removed from land on which has previously been deposited and any soil with which such waste has been in contact, other than—
   (a) waste collected under s.22(3) of the Control of Pollution Act 1974 (see (8) above); or
   (b) waste collected under ss.89, 92(9) or 93 (see (8) above).
(12) leachate from a deposit of waste;
(13) poisonous or noxious waste arising from any of the following processes undertaken on premises used for the purposes of a trade or business—
   (a) mixing or selling paints;
   (b) sign writing;
   (c) laundering or dry cleaning;
   (d) developing photographic film or making photographic prints;
   (e) selling petrol, diesel fuel, paraffin kerosene, heating oil or similar substances; or
   (f) selling pesticides, herbicides or fungicides.
(14) premises used for the purpose of breedings boarding, stabling or exhibiting animals;
(15) waste oil, waste solvent, or (subject to reg. 7(2)) scrap metal, other than—
   (a) waste from a domestic property, caravan or residential house;
   (b) waste falling within paras. 3 to 6 of Sched. 1 (see further notes to subs. (5)).
(16) waste arising from the discharge by the Secretary of State of his duty under s.89(2) (duty to keep clean any trunk road which is a special road and relevant highways or roads for which he is responsible);
(17) waste imported into Great Britain;
(18) tank washings and garbage landed in Great Britain.

Subs. (7)
Commercial waste
Premises used for trade or business. As to case law on this phrase, see annotations to ss.79 and 80.

Waste to be treated as commercial waste. By reg. 6 of the Controlled Waste Regulations 1992, waste of the descriptions set out in Sched. 4 is to be treated as commercial waste. This is waste from—
  (1) an office or showroom;
  (2) a hotel within the meaning of—
     (a) in England and Wales, s.1(3) of the Hotel Proprietors Act 1956; and
     (b) in Scotland, s.139(1) of the Licensing (Scotland) Act 1976.
  (3) any part of a composite hereditament or, in Scotland, part residential subject, which is used for the purposes of a trade or business;
  (4) a private garage which either has a floor area exceeding 25 square metres or is not used wholly or mainly for accommodation of a private motor vehicle;
  (5) premises occupied by a club, society or any association of persons (whether incorporated or not) in which activities are conducted for the benefit of the members;
  (6) premises (not being premises from which waste is by virtue of the Act or any other provision of these regulations to be treated as household waste or industrial waste) occupied by—
     (a) a court;
     (b) a government department;
     (c) a body corporate or an individual appointed by or under any enactment to discharge any public functions; or
     (d) a body incorporated by a Royal Charter.
  (7) waste from a tent pitched on land other than a camp site;
  (8) a market or fair;
  (9) waste collected under s.22(3) of the Control of Pollution Act 1974 (local authority's power to collect waste under an arrangement with the person who has an interest in or is the occupier of relevant land).

Waste not to be treated as industrial or commercial waste
Waste of the following descriptions is not to be treated as industrial or commercial waste (Controlled Waste Regulations 1992, reg. 7(1)):
  (a) sewage, sludge or septic tank sludge which is treated, kept or disposed of (otherwise than by mobile plant) within the curtilage of a sewage treatment works as an integral part of the operation of those works;
  (b) sludge supplied or used in accordance with the Sludge (Use in Agriculture) Regulations 1989 (S.I. 1989 No. 1263), amended by S.I. 1990 No. 880); and
  (c) septic tank sludge used in accordance with the same regulations.
Also, by reg. 7(2) scrap metal is not to be treated as industrial or commercial waste for the purposes of the s.34 duty of care at any time before the coming into force of the waste management licensing provisions under Pt. II of the EPA 1990.

Non-controlled wastes
By s.75(7)(c) two categories of waste are specifically excluded from the definition of commercial waste and consequently from control. These are:
  (a) waste from any mine or quarry; and
  (b) waste from premises used for agriculture.
The definition of "agriculture" in the Agriculture Act 1947, s.109(3) includes:
   "horticulture, fruit growing, seed growing, dairy farming and livestock breeding and keeping, the use of land as grazing land, meadow land, osier land, market gardens and nursery grounds, and the use of land for woodlands where that use is ancillary to the farming of land for other agricultural purposes ... and 'agricultural' shall be construed accordingly."
However, as mentioned by the DoE in its introduction to the Consultation Paper on Waste Management Licensing issued in August 1992, Directive 91/156/EEC appears to contain no exemptions equating to these two categories (unlike 75/442/EEC which excluded waste from mineral extraction and quarry working and agricultural wastes). The Government is seeking further clarification on the point.

Subs. (8)
Sewage. Subsection (8) excludes "sewage" from the definition of commercial waste; nor can such waste be prescribed as being within one or other of the other categories of waste by regulations unless the regulations expressly so provide. However, it appears there is nothing to prevent sewage being classified as household or industrial waste. The treatment, keeping and disposal of sewage within the curtilage of a sewage treatment works as an integral part of the operation of those works is dealt with by reg. 7(1)(a) of the Controlled Waste Regulations 1992, which provides that such sewage shall not be treated as industrial or commercial waste. It seems doubtful whether that exemption would apply to liquid effluent conveyed to the works by means other than a sewer, *e.g.* road tanker.

Subs. (9)
Special waste. See notes to s.62.

Application of this Part to Isles of Scilly

76. This Part shall have effect in its application to the Isles of Scilly with such modifications as the Secretary of State may by order specify.

COMMENCEMENT
Not yet in force.

Transition from Control of Pollution Act 1974 to this Part

77.—(1) This section has effect for the purposes of the transition from the provisions of Part I of the Control of Pollution Act 1974 ("the 1974 Act") to the corresponding provisions of this Part of this Act and in this section—

"existing disposal authority" has the same meaning as in section 32 above;

"existing disposal licence" means a disposal licence under section 5 of the 1974 Act subsisting on the day appointed under section 164(3) below for the repeal of sections 3 to 10 of the 1974 Act and "relevant appointed day for licences" shall be construed accordingly;

"existing disposal plan" means a plan under section 2 of the 1974 Act subsisting on the day appointed under section 164(3) below for the repeal of that section and "relevant appointed day for plans" shall be construed accordingly;

"relevant part of its undertaking," in relation to an existing disposal authority, has the same meaning as in section 32 above; and

"the vesting date," in relation to an existing disposal authority and its waste disposal contractors, means the vesting date under Schedule 2 to this Act.

(2) An existing disposal licence shall, on and after the relevant appointed day for licences, be treated as a site licence until it expires or otherwise ceases to have effect; and accordingly it shall be variable and subject to revocation or suspension under this Part of this Act and may not be surrendered or transferred except under this Part of this Act.

(3) The restriction imposed by section 33(1) above shall not apply in relation to land occupied by an existing disposal authority for which a resolution of the authority subsists under section 11 of the 1974 Act on the relevant appointed day for licences until the following date, that is to say—

   (a) in the case of an authority which transfers the relevant part of its undertaking in accordance with a scheme under Schedule 2 to this Act, the date which is the vesting date for that authority; and

   (b) in any other case, the date on which the authority transfers, or ceases itself to carry on, the relevant part of its undertaking or ceases to provide places at which and plant and equipment by means of which controlled waste can be disposed of or deposited for the purposes of disposal.

(4) Any existing disposal plan of an existing disposal authority shall, on and after the relevant appointed day for plans, be treated as the plan of that authority under section 50 above and that section shall accordingly have effect as if references in it to "the plan" included the existing disposal plan of that authority.

(5) Subs. (4) above applies to Scotland and, for the purposes of that application, "existing disposal authority" means any authority constituted as a disposal authority for any area before the day appointed for this section to come into force and "that authority" means the waste disposal authority for that area under section 30(2) above.

(6) Subject to subsection (7) below, as respects any existing disposal authority—

   (a) the restriction imposed by section 51(1) of this Act on the means

whereby the authority arranges for the disposal of controlled waste shall not apply to the authority—
  (i) in the case of an authority which transfers the relevant part of its undertaking in accordance with a scheme under Schedule 2 to this Act, until the date which is the vesting date for that authority; and
  (ii) in any other case, until the date on which the authority transfers, or ceases itself to carry on, the relevant part of its undertaking or ceases to provide places at which and plant and equipment by means of which controlled waste can be disposed of or deposited for the purposes of disposal; and
 (b) on and after that date, section 14(4) of the 1974 Act shall not authorise the authority to arrange for the disposal of controlled waste except by means of arrangements made (in accordance with Part II of Schedule 2 to this Act) with waste disposal contractors.

(7) The Secretary of State may, as respects any existing disposal authority, direct that the restriction imposed by section 51(1) above shall not apply in the case of that authority until such date as he specifies in the direction and where he does so paragraph (a) of subsection (6) above shall not apply and paragraph (b) shall be read as referring to the date so specified.

(8) In section 14(4) of the 1974 Act, after the words "this subsection," there shall be inserted the words "but subject to subsection (6) of section 77 of the Environment Protection Act 1990 as respects any time after the date applicable to the authority under paragraph (a) or (b) of that subsection."

(9) As respects any existing disposal authority, until the date which is, under subsection (6)(a) above, the date until which the restriction imposed by section 51(1) of this Act is disapplied,—
 (a) the powers conferred on a waste disposal authority by section 55(2)(a) and (b) of this Act as respects the recycling of waste and the use of waste to produce heat or electricity shall be treated as powers which the authority may exercise itself; and
 (b) the power conferred on a waste disposal authority by section 48(4) of this Act to object to a waste collection authority having waste recycled where the disposal authority has made arrangements with a waste disposal contractor for the contractor to recycle the waste shall be available to the waste disposal authority where it itself has the waste recycled.

DEFINITIONS
 "controlled waste": s.75(4).
 "disposed of": s.29(6).
 "site licence": s.35(12).
 "waste disposal contractors": s.30(5).

COMMENCEMENT
 Not yet in force.

GENERAL NOTE
 This section makes various transitional provisions as to site licences and disposal authorities.

Subs. (2)
 Existing disposal licences. Disposal licences granted under COPA effectively become site licences under Pt. II of the Act as from the appointed day, and therefore are subject to the same provisions on variation, revocation, suspension, transfer and surrender.

Subs. (3)
 Land occupied by existing disposal authorities. This subsection ensures that until the date of transfer of its disposal undertaking to a waste disposal company, or until the date of cessation of that part of its undertaking, a waste disposal authority may continue to carry on its disposal activities lawfully under a resolution granted under s.11 of COPA.

Subs. (6)
Existing disposal authorities. This subsection allows for the transition of disposal functions from disposal authorities to waste disposal contractors. The relevant date is the vesting date under a Sched. 2 scheme of transfer or alternatively, if there is no such scheme, the date of actual transfer. Until that date the authority is not restricted from dealing with the waste itself, but after that date the waste may only be disposed of by waste disposal contractors. Further, until that date, the disposal authority enjoys the ancillary powers related to disposals referred to in subs. (9).

This Part and radioactive substances

78. Except as provided by regulations made by the Secretary of State under this section, nothing in this Part applies to radioactive waste within the meaning of the Radioactive Substances Act 1960; but regulations may—
  (a) provide for prescribed provisions of this Part to have effect with such modifications as the Secretary of State considers appropriate for the purposes of dealing with such radioactive waste;
  (b) make such modifications of the Radioactive Substances Act 1960 and any other Act as the Secretary of State considers appropriate.

COMMENCEMENT
December 13, 1991 (S.I. 1991 No. 2829).

GENERAL NOTE
The effect of s.78 is that Pt. II of the Act does not apply to radioactive waste as defined in the Radioactive Substances Act 1960 save to the extent the Secretary of State so provides in regulations.
The definition of radioactive waste in the 1960 Act, s.18(4) is:
"Waste which consists wholly or partly of—
  (a) a substance or article which, if it were not waste, would be radioactive material, or
  (b) a substance or article which has been contaminated in the course of the production, keeping or use of radioactive material, or by contact with a proximity to other waste falling within [para. (a)] or [para. (b)]."
"Radioactive material" is defined by ss.19(1) and (2) and by reference to the elements specified in the Third Schedule. The definition of "waste" in s.19(1) of the 1960 Act is consistent with that in s.75 of the 1990 Act.
Note that as from August 27, 1993 the relevant statute will be the Radioactive Substances Act 1993 which is a consolidating statute.

PART III

STATUTORY NUISANCES AND CLEAN AIR

COMMENCEMENT
Sections 79–85 came into force on January 1, 1991 (s.164(2)).

GENERAL NOTE
Part III of the Act deals with statutory nuisances, clean air, and controls over offensive trades. In relation to statutory nuisances, ss.79–82 replace the provisions of the Public Health Act 1936 and the Public Health (Recurring Nuisances) Act 1969 with a more streamlined system of summary procedures. The new procedures are similar to those contained in Pt. III of the Control of Pollution Act 1974 relating to noise nuisances, and the differences between the former procedures and those of the 1990 Act are perhaps best demonstrated diagrammatically.
The changes do not apply to Scotland (s.83) but the definition of statutory nuisances contained in the Public Health (Scotland) Act 1897 is extended by the addition of two further categories.
Section 84 deals with the provisions contained in the Public Health Act 1936 and the Public Health (Scotland) Act 1897 for control over "offensive trades." Such controls are disapplied in the case of processes designated for local authority air pollution control under Pt. I of the Act. The Secretary of State is given power when it appears expedient to do so to repeal the relevant provisions entirely, leaving control to be provided by Pt. I of the Act and the statutory nuisance provisions of Pt. III.

PROCEDURE UNDER PUBLIC HEALTH ACT 1936 (PHA 1936) AND PUBLIC HEALTH (RECURRING NUISANCES) ACT 1969 (PH(RN)A 1969)

Local authority satisfied of existence of statutory nuisance or of likely recurrence ↓ Service of abatement notice or prohibition notice	s.93 of the PHA 1936 or s.1 of the PH(RN)A 1969
↓ Complaint to magistrates if default in compliance with notice or if abated nuisance likely to recur ↓ Magistrates' summons	s.94(1) of the PHA 1936 or s.2 of the PH(RN)A 1969
↓ Hearing of complaint ↓ Court makes nuisance order and/or imposes fine	s.94(2) of the PHA 1936
↓ Failure to comply with nuisance order is an offence and local authority may abate nuisance and recover costs	s.95(1) and (2) of the PHA 1936

NOTE:
1. Commencement of summary proceedings requires consent of the Secretary of State in certain cases: s.92(2) of the PHA 1936.
2. Complaint may be made direct to a magistrates' court by any person aggrieved by the nuisance: s.99 of the PHA 1936. This does not apply to nuisances which have occurred and are likely to recur: s.3(1) of the PH(RN)A 1969.
3. Local authorities may take abatement or prohibition proceedings in the High Court if of the opinion that summary proceedings would not provide an adequate remedy: s.100 of the PHA 1936. This applies also to recurring nuisances: s.3(1) of the PH(RN)A 1969.

PROCEDURE UNDER PART III OF ENVIRONMENTAL PROTECTION ACT 1990 (EPA 1990)

Local authority satisfied that statutory nuisance exists or is likely to occur or recur ↓ Service of abatement notice	s.80(1) of the EPA 1990
↓ Person served may appeal to magistrates within 21 days	s.80(3) of the EPA 1990
↓ Failure to comply with abatement notice is an offence and local authority may abate nuisance and recover expenses	ss.80(4) and 81(3) and (4) of the EPA 1990

NOTE:
1. Commencement of summary proceedings requires consent of the Secretary of State in certain cases: s.79(10).

2. A complaint may be made to a magistrates' court by any person aggrieved by the existence of a statutory nuisance. The court must make an order requiring abatement or prohibiting recurrence, if satisfied the nuisance exists or, if abated, is likely to recur and may also impose a fine. Breach of such an order is an offence: s.82.
3. Local authorities may take abatement, prohibition or restriction proceedings in the High Court if of the opinion that a prosecution for failure to comply with the authority's abatement notice would afford an inadequate remedy: s.81(5).

Section 85 enables the Secretary of State to make regulations to control the emission of specified gases from furnaces, thus extending the controls of the Clean Air Acts 1956 and 1968 to such emissions and beyond the grit, dust and smoke presently controlled by those Acts. This provision applies throughout Great Britain.

Statutory nuisances: England and Wales

Statutory nuisances and inspections therefor

79.—(1) Subject to subsections (2) to (6) below, the following matters constitute "statutory nuisances" for the purposes of this Part, that is to say—
  (a) any premises in such a state as to be prejudicial to health or a nuisance;
  (b) smoke emitted from premises so as to be prejudicial to health or a nuisance;
  (c) fumes or gases emitted from premises so as to be prejudicial to health or a nuisance;
  (d) any dust, steam, smell or other effluvia arising on industrial, trade or business premises and being prejudicial to health or a nuisance;
  (e) any accumulation or deposit which is prejudicial to health or a nuisance;
  (f) any animal kept in such a place or manner as to be prejudicial to health or a nuisance;
  (g) noise emitted from premises so as to be prejudicial to health or a nuisance;
  (h) any other matter declared by any enactment to be a statutory nuisance;
and it shall be the duty of every local authority to cause its area to be inspected from time to time to detect any statutory nuisances which ought to be dealt with under section 80 below and, where a complaint of a statutory nuisance is made to it by a person living within its area, to take such steps as are reasonably practicable to investigate the complaint.
  (2) Subs. (1)(b) and (g) above do not apply in relation to premises—
  (a) occupied on behalf of the Crown for naval, military or air force purposes or for the purposes of the department of the Secretary of State having responsibility for defence, or
  (b) occupied by or for the purposes of a visiting force;
and "visiting force" means any such body, contingent or detachment of the forces of any country as is a visiting force for the purposes of any of the provisions of the Visiting Forces Act 1952.
  (3) Subs. (1)(b) above does not apply to—
  (i) smoke emitted from a chimney of a private dwelling within a smoke control area,
  (ii) dark smoke emitted from a chimney of a building or a chimney serving the furnace of a boiler or industrial plant attached to a building or for the time being fixed to or installed on any land,
  (iii) smoke emitted from a railway locomotive steam engine, or
  (iv) dark smoke emitted otherwise than as mentioned above from industrial or trade premises.
  (4) Subs. (1)(c) above does not apply in relation to premises other than private dwellings.

(5) Subs. (1)(d) above does not apply to steam emitted from a railway locomotive engine.

(6) Subs. (1)(g) above does not apply to noise caused by aircraft other than model aircraft.

(7) In this Part—

"chimney" includes structures and openings of any kind from or through which smoke may be emitted;

"dust" does not include dust emitted from a chimney as an ingredient of smoke;

"fumes" means any airborne solid matter smaller than dust;

"gas" includes vapour and moisture precipitated from vapour;

"industrial, trade or business premises" means premises used for any industrial, trade or business purposes or premises not so used on which matter is burnt in connection with any industrial, trade or business process, and premises are used for industrial purposes where they are used for the purposes of any treatment or process as well as where they are used for the purposes of manufacturing;

"local authority" means, subject to subsection (8) below,—
- (a) in Greater London, a London borough council, the Common Council of the City of London and, as respects the Temples, the Sub-Treasurer of the Inner Temple and the Under-Treasurer of the Middle Temple respectively;
- (b) outside Greater London, a district council; and
- (c) the Council of the Isles of Scilly;

"noise" includes vibration;

"person responsible," in relation to a statutory nuisance, means the person to whose act, default or sufferance the nuisance is attributable;

"prejudicial to health" means injurious, or likely to cause injury, to health;

"premises" includes land and, subject to subsection (12) below, any vessel;

"private dwelling" means any any building, or part of a building, used or intended to be used, as a dwelling;

"smoke" includes soot, ash, grit and gritty particles emitted in smoke;

and any expressions used in this section and in the Clean Air Act 1956 or the Clean Air Act 1968 have the same meaning in this section as in that Act and section 34(2) of the Clean Air Act 1956 shall apply for the interpretation of the expression "dark smoke" and the operation of this Part in relation to it.

(8) Where, by an order under section 2 of the Public Health (Control of Disease) Act 1984, a port health authority has been constituted for any port health district, the port health authority shall have by virtue of this subsection, as respects its district, the functions conferred or imposed by this Part in relation to statutory nuisances other than a nuisance falling within paragraph (g) of subsection (1) above and no such order shall be made assigning those functions, and "local authority" and "area" shall be construed accordingly.

(9) In this Part "best practicable means" is to be interpreted by reference to the following provisions—
- (a) "practicable" means reasonably practicable having regard among other things to local conditions and circumstances, to the current state of technical knowledge and to the financial implications;
- (b) the means to be employed include the design, installation, maintenance and manner and periods of operation of plant and machinery, and the design, construction and maintenance of buildings and structures;
- (c) the test is to apply only so far as compatible with any duty imposed by law;

(d) the test is to apply only so far as compatible with safety and safe working conditions, and with the exigencies of any emergency or unforeseeable circumstances;

and, in circumstances where a code of practice under section 71 of the Control of Pollution Act 1974 (noise minimisation) is applicable, regard shall also be had to guidance given in it.

(10) A local authority shall not without the consent of the Secretary of State institute summary proceedings under this Part in respect of a nuisance falling within paragraph (b), (d) or (e) of subsection (1) above if proceedings in respect thereof might be instituted under Part I or the Alkali &c. Works Regulation Act 1906 or section 5 of the Health and Safety at Work etc. Act 1974.

(11) The area of a local authority which includes part of the seashore shall also include for the purposes of this Part the territorial sea lying seawards from that part of the shore; and subject to subsection (12) below, this Part shall have effect, in relation to any area included in the area of a local authority by virtue of this subsection—

(a) as if references to premises and the occupier of premises included respectively a vessel and the master of a vessel; and
(b) with such other modifications, if any, as are prescribed in regulations made by the Secretary of State.

(12) A vessel powered by steam reciprocating machinery is not a vessel to which this Part of this Act applies.

GENERAL NOTE

This section has various functions. Subsections (1)–(6) provide the definition of "statutory nuisances" for the purposes of the Part. By subs. (1), every local authority is under a duty to cause its area to be inspected for statutory nuisances. Subs. (7) gives a series of other definitions. Subs. (8) deals with the position of certain port health authorities, and subs. (9) provides the important definition of "best practicable means." Subsections (10)–(12) contain ancillary provisions.

Subs. (1)

Definition of "statutory nuisance". This subsection draws together various statutory nuisances which were formerly to be found in a number of different pieces of legislation. In some cases the opportunity has been taken to amend or clarify the definition and, in particular, noise nuisance which was formerly covered by ss.58 and 59 of the Control of Pollution Act 1974 has been defined as a statutory nuisance. However, given the many similarities of expression with the previous legislation, no doubt much of the substantial body of case law that has built up around the Public Health Act 1936, and other legislation, will remain relevant.

(a) *Any premises in such a state as to be prejudicial to health or a nuisance.* This is a straight re-enactment of s.91(1)(a) of the Public Health Act 1936.

Premises. This is defined so as to include land and vessels other than those powered by steam reciprocating machinery (subss. (7) and (12)). There can therefore be no doubt that, for example, houseboats (*West Mersea Urban District Council* v. *Fraser* [1950] 2 K.B. 119) and caves (*Gardiner* v. *Sevenoaks Rural District Council* [1950] W.N. 260) would potentially be covered. Section 109 of the Public Health Act 1936 contained a saving provision excluding mines and smelting works, but the 1990 Act gives no such exemption. As to the case of premises rendered prejudicial to health by problems emanating from other premises, see *Pollway Nominees* v. *Havering London Borough Council* (1989) 21 H.L.R. 462. A limited Crown exemption applies by subs. (2).

Prejudicial to health. The definition (subs. (7)) repeats that in the 1936 Act, s.343(1). It is not necessary to show that the activity is prejudicial to health in order for it to constitute a statutory nuisance: in *Betts* v. *Penge Urban District Council* [1942] 2 K.B. 154 (D.C.) it was held that it is sufficient to show that the premises in question are such as to interfere with personal comfort and thus constitute a nuisance. The case appears to remain good authority for that proposition, though it has been argued in relation to the Public Health Acts that the "nuisance" limb is itself to be qualified by reference to the general spirit and intention of the legislation as dealing with matters appertaining to health, disease or vermin: see *Salford City Council* v. *McNally* [1976] A.C. 379, 389, 394; *Coventry City Council* v. *Cartwright* [1975] 1 W.L.R. 845 at 848 and

National Coal Board v. *Neath Borough Council* [1976] 2 All E.R. 478 at 482; and *cf. Wivenhoe Port* v. *Colchester Borough Council* [1985] J.P.L. 175, 178 (affirmed [1985] J.P.L. 396).

Nuisance. In *Betts* v. *Penge Urban District Council* (above) it was held that premises which were in such a state as to interfere with the reasonable comfort of the occupier (the front door and some of the window-sashes having been removed by the landlord) constituted a statutory nuisance. However, the decision was not followed in *National Coal Board* v. *Neath Borough Council* (above) on the basis that a "nuisance" coming within the meaning of the Public Health Act must be either a private or public nuisance as understood by common law. On that basis, interference with the enjoyment of neighbouring property is a prerequisite, and "a nuisance cannot arise if what has taken place affects only the person or person occupying the premises where the nuisance is said to have taken place" (p. 482). See also *Bishop Auckland Local Board* v. *Bishop Auckland Iron and Steel Co.* (1882) 10 Q.B.D. 138, 140–141 and *Salford City Council* v. *McNally* [1976] A.C. 379, 389, 392. See also the discussion of "nuisance" below in the context of dust (para. (d)).

(b) *Smoke emitted from premises so as to be prejudicial to health or or a nuisance*. This is a category of statutory nuisance which does not appear in the Public Health Act 1936, which by s.110(1) excluded from the meaning of "dust," dust emitted from a chimney as an ingredient of smoke. For the meaning of "premises," "prejudicial to health" and "nuisance," see (a) above. "Smoke" is defined at subs. (7).

(c) *Fumes or gases emitted from premises so as to be prejudicial to health or a nuisance*. Again, this is a new category of statutory nuisance. "Dust" and "fumes" are defined in subs. (7), and see (a) above generally. The category applies only to fumes and gases from private dwellings (subs. (4)). Emissions from commercial or industrial premises might well be caught under (d) below and in any event, may be subject to local authority air pollution control under Pt. I.

(d) *Any dust, steam, smell or other effluvia arising on industrial, trade or business premises and being prejudicial to health or a nuisance*. This corresponds broadly, though not exactly, to para. (d) of s.92(1) of the 1936 Act ("any dust or effluvia caused by any trade, business, manufacture or process and injurious, or likely to cause injury, to the public health or a nuisance"). "Dust" does not include chimney smoke, that being dealt with under para. (b) above.

Section 92(1)(d) of the 1936 Act was considered in *Wivenhoe Port* v. *Colchester Borough Council* [1985] J.P.L. 175 (Chelmsford Crown Court) (affirmed [1985] J.P.L. 396) in relation to an alleged statutory nuisance by dust arising from the handling of soya meal. Whilst recognising the great uncertainty of this area of law, Butler J. said that:

"To be within the spirit of the Act a nuisance to be statutory nuisance had to be one interfering materially with the personal comfort of the residents, in the sense that it materially affected their wellbeing although it might not be prejudicial to their health. Thus, dust falling on motor cars might cause inconvenience to their owners; it might even diminish the value of their motor car; but this would not be a statutory nuisance. In the same way, dust falling on gardens or trees, or on stock held in shop would not be a statutory nuisance. But dust in eyes or hair, even if not shown to be prejudicial to health, would be so as an interference with personal comfort."

How far the reference to "the spirit of the Act" is relevant now that the relevant provisions are contained in Pt. III of a general environmental protection statute is open to question, but certainly if the above statement of the law is correct, the use of the provisions to effect environmental quality improvements or to protect flora or fauna would, in the absence of interference with human comfort, be limited.

Paragraph (d) is the only category of statutory nuisance specifically confined to "industrial, trade or business premises." The expression is defined in subs. (7).

Trade. This has been the subject of the following judicial definitions:

"No doubt in many contexts the word "trade" indicates a process of buying and selling, but that is by no means an exchaustive definition of its meaning. It may also mean a calling or industry or class of skilled labour." (*Skinner* v. *Jack Breach* [1927] 2 K.B. 220, 225–227).

"A trade is an organised seeking after profits as a rule with the aid of physical assets" (*Aviation & Shipping Co.* v. *Murray* [1961] 1 W.L.R. 974).

It seems clear that in the context of Pt. III the term would not be confined to buying and selling, but would include manufacture and processing.

Business. This again must be construed in its context, but has been said to be a wider term than "trade": see, *e.g. Debtor, A Re* (*No. 490 of 1935*) [1936] Ch. 237. It has been said to mean:

"... almost anything which is an occupation, as distinguished from a pleasure—anything which is an occupation or duty which requires attention is a business" (*Rolls* v. *Miller* (1894) 27 Ch.D. 71, 88).

It seems clear that the term can include professional activities: *Wilkinson, Re* [1922] 1 K.B. 584, 587; *Williams' Will Trusts, Re*; *Chartered Bank of India, Australia and China* v. *Williams* [1953] Ch. 138, 141; *R.* v. *Breeze* [1973] 1 W.L.R. 994. Purely domestic or recreational activities would not appear to fall within the term: see *Abernethie* v. *Kleiman* [1970] 1 Q.B. 10; *Town Investments* v. *Department of Environment* [1976] 3 All E.R. 479, 496 (C.A.); *Customs & Excise Commissioners* v. *Fisher* (*Lord*) [1981] 2 All E.R. 147; neither would an isolated transaction undertaken with no intention that it be repeated: *Griffin, Re*, ex p. *Board of Trade* (1890) 60 L.J. Q.B. 235, 237.

(e) *Any accumulation or deposit which is prejudicial to health or a nuisance.* This paragraph corresponds verbatim with s.93(1)(c) of the 1936 Act. In *Coventry City Council* v. *Cartwright* [1975] 1 W.L.R. 845 this paragraph was held by the Divisional Court to have the underlying concept of "an accumulation of something which produces a threat to health in the sense of a threat of disease, vermin or the like." It was held therefore not to extend the meaning to an accumulation of inert matter (building materials, scrap iron, broken glass and tin cans) merely because that matter may cause physical injury to persons who come into the land and walk on it.

As to "prejudicial to health" and "nuisance," see (a) above.

(f) *Any animal kept in such a place or manner as to be prejudicial to health or a nuisance.* The corresponding provision of the 1936 Act, with identical wording, is s.92(1)(b). In *Morrisey* v. *Galer* [1955] 1 W.L.R. 110 Lord Goddard C.J., in considering a case concerning noise from the keeping of greyhounds, suggested that statutory nuisance provisions would not apply to such a noise nuisance, though they would cover smell from animals. However, Lord Widgery C.J. in *Coventry City Council* v. *Cartwright* (above) thought the wording was equally apt to catch noise made by animals.

See generally para. (a) as to "prejudicial to health" and "nuisance."

(g) *Noise emitted from premises so as to be prejudicial to health or a nuisance.* This paragraph defines noise, previously covered by ss.58 and 59 of the Control of Pollution Act 1974, as a statutory nuisance. "Noise" includes vibration (subs. (7)). As with other categories of statutory nuisance, it appears that noise may fall into this category either because it is prejudicial to health or because it is a nuisance in the sense of interfering unduly with the comfort and convenience of neighbouring occupiers (see Note to para. (a) above).

The noise must be emitted from premises. In a case decided under s.58 of COPA, the word "premises" was held not to cover noise made in streets or public places (see *Tower Hamlets London Borough Council* v. *Manzoni and Walder* (1984) J.P. 123 and the article by Macrory at [1984] J.P.L. 388). However, "premises" is now expressly defined to include land (s.79(7)), though it might still be arguable whether noise made by a person or group of persons at large in a public place could be said to be "emitted from land." There is an important exception by subs. (6), which is that the provision does not apply to aircraft noise other than model aircraft.

Noise which affects premises, though emanating elsewhere, can make the premises affected themselves a statutory nuisance under para. (a) if the noise is such as to be injurious to health: *Southwark London Borough Council* v. *Ince* (1989) 153 J.P. 597.

(h) *Any other matter declared by any enactment to be a statutory nuisance.* This paragraph widens the category in para. (f) of s.92(1) of the 1936 Act which was limited to matters declared by provisions of that Act to be a statutory nuisance. The matters now covered include: s.141 of the Public Health Act 1936 (insanitary cisterns, etc.); s.259 of the 1936 Act (nuisances in connection with watercourses, etc.); s.268 of the 1936 Act (nuisances relating to tents, vans, etc.); and s.151 of the Mines and Quarries Act 1954 (fencing of abandoned and disused mines and quarries).

Nuisance at workplaces

Subs. (1) does not re-enact the provisions of s.92(1)(e) of the 1936 Act relating to nuisance at workplaces. Such matters are now covered adequately by health and safety at work legislation.

Duty to inspect area. By subs. (1), local authorities are under a duty to cause their areas to be inspected from time to time to detect statutory nuisances which ought to be dealt with according to the summary procedures under s.80. Schedule 3, para. 4 contains procedures to be followed in the event of default in this duty, which may lead to an order of direction by the Secretary of State enforceable by mandamus, or an order of the Secretary of State transferring the relevant functions to himself (para. 4(4)). In the light of these special procedures it is questionable whether other remedies are available: see, *e.g. Pasmore* v. *Oswaldtwistle Urban District Council* [1898] A.C. 387; *Clark* v. *Epsom Rural District Council* [1929] 1 Ch. 287; *R.* v. *Kensington and Chelsea (Royal) London Borough Council,* ex p. *Birdwood* (1976) 74 L.G.R. 424.

Subs. (9)
Defence of Best Practicable Means. This subsection defines the defence of best practicable means (bpm) which applies to some categories of statutory nuisance (see s.80(7) and (9)). The defence existed under s.94(5) of the Public Health Act 1936 and s.58(5) of the Control of Pollution Act 1974. The definition in subs. (8) follows that in s.72 of COPA.

The defence was raised in *Wivenhoe Port* v. *Colchester Borough Council* [1985] J.P.L. 175 (affirmed [1985] J.P.L. 396), where it was argued that the avoidance of dust nuisance by vacuum machinery was not practicable because it would render the operation uneconomic. It was accepted by the Crown Court that profitability was a relevant factor, but that it was for the company to establish the defence, the onus of proof as to practicability lying on them. The mere fact of increased expenditure, or even unprofitability, was not sufficient to establish the defence.

In the case of noise nuisance, any codes of practice promulgated under s.71 of COPA will be relevant. These include codes on:

Construction and open sites	— S.I. 1984 No. 1992
	— S.I. 1987 No. 1730
Construction and open sites (Scotland)	— S.I. 1982 No. 601
Audible intruder alarms	— S.I. 1981 No. 1829
Ice cream van chimes	— S.I. 1981 No. 1828
Model aircraft	— S.I. 1981 No. 1830.

Summary proceedings for statutory nuisances

80.—(1) Where a local authority is satisfied that a statutory nuisance exists, or is likely to occur or recur, in the area of the authority, the local authority shall serve a notice ("an abatement notice") imposing all or any of the following requirements—
   (a) requiring the abatement of the nuisance or prohibiting or restricting its occurrence or recurrence;
   (b) requiring the execution of such works, and the taking of such other steps, as may be necessary for any of those purposes,
and the notice shall specify the time or times within which the requirements of the notice are to be complied with.
   (2) The abatement notice shall be served—
   (a) except in a case falling within paragraph (b) or (c) below, on the person responsible for the nuisance;
   (b) where the nuisance arises from any defect of a structural character, on the owner of the premises;
   (c) where the person responsible for the nuisance cannot be found or the nuisance has not yet occurred, on the owner or occupier of the premises.
   (3) The person served with the notice may appeal against the notice to a magistrates' court within the period of 21 days beginning with the date on which he was served with the notice.
   (4) If a person on whom an abatement notice is served, without reasonable excuse, contravenes or fails to comply with any requirement or prohibition imposed by the notice, he shall be guilty of an offence.
   (5) Except in a case falling within subsection (6) below, a person who commits an offence under subsection (4) above shall be liable on summary conviction to a fine not exceeding level 5 on the standard scale together with a further fine of an amount equal to one-tenth of that level for each day on which the offence continues after the conviction.

(6) A person who commits an offence under subsection (4) above on industrial, trade or business premises shall be liable on summary conviction to a fine not exceeding £20,000.

(7) Subject to subsection (8) below, in any proceedings for an offence under subsection (4) above in respect of a statutory nuisance it shall be a defence to prove that the best practicable means were used to prevent, or to counteract the effects of, the nuisance.

(8) The defence under subsection (7) above is not available—
   (a) in the case of a nuisance falling within paragraph (a), (d), (e), (f) or (g) of section 79(1) above except where the nuisance arises on industrial, trade or business premises;
   (b) in the case of a nuisance falling within paragraph (b) of section 79(1) above except where the smoke is emitted from a chimney; and
   (c) in the case of a nuisance falling within paragraph (c) or (h) of section 79(1) above.

(9) In proceedings for an offence under subsection (4) above in respect of a statutory nuisance falling within paragraph (g) of section 79(1) above where the offence consists in contravening requirements imposed by virtue of subsection (1)(a) above is shall be a defence to prove—
   (a) that the alleged offence was covered by a notice served under section 60 or a consent given under section 61 or 65 of the Control of Pollution Act 1974 (construction sites, etc.); or
   (b) where the alleged offence was committed at a time when the premises were subject to a notice under section 66 of that Act (noise reduction notice), that the level of noise emitted from the premises at that time was not such as to a constitute a contravention of the notice under that section; or
   (c) where the alleged offence was committed at a time when the premises were not subject to a notice under section 66 of that Act, and when a level fixed under section 67 of that Act (new buildings liable to abatement order) applied to the premises, that the level of noise emitted from the premises at that time did not exceed that level.

(10) Paragraphs (b) and (c) of subsection (9) above apply whether or not the relevant notice was subject to appeal at the time when the offence was alleged to have been committed.

DEFINITIONS
"best practicable means": s.79(9).
"chimney": s.79(7).
"industrial trade or business premises": s.79(7).
"local authority": s.79(7).
"premises": s.79(7).
"smoke": s.79(7).
"statutory nuisance": s.79(1).

GENERAL NOTE
This section deals with the procedures for action by local authorities for the abatement of statutory nuisances. The new procedure draws together those contained in the Public Health Act 1936 and in the Public Health (Recurring Nuisances) Act 1969. The procedures are amended by the 1990 Act in three chief respects:
   (1) The procedure is streamlined. Under the former legislation, the local authority had first to serve an abatement notice. If that notice was not complied with, the authority then had to obtain a nuisance order in the Magistrates' Court. If that order was not complied with, the authority then had to go back to court and prosecute for non-compliance. Complaints were made by local authorities that this procedure was cumbersome, time-consuming and ineffective. The new procedure is modelled on that found in s.58 of the Control of Pollution Act 1974 for noise nuisances. This procedure cuts out the middle nuisance order stage, so that the abatement notice becomes the main step, on which a prosecution may be founded. See also the comparative diagrams at the General Note to Pt. III.

(2) The new section gives local authorities a power, similar to that existing in s.58 of the Control of Pollution Act 1974 in relation to noise nuisances, to take action in anticipation of a statutory nuisance occurring. The Government envisages that this power will be particularly useful in dealing with transient nuisances, such as dust from construction, demolition or cleaning operations, or certain agricultural operations such as the spreading of slurry.

(3) The availability of the defence of best practicable means is widened so as to make it available for nuisances arising on industrial, trade or business premises where the nuisance falls within paras. (a), (d), (e), (f) and (g) of s.79(1). Under the 1936 Act, the defence was only available in trade, business and manufacturing cases for two categories of statutory nuisance, *i.e.* accumulations or deposits (s.92(1)(c)) and dust or effluvia (s.92(1)(d)). The effect of the change is to remove the anomaly whereby a business had the bpm defence available to it if the proceedings related to a smell nuisance under s.92(1)(d) relating to "effluvia," but not if the proceedings were taken under s.92(1)(a) relating to premises in such a state as to be a nuisance.

(4) A distinction is drawn between statutory nuisances committed on industrial, trade or business premises, and those arising on other premises. The maximum fine on summary conviction for the former is increased to £20,000.

Service of notice. The wording of subs. (1) appears to impose a duty on local authorities to serve an abatement notice when satisfied that a statutory nuisance exists or is likely to occur or recur. However, in the housing context it has been suggested that where alternative remedies are open to a local authority, the word "shall" does not mean that the authority are bound to follow the abatement notice route in preference to all others open to them: *Nottinghamshire City District Council* v. *Newton* [1974] 1 W.L.R. 923. The notice should be served in accordance with s.233 of the Local Government Act 1972 or s.192 of the Local Government (Scotland) Act 1973.

Form of notice. No form of notice is prescribed, nor is there provision for regulations to prescribe the form. However, the notice must include a statement informing the recipient of his right of appeal under s.80(3) and giving the time limit for such appeal (Sched. 3, para. 6). It appears, on general principles, that the notice must at least identify clearly and precisely the nuisance complained of and tell the recipient clearly what is required of him. Thus, if works or steps are necessary to abate or prevent the recurrence of the nuisance, those works or steps must be specified with some particularity: see *Salford City Council* v. *McNally* [1976] A.C. 379, 389, *Millard* v. *Wastall* [1898] 1 Q.B. 342; *Whatling* v. *Rees* (1914) 84 L.J.K.B. 1122. If the nuisance can be abated without taking steps or executing works, then none need be specified (*ibid.*).

It is arguable whether a notice can direct the recipient how to carry on day-to-day operations: see *Wivenhoe Port* v. *Colchester Borough Council* [1985] J.P.L. 175, 178; affirmed [1985] J.P.L. 396.

By analogy with the abatement orders made by magistrates under the old procedure, it can by suggested that any notice should be: (a) practical in its effect; (b) easily understood by the recipient and by persons aggrieved by the notice; and (c) specify, where appropriate, the action to be taken to comply (see *R.* v. *Fenny Stratford Justices,* ex p. *Watney Mann (Midlands)* [1976] 1 W.L.R. 110, 1106). Where modern science allows requirements to be stated precisely, *e.g.* by giving decibel levels, this should be done (*ibid.,* p. 1107) but a notice specifying decibel levels without saying where they are to be measured will be void for uncertainty (*ibid.*).

Time for compliance

In cases under s.58 of the Control of Pollution Act, on identical wording as to notices, it has been held that there is no necessity to specify a time for compliance and that in appropriate cases an extremely short time may suffice: see *Strathclyde Regional Council* v. *Tudhope* [1983] J.P.L. 536. In that case the notice required road-breaking equipment not to be used until fitted with effective dampeners. In the absence of a stated date for compliance, the notice was held to come into effect at midnight following the day of service. It was not unreasonable that the equipment should not be used thereafter unless fitted with dampeners. The prohibition of recurrence continues in effect indefinitely: see *R.* v. *Birmingham Justices,* ex p. *Guppy* (1988) 152 J.P. 159.

Subs. (2)

On whom notice may be served. The notice will in most cases be served on the "person responsible" for the nuisance: this means the person to whose act, default or sufferance the nuisance is attributable (s.79(7)). The wording in s.93 of the Public Health Act 1936 referred to the person by whose act default or sufferance the nuisance "arises or continues." In *Clayton* v.

Sale Urban District Council [1926] 1 K.B. 415 it was held that an owner of land may be liable under those words for failure to abate a nuisance existing on his land in consequence of the activities or defaults of another, and regardless of whether the owner is under any contractual or other obligation to take remedial action. An analogy may possibly be drawn with the cases on "continuation" of nuisances in private law: see *Sedleigh-Denfield* v. *O'Callaghan* [1940] A.C. 880; *Leanse* v. *Lord Egerton* [1943] 1 K.B. 323.

If the nuisance arises from a defect "of a structural character" the notice is to be served on the owner of the premises. This appears to mean some defect which affects a structure: *Granada Theatres* v. *Freehold Investment (Leytonstone)* [1958] 2 All E.R. 551, 552, 553. "Structure" has been said to mean "... something which is constructed in the way of being built up as is a building; it is in the nature of a building" (*South Wales Aluminium Co.* v. *Neath Assessment Committee* [1943] 2 All E.R. 587, 592) and "... something which is constructed. It is not everything which is 'constructed' that would ordinarily be called a building, but every building is a structure" (*Mills & Rochleys* v. *Leicester City Council* [1946] 1 All E.R. 424, 427). See also *Cardiff Rating Authority* v. *Guest Keen Baldwin's Iron and Steel Co.* [1949] 1 K.B. 385, 396.

Also, where the person who is responsible for the nuisance cannot be found, the notice may be served on the owner or occupier of the premises. "Owner" was defined at length in the 1936 Act by reference to the person receiving or entitled to receive the rack rent of the premises, but no such definition is found in the 1990 Act. For cases under the old legislation on "owner," see *Walford* v. *Hackney Board of Works* (1894) 43 W.R. 110 (mesne tenant); *Kensington London Borough Council* v. *Allen* [1926] 1 K.B. 576 (mesne tenant); *St. Helen's Corporation* v. *Kirkham* (1885) 16 Q.B.D. 403 (agent); *Bacup Corporation* v. *Smith* (1890) 44 Ch.D. 395 (receiver); *Midland Bank* v. *Conway Corporation* [1965] 1 W.L.R. 1165 (bank); *Poplar Board of Works* v. *Love* (1874) 29 L.T. 915 (lessee at ground rent); *Holland (Lady)* v. *Kensington Vestry* (1867) L.R. 2 C.P. 565 (tenant under building agreement); *Blackburn Corporation* v. *Micklethwaite* (1886) 54 L.T. 539 (mortgagee); *Ebor Land & Development Co.* v. *Benfield* (1969) 68 L.G.R. 237 (vendor under Law Society's Conditions of Sale). See also *Environment Law Brief* (1990) Vol. 1, No. 9, p. 102 (owner responsible for noise nuisance by trespassers).

As to grounds of appeal based on service on the wrong person, see the Statutory Nuisance (Appeals) Regulations 1990 (S.I. 1990 No. 2276), reg. 2(2)(g)–(i) (See Note to s.81).

It appears from one case that a person who converts a building into flats may be a "person responsible" for nuisance resulting from inadequate soundproofing: see article by Bettle [1988] J.P.L. 79 and the case of *Russell* v. *London Borough of Southwark* (November 1985, unreported) referred to therein.

Subs. (4)

Failure to comply with notice. Failure to comply with an abatement notice without reasonable excuse is an offence.

"Reasonable excuse" was argued as a defence in a case under the 1936 Act in *Saddleworth Urban District Council* v. *Aggregate and Sand* (1970) 114 S.J. 931. The argument was that an expert had advised certain works be carried out but funds were exhausted before the work could be completed. The Divisional Court held that lack of finance was not a reasonable excuse and that it would be difficult to rely on the advice of an independent expert as a defence when his recommendations had not been fully implemented. As to the distinction between the defence of reasonable excuse and matters of mitigation, see *Wellingborough Borough Council* v. *Gordon*, *The Times*, November 9, 1990 (birthday celebration held not to be "reasonable excuse" to offence caused by loud reggae music, air horns and whistles).

Where premises are in such a state as to be prejudicial to health or a nuisance, it has been suggested that simply removing the occupants does not constitute abatement of the nuisance: *Coventry City Council* v. *Doyle* [1981] 1 W.L.R. 1325. However, in the same case it was held that different considerations might apply if the premises had effectively been rendered incapable of being occupied.

Although the procedure for statutory nuisances is now different, on the principles discussed in *Coventry City Council* v. *Doyle*, it appears that the relevant date for deciding whether the nuisance has been abated and the notice complied with is the date of the information being laid, not the date of the hearing: see also *Northern Ireland Trailers* v. *Preston Corporation* [1972] 1 W.L.R. 203 and *Lambeth London Borough Council* v. *Stubbs* [1980] J.P.L. 517.

As to proof in noise cases, see *Cooke* v. *Adatia* (1989) J.P. 129 D.C.—it may be sufficient to present evidence of decibel levels from an environmental health officer without calling neighbouring occupiers to testify as to interference with their reasonable comfort or enjoyment.

Subss. (5) and (6)

Penalties. The current maximum penalty for nuisance offences on non-industrial, trade or business premises is £5,000, plus £500 for each day the offence continues after conviction. For nuisances arising on industrial, trade or business premises, the maximum penalty is £20,000 and there is no provision for further daily fines. For the definition of "industrial, trade or business premises," see s.79(7). The definition includes land on which matter is burnt in connection with any trade or business process, and so would catch, for example, construction site bonfires or cable-burning. For the meaning of "trade" and "business" see Note to s.79.

Subs. (8)
This subsection states in what circumstances the defence of best practicable means (bpm) is available (see s.79(9)). The defence is not available at all in the case of fumes or gases emitted from premises (s.79(1)(c)) and any matters declared by other enactments to be a statutory nuisance (s.79(1)(h)). In relation to smoke nuisances it is only available where smoke is emitted from a chimney as defined in s.79 (*cf.* s.16 of the Clean Air Act 1956). In other cases it is only available where the nuisance arises on industrial, trade or business premises (see above).

Subs. (9)
This subsection contains provisions, relating to noise nuisance only, which reproduce the provisions of s.58(6) of the Control of Pollution Act 1974. It provides three further defences, all of which are based on the principle that it is unreasonable for the local authority to institute statutory noise nuisance proceedings where under some other provision they have effectively given consent for a particular level of noise, and the person concerned is not exceeding that level. The particular cases are:
  (a) noise covered by a notice served under s.60 of the Control of Pollution Act 1974 (specifying maximum levels of noise for construction works) and consents given under ss.61 or 65 of COPA (s.61 relates to orders under which local authorities agree to specified noise levels from construction works and s.65 relates to orders under which premises may be allowed to increase their noise levels above the originally measured level with the written consent of the local authority);
  (b) noise where the premises are subject to a notice under s.66 of COPA, not constituting a contravention of that notice (s.66 of COPA deals with notices requiring a reduction in the levels of noise emanating from premises); and
  (c) noise from premises in respect of which a level has been fixed under s.67 of COPA where the noise does not exceed that level (s.67 allows a local authority to determine the noise level for a new building before the building is complete).

Paragraphs (b) and (c) apply whether or not the relevant notice was subject to appeal at the time (subs. (10)).

Additionally, the High Court decision in *Gillingham Borough Council* v. *Medway (Chatham) Dock Co. Ltd.* [1991] NPC 97 is particularly relevant to the potential availability of the statutory nuisance provisions although it dealt with a common law action based on public nuisance. Residents in the area complained to the environmental health officer about the noise associated with the use of the access roads to the dockyard and the Council sought an injunction to restrict night-time lorry movements on the grounds that the disturbance amounted in law to a public nuisance. The Council were unsuccessful as the Court found that the planning permission granted by Gillingham Borough Council for the dockyard use in 1983 had changed the character of the neighbourhood. Instead of considering the nuisance in the context of a residential area the Court considered it in the context of a commercial port and concluded that the noise and disturbance could not be a nuisance in law.

Supplementary provisions

81.—(1) Where more than one person is responsible for a statutory nuisance section 80 above shall apply to each of those persons whether or not what any one of them is responsible for would by itself amount to a nuisance.

(2) Where a statutory nuisance which exists or has occurred within the area of a local authority, or which has affected any part of that area, appears to the local authority to be wholly or partly caused by some act or default committed or taking place outside the area, the local authority may act under section 80 above as if the act or default were wholly within that area, except that any appeal shall be heard by a magistrates' court having jurisdiction where the act or default is alleged to have taken place.

(3) Where an abatement notice has not been complied with the local authority may, whether or not they take proceedings for an offence under section 80(4) above, abate the nuisance and do whatever may be necessary in execution of the notice.

(4) Any expenses reasonably incurred by a local authority in abating, or preventing the recurrence of, a statutory nuisance under subsection (3) above may be recovered by them from the person by whose act or default the nuisance was caused and, if that person is the owner of the premises, from any person who is for the time being the owner thereof; and the court may apportion the expenses between persons by whose acts or defaults the nuisance is caused in such manner as the court consider fair and reasonable.

(5) If a local authority is of opinion that proceedings for an offence under section 80(4) above would afford an inadequate remedy in the case of any statutory nuisance, they may, subject to subsection (6) below, take proceedings in the High Court for the purpose of securing the abatement, prohibition or restriction of the nuisance, and the proceedings shall be maintainable notwithstanding the local authority have suffered no damage from the nuisance.

(6) In any proceedings under subsection (5) above in respect of a nuisance falling within paragraph (g) of section 79(1) above, it shall be a defence to prove that the noise was authorised by a notice under section 60 or a consent under section 61 (construction sites) of the Control of Pollution Act 1974.

(7) The further supplementary provisions in Schedule 3 to this Act shall have effect.

DEFINITIONS
"local authority": s.79(6).
"premises": s.79(6).
"statutory nuisance": s.79(1).

GENERAL NOTE
This section, together with Sched. 3, contains various supplementary provisions.

Subs. (1)
This provision, modelled on s.73(3) of the Control of Pollution Act 1974, provides for the situation where more than one person is responsible for a statutory nuisance. Action may be taken against each such person regardless of whether or not the matters for which each is responsible would, taken in isolation, constitute a statutory nuisance.

Subs. (2)
This provision allows a local authority to take action in respect of a statutory nuisance wholly or partly caused by some act or default outside their area, but which affects their area. The provision replaces s.98 of the Public Health Act 1936 and is modelled on s.58(7) of the Control of Pollution Act 1974. If any appeal is made against the abatement notice in such cases, it is the magistrates' court for the area in which the relevant act or default took place that has jurisdiction.

Subss. (3) and (4)
These subsections give authorities powers comparable to those in ss.95 and 96 of the Public Health Act 1936 to take action themselves to abate statutory nuisances and to recover reasonable expenses incurred in so doing. The power arises where an abatement notice has not been complied with, whether or not criminal proceedings are taken under s.80(4).

The expenses of abating the nuisance or preventing its recurrence are to be recovered from the person by whose act or default the nuisance was caused. If that person happens to have been the owner of the premises, the expenses may be recovered from any person who is the owner for the time being. As to the meaning of "owner," see notes to s.80.

The court has wide power to apportion expenses between persons by whose acts or defaults the nuisance arose, in such manner as it considers fair and reasonable. For a recent apportionment case in a different statutory context, see *Watney Combe Reid & Co.* v. *Westminster (City) Council* (1970) 214 E.G. 1631 (fire precautions). On the question as to how far the power of apportionment can be excluded by agreement, for example in a lease, see *Monk* v. *Arnold* [1902] 1 K.B. 761, *Monro* v. *Lord Burghclere* [1918] 1 K.B. 291 and *Horner* v. *Franklin* [1905] 1 K.B. 479.

Subs. (5)
This subsection enables High Court proceedings to be taken by local authorities to secure

abatement, prohibition or restriction of statutory nuisances. The precondition is that the authority must be satisfied that proceedings for an offence under s.80(4) would afford an inadequate remedy. The provision follows s.100 of the Public Health Act 1936 and s.58(8) of the Control of Pollution Act 1974.

For an example of successful injunctive proceedings in relation to noise, see *Hammersmith London Borough Council* v. *Magnum Automated Forecourts* [1978] 1 W.L.R. 50, where the criteria for granting such relief were discussed. It was held there that the remedy is in addition to summary proceedings and that it is not a bar to relief that summary remedies have not been exhausted. Interlocutory injunctive relief may be obtained where appropriate on the principles of *American Cyanamid Co.* v. *Ethicon* [1975] A.C. 396. See also *Lloyds Bank* v. *Guardian Assurance and Trollope & Colls* (1987) 35 Build.L.R. 34 (C.A.) for the relationship between statutory procedures and private nuisance actions. Civil proceedings may also be instituted by a local authority under s.222 of the Local Government Act 1972: see *Mayor and Commonalty of the City of London* v. *Bovis Construction* [1989] J.P.L. 263.

Subs. (6)
This re-enacts the proviso to s.58(8) of the Control of Pollution Act 1974. In relation to noise nuisances it is a defence to proceedings in the High Court under subs. (5) to prove that the noise was authorised by a notice under s.60 of COPA (control of noise on construction sites) or a consent under s.61 (prior consent for work on construction sites).

Subs. (7) and Sched. 3
Schedule 3 contains further ancillary provisions dealing with the procedure for appeals against abatement notices, powers of entry and related powers, offences of obstructing entry, procedures where local authorities default in their duties under Pt. III and protection of officers against personal liability.

Regulations on appeals against abatement notices have now been made: the Statutory Nuisance (Appeals) Regulations 1990 (S.I. 1990 No. 2276) as amended by S.I. 1990 No. 2483. These Regulations follow in many respects those under COPA in relation to noise: the Control of Noise (Appeals) Regulations 1975 (S.I. 1975 No. 2116) and the Control of Noise (Appeals) (Scotland) Regulations 1983 (S.I. 1983 No. 1455). The grounds of appeal are identical in many respects. The 1990 Regulations give some nine separate grounds of appeal (reg. 2(2)) and give the court wide discretion in dealing with appeals (reg. 2(3)–(7)). By reg. 3 the effect of an appeal does not in general have the effect of suspending the notice unless compliance with it would require expenditure on carrying out works before the hearing of the appeal, or where the alleged nuisance is noise caused in the course of the appellant performing some duty imposed by law. For cases on the 1975 Regulations, see *Wycombe District Council* v. *Jeffways and Pilot Coaches* (1983) 81 L.G.R. 662 (C.A.) and *Johnsons News of London* v. *Ealing London Borough Council* (1989) 154 J.P. 33. In the latter case it was held that where an appeal is made on ground (e) (use of best practicable means), steps taken by the appellant to abate the nuisance after the issue of the notice must be taken into account.

Paragraph 6 was introduced as a House of Lords amendment, and requires local authorities to include in notices served under Pt. III a statement (if that be the case) that appeal lies to a magistrates' court and to specify the time within which such an appeal must be brought.

Summary proceedings by person aggrieved by statutory nuisances

82.—(1) A magistrates' court may act under this section on a complaint made by any person on the ground that he is aggrieved by the existence of a statutory nuisance.

(2) If the magistrates' court is satisfied that the alleged nuisance exists, or that although abated it is likely to recur on the same premises, the court shall make an order for either or both of the following purposes—
  (a) requiring the defendant to abate the nuisance, within a time specified in the order, and to execute any works necessary for that purpose;
  (b) prohibiting a recurrence of the nuisance, and requiring the defendant, within a time specified in the order, to execute any works necessary to prevent the recurrence,
and may also impose on the defendant a fine not exceeding level 5 on the standard scale.

(3) If the magistrates' court is satisfied that the alleged nuisance exists and is such as, in the opinion of the court, to render premises unfit for human habitation, an order under subsection (2) above may prohibit the use of the

premises for human habitation until the premises are, to the satisfaction of the court, rendered fit for that purpose.

(4) Proceedings for an order under subsection (2) above shall be brought—
   (a) except in a case falling within paragraph (b) or (c) below, against the person responsible for the nuisance;
   (b) where the nuisance arises from any defect of a structural character, against the owner of the premises;
   (c) where the person responsible for the nuisance cannot be found, against the owner or occupier of the premises.

(5) Where more than one person is responsible for a statutory nuisance, subsections (1) to (4) above shall apply to each of those persons whether or not what any one of them is responsible for would by itself amount to a nuisance.

(6) Before instituting proceedings for an order under subsection (2) above against any person, the person aggrieved by the nuisance shall give to that person such notice in writing of his intention to bring the proceedings as is applicable to proceedings in respect of a nuisance of that description and the notice shall specify the matter complained of.

(7) The notice of the bringing of proceedings in respect of a statutory nuisance required by subsection (6) above which is applicable is—
   (a) in the case of a nuisance falling within paragraph (g) of section 79(1) above, not less than three days' notice; and
   (b) in the case of a nuisance of any other description, not less than 21 days' notice;
but the Secretary of State may, by order, provide that this subsection shall have effect as if such period as is specified in the order were the minimum period of notice applicable to any description of statutory nuisance specified in the order.

(8) A person who, without reasonable excuse, contravenes any requirement or prohibition imposed by an order under subsection (2) above shall be guilty of an offence and liable on summary conviction to a fine not exceeding level 5 on the standard scale together with a further fine of an amount equal to one-tenth of that level for each day on which the offence continues after the conviction.

(9) Subject to subsection (10) below, in any proceedings for an offence under subsection (8) above in respect of a statutory nuisance it shall be a defence to prove that the best practicable means were used to prevent, or to counteract the effects of, the nuisance.

(10) The defence under subsection (9) above is not available—
   (a) in the case of a nuisance falling within paragraph (a), (d), (e), (f) or (g) of section 79(1) above except where the nuisance arises on industrial, trade or business premises;
   (b) in the case of a nuisance falling within paragraph (b) of section 79(1) above except where the smoke is emitted from a chimney; and
   (c) in the case of a nuisance falling within paragraph (c) or (h) of section 79(1) above; and
   (d) in the case of a nuisance which is such as to render the premises unfit for human habitation.

(11) If a person is convicted of an offence under subsection (8) above, a magistrates' court may, after giving the local authority in whose area the nuisance has occurred an opportunity of being heard, direct the authority to do anything which the person convicted was required to do by the order to which the conviction relates.

(12) Where on the hearing of proceedings for an order under subsection (2) above it is proved that the alleged nuisance existed at the date of the making of the complaint, then, whether or not at the date of the hearing it still exists or is likely to recur, the court shall order the defendant (or

defendants in such proportions as appears fair and reasonable) to pay to the person bringing the proceedings such amount as the court considers reasonably sufficient to compensate him for any expenses properly incurred by him in the proceedings.

(13) If it appears to the magistrates' court that neither the person responsible for the nuisance nor the owner or occupier of the premises can be found the court may, after giving the local authority in whose area the nuisance has occurred an opportunity of being heard, direct the authority to do anything which the court would have ordered that person to do.

DEFINITIONS
"best practicable means": s.79(9).
"chimney": s.79(6).
"local authority": s.79(6).
"premises": s.79(6).
"smoke": s.79(6).
"statutory nuisance": s.79(1).

GENERAL NOTE
This section provides a right for any person aggrieved by the existence of a statutory nuisance to make a complaint direct to a magistrates' court. A similar right existed under s.99 of the Public Health Act 1936; s.81 is, however, based on the model of s.59 of the Control of Pollution Act 1974 which applies to noise nuisance. The magistrates may, by subs. (2), make an order either requiring abatement of the nuisance or prohibiting its recurrence; they may also impose a fine. In each case, the defendant may be required to execute necessary works. Failure to comply with the order without reasonable excuse is an offence (subs. (8)). The section contains ancillary provisions similar to those relating to proceedings by local authorities, including the defence of best practicable means (subss. (9) and (10)).

Person aggrieved. There is an important difference from s.59 of the Control of Pollution Act, under which the remedy was available only to an occupier of premises aggrieved by the noise in his capacity as occupier. Under s.82 the complainant merely has to be a person aggrieved by the existence of the nuisance.

Clearly a person whose own health, or that of their family, is being prejudicially affected by the nuisance would be a person aggrieved: see *Sandwell Metropolitan Borough Council* v. *Bujok* [1990] 3 All E.R. 385. A person whose reasonable enjoyment of their property is materially affected would similarly be a person aggrieved, and there seems no reason why interference with commercial interests should not similarly provide standing.

One of the best known definitions of "person aggrieved" is that given by Lord Denning M.R. in *Att.-Gen. (Gambia)* v. *N'Jie* [1961] 2 All E.R. 504 at 511:

"The words 'person aggrieved' are of wide import and should not be subjected to a restricted interpretation. They do not include, of course, a mere busybody who is interfering in things that do not concern him; but they do include a person who has a genuine grievance because an order has been made which prejudicially affects his interest."

In *Birmingham District Council* v. *McMahon* (1987) 151 J.P. 709 (D.C.) it was held that a council tenant in a block of flats who complained of a statutory nuisance affecting the block in general, but not his flat, was not a "person aggrieved." It appears that the important consideration is to relate the grievance to the existence of the relevant category of statutory nuisance and the interpretation to be placed on the qualifying words in s.79(1)(a)–(g) "prejudicial to health or a nuisance": see note to s. 79.

In *Sandwell Metropolitan Borough Council* v. *Bujok* (above) the House of Lords held (p. 391) that an adversely affected individual is a person aggrieved under s.99 of the Public Health Act 1936, irrespective of whether or not he has given prior notice of the nuisance to the proposed defendant. See, however, the new requirement to give notice under subss. (6) and (7) (below).

Use of provisions against local authorities
It became well established that s.99 of the Public Health Act could be used against local authorities responsible for statutory nuisances: *R.* v. *Epping (Waltham Abbey) JJ.*, ex p. *Burlinson* [1948] 1 K.B. 79. The section came to be used extensively in housing cases as a means of forcing local authority landlords to carry out repairs or to remedy defects resulting in problems such as excessive condensation or inadequate sound insulation. In *Sandwell Metropolitan Borough Council* v. *Bujok* [1990] 3 All E.R. 385, 392 the House of Lords was told that

the authority in question had been served with no less than 632 summonses under s.99 in just over two years since June 1988.

Procedure
Procedure under s.99 of the Public Health Act 1936 has been considered in a number of recent reported cases. Proceedings under s.99, read in conjunction with s.94(2), could result in a fine being imposed in addition to the making of a nuisance order. On that basis such proceedings have been held to be criminal in nature, and as such to be commenced by information and summons rather than complaint: see *Northern Ireland Trailers* v *Preston Corporation* [1972] 1 W.L.R. 203; *R.* v. *Newham East Justices*, ex p. *Hunt*; *R.* v. *Oxted Justices*, ex p. *Franklin* [1976] 1 W.L.R. 420; *R.* v. *Inner London Crown Court*, ex p. *Bentham* [1989] 1 W.L.R. 408.

Proceedings under s.59 of the Control of Pollution Act, however, could not lead to an immediate fine and so on the same test were of the nature of civil proceedings, instigated by complaint. As originally drafted, s.82 of the 1990 Act like s.59 of COPA, contained no reference to a fine and indeed an express Government amendment altered the reference to an "information laid" to "complaint made." However, the section was subject to a late amendment on Third Reading in the Lords to allow magistrates to impose a fine in conjunction with the abatement order. The amended reference to "complaint made," however, anomalously remains. The reason for the amendment to "criminalise" the complaint was expressed as follows by Lord Byron in moving the amendment:

"Where a landlord is convicted of an offence under that section, the court may, and in most cases will, award compensation to the tenant for any personal injury, loss or damage caused by the offence. The magistrates will also order necessary work to be done. As drafted, the Bill will replace the current criminal procedure with a civil one, although still in the magistrates' court. No offence will be committed until a nuisance order made by the court has been breached, which issue will be determined by a second, later hearing. The power to award compensation to tenants will therefore be severely limited.

The purpose of the amendment is to restore the current power in relation to proceedings brought by individuals where, by ss.99 and 94 of the 1936 Act, the existence of a statutory nuisance amounts to an offence and a court may fine a defendant and make an award of compensation in favour of the tenant under s.35 of the Powers of Criminal Courts Act 1973. The amendment will reproduce those arrangements in the Bill. Thus, under Clause 81, where the court is satisfied that a nuisance exists, the court shall make an order and, if the amendment is accepted, may impose a fine. The court may also in those circumstances make an award of compensation in favour of the tenant under s.35 of the Powers of Criminal Courts Act. That is possible only if, as is currently the case, a criminal offence has been committed.

It is the power to award compensation which will be lost, or at least substantially diminished, unless the amendment is accepted. There is no doubt that as the law stands at present the nature of proceedings under s.99 is criminal and the offence is that of permitting the nuisance of exist. Magistrates' courts throughout England and Wales, especially in the metropolitan areas, are familiar with the criminal proceedings brought by individuals under s.99 and would similarly be able to apply the law as set out in Clause 82 if the amendment were accepted.

The issue raised by the amendment is of great importance to tenants and other individual occupiers. Under the present arrangement, where a defendant is convicted in proceedings brought under s.99 of the 1936 Act, the power to award compensation is used widely by the courts. In many of the busy magistrates' courts in metropolitan areas it is now common for awards of between £1,500 and £2,000 to be made in favour of individuals aggrieved by nuisance.

As presently drafted, the clause will reduce substantially the sums available for compensation in the event of the court choosing to exercise its discretion. This is because no offence is committed other than under Clause 81(5) where a nuisance order made at the first hearing has been breached and a tenant has proved the breach at the second subsequent hearing, once the time allowed for the work has expired. The time usually available for works in nuisance orders currently made depends on the nature of the works ordered. It could perhaps be eight weeks if the works are simple and up to six months for substantial works. The tenant having brought the matter back to court, there may be conviction at the second hearing. The individual may then seek to persuade the court to exercise its discretion to make an award of compensation in his favour.

However, in contrast to the present arrangements, the courts can have in mind only any personal injury, loss or damage flowing from the offence: that is, any such loss occurring as a result of the breach of the order. The court will have no choice about that. It will be unlawful to relate an award of compensation to any period of time before the commission of the offence. Evidence relating to injury and loss during the period before conviction in which the premises are prejudicial to health and nuisance will be inadmissible.

There are other reasons for and other major advantages to the present criminal process. Briefly, these are that the conviction and the discretion of the court to impose a fine allows the court to show its disapproval to the community. Further, landlords who allow premises to become dangerously unhealthy—and unhappily this also includes landlords in the public sector—take criminal proceedings seriously. The response to what is initially a civil claim may simply be to treat the matter as a commercial risk.

Finally, the powers to fine and make an award of compensation are entirely discretionary. It is therefore hard to identify any objection in principle to the amendment. Furthermore—and perhaps the most powerful point—there is no case for a change in the law. Proceedings by individuals for statutory nuisance have been criminal in nature for over 50 years. Lawyers, advisers and all other organisations involved in this type of matter all favour the retention of the existing criminal procedures. I beg to move." (*Hansard*, H.L. Vol. 522, cols. 1279–1280.)

It has been held that an information laid under s.99 of the 1936 Act should disclose, at least in summary form, the same details was would have been contained in a s.93 abatement notice, as to the capacity in which the defendant is being served and the steps it is alleged he should take in order to abate the nuisance: *Warner* v. *Lambeth London Borough Council* (1984) 15 H.L.R. 42. The same principles may well apply to proceedings under s.82.

Notice before action
In *Sandwell Metropolitan Borough Council* v. *Bujok* [1990] 3 All E.R. 385 (H.L.) it was held that s.99 of the 1936 Act did not require an aggrieved person to give notice equivalent to an abatement notice before commencing summary proceedings. However, the House of Lords made it clear that failure to give reasonable notice requiring the defect or nuisance to be remedied is to be deplored, endorsing the following passage from the judgment of Watkins L.J. at (1989) 88 L.G.R. 521, 534:

". . . it is surely repugnant to common sense that in the area of legal activity a local authority should be prosecuted by one of its tenants without first being given the opportunity by that tenant to remedy the consequences of a neglect to repair the dwelling that tenant occupies. In law there is no doubt that [the respondent] was entitled to commence proceedings without giving notice of the state of the dwelling to the local authority. But in every other conceivable way I regard that action as entirely wrong. Endless trouble to many people in courts and local authority offices and much money could be saved by the giving of notice of disrepair which it is to be supposed a local authority would appropriately react to. If they did not, then would be the time for a tenant to exercise the right to prosecute. I doubt whether there is anyone, a ratepayer especially, giving proper thought to such a situation as we have been confronted with who would disagree with that approach to what surely is a commonplace problem."

That problem has now been addressed by late amendments to the Bill, forming subss. (6) and (7). These provisions require the person aggrieved to give at least 21 days' written notice (three days' in the case of noise nuisance) of intention to bring proceedings.

Abatement order by magistrates
If satisfied as to the matters stated in subs. (2), the magistrates have a duty to make an abatement order, but have wide discretion as to the terms of such order: *Nottingham Corporation* v. *Newton* [1974] 1 W.L.R. 923; *Salford City Council* v. *McNally* [1976] A.C. 379. In particular, in housing cases, any relevant proceedings under the Housing Acts may be taken into consideration: *ibid.*

As to the precision and clarity required in an order, see *R.* v. *Fenny Stratford Justices, ex p. Watney Mann (Midlands)* [1976] 1 W.L.R. 1101 (D.C.) noted under s.80 above. As to whether an order may regulate day to day operational matters, see *Wivenhoe Port* v. *Colchester Borough Council* [1985] J.P.L. 396 (also noted above).

Where a person is convicted of contravention of the abatement notice, there is a residual power under subs. (11) for the court to direct the local authority for the area to do what is required to abate the nuisance, rather than the person convicted.

Subs. (3)
Unfit dwellings. Where the magistrates are satisfied that the alleged nuisance is such as to render premises unfit for human habitation, the abatement order may prohibit the use of the premises for human habitation until rendered fit for that purpose. Whether a house is unfit for habitation is a question of fact for the magistrates: see *Hall* v. *Manchester Corporation* (1915) 84

L.J. Ch. 732, 741 and 742. Nor does it appear that non-compliance with any statutory requirements or standards means that premises are necessarily unfit: *Birchall* v. *Wirrall Urban District Council* (1953) 117 J.P. 384. In the context of the implied statutory obligation on landlords that dwelling-houses should be reasonably fit for human habitation it has been said that:

> "If the state . . . of a house is such that by ordinary use damage may naturally be caused to the occupier, either in respect of personal injury to life or limb or injury to health, then the house is not in all respects reasonably fit for human habitation" (*Morgan* v. *Liverpool Corporation* [1927] 2 K.B. 131, 144 and 145 (C.A., *per* Atkin L.J.)).

Subs. (12)
Costs. The summary procedure under s.99 of the Public Health Act contained no provision as to costs, which were at the discretion of the court: see *Sandwell Metropolitan Borough Council* v. *Bujok* [1990] 3 All E.R. 385, 392.

However, subs. (12) now provides that costs must be awarded in favour of the complainant where it is proved that the alleged nuisance existed at the date of the complaint, whether or not it has ceased or been abated by the time of the hearing. It is the "alleged nuisance" that must be proved, *i.e.* the nuisance alleged in the complaint and specified in the notice before proceedings. If some different nuisance is found to exist rather than the one alleged, it would appear that subs. (12) does not apply and that costs are at the discretion of the court.

Statutory nuisances: Scotland

Statutory nuisances: Scotland

83.—(1) Sections 79 to 82 above do not apply to Scotland.

(2) In section 16 of the Public Health (Scotland) Act 1897 (definition of nuisances), after paragraph (5) there shall be inserted the following paragraphs—

> "(5A) Any fumes ("fumes" meaning airborne solid matter smaller than dust), gases or vapours emitted, so as to be a nuisance or injurious or dangerous to health, from any premises, or part thereof, used or intended to be used as a dwelling house."
>
> (5B) Any dust caused by any trade, business, manufacture or process, being a nuisance or injurious or dangerous to health."

GENERAL NOTE
Subsection (1) states that the statutory nuisance provisions of Pt. III do not apply to Scotland.
Subsection (2) amends s.16 of the Public Health (Scotland) Act 1897 (which defines nuisances) so as to extend the definition to fumes, gases or vapours emitted from dwellings, and also to dust caused by any trade, business, manufacture or process.

Termination of existing controls over offensive trades and businesses

Termination of Public Health Act controls over offensive trades etc.

84.—(1) Where a person carries on, in the area or part of the area of any local authority—
  (a) in England or Wales, a trade which—
    (i) is an offensive trade within the meaning of section 107 of the Public Health Act 1936 in that area or part of that area, and
    (ii) constitutes a prescribed process designated for local control for the carrying on of which an authorisation is required under section 6 of this Act; or
  (b) in Scotland, a business which—
    (i) is mentioned in section 32(1) of the Public Health (Scotland) Act 1897 (or is an offensive business by virtue of that section) in that area or part of that area; and
    (ii) constitutes a prescribed process designated for local control for the carrying on of which an authorisation is required under the said section 6,

subsection (2) below shall have effect in relation to that trade or business as from the date on which an authorisation is granted under section 6 of this Act or, if that person has not applied for such an authorisation within the period allowed under section 2(1) above for making applications under that section, as from the end of that period.

(2) Where this subsection applies in relation to the trade or business carried on by any person—
   (a) nothing in section 107 of the Public Health Act 1936 or in section 32 of the Public Health (Scotland) Act 1897 shall apply in relation to it, and
   (b) no byelaws or further byelaws made under section 108(2) of the said Act of 1936, or under subsection (2) of the said section 32, with respect to a trade or business of that description shall apply in relation to it;

but without prejudice to the continuance of, and imposition of any penalty in, any proceedings under the said section 107 or the said section 32 which were instituted before the date as from which this subsection has effect in relation to the trade or business.

(3) Subsection (2)(b) above shall apply in relation to the trade of fish frying as it applies in relation to an offensive trade.

(4) When the Secretary of State considers it expedient to do so, having regard to the operation of Part I and the preceding provisions of this Part of this Act in relation to offensive trades or businesses, he may by order repeal—
   (a) sections 107 and 108 of the Public Health Act 1936; and
   (b) section 32 of the Public Health (Scotland) Act 1897;

and different days may be so appointed in relation to trades or businesses which constitute prescribed processes and those which do not.

(5) In this section—
   "prescribed process" has the same meaning as in Part I of this Act; and
   "offensive trade" or "trade" has the same meaning as in section 107 of the Public Health Act 1936.

DEFINITIONS
"local authority": s.79(6).

GENERAL NOTE
Existing controls over "offensive trades". This section makes provision for the gradual disapplication and eventual termination of existing statutory controls over the so-called "offensive trades" in ss.107 and 108 of the Public Health Act 1936 and s.32 of the Public Health (Scotland) Act 1897. Under s.107 of the 1936 Act, the consent of the local authority is required for offensive trades carried on within their area. No such trade may be lawfully established without such consent in writing: *Epping Forest District Council* v. *Essex Rendering* [1983] 1 W.L.R. 158 (H.L.). Such trades are defined by s.107 of the 1936 Act, as amended by Sched. 14, para. 11 of the Local Government Act 1972. As well as the list of trades given there, other trades or processes may come under control by designation by the local authority, confirmed by the Secretary of State. Local authorities may make by-laws relating to offensive trades under s.108(2) of the 1936 Act and s.32(3) of the 1897 Scotland Act, for the purpose of preventing or diminishing the noxious or injurious effects of the trade.

Subss. (1) and (2)
Disapplication of present controls. The subsections together provide for the disapplication of the controls described above. The general effect is that the offensive trade or offensive business controls cease to have effect in relation to trades or businesses as they fall under the local authority air pollution controls of Pt. I of the Act. The relevant date is that on which the individual trade or business is granted an authorisation under Pt. I, or if no application is made, the end of the period allowed for such applications. By subs. (2) the requirements for consent mentioned above cease to have effect in relation to the trade or business, as do any by-laws made by the authority. This does not, however, affect proceedings instituted under the previous controls in relation to the trade or business before the relevant date.

Subs. (3)
Fish frying. This subsection has the same effect of disapplication in relation to by-laws made under s.108(1) of the 1936 Act in relation to fish frying. Fish frying is not an offensive trade in England and Wales, but can be the subject of analogous by-laws. In Scotland, fish frying may be declared an offensive trade under s.32(1) of the 1897 Act.

Subs. (4)
Termination of controls. This subsection gives the Secretary of State power, when he considers it expedient to do so, to repeal entirely the offensive trade provisions in England and Wales and in Scotland. The Secretary of State must have regard to the operation of Pts. I and III of the 1990 Act in making this decision, the intention being that such activities will in future be controlled under those provisions. The majority of such processes will no doubt be scheduled for control under Pt. I.

Application to gases of certain Clean Air Act provisions

Application to gases of certain Clean Air Act provisions

85. After section 7 of the Clean Air Act 1968 there shall be inserted the following section—

> **"Application to gases of certain provisions as to grit and dust**
>
> 7A.—(1) The Minister may by regulations—
> (a) apply all or any the provisions of sections 2, 3, 4 and 5 of this Act and of sections 7, 18(2), 19(3), 20(4) and 22(1) of the principal Act (provisions relating to grit and dust or smoke) to prescribed gases as they apply to grit and dust; and
> (b) apply all or any of the provisions of section 3 of the principal Act (requirement that new furnaces shall be so far as practicable smokeless) to prescribed gases as they apply to smoke;
> subject, in either case, to such exceptions and modifications as the Minister thinks expedient.
>
> (2) Regulations under this section may make different provision for different cases.
>
> (3) No regulations shall be made under this section unless a draft of the regulations has been laid before Parliament and approved by each House of Parliament.
>
> (4) In the application of any provision of the principal Act or this Act to prescribed gases by virtue of regulations under this section, any reference to the rate of emission of any substance shall be construed as a reference to the percentage by volume or by mass of the gas which may be emitted during a period specified in the regulations.
>
> (5) In this section—
> 'gas' includes vapour and moisture precipitated from vapour; and
> 'prescribed' means prescribed in regulations under this section."

GENERAL NOTE
This is an enabling measure which allows the Secretary of State to make regulations to control the emission of prescribed gases from furnaces controlled under the Clean Air Acts 1956 and 1968. The power applies generally throughout Great Britain. The effect of such regulations is to apply all or any of the listed sections of the 1956 and 1968 Acts to prescribed gases in the same way that they presently apply to dust, grit and smoke.

The relevant sections that may be so applied (with references to "prescribed gases" inserted for ease of reference) are:

Clean Air Act 1956

S.3	—	Requiring new furnaces to be as far as practicable capable of being operated without emitting [prescribed gases].
S.7	—	Requiring measurement of [prescribed gases] emitted from certain furnaces.

S.18(2)	—	Exempting emission of [prescribed gases] from colliery spoilbanks from the provisions of the Public Health Act 1936 and of the Clean Air Acts. (Emissions of "Smoke and Fumes" from such spoilbanks are already controlled under s.18(1) of the 1956 Act).
S.19(3)	—	Exempting [prescribed gas] emissions from railway locomotives from the other provisions of the Clean Air Acts ("Dark smoke" emissions from such engines are controlled under s.19 of the 1956 Act).
S.20(4)	—	Exempting [prescribed gas] emissions from vessels from the other provisions of the Clean Air Acts ("Dark Smoke" emissions are controlled under s.20 of the 1956 Act).
S.22(1)	—	Emissions of [prescribed gases] from Crown premises.

Clean Air Act 1968

S.2	—	Limits on rates of emission of [prescribed gases] from certain furnaces.
S.3	—	Requirements of provision of plant for arresting [prescribed gases] from certain furnaces.
S.4	—	Allowing exemptions from requirements to fit arrestment plant.
S.5	—	Concerning measurement of emissions of [prescribed gases] from certain furnaces.

See now the Clean Air Act 1993, which is a consolidating measure.

PART IV

LITTER ETC.

GENERAL NOTE

Part IV of the Act contains new provisions relating to litter and to abandoned shopping and luggage trolleys. The Government issued a Consultation Paper on July 20, 1989, *Action on Litter: The Government's Proposals for Legislation* (DoE, Department of Transport and Welsh Office). The Paper pointed out (paras. 2 and 3):

"More and more people are concerned that in spite of increased efforts by many local authorities, private land owners, voluntary groups and individuals, the problem of litter shows no signs of abating. At the same time, public awareness, and the demand from both local authorities and individuals for tougher action, are growing. The Government shares this concern, and is determined to take the measures needed to ensure that the problem can be, and is, tackled effectively."

Various initiatives were mooted in the paper, a number of which are included in Pt. IV of the Act, with or without subsequent amendments:
 (1) an increase in the maximum fine for littering to £1,000;
 (2) power to introduce fixed penalty schemes for littering offences;
 (3) a duty on local authorities to clean and keep clean of litter "all land in their beneficial occupancy or control, open to the air and to which the public have access";
 (4) a rationalisation of the current division of responsibility for road cleaning between different tiers of authority;
 (5) the issue of a Code of Practice on cleaning, to which local authorities would be required to have regard in discharging their duties;
 (6) the ability for any "person aggrieved" by failure of a local authority to keep land clean to apply to the magistrates' court for a "litter abatement order" directed to the authority;
 (7) obligations on statutory undertakers and private owners or occupiers of land to which the public have access (*e.g.* car parks, shopping precincts and sports grounds) to keep the land clean, and extension of littering offences to such areas;
 (8) a reserve power to require local authorities to remove graffiti in public places, for possible implementation when the necessary technology is proven and the financial implications clearer; and
 (9) cleaning up dog faeces to be included within the duty on local authorities to keep public areas clean.
These proposals have been translated into the following provisions of the Act:

43–227

(1) a widened offence of leaving litter, subject to a maximum £1,000 fine on summary conviction (s.87);
(2) power to issue fixed penalty notices to a person believed to have committed the new littering offence (s.88);
(3) duties on the Crown, local authorities, highway authorities designated statutory undertakers and the occupiers of "relevant land" to ensure land is, so far as practicable, kept clear of litter and refuse (s.89);
(4) power for the Secretary of State to issue a Code or Codes of Practice on the duty (s.89(7)–(13)). The Code was issued in November 1990: see Note to s.89. The operative (statutory) part of the Code is reproduced, without the non-statutory Appendix, as Appendix 8 at the end of these annotations;
(5) power to designate "litter control areas" (s.90);
(6) provision for summary proceedings by persons aggrieved by litter on highways, Crown and local authority land, other relevant land, and litter control areas designated under s.90 (s.91). The proceedings may lead to a "litter abatement order" under s.91(6), non-compliance with which is an offence;
(7) provision for summary proceedings by litter authorities, with power to serve litter abatement notices (s.92);
(8) power for litter authorities to issue "street litter control notices" on occupiers of premises adjacent to streets or fronting on to streets (s.93);
(9) power to apply provisions as to the seizure, removal, retention, return and disposal of abandoned shopping and luggage trolleys, with power to levy charges on the return of the trolleys (s.99 and Sched. 4).

Territorial extent
Part IV does not extend to Northern Ireland (s.164(4)).

Commencement
Section 97 (transitional provisions) and s.99 (shopping and luggage trolleys) come into force after two months from passage of the Act, *i.e.* on January 1, 1991 (s.156(2)). The remainder of the provisions come into force on an appointed day or days. Section 89(7), (8), (9), (11), (12) and (13) came into force on November 13, 1990 (S.I. 1990 No. 2243). Sections 86(2), (6)–(8), (11), (14) and (15), 88(5), (7) and (9)(b), 89(4), 90(1), (2) and (7), 94(1) and (2) and 96(2) and (3) came into force in England and Wales and Scotland on January 14, 1991 (S.I. 1991 No. 96). Sections 86(1), (4), (5), (9) and (13), 87(1)(2)(3)(a)–(e) and (4)–(6), 88(1)–(4), (6), (8), (9)(a) and (c)–(e) and (10) came into force in England and Wales only on February 13, 1991 (S.I. 1991 No. 96). The new duties on local authorities have been brought into force (Commencement Order No. 7 (S.I. 1991 No. 1042) and Commencement Order No. 5 (S.I. 1991 No. 96). Orders have also been made designating statutory undertakers and prescribing relevant land for litter control purposes. The Litter (Statutory Undertakers) (Designation and Relevant Land) Order 1991 (S.I. 1991 No. 1043) as amended by S.I. 1992 No. 406; the Litter Control Areas Order 1991 (S.I. 1991 No. 1325); and the Street Litter Control Notices Order 1991 (S.I. No. 1991 No. 1324). For the full list of sections in force see the Table of Sections In Force in the General Note to Pt. I.

Provisions relating to litter

Preliminary

86.—(1) The following provisions have effect for the purposes of this Part.
(2) In England and Wales the following are "principal litter authorities"—
(a) a county council,
(b) a district council,
(c) a London borough council,
(d) the Common Council of the City of London, and
(e) the Council of the Isles of Scilly;
but the Secretary of State may, by order, designate other descriptions of local authorities as litter authorities for the purposes of this Part; and any such authority shall also be a principal litter authority.
(3) In Scotland the following are "principal litter authorities"—
(a) a regional council;
(b) a district or islands council; and
(c) a joint board.

(4) Subject to subsection (8) below, land is "relevant land" of a principal litter authority if, not being relevant land falling within subsection (7) below, it is open to the air and is land (but not a highway or in Scotland a public road) which is under the direct control of such an authority to which the public are entitled or permitted to have access with or without payment.

(5) Land is "Crown land" if it is land—
(a) occupied by the Crown Estate Commissioners as part of the Crown Estate,
(b) occupied by or for the purposes of a government department or for naval, military or air force purposes, or
(c) occupied or managed by any body acting on behalf of the Crown;

is "relevant Crown land" if it is Crown land which is open to the air and is land (but not a highway or in Scotland a public road) to which the public are entitled or permitted to have access with or without payment; and "the appropriate Crown authority" for any Crown land is the Crown Estate Commissioners, the Minister in charge of the government department or the body which occupies or manages the land on the Crown's behalf, as the case may be.

(6) Subject to subsection (8) below, land is "relevant land" of a designated statutory undertaker if it is land which is under the direct control of any statutory undertaker or statutory undertaker of any description which may be designated by the Secretary of State, by order, for the purposes of this Part, being land to which the public are entitled or permitted to have access with or without payment or, in such cases as may be prescribed in the designation order, land in relation to which the public have no such right or permission.

(7) Subject to subsection (8) below, land is "relevant land" of a designated educational institution if it is open to the air and is land which is under the direct control of the governing body of or, in Scotland, of such body or of the education authority responsible for the management of, any educational institution or educational institution of any description which may be designated by the Secretary of State, by order, for the purposes of this Part.

(8) The Secretary of State may, by order, designate descriptions of land which are not to be treated as relevant Crown land or as relevant land of principal litter authorities, of designated statutory undertakers or of designated educational institutions or of any description of any of them.

(9) Every highway maintainable at the public expense other than a trunk road which is a special road is a "relevant highway" and the local authority which is, for the purposes of this Part, "responsible" for so much of it as lies within its area is, subject to any order under subsection (11) below—
(a) in Greater London, the council of the London borough or the Common Council of the City of London;
(b) outside Greater London, the council of the district; and
(c) the Council of the Isles of Scilly.

(10) In Scotland, every public road other than a trunk road which is a special road is a "relevant road" and the local authority which is, for the purposes of this Part, "responsible" for so much of it as lies within its area is, subject to any order under subsection (11) below, the district of islands council or (in the case of a special road) the regional or islands council.

(11) The Secretary of State may, by order, as respects relevant highways or relevant roads, relevant highways or relevant roads of any class or any part of a relevant highway or relevant road specified in the order, transfer the responsibility for the discharge of the duties imposed by section 89 below from the local authority to the highway or roads authority; but he shall not make an order under this subsection unless—
(a) (except where he is the highway or roads authority) he is requested to do so by the highway or roads authority;
(b) he consults the local authority; and

(c) it appears to him to be necessary or expedient to do so in order to prevent or minimise interference with the passage or with the safety of traffic along the highway or, in Scotland, road in question.

and where, by an order under this subsection, responsibility for the discharge of those duties is transferred, the authority to which the transfer is made is, for the purposes of this Part, "responsible" for the highway, road or part specified in the order.

(12) Land is "relevant land within a litter control area of a local authority" if it is land included in an area designated by the local authority under section 90 below to which the public are entitled or permitted to have access with or without payment.

(13) A place on land shall be treated as "open to the air" notwithstanding that it is covered if it is open to the air on at least one side.

(14) The Secretary of State may, by order, apply the provisions of this Part which apply to refuse to any description of animal droppings in all or any prescribed circumstances subject to such modifications as appear to him to be necessary.

(15) Any power under this section may be exercised differently as respects different areas, different descriptions of land or for different circumstances.

DEFINITIONS
"educational institution": s.98(2) and (3).
"highway": s.98(5).
"public road": s.98(5).
"special road": s.98(5).
"statutory undertaker": s.98(5).
"trunk road": s.98(5).

GENERAL NOTE

Subs. (4)
"Relevant land" of principal litter authorities. Essentially there are three ingredients of such land:
(a) it must be open to the air (see subs. (13)), but not a highway or public road;
(b) it must be "under the direct control" of the principal litter authority. "Control" appears to be a wide expression including many types of possession not commensurate with full ownership: *Johnstone Fear & Kingham* v. *Commonwealth* (1943) 67 C.L.R. 314 at 324. It would seem to include land under the superintendence and management of, though not owned by, the authority: see *Pardoe* v. *Pardoe* (1900) 82 L.T. 547 at 549; and
(c) the public are entitled or permitted to have access to it with or without payment.

Subs. (6)
"Relevant land" of statutory undertakers. This comprises land "under the direct control" of a statutory undertaker designated by the Secretary of State (see above). As well as land to which the parties have access, land to which there is no such access may be prescribed in the relevant order: this is to leave open the ability to extend the regime to areas such as railway embankments which are highly visible and particularly prone to litter. The Government's July 1989 Consultative Paper (para. 30) states that only railway embankments and canal banks are currently proposed for designation, "but there may be a case for considering additional categories of land where problems of a similar order occur." It is recognised that the burden on the landowners concerned "may not be a light one." See the Litter (Statutory Undertakers) (Designation and Relevant Land) Order 1991 (S.I. 1991 No. 1043). This designates the following statutory undertakers:
— the British Railways Board and London Regional Transport, and certain other specified railway operators;
— persons authorised to carry on any road transport undertaking other than taxi or car hire operators;
— persons authorised to carry on canal, inland navigation, dock, harbour or pier undertakings; and
— any relevant airport operator. The Regulations prescribe operational land which is within a 100 metres of a railway station platform to which the public is permitted or entitled to have access. The Regulations also prescribe land which is not to be treated as relevant land for

these purposes notwithstanding that the public are permitted or entitled to have access to it.

Subs. (7)
"*Relevant land" of educational institutions.* This covers land under the direct control of designated educational institutions and which is open to the air (see subs. (13)) whether or not the public has access thereto. See the Litter (Designated Educational Institutions) Order 1991 (S.I. 1991 No. 561) designating the institutions in s.98(2) and (3).

Subss. (9)–(11)
Highways and public roads. In England and Wales, responsibility for litter on highways falls to district and London Borough Councils (subs. (9)). In Scotland, district or islands councils are responsible (subs. (10)). In both cases, motorways are excluded, responsibility lying with the Department of Transport in England and Wales and regional or islands councils in Scotland. Also, in each case the Secretary of State may, by order, transfer responsibility to highway or roads authorities (subs. (11)). The duties to keep highways and roads clean of litter are created by s.89(1)(a) and (b). See the Highway Litter Clearance and Cleaning (Transfer of Duties) Order 1991 (S.I. 1991 No. 337) which transfers responsibility from named councils to the Secretary of State for Transport.

Subs. (12)
Litter control area. This subsection defines "relevant land within a litter control area," to which duties under Pt. IV apply: see ss. 89(1)(g) and 91(1)(g). Designation of such areas is under s.90.

Subs. (13)
Open to the air. This provision was added on amendment to make it clear that partially covered areas, such as bus stations, precincts and sports stadiums, can still be regarded as open to the air.

Subs. (14)
Animal droppings. This subsection, much debated in the House of Lords, allows the Secretary of State to apply any of the provisions of the Act on litter to animal droppings. The mischief prompting this provision is that of dog faeces (see para. 41 of the July 1989 Consultative Paper) or, as less delicately put by Lord Macintosh of Haringey in the House of Lords, "dogshit." An assurance has been given by the Government that the subsection will be used to deal with that problem: *Hansard*, H.L. Vol. 522, col. 631. See the Litter (Animal Droppings) Order 1991 (S.I. 1991 No. 961) which applies the litter control provisions of this part to dog faeces on prescribed land such as public walks, pleasure grounds, frequented sea shores and picnic sites. For discussion of the existing law on this problem, see Peter Alldridge, *Incontinent Dogs and the Law* [1990] New L.J. 1067: see also the report in the same issue of the New L.J. of the first prosecution of a dog owner under by-laws by Westminster City Council for dog fouling: [1990] New L.J. 1063. The Home Office has produced model by-laws on dog fouling.

Offence of leaving litter

87.—(1) If any person throws down, drops or otherwise deposits in, into or from any place to which this section applies, and leaves, any thing whatsoever in such circumstances as to cause, or contribute to, or tend to lead to, the defacement by litter of any place to which this section applies, he shall, subject to subsection (2) below, be guilty of an offence.

(2) No offence is committed under this section where the depositing and leaving of the thing was—
  (a) authorised by law, or
  (b) done with the consent of the owner occupier or other person or authority having control of the place in or into which that thing was deposited.

(3) This section applies to any public open place and, in so far as the place is not a public open place, also to the following places—
  (a) any relevant highway or relevant road and any trunk road which is a special road;
  (b) any place on relevant land of a principal litter authority;
  (c) any place on relevant Crown land;

(d) any place on relevant land of any designated statutory undertaker;
(e) any place on relevant land of any designated educational institution;
(f) any place on relevant land within a litter control area of a local authority.

(4) In this section "public open place" means a place in the open air to which the public are entitled or permitted to have access without payment; and any covered place open to the air on at least one side and available for public use shall be treated as a public open place.

(5) A person who is guilty of an offence under this section shall be liable on summary conviction to a fine not exceeding level 4 on the standard scale.

(6) A local authority, with a view to promoting the abatement of litter, may take such steps as the authority think appropriate for making the effect of subsection (5) above known to the public in their area.

(7) In any proceedings in Scotland for an offence under this section it shall be lawful to convict the accused on the evidence of one witness.

DEFINITIONS
"educational institution": s.98(2) and (3).
"highway": s.98(5).
"principal litter authority": s.86(2).
"relevant Crown land": s.86(5).
"relevant highway": s.86(9).
"relevant land of any designated educational institution": s.86(7).
"relevant land of any designated statutory undertaker": s.86(6).
"relevant land within a litter control area of a local authority": s.86(12).
"relevant road": s.86(10).
"special road": s.98(5).
"statutory undertaker": s.98(6).
"trunk road": s.98(5).

GENERAL NOTE
The offence created by the section is similar in effect to that of s.1 of the Litter Act 1983, as are the specific circumstances described in subs. (2) where the offence is not committed. The land in relation to which an offence is committed is extended beyond the "free public open place" to which the Litter Act 1983 applied: the relevant places are defined in subs. (3) as any public open place (see subs. (4)) and also a list of other places paras. (a)–(f) in so far as they are not public open places. The definition can include land in the open air to which the public have access by permission or entitlement without making payment. This covers land in private as well as public ownership, and by subs. (4) can include covered places open to the air on at least one side such as railway stations, concert arenas and sports grounds and stadiums.

Subs. (5)
Penalties. The maximum penalty is a fine of £2,500.

Subs. (6)
Public awareness. The power to take steps for making the penalties for littering known to the public extends to all local authorities, not just principal litter authorities under Pt. IV. It replaces s.2 of the Litter Act 1983.

Fixed penalty notices for leaving litter

88.—(1) Where on any occasion an authorised officer of a litter authority finds a person who he has reason to believe has on that occasion committed an offence under section 87 above in the area of that authority, he may give that person a notice offering him the opportunity of discharging any liability to conviction for that offence by payment of a fixed penalty.

(2) Where a person is given a notice under this section in respect of an offence—

(a) no proceedings shall be instituted for that offence before the expiration of 14 days following the date of the notice; and
(b) he shall not be convicted of that offence if he pays the fixed penalty before the expiration of that period.

(3) A notice under this section shall give such particulars of the circumstances alleged to constitute the offence as are necessary for giving reasonable information of the offence and shall state—
   (a) the period during which, by virtue of subsection (2) above, proceedings will not be taken for the offence;
   (b) the amount of the fixed penalty; and
   (c) the person to whom and the address at which the fixed penalty may be paid;

and, without prejudice to payment by any other method, payment of the fixed penalty may be made by pre-paying and posting to that person at that address a letter containing the amount of the penalty (in cash or otherwise).

(4) Where a letter is sent in accorance with subsection (3) above payment shall be regarded as having been made at the time at which that letter would be delivered in the ordinary course of post.

(5) The form of notices under this section shall be such as the Secretary of State may by order prescribe.

(6) The fixed penalty payable to a principal litter authority in pursuance of a notice under this section shall, subject to subsection (7) below, be £10; and as respects the sums received by the authority, those sums—
   (a) if received by an authority in England and Wales, shall be paid to the Secretary of State;
   (b) if received by an authority in Scotland, shall be treated as if the penalty were a fine imposed by a district court.

(7) The Secretary of State may by order substitute a different amount for the amount for the time being specified as the amount of the fixed penalty in subsection (6) above.

(8) In any proceedings a certificate which—
   (a) purports to be signed by or on behalf of—
      (i) in England and Wales, the chief finance officer of the litter authority; or
      (ii) in Scotland, the proper officer; and
   (b) states that payment of a fixed penalty was or was not received by a date specified in the certificate,
shall be evidence of the facts stated.

(9) For the purposes of this section the following are "litter authorities"—
   (a) any principal litter authority, other than a county council, a regional council or a joint board;
   (b) any county council, regional council or joint board designated by the Secretary of State, by order, in relation to such area as is specified in the order (not being an area in a National Park);
   (c) any National Park Committee;
   (d) any Park board for any area in a National Park; and
   (e) the Broads Authority.

(10) In this section—
   "authorised officer" means an officer of, or in the case of any Park board or National Park Committee, an officer acting on behalf of, a litter authority who is authorised in writing by the authority for the purpose of issuing notices under this section;
   "chief finance officer", in relation to a litter authority, means the person having responsibility for the financial affairs of the authority;
   "National Park Committee" means a committee appointed to perform functions under paragraph 5 of Schedule 17 to the Local Government Act 1972;

"Park board," in relation to a National Park, means—
  (a) a joint planning board reconstituted under paragraph 1 of Schedule 17 to the Local Government Act 1972; or
  (b) a board reconstituted as a special planning board under paragraph 3 of that Schedule;
"proper officer" means the officer who has, as respects the authority, the responsibility mentioned in section 95 of the Local Government (Scotland) Act 1973 (financial administration).

GENERAL NOTE

This section gives power to litter authorities, as defined in subs. (9), to operate fixed penalty schemes for littering. National Park authorities and the Broads Authority are included within the definition of litter authorities. By subs. (6), the fixed penalty is £10, but may be reviewed by the Secretary of State under subs. (7).

The period for payment of the penalty is 14 days (subs. (2)) and payment means the person concerned cannot then be convicted of a litter offence (subs. (2)(b)).

The 1989 Consultation Paper gives details of the Government's background thinking on this issue (paras. 6 and 7):

"6. The model for such a scheme already exists in the City of Westminster, as provided for by the City of Westminster Act 1988. Many other local authorities are anxious to adopt this model. Following close monitoring of the Westminster scheme's first year of operation the Government concurs in Westminster's view that the scheme is a helpful and workable tool in the authority's efforts to fight litter and improve public awareness of the problem. Almost all approaches made by authorised officers resulted in the person concerned picking up the litter rather than the officer issuing a ticket. This bears out that the value of the scheme is above all one of education and persuasion, and that the demand of operating the scheme on the resources of the local authority and, ultimately, the courts is modest.

7. The Government has considered the case for retention of fines by the local authority, but does not accept that this particular instance merits a departure from the general principle that all such fines should be passed on to the Exchequer. Similarly, the Government has concluded that the Police should not be given the same power as authorised officers of the local authority to issue fixed penalty tickets, since this additional burden would effectively detract resources from serious crime prevention and detection."

The form of notice to be given to a person believed to have committed an offence has now been prescribed under subs. (5) by the Litter (Fixed Penalty Notices) Order 1991 (S.I. 1991 No. 111).

Duty to keep land and highways clear of litter etc.

89.—(1) It shall be the duty of—
  (a) each local authority, as respects any relevant highway or, in Scotland, relevant road for which it is responsible,
  (b) the Secretary of State, as respects any trunk road which is a special road and any relevant highway or relevant road for which he is responsible,
  (c) each principal litter authority, as respects its relevant land,
  (d) the appropriate Crown authority, as respects its relevant Crown land,
  (e) each designated statutory undertaker, as respects its relevant land,
  (f) the governing body of each designated educational institution or in Scotland such body or, as the case may be, the education authority responsible for the management of the institution, as respects its relevant land, and
  (g) the occupier of any relevant land within a litter control area of a local authority,
to ensure that the land is, so far as is practicable, kept clear of litter and refuse.

(2) Subject to subsection (6) below, it shall also be the duty of—
  (a) each local authority, as respects any relevant highway or relevant road for which it is responsible,
  (b) the Secretary of State, as respects any trunk road which is a special

road and any relevant highway or relevant road for which he is responsible,
to ensure that the highway or road is, so far as is practicable, kept clean.

(3) In determining what standard is required, as respects any description of land, highway or road, for compliance with subsections (1) and (2) above, regard shall be had to the character and use of the land, highway or road as well as the measures which are practicable in the circumstances.

(4) Matter of any description prescribed by regulations made by the Secretary of State for the purposes of subsections (1)(a) and (2) above shall be litter or refuse to which the duties imposed by those subsections apply as respects relevant highways or relevant roads whether or not it would be litter or refuse apart from this subsection.

(5) It shall be the duty of a local authority, when discharging its duty under subsection (1)(a) or (2) above as respects any relevant highway or relevant road, to place and maintain on the highway or road such traffic signs and barriers as may be necessary for giving warning and preventing danger to traffic or for regulating it and afterwards to remove them as soon as they cease to be necessary for those purposes; but this subsection has effect subject to any directions given under subsection (6) below.

(6) In discharging its duty under subsection (1)(a) or (2) above to keep clear of litter and refuse or to clean any relevant highway or relevant road for which it is responsible, the local authority shall comply with any directions given to it by the highway or roads authority with respect to—

(a) the placing and maintenance of any traffic signs or barriers;
(b) the days or periods during which clearing or cleaning shall not be undertaken or undertaken to any extent specified in the direction;

and for the purpose of enabling it to discharge its duty under subsection (1)(a) or (2) above as respects any relevant highway or relevant road the local authority may apply to the highway authority or roads authority for that authority to exercise its powers under section 14(1) or (3) of the Road Traffic Regulation Act 1984 (temporary prohibition or restriction of traffic).

(7) The Secretary of State shall prepare and issue a code of practice for the purpose of providing practical guidance on the discharge of the duties imposed by subsections (1) and (2) above.

(8) Different codes of practice may be prepared and issued under subsection (7) above for different areas.

(9) The Secretary of State may issue modifications of, or withdraw, a code issued under subsection (7) above; but where a code is withdrawn, he shall prepare and issue a new code under that subsection in substitution for it.

(10) Any person subject to any duty imposed by subsection (1) or (2) above shall have regard to the code of practice in force under subsection (7) above in discharging that duty.

(11) A draft code prepared under subsection (7) above shall be laid before both Houses of Parliament and shall not be issued until after the end of the period of 40 days beginning with the day on which the code was so laid, or if the draft is laid on different days, the later of the two days.

(12) If, within the period mentioned in subsection (11) above, either House resolves that the code the draft of which was laid before it should not be issued, the Secretary of State shall not issue that code.

(13) No account shall be taken in reckoning any period of 40 days for the purposes of this section of any time during which Parliament is dissolved or prorogued or during which both Houses are adjourned for more than four days.

(14) In this section "traffic sign" has the meaning given in section 64(1) of the Road Traffic Regulation Act 1984.

DEFINITIONS
"appropriate Crown authority": s.86(5).

"educational institution": s.98(2) and (3).
"highway"' s.98(5).
"principal litter authority": s.86(2) and (3).
"relevant Crown land": s.86(5).
"relevant highway": s.86(9).
"relevant land": s.86(4).
"relevant land of designated educational institution": s.86(6).
"relevant land of designated statutory undertaker": s.86(6).
"relevant land within a litter control area of a local authority": s.86(12).
"relevant road": s.86(10).
"special road": s.98(5).
"statutory undertaker": s.98(6).
"trunk road": s.98(5).

GENERAL NOTE
This section creates a new duty on the authorities and persons specified to ensure that their land is so far as practicable kept clear of litter and refuse (subs. (1)). A further duty is created by subs. (2) on district councils and trunk road authorities to keep highways and roads clean, so far as is practicable.

Standard of cleanliness
Two matters are relevant in relation to the standard of cleanliness and freedom from litter to be excepted. These are: (a) the character and use of the land, highway or road and the measures which are practicable in the circumstances (subs. (3)): (b) the Code of Practice prepared by the Secretary of State under subs. (7), to which regard must be had under subs. (10).

A draft code was issued for consultation on February 23, 1990, after work by an Advisory Group comprising representatives from local authority associations, statutory undertakers, commercial property owners and cleaning contractors. The Code was formally laid before Parliament in November 1990 and is reproduced as Appendix 7 to the annotations. The Code, which was published in January 1991, falls into two parts. The first part, the Statutory Code, describes four standards of cleanliness from Grade A (litter free) to Grade D (heavily littered) and divides land into 11 zones according to use and volume of traffic, describing the expected standards and the time by which those standards should be restored if the standard falls. Photographic examples are given. It will be for local authorities or the other body under the relevant duty to allocate to the various zones and to publicise such allocations. The second, non-statutory, part of the Code contains advice on "best practice" dealing with appraisal, implementation, campaigning, education and community involvement, litter bins, fly-tipping and grass cutting.

Special criteria have been applied to beaches, taking into account matters such as action of the tides, difficult access for machinery, unsuitability of terrain for mechanical cleaning and ecological sensitivity.

Highways
As mentioned above, the new duties apply to roads and highways. The two duties are (a) to ensure that highways and roads (including motorways and trunk roads) are, so far as is practicable, kept clear of litter and refuse (s.89(1)(a) and (b)); and (b) to ensure that highways and roads (including motorways and trunk roads) are, so far as is practicable, kept clean (s.89(2)).

The duties fall to the Secretary of State in relation to motorways and trunk roads for which he is responsible. Otherwise, the responsibility is that of district and London borough councils in England and Wales and district and islands councils (or regional or islands councils for special roads) in Scotland (s.86(10) and (11)). The object is to achieve a clear allocation of responsibility for street and road cleaning. The system of divided responsibility under s.22(1) and (2) of the Control of Pollution Act 1974 had proved to cause friction and to have blurred accountability.

Under the new provisions, the responsibilities of highway and roads authorities are limited to their duties to maintain the highway under s.41 of the Highways Act 1980. The only exception is where responsibility is transferred to the highway authority by order under s.86(11). The local authority must, in discharging its cleaning duties, take the necessary traffic warning precautions (subs. (5)) and comply with any directions as to such matters given by the highway authority under subs. (6). Compliance with such directions is a defence to summary proceedings in respect of the s.89 duty, under s.91 (see s.91(8)). Additional powers of temporary prohibition or restriction of traffic are given by Sched. 15, para. 23, amending the Road Traffic Regulation Act 1984.

Subs. (4)

Matter to be treated as litter or refuse. The Secretary of State may make regulations as to whether any matter is litter or refuse for the purpose of the provisions on highways and roads. This is a reserve power intended to enable the Secretary of State to resolve disputes as to whether specific matter (for example leaves) falls to the highway authority as a road safety issue or is also a litter issue for the district councils.

Costs

In DoE News Release No. 418 (July 11, 1990) the Government, in commenting on a report prepared by Coopers & Lybrand Deloitte on the new litter duties, suggested that the additional costs involved for local authorities are likely to be in the range of 7–30 per cent. But *cf. Hansard*, H.L. Vol. 522, cols. 622–3. The Government is committed to considering the resource implications of the new controls in the next round of Rate Support Grant.

Implementation

In issuing the Consultative Code of Practice in February 1990 the Department of the Environment indicated that the relevant provisions would not come into force before April 1, 1991. The intention was to give authorities and others concerned sufficient time to make any necessary arrangements.

The following comments were also made on the implications of the provisions for street-cleaning contracts (letter from DoE Local Environment Quality Division, February 23, 1990):

"Authorities will need to take account of the proposed rationalisation of street cleaning responsibilities when inviting tenders for this work. Existing street cleaning contracts let by highway authorities or their agents will generally run until the expiry date, unless the contracts have provided for external factors such as legislative changes, or unless authorities can negotiate amendment or termination of the contract. Highway authorities should find it easier to wind down their street cleaning activities in those cases where the work is carried out by the respective DSO, either following competitive tendering or because the authority has not yet been required to put the work out to tender under the Local Government Act 1988. Any overlap between a particular highway authority's street cleaning activities and those of district councils in its area will be minimised where highway authorities have already taken a strict interpretation of their existing duty under section 22(1) of the Control of Pollution Act 1974 and where they allow for proposed legislative changes when drawing up future contracts. The Department would welcome comments from local authorities on the implications for competitive tendering of the proposed rationalisation of street cleaning responsibilities."

Litter control areas

90.—(1) The Secretary of State may, by order, prescribe descriptions of land which may be designated under subsection (3) below as, or as part of, a litter control area.

(2) The power of the Secretary of State to prescribe descriptions of land under subsection (1) above includes power to describe land by reference to the ownership or occupation of the land or the activities carried on on it.

(3) Any principal litter authority other than a county council, regional council or joint board may, in accordance with the following provisions of this section, by order designate any land in their area as, or as part of, a litter control area.

(4) No order under subsection (3) above designating any land shall be made unless the authority is of the opinion that, by reason of the presence of litter or refuse, the condition of the land is, and unless they make a designation order is likely to continue to be, such as to be detrimental to the amenities of the locality.

(5) The power to make a designation order under subsection (3) above shall be excluded from the functions to which section 101 of the Local Government Act 1972 (functions capable of delegation) applies.

(6) An authority proposing to make a designation order in relation to any land shall—
 (a) notify persons who appear to the authority to be persons who will be affected by the proposed order;

(b) give them an opportunity to make representations about it within the period of 21 days beginning with the service of the notice; and
(c) take any representations so made into account in making their decision.

(7) A designation order under subsection (3) above shall identify the land to which it applies and shall be in such form as the Secretary of State may by order prescribe.

DEFINITIONS
"principal litter authority": s.86(2) and (3).

GENERAL NOTE
This section makes provision for the designation of litter control areas. The Secretary of State may prescribe descriptions of land under subs. (1) which may be designated as such. The descriptions of such land could include, for example, car parks, beaches, shopping precincts, and industrial estates. Alternatively the land may be designated by reference to its ownership or occupation or the activities carried out on it (subs. (2)). Principal litter authorities may then make orders designating any land in their area as, or as part of, a litter control area (subs. (3)). County councils cannot make such orders, nor can the power to make orders be delegated (subs. (5)).

The condition precedent to making an order is by reference to detriment to the amenities of the area caused by the condition of the land due to the presence of litter or refuse (subs. (4)).

Persons who appear to be affected by any prospective order must be notified and given an opportunity to comment (subs. (6)). See the Litter Control Areas Order 1991 (S.I. 1991 No. 1325) which prescribes the descriptions of land which may be designated as litter control areas under subs. (3). These include car parks, shopping areas, cinemas, theatres, amusement centres, frequented beaches, motorway service stations, markets, camping and caravan sites, and a trunk road picnic area. The Regulations also prescribe the form of designation orders.

Summary proceedings by persons aggrieved by litter

91.—(1) A magistrates' court may act under this section on a complaint made by any person on the ground that he is aggrieved by the defacement, by litter or refuse, of—
(a) any relevant highway;
(b) any trunk road which is a special road;
(c) any relevant land of a principal litter authority;
(d) any relevant Crown land;
(e) any relevant land of a designated statutory undertaker;
(f) any relevant land of a designated educational institution; or
(g) any relevant land within a litter control area of a local authority.

(2) A magistrates' court may also act under this section on a complaint made by any person on the ground that he is aggrieved by the want of cleanliness of any relevant highway or any trunk road which is a special road.

(3) A principal litter authority shall not be treated as a person aggrieved for the purposes of proceedings under this section.

(4) Proceedings under this section shall be brought against the person who has the duty to keep the land clear under section 89(1) above or to keep the highway clean under section 89(2) above, as the case may be.

(5) Before instituting proceedings under this section against any person, the complainant shall give to the person not less than five days' written notice of his intention to make the complaint and the notice shall specify the matter complained of.

(6) If the magistrates' court is satisfied that the highway or land in question is defaced by litter or refuse or, in the case of a highway, is wanting in cleanliness, the court may, subject to subsections (7) and (8) below, make an order ("a litter abatement order") requiring the defendant to clear the litter or refuse away or, as the case may be, clean the highway within a time specified in the order.

(7) The magistrates' court shall not make a litter abatement order if the defendant proves that he has complied, as respects the highway or land in question, with his duty under section 89(1) and (2) above.

(8) The magistrates' court shall not make a litter abatement order where it appears that the matter complained of is the result of directions given to the local authority under section 89(6) above by the highway authority.

(9) A person who, without reasonable excuse, fails to comply with a litter abatement order shall be guilty of an offence and liable on summary conviction to a fine not exceeding level 4 on the standard scale together with a further fine of an amount equal to one-twentieth of that level for each day on which the offence continues after the conviction.

(10) In any proceedings for an offence under subsection (9) above it shall be a defence for the defendant to prove that he has complied, as respects the highway or land in question, with his duty under section 89(1) and (2) above.

(11) A code of practice under section 89(7) above shall be admissible in evidence in any proceedings under this section and if any provision of such a code appears to the court to be relevant to any question in the proceedings it shall be taken into account in determining that question.

(12) Where a magistrates' court is satisfied on the hearing of a complaint under this section—
- (a) that, when the complaint was made to it, the highway or land in question was defaced by litter or refuse or, as the case may be, was wanting in cleanliness, and
- (b) that there were reasonable grounds for bringing the complaint,

the court shall order the defendant to pay such reasonable sum to the complainant as the court may determine in respect of the expenses incurred by the complainant in bringing the complaint and the proceedings before the court.

(13) In the application of this section to Scotland—
- (a) for any reference to a magistrates' court there shall be substituted a reference to the sheriff;
- (b) for any reference to a complaint there shall be substituted a reference to a summary application, and "complainant" shall be construed accordingly;
- (c) for any reference to the defendant there shall be substituted a reference to the person against whom the proceedings are taken;
- (d) for any reference to a highway and a relevant highway there shall be substituted a reference to a road and a relevant road; and
- (e) for any reference to a highway authority there shall be substituted a reference to a roads authority.

and any person against whom proceedings are brought may appeal on a point of law to the Court of Session against the making of a litter abatement order.

DEFINITIONS
"educational institution": s.98(2) and (3).
"highway": s.98(5).
"principal litter authority": s.86(2) and (3).
"relevant Crown land": s.86(5).
"relevant highway": s.86(9).
"relevant land of a designated educational institution": s.86(7).
"relevant land of a designated statutory undertaker": s.86(6).
"relevant land of a principal litter authority": s.86(4).
"relevant land within a litter control area of a local authority": s.86(12).
"special road": s.98(5).
"statutory undertaker": s.98(6).
"trunk road": s.98(5).

GENERAL NOTE
This section provides a remedy for members of the public aggrieved by breach of the duties imposed by s.89. The remedy is by way of complaint to magistrates' courts in England and

Wales, or by summary application to the sheriff in Scotland (subs. (13)). The proceedings must be preceded by not less than five days' written notice to the authority or other person alleged to be in breach of duty of intention to make the complaint, specifying the nature of the complaint (subs. (5)).

The Code of Practice (see s.89 above) is admissible in evidence (subs. (11)). If the complaint is successful, a litter abatement order will be made, failure to comply with which is an offence (subss. (6)–(9)). No offence can result in the case of the Crown (s.159(2)). Compliance with the relevant duty under s.89 is a defence to the original complaint (subs. (7)) and also to subsequent proceedings for non-compliance with a litter abatement order (subs. (10)).

Subs. (1)

Person aggrieved. In the context of duties relating to the state and cleanliness of public places, this expression is naturally likely to be construed widely and might therefore cover local residents, visitors, travellers, persons occupying property overlooking the relevant land, pupils at the relevant educational institutions, and no doubt their parents.

The Government's view, in some respects rather narrower, is expressed in the July 1989 Consultation Paper (para. 26):

"The Government's view is that a 'person aggrieved' might be a local resident, someone who worked in the area, or a regular visitor to it—in other words, anyone who had a bona fide interest in that locality and hence a particular right to demand proper standards of cleanliness there. The person could equally be an individual representing a local community organisation or voluntary body with such an interest in the locality."

Subs. (12)

Costs. Where, on hearing a complaint, the court is satisfied that there was cause for complaint at the time the complaint was made, and that there were reasonable grounds for bringing the complaint, the court may order the defendant to pay a reasonable sum in respect of the complainant's costs. This is necessary because, if by the time the complaint was heard, the litter had been cleared away or the lack of cleanliness rectified, no order could be made under subs. (6), and there would be no power to award costs.

Summary proceedings by litter authorities

92.—(1) Where a principal litter authority other than a county council, regional council or joint board are satisfied as respects—
   (a) any relevant Crown land,
   (b) any relevant land of a designated statutory undertaker,
   (c) any relevant land of a designated educational institution, or
   (d) any relevant land within a litter control area of a local authority,
that it is defaced by litter or refuse or that defacement of it by litter or refuse is likely to recur, the authority shall serve a notice (a "litter abatement notice") imposing either the requirement or the prohibition or both the requirement and the prohibition specified in subsection (2) below.

(2) The requirement and prohibition referred to in subsection (1) above are as follows, namely—
   (a) a requirement that the litter or refuse be cleared within a time specified in the notice;
   (b) a prohibition on permitting the land to become defaced by litter or refuse.

(3) The litter abatement notice shall be served—
   (a) as respects relevant Crown land, on the appropriate Crown authority;
   (b) as respects relevant land of a designated statutory undertaker, on the undertaker;
   (c) as respects relevant land of a designated educational institution, on the governing body of the institution or in Scotland on such body or, as the case may be, on the education authority responsible for the management of the institution;
   (d) in any other case, on the occupier of the land or, if it is unoccupied, on the owner of the land.

(4) The person served with the notice may appeal against the notice to a magistrates' court or, in Scotland, to the sheriff by way of summary applica-

tion within the period of 21 days beginning with the date on which the notice was served.

(5) If, on any appeal under subsection (4) above, the appellant proves that, as respects the land in question, he has complied with his duty under section 89(1) above, the court shall allow the appeal.

(6) If a person on whom a litter abatement notice is served, without reasonable excuse, fails to comply with or contravenes the requirement or prohibition imposed by the notice, he shall be guilty of an offence and liable on summary conviction to a fine not exceeding level 4 on the standard scale together with a further fine of an amount equal to one-twentieth of that level for each day on which the offence continues after the conviction.

(7) In any proceedings for an offence under subsection (6) above it shall be a defence for the person charged to prove that he has complied, as respects the land in question, with this duty under section 89(1) above.

(8) A code of practice under section 89(7) above shall be admissible in evidence in any proceedings under this section and if any provision of such a code appears to the court to be relevant to any question in the proceedings it shall be taken into account in determining that question.

(9) If a person on whom a litter abatement notice is served fails to comply with the requirement imposed by the notice in respect of any land, the authority may, subject to subsection (10) below—
   (a) enter on the land and clear the litter or refuse; and
   (b) recover from that person the expenditure attributable to their having done so, except such of the expenditure as that person shows was unnecessary in the circumstances.

(10) Subsection (9) above does not apply in relation to relevant Crown land or relevant land of statutory undertakers.

DEFINITIONS
  "appropriate Crown authority": s.86(5).
  "education institution": s.98(2) and (3).
  "joint board": s.98(4).
  "principal litter authority": s.86(2) and (3).
  "relevant Crown land": s.86(5).
  "relevant land of a designated educational institution": s.86(7).
  "relevant land of a designated statutory undertaker": s.86(6).
  "relevant land within a litter control area of a local authority": s.86(12).
  "statutory undertaker": s.98(6).

GENERAL NOTE
Principal litter authorities have no right to take summary action under s.91 in respect of litter, refuse or want of cleanliness (s.91(3)). However, s.92 provides a specific remedy for such authorities (except county councils, regional councils or joint boards) in respect of some categories of land as listed in subs. (1). Such land does not include, for obvious reasons, principal litter authorities' own land; nor does it include highway land.

The procedure is that the authority may serve notice (a litter abatement notice) on the relevant authority or in the case of private land on the occupier or, if the land is unoccupied, the owner. There is a right of appeal against the notice to a magistrates' court or to the sheriff in Scotland (subs. (4)).

Failure to comply with the notice is an offence (subs. (6)). The maximum penalty is a £2,500 fine, plus a daily fine of £175 for each day the offence continues after conviction. No offence is committed in the case of the Crown, but a declaration of unlawfulness may be obtained from the High Court or Court of Session (s.159(2)).

Default powers are given to enter and clear the relevant land of litter in the event of non-compliance, and to recover the costs from the person served with the notice (subs. (9)). This power does not, however, apply in relation to Crown land or land of statutory undertakers (subs. (10)).

Street litter control notices

    93.—(1) A principal litter authority other than a county council, regional council or a joint board may, with a view to the prevention of accumulations of litter or refuse in and around any street or open land adjacent to any street, issue notices ("street litter control notices") imposing requirements on occupiers of premises in relation to such litter or refuse, in accordance with this section and section 94 below.

(2) If the authority is satisfied, in respect of any premises which are of a description prescribed under section 94(1)(a) below and have a frontage on a street in their area, that—
  (a) there is recurrent defacement by litter or refuse of any land, being part of the street or open land adjacent to the street, which is in the vicinity of the premises, or
  (b) the condition of any part of the premises which is open land in the vicinity of the frontage is, and if no notice is served is likely to continue to be, detrimental to the amenities of the locality by reason of the presence of litter or refuse, or
  (c) there is produced, as a result of the activities carried on on the premises, quantities of litter or refuse of such nature and in such amounts as are likely to cause the defacement of any part of the street, or of open land adjacent to the street, which is in the vicinity of the premises,

the authority may serve a street litter control notice on the occupier or, if the premises are unoccupied, on the owner of the premises.

(3) A notice shall, subject to section 94(2), (3) and (4) below—
  (a) identify the premises and state the grounds under subsection (2) above on which it is issued;
  (b) specify an area of open land which adjoins or is in the vicinity of the frontage of the premises on the street;
  (c) specify, in relation to that area or any part of it, such reasonable requirements as the authority considers appropriate in the circumstances;

and, for the purposes of paragraph (b) above, an area which includes land on both sides of the frontage of the premises shall be treated as an area adjoining that frontage.

(4) In this section and section 94 below—
  "notice" means a street litter control notice;
  "open land" means land in the open air;
  "the premises," in relation to a notice, means the premises in respect of which the notice is issued;
  "specified area" means the area specified in a notice under subsection (3)(b) above; and
  "street" means a relevant highway, a relevant road or any other highway or road over which there is a right of way on foot.

DEFINITIONS
  "highway": s.96(5).
  "joint board": s.98(4).
  "principal litter authority": s.86(2) and (3).
  "relevant highway": s.86(9).
  "relevant road": s.86(10).
  "road": s.96(5).

GENERAL NOTE

This section gives new powers to principal litter authorities (but not county councils, regional councils or joint boards) to issue street litter control notices, with a view to preventing accumulations of litter or refuse in and around any street or open land adjacent to any street. Such notices are served on the occupier of premises which could loosely be described as being connected with street litter problems. The case for imposing a duty on the owners of commercial premises to keep clean any frontage land within their ownership and also the adjoining pavement was considered and rejected in the July 1989 Consultation Paper, para. 38. The provisions in s.93 directly address that problem.

The types of premises on which, and the conditions under which, notice can be served are set out in subs. (2) and are essentially:
  (a) premises having a frontage to a street where there is a recurrent defacement by litter or refuse of part of the street or of open land adjacent to the street, which is in the vicinity of the premises;
  (b) premises having a frontage to a street, where open land forming part of the premises in the vicinity of the frontage is in a condition detrimental to the amenities of the locality because of litter or refuse, and is likely to continue to be so;
  (c) premises having a frontage to a street, on which activities are carried on so as to produce litter or refuse likely in nature, quantities or amounts to cause the defacement of the street or of open land in the vicinity of the premises and adjacent to the street. The obvious examples are fast-food retail outlets.

The notice is served on the occupier or, in the case of unoccupied premises, on the owner. The notice must specify appropriate and reasonable requirements in relation to an area of open land which adjoins or is in the vicinity of the frontage of the premises on the street (subs. (3)), and for this purpose land on both sides of the frontage can be included as an area adjoining the frontage. It is not clear how the provisions apply to first floor premises, perhaps with simply a common entrance at ground level: would such premises "have a frontage on a street"?

Further provisions and requirements as to such notices are contained in s.94.

Street litter: supplementary provisions

94.—(1) The Secretary of State may by order prescribe—
  (a) the descriptions of commercial or retail premises in respect of which a street litter control notice may be issued;
  (b) the descriptions of land which may be included in a specified area; and
  (c) the maximum area of land which may be included in a specified area;
and different descriptions or maximum dimensions may be prescribed under paragraph (b) or (c) above for different cases or circumstances.

(2) The power to describe premises or land under subsection (1)(a) or (b) above includes power to describe the premises or land by reference to occupation or ownership or to the activities carried on there.

(3) The land comprised in a specified area—
  (a) shall include only land of one or more of the descriptions prescribed under subsection (1)(b) above;
  (b) shall not include any land which is not—
     (i) part of the premises,
     (ii) part of a street,
     (iii) relevant land of a principal litter authority, or
     (iv) land under the direct control of any other local authority; and
  (c) shall not exceed any applicable maximum area prescribed under subsection (1)(c) above;
but a specified area shall not include any part of the premises which is or is part of a litter control area.

(4) The requirements which may be imposed by a notice shall relate to the clearing of litter or refuse from the specified area and may in particular require—
  (a) the provision or emptying of receptacles for litter or refuse;
  (b) the doing within a period specified in the notice of any such thing as may be so specified; or
  (c) the doing (while the notice remains in force) at such times or intervals, or within such periods, of any such thing as may be so specified;
but a notice may not require the clearing of litter or refuse from any carriageway, except at a time when the carriageway is closed to all vehicular traffic.

(5) In relation to so much of the specified area as is not part of the premises the authority shall take account, in determining what requirements to impose, of their own duties under this Part or otherwise, and of any similar duties of any other local authority, in relation to that land.

(6) An authority proposing to serve a notice shall—
  (a) inform the person on whom the notice is to be served;

(b) give him the opportunity to make representations about the notice within the period of 21 days beginning with the day on which he is so informed; and
(c) take any representations so made into account in making their decision.

(7) A person on whom a notice is served may appeal against the notice to a magistrates' court or, in Scotland, to the sheriff by way of summary application; and the court may quash the notice or may quash, vary or add to any requirement imposed by the notice.

(8) If it appears to the authority that a person has failed or is failing to comply with any requirement imposed by a notice the authority may apply to a magistrates' court or, in Scotland, to the sheriff by way of summary application for an order requiring the person to comply with the requirement within such time a may be specified in the order.

(9) A person who, without reasonable excuse, fails to comply with an order under subsection (8) above shall be guilty of an offence and liable on summary conviction to a fine not exceeding level 4 on the standard scale.

DEFINITIONS
"notice": s.93(4).
"relevant land of a principal litter authority": s.86(4).
"specified area": s.93(4).
"street": s.93(4).

GENERAL NOTE
This section contains further and supplementary provisions as to street litter notices as set out below:

Matters to be prescribed
Various matters are to be prescribed by the Secretary of State including the types of commercial and retail premises that may be issued with a notice, and the descriptions and maximum areas of land that may be included within specified areas in notices (subs. (1)).

Subs. (3)
Land to be comprised in specified area. As well as the prescribed limitations as to description and area of land to be comprised in a specified area, such land may not include any land unless it is either: (a) part of the premises; or (b) part of a street; or (c) relevant land of a principal litter authority; or (d) land under the direct control of any other local authority. Nor can such areas include any land which is part of a litter control area (see s.90).

Subs. (4)
Requirements of the notice. Such requirements relate to the clearing of litter or refuse from the specified area and may contain the specific requirements listed in subs. (4).
Rights of occupier/owner. The occupier or owner has the right under subs. (6) to be informed of the authority's intention to serve a notice, and to make representations. There is a right of appeal to the magistrates' court or to the sheriff under subs. (7) against a notice served.
Enforcement. This is by way of application to the magistrates' court or to the sheriff for an order requiring compliance with the notice (subs. (8)). It appears that objections to the notice may not be raised at this stage, but should be the subject of an appeal under subs. (7). Breach of an order is an offence punishable with a maximum £2,500 fine on summary conviction (subs. (9)).

Public registers

95.—(1) It shall be the duty of each principal litter authority other than a county council, regional council or joint board to maintain, in accordance with this section, a register containing copies of—
(a) all orders made by the authority under section 90(3)) above; and
(b) all street litter control notices issued under section 93(1) above.
(2) Where the requirements of a street litter control notice are varied or added to on an appeal under section 94(7) above a copy of the order making the variation or addition shall be included in the register.

(3) Copies of the orders and notices required to be kept in the register shall be so kept for so long as the order or notice is in force.

(4) It shall be the duty of each authority maintaining a register under this section—
  (a) to secure that the register is available, at all reasonable times, for inspection by the public free of charge; and
  (b) to afford to members of the public facilities for obtaining copies of the documents kept in the register, on payment of reasonable charges.

(5) A register under this section need not be kept in documentary form.

DEFINITIONS
"principal litter authority": s.86(2) and (3).

GENERAL NOTE
This section imposes an obligation on district and London borough councils, and district and islands councils in Scotland, to keep public registers of: (a) orders designating litter control areas; and (b) street litter control notices.

Application of Part II

96.—(1) This section applies to litter and refuse collected—
  (a) by an authority or person in pursuance of section 89(1) above;
  (b) by a principal litter authority in pursuance of section 92(9) above; or
  (c) by any person in pursuance of section 93 above.

(2) The Secretary of State may make regulations providing that prescribed provisions of Part II shall have effect, with such modifications (if any) as may be prescribed—
  (a) as if references to controlled waste or controlled waste of a prescribed description included references to litter and refuse to which this section applies or any description of such litter and refuse;
  (b) as if references to controlled waste or controlled waste of a prescribed description collected under section 45 above included references to litter and refuse collected as mentioned in subsection (1) above or any description of such litter and refuse.

(3) The powers conferred by this section are exercisable in relation to litter and refuse to which it applies whether or not the circumstances are such that the litter or refuse would be treated as controlled waste apart from this section and this section is not to affect the interpretation of the expressions defined in section 75 above.

DEFINITIONS
"principal litter authority": s.86(2) and (3).

GENERAL NOTE
This section applies to litter and refuse collected by litter authorities and other persons pursuant to the duties and power in Pt. IV. It allows the Secretary of State to make regulations applying provisions of Pt. II of the Act (with or without modifications) to such litter or refuse as if it were controlled waste and as if it were such waste collected by the waste collection authority. Such waste might not otherwise fall within any of the categories of controlled waste in s.75(4)–(7), which are concerned essentially with waste from premises. The provisions would, for example, make it clear that such items belong to the litter authority and may be recycled or otherwise dealt with under Pt. II.

Transitional provision relating to section 89

97.—(1) The Secretary of State may, for the purposes of the transition to the duties imposed by section 89 above on local authorities and educational bodies, by regulations, make provision—
  (a) modifying that section, or
  (b) modifying Part I of the Local Government Act 1988 (competition rules for functional work or works contracts).

(2) Regulations under this section may make different provision for different descriptions of authorities, different areas or other different circumstances or cases.

(3) In this section—

"educational bodies" means the governing bodies and education authorities mentioned in section 89(1)(f) above; and

"local authorities" means the local authorities mentioned in section 89(1)(a) and (c) and (2)(a) above.

GENERAL NOTE

This section is designed to assist the transition to the new duties as to litter and public cleanliness contained in s.89. The Secretary of State is given power to make regulations: (a) modifying those duties: and (b) modifying the provisions on competitive tendering in Pt. I of the Local Government Act 1988. The Regulations may make different provisions for different authorities or for different cases. The purpose of the provision was explained by Baroness Blatch in the House of Lords at Report Stage as follows:

"The new clause gives the Secretary of State the power to make transitional provisions to protect the position of authorities who had already assigned contracts for the provision of the relevant services under the competitive tendering legislation before the new litter code was published.

We appreciate that such contracts are likely to have to be modified in many cases to take account of the standards of litter clearance now required by the code. Indeed, so far as concerns future contracts, we have already taken action by postponing the rounds of competition due to be completed by January 1 and August 1 next year to August 1, 1991 and January 1, 1992 respectively, so as to make it possible for authorities to take full account of the code when drawing up their specifications.

Where contracts had already been let before the code was promulgated, the new clause will give the Secretary of State the power to make the necessary transitional arrangements. These will provide for any additional work which may be necessary to be taken on board. They will also protect the position of authorities until such time as this can be done. They will cover cases in which contracts have been let to the private sector and also those in which work has been assigned to the authority's own direct service organisation following competition under the terms of the Local Government Act 1988. We intend to announce the nature of the provision to be made as soon as possible, once the details have been finalised" (*Hansard*, H.L. Vol. 522, cols. 667–668).

Definitions

98.—(1) The following definitions apply for the interpretation of this Part.

(2) "Educational institution," in relation to England and Wales, means—
(a) any university (within the meaning of the Education Reform Act 1988) funded by the Universities Funding Council under section 131 of that Act;
(b) the Open University;
(c) any institution which provides higher education or further education (or both) which is full-time education being an institution which—
  (i) is maintained by grants made by the Secretary of State under section 100(1)(b) of the Education Act 1944;
  (ii) is designated by or under regulations under section 218 of the Education Reform Act 1988 as an institution dependent for its maintenance on assistance from local education authorities; or
  (iii) is maintained by a local education authority;
(d) any higher education institution funded by the Polytechnics and Colleges Funding Council under section 132 of the Education Reform Act 1988;
(e) any city technology college or city college for the technology of the arts (within the meaning of section 105 of the Education Reform Act 1988);
(f) any county school, voluntary school or maintained special school;
(g) any grant-maintained school.

(3) "Educational institution," in relation to Scotland, means—
(a) any university within the meaning of the Education Reform Act 1988 funded by the Universities Funding Council under section 131 of that Act;
(b) the Open University;
(c) a college of further education—
  (i) as defined in section 80(1) of the Self Governing Schools (Scotland) Act 1989 ("the 1989 Act"); or
  (ii) managed by a company by virtue of section 65(1) of the 1989 Act;
(d) a grant-aided college within the meaning of section 77(5) of the Education (Scotland) Act 1980 ("the 1980 Act");
(e) a technology academy within the meaning of section 68(1) of the 1989 Act;
(f) a public school as defined in section 135(1) of the 1980 Act;
(g) a grant-aided school as defined in section 135(1) of the 1980 Act;
(h) a self-governing school within the meaning of section 1(3) of the 1989 Act.
(4) "Joint board", in relation to Scotland, has the meaning given by section 235(1) of the Local Government (Scotland) Act 1973.
(5) "Highway" (and "highway maintainable at the public expense"), "special road" and "trunk road," in relation to England and Wales, have the same meaning as in the Highways Act 1980 and "public road," "special road" and "trunk road," in relation to Scotland, have the same meaning as in the Roads (Scotland) Act 1984.
(6) "Statutory undertaker" means—
(a) any person authorised by any enactment to carry on any railway, light railway, tramway or road transport undertaking;
(b) any person authorised by any enactment to carry on any canal, inland navigation, dock, harbour or pier undertaking; or
(c) any relevant airport operator (within the meaning of Part V of the Airports Act 1986).

GENERAL NOTE

Subs. (4)
  Joint board. Section 235(1) of the Local Government (Scotland) Act 1973 defines this term as any body set up by two or more local authorities to further their purposes and consisting entirely of members appointed by them. Examples are the Board for Lothian and Borders Police and the Board for the Forth Road Bridge.

Subs. (5)
  Highways. The relevant definitions from the Highways Act 1980 are as follows:
  (1) "Highway" means the whole or part of a highway other than a ferry or waterway.
  (2) Where a highway passes over a bridge or through a tunnel, that bridge or tunnel is to be taken ... to be a part of the highway (s.328).
    "Special road" means a highway, or a proposed highway, which is a special road in accordance with s.16 [of the 1980 Act].
    "Trunk road" means a highway, or a proposed highway, which is a trunk road by virtue of s.10(1) or s.19 [of the 1980 Act] or by virtue of an order or direction under s.10 [of the 1980 Act] or under any other enactment (s.239(1)).
  Privately-maintained or "unadopted" roads are therefore not included in the relevant litter clearing and cleaning duties of Pt. IV.

Statutory undertakers
  The relevant classes of statutory undertakers are all those with transport-related functions: *e.g.* railways, underground railways, ports, harbours, airports, bus stations and canals.

Abandoned trolleys

Powers in relation to abandoned shopping and luggage trolleys

99.—(1) A local authority may, subject to subsection (3) below, resolve that Schedule 4 to this Act is to apply in its area; and if a local authority does so resolve, that Schedule shall come into force in its area on the day specified in the resolution, which must not be before the expiration of the period of three months beginning with the day on which the resolution is passed.

(2) A local authority shall publish in at least one newspaper circulating in its area a notice that the authority has passed a resolution under this section and indicating the general effect of that Schedule.

(3) It shall be the duty of the local authority, before making any resolution for the application of Schedule 4 to this Act in its area, to consult with the persons or representatives of persons who appear to the authority to be persons who will be affected by the application of that Schedule.

(4) It shall be the duty of a local authority from time to time to consult about the operation of Schedule 4 to this Act with the persons or representatives of persons who appear to be affected by its operation.

(5) In this section "local authority" means—
(a) the council of a district;
(b) the council of a London borough;
(c) the Common Council of the City of London;
(d) the council of the Isles of Scilly; and
(e) in Scotland, an islands or district council.

(6) In Schedule 4 to this Act "the local authority" means any local authority which has resolved that that Schedule is to apply in its area.

GENERAL NOTE

This section allows local authorities at district level to resolve to apply to their area the provisions of Sched. 4, relating to abandoned shopping and luggage trolleys.

There is a general duty to consult about the operation of Sched. 4 from time to time with persons or representatives of persons who appear to be affected by its operation (subs. (3)). The main elements of Sched. 4 are:
(1) it applies to any shopping or luggage trolley (defined in para. 5) found on any land in the open air by an authorised officer of the authority and appearing to him to be abandoned (para. 1);
(2) it does not apply to trolleys found on land within the descriptions of para. 1(2);
(3) trolleys to which the Schedule applies may be seized and removed to a place under the control of the authority (para. 2(1));
(4) the power of removal is subject to consent or notification requirements where the trolley is found on land which appears to be occupied (para. 2(2));
(5) trolleys seized must be kept for six weeks and may then be sold or otherwise disposed of (para. 3(1));
(6) this is subject to the obligation to serve notice on any person believed to be the owner (para. 3(2)) and to make reasonable enquiries to ascertain who owns it (para. 3(5));
(7) owners have the right to delivery of their trolleys, subject to payment of such charge as the authority requires (para. 3(3) and (4));
(8) the authority, in setting charges, shall secure that the sums payable are sufficient, taking one year with another, to cover the cost of removal, storage and disposal (para. 4(1));
(9) the authority may agree a scheme for collection with owners of trolleys, and in such cases no charge may be demanded under para. 3 (para. 4(2)).

For a case on obstruction of the highway by supermarket trolleys (parked rather than abandoned), see *Devon County Council* v. *Gateway Foodmarkets* [1990] LMELR Issue 3, Vol. 21, p. 96; *The Daily Telegraph*, March 22, 1990, D.C.

PART V

AMENDMENT OF THE RADIOACTIVE SUBSTANCES ACT 1960

Part V was repealed by the Radioactive Substances Act 1993 with effect from August 27, 1993

Part VI

Genetically Modified Organisms

This part of the Act contains new provisions imposing control over various activities involving genetically modified organisms (GMOs). Section 106(1) states the purpose of the provision as "preventing or minimising any damage to the environment which may arise from the escape or release from human control of genetically modified organisms."

Royal Commission Report

The issues raised by the possibility of genetically modified or engineered organisms being released into the environment were considered by the Royal Commission on Environmental Pollution in its Thirteenth Report, *The Release of Genetically Engineered Organisms into the Environment* (Cm. 720, July 1989). The benefits and risks of the new technology were stated by the Royal Commission as follows (paras. 1.2, 1.3, 4.2 and 5.8).

"1.2 Genetic engineering offers the prospect of major improvements in medicine, in industry and in agricultural quality and efficiency. It is also likely to help in dealing with problems of environmental pollution and to lead to new commercial products. The UK is well fitted scientifically to make advances in genetic engineering.

1.3 As in many other fields of technological innovation, potential benefits bring potential risks. The risks that genetic engineering may entail, and the associated ethical considerations, have been debated since the technology came into existence in the early 1970s. There can rarely have been a new technology which has attracted so much intense discussion of its potential risks from such an early point in its development. To some extent this reflects the nature of the science. There is a natural apprehension stemming from the belief that scientists are now manipulating something as fundamental as life itself. The discussion also reflects an awareness that the relationship between living things and their environment is complex and imperfectly understood. Changes to one may have unknown, widespread and lasting effects on the other. Consideration of the environmental implications of releasing GEOs forms the main thrust of this Report.

4.2 Organisms which survive and become established could affect the environment in a variety of ways—both beneficial and undesirable. Some releases may alter the diversity of species in the environment, including changing the composition of existing communities. Such effects could produce noticeable changes in the countryside, locally or more widely, and could also have an economic impact, for example if the new organisms proved to be successful predators, competitors, parasites or pathogens of crop plants. Some organisms could pose a threat to human health. At the most extreme, new organisms could conceivably affect major environmental processes such as weather patterns, the nitrogen cycle or other regenerative soil processes.

5.8 We conclude that, although the environment is generally resilient, resistant to invasion by alien organisms and robust to biological perturbations, it is probable that some organisms, once released to the environment will become established. Most are likely to pose no hazard but others may cause varying degrees of disturbances which, in the extreme, could have serious environmental consequences."

The Commission, in the light of these conclusions, proposed "a precautionary but realistic system of regulation" (para. 5.4.7). The Commission's main recommendations were:

(1) statutory control of releases of genetically engineered organisms (GEOs) to the environment;
(2) involvement of both the Secretary of State for the Environment and the Health and Safety Commission (acting on behalf of the Secretary of State for Employment) in decisions on release but with the Secretary of State for the Environment taking primary responsibility with regard to the environmental consequences of releases;
(3) a general statutory duty of care on all those responsible for release of a GEO to take all reasonable steps for protection of human health and safety and that of the environment;
(4) a "release licence" to be required before release of a GEO could take place, with powers of revocation and amendment of licences;
(5) proposed releases of GEOs to be notified to the licensing authorities, with full details including the results of a safety assessment;
(6) each stage in the development of a GEO to be the subject of a licence with the appropriate licensing authorities to be informed and consulted in relation to applications for product licensing involving GEOs;
(7) wide additional and ancillary regulatory powers to be given to the Secretary of State for the Environment;

(8) every proposed release to be screened by a local committee and then, if passed, thoroughly scrutinised by a national committee of experts;
(9) referral of each application for a release licence or product approval to a committee of experts for assessment with regard to environmental protection and human health and safety;
(10) arrangements to be made for the registration of companies or other organisations carrying out trial releases;
(11) statutory strict liability on any person, or the directors of any company or other organisation, responsible for carrying out the release of a GEO without the necessary licence and registration;
(12) power to impose licence conditions as to monitoring the released GEOs and their environmental impacts;
(13) public registers of applications and licences and authorised releases, and general public access to information forming the basis of decisions on release;
(14) extension of controls over contained work on GEOs to minimise the risk of damage to the environment, for example in relation to waste disposal, storage and transport.

Some, but by no means all, of these recommendations are embodied in Pt. VI of the Act.

Previous arrangements

Prior to the introduction of statutory controls in Pt. VI of the Act, release of GMOs was covered by a variety of arrangements, some statutory and some non-statutory. Following the reports of two working parties on *Experimental Manipulation of the Genetic Composition of Micro-Organisms* (Cm. 5880, 1975, "the Ashby Working Party") and *The Laboratory Use of Dangerous Pathogens* (Cm. 6054, 1975, "the Godber Working Party"), a further working party was established "to draft a central code of practice and to make recommendations for the establishment of a central advisory service for laboratories using the techniques available for genetic manipulation." This working party reported in 1976: *Report of the Working Party on the Practice of Genetic Manipulation* (Cm. 6600, "the Williams Working Party"). The recommendations of this report led to the establishment of the Genetic Manipulation Advisory Group (GMAG) with a risk assessment and advisory rôle. GMAG produced various reports and a series of guidance notes.

At that stage, concern was mainly focused upon the risks arising from contained work with GMOs, primarily in the laboratory. The relevant statutory powers were therefore those under the Health and Safety at Work, etc. Act 1974, and in 1978 regulations were made under that Act requiring notification to the HSE of intention to carry out genetic manipulation: Health and Safety (Genetic Manipulation) Regulations 1978 (S.I. 1978 No. 752). Using Health and Safety at Work Act powers, HSE inspectors could therefore exercise control over work activities involving GMOs including, where appropriate, their release. The HSE took the view, however, that because their powers derived from health and safety at work legislation, they could not be used to prevent damage to the natural environment.

In 1984 the Health and Safety Commission established an Advisory Committee on Genetic Manipulation (ACGM) to replace GMAG. ACGM was given an advisory rôle to the Health and Safety Commission and Executive, and to related Ministers, including environment, on various aspects of genetic manipulation. Again, the main concern of the Committee was on contained experimental and industrial work and the health and safety aspects. However, the ACGM also took a close interest in the planned release of GMOs and established a working group on that subject which later became the Planned Release Sub-Committee (later the Intentional Introductions Sub-Committee or IISC). In 1986, guidance prepared by that Sub-Committee was issued as ACGM/HSE/Note 3, *The Planned Release of Genetically Manipulated Organisms for Agricultural and Environmental Purposes: Guidelines for Risk Assessment and for the Notification of Proposals for Such Work*. The recommendations of ACGM in the Guidelines were that:

(1) in the absence of any statutory requirements, all proposals for the release of GMOs should nonetheless be notified to the ACGM for its consideration;
(2) the notifier should be advised on the possible environmental consequences of release by an appropriately constituted local body including relevant scientific expertise and, where appropriate, a local environmental health officer;
(3) various listed factors should be taken into account when making the initial local risk assessment;
(4) it was premature to devise a single, broadly applicable risk assessment scheme, though material was available to achieve a measure of consistency. All proposals to release GMOs should therefore be considered by ACGM on a case-by-case basis.

These arrangements were originally implemented by the HSE on a voluntary basis. However, the arrangements were put on to a statutory basis by the Genetic Manipulation

Regulations 1989 (S.I. 1989 No. 1810), in force from November 1, 1989 (see also the HSE Guidance Notes on the Regulations). The effect of the Regulations is to require at least 30 days' advance notice of intention to carry out activities involving genetic manipulation to be given to the HSE (reg. 5(1)). In the case of activities involving an intentional introduction into the environment, the period is 90 days. The Regulations also require the establishment by persons carrying out such activities of a risk assessment committee (reg. 6(2)). The risk assessment of the activity determines the type of notification required, according to the hazard groupings of Sched. 1 (reg. 5(4) and (5)). Further work of ACGM involving release to the environment includes ACGM/HSE/Note 6—*Large Scale Use of Genetically Manipulated Organisms* (October, 1990), Appendix IV of which deals with environmental aspects of risk assessment in arriving at "good large-scale practice."

In addition to these controls, specific legislation applicable to products comprising or including GMOs include the Food and Environment Protection Act 1985 (pesticides), the Medicines Acts 1968 and 1971, the Plant and Health (Great Britain) Act 1967, the Animals (Scientific Procedures) Act 1986, the Food and Environment Protection Act 1985, Part II (deposits at sea), the Food Act 1984 and the Consumer Protection Act 1987.

The conclusion of the Royal Commission, in considering these measures, was that, whilst many could in principle be used to control the release of GMOs to the environment, even taken together all the measures did not appear to cover all possible circumstances. Even the regulations made under the Health and Safety at Work, etc. Act 1974, whilst referring specifically to GMOs, presented problems in controlling releases which presented a risk to the natural environment but which do not affect human health or safety. The Commission's conclusion was that "there is a clear need for fresh legislation to provide specifically for the control of releases of all categories of genetically engineered organism" (para. 7.23).

See also Neil Hawke, *Man-made micro-organisms and the environment* [1988] New L.J. 628.

Proposals for further legislation

In June 1989 the DoE, Welsh Office and Scottish Office issued a Consultation Paper on *Proposals for Additional Legislation on the Intentional Release of Genetically Modified Organisms*. The Paper was published in advance of the Royal Commission's Report. In the light of existing controls, the Government concluded that there were good reasons for considering further environmental safety measures to control the release of GMOs; any such system, it was suggested, would need to be compatible both with general environmental protection measures and the human health and safety regulatory system.

Various approaches were canvassed and it was proposed (para. 6) that the augmented system should provide a comprehensive régime for environmental protection with four main elements: (1) a general duty of care on those releasing GMOs to protect the environment; (2) notification to Ministers by those proposing to release GMOs; (3) authorisation by Ministers of proposed releases; and (4) appropriate enforcement of the provisions.

At the stage of the Government introducing such measures in the Environmental Protection Bill, the Health and Safety Executive and DOE issued an explanatory leaflet on *Biotechnology and Genetically Modified Organisms: The Proposed New Controls*. This provides valuable guidance as to how the new system is likely to operate in practice.

The Scheme of Pt. VI

The main features of Pt. VI of the Act are as follows:—
(1) Sections 106 and 107 contain a series of definitions of key terms and concepts.
(2) Section 108 contains a general prohibition on importation, acquisition, release and marketing of GMOs without carrying out a risk assessment of possible damage to the environment and notifying the Secretary of State of the intention to carry out the activity. Persons keeping GMOs are also under an obligation to carry out a risk assessment and to notify the Secretary of State of the keeping of the GMOs.
(3) Section 109 places a series of duties of care relating to the risk of environmental damage on persons proposing to import or acquire GMOs, persons keeping GMOs and persons proposing to release GMOs.
(4) Section 110 gives the Secretary of State power to serve prohibition notices in relation to acts or activities involving GMOs which would entail a risk of causing damage to the environment.
(5) By s.111, in certain cases to be prescribed, the importation, acquisition, keeping, release or marketing of GMOs is prohibited, except in pursuance of a consent granted by the Secretary of State and in accordance with any limitations and conditions to which the consent is subject. In such cases the requirements of ss.108 and 109 do not apply. Section 112 contains provisions as to express and implied conditions and limitations on such consents. Such conditions may not be imposed for the sole purpose of securing the

health and safety of workers (s.112(1)). Consents will contain a series of conditions implied by statute as to reasonable measures for risk assessment, notification and use of best available techniques not entailing excessive cost for the purpose of preventing damage to the environment.
(6) By s.113 a scheme of fees and charges for consents may be instituted.
(7) Sections 114–117 provide for the appointment of inspectors and give various powers of entry, inspection, obtaining information, and dealing with imminent dangers.
(8) Section 118 creates various offences in relation to contravention of the requirements of Pt. VI.
(9) Sections 119–121 contain ancillary provisions on offences, including the onus of proof and powers to order matters to be remedied, or to recover the costs of remedial steps.
(10) Sections 122 and 123 make provision for public registers of information relating to matters under Pt. VI of the Act.
(11) Section 124 provides for the appointment of a committee to advise the Secretary of State on the exercise of his powers.
(12) Section 125 allows the delegation of certain enforcement functions to officers of public authorities.

Public access to information
Originally Pt. VI did not provide on its face for public access to information, save in relation to the advertising of applications for consent. However, the Government gave an assurance (DoE News Release No. 140, March 1, 1990) that it was committed to allowing access to information as for other Parts of the Act under the Secretary of State's inherent powers of disclosure. In the event, express statutory provisions to that effect were inserted as ss.122 and 123.

Strict liability
The Government has not followed the suggestions of the RCEP on strict liability for activities involving GMOs (see above). This is regarded as a wider and more complex issue than general regulation, and one that needs to be considered on an international basis: *Hansard*, H.L. Vol. 522, cols. 704–706.

Expert committee
The Government has acknowledged the need of expert advice as to questions both of environmental and human safety in relation to GMOs. The Government announced its intention (DoE News Release No. 140, March 1, 1990) to establish a single expert committee to advise on both aspects in relation to the introduction of GMOs to the environment. The committee is known as the Advisory Committee on Releases to The Environment (ACRE). Section 124 deals with the appointment of that committee. The Government announced that the new committee would be chaired by Professor John Beringer of the Unit of Molecular Genetics at the University of Bristol and that it will have representatives from various areas of expertise (see further, note to s.124).

Relationship to Royal Commission proposals
At the House of Lords Second Reading stage, the Chairman of the RCEP, Lord Lewis of Newnham, voiced the following reservation about how the Act might operate in practice:
"I have a certain reservation. The Bill makes provision for releases and other activities not involved in releases to be the subject of one of three different levels of control. First, it involves specific consent of the authorities. That is very much a recommendation for the Beringer Committee which we are all very happy to see enforced. However, there are two other possibilities: namely, notifying the authorities in advance of a release or following a special procedure for risk assessment. I have no quarrel with those in principle. However, I am anxious as to whether the Government, when drawing up regulations under the Bill may immediately allow certain classes of releases to be subject only to the second and third categories.
My belief—and it is also the belief of the Royal Commission—is that that would be premature. At present, every prospective release of a GMO should be subject to the full consultative procedure. I believe that to be very important not only for the safety of the community but also for the sensitivity of industry as a whole. We have not enough knowledge of the possible impact of such organisms on the environment to allow exceptions to that rule." (*Hansard*, H.L. Vol. 519, cols. 517–518).

European Community and international obligations
The Council of the European Community has promulgated two directives on GMOs.

Directive 90/219/EEC (O.J. L117, May 8, 1990, p. 1) deals with *The Contained Use of Genetically Modified Organisms*. This Directive lays down common measures for the "contained use" of GMOs with a view to protecting human health and the environment. The measures include prior risk assessment based on a list of "parameters" set out in the Directive. Others relate to the observation of "good microbiological practice," containment measures, information and notification, emergency plans and reporting of accidents.

Directive 90/220/EEC (O.J. L117, May 8, 1990, p. 15) on *The Deliberate Release into the Environment of Genetically Modified Organisms* deals with deliberate releases of GMOs and the marketing of products containing GMOs. In the case of GMOs released in the course of research and development (as opposed to marketing) the release must be pre-notified to the competent authority, together with information specified in the Directive and a risk evaluation statement in relation to human health and the environment. The authority is then under an obligation to check the notification, carry out its own evaluation and any necessary tests, and record its decision in writing. Release may not take place without the authority's written consent. Products containing GMOs must similarly be pre-notified before being placed on the market. Written consent of the competent authority must be obtained and the product must comply with all other applicable Community legislation. The dossiers relating to approved products must be forwarded to the Commission and circulated to all member states.

The date by which the Directives must be implemented in national legislation was October 23, 1991.

Work on safety issues relating to GMOs in the workplace and in the environment has also been carried out by an ad hoc group of government, scientific and industry experts under the OECD. This group made recommendations on risk assessment criteria in its 1986 Report, *R—DNA Safety Considerations*.

Further discussion on the international aspects of the control and regulation of GMOs can be found in the article by Richard B. Stewart and Maria A. Martinez, *Internaional Aspects of Biotechnology: Implications for Environmental Law and Policy* [1989] J.E.L. Vol. 1, No. 2, p. 157.

Territorial extent

By s.127(2), Pt. VI, except as to importation of GMOs, applies to the territorial sea adjacent to Great Britain, and to the designated British Continental Shelf. Pt. VI applies to Northern Ireland so far as it relates to importation of GMOs. Section 127(2) applies to Northern Ireland without that restriction, in so far as it relates to the Continental Shelf (s.164(4)). It is intended in due course to make an Order in Council replicating Pt. VI in Northern Ireland (*Hansard*, H.L. Vol. 522, col. 716).

Commencement

Part VI came into force on January 1, 1993 and February 1, 1993 (S.I. 1992 No. 3253). The Government's intention was to bring the regime into effect by October 1991, in order to comply with the relevant E.C. Directives (*Hansard*, H.L. Vol. 522, col. 1261). However that was not done. In October 1991 the Government issued for consultation a document titled *Genetically Modified Organisms (GMOs): Proposed New Regulations*. These set out the text of two proposed statutory instruments to implement the new regime: The Genetically Modified Organisms (Environmental Protection) Regulations and the Genetically Modified Organisms (Health and Safety) Regulations. The consultation process identified many problems with the Regulations as proposed and the DoE undertook to redraft them.

Second Consultation Paper

On August 14, 1992 the Government issued a second consultation paper setting out revised draft proposals for new regulations on genetically modified organisms and draft guidance on implementing the two European directives on genetically modified organisms. These revised proposals followed earlier consultation on drafts issued in October 1991. The two Directives that these regulations implement are 90/219/EEC which deals with the contained use of genetically modified micro-organisms and 90/2020/EEC which deals with the deliberate release into the environment and the marketing of GMOs. These were due to be implemented into UK legislation by October 23, 1991, but this deadlline was not met. The regulations did not come into force until the start of 1993.

Two hundred responses were received by the Government following the issue of its original consultation paper in October 1991. These responses mainly centred on the complex structure of the regulations and ambiguous points of detail. The newly issued regulations were redrafted to account for these criticisms.

A major change from the first proposals was that the regulations were split into the control of contained use and the control of deliberate release and marketing of genetically modified organisms.

The Genetically Modified Organisms (Contained Use) Regulations 1992 (S.I. 1992 No. 3217) were made under the Health and Safety at Work etc. Act 1974 and the European Communities Act 1972. The Genetically Modified Organisms (Deliberate Release) Regulations 1992 (S.I. 1992 No. 3280) were made pursuant to the EPA 1990 and the European Communities Act. See Appendices 8 and 9 for the text of these Regulations. See also the Genetically Modified Organisms (Contained Use) Regulations (S.I. 1993 No. 15) which restrict the application of s.108(1)(a) of the 1990 Act with reference to both 1992 regulations.

The Contained Use Regulations were made without reference to EPA 1990 in order to avoid the use of the EPA definition which caused problems when applied to contained use of genetically modified organisms and has thus been omitted. Although the directive on contained use of GMOs does not cover non-micro-organisms such as plants or animals in relation to human health and safety these non-micro-organisms are covered by the new regulations. In relation to Environmental Protection, s.108(1)(a) of EPA 1990 was brought in to ensure that anyone intending to make or acquire from another person a genetically modified non-micro-organism which is not an approved product will have to carry out a risk assessment and keep it available for inspection.

Preliminary

Purpose of Part VI and meaning of "genetically modified organisms" and related expressions

106.—(1) This Part has effect for the purpose of preventing or minimising any damage to the environment which may arise from the escape or release from human control of genetically modified organisms.

(2) In this Part the term "organism" means any acellular, unicellular or multicellular entity (in any form), other than humans or human embryos; and, unless the context otherwise requires, the term also includes any article or substance consisting or including biological matter.

(3) For the purpose of subsection (2) above "biological matter" means anything (other than an entity mentioned in that subsection) which consists of or includes—

(a) tissue or cells (including gametes or propagules) or subcellular entities, of any kind, capable of replication or of transferring genetic material, or

(b) genes or other genetic material, in any form, which are so capable,

and it is immaterial, in determining if something is or is not an organism or biological matter, whether it is the product of natural or artificial processes of reproduction and, in the case of biological matter, whether it has ever been part of a whole organism.

(4) For the purposes of this Part an organism is "genetically modified" if any of the genes or other genetic material in the organism—

(a) have been modified by means of an artificial technique prescribed in regulations by the Secretary of State; or

(b) are inherited or otherwise derived, through any number of replications, from genes or other genetic material (from any source) which were so modified.

(5) The techniques which may be prescribed for the purposes of subsection (4) above include—

(a) any technique for the modification of any genes or other genetic material by the recombination, insertion or deletion of, or of any component parts of, that material from its previously occurring state, and

(b) any other technique for modifying genes or other genetic material which in the opinion of the Secretary of State would produce organisms which should for the purposes of this Part be treated as having been genetically modified, but do not include techniques which involve no more than, or no more than the assistance of, naturally occurring processes of reproduction (including selective breeding techniques or *in vitro* fertilisation).

(6) It is immaterial for the purposes of subsections (4) and (5) above whether the modifications of genes or other genetic material effected by a prescribed technique are produced by direct operations on that genetic material or are induced by indirect means (including in particular the use of viruses, microbial plasmids or other vector systems or of mutation inducing agents).

(7) In this Part, where the context permits, a reference to "reproduction", in relation to an organism, includes a reference to its replication or its transferring genetic material.

GENERAL NOTE

Subsection (1) states the purpose of Pt. VI, whilst subss. (2)–(7) provide a series of highly technical definitions dealing with what constitutes a "genetically modified organism."

Subs. (2)

Organism. The term is defined to include all living things, except humans or human embryos. It also includes "biological matter," which is defined in subs. (3) to include tissues, cells, subcellular material, genes or genetic material, which in each case is capable of replication or of transferring genetic material. The qualification in respect of replication or transfer is to ensure that matter is covered in situations where it might spontaneously hand on genetic material to other organisms which in turn might damage the environment. It is expressly provided that the origin of the organism or biological matter is immaterial, so that an organism reproduced by artificial processes is still an organism for the purposes of Pt. VI.

Subs. (4)

Genetically modified. Genetic modification means the modification of any genes or genetic material in the organism by the various artificial techniques to be prescribed in regulations made by the Secretary of State. By subs. (4)(b) the definition also extends to cases where the genes or genetic material in the organism have not been directly modified but were inherited or otherwise derived from genes or genetic material which were so modified. This provision as to the inheritance of modified genes is crucial because the effects of genetic modification on the properties of an organism might not become apparent for several generations after the original modification. Subsection (5) describes the techniques which may be prescribed for the purposes of subs. (4) and, importantly, excludes techniques involving only naturally occurring processes of reproduction (including selective breeding and *in vitro* fertilisation). By subs. (6) it is immaterial whether the genetic modification operations are direct or indirect, so for example including the introduction of genetic material by means of vector viruses.

Subs. (7)

Reproduction. This term is given an extended meaning to include not only the replication of an organism, but also the transferral of genetic material.

Scientific terms

Section 106 uses a number of scientific terms which are not defined and the meaning of which as terms of art may not be familiar to all lawyers. The following definitions are therefore set out below for convenience (adapted from *Chambers Science and Technology Dictionary*, Cambridge 1988).

Acellular. Not partitioned into cells.

Cell. The unit, consisting of nucleus and cytoplasm, of which plants and animals are composed.

Gametes. Reproductive cells which will unite in pairs to form zygotes; germ cells.

Microbial plasmid. A plasmid is a genetic element containing nucleic acid and able to replicate independently of its host's chromosome. "Microbial" connotes that the plasmid is sub-microscopic and would therefore include, for example, bacteria and yeasts.

Multicellular. Consisting of a number of cells.

Organisms. Animals, plants, fungi and micro-organisms.

Propagule. Any structure, sexual or asexual, and independent from the parent, which serves as a means of reproduction.

Tissue. An aggregate of similar cells forming a definite and continuous fabric, and usually having a comparable and definable function.

Unicellular. Consisting of a single cell.

Vector systems. A vector is an agent of transmission; in the context of genetic engineering it means a DNA molecule that can accept inserted DNA and can be used to transfer it from one organism to another. "Systems" appears to be used to incorporate the various types of vectors used in practice.

Meaning of "damage to the environment", "control" and related expressions in Part VI

107.—(1) The following provision have effect for the interpretation of this Part.

(2) The "environment" consists of land, air and water or any of those media.

(3) "Damage to the environment" is caused by the presence in the environment of genetically modified organisms which have (or of a single such organism which has) escaped or been released from a person's control and are (or is) capable of causing harm to the living organisms supported by the environment.

(4) An organism shall be regarded as present in the environment notwithstanding that it is present in or on any human or other organism, or any other thing, which is itself present in the environment.

(5) Genetically modified organisms present in the environment are capable of causing harm if—
   (a) they are individually capable, or are present in numbers such that together they are capable, of causing harm; or
   (b) they are able to produce descendants which will be capable, or which will be present in numbers such that together they will be capable, of causing harm;

and a single organism is capable of causing harm either if it is itself capable of causing harm or if it is able to produce descendants which will be so capable.

(6) "Harm" means harm to the health of humans or other living organisms or other interference with the ecological systems of which they form part and, in the case of many, includes offence caused to any of his senses or harm to his property.

(7) "Harmful" and "harmless" mean respectively, in relation to genetically modified organisms, their being capable or their being incapable of causing harm.

(8) The Secretary of State may by regulations provide, in relation to genetically modified organisms of any description specified in the regulations, that—
   (a) the capacity of those organisms for causing harm of any description so specified, or
   (b) harm of any description so specified,

shall be disregarded for such purpose of this Part as may be so specified.

(9) Organisms of any description are under the "control" of a person where he keeps them contained by any system of physical, chemical or biological barriers (or combination of such barriers) used for either or both of the following purposes, namely—
   (a) for ensuring that the organisms do not enter the environment or produce descendants which are not so contained; or
   (b) for ensuring that any of the organisms which do enter the environment, or any descendants of the organisms which are not so contained, are harmless.

(10) An organism under a person's control is "released" if he deliberately causes or permits it to cease to be under his control or the control of any other person and to enter the environment; and such an organism "escapes" if, otherwise than by being released, it ceases to be under his control or that of any other person and enters the environment.

(11) Genetically modified organisms of any description are "marketed" when products consisting of or including such organisms are placed on the market.

DEFINITIONS
"descendant": s.127(1).
"genetically modified organisms": s.106.
"organism": s.106.

Subs. (3)
Damage to the environment. A number of components make up the definition of "damage to the environment." These are: (1) the presence of GMOs in the environment (see subs. (4)); (2) such GMOs have either been released from or have escaped from a person's control (see subs. (9)); (3) such GMOs are capable of causing harm to the living organisms supported by the environment (see subs. (5)).

Subs. (5)
Capable of causing harm. It is the capability of GMOs to cause harm rather than actual harm which is the crucial concept, in view of the difficulty or impossibility of recovering or rendering harmless many forms of GMO once they are outside human control. GMOs can be capable of causing harm either individually, collectively, or in their ability to produce descendants capable of causing such harm.

Subs. (6)
Harm. The expression is given an extended meaning consistent with that given in other parts of the Act. It appears that the harm could be direct or indirect, so that, for example, it would cover the situation where material produced by a GMO reached a watercourse and thus affected organisms present in or dependent on the water.

Subs. (8)
The Secretary of State has power to provide by regulations that certain descriptions of harm are to be disregarded for the purposes of Pt. VI.

Subs. (9)
Control. This subsection deals with the crucial distinction between GMOs which are under human control and GMOs which have entered the environment at large. "Control" means that the GMOs are contained by physical, chemical or biological barriers so as to ensure that: (a) they or their descendants do not enter the environment; or (b) if they or their descendants do enter the environment, they are harmless. A simple example of the first type of control would be a fence or cage preventing the escape of a genetically modified animal. An example of the second type of control would be the insertion of a gene that would ensure the death of the GMO on exposure to sunlight, so that the organism would not survive in the open.

Subs. (10)
Release/escape. This subsection distinguishes the two means by which a GMO may cease to be under human control and enter the environment. The first is deliberate "release", and the second is non-intentional "escape." "Release" would include the discharge of waste from an industrial process which contains GMOs.

General controls

Risk assessment and notification requirements

108.—(1) Subject to subsections (2) and (7) below, no person shall import or acquire, release or market any genetically modified organisms unless, before that act—
 (a) he has carried out an assessment of any risks there are (by reference to the nature of the organisms and the manner in which he intends to keep them after their importation or acquisition or, as the case may be, to release or market them) of damage to the environment being caused as a result of doing that act; and
 (b) in such cases and circumstances as may be prescribed, he has given the

Secretary of State such notice of his intention of doing that act and such information as may be prescribed.

(2) Subsection (1) above does not apply to a person proposing to do an act mentioned in that subsection who is required under section 111(1)(a) below to have a consent before doing that act.

(3) Subject to subsections (4) and (7) below, a person who is keeping genetically modified organisms shall, in such cases or circumstances and at such times or intervals as may be prescribed—
- (a) carry out an assessment of any risks there are of damage to the environment being caused as a result of his continuing to keep them;
- (b) give the Secretary of State notice of the fact that he is keeping the organisms and such information as may be prescribed.

(4) Subsection (3) above does not apply to a person who is keeping genetically modified organisms and is required under section 111(2) below to have a consent authorising him to continue to keep the organisms.

(5) It shall be the duty of a person who carries out an assessment under subsection (1)(a) or (3)(a) above to keep, for the prescribed period, such a record of the assessment as may be prescribed.

(6) A person required by subsection (1)(b) or (3)(b) above to give notice to the Secretary of State shall give the Secretary of State such further information as the Secretary of State may by notice in writing require.

(7) Regulations under this section may provide for exemptions, or for the granting by the Secretary of State of exemptions to particular persons or classes of person, from the requirements of subsection (1) or (3) above in such cases or circumstances, and to such extent, as may be prescribed.

(8) The Secretary of State may at any time—
- (a) give directions to a person falling within subsection (1) above requiring that person to apply for a consent before doing the act in question; or
- (b) give directions to a person falling within subsection (3) above requiring that person, before such date as may be specified in the direction, to apply for a consent authorising him to continue keeping the organisms in question;

and a person given directions under paragraph (a) above shall then, and a person given directions under paragraph (b) above shall from the specified date, be subject to section 111 below in place of the requirements of this section.

(9) Regulations under this section may—
- (a) prescribe the manner in which assessments under subsection (1) or (3) above are to be carried out and the matters which must be investigated and assessed;
- (b) prescribe minimum periods of notice between the giving of a notice under subsection (1)(b) above and the doing of the act in question;
- (c) make provision allowing the Secretary of State to shorten or to extend any such period;
- (d) prescribe maximum intervals at which assessments under subsection (3)(a) above must be carried out;

and the regulations may make different provision for different cases and different circumstances.

(10) In this section "prescribed" means prescribed by the Secretary of State in regulations under this section.

DEFINITIONS
"acquire": s.127(1).
"consent": s.127(1).
"damage to the environment": s.107(3).
"genetically modified organisms": s.106.
"import": s.127(1).

"market": s.107(11).
"release": s.107(10).

GENERAL NOTE

The effect of this section is that all persons proposing to import, acquire, keep, release or market GMOs (other than those who require express consent under s.111) must assess the risks to the environment. The risks are to be assessed by reference to the nature of the GMOs and the proposed activity (subs. (1)(a)). In addition, in prescribed cases notice must be given to the Secretary of State of intention to carry out the activity, together with such information as may be prescribed (subs. (1)(b)). Similar obligations apply to persons keeping, or continuing to keep, GMOs (subs. (3)).

It is possible for the Secretary of State to give directions requiring express consent to be applied for and obtained (subs. (8)), in which case the requirements of s.111 as to consent will apply, and conditions may be imposed. If no such direction is given, then after a prescribed period from notification the act in question may be carried out (subs. (9)(b)).

General duties relating to importation, acquisition, keeping, release or marketing of organisms

109.—(1) A person who—
  (a) is proposing to import or acquire any genetically modified organisms, or
  (b) is keeping any such organisms, or
  (c) is proposing to release or market any such organisms,
shall, subject to subsection (5) below, be subject to the duties specified in subsection (2), (3) or (4) below, as the case may be.

(2) A person who proposes to import or acquire genetically modified organisms—
  (a) shall take all reasonable steps to identify, by reference to the nature of the organisms and the manner in which he intends to keep them (including any precautions to be taken against their escaping or causing damage to the environment), what risks there are of damage to the environment being caused as a result of their importation or acquisition; and
  (b) shall not import or acquire the organisms if it appears that, despite any precautions which can be taken, there is a risk of damage to the environment being caused as a result of their importation or acquisition.

(3) A person who is keeping genetically modified organisms—
  (a) shall take all reasonable steps to keep himself informed of any damage to the environment which may have been caused as a result of his keeping the organisms and to identify what risks there are of damage to the environment being caused as a result of his continuing to keep them;
  (b) shall cease keeping the organisms if, despite any additional precautions which can be taken, it appears, at any time, that there is a risk of damage to the environment being caused as a result of his continuing to keep them; and
  (c) shall use the best available techniques not entailing excessive cost for keeping the organisms under his control and for preventing any damage to the environment being caused as a result of his continuing to keep the organisms;
and where a person is required by paragraph (b) above to cease keeping the organisms he shall dispose of them as safely and as quickly as practicable and paragraph (c) above shall continue to apply until he has done so.

(4) A person who proposes to release genetically modified organisms—
  (a) shall take all reasonable steps to keep himself informed, by reference to the nature of the organisms and the extent and manner of the release (including any precautions to be taken against their causing

damage to the environment), what risks there are of damage to the environment being caused as a result of their being released;
(b) shall not release the organisms if it appears that, despite the precautions which can be taken, there is a risk of damage to the environment being caused as a result of their being released; and
(c) subject to paragraph (b) above, shall use the best available techniques not entailing excessive cost for preventing any damage to the environment being caused as a result of their being released;

and this subsection applies, with the necessary modifications, to a person proposing to market organisms as it applies to a person proposing to release organisms.

(5) This section does not apply—
(a) to persons proposing to import or acquire, to release or to market any genetically modified organisms, in cases or circumstances where, under section 108 above, they are not required to carry out a risk assessment before doing that act;
(b) to persons who are keeping any genetically modified organisms and who—
   (i) were not required under section 108 above to carry out a risk assessment before importing or acquiring them;
   (ii) have not been required under that section to carry out a risk assessment in respect of the keeping of those organisms since importing or acquiring them; or
(c) to holders of consents, in the case of acts authorised by those consents.

DEFINITIONS
"acquire": s.127(1).
"consent": s.127(1).
"control": s.107(9).
"damage to the environment": s.107(3).
"escaping": s.107(10).
"genetically modified organisms": s.106.
"import": s.127(1).
"market": s.107(11).
"release": s.107(10).

GENERAL NOTE
This section imposes separate duties on: (a) persons proposing to import or acquire GMOs; (b) persons keeping GMOs; (c) persons proposing to release or market GMOs.

Subs. (2)
Persons importing or acquiring GMOs. Such persons are: (a) under a duty to take reasonable steps to identify the risks of damage to the environment from the import or acquisition; and (b) may not import or acquire the GMOs if it appears there are such risks despite any precautions that could be taken.

Subs. (3)
Persons keeping GMOs. Such persons are under a duty: (a) to take all reasonable steps to identify past damage to the environment and what risks there are of damage being caused as a result of their continuing to keep the GMOs; (b) to cease keeping the organisms if it appears at any time that there is a risk of damage to the environment despite any additional precautions that can be taken; and (c) to use the best available techniques not entailing excessive cost (BATNEEC) for keeping the GMOs under their control and preventing damage to the environment.

Subs. (4)
Persons proposing to release or market GMOs. Such a person: (a) is under a duty to take all reasonable steps to identify the risks of damage from the release or marketing; (b) shall not release or market the GMOs if it appears there is a risk of such damage; and (c) shall, if the GMOs are released or marketed, use BATNEEC for preventing any such damage.

BATNEEC

This term is not defined, though by s.119(1) in any proceedings for the offence of failing to use BATNEEC, the onus of showing there was no better available technique not entailing excessive cost than that used lies with the defendant. It appears that the expression is likely to be interpreted by the Secretary of State in the same way as in Pt. I of the Act (see General Note to Pt. I) in that it involves not only technology but also the way in which the technology is applied, for example training of personnel and the layout of premises. Similarly, what is "excessive cost" seems likely to be judged objectively, balancing the benefits of risk reduction against the costs. It will not depend on the financial resources of the person involved, the philosophy being that persons who cannot afford to apply the approximate techniques should not operate with GMOs. It is intended that the Advisory Committee on Releases to the Environment (ACRE) will issue expert guidance on good practice "in an easily-updated form": see *Hansard*, H.L. Vol. 520, col. 1983.

Subs. (5)

Exclusions. The subsection disapplies the requirements of the section: (a) to persons who are not, and have not been, required to carry out a risk assessment under s.108; and (b) to persons holding consents under s.111, in relation to acts authorised by such consents.

Prohibition notices

110.—(1) The Secretary of State may serve a notice under this section (a "prohibition notice") on any person he has reason to believe—
 (a) is proposing to import or acquire, release or market any genetically modified organisms; or
 (b) is keeping any such organisms;
if he is of the opinion that doing any such act in relation to those organisms or continuing to keep them, as the case may be, would involve a risk of causing damage to the environment.

(2) A prohibition notice may prohibit a person from doing an act mentioned in subsection (1)(a) above in relation to any genetically modified organisms or from continuing to keep them; and the prohibition may apply in all cases or circumstances or in such cases or circumstances as may be specified in the notice.

(3) A prohibition notice shall—
 (a) state that the Secretary of State is, in relation to the person on whom it is served, of the opinion mentioned in subsection (1) above;
 (b) specify what is, or is to be, prohibited by the notice; and
 (c) if the prohibition is not to be effective on being served, specify the date on which the prohibition is to take effect;
and a notice may be served on a person notwithstanding that he may have a consent authorising any act which is, or is to be, prohibited by the notice.

(4) Where a person is prohibited by a prohibition notice from continuing to keep any genetically modified organisms, he shall dispose of them as quickly and safely as practicable or, if the notice so provides, as may be specified in the notice.

(5) The Secretary of State may at any time withdraw a prohibition notice served on any person by notice given to that person.

DEFINITIONS
 "acquire": s.127(1).
 "consent": s.127(1).
 "damage to the environment": s.107(3).
 "genetically modified organisms": s.106.
 "import": s.127(1).
 "market": s.107(11).
 "release": s.107(10).

GENERAL NOTE

This section empowers the Secretary of State to prohibit a person from importing, acquiring, continuing to keep, releasing or marketing GMOs, if he is of the opinion that there is a risk of causing damage to the environment. The notice of prohibition may forbid the doing of the proposed act, or may prohibit the continued keeping of the GMOs (subs. (2)): in the latter case the person must then dispose of the GMOs as quickly and safely as possible, or in accordance with any requirements specified in the notice (subs. (4)).

The Secretary of State regards the power to prohibit the import of GMOs as being potentially of particular value in cases involving especially hazardous GMOs.

Consents

Consents required by certain persons

111.—(1) Subject to subsection (7) below, no person shall import or acquire, release or market any genetically modified organisms—
  (a) in such cases or circumstances as may be prescribed in relation to that act, or
  (b) in any case where he has been given directions under section 108(8)(a) above,
except in pursuance of a consent granted by the Secretary of State and in accordance with any limitations and conditions to which the consent is subject.

(2) Subject to subsection (7) below, no person who has imported or acquired any genetically modified organisms (whether under a consent or not) shall continue to keep the organisms—
  (a) in such cases or circumstances as may be prescribed, after the end of the prescribed period, or
  (b) if he has been given directions under section 108(8)(b) above, after the date specified in the directions,
except in pursuance of a consent granted by the Secretary of State and in accordance with any limitations or conditions to which the consent is subject.

(3) A person who is required under subsection (2) above to cease keeping any genetically modified organisms shall dispose of them as quickly and safely as practicable.

(4) An application for a consent must contain such information and be made and advertised in such manner as may be prescribed and shall be accompanied by the fee required under section 113 below.

(5) The applicant shall, in prescribed circumstances, give such notice of his application to such persons as may be prescribed.

(6) The Secretary of State may by notice to the applicant require him to furnish such further information specified in the notice, within such period as may be so specified, as he may require for the purpose of determining the application; and if the applicant fails to furnish the information within the specified period the Secretary of State may refuse to proceed with the application.

(6A) Where an applicant for consent for releasing or marketing genetically modified organisms becomes aware, before his application is either granted or rejected, of any new information with regard to any risks there are of damage to the environment being caused as a result of the organisms being released or marketed, he shall notify the Secretary of State of that new information forthwith.

(7) Regulations under this section may provide for exemptions, or for the granting by the Secretary of State of exemptions to particular persons or classes of person, from—
  (a) any requirement under subsection (1) or (2) above to have a consent, or

(b) any of the requirements to be fulfilled under the regulations by an applicant for a consent,

in such cases or circumstances as may be prescribed.

(8) Where an application for a consent is duly made to him, the Secretary of State may grant the consent subject to such limitations and conditions as may be imposed under section 112 below or he may refuse the application.

(9) The conditions attached to a consent may include conditions which are to continue to have effect notwithstanding that the holder has completed or ceased the act or acts authorised by the consent.

(10) The Secretary of State may at any time, by notice given to the holder of a consent, revoke the consent or vary the consent (whether by attaching new limitations and conditions or by revoking or varying any limitations and conditions to which it is at that time subject).

(11) Regulations under this section may make different provision for different cases and different circumstances; and in this section "prescribed" means prescribed in regulations under this section.

DEFINITIONS
"acquire": s.127(1).
"consent": s.127(1).
"genetically modified organisms": s.106.
"import": s.127(1).
"market": s.107(11).
"release" s.107(10).

AMENDMENTS
Section 6A was inserted by the Genetically Modified Organisms (Deliberate Release) Regulations 1992 (S.I. 1992 No. 3280), reg. 13.

GENERAL NOTE
This section contains provisions as to the requirement of consent for the import, acquisition, keeping, release or marketing of GMOs. The consent requirements apply in two circumstances: (a) cases or circumstances prescribed in regulations; and (b) where the Secretary of State has given a direction under s.108(8) requiring consent to be applied for. In such cases the activity or keeping may only be carried out or continued, as the case may be, in pursuance of the consent and in accordance with any condition or limitations to which it is subject. The consent requirements might well apply to the release of GMOs as waste or as a part of waste, as well as to releases for commercial or trial purposes.

Matters to be dealt with by regulations include: (a) the cases or circumstances in which consent is required; (b) information to be contained in an application for consent; (c) requirements as to advertisement of consents; (d) circumstances in which notification of applications are required and the persons to whom such notice should be given; and (e) exemptions from the consent requirement or from the requirements of regulations as to applications.

Fees
Applications must be accompanied by the appropriate fee (subs. (5) and s.113) and will not be regarded as "duly made" unless the fee is paid (subs. (8)).

Conditions
The consent may be granted subject to conditions or limitations (subs. (8)). The detailed requirements or conditions are contained in s.112.

Revocation and variation
The Secretary of State is given wide powers by subs. (10) to give notice revoking or varying consents.

Appeals
There is no appeal from decisions of the Secretary of State (see *Hansard*, H.L. Vol. 520, cols. 1989–1993). The Government proposes that the advice of ACRE to the Secretary of State should be made public and that there should be a period for the applicant and the public to make representations thereon to the Secretary of State before he reaches a decision.

Consents: limitations and conditions

112.—(1) The Secretary of State may include in a consent such limitations and conditions as he may think fit; [...].
(2) Without prejudice to the generality of subsection (1) above, the conditions included in a consent may—
  (a) require the giving of notice of any fact to the Secretary of State; or
  (b) prohibit or restrict the keeping, releasing or marketing of genetically modified organisms under the consent in specified cases or circumstances;
and where, under any condition, the holder of a consent is required to cease keeping any genetically modified organisms, he shall dispose of them, if no manner is specified in the conditions, as quickly and safely as practicable.
(3) Subject to subsection (6) below, there is implied in every consent for the importation or acquisition of genetically modified organisms a general condition that the holder of the consent shall—
  (a) take all reasonable steps to keep himself informed (by reference to the nature of the organisms and the manner in which he intends to keep them after their importation or acquisition) of any risks there are of damage to the environment being caused as a result of their importation or acquisition; and
  (b) if at any time it appears that any such risks are more serious than were apparent when the consent was granted, notify the Secretary of State forthwith.
(4) Subject to subsection (6) below, there is implied in every consent for keeping genetically modified organisms a general condition that the holder of the consent shall—
  (a) take all reasonable steps to keep himself informed of any damage to the environment which may have been caused as a result of his keeping the organisms and of any risks there are of such damage being caused as a result of his continuing to keep them;
  (b) if at any time it appears that any such risks are more serious than were apparent when the consent was granted, notify the Secretary of State forthwith; and
  (c) use the best available techniques not entailing excessive cost for keeping the organisms under his control and for preventing any damage to the environment being caused as a result of his continuing to keep them.
(5) Subject to subsection (6) below, there is implied in every consent for releasing or marketing genetically modified organisms a general condition that the holder of the consent shall—
  (a) take all reasonable steps to keep himself informed (by reference to the nature of the organisms and the extent and manner of the release or marketing) of any risks there are of damage to the environment being caused as a result of their being released or, as the case may be, marketed;
  [(b) notify the Secretary of State of—
    (i) any new information which becomes available with regard to any risks there are of damage to the environment being so caused, and
    (ii) the effects of any releases by him for the assessment of any risks there are of damage to the environment being so caused by such organisms being released or marketed;]
  (c) use the best available techniques not entailing excessive cost for preventing any damage to the environment being caused as a result of their being released or, as the case may be, marketed.
(6) The general condition implied into a consent under subsection (3), (4) or (5) above has effect subject to any conditions imposed under subsection

(1) above; and the obligations imposed by virtue of subsection (4)(c) or (5)(c) above shall not apply to any aspect of an act authorised by a consent which is regulated by such a condition.

(7) There shall be implied in every consent for keeping, releasing or marketing genetically modified organisms of any description a general condition that the holder of the consent—
- (a) shall take all reasonable steps to keep himself informed of developments in the techniques which may be available in his case for preventing damage to the environment being caused as a result of the doing of the act authorised by the consent in relation to organisms of that description; and
- (b) if it appears at any time that any better techniques are available to him than is required by any condition included in the consent under subsection (1) above, shall notify the Secretary of State of the fact forthwith.

But this general condition shall have effect subject to any conditions imposed under subsection (1) above.

DEFINITIONS
    "acquire": s.127(1).
    "consent": s.127(1).
    "control": s.107(9).
    "damage to the environment": s.107(3).
    "genetically modified organisms": s.106.
    "import": s.127(1).
    "market": s.107(1).
    "release": s.107(10).

AMENDMENTS
    The words missing in the square brackets in subs. (1) were deleted by the Environmental Protection Act 1990 (Modification of s.112) Regulations 1992 (S.I. 1992 No. 2617). The words in square brackets in subs. (5)(b) were substituted by the Genetically Modified Organisms (Deliberate Release) Regulations 1992 (S.I. 1992 No. 3280).

GENERAL NOTE
    This section contains detailed provisions on conditions or limitations imposed on consents under s.111 (see s.111(8)). These may be express or implied. Such express limitations or conditions may be included as the Secretary of State thinks fit, save that they may not be imposed for the purpose only of securing the health of persons at work (subs. (1)). By s.111(9) such conditions may include those which continue to have effect notwithstanding completion or cessation of the acts authorised by the consent: this could allow, for example, a condition requiring continued monitoring following a release.
    Further general conditions are implied by subss. (3)–(7). These in general correspond with the obligations as to risk identification and use of BATNEEC contained in s.109, which do not apply to authorised acts done under consents.
    Subs. (3) contains the implied conditions for consents for the import or acquisition of GMOs, subs. (4) those on the keeping of GMOs, and subs. (5) those on release or marketing.
    Subs. (6) makes clear that such general conditions have effect subject to any express conditions and that the obligations as to BATNEEC are disapplied in the case of aspects of activities dealt with by express conditions.
    There is also by subs. (7) a general duty in the case of keeping, releasing or marketing GMOs to take reasonable steps to remain informed as to developments in the relevant techniques for preventing harm to the environment and to notify the Secretary of State where it appears that better techniques than those specified in conditions have become available. This unusual provision reflects the fact that those carrying out work on GMOs are likely to be at the forefront of developing techniques for control and containment in their own specialist fields.

Fees and charges

113.—(1) The Secretary of State may, with the approval of the Treasury, make and from time to time revise a scheme prescribing—
    (a) fees payable in respect of applications for consents; and

(b) charges payable by persons holding consents in respect of the subsistence of their consents;

and it shall be a condition of any such consent that any applicable prescribed charge is paid in accordance with that scheme.

(2) A scheme under this section may, in particular—
  (a) provide for different fees or charges to be payable in different cases or circumstances;
  (b) provide for the times at which and the manner in which payments are to be made; and
  (c) make such incidental, supplementary and transitional provision as appears to the Secretary of State to be appropriate.

(3) The Secretary of State shall so frame a scheme under this section as to secure, so far as practicable, that the amounts payable under it will be sufficient, taking one financial year with another, to cover the expenditure of the Secretary of State in discharging his functions under this Part in relation to consents.

(4) The Secretary of State shall, on making or revising a scheme under this section, lay a copy of the scheme or of the scheme as revised before each House of Parliament.

DEFINITIONS
"consent": s.127.

GENERAL NOTE
This section provides for a scheme of fees for applications for consents and of charges for the subsistence of consents. It accords with the general policy, apparent in the Act, that the cost of regulatory functions should be borne by the persons regulated rather than by the public at large.

Inspectors

Appointment etc. of inspectors

114.—(1) The Secretary of State may appoint as inspectors, for carrying this Part into effect, such number of persons appearing to him to be qualified for the purpose as he may consider necessary.

(2) The Secretary of State may make to or in respect of any person so appointed such payments by way of remuneration, allowances or otherwise as he may with the approval of the Treasury determine.

(3) An inspector shall not be personally liable in any civil or criminal proceedings for anything done in the purported exercise of any power under section 115 or 117 below if the court is satisfied that the act was done in good faith and that there were reasonable grounds for doing it.

(4) In England and Wales an inspector, if authorised to do so by the Secretary of State, may, although not of counsel or a solicitor, prosecute before a magistrates' court proceedings for an offence under section 118(1) below.

(5) In this Part "inspector" means, subject to section 125 below, a person appointed as an inspector under subsection (1) above.

GENERAL NOTE
This section allows the Secretary of State to appoint suitably qualified inspectors for the purposes of Pt. VI. Provision is made for remuneration, immunity from suit and standing to prosecute in magistrates' courts.

Rights of entry and inspection

115.—(1) An inspector may, on production (if so required) of his authority, exercise any of the powers specified in subsection (3) below for the purposes of the discharge of the functions of the Secretary of State under this Part.

(2) Those powers are exercisable—

(a) in relation to premises—
  (i) on which the inspector has reason to believe a person is keeping or has kept any genetically modified organisms, or
  (ii) from which he has reason to believe any such organisms have been released or have escaped; and
(b) in relation to premises on which the inspector has reason to believe there may be harmful genetically modified organisms or evidence of damage to the environment caused by genetically modified organisms;

but they are not exercisable in relation to premises used wholly or mainly for domestic purposes.

(3) The powers of an inspector are—
(a) At any reasonable time (or, in a situation in which in his opinion there is an immediate risk of damage to the environment, at any time)—
  (i) to enter premises which he has reason to believe it is necessary for him to enter and to take with him any person duly authorised by the Secretary of State and, if the inspector has reasonable cause to apprehend any serious obstruction in the execution of his duty, a constable; and
  (ii) to take with him any equipment or materials required for any purpose for which the power of entry is being exercised;
(b) to carry out such tests and inspections (and to make such recordings), as may in any circumstances be necessary;
(c) to direct that any, or any part of, premises which he has power to enter, or anything in or on such premises, shall be left undisturbed (whether generally or in particular respects) for so long as is reasonably necessary for the purpose of any test or inspection;
(d) to take samples of any organisms, articles or substances found in or on any premises which he has power to enter, and of the air, water or land in, on, or in the vicinity of, the premises;
(e) in the case of anything found in or on any premises which he has power to enter, which appears to him to contain or to have contained genetically modified organisms which have caused or are likely to cause damage to the environment, to cause it to be dismantled or subjected to any process or test (but not so as to damage or destroy it unless this is necessary);
(f) in the case of anything mentioned in paragraph (e) above or anything found on premises which he has power to enter which appears to be a genetically modified organism or to consist of or include genetically modified organisms, to take possession of it and detain it for so long as is necessary for all or any of the following purposes, namely—
  (i) to examine it and do to it anything which he has power to do under that paragraph;
  (ii) to ensure that it is not tampered with before his examination of it is completed; and
  (iii) to ensure that it is available for use as evidence in any proceedings for any offence under section 118 below;
(g) to require any person whom he has reasonable cause to believe to be able to give any information relevant to any test or inspection under this subsection to answer (in the absence of persons other than a person nominated to be present and any persons whom the inspector may allow to be present) such questions as the inspector thinks fit to ask and to sign a declaration of the truth of his answers;
(h) to require the production of, or where the information is recorded in computerised form, the furnishing of extracts from, any records which are required to be kept under this Part or it is necessary for him to see for the purposes of any test or inspection under this subsection and to inspect, and take copies of, or of any entry in, the records;

(i) to require any person to afford him such facilities and assistance with respect to any matters or things within that person's control or in relation to which that person has responsibilities as are necessary to enable the inspector to exercise any of the powers conferred on him by this section;

(j) any other power for the purpose mentioned in subsection (1) above which is conferred by regulations made by the Secretary of State.

(4) The Secretary of State may by regulations make provision as to the procedure to be followed in connection with the taking of, and the dealing with, samples under subsection (3)(d) above.

(5) Where an inspector proposes to exercise the power conferred by subsection (3)(e) above, he shall, if so requested by a person who at the time is present on and has responsibilities in relation to those premises, cause anything which is to be done by virtue of that power to be done in the presence of that person.

(6) Before exercising the power conferred by subsection (3)(e) above, an inspector shall consult such persons as appear to him appropriate for the purpose of ascertaining what dangers, if any, there may be in doing anything which he proposes to do under the power.

(7) Where under the power conferred by subsection (3)(f) above an inspector takes possession of anything found on any premises, he shall leave there, either with a responsible person or, if that is impracticable, fixed in a conspicuous position, a notice giving particulars sufficient to identify what he has seized and stating that he has taken possession of it under that power; and before taking possession under that power of—

(a) any thing that forms part of a batch of similar things, or

(b) any substance,

an inspector shall, if it is practical and safe for him to do so, take a sample of it and give to a responsible person at the premises a portion of the sample marked in a manner sufficient to identify it.

(8) No answer given by a person in pursuance of a requirement imposed under subsection (3)(g) above shall be admissible in evidence—

(a) in any proceedings in England and Wales against that person; or

(b) in any criminal proceedings in Scotland against that person.

(9) The powers conferred by subsection (3)(a), (b), (c), (d), (e) and (h) above shall also be exercisable (subject to subsections (4), (5) and (6) above) by any person authorised for the purpose in writing by the Secretary of State.

(10) Nothing in this section shall be taken to compel the production by any person to a document of which he would on grounds of legal professional privilege be entitled to withhold production on an order for discovery in an action in the High Court or, in relation to Scotland, on an order for the production of documents in an action in the Court of Session.

DEFINITIONS
"damage to the environment": s.107(3).
"escape": s.107(10).
"genetically modified organisms": s.106.
"harmful": s.107(7).
"inspector": s.114(5).
"premises": s.127(1).
"release": s.107(10).

GENERAL NOTE
The section confers wide powers on inspectors including powers of entry, testing, sampling, seizure, requesting information and the production of records. The powers are exercisable in relation to premises (including any land) where the inspector has reason to believe GMOs are being or have been kept, or from which they have been released or have escaped (subs. (2)(a)). They are also exercisable in relation to premises on which there may be harmful released or escaped GMOs or where there may be evidence of damage to the environment caused by

GMOs (subs. (2)(b)). In either event, they are not exercisable in relation to premises used wholly or mainly for domestic purposes.

Enforcement powers and offences

Obtaining of information from persons

116.—(1) For the purposes of the discharge of his functions under this Part, the Secretary of State may, by notice in writing served on any person who appears to him—
   (a) to be involved in the importation, acquisition, keeping, release or marketing of genetically modified organisms; or
   (b) to be about to become, or to have been, involved in any of those activities;
require that person to furnish such relevant information available to him as is specified in the notice, in such form and within such period following service of the notice as is so specified.

(2) For the purposes of this section "relevant information" means information concerning any aspects of the activities in question, including any damage to the environment which may be or have been caused thereby; and the discharge by the Secretary of State of an obligation of the United Kingdom under the Community Treaties or any international agreement concerning the protection of the environment from harm caused by genetically modified organisms shall be treated as a function of his under this Part.

DEFINITIONS
   "acquisition": s.127(1).
   "damage to the environment": s.107(3).
   "genetically modified organisms": s.106.
   "harm": s.107(6).
   "importation": s.127(1).
   "marketing ": s.107(11).
   "release": s.107(10).

GENERAL NOTE
This section provides that the Secretary of State may, by notice in writing, obtain information from persons involved or about to be involved in activities relating to GMOs. It should be noted that this power is not restricted to the actual or proposed keeper, importer, releaser, marketer, etc. but applies to anyone involved in, or connected with, such operations.

By subs. (2) the power may be used not only in the discharge of functions under Pt. VI but in fulfilment of any E.C. or international obligation concerning the protection of the environment from damage caused by GMOs. For the Community and international aspects, see the General Note to Pt. VI.

Power to deal with cause of imminent danger of damage to the environment

117.—(1) Where, in the case of anything found by him on any premises which he has power to enter, an inspector has reason to believe that it is a genetically modified organism or that it consists of or includes genetically modified organisms and that, in the circumstances in which he finds it, it is a cause of imminent danger of damage to the environment, he may seize it and cause it to be rendered harmless (whether by destruction, by bringing it under proper control or otherwise).

(2) Before there is rendered harmless under this section—
   (a) any thing that forms part of a batch of similar things; or
   (b) any substance,
the inspector shall, if it is practicable and safe for him to do so, take a sample of it and give to a responsible person at the premises a portion of the sample marked in a manner sufficient to identify it.

(3) As soon as may be after anything has been seized and rendered harmless under this section, the inspector shall prepare and sign a written

report giving particulars of the circumstances in which it was seized and so dealt with by him, and shall—
  (a) give a signed copy of the report to a responsible person at the premises where it was found by him; and
  (b) unless that person is the owner of it, also serve a signed copy of the report on the owner;
and if, where paragraph (b) above applies, the inspector cannot after reasonable inquiry ascertain the name or address of the owner, the copy may be served on him by giving it to the person to whom a copy was given under paragraph (a) above.

DEFINITIONS
"damage to the environment": s.107(3).
"genetically modified organism": s.106.
"harmless": s.107(3).
"inspector": s.114(5).
"premises": s.127(1).

GENERAL NOTE
This section is complementary to the power to serve prohibition notices contained in s.110, in that it enables speedy action to be taken to seize and render harmless GMOs which present an imminent danger to the environment. The power could be used either in situations where GMOs presently under control appear to be a cause of danger, or where GMOs are at large in the environment.

Offences

118.—(1) It is an offence for a person—
  (a) to do anything in contravention of section 108(1) above in relation to something which is, and which he knows or has reason to believe is, a genetically modified organism;
  (b) to fail to comply with section 108(3) above when keeping something which is, and which he knows or has reason to believe is, a genetically modified organism;
  (c) to do anything in contravention of section 111(1) or (2) above in relation to something which is, and which he knows or has reason to believe is, a genetically modified organism;
  (d) to fail to comply with any requirement of subsection (2), (3)(a), (b) or (c) or (4) of section 109 above in relation to something which is, and which he knows or has reason to believe is, a genetically modified organism;
  (e) to fail, without reasonable excuse, to comply with section 108(5) or (6) [or section 111(6A)] above;
  (f) to contravene any prohibition imposed on him by a prohibition notice;
  (g) without reasonable excuse, to fail to comply with any requirement imposed under section 115 above;
  (h) to prevent any other person from appearing before or from answering any question to which an inspector may, by virtue of section 115(3) above, require an answer;
  (i) intentionally to obstruct an inspector in the exercise of performance of his powers or duties, other than his powers or duties under section 117 above;
  (j) intentionally to obstruct an inspector in the exercise of his powers or duties under section 117 above;
  (k) to fail, without reasonable excuse, to comply with any requirement imposed by a notice under section 116 above;
  (l) to make a statement which he knows to be false or misleading in a

material particular, or recklessly to make a statement which is false or misleading in a material particular, where the statement is made—
      (i) in purported compliance with a requirement to furnish any information imposed by or under any provision of this Part; or
     (ii) for the purpose of obtaining the grant of a consent to himself or any other person or the variation of a consent;
 (m) intentionally to make a false entry in any record required to be kept under section 108 or 111 above;
 (n) with intent to deceive, to forge or use a document purporting to be issued under section 111 above or required for any purpose thereunder or to make or have in his possession a document so closely resembling any such document as to be likely to deceive;
 (o) falsely to pretend to be an inspector.

(2) It shall be a defence for a person charged with an offence under paragraph (a), (b), (c), (d) or (f) of subsection (1) above to prove that he took all reasonable precautions and exercised all due diligence to avoid the commission of the offence.

(3) A person guilty of an offence under paragraph (c) or (d) of subsection (1) above shall be liable—
 (a) on summary conviction, to a fine not exceeding £20,000 or to imprisonment for a term not exceeding six months, or to both;
 (b) on conviction on indictment, to a fine or to imprisonment for a term not exceeding five years, or to both.

(4) A person guilty of an offence under paragraph (f) of subsection (1) above shall be liable—
 (a) on summary conviction, to a fine not exceeding £20,000 or to imprisonment for a term not exceeding six months, or to both;
 (b) on conviction on indictment, to a fine or to imprisonment for a term not exceeding two years, or to both.

(5) A person guilty of an offence under paragraph (a) or (b) of subsection (1) above shall be liable—
 (a) on summary conviction, to a fine not exceeding the statutory maximum or to imprisonment for a term not exceeding six months, or to both;
 (b) on conviction of indictment, to a fine or to imprisonment for a term not exceeding five years, or to both.

(6) A person guilty of an offence under paragraph (e), (j), (k), (l), (m) or (n) of subsection (1) above shall be liable—
 (a) on summary conviction, to a fine not exceeding the statutory maximum or to imprisonment for a term not exceeding six months, or to both;
 (b) on conviction on indictment, to a fine or to imprisonment for a term not exceeding two years, or to both.

(7) A person guilty of an offence under paragraph (g), (h) or (i) of subsection (1) above shall be liable on summary conviction to a fine not exceeding the statutory maximum or to imprisonment for a term not exceeding three months, or to both.

(8) A person guilty of an offence under paragraph (o) of subsection (1) above shall be liable on summary conviction to a fine not exceeding level 5 on the standard scale.

(9) Where a person is convicted of an offence under paragraph (b) of subsection (1) above in respect of his keeping any genetically modified organism, then, if the contravention in respect of which he was convicted is continued after he was convicted he shall be guilty of a further offence and liable on summary conviction to a fine of one-fifth of level 5 on the standard scale for each day on which the contravention is so continued.

(10) Proceedings in respect of an offence under this section shall not be instituted in England and Wales except by the Secretary of State or with the

consent of the Director of Public Prosecutions or in Northern Ireland except with the consent of the Director of Public Prosecutions for Northern Ireland.

DEFINITIONS
"genetically modified organism": s.106.
"inspector": s.114(5).
"prohibition notice": s.127(1).

AMENDMENTS
The words in square brackets in s.118(1)(e) were inserted by the Genetically Modified Organisms (Deliberate Release) Regulations 1992 (S.I. 1992 No. 3280), reg. 13(2).

GENERAL NOTE
Subsection (1) establishes the various offences in relation to the requirements of Pt. VI. Subsections (3)–(9) prescribe the various penalties, which reflect the relative seriousness of the separate offences.

The most serious offences are those of engaging in GMO activities without the necessary consent or in breach of consent conditions (s.111(1) and (2)), failure to comply with general duties as to risk assessment and use of BATNEEC (s.109(2), (3) and (4)) and contravention of a prohibition notice (s.118(1)(f)). Such offences are subject to a maximum fine of £20,000 or to imprisonment for a term not exceeding six months on summary conviction. On conviction on indictment the fine may be unlimited, and the maximum term of imprisonment is five years, or two years for breach of a prohibition notice (subss. (3) and (4)).

Subs. (10)
Restriction on prosecutions. Prosecutions under s.118 may only be brought by the Secretary of State in England and Wales or with the consent of the Director of Public Prosecutions.

Defence of all reasonable precautions and all due diligence
This defence is available in relation to certain offences (subs. (2)). "All reasonable precautions" has been said to be related to those risks of harm reasonably foreseeable when a prudent and competent person applies his mind seriously to the situation: see *Colpron* v. *Canadian National Rly. Co.* [1934] S.C.R. 189 and 192.

An obligation to exercise due diligence has been said to be "indistinguishable from an obligation to exercise reasonable care": *Riverstone Meat Co. Pty.* v. *Lancashire Shipping Co.* [1960] 1 All E.R. 193 at 219, Willmer L.J.; reversed [1961] A.C. 807.

Onus of proof as regards techniques and evidence

119.—(1) In any proceedings for either of the following offences, that is to say—
  (a) an offence under section 118(1)(c) above consisting in a failure to comply with the general condition implied by section 112(4)(c) or (5)(c) above; or
  (b) an offence under section 118(1)(d) above consisting in a failure to comply with section 109(3)(c) or (4)(c) above;
it shall be for the accused to prove that there was no better available technique not entailing excessive cost than was in fact used to satisfy the condition or to comply with that section.

(2) Where an entry is required by a condition in a consent to be made in any record as to the observance of any other condition and the entry has not been made, that fact shall be admissible as evidence that that other condition has not been observed.

DEFINITIONS
"consent": s.127(1).

GENERAL NOTE
The effect of this provision is to put the onus of proof as to the use of BATNEEC on the accused and to make admissible as evidence the failure of the accused to produce appropriate records in respect of compliance with conditions, where such records are required by conditions.

Power of court to order cause of offence to be remedied

120.—(1) Where a person is convicted of an offence under section 118(1) (a), (b), (c), (d), (e) or (f) above in respect of any matters which appear to the court to be matters which it is in his power to remedy, the court may, in addition to or instead of imposing any punishment, order him, within such time as may be fixed by the order, to take such steps as may be specified in the order for remedying those matters.

(2) The time fixed by an order under subsection (1) above may be extended or further extended by order of the court on an application made before the end of the time as originally fixed or as extended under this subsection, as the case may be.

(3) Where a person is ordered under subsection (1) above to remedy any matters, that person shall not be liable under section 118 above in respect of those matters, in so far as they continue during the time fixed by the order or any further time allowed under subsection (2) above.

GENERAL NOTE

This section enables a court to order a person convicted of certain offences under Pt. VI to take specified steps to remedy such matters as it appears to be within his power to remedy.

By subs. (3) where such an order is made, no further criminal liability may arise during the period allowed by the order for taking the steps.

Power of Secretary of State to remedy harm

121.—(1) Where the commission of an offence under section 118(1)(a), (b), (c), (d), (e) or (f) above causes any harm which it is possible to remedy, the Secretary of State may, subject to subsection (2) below—
   (a) arrange for any reasonable steps to be taken towards remedying the harm; and
   (b) recover the cost of taking those steps from any person convicted of that offence.

(2) The Secretary of State shall not exercise his powers under this section, where any of the steps are to be taken on or will affect land in the occupation of any person other than a person convicted of the offence in question, except with the permission of that person.

DEFINITIONS

"harm": s. 107(6).

GENERAL NOTE

By this section, where commission of certain offences under Pt. VI has caused harm, which it is possible to remedy, the Secretary of State may arrange for reasonable steps to be taken towards remedying the harm, and may recover the cost from any person convicted of the offence. Where the steps have to be taken on land occupied by a person other than the offender, the permission of that person must be obtained.

Publicity

Public register of information

122.—(1) The Secretary of State shall maintain a register ("the register") containing prescribed particulars of or relating to—
   (a) notices given or other information furnished under section 108 above;
   (b) directions given under section 108(8) above;
   (c) prohibition notices;
   (d) applications for consents (and any further information furnished in connection with them) and any advice given by the committee appointed under section 124 below in relation to such applications;
   (e) consents granted by the Secretary of State and any information furnished to him in pursuance of consent conditions;

(f) any other information obtained or furnished under any provision of this Part;
(g) convictions for such offences under section 118 above as may be prescribed;
(h) such other matters relating to this Part as may be prescribed;

but that duty is subject to section 123 below.

(2) It shall be the duty of the Secretary of State—
(a) to secure that the register is open to inspection by members of the public free of charge at all reasonable hours; and
(b) to afford to members of the public facilities for obtaining copies of entries, on payment of reasonable charges.

(3) The register may be kept in any form.

(4) The Secretary of State may make regulations with respect to the keeping of the register; and in this section "prescribed" means prescribed in regulations made by the Secretary of State.

DEFINITIONS
"consents": s.127(1).
"prohibition notices": s.127(1).

GENERAL NOTE
This section makes provision for public registers of information as to consent, notices and other matters under Pt. VI. See also General Note to Pt. VI.

Exclusion from register of certain information

123.—(1) No information shall be included in the register under section 122 above if and so long as, in the opinion of the Secretary of State, the inclusion of the information would be contrary to the interests of national security.

(2) No information shall be included in the register if and so long as, in the opinion of the Secretary of State, it ought to be excluded on the ground that its inclusion might result in damage to the environment.

(3) No information relating to the affairs of any individual or business shall be included in the register without the consent of that individual or the person for the time being carrying on that business, if the Secretary of State has determined that the information—
(a) is, in relation to him, commercially confidential; and
(b) is not information of a description to which subsection (7) below applies;

unless the Secretary of State is of the opinion that the information is no longer commercially confidential in relation to him.

(4) Nothing in subsection (3) above requires the Secretary of State to determine whether any information is or is not commercially confidential except where the person furnishing the information applies to have it excluded on the ground that it is (in relation to himself or another person) commercially confidential.

(5) Where an application has been made for information to be excluded under subsection (3) above, the Secretary of State shall make a determination and inform the applicant of it as soon as is practicable.

(6) Where it appears to the Secretary of State that any information (other than information furnished by the person to whom it relates) which has been obtained under or by virtue of any provision of this Part might be commercially confidential, the Secretary of State shall—
(a) give to the person to whom or to whose business it relates notice that the information is required to be included in the register unless excluded under subsection (3) above; and
(b) give him a reasonable opportunity—

(i) of objecting to the inclusion of the information on the ground that it is commercially confidential; and
(ii) of making representations to the Secretary of State for the purpose of justifying any such objection;

and the Secretary of State shall take any representations into account before determining whether the information is or is not commercially confidential.

(7) The prescribed particulars of or relating to the matters mentioned in section 122(1)(a), (d) and (e) above shall be included in the register notwithstanding that they may be commercially confidential if and so far as they are of any of the following descriptions, namely—
(a) the name and address of the person giving the notice or furnishing the information;
(b) the description of any genetically modified organisms to which the notice or other information relates;
(c) the location at any time of those organisms;
(d) the purpose for which those organisms are being imported, acquired, kept, released or marketed (according to whichever of those acts the notice or other information relates);
(e) results of any assessment of the risks of damage to the environment being caused by the doing of any of those acts;
(f) notices under section 112(3), (4), (5) or (7) above;

and the Secretary of State may by regulations prescribe any other description of information as information which the public interest requires to be included in the register notwithstanding that it may be commercially confidential.

(8) Information excluded from the register under subsection (3) above shall be treated as ceasing to be commercially confidential for the purposes of that subsection at the expiry of a period of four years beginning with the date of the determination by virtue of which it was excluded; but the person who furnished it or to whom or to whose business it relates may apply to the Secretary of State for the information to remain excluded on the ground that it is still commercially confidential.

(9) The Secretary of State may by order substitute for the period for the time being specified in subsection (8) above such other period as he considers appropriate.

DEFINITIONS
"damage to the environment": s.107(3).

GENERAL NOTE
This section provides for the categories of information to be excluded from the register kept under s.122. Broadly, these are:
(1) information the inclusion of which would, in the opinion of the Secretary of State, be contrary to the interests of national security (subs. (1));
(2) information the inclusion of which might result in damage to the environment (subs. (2)), *e.g.* by giving information which could facilitate sabotage or other illegal action (see *Hansard*, H.L. Vol. 522, col. 711);
(3) information which is commercially confidential (subs. (3)). Applications for the commercial confidentiality exemption will no doubt be scrutinised closely: see note to s.22. Further, even where the confidentiality exemption is successfully claimed, certain information will still be included (subs. (7)) and the confidentiality lapses after four years, so a fresh application for exemption must be made (subs. (8)).

Supplementary

Advisory committee for purposes of Part VI

124.—(1) The Secretary of State shall appoint a committee to provide him with advice—
(a) on the exercise of his powers under sections 111, 112 and 113 above;

(b) on the exercise of any power under this Part to make regulations; and on such other matters concerning his functions under this Part as he may from time to time direct.

(2) The chairman and other members of the committee shall hold and vacate office in accordance with the terms of their appointment.

(3) The Secretary of State shall pay to the members of the committee such remuneration (if any) and such allowances as he may, with the consent of the Treasury, determine.

GENERAL NOTE

This section provides for the appointment of an expert committee to provide the Secretary of State with advice as to his consent and regulation-making functions, and on any other matters as he may from time to time direct. The Committee, which already existed but is put on to a statutory footing by s.124 (see *Hansard*, H.L. Vol. 520, col. 1964), is known as the Advisory Committee on Releases to the Environment (ACRE). It is proposed that the Committee will offer integrated advice on both the environmental and health and safety aspects of activities involving GMOs. See also General Note to Pt. VI. The first chairman of the Committee is Professor John Beringer of the Unit of Molecular Genetics at the University of Bristol. Membership includes representatives of scientists in the fields of ecology, molecular biology, virology, microbiology and medicine, the bio-technology industry, agriculture and environmental groups. It is not proposed that the Committee will consider the ethical aspects of genetic engineering, though the Government intends that this issue will be considered by some other body: see *Hansard*, H.L. Vol. 522, col. 701.

As to the relationship between ACRE and the ACGM, see *Hansard*, H.L. Vol. 522, col. 702, where Baroness Blatch put the matter as follows:

"ACGM and ACRE serve distinct purposes. Both committees have the advantage of having not only pure scientists as representatives but also representatives from both sides of industry. Of course the main function of ACGM is to advise on general standards of safe working with GMOs and in particular on the suitability of facilities in which they are produced and the competence of the individuals handling them.

Since the committee is established under the health and safety legislation, its remit concentrates on the protection of human health and safety. On the other hand, ACRE is specifically concerned with the effect of GMOs on the environment. The expertise and experience of those composing ACRE reflect that particular and distinct function."

Delegation of enforcement functions

125.—(1) The Secretary of State may, by an agreement made with any public authority, delegate to that authority or to any officer appointed by an authority exercising functions on behalf of that authority any of his enforcement functions under this Part, subject to such restrictions and conditions as may be specified in the agreement.

(2) For the purposes of this section the following are "enforcement functions" of the Secretary of State, that is to say, his functions under—
section 110;
section 114(1) and (4);
section 116;
section 118(10); and
section 121;
and "inspector" in sections 115 and 117 includes, to the extent of the delegation, any inspector appointed by an authority other than the Secretary of State by virtue of an agreement under this section.

(3) The Secretary of State shall, if and so far as an agreement under this section so provides, make payments to the authority to reimburse the authority the expenses incurred in the performance of functions delegated under this section; but no such agreement shall be made without the approval of the Treasury.

DEFINITIONS

"inspector": s.114(5).

GENERAL NOTE
This section allows "enforcement functions" of the Secretary of State under Pt. VI to be delegated by agreement to any public authority or to an officer of such authority. The relevant functions that may be delegated are prohibitions notices (s.110), appointment of inspectors and authorisation of inspectors to prosecute (s.114), obtaining information (s.116), prosecuting (s.118(10)) and remedying harm (s.121). Functions of direction under s.108(8) and determination of consents under ss.111 and 112 are not amongst those that may be delegated.

The expression "inspector" in ss.115 and 117 applies to public authorities' inspectors where functions have been delegated (subs. (2)), so that such inspectors have the same powers of entry, etc. as those enjoyed by inspectors appointed by the Secretary of State.

It is intended that the Health and Safety Executive will be the enforcing agency for Pt. VI initially, by arrangements made under this section. It is proposed that a five year agreement will be entered into between the Secretary of State and the HSE to that effect, on a similar basis to other agency arrangements with the HSE.

Exercise of certain functions jointly by Secretary of State and Minister of Agriculture, Fisheries and Food

126.—(1) Subject to subsection (2) below, any reference in this Part to a function exercisable by the Secretary of State shall, in any case where the function is to be exercised in relation to a matter with which the Minister of Agriculture, Fisheries and Food is concerned, be exercisable by the Secretary of State and that Minister acting jointly.

(2) The validity of anything purporting to be done in pursuance of the exercise of any such function shall not be affected by any question whether that thing fell, by virtue of this section, to be done by the Secretary of State and the Minister of Agriculture, Fisheries and Food.

GENERAL NOTE
Powers under Pt. VI are to be exercisable jointly by the Secretary of State for the Environment and the Minister of Agriculture, Fisheries and Food in relation to matters with which the latter is concerned. Activities with GMOs will frequently be connected with matters of agriculture, plants, animals, pest control and fisheries.

By subs. (2) the question as to whether a function should have been exercised jointly does not affect the validity of anything done under Pt. VI.

Definitions

127. In this Part—
"acquire," in relation to genetically modified organisms, includes any method by which such organisms may come to be in a person's possession, other than by their being imported;
"consent" means a consent granted under section 111 above, and a reference to the limitations or conditions to which a consent is subject is a reference to the limitations or conditions subject to which the consent for the time being has effect;
"descendant", in relation to a genetically modified organism, means any other organism whose genes or other genetic material is derived, through any number of generations, from that organism by any process of reproduction;
"import" means import into the United Kingdom;
"premises" includes any land;
"prohibition notice" means a notice under section 110 above.

(2) This Part, except in so far as it relates to importations of genetically modified organisms, applies to the territorial sea adjacent to Great Britain, and to any area for the time being designated under section 1(7) of the Continental Shelf Act 1964, as it applies in Great Britain.

GENERAL NOTE

Subs. (2)
Territorial application. Pt. VI applies to the territorial sea adjacent to Great Britain and to

any area designated under the Continental Shelf Act 1964. This provision does not however apply in relation to imports of GMOs.

Part VII

Nature Conservation in Great Britain and Countryside Matters in Wales

General Note
Part VII was undoubtedly the most politically controversial part of the Environmental Protection Bill. Its effect is to reorganise the institutional structure for nature conservation matters in England, Scotland and Wales.

The Nature Conservancy Council was the statutory body with responsibility for nature conservation throughout Great Britain until the reforms under Pt. VII. The NCC was created by the Nature Conservancy Council Act 1973 to replace the committee of the National Environment Research Council known as the Nature Conservancy. Under that Act (s.1) the NCC had the following main functions: (1) establishment, maintenance and management of nature reserves; (2) provision of advice on nature conservation matters to ministers; (3) provision of advice and dissemination of knowledge about nature conservation matters generally; and (4) the commissioning or support of research on nature conservation matters.

The NCC also fulfilled important functions under the later Wildlife and Countryside Act 1981, including the notification of sites of special scientific interest (s.28) and entering into management agreements relating to such sites.

The NCC also had a role as a statutory consultee in a variety of statutory contexts, most importantly in relation to certain applications for planning permission under the Town and Country Planning Act 1990, including development proposals subject to the requirements of environmental assessment.

The background to the proposals for reorganisation was considered in depth by the House of Lords Select Committee on Science and Technology in its report, *Nature Conservancy Council* (H.L. Paper 33–I and II, Session 1989–90, Second Report, March 1, 1990) under the Chairmanship of Lord Carver ("the Carver Report"). The Carver Report summarised this background as follows (paras. 1.2–1.9):

"1.2 On July 11, 1989 the Nature Conservancy Council (NCC) met to put the final touches to a proposal for reorganising itself on a federal model. The object was to devolve more of the executive functions for nature conservation to its three regions, England, Scotland and Wales. On the same day the Government announced, without consultation and to the surprise of the NCC and everyone else, that the NCC would be split into three autonomous country agencies.

1.3 The Government statements also announced that nature conservation and countryside responsibilities would be integrated in a single body in Scotland and in Wales.

1.4 The reasons for the reorganisation were the 'increasing feelings that [existing] arrangements are inefficient, insensitive and mean that conservation issues in both Scotland and Wales are determined with too little regard for the particular requirements in these countries.' The new arrangements, combining the functions of the NCC and the Countryside Commission in Scotland and Wales will, according to the Government, 'allow a more comprehensive approach to pursuing the special inheritances of wildlife and natural beauty in those two countries.' (H.C. Deb. July 11, 1989, c.482W).

1.5 The then Secretary of State for the Environment, Mr Ridley, stated that he would continue to be responsible for representing the United Kingdom's interests on nature conservation matters within the European Community and under international conventions.

1.6 He also said that in England the NCC and Countryside Commission would remain separate 'in view of the much greater density of population and consequent pressure upon the land.'

1.7 The Secretary of State for Scotland, Mr Rifkind, stated (H.C. Deb. July 11, 1989, c.436W) that Scottish reorganisation would take place in two stages. First a separate NCC in Scotland would be set up, and then it would be merged later with the Countryside Commission for Scotland into a single national heritage body, reporting directly to him. The new body would have full executive responsibility for its work in Scotland and the Government's proposals would 'result in substantial improvements in the effectiveness, accountability and, most important of all, in the sensitivity of administration in the vital task of conserving and managing Scotland's national heritage.' A consultation paper for Scotland, in broad terms, was issued after the announcement.

1.8 The Secretary of State for Wales, Mr Walker, announced (H.C. Deb. July 11, 1989, c.433W) that he would be appointing an executive Countryside Council for Wales, taking on the functional responsibilities of the offices in Wales of the NCC and Countryside Commission (whose present remit covers England and Wales). 'Decisions affecting Wales will in future be taken in Wales [by] a single body attuned to the needs of the Principality.' No consultation paper was issued.

1.9 No mention was made of the scientific base for these new agencies. Subject to parliamentary approval, the changes proposed for England and Wales, and the establishment of the new Scottish NCC, were to take effect in April 1991."

Discussion then followed on how best to secure the ability to take "a Great Britain overview," and to ensure that the work of the new national councils continued to be underpinned by a sound science base, utilising the data and experience accumulated by the NCC. The proposed solution was a duty on the successor councils to form a joint advisory committee for that purpose.

The Carver Committee did not take up a position on the merits of reorganising the NCC but felt obliged to say that 'the reorganisation could have been better handled' (para. 3.2). A number of recommendations were made as to the new structure, with the object of ensuring scientific effectiveness, maintaining a national as well as a local perspective and supporting the independent commitment to nature conservation of the successor councils.

The Government's response to the Carver Report was published in May 1990 (H.L. Paper 60, Session 1989–90, 6th Report, May 17, 1990). The Government expressed agreement with or accepted, many of the Carver Committee's recommendations and in some cases assurances were given to introduce amendments to the Bill. The only significant reservation expressed by the Government was that it saw no need to extend the statutory remit of the Joint Committee to cover countryside and landscape conservation matters under the Countryside Acts:

"In the Government's view that remit should remain focused firmly on nature conservation. But the presence of the Chairman of the Countryside Commission will ensure that the Committee is well placed to take account of countryside matters in its deliberations." (DoE News Release No. 306, May 17, 1990.)

Nevertheless, in the debates on Second Reading of the Bill in the House of Lords, Lord Carver expressed continued reservations, the main ones being as to the cost and resourcing of the new arrangements, and the power of the Joint Committee to settle decisively conflicts with the County Councils over jurisdiction (*Hansard*, H.L. Vol. 519, cols. 502–503, May 18, 1990).

Lord Hesketh, on introducing Pt. VII on Second Reading and in Committee in the House of Lords, referred to "six fundamental objectives which lie at the root of reorganisation" (*Hansard*, H.L. Vol. 520, cols, 2119–2120, July 4, 1990).

"First, clearer accountability to Ministers; secondly, improved sensitivity to local circumstances; thirdly, a reduction in bureaucracy; fourthly, retention of the existing legal framework for wildlife conservation created by the 1981 Act; fifthly, effective coverage of national and global nature conservation issues, and, finally, protection of the Nature Conservancy Council's science base built up over 40 years."

The basic scheme of the reorganisation, as effected by Pt. VII, is as follows:—
(1) creation of three councils, the Nature Conservancy Council for England, the Nature Conservancy Council for Scotland and the Countryside Commission for Wales ("the Councils") (s.128);
(2) transfer of nature conservation functions from the NCC to the Councils (ss.131–133);
(3) establishment by the Councils of the Joint Nature Conservation Committee ("the Joint Committee") (s.128(4)), to whose advice the Councils must have regard (s.132(1) and (3));
(4) the making of a transfer scheme or schemes by the NCC for the division of property, rights and liabilities between the Councils (s.135);
(5) entitlement by employees of the NCC to an offer of employment with one of the Councils (s.137); and
(6) dissolution of the NCC (s.138).

SSSIs

Some substantive amendments are also made to the law relating to sites of special scientific interest by Sched. 9: see note to s.132.

Wales

The Countryside Council for Wales takes over not only the functions of the NCC, but also a number of countryside functions of the Countryside Commission so far as concerns Wales (s.130 and Sched. 8).

Scotland
Nature conservation and countryside functions remain separate in Scotland under Pt. VII of the Act, but it was announced in the Queen's Speech on November 7, 1990 that legislation will follow to integrate such functions within a single body, Scottish Natural Heritage, as from April 1, 1992. This will complete the Government's strategy for integrated agencies in Scotland and Wales. It is proposed that funding of the new body will move from the Department of Environment to the Scottish Office. See Scottish Development Department, *Scotland's Natural Heritage: The Way Ahead* (1990).

Territorial extent
Part VII applies to England, Scotland and Wales (s.164(4)).

Commencement
Part VII came into force, save for the amendments made by ss.128, 130 and 132 on November 5, 1990 (The Environmental Protection Act 1990 (Commencement No. 1) Order 1990 No. 2226). The Environmental Protection Act 1990 (Commencement No. 6 and Appointed Day) Order 1991 (S.I. 1991 No. 685) brought the amendments made by ss.128, 130 and 132 and s.162(2) relating to the repeals of the Countryside Act 1968 and the Wildlife and Countryside Act 1981 into force on April 1, 1991. It also appointed April 1, 1991 as the day for the discharge of the respective functions of the Countryside Council for Wales and the Countryside Commission and the Nature Conservancy Council for England and the Nature Conservancy Council for Scotland. The Nature Conservancy Council was accordingly dissolved on December 21, 1991 by the Nature Conservancy Council (Dissolution) Order 1991 (S.I. 1991 No. 2923).

New Councils for England, Scotland and Wales

Creation and constitution of new Councils

128.—(1) There shall be three councils, to be called the Nature Conservancy Council for England, the Nature Conservancy Council for Scotland, and the Countryside Council for Wales (in this Part referred to as "the Councils").

(2) The Councils shall have the following membership, that is to say—
   (a) the Nature Conservancy Council for England shall have not less than 10 nor more than 14 members;
   (b) the Nature Conservancy Council for Scotland shall have not less that 8 nor more than 12 members; and
   (c) the Countryside Council for Wales shall have not less than 8 nor more than 12 members;
and those members shall be appointed by the Secretary of State.

(3) The Secretary of State may by order amend paragraph (a), (b) or (c) of subsection (2) above so as to substitute for the number for the time being specified as the maximum membership of a Council such other number as he thinks appropriate.

(4) The Councils shall establish a committee to be called the Joint Nature Conservation Committee (in this Part referred to as "the joint committee").

(5) Schedules 6 and 7 to this Act shall have effect with respect to the constitution and proceedings of the Councils and of the joint committee and related matters.

GENERAL NOTE

The Councils
This section creates the three new Country Councils in England, Scotland and Wales to take over nature conservation functions from the NCC. Members of the Councils are appointed by the Secretary of State (subs. (3)). Sched. 6 contains the detailed provisions as to constitution and membership, remuneration of members, staff, committees, reports and accounts, and similar practical matters.

The first Chairman of the NCC for England is the Earl of Cranbrook. For Scotland the first chairman is Mr Magnus Magnusson and for Wales Mr Michael Griffith.

The Joint Nature Conservation Committee: By subs. (4) the Councils are under a duty to establish a committee to be called the Joint Nature Conservation Committee. Detailed provisions as to the constitution of that Committee are contained in Sched. 7. Paragraphs 2–4 of the Schedule deal with the membership, which consists of a chairman appointed by the Secretary of State, three members appointed by the Secretary of State, the Chairman and one member of each Council, the chairman of the Countryside Commission, plus two non-voting members appointed by the Development of the Environment for Northern Ireland. The first Chairman of the Joint Council is Professor Fred Holiday. The three Secretary of State appointees as proposed are Professor John Knill (earth science), Professor Robert May (zoology) and Professor John Harper (botany).

The statutory remit of the Joint Committee will not extend to countryside matters, but it is proposed by the Government that the Committee should be in a position to take account of countryside interests by reason of its membership. The Chairman of the Scottish Countryside Commission will be invited to be a non-voting assessor until completion of the merger of functions within Scotland referred to above (see *Hansard*, H.L. Vol. 519, col. 486).

As to proposals for staffing and resourcing the Joint Committee, see *Hansard*, H.L. Vol. 522, col. 896.

Grants by Secretary of State to new Councils

129.—(1) The Secretary of State may with the approval of the Treasury make to the Councils grants of such amounts as the Secretary of State thinks fit.

(2) A grant under this section may be made subject to such conditions (including in particular conditions as to the use of the money for purposes of the joint committee) as the Secretary of State may with the approval of the Treasury think fit.

Countryside matters

Countryside functions of Welsh Council

130.—(1) The Countryside Council for Wales shall, in place of the Commission established under section 1 of the National Parks and Access to the Countryside Act 1949 (so far as concerns Wales), have such of the functions under the Acts amended by Schedule 8 to this Act (which relates to countryside matters) as are assigned to them in accordance with the amendments effected by that Schedule.

(2) The Countryside Council for Wales shall discharge those functions—
  (a) for the conservation and enhancement of natural beauty in Wales and of the natural beauty and amenity of the countryside in Wales, both in the areas designated under the National Parks and Access to the Countryside Act 1949 as National Parks or as areas of outstanding natural beauty and elsewhere;
  (b) for encouraging the provision or improvement, for persons resorting to the countryside in Wales, of facilities for the enjoyment thereof and for the enjoyment of the opportunities for open-air recreation and the study of nature afforded thereby;

and shall have regard to the social and economic interests of rural areas in Wales.

(3) The reference in subsection (2) above to the conservation of the natural beauty of the countryside includes the conservation of its flora, fauna and geological and physiographical features.

(4) The Countryside Council for Wales and the Countryside Commission shall discharge their respective functions under those Acts (as amended by Schedule 8) on and after a day to be appointed by an order made by the Secretary of State.

GENERAL NOTE

This section makes special arrangements for countryside matters in Wales. The Countryside Council for Wales is to exercise functions not only of the NCC but also of the Countryside

Commission so far as concern Wales. The relevant functions are those set out at Sched. 8, which also makes the amendments to the relevant provisions necessary to substitute the name of the Countryside Council for Wales. The transfer of functions is effective on a day to be appointed by the Secretary of State (subs. (4)). The Environmental Protection Act 1990 (Commencement No. 6 and Appointed Day) Order 1991 (S.I. 1991 No. 685) appointed April 1, 1991 as the day for the transfer of functions.

Subsection (2) contains provisions as to the purposes for which the Welsh Council shall exercise its functions and the matters to which it shall have regard. The subsection as originally introduced by the Government on amendment at Lords' Report Stage qualified the reference to National Parks with the word "particularly," corresponding to the relevant wording in the National Parks and Access to the Countryside Act 1949, s.1. The word "particularly" was dropped at Third Reading stage and amendments have been made to the 1949 Act to achieve consistency: see Sched. 8, para. 1(2).

The Welsh Council has issued a "Statement of Policy" (1991). The Statement sets out the functions and responsibilities of the Council. The Council is responsible for undertaking in Wales the previously separate functions of the Countryside Commission in relation to conservation of the natural beauty of the countryside and its public enjoyment, and of the Nature Conservancy Council in relation to the conservation of nature. The Statement highlights the Council's duty to ensure that an appropriate balance is maintained between these functions in accordance with its statutory obligations. Much of the effectiveness of this work depends upon good relationships with organisations in both the public and private sector and with voluntary organisations both national and international.

The Council is expected to develop policies based upon research that it has carried out, commissioned or supported, on all matters affecting its function and to advise Ministers, local authorities and other organisations accordingly. It is also its function to participate fully in the development of policies falling under the Statutory Joint Nature Conservancy Council, that is, policies with a UK or international element. The Statement points out that the Council must not lose sight of economic or social considerations when formulating its policies, paying particular regard to the needs of agriculture, forestry and rural areas. Accordingly, the Council will encourage those social and economic activities that conserve or enhance the natural beauty of the countryside. The Council is responsible for the dissemination of information about conservation and public enjoyment of the countryside in Wales and education to increase public awareness. Within Wales, the council has the authority, with the approval of the Secretary of State, to designate areas as National Parks, areas of outstanding beauty, etc. and to maintain and manage designated sites, providing advice on management matters and financial support when appropriate. Another function is to develop a comprehensive Welsh language policy.

It is anticipated by the Council that more use will be made of the powers to grant aid to organisations wishing to acquire land for conservation or recreational purposes rather than acquire extensive areas itself as was the case under the Nature Conservancy Council.

Nature conservation in Great Britain

Nature conservation functions: preliminary

131.—(1) For the purposes of nature conservation, and fostering the understanding thereof, the Councils shall, in place of the Nature Conservancy Council established under the Nature Conservancy Council Act 1973, have the functions conferred on them by sections 132 to 134 below (which are in this Part referred to as "nature conservation functions").

(2) It shall be the duty of the Councils in discharging their nature conservation functions to take appropriate account of actual or possible ecological changes.

(3) The Councils shall discharge their nature conservation functions on and after a day to be appointed by an order made by the Secretary of State.

(4) The Secretary of State may give the Councils, or any of them, directions of a general or specific character with regard to the discharge of any of their nature conservation functions other than those conferred on them by section 132(1)(a) below.

(5) Any reference in this section to the Councils includes a reference to the joint committee and, accordingly, directions under subsection (4) above may be given to the joint committee as respects any of the functions dischargeable by them (other than under section 133(2)(a)).

(6) In this Part "nature conservation" means the conservation of flora, fauna or geological or physiographical features.

GENERAL NOTE
This section confers upon the new Councils the "nature conservation functions" referred to in ss.132 and 133 as from a date to be appointed by the Secretary of State (subs. (3)). The Environmental Protection Act 1990 (Commencement No. 6 and Appointed Day) Order 1991 (S.I. 1991 No. 685) appoints April 1, 1991 as the relevant day. The functions are conferred for "the purposes of nature conservation" (defined in subs. (6) as the conservation of flora, fauna or geological or physiographical features) and the Councils and Joint Council are under a statutory duty by subs. (2) to "take appropriate account of actual or possible ecological changes" in exercising their functions.
By subs. (4), except in relation to the functions conferred by s.132(1)(a), the Councils can be subject to directions of the Secretary of State as to the discharge of their functions.

General functions of the Councils

132.—(1) The Councils shall each have the following functions, namely—
(a) such of the functions previously discharged by the Nature Conservancy Council under the Acts amended by Schedule 9 to this Act as are assigned to them in accordance with the amendments effected by that Schedule;
(b) the establishment, maintenance and management of nature reserves (within the meaning of section 15 of the National Parks and Access to the Countryside Act 1949) in their area;
(c) the provision of advice for the Secretary of State or any other Minister on the development and implementation of policies for or affecting nature conservation in their area;
(d) the provision of advice and the dissemination of knowledge to any persons about nature conservation in their area or about matters arising from the discharge of their functions under this section or section 134 below;
(e) the commissioning or support (where by financial means or otherwise) of research which in their opinion is relevant to any of their functions under this section or section 134 below,
and the Councils shall, in discharging their functions under this section, have regard to any advice given to them by the joint committee under section 133(3) below.
(2) The Councils shall each have power—
(a) to accept any gift or contribution made to them for the purposes of any of the functions conferred on them by subsection (1) above or section 134 below and, subject to the terms of the gift or contribution, to apply it to those purposes;
(b) to initiate and carry out such research directly related to those functions as it is appropriate that they should carry out instead of commissioning or supporting other persons under paragraph (e) of that subsection;
and they may do all such other things as are incidental or conducive to those functions including (without prejudice to the generality of this provision) making charges and holding land or any interest in or right over land.
(3) Nothing in this section shall be taken as preventing any of the Councils—
(a) if consulted by another of the Councils about a matter relating to the functions of that other Council, from giving that other Council any advice or information which they are able to give; or
(b) from giving advice or information to the joint committee about any matter relating to any of the functions conferred by section 133(2) and (3) below.

DEFINITIONS
"nature conservation": s.131(6).

GENERAL NOTE
This section states the general functions of the Councils. As well as the functions previously discharged by the NCC under the provisions set out in Sched. 9 (which also makes the necessary consequential amendments), the functions include: advice to the Secretary of State or any other Minister (subs. (1)(c)); the provision of advice and the dissemination of knowledge generally (subs. (1)(d)); the commissioning or support of research (subs. (1)(e)); the acceptance of gifts (subs. (2)(a)); direct research activities (subs. (2)(b)); and the provision of advice and information to another of the Councils or to the Joint Committee (subs. (3)).

Schedule 9
Substantive amendments. Schedule 9 in the main consists simply of consequential amendments. However, para. 4(2) of the Schedule makes an important substantive amendment to s.15(2) of the Countryside Act 1968 (dealing with agreements for the management of sites of special scientific interest or SSSIs) by (a) deleting the reference to be "in the national interest"; and (b) making it clear that agreements may be entered into with owners of land adjacent to the SSSI.

This second amendment is particularly important, since, as was pointed out by Lord Cranbrook (*Hansard*, H.L. Vol. 520, col. 2224), operations on land adjoining SSSIs can frequently affect the conservation value of the SSSI itself.

It was also suggested by Lord Cranbrook that an amendment should be made to clarify that the power to enter management agreement extends to owners and occupiers with a lesser interest in land, such as crofters or commoners. The Government, however, took the view that this was already clearly the case (*Hansard*, H.L. Vol. 522, col. 973).

Schedule 9, para. 11(9) makes a further unobtrusive but substantive amendment to correct defective working in s.29 of the Wildlife and Countryside Act 1981. It makes it clear that the owner or occupier of land subject to a nature conservation order under s.29 must *after the making of the Order*, give notice of any intention to carry out a potentially damaging operation (*Hansard*, H.L. Vol. 522, cols. 2232–3).

The Government also in the course of debate on Pt. VII clarified the position as to its views on the scope of existing powers to support positive conservation works in the wider countryside outside SSSIs, the Government's view being that grant schemes to that effect are already permissible under existing legislation (*Hansard*, H.L. Vol. 522, col. 981).

Special functions of Councils

133.—(1) The Councils shall jointly have the following functions which may, however, be discharged only through the joint committee; and in this section the functions so dischargeable are referred to as "special functions."
(2) The special functions of the Council are—
(a) such of the functions previously discharged by the Nature Conservancy Council under the Wildlife and Countryside Act 1981 as are assigned to the Councils jointly as special functions in accordance with the amendments to that Act effected by Schedule 9 to this Act;
(b) the provision of advice for the Secretary of State or any other Minister on the development and implementation of policies for or affecting nature conservation for Great Britain as a whole or nature conservation outside Great Britain;
(c) the provision of advice and the dissemination of knowledge to any persons about nature conservation for Great Britain as a whole or nature conservation outside Great Britain;
(d) the establishment of common standards throughout Great Britain for the monitoring of nature conservation and for research into nature conservation and the analysis of the resulting information;
(e) the commissioning or support (whether by financial means or otherwise) of research which in the opinion of the joint committee is relevant to any matter mentioned in paragraphs (a) to (d) above;
and section 132(2) above shall apply to the special functions as it applies to the functions conferred by subsection (1) of that section.

(3) The joint committee may give advice or information to any of the Councils on any matter arising in connection with the functions of that Council under section 132 above which, in the opinion of the committee, concerns nature conservation for Great Britain as a whole or nature conservation outside Great Britain.

(4) For the purposes of this section, references to nature conservation for Great Britain as a whole are references to—
  (a) any nature conservation matter of national or international importance or which otherwise affect the interests of Great Britain as a whole; or
  (b) any nature conservation matter which arises throughout Great Britain and raises issues common to England, Scotland and Wales,
and it is immaterial for the purposes of paragraph (a) above that a matter arises only in relation to England, to Scotland or to Wales.

(5) The Secretary of State may, as respects any matters arising in connection with—
  (a) any special function of the Councils, or
  (b) the function of the joint committee under subsection (3) above,
give directions to any of the Councils requiring that Council (instead of the joint committee) to discharge that function in relation to that matter.

DEFINITIONS
"nature conservation": s.131(6).

GENERAL NOTE
This important section provides the demarcation line between the functions exercisable by each of the Councils independently and those "special functions" that may only be discharged jointly through the Joint Committee. These "special functions" are listed at subs. (2) and include: the provision of advice to Ministers on policies for nature conservation in Great Britain as a whole or nature conservation outside Great Britain; the dissemination of knowledge and the giving of general advice on such matters; the commissioning or support of research on such matters; and the establishment of common standards for monitoring, research and analysis.

Under subs. (3) the Joint Committee may give advice to the Councils on any matter which, in the opinion of the Joint Committee, concerns nature conservation for Great Britain as a whole or nature conservation outside Great Britain. Subsection (4) defines "nature conservation for Great Britain as a whole" by reference to (a) matters of national or international importance, or which otherwise affect the interests of Great Britain as a whole whether arising in England, Scotland or Wales; and (b) matters arising throughout Great Britain and raising issues common to England, Scotland and Wales.

Presumably the first of these categories would include the designation or conservation of sites which are of national or international importance, whether or not designated as such by E.C. or international law. The second category is intended to enable data, for example on nationally or internationally important species or habitats, to be collected and analysed in a form which meets the requirements of the Government, Joint Committee and, where relevant, the European Community or other international bodies. It will also enable the scientific and research standards of the new Councils to be monitored by the Joint Committee.

Concern was expressed by the Carver Committee on how possible disputes between the Councils and the Joint Committee as to whether a matter fell within the Council's special functions should be resolved. The Government's view expressed in its response to the Carver Committee is that such issues are, in the last analysis, matters of interpretation for the courts and so the views of the Joint Committee cannot be conclusive, though the reference on the opinion of the Joint Committee in subs. (3) inevitably introduces a considerable element of subjectivity.

By s.132(1) the Councils must have regard to any advice given by the Joint Committee under s.133(3).

Grants and loans by the Councils

134.—(1) The Councils may each, with the consent of or in accordance with a general authorisation given by the Secretary of State, give financial assistance by way of grant or loan (or partly in one way and partly in the other) to any person in respect of expenditure incurred or to be incurred by him in doing anything which in their opinion is conducive to nature conservation or fostering the understanding of nature conservation.

(2) No consent or general authorisation shall be given by the Secretary of State under subsection (1) above without the approval of the Treasury.

(3) On making a grant or loan a Council may impose such conditions as they think fit, including (in the case of a grant) conditions for repayment in specified circumstances.

(4) The Councils shall exercise their powers under subsection (3) above so as to ensure that any person receiving a grant or loan under this section in respect of premises to which the public are to be admitted (on payment or otherwise) shall, in the means of access both to and within the premises, and in the parking facilities and sanitary conveniences to be available (if any), make provision, so far as it is in the circumstances both practicable and reasonable, for the needs of members of the public visiting the premises who are disabled.

DEFINITION
"nature conservation": s.131(6).

GENERAL NOTE
This section gives power to the Councils to provide financial assistance by grant or loan to any person incurring, or proposing to incur, expenditure on any activity which in their opinion is conducive to nature conservation or the understanding of it. It retains for the new Councils the enlarged powers of grants and loans given to the NCC by s.38 of the Wildlife and Countryside Act 1981 and follows closely the drafting of that section.

Transfer of property, rights and liabilities to new Councils

Schemes for the transfer of property etc. of the Nature Conservancy Council

135.—(1) The Nature Conservancy Council shall make one or more schemes ("transfer schemes") for the division of all their property, rights and liabilities (other than rights and liabilities under the contracts of employment of their staff and in respect of the provision of pensions, allowances or gratuities) between the Councils.

(2) On the date appointed to a transfer scheme, the property, rights and liabilities of the Nature Conservancy Council which are the subject of the scheme shall, by virtue of this subsection, become property, rights and liabilities of the Council to which they are allocated by the Scheme.

(3) Part I of Schedule 10 to this Act shall have effect in relation to transfer schemes under this section.

(4) The rights and liabilities of the Nature Conservancy Council in respect of the provision of pensions, allowances and gratuities for or in respect of their members and employees or their former members or employees shall, on the date appointed under section 131(3) above, by virtue of this subsection, become rights and liabilities of the Secretary of State.

GENERAL NOTE
The NCC is placed under a duty by this section to draw up a scheme or schemes for the division and transfer of the NCC's property, rights and liabilities as between the Councils.

Subsection (2) has the effect of vesting such property, rights and liabilities in the new Councils in accordance with the transfer schemes. Schedule 10, Pt. I makes detailed provision for the scheme-making procedure and as to the contents of schemes.

Matters of employment and pension rights cannot be dealt with by such schemes, and the rights and liabilities of the NCC in relation to such matters become rights and liabilities of the Secretary of State by virtue of subs. (4).

Transfer to Welsh Council of certain property etc. of Countryside Commission

136.—(1) The Countryside Commission shall make one or more schemes ("transfer schemes") for allocating to the Countryside Council for Wales so much of their property, rights and liabilities (other than rights and liabilities under the contracts of employment of their staff) as the Commission consider appropriate having regard to the countryside functions conferred on the Council by section 130 above.

(2) On the date appointed by a transfer scheme, the property, rights and liabilities of the Countryside Commission which are the subject of the scheme shall, by virtue of this subsection, become property, rights and liabilities of the Countryside Council for Wales.

(3) Part II of Schedule 10 to this Act shall have effect in relation to transfer schemes under this section.

GENERAL NOTE

This section contains equivalent provisions to s.135 in relation to the property, rights and liabilities of the Countryside Commission to be transferred to the Countryside Council for Wales (see s.130). Sched. 10, Pt. II contains the detailed provisions on the necessary schemes of transfer.

Employment by new Councils of staff of existing bodies

Offers of employment to employees of Nature Conservancy Council and certain employees of Countryside Commission

137.—(1) Any person who immediately before the date appointed under section 131(3) above is employed by the Nature Conservancy Council shall be entitled to receive an offer of employment from one of the Councils (to be determined in accordance with proposals made by the Nature Conservancy Council).

(2) Subsection (1) above does not apply to a person whose contract of employment with the Nature Conservancy Council terminates on the day immediately preceding the date appointed under section 131(3) above.

(3) The Countryside Council for Wales shall also make an offer of employment to any person who—
 (a) is, immediately before the date appointed under section 130(4) above, employed by the Countryside Commission; and
 (b) is a person the Commission has proposed should receive such an offer.

(4) Part III of Schedule 10 to this Act shall have effect with respect to the offers and proposals under this section.

GENERAL NOTE

This section ensures that all staff employed by the NCC immediately before the appointed day (see s.131(3)) are entitled to receive an offer of employment from one of the new Councils. The terms of the offers are to be determined in accordance with proposals made by the NCC under Sched. 10, Pt. III (para. 10). The Secretary of State may approve the proposals submitted or substitute his own proposals, in each case after consultation with the new Councils (Sched. 10, para. 11).

The terms offered must be such that, taken as a whole, they are not less favourable to the person to whom the offer is made than the terms on which he is employed at the date of the offer (Sched. 10, para. 14(3)). Any dispute as to whether the offer complies with this requirement is to be referred to an industrial tribunal (Sched. 10, para. 17(1)).

Offers may not be revoked for a period of three months (Sched. 10, para. 14(4)) and unreasonable refusal of an offer results in loss of redundancy rights (Sched. 10, para. 16). Where an offer is accepted, continuity of employment is preserved (Sched. 10, para. 15).

Equivalent provisions apply to employees of the Countryside Commission in relation to any person to whom the Commission proposes an offer of employment with the Countryside Council for Wales should be made (subs. (3)).

Dissolution of Nature Conservancy Council

Winding up and dissolution of Nature Conservancy Council

138.—(1) On the date appointed under section 131(3) above the chairman and other members of the Nature Conservancy Council shall cease to hold office and after that date—
  (a) the Council shall consist only of a chairman appointed by the Secretary of State and such one or more other persons as may be so appointed; and
  (b) the Council shall have only the following functions, namely—
    (i) anything which falls to be done by the Council under any transfer scheme under section 135 above;
    (ii) the preparation of such accounts and reports as the Secretary of State may direct;
and such other functions as are necessary for winding up their affairs.

(2) The Secretary of State may, by order, after consultation with the Nature Conservancy Council and the Councils, dissolve the Nature Conservancy Council on a day specified in the order as soon as he is satisfied that nothing remains to be done by that Council.

(3) The Secretary of State may pay to persons who cease to hold office by virtue of subsection (1) above such sums by way of compensation for loss of office, or loss or diminution of pension rights as the Secretary of State may, with the approval of the Treasury, determine.

GENERAL NOTE
  This section provides for the winding up and ultimate dissolution of the NCC. Provision is made for fulfilment of residual functions of transfer, accounting and reporting.

Transitional provisions and savings

Transitional Provisions and Savings

139. Schedule 11 of this Act (which contains transitional provisions and savings relating to this Part) shall have effect.

GENERAL NOTE
  This section applies the detailed transitional provisions of Sched. 11. These provisions deal with continuity of functions and construction of documents.
  Paragraph 5 of the Schedule deals with existing designated areas of outstanding natural beauty and long-distance routes which straddle the English and Welsh border. The English and Welsh parts of such AONBs are to be treated as distinct AONBs, whereas long-distance routes continue to be single routes for the purposes of Pt. IV of the National Parks and Access to the Countryside Act 1949, but with the relevant Council exercising their functions over their relevant part. The relevant Councils may only exercise their respective functions in relation to their part of the area or route after consultation with the other Council concerned, and arrangements may be made for joint exercise of functions (para. 5(4)). Similarly, by para. 11, nature reserves or SSSIs which straddle the English-Welsh border are to be treated as distinct reserves or sites, but the new Councils concerned may only exercise their functions in consultation with each other or jointly by arrangement (para. 11(3)).

PART VIII

MISCELLANEOUS

GENERAL NOTE
  Part VIII contains a number of miscellaneous provisions of varying importance. The most significant are:
  (1) power to restrict the importation, use, supply or storage of substances or articles for the purpose of avoiding pollution, or harm to man, animals or plants (s.140);
  (2) power to restrict the importation or exportation of waste for the purpose of preventing pollution or harm to human health or for conserving facilities or resources for dealing with waste (s.141);
  (3) powers to make provision for the obtaining of information about substances with potential to cause pollution or harm to human health (s.142);

(4) provision for public registers of potentially contaminated land (s.143);
(5) amendments of the legislation of control of hazardous substances (s.144 and Sched. 13);
(6) increase of maximum penalties in respect of water pollution offences (s.145);
(7) amendments to legislation relating to marine deposits (s.146) and creation of public registers as to such deposits and marine incineration (s.147);
(8) amendments of the provisions as to oil pollution offences from ships (s.148);
(9) provisions for the control of stray dogs (ss.149–151);
(10) provision as to banning the burning of straw, stubble and other crop residues (s.152).

Other controls on substances, articles or waste

Power to prohibit or restrict the importation, use, supply or storage of injurious substances or articles

140.—(1) The Secretary of State may by regulations prohibit or restrict—
 (a) the importation into and the landing and unloading in the United Kingdom,
 (b) the use for any purpose,
 (c) the supply for any purpose, and
 (d) the storage,
of any specified substance or article if he considers it appropriate to do so for the purpose of preventing the substance or article from causing pollution of the environment or harm to human health or to the health of animals or plants.
 (2) Any such prohibition or restriction may apply—
 (a) in all, or only in specified, areas;
 (b) in all, or only in specified, circumstances or if conditions imposed by the regulations are not complied with; and
 (c) to all, or only to specified descriptions of, persons.
 (3) Regulations under this section may—
 (a) confer on the Secretary of State power to direct that any substance or article whose use, supply or storage is prohibited or restricted is to be treated as waste or controlled waste of any description and in relation to any such substance or article—
  (i) to apply, with or without modification, specified provisions of Part II; or
  (ii) to direct that it be disposed of or treated in accordance with the direction;
 (b) confer on the Secretary of State power, where a substance or article has been imported, landed or unloaded in contravention of a prohibition or restriction imposed under subsection (1)(a) above, to require that the substance or article be disposed of or treated in or removed from the United Kingdom;
 (c) confer powers corresponding to those conferred by section 17 above on persons authorised for any purpose of the regulations by the Secretary of State or any local or other authority; and
 (d) include such other incidental and supplemental, and such transitional provisions, as the Secretary of State considers appropriate.
 (4) The Secretary of State may, by regulations under this section, direct that, for the purposes of any power conferred on him under subsection (3)(b) above, any prohibition or restriction on the importation into or the landing and unloading in the United Kingdom imposed—
 (a) by or under any Community instrument, or
 (b) by or under any enactment,
shall be treated as imposed under subsection (1)(a) above and any power conferred on him under subsection (3)(b) above shall be exercisable accordingly.
 (5) The Secretary of State may by order establish a committee to give him advice in relation to the exercise of the power to make regulations under this section and Schedule 12 to this Act shall have effect in relation to it.

(6) Subject to subsection (7) below, it shall be the duty of the Secretary of State before he makes any regulations under this section other than regulations under subsection (4) above—
  (a) to consult the committee constituted under subsection (5) above about the proposed regulations;
  (b) having consulted the committee, to publish in the London Gazette and, if the regulations apply in Scotland or Northern Ireland, the Edinburgh Gazette or, as the case may be, Belfast Gazette and in any other publication which he considers appropriate, a notice indicating the effect of the proposed regulations and specifying—
    (i) the date on which it is proposed that the regulations will come into force;
    (ii) a place where a draft of the proposed regulations may be inspected free of charge by members of the public during office hours; and
    (iii) a period of not less than 14 days, beginning with the date on which the notice is first published, during which representations in writing may be made to the Secretary of State about the proposed regulations; and
  (c) to consider any representations which are made to him in accordance with the notice.

(7) The Secretary of State may make regulations under this section in relation to any substance or article without observing the requirements of subsection (6) above where it appears to him that there is an imminent risk, if those requirements are observed, that serious pollution of the environment will be caused.

(8) The Secretary of State may, after performing the duty imposed on him by subsection (6) above with respect to any proposed regulations, make the regulations either—
  (a) in the form of the draft mentioned in subsection (6)(b) above, or
  (b) in that form with such modifications as he considers appropriate;
but the Secretary of State shall not make any regulations incorporating modifications unless he is of opinion that it is appropriate for the requirements of subsection (6) above to be disregarded.

(9) Regulations under this section may provide that a person who contravenes or fails to comply with a specified provision of the regulations or causes or permits another person to contravene or fail to comply with a specified provision of the regulations commits an offence and may prescribe the maximum penalty for the offence.

(10) No offence under the regulations shall be made punishable with imprisonment for more than two years or punishable on summary conviction with a fine exceeding level 5 on the standard scale (if not calculated on a daily basis) or, in the case of a continuing offence, exceeding one-tenth of the level on the standard scale specified as the maximum penalty for the original offence.

(11) In this section—
  "the environment" means the air, water and land, or any of those media, and the medium of air includes the air within buildings and the air within other natural or man-made structures above or below ground;
  "specified" means specified in the regulations; and
  "substance" means any natural or artificial substance, whether in solid or liquid form or in the form of a gas or vapour and it includes mixtures of substances.

COMMENCEMENT
January 1, 1991 (s.164(2)).

GENERAL NOTE
This section replaces and expands the powers previously contained in s.100 of the Control of

Pollution Act 1974, which empowered the Secretary of State to prohibit or restrict the importation, exportation, use and supply of hazardous substances. The new powers are wider than s.100 in a number of respects. "Articles" are covered as well as "substances"; there is an express power to require re-exportation; storage may now be restricted or prohibited; and use "for any purpose" may now be controlled (as opposed to use "in connection with any trade or business or manufacturing process" under the 1974 Act, s.100(1)(b)).

Three statutory instruments have so far been made under this section.

The Environmental Protection (Controls on Injurious Substances) Regulations 1992 (S.I. 1992 No. 31) have been made under these powers to control the supply or use of preparations or waste with a specified content of PCB or PCT; the supply and use of certain lead paint; and the supply and use of mercury compounds.

The Environmental Protection (Controls on Injurious Substances) (No. 2) Regulations 1992 (S.I. 1992 No. 1583) have been made prohibiting the marketing and use of Ugilec 141 as from June 18, 1994, and Ugilec 121 and DBBT as from July 31, 1992.

The Environmental Protection (Controls on Injurious Substances) Regulations 1993 (S.I. 1993 No. 1) have been made to prohibit the marketing and use of PCPs, with a few specific exemptions.

Subs. (3)

This subsection gives some important ancillary powers including the power to direct that relevant substances or articles be treated as controlled waste and so subjected to the regime of Pt. II of the Act. There is also the power to direct how substances or articles landed in breach of a prohibition or restriction are to be dealt with, whether by treatment or disposal within the UK or by re-exportation.

Subs. (5)

Advisory committee. The Secretary of State is given express power to constitute an advisory committee which must then be consulted by him in exercising his powers under the section (subs. (6)). Sched. 12 contains provisions as to membership, terms of office, facilities and remuneration. The Secretary of State established the Advisory Committee on July 25, 1991 by the Advisory Committee on Hazardous Substances Order 1991 (S.I. 1991 No. 1487) and specified the terms of office of its Members by the Advisory Committee on Hazardous Substances (Terms of Office) Regulations 1991 (S.I. 1991 No. 1488).

Territorial extent

The section applies to imports and exports to and from England, Scotland and Wales and imports to Northern Ireland (s.164(4)).

Power to prohibit or restrict the importation or exportation of waste

141.—(1) The Secretary of State may, for the purpose of preventing any risk of pollution of the environment or of harm to human health arising from waste being imported or exported or of conserving the facilities or resources for dealing with waste, make regulations prohibiting or restricting, or providing for the prohibition or restriction of—

(a) the importation into and the landing and unloading in the United Kingdom, or

(b) the exportation, or the loading for exportation, from the United Kingdom,

of waste of any description.

(2) Regulations under this section may make different provision for different descriptions of waste or waste of any description in different circumstances.

(3) Regulations under this section may, as respects any description of waste, confer or impose on waste regulation authorities or any of them such functions in relation to the importation of waste as appear to be appropriate to the Secretary of State, subject to such limitations and conditions as are specified in the regulations.

(4) Regulations under this section may confer or impose on waste regulation authorities or any of them functions of enforcing any of the regulations on behalf of the Secretary of State whether or not the functions fall within subsection (3) above.

(5) Regulations under this section may—
(a) as respects functions conferred or imposed on waste regulation authorities—
  (i) make them exercisable in relation to individual consignments or consignments in a series by the same person but not in relation to consignments or descriptions of consignments generally; and
  (ii) confer on the Secretary of State power, by direction to the authorities or any of them, to make the functions or any of them exercisable instead by him whether indefinitely or for any period;
(b) impose or provide for the imposition of prohibitions either absolutely or only if conditions or procedures prescribed in or under the regulations are not complied with;
(c) impose duties to be complied with before, on or after any importation or exportation of waste by persons who are, or are to be, consignors, consignees, carriers or holders of the waste or any waste derived from it;
(d) confer powers corresponding to those conferred by section 69(3) above;
(e) provide for appeals to the Secretary of State from determinations made by authorities under the regulations;
(f) provide for the keeping by the Secretary of State, waste regulation authorities and waste collection authorities of public registers of information relating to the importation and exportation of waste and for the transmission of such information between any of those persons;
(g) create offences, subject to the limitation that no offence shall be punishable with imprisonment for more than two years or punishable on summary conviction with imprisonment for more than six months or a fine exceeding level 5 on the standard scale (if not calculated on a daily basis) or, in the case of a continuing offence, exceeding one-tenth of the level on the standard scale specified as the maximum penalty for the original offence.

(6) In this section—
"the environment" means land, water and air or any of them;
"harm" includes offence to any of man's senses;
"waste", "waste collection authority", and "waste regulation authority" have the same meaning as in Part II; and
"the United Kingdom" includes its territorial sea.

(7) In the application of this section to Northern Ireland and the territorial sea of the United Kingdom adjacent to Northern Ireland "waste regulation authority" means a district council established under the Local Government Act (Northern Ireland) 1972.

DEFINITIONS
"waste": s.75(2) and (3).
"waste collection authority": s.30(3).
"waste regulation authority": s.30(1).

COMMENCEMENT
January 1, 1991 (s.164(2)).

GENERAL NOTE
This section contains a new power to control imports and exports of waste by way of regulations. The provisions no doubt stem, to some degree, from public concern as to the importation of waste for incineration or treatment within the UK. The Second Report of HMIP (August 1990) contains information on waste imports for the period 1988/89 (para. 5.20 *ff*). In the relevant period it is estimated that some 52,000 tonnes of special waste were imported into

England and Wales, the majority going to plants in Pontypool, Manchester and the West Midlands. No special waste was exported during the period.

However, as the HMIP report points out, to put the matter in context, only about three per cent. of special waste disposed of in the UK was imported, a figure scarcely justifying the description applied by some environmental groups and M.P.s of the "dustbin of Europe" (para. 5.22). The HMIP Report also refers to two incidents involving proposals for the landing of imported waste, which "caused considerable public anxiety and took up a significant amount of the Inspectorate's time." These were the "Karin B" incident and a proposal to import two million tonnes of household waste from the USA for landfill in a site in Cornwall. Since the reporting period for the HMIP Report, there have been further similar incidents which have received media coverage, in particular the proposed import in 1990 of Canadian PCBs for incineration.

The relevant regulations under subs. (1) may be made for the following purposes:
   (a) preventing any risk of pollution of the environment or of harm to human health. It appears this could cover, for example, the import of waste of unknown composition or characteristics so that safe treatment or handling could not be assured, or the export of waste to countries with no facilities for dealing with it safely. Such exports are intended to be avoided by the Basel Convention on *The Control of Transboundary Movements of Hazardous Waste* (Cm. 984), to which the UK is a signatory but which is not yet in force. The Government's general stance is in favour of national self-sufficiency in waste disposal facilities (see Cm. 1200, *This Common Inheritance*, paras. 14.60–14.62);
   (b) conserving the facilities or resources for dealing with waste. In particular the Government's policy is that waste should not be imported to Britain for direct landfill (Cm. 1200, para. 14.64); and see also HMIP Second Report, August 1990, para. 47, and the Report of the House of Commons Environment Committee, Session 1988–89, Second Report, *Toxic Waste* (February 1989, para. 255).

Enforcement of any regulations made will, by subs. (4), fall to waste regulation authorities. The regulations may include provision as to public registers of information as to the importation and exportation of waste (subs. (5)(f)).

Territorial extent
The section applies to England, Scotland, Wales and Northern Ireland (s.164(4)).

Powers to obtain information about potentially hazardous substances

142.—(1) The Secretary of State may, for the purposes of assessing their potential for causing pollution of the environment or harm to human health, by regulations make provision for and in connection with the obtaining of relevant information relating to substances which may be specified by him by order for the purposes of this section.

(2) The Secretary of State shall not make an order under subsection (1) above specifying any substance—
   (a) which was first supplied in any member State on or after September 18, 1981; or
   (b) in so far as it is a regulated substance for the purposes of any relevant enactment.

(3) The Secretary of State shall not make an order under subsection (1) above specifying any substance without consulting the committee established under section 140(5) except where it appears to him that information about the substance needs to be obtained urgently under this section.

(4) Regulations under this section may—
   (a) prescribe the descriptions of relevant information which are to be furnished under this section in relation to specified substances;
   (b) impose requirements on manufacturers, importers or suppliers generally to furnish information prescribed under paragraph (a) above;
   (c) provide for the imposition of requirements on manufacturers, importers or suppliers generally to furnish relevant information relating to products or articles containing specified substances in relation to which information has been furnished in pursuance of paragraph (b) above;

(d) provide for the imposition of requirements on particular manufacturers, importers or suppliers to furnish further information relating to specified substances in relation to which information has been furnished in pursuance of paragraph (b) above;
(e) provide for the imposition of requirements on particular manufacturers or importers to carry out tests of specified substances and to furnish information of the results of the tests;
(f) authorise persons to comply with requirements to furnish information imposed on them by or under the regulations by means of representative persons or bodies;
(g) impose restrictions on the disclosure of information obtained under this section and provide for determining what information is, and what information is not, to be treated as furnished in confidence;
(h) create offences, subject to the limitation that no offence shall be punishable with imprisonment or punishable on summary conviction with a fine exceeding level 5 on the standard scale;
(i) make any public authority designated by the regulations responsible for the enforcement of the regulations to such extent as may be specified in the regulations;
(j) include such other incidental and supplemental, and such transitional, provisions as the Secretary of State considers appropriate.

(5) The Secretary of State shall have regard, in imposing or providing for the imposition of any requirement under subsection (4)(b), (c), (d) or (e) above, to the cost likely to be involved in complying with the requirement.

(6) In this section—
"the environment" means the air, water and land or any of them;
"relevant information", in relation to substances, products or articles, means information relating to their properties, production, distribution, importation or use or intended use and, in relation to products or articles, to their disposal as waste;
"substance" means any natural or artificial substance, whether in solid or liquid form or in the form of a gas or vapour and it includes mixtures of substances.

(7) The enactments which are relevant for the purposes of subsection (2)(b) above are the following—
the Explosive Substances Act 1875;
the Radioactive Substances Act 1960;
Parts II, III and VIII of the Medicines Act 1968;
Part IV of the Agriculture Act 1970;
the Misuse of Drugs Act 1971;
Part III of the Food and Environment Protection Act 1985; and
the Food Safety Act 1990;
and a substance is a regulated substance for the purposes of any such enactment in so far as any prohibition, restriction or requirement is imposed in relation to it by or under the enactment for the purposes of that enactment.

COMMENCEMENT
January 1, 1991 (s.164(2)).

GENERAL NOTE
This provision enables the Secretary of State to make regulations to require manufacturers, importers, or suppliers of specified substances, natural or artificial, to provide information on those substances. The intention is to use such information to evaluate possible hazards to human health or to the environment caused by the use, storage or disposal of the substance. Information may also be required under the regulations as to products or articles containing such substances (subs. (4)(c)).

By subs. (2) no substance first supplied in any European Community member state on or after September 18, 1981 may be specified, nor may any substance regulated under the other enactments listed in subs. (7). The definitive list of substances on the EEC market before September 18, 1981, is set out at O.J. C146A, June 15, 1990. "New" substances outside that list are subject to the testing and notification requirements of the so-called "Sixth Amendment" Directive 79/831/EEC and related Directives (Directive amending the Sixth Time Directive 67/548/EEC on the approximation of the laws, regulations and administrative provisions relating to the classification, packaging and labelling of dangerous substances; O.J. L259, October 15, 1979). Implementation of this Directive is by means of the Notification of New Substances Regulations 1982 (S.I. 1982 No. 1496).

Section 142 is therefore to be seen in conjunction with this legislation, and it should also be noted that the European Commission has announced its intention of proposals for action on existing chemicals (pre-September 18, 1981) at Community level. The section and regulations under it may well therefore be the vehicle for implementing any such Directive or Directives in due course.

Consultation

Except in an emergency the exercise of the order-making powers must, by subs. (3), be the subject of consultation with any advisory committee established in relation to hazardous substances under s.140(5).

Content of regulations

Subsection (4) deals with the content of regulations made under the section. As well as furnishing information (under subs. (4)(a)–(d)), manufacturers or importers (but not suppliers) can be required to carry out tests on specified substances and furnish the resulting information. In these cases, the Secretary of State must, in formulating the requirements, have regard to the likely costs of compliance (subs. (5)).

Territorial extent

The section applies fully to England, Scotland and Wales and applies to Northern Ireland in respect of importation only (s.164(4)).

Public registers of land which may be contaminated

143.—(1) For the purposes of the registers to be maintained under this section, the Secretary of State may, by regulations—
 (a) specify contaminative uses of land;
 (b) prescribe the form of the registers and the particulars to be included in them; and
 (c) make such other provision as appears to him to be appropriate in connection with the maintenance of the registers.

(2) It shall be the duty of a local authority, as respects land in its area subject to contamination, to maintain, in accordance with the regulations, a register in the prescribed form and containing the prescribed particulars.

(3) The duty imposed by subsection (2) above on a local authority is a duty to compile and maintain the register from the information available to the authority from time to time.

(4) A local authority shall secure that the register is open to inspection at its principal office by members of the public free of charge at all reasonable hours and shall afford to members of the public reasonable facilities for obtaining, on payment of reasonable charges, copies of entries in the register.

(5) Regulations under subsection (1)(c) above may prescribe the measures to be taken by local authorities for informing persons whose land is the subject of entries in a register about the entries or for enabling them to inform themselves about them.

(6) In this section—
"contaminative use" means any use of land which may cause it to be contaminated with noxious substances;
"land subject to contamination" means land which is being or has been put to a contaminative use;
"local authority" means—
(a) in Greater London, a London borough council or the Common Council of the City of London;
(b) in England and Wales outside Greater London, a district council;
(c) in Scotland, a planning authority; and
(d) the Council of the Isles of Scilly; and
"substance" means any natural or artificial substance, whether in solid or liquid form or in the form of a gas or vapour.

COMMENCEMENT
The section comes into force on a day to be appointed (s.164(3)).

GENERAL NOTE
This section, introduced by the Government at the Lords' Committee stage, makes provision for public registers of potentially contaminated land. The issue of contaminated land has not to date received great attention at European Community level, but was considered in depth by the House of Commons' Environment Committee under the Chairmanship of Sir Hugh Rossi, M.P. in its Report, *Contaminated Land* (Session 1989–90, First Report, 170 I–III). Among the recommendations of that Committee were the creation of registers of contaminated land compiled by local authorities and using common methodology and compatible computer hardware and software (paras. 78–85).

The Government's response to the Select Committee was published in July 1990 (Cm. 1161) by which time the intention to set up registers had already been announced. The Government announced its intention to insert the relevant provision in the Bill on April 30, 1990 (DoE News Release No. 279). The Minister of State for the Environment and Planning, Mr David Trippier, said in making the announcement:

"We envisage that these registers will identify sites of potential contamination, based on past land use. In this way, they will provide a means of alerting interested parties to the potential for contamination so that, where necessary, more detailed site surveys can be undertaken. At the same time, I want to ensure that we avoid extending planning blight in those areas of the country with a legacy of industrial land use."

Introducing the new clause in the House of Lords, the Parliamentary Under-Secretary of State, Lord Hesketh, gave a further indication of the Government thinking behind the provision:

"The new clause deals with the serious and difficult problems of contaminated land. Contamination of land can come in a wide range of forms indicative of this country's long industrial history. It cannot be the subject of a single definition but, where it is found to exist, there is a need to make working assessments of the hazards that may be involved and to consider suitable remedial and protective action at specific sites, particularly when changes of land use are proposed.

Such action needs to be based upon the best possible information and knowledge. We provide technical guidance for dealing with contamination. But an essential element in any policies must be to consider ways of gathering information and to see how this might most usefully be supplied for public use. This has been a vexed question for some time. Any attempt to compile information can begin to involve the compiler in making judgments on the condition of land which might affect its value. This difficulty of blight on prospective sale or development requires careful consideration. Information needs to be available to landowners and to regulating authorities where there are genuine problems concerning safety and environmental hazard. But we have to find a basis for alerting those concerned to the need for further assessment so that the dangers are properly understood and remedied or fears about contamination are refuted on valid grounds.

As a result of our own pilot studies and several pilot registers by local authorities we have concluded that suitable registers can be compiled from desk studies of historic land-uses from which the potential for contamination might be inferred and further investigated where necessary, but without placing onerous responsibilities of judgment on those compiling the registers.

Consequently we have decided to introduce a statutory responsibility upon local authorities to compile and maintain registers of potentially contaminating land uses. We consider that the most appropriate level of local government for doing this is the district council in England and Wales; that is the level at which local environmental monitoring is undertaken and at which local planning decisions are taken. In doing so we are acting in accord with a recently published report by the Association of District Councils which recommended that district councils should have powers to survey and register contaminated land. As regards Scotland, we see planning authorities as the equivalent level.

The particular land uses to be plotted and the form of the register will be specified in subsequent regulations on which there will be the fullest possible consultation. We shall be publishing the report of the Cheshire study later this month to show the kind of methods [that] are likely to be needed. Some further research and studies might be required to verify the full range of land-uses involved and to produce profiles of suspected contaminants. But we intend to work closely with the local authority associations in deciding on the form and content of the proposed registers.

An important feature of the proposed system will be public accessibility of the registers. We shall also need to consider how far, and in what way, owners of sites on the registers should be specifically informed. The proposed new clause makes provision for free access by members of the public and also provides for regulations to set out measures for informing those whose land is directly affected.

This may sound an extremely onerous set of tasks for local authorities. In fact, it has been our experience from the various studies and pilot local authority exercises that such registers can be set up and maintained with minimal demands on resources, using those staff already engaged in such activities for planning or environmental purposes" (*Hansard*, H.L. Vol. 520, cols. 2268–9).

The consultation process

The regulations to be made by the Secretary of State will specify uses of land which may cause land to be contaminated with noxious substances ("contaminative uses") and the form of the registers. The Government proposed to issue draft proposals for consultation in early summer 1991 and to lay implementing regulations late in 1991. But following a consultation exercise it announced on March 10, 1992 that it was postponing the introduction of the registers in view of the concerns that had been expressed over them, most relating to the likelihood of blight. The DoE published the second consultation paper on the s.143 EPA registers of contaminative uses on July 31, 1992. The consultation paper accompanied a set of draft regulations which suggested the form and nature of the proposed registers. Subject to the results of the consultation process, the Government hoped to lay the regulations by the end of 1992. Authorities would be given 15 months to compile the registers. This meant that the registers would have been open to the public in about April 1994.

This consultation process was no less thorny than the consultation on the first proposals. In a letter to *The Times*, for example, the Chief Executive of the Royal Institute of Chartered Surveyors reiterated the fears expressed in the first consultation about blight being caused by an aversion to urban sites at the expense of greenfield sites, the likely reluctance on the part of lenders to lend on the security of registered sites and the effect of registration of domestic homeowners who find their houses registered on a s.143 register. As a result of these misgivings Michael Howard, Secretary of State for the Environment, announced on March 24, 1993 that the Government was to withdraw its proposal to set up statutory registers of contaminative uses of land under s.143 of the EPA 1990. Mr Howard also announced a review of the legal powers of regulatory public bodies to control and tackle land pollution.

Three grounds for criticism of the proposals for registers were identified by the Government:
  (a) the proposed registers would have been based on the criterion of use or former use by a limited range of potentially contaminating activities and would therefore include a large number of sites not actually contaminated, whilst omitting other sites which were contaminated;
  (b) because the register would record past potentially contaminative uses of land there would be no way of removing such sites from the register even if any contamination had been satisfactorily dealt with;
  (c) where sites are identified as actually contaminated, it remains unclear what action should be taken and by whom, *i.e.* whether the site should be cleaned up and, if so, who should pay and how much.

Michael Howard also announced a wide ranging review of the appropriate treatment or control of land that could cause pollution of the environment or harm human health, to be conducted by an inter-departmental group of officials under the Chairmanship of the DoE. The group's remit is to review the powers and duties of public authorities in this area, having regard to the need to minimise regulatory costs and to consider the implications for the role of the Environment Agency. As part of this task, the group is to report on any short term statutory changes it considers appropriate and is to carry out long term studies as and when these are required.

Duty of local authorities
Local authorities, at district level, would be under a duty to maintain registers in the prescribed form of "land subject to contamination" (subs. (2)). This phrase does not connote actual contamination, but merely that the land has been or is being put to a "contaminative use." The duty is to compile and maintain the register from the information available to the authority from time to time (subs. (3)).

Territorial extent
The section does not apply to Northern Ireland (s.164(4)).

Amendments of hazardous substances legislation

144. Schedule 13 to this Act (which contains miscellaneous amendments to the legislation relating to hazardous substances) shall have effect.

COMMENCEMENT
The section comes into force on a day to be appointed (s.164(3)).

GENERAL NOTE
This section was inserted by amendment at Committee stage in the Lords. Sched. 13 of the Act contains various amendments to the Planning (Hazardous Substances) Act 1990 and to the equivalent Scottish legislation. The Parliamentary Under-Secretary of State for the Environment (Lord Hesketh) in moving the amendment, described it as being to rectify shortcomings in the legislation controlling the location of hazardous substances, and to enable "this important new control system, which is not yet in force, to be introduced on a much more satisfactory basis than would be possible under existing provisions." Lord Hesketh summarised the main effects of the amendments as follows (*Hansard*, Vol. 520, col. 2267, July 5, 1990):

> "The legislation concerns the storage and use of substances which could present major hazards to people in the surrounding area. Hazardous substances consent will be required where named substances are present at or above specified amounts. There are transitional provisions designed to give existing users of hazardous substances an entitlement to a deemed consent in respect of their existing operations. The intention was that these deemed consents would relate to the situation in the 12-month period preceding the introduction of the new controls.
>
> After considering representations from industry, we have concluded that the standard conditions which would attach to all these deemed consents under the existing legislation are effectively unworkable. They would mean that a substance would have to be kept and used in the same place and manner as it was immediately before the new controls came into force. This would contradict the objective of basing deemed consents on activity in the whole of the 12 months prior to the commencement date. Indeed, a substance used regularly during these 12 months may not even be present immediately before the commencement date. Therefore, paragraph 4 of Part I of the new Schedule deletes the two offending conditions and enables revised conditions to be prescribed in regulations.
>
> This is the most crucial defect. But there are other shortcomings in the legislation which we should like to remedy. These concern the position of statutory undertakers, arrangements for charging fees for applications, and technical points relating to conditions and compensation. Similar amendments are made in Part II to the equivalent Scottish provisions."

Territorial extent
The section does not apply to Northern Ireland (s.164(4)).

Penalties for offences of polluting controlled waters etc.

145.—(1) In section 107(6) of the Water Act 1989 (penalties for offences of polluting controlled waters or contravening consent conditions), in paragraph (a), for the words "the statutory maximum" there shall be substituted "£20,000."

(2) In sections 31(7)(a), 31A(2)(c)(i) and 32(7)(a) of the Control of Pollution Act 1974 (corresponding penalties for Scotland), for the words "the statutory maximum" there shall be substituted "£20,000."

COMMENCEMENT
January 1, 1991 (s.164(2)).

GENERAL NOTE
This section raises the maximum fines on summary conviction for water pollution offences in relation to controlled waters in England and Wales and Scotland from £2,000 to £20,000.

Territorial extent
The section does not apply to Northern Ireland (s.164(4)).

Pollution at sea

Deposits of substances and articles in the sea, etc.

146.—(1) Part II of the Food and Environment Protection Act 1985 (under which licences are required for deposits by British vessels etc. at sea anywhere or by foreign vessels etc. in United Kingdom waters or, in certain circumstances, within British fishery limits) shall be amended as follows.

(2) In section 5 (licences for depositing at sea)—
 (a) in paragraph (a), after the words "United Kingdom waters" there shall be inserted the words "or United Kingdom controlled waters";
 (b) paragraphs (c) and (d) shall be omitted;
 (c) in paragraph (e)—
  (i) in sub-paragraph (i), after the words "United Kingdom waters" there shall be inserted the words "or United Kingdom controlled waters" and at the end there shall be inserted the word "or"; and
  (ii) sub-paragraph (iii) shall be omitted.

(3) In section 6 (licences for incineration at sea), in subsection (1)(a)—
 (a) in sub-paragraph (i), after the words "United Kingdom waters" there shall be inserted the words "or United Kingdom controlled waters" and at the end there shall be inserted the word "or"; and
 (b) sub-paragraph (iii) shall be omitted.

(4) In section 9(5) (Convention State defence to offence of acting without or in contravention of a licence), in paragraph (b), for the word "waters" there shall be substituted the words "controlled waters (and not within United Kingdom waters)."

(5) In section 11 (powers of officers)—
 (a) in subsection (2)(b), for the words "British fishery limits" there shall be substituted the words "United Kingdom waters or United Kingdom controlled waters;"; and
 (b) in subsection (3)(a), for the words "British fishery limits" there shall be substituted the words "United Kingdom waters or United Kingdom controlled waters;".

(6) In section 21 (penalties for offences)—
 (a) in subsection (2), for the words "2(4) and 9(1)" there shall be substituted the words "and 2(4)"; and
 (b) after that subsection, there shall be inserted the following subsection—

 "(2A) A person guilty of an offence under section 9(1) shall be liable—
 (a) on summary conviction, to a fine of an amount not exceeding £50,000; and
 (b) on conviction on indictment, to a fine or to imprisonment for a term not exceeding two years or to both."

(7) In section 24(1) (definitions) at the end of the definition of "United Kingdom waters" there shall be inserted the words "and 'United Kingdom controlled waters' means any part of the sea within the limits of an area designated under section 1(7) of the Continental Shelf Act 1964."

(8) In Schedule 2 (powers in relation to vessels, aircraft, etc. for the purposes of Part I or Part II or both Parts of the Act), in paragraph 3(3) (removal to United Kingdom), after the words "Part I" there shall be inserted the words "or II."

COMMENCEMENT
January 1, 1991 (s.164(2)).

GENERAL NOTE
The main effect of this section is to widen the scope of the prohibition on deposits at sea and incineration at sea in the absence of a licence granted under Pt. II of the Food and Environmental Protection Act 1985. Under FEPA this prohibition applied to British vessels anywhere in the world (s.5(b)), to foreign vessels loaded in Britain within British fishery limits (s.5(c)(i)) and to other foreign vessels within UK 12-mile territorial waters (s.5(a)). The Parliamentary secretary to the Ministry of Agriculture Fisheries and Food, Mr David Curry, described the objects of the section as follows in the Commons Committee stage:

"The clause is disappointingly devoid of conspiracy. It has virtually nothing to do with the issue discussed by the hon. Gentleman. Its purpose is to plug a gap in our existing ability to control dumping at sea. At present we control the fisheries limits of our vessels in international waters, but we cannot control a foreign vessel that loads abroad and dumps outside our territorial waters. If it dumps at 11¾ miles, we can control it, but if it dumps at 12 miles 100 yards, we cannot. So it can dump whatever it wants and we can do nothing.

The clause aims to give us enforcement measures to control dumping by foreign vessels. It extends United Kingdom control to all vessels inside the continental shelf. A change is necessary, which is why that measure is riding piggy back upon this Bill. It can do so because we have agreed with states that share coastal waters on the location of the continental shelf. We could not do that in the past, but we can now take the powers offered by international convention. We are entitled to plug that gap under the E.C. convention. We shall probably not be in a position to issue licences. We have not taken this path in order to do that but to get to grips with people who dump waste illegally in waters that we control. That is the sole purpose of the amendment . . . We made it clear that we would cease dumping except in the case of toxic substances and where there was no other safe alternative. We have taken a precautionary approach. A hundred licences were issued a decade ago, only 20 in 1987 and nine now. Five of those will go this year, leaving four. By the end of 1992, all will have disappeared, except those mentioned by the hon. Gentleman. They will also go in a matter of months—there will be no indefinite extension of those licences. Large quantities of waste cannot be stored on land, as that would be environmentally dangerous" (SCH, 31st sitting, March 15, 1990, col. 1280).

The amendments contained in the section have the effect of extending the prohibition on unlicensed dumping and incineration for foreign vessels loaded in foreign ports from the 12-mile limit out to any UK controlled waters, *i.e.* any part of the sea within limits designated under the Continental Shelf Act 1964 (subs. (7)). Continental Shelf limits accord with the limits laid down by international law for jurisdiction for the purposes of sea deposits. The distinction between foreign vessels loaded in the UK and those loaded elsewhere is ended, so that foreign vessels loaded in the UK are also subject to the Continental Shelf limits. For policy on waste disposal at sea generally, see the White Paper of September 1990, *This Common Inheritance* (Cm. 1200), para. 12.35.

Subs. (2)
This makes the relevant jurisdictional changes for the deposit of articles from foreign vessels. A single limit (UK-controlled waters, as defined above) is created for the scuttling of vessels.

Subs. (3)
This subsection makes the relevant jurisdictional changes for incineration at sea. A licence is needed for incineration on British vessels anywhere in the world and for other vessels within the UK Continental Shelf limits.

Subs. (4)
This removes the Convention state defence to a charge of unlicensed incineration or deposit in cases where the operation takes place within UK-controlled (*i.e.* Continental Shelf) waters. Thus all deposits within such waters now require a licence.

Subs. (5)
This extends the relevant powers of enforcement to the new jurisdictional limits.

Subs. (6)
This subsection increases the maximum fine on summary conviction for unlicensed deposits from £2,000 to £50,000.

Subs. (8)
This extends the powers of enforcement officers under Pt. II of the 1985 Act to allow them to order a vessel to be taken to the nearest convenient port, or to take the vessel to port themselves.

Territorial extent
The section extends to Northern Ireland (s.164(4)).

Public registers relating to deposits in the sea and incineration at sea

147. In Part II of the Food and Environment Protection Act 1985, for section 14 (registers of licences) there shall be substituted the following section—

"Duty of licensing authority to keep public registers of information

14.—(1) It shall be the duty of each licensing authority, as respects licences for which it is the licensing authority, to maintain, in accordance with regulations, a register containing prescribed particulars of or relating to—
(a) applications for licences made to that authority;
(b) the licences issued by that authority;
(c) variations of licences effected by that authority;
(d) revocations of licences effected by that authority;
(e) convictions for any offences under section 9 above;
(f) information obtained or furnished in pursuance of section 8(3), (4) or (5) above;
(g) the occasions on which either of the Ministers has carried out any operation under section 10 above; and
(h) such other matters relating to operations for which licences are needed under this Part of this Act as may be prescribed.

(2) No information shall be included in any register which, in the opinion of either of the Ministers, is such that its disclosure on the register—
(a) would be contrary to the interests of national security, or
(b) would prejudice to an unreasonable degree some person's commercial interests.

(3) Information excluded from a register by virtue of subsection (2)(b) above shall be treated as ceasing to prejudice a person's commercial interests at the expiry of the period of four years beginning with the date on which the Minister made his decision under that subsection; but, on the application of any person to whom it relates, the Minister shall decide whether the information should be included or continue to be excluded from the register.

(4) Where information of any description is excluded from a register by virtue of subsection (2)(b) above, a statement shall be entered in the register indicating the existence of information of that description.

(5) It shall be the duty of each licensing authority—
(a) to secure that the register maintained by the authority under this section is available, at all reasonable times, for inspection by the public free of charge; and
(b) to afford to members of the public facilities for obtaining copies of entries, on payment of reasonable charges.

(6) Registers under this section may be kept in any form.
(7) In this section "prescribed" means prescribed in regulations.
(8) Either of the Ministers may exercise any power to make regulations under this section and any such power shall be exercisable by

statutory instrument, subject to annulment in pursuance of a resolution of either House of Parliament."

COMMENCEMENT
May 31, 1991: S.I. 1991 No. 1319.

GENERAL NOTE
This is another provision introduced by amendment at Lords' Committee stage. The object is simply to make the same provision for public registers in relation to licensing activities under Pt. II of the Food and Environment Protection Act 1985 (dumping and incineration at sea) as appear in Pt. I of the 1990 Act. The same exclusions as to national security and commercial confidentiality apply.

Territorial extent
The section applies to Northern Ireland (s.164(4)).

Oil pollution from ships

148.—(1) Schedule 14 to this Act (which amends the provisions of the Prevention of Oil Pollution Act 1971) shall have effect.

(2) Without prejudice to the generality of subsections (1), (3) and (4) of section 20 of the Merchant Shipping Act 1979, an Order under subsection (1) of that section may make in connection with offences created by or under any such Order provision corresponding to that made in connection with offences under section 2(2A) of the Prevention of Oil Pollution Act 1971 by any provision of—
  (a) section 19(4A) of that Act, and
  (b) sections 19A and 20 of that Act,
and may do so whether by applying (or making provision for the application of) any of those provisions, subject to such modifications as may be specified by or under the Order, or otherwise.

(3) This section (and Schedule 14) shall not apply in relation to any offence committed before this section comes into force.

COMMENCEMENT
January 1, 1991 (s.164(2)).

GENERAL NOTE
This section results from amendments moved by Mr Roger Knapman M.P. The purpose of the provisions were fully summarised by Mr Knapman in Committee in terms which the Government found "overwhelming," agreeing to the amendments in their entirety:

"The new clause and new schedule relate to the vital environmental matter of the pollution of the sea by oil. They may seem fairly complicated, but their essential purpose is simple. They would enable owners, as well as masters, of foreign-registered ships to be prosecuted when their ships spill oil into navigable [waters], which are landward of the baseline for measuring the breadth of the territorial waters of the United Kingdom.

Under s.2(2A) of the Prevention of Oil Pollution Act 1971, if oil or oily mixture is discharged from a vessel into those waters, which include almost all the statutory limits of jurisdiction of British harbour authorities then subject to certain defences specified in the Act, for example, that the discharge was for the purpose of securing the safety of any vessel or of saving life, the owner or master of the vessel is guilty of an offence. The maximum penalty for that offence on summary conviction is a fine of £50,000 and, on conviction on indictment, an unlimited fine.

Either the owner or the master of the vessel that spills oil may be prosecuted. However, the courts have held that, if the master is convicted, the amount of the fine imposed must be fixed having regard to his personal income and resources, and that the probability that he will be reimbursed by his owners cannot be taken into account.

The result is that fines imposed on masters are usually only a few thousand pounds and a fine imposed on a master by a magistrates' court is often reduced on appeal to the Crown Court for the reasons that I have mentioned.

As a result, when there is a serious leakage or discharge of oil from a British ship into a harbour, the harbour authority, which in England and Wales has the exclusive right— except for the Attorney-General or a person authorised by him or, in Scotland, the

Procurator Fiscal—to prosecute for this offence, normally institutes proceedings against the owner of the vessel.

When a foreign ship is involved, in practice only the master can usually be prosecuted because the owner is not normally within British jurisdiction. He cannot therefore be served with a summons or be compelled to appear before the court. As a result, the fine imposed on a foreign ship for a serious spillage of oil is often far smaller than it should be having regard to the gravity of the offence.

That unsatisfactory state of affairs has caused concern for some time. The Royal Commission on environmental pollution recommended in its eighth report issued in 1981 that serious consideration should be given to changing the law to overcome those difficulties. The matter has also been the subject of judicial comment. In Maidstone Crown Court in September 1988 the judge decided, because of the master's modest personal income, to reduce to £2,000 a fine of £10,000 imposed by Medway magistrates' court on the master of a foreign ship that had discharged oil into the Medway. He observed that, having regard to the gravity of the offence, even the original fine was, objectively too low and that the law appeared to be unsatisfactory.

It is important that the law should be changed to overcome that problem. One has only to think of what the public reaction would be if a foreign tanker spilled oil in a British port on the scale of the recent Alaskan disaster and if the maximum penalty that could be imposed was, in practice, a fine of only £2,000." (SCH, 31st sitting, March 15, 1990, cols. 1304–1306.)

The effect of s.148 and Sched. 14 is that the Prevention of Oil Pollution Act 1971 is amended to enable the owner of a foreign vessel to be prosecuted for oil pollution offences committed by the ship in harbour areas.

Schedule 14, para. 2, enables documents in connection with proceedings under the Act to be served on the foreign company owning the vessel by way of service on the ship's master. The right to board the vessel for that purpose is given. Paragraph 3 gives new powers to harbourmasters to detain vessels where it is believed that the master or owner has committed an offence by discharging oil into the harbour. The vessel must be released immediately if: (a) proceedings are not commenced within seven days of detention; or (b) such proceedings are concluded without a conviction; or (c) satisfactory security of at least £55,000 is given; or (d) any fines, costs or expenses are paid on conviction.

Subs. (2)
This amends s.20 of the Merchant Shipping Act 1979 to allow orders to be made with provisions equivalent to those referred to above on service of foreign companies and detention of vessels where offences are committed involving discharge of oil into territorial sea waters in contravention of the Merchant Shipping (Prevention of Oil Pollution) Regulations 1983, or any like regulations.

Territorial extent
The section applies to Northern Ireland (s.164(4)).

Control of Dogs

Seizure of stray dogs

149.—(1) Every local authority shall appoint an officer (under whatever title the authority may determine) for the purpose of discharging the functions imposed or conferred by this section for dealing with stray dogs found in the area of the authority.

(2) The officer may delegate the discharge of his functions to another person but he shall remain responsible for securing that the functions are properly discharged.

(3) Where the officer has reason to believe that any dog found in a public place or on any other land or premises is a stray dog, he shall (if practicable) seize the dog and detain it, but, where he finds it on land or premises which is not a public place, only with the consent of the owner or occupier of the land or premises.

(4) Where any dog seized under this section wears a collar having inscribed thereon or attached thereto the address of any person, or the owner of the dog is known, the officer shall serve on the person whose address is given on the collar, or on the owner, a notice in writing stating that

the dog has been seized and where it is being kept and stating that the dog will be liable to be disposed of if it is not claimed within seven clear days after the service of the notice and the amounts for which he would be liable under subsection (5) below are not paid.

(5) A person claiming to be the owner of a dog seized under this section shall not be entitled to have the dog returned to him unless he pays all the expenses incurred by reason of its detention and such further amount as is for the time being prescribed.

(6) Where any dog seized under this section has been detained for seven clear days after the seizure or, where a notice has been served under subsection (4) above, the service of the notice and the owner has not claimed the dog and paid the amounts due under subsection (5) above the officer may dispose of the dog—
- (a) by selling it or giving it to a person who will, in his opinion, care properly for the dog;
- (b) by selling it or giving it to an establishment for the reception of stray dogs; or
- (c) by destroying it in a manner to cause as little pain as possible;

but no dog seized under this section shall be sold or given for the purposes of vivisection.

(7) Where a dog is disposed of under subsection (6)(a) or (b) above to a person acting in good faith, the ownership of the dog shall be vested in the recipient.

(8) The officer shall keep a register containing the prescribed particulars of or relating to dogs seized under this section and the register shall be available, at all reasonable times, for inspection by the public free of charge.

(9) The officer shall cause any dog detained under this section to be properly fed and maintained.

(10) Notwithstanding anything in this section, the officer may cause a dog detained under this section to be destroyed before the expiration of the period mentioned in subsection (6) above where he is of the opinion that this should be done to avoid suffering.

(11) In this section—
"local authority," in relation to England and Wales, means a district council, a London borough council, the Common Council of the City of London or the Council of the Isles of Scilly and, in relation to Scotland, means an islands or district council;
"officer" means an officer appointed under subsection (1) above;
"prescribed" means prescribed in regulations made by the Secretary of State; and
"public place" means—
- (i) as respects England and Wales, any highway and any other place to which the public are entitled or permitted to have access;
- (ii) as respects Scotland, any road (within the meaning of the Roads (Scotland) Act 1984) and any other place to which the public are entitled or permitted to have access;

and, for the purposes of section 160 below in its application to this section, the proper address of the owner of a dog which wears a collar includes the address given on the collar.

COMMENCEMENT

April 1, 1992: Environmental Protection Act (Commencement Order No. 11) 1992 (S.I. 1992 No. 266). Under the Environmental Protection (Stray Dogs) Regulations 1992 (S.I. 1992 No. 288), the Secretary of State prescribed £25 as the amount of to be paid by a person claiming to be the owner of a seized dog. It prescribes particulars to be contained in a register of seized dogs, *i.e.*, its details, particulars of seizure such as time and place and date, and if disposed of, details of the disposal. Finally the regulations prescribe the procedure to be followed where a dog is found by a member of the public who wishes to keep it.

GENERAL NOTE

The problem of uncontrolled dogs was recognised by the Government, both in the Consultation Paper, *Action on Dogs: the Government's Proposals for Legislation* (DoE/Welsh Office, August 1989) and in the subsequent Consultative Paper of the Home Office, Scottish Office, Welsh Office and DoE, *The Control of Dogs* (June 1990). The first paper identified three main problems: (1) the numbers of stray dogs; (2) the high incidence of dog fouling in public places; and (3) an increase in the number of reports of attacks by dangerous dogs, which Lord Mancroft in debate somewhat unfortunately described as "large and rather unpleasant dogs biting small and almost as unpleasant children" (*Hansard*, H.L. Vol. 520, col. 2278, July 4, 1990).

The problem of fouling was considered at length in relation to the provisions of Part IV of the Act on litter in public places. The third problem, dangerous dogs, is to some extent addressed by the greater powers and penalties introduced by the Dangerous Dogs Act 1989. The second consultation paper rejected the creation of a dog registration scheme and canvassed a package of other measures including a new offence of allowing a dog to be dangerously out of control, additional powers of control by the courts, a ban on the keeping or ownership of certain breeds of dog, an offence of allowing a dog to stray (coining the memorable phrase "latch-key dogs" in the process) a fixed penalty scheme for failure to ensure a dog wears a collar and identification tag in a public place, and a review of by-laws and by-law-making powers.

Section 149, together with ss.150 and 151, is an attempt to tackle the problem of stray dogs. The provisions represent a defeat for proponents of a scheme for the compulsory registration of dogs. Such a scheme was tabled on a Commons amendment and defeated by 12 votes. A similar amendment was put forward in the House of Lords by Lord Stanley of Alderley and was carried. Lord Stanley's amendment caused the Government considerable difficulty in the closing stages of the Bill (see General Note to the Act) but was ultimately defeated and replaced by the Government's package of measures now contained in ss.149–151. The Government's view was that a dog registration scheme would be "an expensive and bureaucratic diversion from the need to act decisively against the actual problems" (*Hansard*, H.C. Vol. 178, col. 795). On the other hand, Dame Janet Fookes, the principal proponent of registration in the Commons, was able to point to the support of the RSPCA and other relevant agencies for a registration scheme and the lack of technical means for the implementation of the Government's package of measures (*Hansard*, H.C. Vol. 178, col. 804).

Section 149 places a duty on district and London borough councils to appoint an officer for the purpose of discharging the functions under the section for dealing with stray dogs. Those functions are as follows:

(1) the seizure and detention (if practicable) of dogs which appear to be strays (subs. (3));
(2) notification of the owner, if known, or of the person whose name and address appears on the dog's collar, if any (subs. (4));
(3) the owner may claim the dog within seven clear days of notification on payment of expenses and a sum prescribed by regulations (subss. (4) and (5));
(4) if not claimed, the dog may be disposed of by sale or gift, either to a person who will care properly for it or to a stray dogs' home, or by destroying it (subss. (4) and (6));
(5) keeping a public register of dogs seized (subs. (8));
(6) properly feeding and maintaining dogs detained after seizure (subs. (9));
(7) destroying any detained dog where necessary to avoid suffering (subs. (10)).

Territorial extent

The section does not apply to Northern Ireland (s.164(4)), where a dog licensing scheme is already in place.

Delivery of stray dogs to police or local authority officer

150.—(1) Any person (in this section referred to as "the finder") who takes possession of a stray dog shall forthwith either—
 (a) return the dog to its owner; or
 (b) take the dog—
  (i) to the officer of the local authority for the area in which the dog was found; or
  (ii) to the police station which is nearest to the place where the dog was found;
and shall inform the officer of the local authority or the police officer in charge of the police station, as the case may be, where the dog was found.

(2) Where a dog has been taken under subsection (1) above to the officer of a local authority, then—

(a) if the finder desires to keep the dog, he shall inform the officer of this fact and shall furnish his name and address and the officer shall, having complied with the procedure (if any) prescribed under subsection (6) below, allow the finder to remove the dog;

(b) if the finder does not desire to keep the dog, the officer shall, unless he has reason to believe it is not a stray, treat it as if it had been seized by him under section 149 above.

(3) Where the finder of a dog keeps the dog by virtue of this section he must keep it for not less than one month.

(4) In Scotland a person who keeps a dog by virtue of this section for a period of two months without its being claimed by the person who has right to it shall at the end of that period become the owner of the dog.

(5) If the finder of a dog fails to comply with the requirements of subsection (1) or (3) above he shall be liable on summary conviction to a fine not exceeding level 2 on the standard scale.

(6) The Secretary of State may, by regulations, prescribe the procedure to be followed under subsection (2)(a) above.

(7) In this section "local authority" and "officer" have the same meaning as in section 149 above.

COMMENCEMENT

April 1, 1992: Environmental Protection (Commencement No. 11) Order 1992 (S.I. 1992 No. 266).

GENERAL NOTE

As a second strand of the Government's package of measures on stray dogs (see s.149 above), this section places obligations on the "finders" of stray dogs. A "finder" is someone who takes possession of a stray dog, and the obligation is to return the dog to its owner, or to take it to the relevant officer of the local authority or to the nearest police station. Failure to do so is an offence.

The finder may indicate to the officer of the authority that he desires to keep the dog and may, following a prescribed procedure, be allowed to do so (subs. (2)(a)). Otherwise the dog is treated as a stray seized under s.149.

Consequential amendments are made by Sched. 15, para. 3, in order to harmonise the similar procedures as to delivery of stray dogs to the police in s.4 of the Dogs Act 1906.

Territorial extent

The section does not apply to Northern Ireland (s.164(4)).

Enforcement of orders about collars and tags for dogs

151.—(1) Section 13 of the Animal Health Act 1981 (orders for control, etc. of dogs) shall be amended by the insertion, after subsection (2), of the following subsections—

"(3) An order under subsection (2)(a) above may include provision for the execution and enforcement of the order by the officers of local authorities (and not by the police force for any area).

(4) In subsection (3) above 'local authority' and 'officer' have the same meaning as in section 149 of the Environmental Protection Act 1990."

(2) In section 50(1) of that Act (meaning of "local authority") at the end there shall be inserted the words "and to section 13(3) above."

(3) In section 60(1) of that Act (enforcement), at the end, there shall be inserted the words "but subject, in the case of orders under section 13, to any provision made under subsection (3) of that section."

GENERAL NOTE

This section amends s.13 of the Animal Health Act 1981 to allow orders made under s.13(2)(a) to be executed and enforced by the local authority officers appointed under s.149 of the Act, rather than by the police. The orders in question are for prescribing and regulating the wearing of collars by dogs, while in highways or "places of public resort," giving the name and address of the owner.

Straw and stubble burning

Burning of straw and stubble etc.

152.—(1) The appropriate Minister may by regulations prohibit or restrict the burning of crop residues on agricultural land by persons engaged in agriculture and he may (by the same or other regulations) provide exemptions from any prohibition or restriction so imposed.

(2) Regulations providing an exemption from any prohibition or restriction may make the exemption applicable—
 (a) in all, or only in specified, areas;
 (b) to all, or only to specified, crop residues; or
 (c) in all, or only in specified, circumstances.

(3) Any power to make regulations under this section includes power—
 (a) to make different provision for different areas or circumstances;
 (b) where burning of a crop residue is restricted, to impose requirements to be complied with before or after the burning;
 (c) to create offences subject to the limitation that no offence shall be made punishable otherwise than on summary conviction and the fine prescribed for the offence shall not exceed level 5 on the standard scale; and
 (d) to make such incidental, supplemental and transitional provision as the appropriate Minister consider appropriate.

(4) Where it appears to the appropriate Minister appropriate to do so in consequence of any regulations made under the foregoing provisions of this section, the appropriate Minister may, by order, repeal any byelaws of local authorities dealing with the burning of crop residues on agricultural land.

(5) In this section—
 "agriculture" and "agricultural land" have, as respects England or as respects Wales, the same meaning as in the Agriculture Act 1947 and, as respects Scotland, the same meaning as in the Agriculture (Scotland) Act 1948;
 "crop residue" means straw or stubble or any other crop residue;
 "the appropriate Minister" means the Minister of Agriculture, Fisheries and Food or the Secretary of State or both of them.

COMMENCEMENT

July 10, 1991: Commencement Order (No. 9) 1991 (S.I. 1991 No. 1577). Under the Crop Residues (Restriction of Burning) (No. 2) Regulations 1991 (S.I. 1991 No. 1590), the Minister with effect from July 12, 1991, restricted the burning of straw from cereal, field beans, linseed, oilseed rape and peas. The regulations also created an offence of burning in contravention of the Regulations.

GENERAL NOTE

This section gives power to make regulations prohibiting or restricting the burning of stubble or other crop residues by farmers. The public nuisance caused by the practice of stubble-burning and the resulting smoke and ash has for some years been a cause of public discontent, and was referred to as a potentially serious problem by the Royal Commission on Environmental Pollution in its Tenth Report, *Tackling Pollution: Experience and Prospects* (Cm. 9149) 1984, paras. 2.7–2.11. The Royal Commission called for immediate legislation banning the practice, to take effect in five years' time, and for greater priority to be given to research and development on alternative uses for straw.

The Government's response to the problem hitherto has been a mixture of urging voluntary restraint by farmers and the use of local authority by-laws. However, the inadequacy of such a regime to prevent major public nuisance and, in some cases, danger to highway users, was becoming increasingly apparent.

Very wide discretion is given to the Secretary of State to frame the controls by reference to different areas and circumstances (subs. (3)). Exemptions may be made applicable to specified areas, crop residues or circumstances. The Government's intention expressed in debates in both Houses, is that such exemptions will be rigidly confined. In the Commons, the Parliamentary Secretary to the Minister of Agriculture, Fisheries and Food said:

"Hon. Members will be interested in the exemptions that we envisage, which are of two sorts. First, exemptions of certain crop residues will be permanent. Secondly, some exemptions will be temporary and apply in particular circumstances.

A candidate for the first sort—this is not yet definitive—would be linseed straw and straw used to protect horticultural crops such as strawberries, carrots and potatoes. Exceptional circumstances might involve a waterlogged field where it is difficult to use normal equipment. We have no intention to exempt heavy land as such, but we are aware of the difficulties trying to follow cereals with oilseed rape crop, especially in very wet or very dry years.

We shall examine the matter carefully, but it will be difficult to monitor and control any general exemption of this sort. We are considering the special circumstances and problems that may demand special provision. I wish to make it clear that fruit pruning, clipping and heather are not crop residues and are not covered by the clause.

The permanent exemptions will permit burning subject only to the regulations that replace the by-law. They will not be subject to any special application or permit, but be under broad general law. They will be specified from the outset. However, the exceptional cases would involve farmers or farmers' organisations applying to the Minister who would introduce a statutory instrument which would determine the area to be exempt. It could be as small as a parish or as large as several counties, depending on circumstances. Details of exemption relating to a specific crop will be set out. The Ministry will publicise applications by press release to the local paper and I give an undertaking that we shall not grant exemptions until a clear opportunity for other interested parties to comment had been given." (SCH, 31st sitting, March 15, 1990, cols. 1288–9.)

Similarly in the Lords, Baroness Trumpington gave the following assurances (*Hansard*, Vol. 520, col. 2311):

"I can assure the noble Lord, Lord McIntosh of Haringey, and this Committee that when we receive applications for exemptions to the ban, where there is evidence of genuine need, we shall take steps to ensure that everyone with an interest is made aware of the position. We have it in mind to issue a press release. This will give organisations such as the National Society for Clean Air and any others an opportunity to make representations, and their views will be considered when Ministers decide whether to grant exemptions. The noble Lord will, I hope, recognise that there will be a degree of urgency, but there will be no secrets in our decision-making.

I can also assure the noble Lord that it is our firm intention only to allow exemptions where there is no practicable alternative method of disposal. Our guiding principle will always be the practicability of alternatives, not their costs."

The intention of the Government is to apply a general prohibition from the 1993 harvest onwards. The Crop Residues (Restrictions on Burning) (No. 2) Regulations 1991 (S.I. 1991 No. 1590) were made under these powers.

On the scheme coming into force, all existing local authority by-laws will have to be repealed under subs. (4). By Sched. 15, para. 21 (when in force), the relevant by-law making power under the Criminal Justice Act 1982, s.43 will be repealed.

Territorial extent
The section does not apply to Northern Ireland (s.164(4)).

Environmental expenditure

Financial assistance for environmental purposes

153.—(1) The Secretary of State may, with the consent of the Treasury, give financial assistance to, or for the purposes of, any of the following—
(a) the United Nations Environment Programme;
(b) the European Environmental Bureau;
(c) the chemicals programme of the Organisation for Economic Co-operation and Development;
(d) the joint inter-Governmental panel on Climate Change of the United Nations Environment Programme and the World Meteorological Organisation;

(e) the International Union for the Conservation of Nature and Natural Resources;
(f) the Convention on International Trade in Endangered Species of Wild Fauna and Flora;
(g) the Convention on Wetlands of International Importance Especially as Waterfowl Habitat;
(h) the Convention on Long-range Transboundary Air Pollution and any protocol to that Convention;
(i) the Convention and Protocol for the Protection of the Ozone Layer;
(j) the Convention on the Conservation of Migratory Species of Wild Animals;
(k) the Groundwork Foundation and Trusts;
(l) the environmental protection technology scheme for research and development in the United Kingdom in relation to such technology;
(m) the programme known as the special grants programme so far as it relates to the protection, improvement or better understanding of the environment of, or of any part of, Great Britain;
[(n) the Royal Society for the Encouragement of Arts, Manufactures and Commerce so far as its activities relate to the protection, improvement or better understanding of the environment;]
[(o) UK 2000 Scotland;]
[(p) the programme known as the Environment Wales programme so far as it relates to the protection, improvement or better understanding of the environment of, or of any part of, Wales;]
[(q) the grant programme known as the Environmental Action Fund;
(r) the programmes or schemes of the United Nations Habitat and Human Settlements Foundation;
(s) the programmes or schemes of the International Federation for Housing and Planning so far as they relate to the protection, improvement or better understanding of the environment;
(t) the programmes or schemes of the INTA.AIVN—International Urban Development Association so far as they relate to the protection, improvement or better understanding of the environment;
(u) the scheme known as the Darwin Initiative for the Survival of Species that provides support for the conservation and sustainable use of biological resources and habitats and for the furtherance of the aims of the Convention on Biological Diversity.]

(2) Financial assistance may be given in respect of particular activities or generally in respect of all or some part of the activities carried on or supported by the recipient.

(3) Financial assistance shall be given in such form and on such terms as the Secretary of State may think fit and, in particular, assistance may be given by making grants (whether or not repayable), loans or guarantees to, or by incurring expenditure, or providing services, staff or equipment for the benefit of, the recipient.

(4) The Secretary of State may, by order, vary subsection (1) above by adding to or deleting from it any description of organisation, scheme, programme or international agreement whose purposes relate to the protection, improvement or better understanding of the environment.

(5) Subject to any Order made after the passing of this Act by virtue of subsection (1)(a) of section 3 of the Northern Ireland Constitution Act 1973, the environmental protection technology scheme for research and development in the United Kingdom in relation to such technology shall not be a transferred matter for the purposes of that Act but shall for the purposes of subsection (2) of that section be treated as specified in Schedule 3 to that Act.

AMENDMENTS
Subsection (1)(n) was added by S.I. 1991 No. 682. Subsection (1)(o) was added by S.I. 1991 No. 1179 (s.118). Subsection (1)(p) was added by S.I. 1992 No. 654. Subsections (1)(q) to (u) were added by S.I. 1993 No. 1062.

COMMENCEMENT
January 1, 1991 (s.164(2)).

GENERAL NOTE
This section expressly authorises the Secretaries of State for the Environment, Wales and Scotland, with Treasury consent, to give financial assistance to a wide range of international environmental programmes and initiatives. Many of the payments are already made under the general authority provided by the annual Appropriation Act, but this practice was criticised by the House of Commons Environment Committee and the DoE undertook to take specified legislative powers at the earliest opportunity.
The list of recipients may be widened or narrowed by orders made under subs. (4). Further detail on research and other initiatives funded by the Government is given throughout the White Paper, *This Common Inheritance* (Cm. 1200, September 25, 1990).

Subs. (5)
This enables the Government's environmental protection technology (EPT) scheme to be treated as a reserved item under the Northern Ireland constitution, thus allowing grants under the scheme to continue to be paid to organisations working in this field in Northern Ireland.

Territorial extent
The section applies to Northern Ireland with the exception of paras. (k) and (m) of subs. (1) (s.164(4)).

The Groundwork Foundation: superannuation

154. Employment with the Groundwork Foundation shall be and shall be deemed always to have been included among the kinds of employment to which a superannuation scheme under section 1 of the Superannuation Act 1972 can apply, and accordingly in Schedule 1 to that Act (in which those kinds of employment are listed) the words "Groundwork Foundation" shall be inserted after the words "Gaming Board for Great Britain."

COMMENCEMENT
January 1, 1991 (s.164(2)).

GENERAL NOTE
This section allows employees of the Groundwork Foundation to remain in the Principal Civil Service Pension Scheme. The Foundation was set up by the Countryside Commission in 1985 with staff seconded from the Commission. On April 1, 1988 the Foundation's Staff became employees of the Foundation when the DoE took over the Foundation's core funding. At that time an undertaking was given by the DoE to obtain statutory cover under the PCSP Scheme as soon as possible.

Territorial extent
The section does not apply to Northern Ireland (s.164(4)).

Remuneration of chairman of Inland Waterways Amenity Advisory Council

155. In section 110 of the Transport Act 1968 (Inland Waterways Amenity Advisory Council) at the end there shall be inserted—
"(7) The Secretary of State may, with the consent of the Treasury, pay the chairman of the Council out of money provided by Parliament

such remuneration as the Secretary of State may determine; and where the chairman is in receipt of such remuneration he shall not be paid any allowance under subsection (6) of this section in respect of loss of remunerative time."

COMMENCEMENT
January 1, 1991 (s.164(2)).

GENERAL NOTE
The section allows the Secretary of State, with Treasury consent, to remunerate the Chairman of the Inland Waterways Amenity Advisory Council. The Council was constituted by s.110 of the Transport Act 1968, which provided for remuneration of expenses by the British Waterways Board, but not for allowances in respect of loss of remunerative time.

Territorial extent
The section does not apply to Northern Ireland (s.164(4)).

PART IX

GENERAL

Power to give effect to Community and other international obligations etc.

156.—(1) The Secretary of State may by regulations provide that the provisions to which this section applies shall have effect with such modifications as may be prescribed for the purpose of enabling Her Majesty's Government in the United Kingdom—
  (a) to give effect to any Community obligation or exercise any related right; or
  (b) to give effect to any obligation or exercise any related right under any international agreement to which the United Kingdom is for the time being a party.
(2) This section applies to the following provisions of this Act—
  (a) Part I;
  (b) Part II;
  (c) Part VI; and
  (d) in Part VIII, sections 140, 141 or 142;
and the provisions of the Radioactive Substances Act 1960.
(3) In this section—
  "modifications" includes additions, alterations and omissions;
  "prescribed" means prescribed in regulations under this section; and
  "related right," in relation to an obligation, includes any derogation or other right to make more onerous provisions available in respect of that obligation.
(4) This section, in its application to Northern Ireland, has effect subject to the following modification, that is to say—
  (a) in its application in relation to Part VI and sections 140, 141, and 142, the reference to Her Majesty's Government in the United Kingdom includes a reference to Her Majesty's Government in Northern Ireland; and
  (b) in its application in relation to the Radioactive Substances Act 1960, the reference to the Secretary of State shall be construed as a reference to the Department of the Environment for Northern Ireland and the reference to Her Majesty's Government in the United Kingdom shall be construed as a reference to Her Majesty's Government in Northern Ireland;

and regulations under it made by that Department shall be a statutory rule for the purposes of the Statutory Rules (Northern Ireland) Order 1979 and shall be subject to negative resolution within the meaning of section 41(6) of the Interpretation Act (Northern Ireland) 1954.

COMMENCEMENT
April 1, 1991: Commencement Order (No. 7) 1991 (S.I. 1991 No. 1042).

GENERAL NOTE
This section gives a general power to the Secretary of State to amend various parts of the Act and the whole of the Radioactive Substances Act 1960 by regulations in order (a) to give effect to any European Community obligation or exercise any "related right"; and (b) to give effect to any obligation under an international agreement to which the UK is a party, or to exercise any "related right."

In each case, by subs. (3), "related right" includes making any derogation from E.C. or international obligations or the exercise of any right to make more onerous provisions at domestic level.

Territorial extent
The section applies to Northern Ireland with modifications (subs. (4)) in so far as it relates to Pt. VI, ss.140–142 and the Radioactive Substances Act 1960.

Offences by bodies corporate

157.—(1) Where an offence under any provision of this Act committed by a body corporate is proved to have been committed with the consent or connivance of, or to have been attributable to any neglect on the part of, any director, manager, secretary or other similar officer of the body corporate or a person who was purporting to act in any such capacity, he as well as the body corporate shall be guilty of that offence and shall be liable to be proceeded against and punished accordingly.

(2) Where the affairs of a body corporate are managed by its members, subsection (1) above shall apply in relation to the acts or defaults of a member in connection with his functions of management as if he were a director of the body corporate.

COMMENCEMENT
January 1, 1991 (s.164(2)).

GENERAL NOTE
Consent. "It would seem that where a director consents to the commission of an offence by his company, he is well aware of what is going on and agrees to it" (*Huckerby* v. *Elliott* [1970] All E.R. 189, 194, Ashworth J.).

Connivance. This term implies acquiescence in a course of conduct reasonably likely to lead to the commission of the offence. "Where he [the director] connives at the offence committed by the company he is equally well aware of what is going on but his agreement is tacit, not actively encouraging what happens but letting it continue and saying nothing about it": *Huckerby* v. *Elliott* (*ibid.*). See also Glanville Williams, *Criminal Law: the General Part*, para. 284, describing connivance in the criminal law context as requiring "knowledge (including wilful blindness) plus negligent failure to prevent."

Neglect. This term implies "failure to perform a duty which the person knows or ought to know": *Hughes, Re* [1943] 2 All E.R. 269. A director's duty is not absolute and some act or omission constituting neglect must be shown: *Huckerby* v. *Elliott* (*ibid.*). As to director's duties, see *City Equitable Fire Insurance Co., Re* [1925] Ch. 407 and as to duties of persons responsible for health and safety policy matters see *Armour* v. *Skeen* [1977] I.R.L.R. 310. Duties may in certain circumstances be properly delegated: "a director may delegate, but each case is one of fact and of the circumstances of the case" (*Hirschler* v. *Birch* (1987) 151 J.P. 396, and see *City Equitable Fire Insurance Co., Re* (*ibid.*)).

Director, manager, secretary or other similar officer. See *Armour* v. *Skeen* (*ibid.*) (held to include a senior officer of a Scottish Regional Council).

Or a person purporting to act in any such capacity. This term will cover directors or officers whose appointment is irregular or defective: see, *e.g. Dean* v. *Hiesler* [1942] 2 All E.R. 340.

The case of *R.* v. *Boal* [1992] 3 All E.R. 177, provides some authority on the meaning of the word "manager" in a directors' and officers' liability provision under the Fire Precautions Act 1971 which is phrased in virtually identical terms to s.157 of the EPA. The Court of Appeal held that the intention of the provision was to fix with criminal liability only those who are in a position of real authority and who were responsible for putting proper procedures into place. In this case, the defendant, an assistant general manager of a bookshop who was placed in charge of the shop whilst the general manager was away on a week's holiday, was found not to be a manager for the purposes of this provision. Whether waste regulation authorities, for example, will adopt this line of reasoning when bringing prosecutions against waste disposal site managers is of some doubt and it is not yet clear that all magistrates' courts will approach the question of who is a manager using the reasoning in *R.* v. *Boal.*

Territorial extent
The section does not extend to Northern Ireland (s.164(4)).

Offences under Parts I, II, IV, VI, etc. due to fault of others

158. Where the commission by any person of an offence under Part I, II, IV, or VI, or section 140, 141 or 142 above is due to the act or default of some other person, that other person may be charged with and convicted of the offence by virtue of this section whether or not proceedings for the offence are taken against the first-mentioned person.

COMMENCEMENT
April 1, 1991: Commencement Order (No. 7) 1991 (S.I. 1991 No. 1042).

GENERAL NOTE
This section allows persons whose acts or defaults result in the commission of certain offences by other persons to be charged and convicted of the offence, whether or not proceedings are taken against the person committing the offence. The section could be used, for example, to prosecute employees whose acts cause offences on the part of their employer or a waste producer who deliberately misdescribed waste so as to cause a waste contractor to commit an offence under Pt. II of the Act.

Territorial extent
The section applies to Northern Ireland in so far as it relates to Pt. VI and ss.140–142 (s.164(4)).

Application to Crown

159.—(1) Subject to the provisions of this section, the provisions of this Act and of regulations and orders made under it shall bind the Crown.

(2) No contravention by the Crown of any provision of this Act or of any regulations or order made under it shall make the Crown criminally liable; but the High Court or, in Scotland, the Court of Session may, on the application of any public or local authority charged with enforcing that provision, declare unlawful any act or omission of the Crown which constitutes such a contravention.

(3) Notwithstanding anything in subsection (2) above, the provisions of this Act and of regulations and orders made under it shall apply to persons in the public service of the Crown as they apply to other persons.

(4) If the Secretary of State certifies that it appears to him, as respects any Crown premises and any powers of entry exercisable in relation to them specified in the certificate that it is requisite or expedient that, in the interests of national security, the powers should not be exercisable in relation to the premises, those powers shall not be exercisable in relation to those premises; and in this subsection "Crown premises" means premises held or used by or on behalf of the Crown.

(5) Nothing in this section shall be taken as in any way affecting Her Majesty in her private capacity; and this subsection shall be construed as if

section 38(3) of the Crown Proceedings Act 1947 (interpretation of references in that Act to Her Majesty in her private capacity) were contained in this Act.

(6) References in this section to regulations or orders are references to regulations or orders made by statutory instrument.

(7) For the purposes of this section in its application to Part II and Part IV the authority charged with enforcing the provisions of those Parts in its area is—

(a) in the case of Part II, any waste regulation authority, and
(b) in the case of Part IV, any principal litter authority.

COMMENCEMENT
January 1, 1991: S.I. 1990 No. 2635.

GENERAL NOTE
Crown premises, notably hospital incinerators, have been subject to much criticism in the past for failure to observe proper environmental standards whilst subject to the doctrine of Crown immunity. This important section provides that the Act and all regulations made under it bind the Crown. The only exception is that powers of entry may be removed in relation to Crown premises in the interests of national security by subs. (4).

Also, the Crown cannot be criminally liable under the legislation. Instead, subs. (2) provides a means by which the relevant enforcing authority may obtain a declaration that the Crown is in contravention of the Act from the High Court or Court of Session.

Territorial extent
The section does not extend to Northern Ireland (s.164(4)).

Service of notices

160.—(1) Any notice required or authorised by or under this Act to be served on or given to an inspector may be served or given by delivering it to him or by leaving it at, or sending it by post to, his office.

(2) Any such notice required or authorised to be served on or given to a person other than an inspector may be served or given by delivering it to him, or by leaving it at his proper address, or by sending it by post to him at that address.

(3) Any such notice may—
(a) in the case of a body corporate, be served on or given to the secretary or clerk of that body;
(b) in the case of a partnership, be served on or given to a partner or a person having the control or management of the partnership business.

(4) For the purposes of this section and of section 7 of the Interpretation Act 1978 (service of documents by post) in its application to this section, the proper address of any person on or to whom any such notice is to be served or given shall be his last known address, except that—
(a) in the case of a body corporate or their secretary or clerk, it shall be the address of the registered or principal office of that body;
(b) in the case of a partnership or person having the control or the management of the partnership business, it shall be the principal office of the partnership;

and for the purposes of this subsection the principal office of a company registered outside the United Kingdom or of a partnership carrying on business outside the United Kingdom shall be their principal office within the United Kingdom.

(5) If the person to be served with or given any such notice has specified an address in the United Kingdom other than his proper address within the meaning of subsection (4) above as the one at which he or someone on his behalf will accept notices of the same description as that notice, that address

shall also be treated for the purposes of this section and section 7 of the Interpretation Act 1978 as his proper address.

(6) The preceding provisions of this section shall apply to the sending or giving of a document as they apply to the giving of a notice.

COMMENCEMENT
January 1, 1991 (s.164(2)).

GENERAL NOTE
Territorial extent. This section does not apply to Northern Ireland (s.164(4)).

Regulations, orders and directions

161.—(1) Any power of the Secretary of State or the Minister of Agriculture, Fisheries and Food under this Act to make regulations or orders shall be exercisable by statutory instrument; but this subsection does not apply to orders under section 72 above or paragraph 4 of Schedule 3.

(2) A statutory instrument containing regulations under this Act shall be subject to annulment in pursuance of a resolution of either House of Parliament.

(3) Except in the cases specified in subsection (4) below, a statutory instrument containing an order under this Act shall be subject to annulment in pursuance of a resolution of either House of Parliament.

(4) Subsection (3) above does not apply to an order under section 130(4), 131(3) or 138(2) above or section 164(3) below.

(5) Any power conferred by this Act to give a direction shall include power to vary or revoke the direction.

(6) Any direction given under this Act shall be in writing.

COMMENCEMENT
January 1, 1991 (s.164(2)).

GENERAL NOTE
Territorial extent: The section does not apply to Northern Ireland (s.164(4)).

Consequential and minor amendments and repeals

162.—(1) The enactments specified in Schedule 15 to this Act shall have effect subject to the amendments specified in that Schedule.

(2) The enactments specified in Schedule 16 are hereby repealed subject to section 77 above, Schedule 11 to this Act and any provision made by way of a note in Schedule 16.

(3) The repeal of section 124 of the Civic Government (Scotland) Act 1982 shall not affect a compulsory purchase order made for the purposes of that section under the Local Government (Scotland) Act 1973 before the coming into force of the repeal and such compulsory purchase order may be proceeded with and shall have effect as if the said section 124 had not been repealed.

(4) The Secretary of State may by order repeal or amend any provision of any local Act passed before this Act (including an Act confirming a provisional order) or of any order or other instrument made under an Act so passed if it appears to him that the provisions is inconsistent with, or has become unnecessary or requires alteration in consequence of, any provision of this Act or corresponds to any provision repealed by this Act.

(5) Any regulations made under section 100 of the Control of Pollution Act 1974 shall have effect after the repeal of that section by subsection (2) above as if made under section 140 of this Act.

COMMENCEMENT
Subsection (1) (partially) by s.164(2). Subsection (1) (partially) on January 14, 1991. S.I.

1991 No. 96. Subsection (1) (partially) on April 1, 1991: S.I. 1991 No. 1042. Subsection (1) (partially) on May 31, 1991: S.I. 1991 No. 1319. Subsection (1) (partially) on April 1, 1992: S.I. 1991 No. 2829. Subsection (1) (partially) on April 1, 1992: S.I. 1992 No. 266. Subsection (1) (partially) on February 18, 1993: S.I. 1993 No. 274. Subsection (2) (partially) by s.164(2). Subsection (2) (partially) on January 1, 1991: S.I. 1990 No. 2565. Subsection (2) (partially) on January 1, 1991: S.I. 1990 No. 2635. Subsection (2) (partially) on April 1, 1991: S.I. 1991 No. 685. Subsection (2) (partially) on April 1, 1991: S.I. 1991 No. 1042. Subsection (2) (partially) on May 31, 1991: S.I. 1991 No. 1319. Subsection (2) (partially) on January 1, 1992: S.I. 1991 No. 2829. Subsection (2) (partially) on April 1, 1992: S.I. 1991 No. 2829. Subsection (2) (partially) on April 1, 1992: S.I. 1992 No. 266. Subsection (2) (partially) on February 18 and May 1, 1993: S.I. 1993 No. 274. Subsection (3) on April 1, 1992: S.I. 1992 No. 266. Subsection (4): not yet in force. Subsection (5) by s.164(2).

GENERAL NOTE

Section 162 introduces Sched. 15, which makes amendments to various Acts. Many of these amendments are of a consequential nature only. Others are intended to clarify the relationship between controls introduced by the Act and other systems of control, for example:
  (a) the exclusion of the Alkali, & C. Works Regulation Act 1906 in relation to processes prescribed under Pt. I of the 1990 Act (para. 2);
  (b) the exclusion of provisions of the Clean Air Acts 1956 and 1968 in relation to prescribed processes (paras. 6 and 12);
  (c) the exclusion of s.5 of the Health and Safety at Work, etc. Act 1974 (general duty in relation to harmful emissions into the air from prescribed premises) in relation to prescribed processes (para. 14);
  (d) the exclusion of control by the Secretary of State over trade effluent discharges to sewers under Pt. IV, Chapter III of the Water Industry Act 1991 in relation to trade effluent produced in prescribed processes designated for central control (para. 28); and
  (e) the exclusion of pollution controls under Pt. III of the Water Resources Act 1991 in relation to discharges from authorised prescribed processes designated for central control (para. 30).

One important substantive amendment (para. 10) relates to the provisions of the Transport Act 1968 on goods vehicle operators' licences. A further ground for suspension or revocation of such licences under s.69 is given, namely conviction of the holder of the licence or of a servant or agent of his (apparently, whether or not acting in the course of employment) of a range of waste-related offences. These include the illegal deposit of waste under the Act or the Control of Pollution Act 1974 and the transport of controlled waste with a view to profit without registration under the Control of Pollution (Amendment) Act 1989. This represents a useful extension of powers for use against persons fly-tipping or dealing with wastes in a similarly irresponsible manner.

Territorial extent
The section does not extend to Northern Ireland (s.164(4)).

Financial provisions

163.—(1) There shall be paid out of money provided by Parliament—
(a) any administrative or other expenses incurred by any Minister of the Crown in consequence of the provisions of this Act; and
(b) any increase attributable to this Act in the sums payable out of money so provided under any other Act.

(2) Any fees or other sums received by any Minister of the Crown by virtue of any provisions of this Act shall be paid into the Consolidated Fund.

COMMENCEMENT
January 1, 1991, (s.164(2)).

GENERAL NOTE
Territorial extent. The section does not extend to Northern Ireland (s.164(4)).

Short title, commencement and extent

164.—(1) This Act may be cited as the Environmental Protection Act 1990.

(2) The following provisions of the Act shall come into force at the end of the period of two months beginning with the day on which it is passed, namely—
    sections 79 to 85;
    section 97;
    section 99;
    section 105 in so far as it relates to paragraphs 7, 13, 14 and 15 of Schedule 5;
    section 140;
    section 141;
    section 142;
    section 145;
    section 146;
    section 148;
    section 153;
    section 154;
    section 155;
    section 157;
    section 160;
    section 161;
    section 162(1) in so far as it relates to paragraphs 4, 5, 7, 8, 9, 18, 22, 24 and 31(4)(b) of Schedule 15; but, in the case of paragraph 22, in so far only as that paragraph inserts a paragraph (m) into section 7(4) of the Act of 1984;
    section 162(2) in so far as it relates to Part III of Schedule 16 and, in Part IX of that Schedule, the repeal of section 100 of the Control of Pollution Act 1974;
    section 162(5);
    section 163.

(3) The remainder of this Act (except this section) shall come into force on such day as the Secretary of State may by order appoint and different days may be appointed for different provisions or different purposes.

(4) Only the following provisions of this Act (together with this section) extend to Northern Ireland, namely—
    section 3(5) to (8);
    section 62(2)(e) in so far as it relates to importation;
    Part V;
    Part VI in so far as it relates to importation and, without that restriction, section 127(2) in so far as it relates to the continental shelf;
    section 140 in so far as it relates to importation;
    section 141;
    section 142 in so far as it relates to importation;
    section 146;
    section 147;
    section 148;
    section 153 except subsection (1)(k) and (m);
    section 156 in so far as it relates to Part VI and sections 140, 141 and 142 in so far as they extend to Northern Ireland and in so far as it relates to the Radioactive Substances Act 1960;
    section 158 in so far as it relates to Part VI and sections 140, 141 and 142 in so far as they extend to Northern Ireland.

(5) Where any enactment amended or repealed by this Act extends to any part of the United Kingdom, the amendment or repeal extends to that part, subject, however, to any express provision in Schedule 15 or 16.

GENERAL NOTE
    Apart from the listed provisions in subs. (2) which come into force after two months, the remainder of the Act comes into force on an appointed day or appointed days.

Where the Government has given an indication of the proposed timetable for implementation, this is referred to in the notes to the relevant Part or section. The information is also given in composite form in the General Note to the Act.

Section 6

SCHEDULE 1

AUTHORISATION FOR PROCESSES: SUPPLEMENTARY PROVISIONS

PART I

GRANT OF AUTHORISATIONS

Applications for authorisations

1.—(1) An application to the enforcing authority for an authorisation must contain such information, and be made in such manner, as may be prescribed in regulations made by the Secretary of State.

(2) An application to the enforcing authority for an authorisation must also, unless regulations made by the Secretary of State exempt applications of that class, be advertised in such manner as may be prescribed in regulations so made.

(3) The enforcing authority may, by notice in writing to the applicant, require him to furnish such further information specified in the notice, within the period so specified, as the authority may require for the purpose of determining the application.

(4) If a person fails to furnish any information required under sub-paragraph (3) above within the period specified thereunder the enforcing authority may refuse to proceed with the application.

(5) Regulations under this paragraph may make different provision for different classes of applications.

Determination of applications

2.—(1) Subject to sub-paragraph (2) below, the enforcing authority shall give notice of any application for an authorisation, enclosing a copy of the application, to the persons who are prescribed or directed to be consulted under this paragraph and shall do so within the specified period for notification.

(2) The Secretary of State may, by regulations, exempt any class of application from the requirements of this paragraph or exclude any class of information contained in applications for authorisations from those requirements, in all cases or as respects specified classes only of persons to be consulted.

(3) Any representations made by the persons so consulted within the period allowed shall be considered by the enforcing authority in determining the application.

(4) For the purposes of sub-paragraph (1) above—
   (a) persons are prescribed to be consulted on any description of application for an authorisation if they are persons specified for the purposes of applications of that description in regulations made by the Secretary of State;
   (b) persons are directed to be consulted on any particular application if the Secretary of State specifies them in a direction given to the enforcing authority;
and the "specified period for notification" is the period specified in the regulations or in the direction.

(5) Any representations made by any other persons within the period allowed shall also be considered by the enforcing authority in determining the application.

(6) Subject to sub-paragraph (7) below, the period allowed for making representation is—
   (a) in the case of persons prescribed or directed to be consulted, the period of 28 days beginning with the date on which notice of the application was given under sub-paragraph (1) above, and
   (b) in the case of other persons, the period of 28 days beginning with the date on which the making of the application was advertised in pursuance of paragraph 1(2) above.

(7) The Secretary of State may, by order, substitute for the period for the time being specified in sub-paragraph (6)(a) or (b) above, such other period as he considers appropriate.

3.—(1) The Secretary of State may give directions to the enforcing authority requiring that any particular application or any class of applications for an authorisation shall be transmitted to him for determination pending a further direction under sub-paragraph (5) below.

(2) The enforcing authority shall inform the applicant of the fact that his application is being transmitted to the Secretary of State.

(3) Where an application for an authorisation is referred to him under sub-paragraph (1) above the Secretary of State may—

(a) cause a local inquiry to be held in relation to the application; or
(b) afford the applicant and the authority concerned an opportunity of appearing before and being heard by a person appointed by the Secretary of State;

and he shall exercise one of the powers under this sub-paragraph in any case where, in the manner prescribed by regulations made by the Secretary of State, a request is made to be heard with respect to the application by the applicant or the local enforcing authority concerned.

(4) Subsections (2) to (5) of section 250 of the Local Government Act 1972 (supplementary provisions about local inquiries under that section) or, in relation to Scotland, subsections (2) to (8) of section 210 of the Local Government (Scotland) Act 1973 (which make similar provision) shall, without prejudice to the generality of subsection (1) of either of those sections, apply to inquiries in pursuance of sub-paragraph (3) above as they apply to inquiries in pursuance of either of those sections and, in relation to England and Wales, as if the reference to a local authority in subsection (4) of the said section 250 included a reference to the enforcing authority.

(5) The Secretary of State shall, on determining any application transferred to him under this paragraph, give to the enforcing authority such a direction as he thinks fit as to whether it is to grant the application and, if so, as to the conditions that are to be attached to the authorisation.

4. The Secretary of State may give the enforcing authority a direction with respect to any particular application or any class of applications for an authorisation requiring the authority not to determine or not to proceed with the application or applications of that class until the expiry of any such period as may be specified in the direction, or until directed by the Secretary of State that they may do so, as the case may be.

5.—(1) Except in a case where an application has been referred to the Secretary of State under paragraph 3 above and subject to sub-paragraphs (3) below, the enforcing authority shall determine an application for an authorisation within the period of four months beginning with the day on which it received the application or within such longer period as may be agreed with the applicant.

(2) If the enforcing authority fails to determine an application for an authorisation within the period allowed by or under this paragraph the application shall, if the applicant notifies the authority in writing that he treats the failure as such, be deemed to have been refused at the end of that period.

(3) The Secretary of State may, by order, substitute for the period for the time being specified in sub-paragraph (1) above such other period as he considers appropriate and different periods may be substituted for different classes of application.

Part II

Variation of Authorisation

Variations by the enforcing authority

6.—(1) The requirements of this paragraph apply where an enforcing authority has decided to vary an authorisation under section 10 and is of the opinion that any action to be taken by the holder of the authorisation in consequence of the variation will involve a substantial change in the manner in which the process is being carried on.

(2) Subject to sub-paragraph (3) below, the enforcing authority shall give notice of the action to be taken by the holder of the authorisation to the persons who are prescribed or directed to be consulted under this paragraph and shall do so within the specified period for notification; and the holder shall advertise the action in the manner prescribed in regulations made by the Secretary of State.

(3) The Secretary of State may, by regulations, exempt any class of variation from all or any of the requirements of this paragraph or exclude any class of information relating to action to be taken by holders of authorisations from all or any of those requirements, in all cases or as respects specified classes only of persons to be consulted.

(4) Any representations made by the persons so consulted within the period allowed shall be considered by the enforcing authority in taking its decision.

(5) For the purposes of sub-paragraph (2) above—
(a) persons are prescribed to be consulted on any description of variation if they are persons specified for the purposes of variations of that description in regulations made by the Secretary of State;
(b) persons are directed to be consulted on any particular variation if the Secretary of State specifies them in a direction given to the enforcing authority;

and the "specified period for notification" is the period specified in the regulations or in the direction.

(6) Any representations made by any other persons within the period allowed shall also be considered by the enforcing authority in taking its decision.

(7) Subject to sub-paragraphs (8) below, the period allowed for making representations is—
  (a) in the case of persons prescribed or directed to be consulted, the period of 28 days beginning with the date on which notice was given under sub-paragraph (2) above, and
  (b) in the case of other persons, the period of 28 days beginning with the date of the advertisement under sub-paragraph (2) above.

(8) The Secretary of State may, by order, substitute for the period for the time being specified in sub-paragraph (7)(a) or (b) above, such other period as he considers appropriate.

Applications for variation

7.—(1) The requirements of this paragraph apply where an application is made to an enforcing authority under section 11(4) for the variation of an authorisation.

(2) Subject to sub-paragraph (3) below, the enforcing authority shall give notice of any such application for a variation of an authorisation, enclosing a copy of the application, to the persons who are prescribed or directed to be consulted under this paragraph and shall do so within the specified period for notification; and the holder of the authorisation shall advertise the application in the manner prescribed in regulations made by the Secretary of State.

(3) The Secretary of State may, by regulations, exempt any class of application from all or any of the requirements of this paragraph or exclude any class of information furnished with applications for variations of authorisation from all or any of those requirements, in all cases or as respects specified classes only of persons to be consulted.

(4) Any representations made by the persons so consulted within the period allowed shall be considered by the enforcing authority in determining the application.

(5) For the purposes of sub-paragraph (2) above—
  (a) persons are prescribed to be consulted on any description of application for a variation if they are persons specified for the purposes of applications of that description in regulations made by the Secretary of State;
  (b) persons are directed to be consulted on any particular application if the Secretary of State specifies them in a direction given to the enforcing authority;
and the "specified period for notification" is the period specified in the regulations or in the direction.

(6) Any representation made by any other persons within the period allowed shall also be considered by the enforcing authority in determining the application.

(7) Subject to sub-paragraph (8) below, the period allowed for making representations is—
  (a) in the case of persons prescribed or directed to be consulted, the period of 28 days beginning with the date on which notice of the application was given under sub-paragraph (2) above; and
  (b) in the case of other persons, the period of 28 days beginning with the date on which the making of the application was advertised in pursuance of sub-paragraph (2) above.

(8) The Secretary of State may, by order, substitute for the period for the time being specified in sub-paragraph (7)(a) or (b) above, such other period as he considers appropriate.

Section 32   SCHEDULE 2

WASTE DISPOSAL AUTHORITIES AND COMPANIES

PART I

TRANSITION TO COMPANIES

Preliminary

1. In this Part of this Schedule—
  "authority" means an existing disposal authority as defined in section 32(1);
  "company" means a waste disposal contractor formed under the Companies Act 1985 by a waste disposal authority as mentioned in section 30(5);
  "direction" means a direction under section 32(2);
  "joint company" means a company in which more than one authority holds securities;
  "securities," in relation to a company included shares, debentures, bonds or other securities of the company, whether or not constituting a charge on the assets of the company; and
  "the vesting date" means the date on which property, rights and liabilities vest in a company by virtue of a transfer scheme under paragraph 6 below.

Notice of direction

2.—(1) The Secretary of State, before giving any directions to any authority or constituent authority, shall give notice of his intention to do so to that authority.

(2) A notice under this paragraph shall give a general indication of the provisions to be included in the direction, indicating in particular whether the proposed direction will require the formation of one or more than one company and the authority or authorities who are to form or control the company or companies and whether any existing disposal authority will be abolished.

(3) A notice under this paragraph shall state that the authority to whom it is given is entitled, within a period specified in the notice, to make to the Secretary of State applications or representations with respect to the proposed direction under paragraph 3 below.

Applications for exemption from and representations about directions

3.—(1) An authority which has been given notice under paragraph 2 above of a proposed direction may, within the period specified in the notice, make to the Secretary of State either an application under sub-paragraph (2) below or representations under sub-paragraph (3) below.

(2) An authority may, under this sub-paragraph, apply to the Secretary of State requesting him not to make a direction in its case on the ground that the authority falls within any of paragraphs (a), (b), (c) or (d) of section 32(3).

(3) An authority may, under this sub-paragraph, make representations to the Secretary of State requesting him to make, in the direction, other provision than that proposed in the notice.

(4) It shall be the duty of the Secretary of State to consider any application duly made under sub-paragraph (2) above and to notify the authority of his decision.

(5) It shall be the duty of the Secretary of State to consider any representations duly made under sub-paragraph (3) above before he gives a direction.

Directions

4.—(1) A direction may require the authority or authorities to whom it is given to form or participate in forming one or more than one company or to form or participate in forming one or more than one joint company and it shall specify the date before which the company or companies is or are to be formed.

(2) Where a direction is to require a joint company to be formed the direction may be given to such of the authorities as the Secretary of State considers appropriate (the "representative authority").

(3) Where a direction is given to an authority as the representative authority it shall be the duty of that representative authority to consult the other authorities concerned before forming a company in accordance with the direction.

(4) The Secretary of State may exercise his powers to vary or revoke a direction and give a further direction at any time before the vesting date, whether before or after a company has been formed in accordance with the direction or previous direction, as the case may be.

Formation and status of companies

5.—(1) An authority which has been directed to form a company shall do so by forming it under the Companies Act 1985 as a company which—
(a) is limited by shares, and
(b) is a wholly-owned subsidiary of the authority or authorities forming it;
and it shall do so before such date as the Secretary of State specifies in the direction.

(2) The authority shall so exercise its control of the company as to secure that, at some time before the vesting date, the conditions specified in section 68(6)(a) to (h) of the Local Government and Housing Act 1989 (conditions for "arm's length companies") apply in relation to the company and shall, at some time before the vesting date, resolve that the company shall be an arm's length company for the purposes of Part V of that Act.

(3) In this paragraph "wholly-owned subsidiary", in relation to a company and an authority, is to be construed in accordance with section 736 of the Companies Act 1985.

Transfer schemes

6.—(1) Where an authority has formed a company or companies in pursuance of a direction, the authority shall, before such date as the Secretary of State may specify in a direction given to the authority under this sub-paragraph, submit to the Secretary of State a scheme providing for the transfer to the company or companies of any property, rights or liabilities of that or that and any other authority, or of any subsidiary of its or theirs, which appear to be appropriate to transfer as representing the relevant part of the undertaking of that authority or of that authority and the other authorities.

(2) In preparing a scheme in pursuance of sub-paragraph (1) above the authority shall take into account any advice given by the Secretary of State as to the provisions he regards as appropriate for inclusion in the scheme (and in particular any advice as to the description of property, rights and liabilities which it is in his view appropriate to transfer to the company).

(3) A scheme under this paragraph shall not come into force until it is has been approved by the Secretary of State and the date on which it is to come into force shall be such date as the Secretary of State may, either in giving his approval or subsequently, specify in writing to the authority; and the Secretary of State may approve a scheme either without modifications or with such modifications as he thinks fit after consulting the authority who submitted the scheme.

(4) If it appears to the Secretary of State that a scheme submitted under sub-paragraph (1) above does not accord with any advice given by him, he may do one or other of the following things, as he thinks fit, namely—
  (a) approve the scheme under sub-paragraph (3) above with modifications; or
  (b) after consulting the authority who submitted the scheme, substitute for it a scheme of his own, to come into force on such date as may be specified in the scheme.

(5) In the case of a scheme for the transfer to a company or joint company of the relevant part of the undertaking of two or more authorities, the representative authority shall consult the other authority or authorities before submitting the scheme under sub-paragraph (1) above; and the Secretary of State shall not approve the scheme (whether with or without modifications), or substitute a scheme of his own unless—
  (a) he has given that other authority or (as the case may be) those other authorities an opportunity of making, within such time as he may allow for the purpose, written representations with respect to the scheme; and
  (b) he has considered any such representations made to him within that time.

(6) The Secretary of State shall not specify the date on which the scheme is to come into force without consulting the authority which submitted the scheme and, where the scheme was submitted by a representative authority, the other authorities concerned.

(7) On the coming into force of a scheme under this paragraph the property, rights and liabilities affected by the scheme shall be transferred and vest in accordance with the scheme.

(8) As a consequence of the vesting by virtue of the scheme of property, rights and liabilities of an authority in a company, that company shall issue to the authority such securities of the company as are specified in the transfer scheme.

Transfer schemes: opportunity provisions

7. A scheme under paragraph 6 above may define the property, rights and liabilities to be transferred by the scheme—
  (a) by specifying the property, rights and liabilities in question; or
  (b) by referring to all the property, rights and liabilities comprised in any specified part of the undertaking or undertakings to be transferred; or
  (c) partly in one way and partly in the other;
and may make such supplemental, incidental and consequential provision as the authority making the scheme considers appropriate.

8.—(1) The provisions of this paragraph apply to the transfer to a company of the property, rights and liabilities representing the relevant part of an authority's undertakings.

(2) Any property, rights or liabilities held or subsisting partly for the purpose of the relevant part of the authority's undertaking and partly for the purpose of another part shall, where the nature of the property, rights or liabilities permits, be divided or apportioned between the authority and the company in such proportions as may be appropriate; and where any estate or interest in land falls to be so divided, any rent payable under a lease in respect of that estate or interest, and any rent charged on that estate or interest, shall be correspondingly apportioned or divided so that the one part is payable in respect of, or charged on, only one part of the estate or interest and the other part is payable in respect of, or charged on, only the other part of the estate or interest.

(3) Any property, rights or liabilities held or subsisting as mentioned in sub-paragraph (2) above the nature of which does not permit their division or apportionment as so mentioned shall be transferred to the company or retained by the authority according to which of them appear at the vesting date likely to make use of the property, or, as the case may be, to be affected by the right or liability, to the greater extent, subject to such arrangements for the protection of the other of them as may be agreed between them.

(4) It shall be the duty of the authority and the company, before or after the vesting date, so far as practicable to enter into such written agreements, and to execute such other instruments

as are necessary or expedient to identify or define the property, rights and liabilities transferred to the company or retained by the authority and as will—
  (a) afford to the authority and the company as against one another such rights and safeguards as they may require for the proper discharge of the authority's functions and the proper carrying on of the company's undertaking; and
  (b) make, as from such date (not being earlier than the vesting date) as may be specified in that agreement or instrument, such clarifications and modifications of the division of the authority's undertaking as will best serve the proper discharge of the authority's functions and the proper carrying on of the company's undertaking.
  (5) Any such agreement shall provide so far as it is expedient—
  (a) for the granting of leases and for the creation of other liabilities and rights over land whether amounting in law to interests in land or not, and whether involving the surrender of any existing interest or the creation of a new interest or not;
  (b) for the granting of indemnities in connection with the severance of leases and other matters;
  (c) for responsibility for complying with any statutory requirements as respects matters to be registered and any licences, authorisations or permissions which need to be obtained.
  (6) If the authority or the company represents to the Secretary of State, or if it appears to him without such a representation, that it is unlikely in the case of any matter on which agreement is required under sub-paragraph (4) above that such agreement will be reached, the Secretary of State may, whether before or after the vesting date, give a direction determining the manner in which the property, rights or liabilities in question are to be divided between the authority and the company, and may include in the direction any provision which might have been included in an agreement under that sub-paragraph; and any property, rights or liabilities required by the direction to be transferred to the company shall be regarded as having been transferred to, and by virtue of the transfer scheme vested in, the company accordingly.

Tax and company provisions

9.—(1) Any shares in a company which are issued as a consequence of the vesting by a transfer scheme of property, rights and liabilities in the company shall—
  (a) be issued as fully paid; and
  (b) treated for the purposes of the application of the Companies Act 1985 in relation to that company as if they had been paid up by virtue of the payment to the company of their nominal value in cash.
  (2) For the purposes of Chapter I of Part II of the Capital Allowances Act 1990 (capital allowance in respect of machinery and plant) property which is vested in a company by virtue of a transfer scheme shall be treated as if—
  (a) it had been acquired by the company on the transfer date for the purposes for which it is used by the company on and after that date; and
  (b) capital expenditure of an amount equal to the price which the property would have fetched if sold in the open market had been incurred on that date by the company on the acquisition of the property for the purposes mentioned in paragraph (a) above.

Benefit of certain planning permission

10.—(1) This paragraph applies in relation to planning permission deemed to have been granted to the authority under Regulation 4 of the Town and Country Planning General Regulations 1976 (deemed planning permission for development by local authorities) which subsists at the vesting date.
  (2) Any planning permission to which this paragraph applies which authorises the use of land by the authority for the treatment, keeping or disposal of waste shall, on the transfer of the land to the company by the scheme, enure for the benefit of the land.

Right to production of documents of title

11. Where on any transfer by virtue of a transfer scheme the authority is entitled to retain possession of any documents relating to the title to, or to the management of, any land or other property transferred to the company, the authority shall be deemed to have given to the company an acknowledgement in writing of the right of the company to production of that document and to delivery of copies thereof; and, in England and Wales, section 64 of the Law of Property Act 1925 shall have effect accordingly, and on the basis that the acknowledgement did not contain any such expression of contrary intention as is mentioned in that section.

Proof of title by certificate

12.—(1) A joint certificate by or on behalf of the authority and the company that any property specified in the certificate, or any such interest in or right over any such property as may be specified in the certificate, is by virtue of the transfer scheme for the time being vested in the authority or in the company shall be conclusive evidence for all purposes of that fact.

(2) If on the expiration of one month after a request from the authority or the company for the preparation of such a joint certificate the authority and the company have failed to agree on the terms of the certificate, they shall refer the matter to the Secretary of State and issue the certificate in such terms as the Secretary of State may direct.

Construction of agreements

13. Where any of the rights or liabilities transferred by a transfer scheme are rights or liabilities under an agreement to which the authority was a party immediately before the vesting date, whether in writing or not, and whether or not of such a nature that rights and liabilities thereunder could be assigned by the authority, that agreement shall have effect on and after the vesting date as if—
   (a) the company had been a party to the agreement; and
   (b) for any reference (however worded and whether express or implied) to the authority there were substituted a reference, as respects anything falling to be done on or after the vesting date, to the company; and
   (c) any reference (however worded and whether express or implied) to any officer or servant of the authority were, as respects anything falling to be done on or after the vesting date, a reference to such person as the company may appoint or, in default of appointment, to the officer or servant of the company who corresponds as nearly as may be to that officer or servant of the authority; and
   (d) where the agreement refers to property, rights or liabilities which fall to be apportioned or divided between the authority and the company, as if the agreement constituted two separate agreements separately enforceable by and against the authority and the company respectively as regards the part of the property, rights and liabilities retained by the authority or, as the case may be, the part of the property, rights and liabilities vesting in the company and not as regards the other part;

and sub-paragraph (d) above shall apply in particular to the covenants, stipulations and conditions of any lease by or to the authority.

14. Without prejudice to the generality of the provisions of paragraph 13 above, the company and any other persons shall, as from the vesting date, have the same rights, powers and remedies (and in particular the same rights and powers as to the taking or resisting of legal proceedings or the making or resisting of applications to any authority) for ascertaining, perfecting or enforcing any right or liability transferred to and vested in the company by a transfer scheme as he would have had if that right or liability had at all times been a right or liability of the company, and any legal proceedings or applications to any authority pending on the vesting date by or against the authority, in so far as they relate to any property, right or liability transferred to the company by the scheme, or to any agreement to any such property, right or liability, shall be continued by or against the company to the exclusion of the authority.

Third parties affected by vesting provisions

15.—(1) Without prejudice to the provisions of paragraphs 13 and 14 above, any transaction effected between the authority and the company in pursuance of paragraph 8(4) above or of a direction under paragraph 8(6) above shall be binding on all other persons, and notwithstanding that it would, apart from this sub-paragraph, have required the consent or concurrence of any other person.

(2) It shall be the duty of the authority and the company, if they effect any transaction in pursuance of paragraph 8(4) above or of a direction under paragraph 8(6) above, to notify any person who has rights or liabilities which thereby become enforceable as to part by or against the authority and as to part by or against the company; and if such a person applies to the Secretary of State and satisfies him that the transaction operated unfairly against him the Secretary of State may give such directions to the authority and the company as appear to him to be appropriate for varying the transaction.

(3) If in consequence of a transfer by a transfer scheme or of anything done in pursuance of paragraphs 8 to 14 above the rights or liabilities of any person other than the authority which were enforceable against or by the authority become enforceable as to part against or by the authority and as to part against or by the company, and the value of any property or interest of that person is thereby diminished, such compensation as may be just shall be paid to that person by the authority, the company or both, and any dispute as to whether and if so how much compensation is payable, or as to the person by whom it shall be paid, shall be referred to, and determined by, the Lands Tribunal.

Transfer of staff

16.—(1) The Transfer of Undertakings (Protection of Employment) Regulations 1981 shall apply in relation to the relevant employees of an authority in accordance with sub-paragraph (2) below.

(2) For the purposes of the application of those regulations in relation to any of the relevant employees of an authority, the relevant part of the undertaking of the authority shall (whether or not it would otherwise be so regarded) be regarded—
  (a) as a part of an undertaking within the meaning of those regulations which is transferred from the authority to the company on the vesting date, and
  (b) as being so transferred by a transfer to which those regulations apply and which is completed on that date.

(3) Where a person is, in pursuance of section 32, to cease to be employed by an authority and to become employed by a company, none of the agreed redundancy procedures applicable to persons employed by waste disposal authorities shall apply to him.

(4) For the purposes of this paragraph persons are "relevant employees" of an authority if they are to become, in pursuance of section 32, employees of a company to which the relevant part of the undertaking of the authority is to be transferred.

Information for purposes of transfer scheme

17.—(1) The Secretary of State may, by directions, prescribe descriptions of information which are to be furnished for purposes connected with the transfer by authorities to companies of the relevant part of the undertakings of authorities.

(2) It shall be the duty of a waste regulation authority or a waste disposal authority, on being requested to do so by a written notice served on it by the Secretary of State, to furnish to the Secretary of State such information of a description prescribed under sub-paragraph (1) above as may be specified in the notice.

Part II

Provisions Regulating Waste Disposal Authorities and Companies

Terms of waste disposal contracts

18. A waste disposal authority shall, in determining the terms and conditions of any contract which the authority proposes to enter into for the keeping, treatment or disposal of waste, so frame the terms and conditions as to avoid undue discrimination in favour of one description of waste disposal contractor as against other descriptions of waste disposal contractors.

19.—(1) A waste disposal authority shall have regard to the desirability of including in any contract which the authority proposes to enter into for the keeping, treatment or disposal of waste terms or conditions designed to—
  (a) minimise pollution of the environment or harm to human health due to the disposal or treatment of the waste under the contract; and
  (b) maximise the recycling of waste under the contract.

(2) A waste disposal authority shall be entitled—
  (a) to invite tenders for any such contract, and
  (b) to accept or refuse to accept any tender for such a contract and accordingly to enter or not to enter into a contract,

by reference to acceptance or refusal of acceptance by persons tendering for the contract of any terms or conditions included in the draft contract in pursuance of sub-paragraph (1) above.

Procedure for putting waste disposal contracts out to tender

20.—(1) A waste disposal authority which proposes to enter into a contract for the keeping, treatment or disposal of controlled waste shall comply with the following requirements before making the contract and if it does not any contract which is made shall be void.

(2) The authority shall publish, in at least two publications circulating among waste disposal contractors, a notice containing—
  (a) a brief description of the contract work;
  (b) a statement that during a specified period any person may inspect a detailed specification of the contract work free of charge at a specified place and time;
  (c) a statement that during that period any person will be supplied with a copy of the detailed specification on request and on payment of the specified charge;
  (d) a statement that any person who wishes to submit a tender for the contract must notify the authority of his wish within a specified period; and

(e) a statement that the authority intend to invite tenders for the contract, in accordance with sub-paragraph (4) below.

(3) The authority shall—
   (a) ensure that the periods, place and time and the charge specified in the notice are such as are reasonable;
   (b) make the detailed specification available for inspection in accordance with the notice; and
   (c) make copies of the detailed specification available for supply in accordance with the notice.

(4) If any persons notified the authority, in accordance with the notice, of their wish to submit tenders for the contract, the authority shall—
   (a) if more than four persons did so, invite at least four of them to tender for the contract;
   (b) if less than four persons did so, invite each of them to tender for the contract.

(5) In this paragraph—
   "the contract work," in relation to a contract for the keeping, treatment or disposal of waste, means the work comprising the services involved in the keeping, treatment or disposal of the waste under the contract; and
   "specified" means specified in the notice under sub-paragraph (2) above.

21. A waste disposal authority, in taking any of the following decisions, namely—
   (a) who to invite to tender for the contract under paragraph 20(4)(a) above, and
   (b) who to enter into the contract with,
shall disregard the fact that any waste disposal contractor tendering for the contract is, or is not, controlled by the authority.

Variation of waste disposal contracts

22. Where a waste disposal authority has entered into a contract with a waste disposal contractor under the authority's control, paragraph 18 above shall, with the necessary modifications, apply on any proposed variation of the contract during the subsistence of that control in relation to the terms and conditions that would result from the variation as it applies to the original contract.

Avoidance of restrictions on transfer of securities of companies

23.—(1) Subject to sub-paragraph (3) below, any provision to which this paragraph applies shall be void in so far as it operates—
   (a) to preclude the holder of any securities of a waste disposal contractor from disposing of those securities; or
   (b) to require the holder of any such securities to dispose, or offer to dispose, of those securities to particular persons or to particular classes of persons; or
   (c) to preclude the holder of any securities from disposing of those securities except—
      (i) at a particular time or at particular times; or
      (ii) on the fulfilment of particular conditions or in other particular circumstances.

(2) This paragraph applies to any provision relating to any securities of a waste disposal contractor which is controlled by a waste disposal authority or to which the authority has transferred the relevant part of its undertaking and contained in—
   (a) the memorandum or articles of association of the company or any other instrument purporting to regulate to any extent the respective rights and liabilities of the members of the company;
   (b) any resolution of the company; or
   (c) any instrument issued by the company and embodying terms and conditions on which any such securities are to be held by persons for the time being holding them.

(3) No provision shall be void by reason of its operating as mentioned in sub-paragraph (1) above if the Secretary of State has given his approval in writing to that provision.

Section 81   **SCHEDULE 3**

STATUTORY NUISANCES: SUPPLEMENTARY PROVISIONS

Appeals to magistrates' court

1.—(1) This paragraph applies in relation to appeals under section 80(3) against an abatement notice to a magistrates' court.

(2) An appeal to which this paragraph applies shall be by way of complaint for an order and the Magistrates' Courts Act 1980 shall apply to the proceedings.

(3) An appeal against any decision of a magistrates' court in pursuance of an appeal to which this paragraph applies shall lie to the Crown Court at the instance of any party to the proceedings in which the decision was given.

(4) The Secretary of State may make regulations as to appeals to which this paragraph applies and the regulations may in particular—
  (a) include provisions comparable to those in section 290 of the Public Health Act 1936 (appeals against notices requiring the execution of works);
  (b) prescribe the cases in which an abatement notice is, or is not, to be suspended until the appeal is decided, or until some other stage in the proceedings;
  (c) prescribe the cases in which the decision on appeal may in some respects be less favourable to the appellant than the decision from which he is appealing;
  (d) prescribe the cases in which the appellant may claim that an abatement notice should have been served on some other person and prescribe the procedure to be followed in those cases.

Powers of entry etc.

2.—(1) Subject to sub-paragraph (2) below, any person authorised by a local authority may, on production (if so required) of his authority, enter any premises at any reasonable time—
  (a) for the purpose of ascertaining whether or not a statutory nuisance exists; or
  (b) for the purpose of taking any action, or executing any work, authorised or required by Part III.

(2) Admission by virtue of sub-paragraph (1) above to any premises used wholly or mainly for residential purposes shall not except in an emergency be demanded as of right unless 24 hours notice of the intended entry has been given to the occupier.

(3) If it is shown to the satisfaction of a justice of the peace on sworn information in writing—
  (a) that admission to any premises has been refused, or that refusal is apprehended, or that the premises are unoccupied or the occupier is temporarily absent, or that the case is one of emergency, or that an application for admission would defeat the object of the entry; and
  (b) that there is reasonable ground for entry into the premises for the purpose for which entry is required,
the justice may by warrant under his hand authorise the local authority by any authorised person to enter the premises, if need be by force.

(4) An authorised person entering any premises by virtue of sub-paragraph (1) or a warrant under sub-paragraph (3) above may—
  (a) take with him such other person and such equipment as may be necessary;
  (b) carry out such inspections, measurements and tests as he considers necessary for the discharge of any of the local authority's functions under Part III; and
  (c) take away such samples or articles as he considers necessary for that purpose.

(5) On leaving any unoccupied premises which he has entered by virtue of sub-paragraph (1) above or a warrant under sub-paragraph (3) above the authorised person shall leave them as effectually secured against trespassers as he found them.

(6) A warrant issued in pursuance of sub-paragraph (3) above shall continue in force until the purpose for which the entry is required has been satisfied.

(7) Any reference in this paragraph to an emergency is a reference to a case where the person requiring entry has reasonable cause to believe that circumstances exist which are likely to endanger life or health and that immediate entry is necessary to verify the existence of those circumstances or to ascertain their cause and to effect a remedy.

Offences relating to entry

3.—(1) A person who wilfully obstructs any person acting in the exercise of any powers conferred by paragraph 2 above shall be liable, on summary conviction, to a fine not exceeding level 3 on the standard scale.

(2) If a person discloses any information relating to any trade secret obtained in the exercise of any powers conferred by paragraph 2 above he shall, unless the disclosure was made in the performance of his duty or with the consent of the person having the right to disclose the information, be liable, on summary conviction, to a fine not exceeding level 5 on the standard scale.

Default powers

4.—(1) This paragraph applies to the following function of a local authority, that is to say its duty under section 79 to cause its area to be inspected to detect any statutory nuisance which ought to be dealt with under section 80 and its powers under paragraph 2 above.

(2) If the Secretary of State is satisfied that any local authority has failed, in any respect, to discharge the function to which this paragraph applies which it ought to have discharged, he may make an order declaring the authority to be in default.

(3) An order made under sub-paragraph (2) above which declares an authority to be in default may, for the purpose of remedying the default, direct the authority ("the defaulting authority") to perform the function specified in the order and may specify the manner in which and the time or times within which the function is to be performed by the authority.

(4) If the defaulting authority fails to comply with any direction contained in such an order the Secretary of State may, instead of enforcing the order by mandamus, make an order transferring to himself the function of the authority specified in the order.

(5) Where the function of a defaulting authority is transferred under sub-paragraph (4) above, the amount of any expenses which the Secretary of State certifies were incurred by him in performing the function shall on demand be paid to him by the defaulting authority.

(6) Any expenses required to be paid by a defaulting authority under sub-paragraph (5) above shall be defrayed by the authority in like manner, and shall be debited to the like account, as if the function had not been transferred and the expenses had been incurred by the authority in performing them.

(7) The Secretary of State may by order vary or revoke any order previously made by him under this paragraph.

(8) Any order under this paragraph may include such incidental, supplemental and transitional provisions as the Secretary of State considers appropriate.

Protection from personal liability

5. Nothing done by, or by a member of, a local authority or by any officer of or other person authorised by a local authority shall, if done in good faith for the purpose of executing Part III, subject them or any of them personally to any action, liability, claim or demand whatsoever (other than any liability under section 19 or 20 of the Local Government Finance Act 1982 (powers of district auditor and court)).

Statement of right of appeal in notices

6. Where an appeal against a notice served by a local authority lies to a magistrates' court by virtue of section 80, it shall be the duty of the authority to include in such a notice a statement indicating that such an appeal lies as aforesaid and specifying the time within which it must be brought.

Section 99 SCHEDULE 4

ABANDONED SHOPPING AND LUGGAGE TROLLEYS

Application

1.—(1) Subject to sub-paragraph (2) below, this Schedule applies where any shopping or luggage trolley is found by an authorised officer of the local authority on any land in the open air and appears to him to be abandoned.

(2) This Schedule does not apply in relation to a shopping or luggage trolley found on the following descriptions of land, that is to say—
  (a) land in which the owner of the trolley has a legal estate or, in Scotland, of which the owner of the trolley is the owner or occupier;
  (b) where an off-street parking place affords facilities to the customers of shops for leaving there shopping trolleys used by them, land on which those facilities are afforded;
  (c) where any other place designated by the local authority for the purposes of this Schedule affords like facilities, land on which those facilities are afforded; and
  (d) as respects luggage trolleys, land which is used for the purposes of their undertaking by persons authorised by an enactment to carry on any railway, light railway, tramway or road transport undertaking or by a relevant airport operator (within the meaning of Part V of the Airports Act 1986).

Power to seize and remove trolleys

2.—(1) Where this Schedule applies in relation to a shopping or luggage trolley, the local authority may, subject to sub-paragraph (2) below,—
  (a) seize the trolley; and
  (b) remove it to such place under its control as the authority thinks fit.

(2) When a shopping or luggage trolley is found on any land appearing to the authorised officer to be occupied by any person, the trolley shall not be removed without the consent of that person unless—
  (a) the local authority has served on that person a notice stating that the authority proposes to remove the trolley; and
  (b) no notice objecting to its removal is served by that person on the local authority within the period of 14 days beginning with the day on which the local authority served the notice of the proposed removal on him.

Retention, return and disposal of trolleys

3.—(1) Subject to the following sub-paragraphs, the local authority, as respects any shopping or luggage trolley it has seized and removed,—
  (a) shall keep the trolley for a period of six weeks; and
  (b) may sell or otherwise dispose of the trolley at any time after the end of that period.

(2) The local authority shall, as respects any trolley it has seized or removed, as soon as reasonably practicable (but not later than 14 days) after its removal, serve on the person (if any) who appears to the authority to be the owner of the trolley a notice stating—
  (a) that the authority has removed the trolley and is keeping it;
  (b) that place where it is being kept; and
  (c) that, if it is not claimed, the authority may dispose of it.

(3) Subject to sub-paragraph (4) below, if, within the period mentioned in sub-paragraph (1)(a) above, any person claims to be the owner of a shopping or luggage trolley being kept by the authority under that sub-paragraph, the local authority shall, if it appears that the claimant is the owner, deliver the trolley to him.

(4) A person claiming to be the owner of a shopping or luggage trolley shall not be entitled to have the trolley delivered to him unless he pays the local authority, on demand, such charge as the authority requires.

(5) No shopping or luggage trolley shall be disposed of by the local authority unless (where it has not been claimed) the authority has made reasonable enquiries to ascertain who owns it.

Charges

4.—(1) The local authority, in fixing the charge to be paid under paragraph 3 above by the claimant of a shopping or luggage trolley, shall secure that the charges so payable by claimants shall be such as are sufficient, taking one financial year with another, to cover the cost of removing, storing and disposing of such trolleys under this Schedule.

(2) The local authority may agree with persons who own shopping or luggage trolleys and make them available for use in its area a scheme for the collection by them of trolleys they make available for use; and where such an agreement is in force with any person, no charge may be demanded under paragraph 3 above by the local authority in respect of any trolley within the scheme in relation to which the provisions of the scheme are complied with.

Definitions

5. In this Schedule—
  "luggage trolley" means a trolley provided by a person carrying on an undertaking mentioned in paragraph 1(2)(d) above to travellers for use by them for carring their luggage to, from or within the premises used for the purposes of his undertaking, not being a trolley which is power-assisted; and
  "shopping-trolley," means a trolley provided by the owner of a shop to customers for use by them for carrying goods purchased at the shop, not being a trolley which is power-assisted.

Section 105   SCHEDULE 5

FURTHER AMENDMENTS OF THE RADIOACTIVE SUBSTANCES ACT 1960

[*Schedule 5 was repealed by the Radioactive Substances Act 1993*]

Section 128   SCHEDULE 6

THE NATURE CONSERVANCY COUNCILS FOR ENGLAND AND SCOTLAND AND THE COUNTRYSIDE COUNCIL FOR WALES: CONSTITUTION

Preliminary

1. In this Part of this Schedule any reference to the council is a reference to each of the Councils established by section 128 of this Act.

Constitution and membership

2. The council shall be a body corporate.

3.—(1) The council shall not be regarded as the servant or agent of the Crown, or as enjoying any status, immunity or privilege of the Crown; and the council's property shall not be regarded as property of, or property held on behalf of, the Crown.

(2) Sub-paragraph (1) above has effect subject to paragraph 18 below.

4.—(1) The Secretary of State shall appoint one of the members of the council to be chairman of the council and may appoint a member to be deputy chairman.

(2) The chairman, deputy chairman and other members of the council shall hold and vacate office in accordance with the terms of their appointment.

(3) A member of the council may, by notice in writing addressed to the Secretary of State, resign his membership, and the chairman and deputy chairman of the council may by such a notice resign their office as such without resigning their membership.

5. A member of the council who ceases to be a member or ceases to be chairman or deputy chairman of the council shall be eligible for reappointment.

6. The Secretary of State may remove a member of the council from membership if he has—
   (a) become bankrupt or made an arrangement with his creditors or, in Scotland, had his estate sequestrated or made a trust deed for behoof of his creditors or a composition contract; or
   (b) been absent from meeting of the council for a period longer than six consecutive months without the permission of the council;
or if he is, in the opinion of the Secretary of State unable or unfit to discharge the functions of a member.

Remuneration and allowances for members of council

7.—(1) The council shall—
   (a) pay to their members such remuneration and allowances (if any); and
   (b) as regards any member or former member in whose case the Secretary of State may so determine, pay such pension, allowance or gratuity to or in respect of him, or make such payments towards the provision of such pension, allowance or gratuity,
as the Secretary of State may with the approval of the Treasury determine.

(2) If a person ceases to be a member of the council, and it appears to the Secretary of State that there are special circumstances which make it right that he should receive compensation, the Secretary of State may require the council to pay to that person a sum of such amount as the Secretary of State may with the approval of the Treasury determine.

Staff

8.—(1) There shall be a chief officer of the council.

(2) The first appointment of a chief officer shall be made by the Secretary of State after consultation with the chairman of the council (if there is a person holding that office when the appointment is made); and the council shall, with the approval of the Secretary of State, make the subsequent appointments.

9. The council may appoint such number of other employees as they may, with the approval of the Secretary of State given with the consent of the Treasury, determine.

10. The council shall pay to the chief officer and their other employees such remuneration and allowances as the council may, with the approval of the Secretary of State given with the consent of the Treasury, determine.

11. The council shall, in the case of such of their employees or former employees as they may, with the approval of the Secretary of State given with the consent of the Treasury, determine—
   (a) pay such pensions, allowances or gratuities to or in respect of those employees,
   (b) make such payments towards provision of such pensions, allowances or gratuities, or
   (c) provide and maintain such schemes (whether contributory or not) for the payment of such pensions, allowances or gratuities,

as they may, with the approval of the Secretary of State given with the consent of the Treasury, determine.

Proceedings

12.—(1) The council may regulate their own procedure (including making provision in relation to quorum).

(2) The proceedings of the council and any committee of the council shall not be invalidated by any vacancy amongst their members or by any defect in the appointment of any such member.

Delegation of powers

13.—(1) Anything authorised or required by or under any enactment to be done by the council may be done by any committee of theirs which, or by any member or employee of the council who, is authorised (generally or specially) for the purpose by the council.

(2) Nothing in sub-paragraph (1) above shall prevent the council from doing anything that a committee, member or employee has been authorised to do.

Committees

14.—(1) The council may appoint persons who are not members of the council to be members of any committee established by the council (in addition to any members of the council).

(2) The council shall pay to a person so appointed such remuneration and allowances (if any) as the Secretary of State may with the approval of the Treasury determine.

(3) The council may regulate the procedure of any committee of theirs.

Documents

15.—(1) This paragraph applies in England and Wales only.

(2) The application of the seal of the council shall be authenticated by the signature of any member or employee of the council who is authorised (generally or specially) for the purpose by the council.

(3) Any document purporting to be an instrument made or issued by the council and to be duly executed under the seal of the council, or to be signed or executed by a person authorised for the purpose by the council, shall be received in evidence and treated, without further proof, as being so made or issued unless the contrary is shown.

16.—(1) Sub-paragraphs (2) and (3) below apply in Scotland only; and they do not apply where an enactment (including an enactment contained in a statutory instrument) provides otherwise.
  (a) is signed by the council if it is signed on their behalf by a member or by the chief officer or by a person authorised to sign the document on behalf of the council; and
  (b) is subscribed by the council if it is subscribed on their behalf by being signed in accordance with the provisions of paragraph (a) above at the end of the last page of the document.

(3) A document shall be presumed, unless the contrary is shown, to have been subscribed in accordance with sub-paragraph (2) above if—
  (a) it bears to have been subscribed on behalf of the council by a member or by the chief officer or by a person bearing to have been authorised to subscribe the document on behalf of the council; and
  (b) it bears to have been signed by a person as a witness of the subscription of the member, chief officer or other person subscribing on behalf of the council or (if the subscription is not so witnessed) to have been sealed with the common seal of the council.

Public records

17. In Schedule 1 to the Public Records Act 1958 (definition of public records), in Part II of the Table at the end of paragraph 3 (organisations whose records are public records) there shall be inserted in the appropriate places entries relating to the Countryside Council for Wales and the Nature Conservancy Council for England.

Land

18.—(1) For the purposes of the application of any enactment or rule of law to land an interest in which belongs to the council, and which is managed as a nature reserve, the council shall be deemed to be a Government department; and any other land occupied by them shall be deemed, for the purpose of any rate on property, to be property occupied by or on behalf of the Crown for public purposes.

(2) In sub-paragraph (1) above "interest" and "land" have the meanings assigned to them by section 114 of the National Parks and Access to the Countryside Act 1949.

Reports, accounts etc.

19. The council shall—
(a) furnish the Secretary of State with such returns, accounts and other information with respect to their property and activities or proposed activities as he may from time to time require;
(b) afford to the Secretary of State facilities for the verification of information so furnished; and
(c) for the purpose of such verification, permit any person authorised in that behalf by the Secretary of State to inspect and make copies of the council's accounts, books, documents or papers and give that person such explanation of anything he is entitled to inspect as he may reasonably require.

20. The council shall—
(a) as soon as possible after the March 31 following the date appointed under section 131(3) of this Act make to the Secretary of State a report on the exercise and performance of their functions down to that date, and
(b) make a similar report to him as to each period of 12 months thereafter as soon as possible after its end;

and a copy of each such report shall be laid before each House of Parliament by the Secretary of State.

(2) Without prejudice to the generality of sub-paragraph (1) above, the report of the Countryside Council for Wales for any year shall include statement of the action taken by the Council to promote the enjoyment of the countryside by members of the public who are disabled.

21.—(1) The council shall keep proper accounts and other records, and shall prepare for each financial year a statement of account in such form as the Secretary of State with the approval of the Treasury may direct and submit those statements of account to the Secretary of State at such time as he may with the approval of the Treasury direct.

(2) The Secretary of State shall, on or before November 30 in any year, transmit to the Comptroller and Auditor General the statements of account of the council for the financial year last ended.

(3) The Comptroller and Auditor General shall examine and certify the statements of account transmitted to him under this paragraph, and lay copies of them together with his report thereon before each House of Parliament.

(4) In this paragraph "financial year" means the period beginning with the day appointed under section 131(3) of this Act and ending with the March 31 following that date and each period of 12 months thereafter.

Superannuation Act 1965 (c.74)

22. In paragraph 7 of section 39(1) of the Superannuation Act 1965 (public offices)—
(a) there shall be inserted in the appropriate place the following entry—
"The Countryside Council for Wales.";
(b) for the entry relating to the Nature Conservancy Council there shall be substituted the following entries—
"The Nature Conservancy Council for England.
The Nature Conservancy Council for Scotland."

Parliamentary Commissioner Act 1967 (c.13)

23. In Schedule 2 to the Parliamentary Act 1967 (departments and authorities subject to investigation)—
(a) after the entry for the Countryside Commission for Scotland there shall be inserted the following entry—
"Countryside Council for Wales.";
(b) for the entry relating to the Nature Conservancy Council there shall be substituted the following entries—
"Nature Conservancy Council for England.
Nature Conservancy Council for Scotland."

House of Commons Disqualification Act 1975 (c.24)

24. In Part III of Schedule 1 to the House of Commons Disqualification Act 1975 (other

disqualifying offices), for the entry relating to members of the Nature Conservancy Council in receipt of remuneration there shall be substituted—

"Any member of the Nature Conservancy Council for England, the Nature Concervancy Council for Scotland or the Countryside Council for Wales in receipt of remuneration."

Inheritance Tax Act 1984 (c.51)

25. In Schedule 3 to the Inheritance Tax Act 1984 (gifts for national purpose), for the entry relating to the Nature Conservancy Council there shall be substituted the following entries—

"Nature Conservancy Council for England.
Nature Conservancy Council for Scotland.
Countryside Council for Wales."

Section 128   SCHEDULE 7

THE JOINT NATURE CONSERVATION COMMITTEE

Preliminary

1. In this Schedule—
"chairman" means (except in paragraph 2(1) below) the chairman of the committee;
"the committee" means the Joint Nature Conservation Committee; and
"council" means a council established by section 128(1) of this Act.

Membership

2.—(1) The committee shall consist of 11 voting members, namely—
(a) a chairman appointed by the Secretary of State;
(b) three members appointed by the Secretary of State;
(c) the chairman of each council and one other member of each council appointed by that council; and
(d) the chairman of the Countryside Commission;
and two non-voting members appointed by the Department of the Environment for Northern Ireland.

(2) The committee may appoint any voting member to be deputy chairman.

(3) The chairman and the three members appointed by the Secretary of State shall be persons who are not members of any of the councils and shall hold and vacate office in accordance with the terms of their appointments.

4.—(1) The three members appointed by the Secretary of State shall be persons appearing to the Secretary of State to have experience in or scientific knowledge of nature conservation; and the Secretary of State shall, in determining who to appoint, have regard to any recommendations made to him by the chairman.

(2) Before appointing such a member the Secretary of State shall consult the chairman and such persons having scientific knowledge of nature conservation as the Secretary of State considers appropriate.

Remuneration and allowances for members

5.—(1) The council shall—
(a) pay to the chairman such remuneration and allowances; and
(b) pay such pension, allowance or gratuity to or in respect of the chairman or make such payments towards the provision of such pension, allowance or gratuity;
as the Secretary of State may with the approval of the Treasury determine.

(2) If a person ceases to be chairman and it appears to the Secretary of State that there are special circumstances which make it right that he should receive compensation, the Secretary of State may require the councils to pay to that person a sum of such amount as the Secretary of State may with the approval of the Treasury determine.

6. The councils shall pay to the three members appointed by the Secretary of State, and to the non-voting members, such remuneration and allowances as the Secretary of State may with the approval of the Treasury determine.

Staff etc. and expenses

7.—(1) The councils shall provide the committee with such staff, accommodation and other facilities, and such financial resources, as the councils, after consultation with the committee, consider appropriate for the proper discharge of the functions conferred by section 133(2) and (3) of this Act.

(2) The expenses of the committee shall be defrayed by the councils in such proportions as the councils may agree.

(3) In default of agreement between the councils as to any question arising under sub-paragraph (1) or (2) above the Secretary of State shall determine that question.

Proceedings

8.—(1) The committee may regulate their own procedure (including making provision in relation to the quorum of voting members).

(2) The proceedings of the committee shall not be invalidated by any vacancy amongst their members or defect in the appointment of any member.

Delegation of functions

9.—(1) Anything authorised or required to be done by the committee may be done by any member of the committee, by any council or by any employee of a council who is authorised (generally or specially) for the purpose by the committee.

(2) Nothing in sub-paragraph (1) above shall prevent the committee from doing anything that another person has been authorised to do.

Annual reports

10.—(1) The committee shall—
 (a) as soon as possible after March 31 following the date appointed under section 131(1) of this Act make to the Secretary of State a report on their activities down to that date; and
 (b) make a similar report to him as to each period of 12 months thereafter as soon as possible after its end;
and a copy of each such report shall be laid before each House of Parliament by the Secretary of State.

(2) The Committee shall, at the same time as they make a report under sub-paragraph (1) above, send a copy of it to each of the councils.

Section 130 SCHEDULE 8

AMENDMENT OF ENACTMENTS RELATING TO COUNTRYSIDE MATTERS

National Parks and Access to the Countryside Act 1949 (c.97)

1.—(1) The National Parks and Access to the Country Act 1949 shall be amended as follows.

(2) For section 1 (the Countryside Commission) there shall be substituted the following section—

 "The Countryside Commission and the Countryside Council for Wales

 1.—(1) There shall be a Countryside Commission which shall exercise functions in relation to England for the purposes specified in subsection (2) below; and the Countryside Council for Wales (established by section 128 of the Environmental Protection Act 1990) shall exercise corresponding functions in relation to Wales for the corresponding purposes specified in section 130(2) of the Environmental Protection Act 1990.

 (2) The purposes for which the functions of the Commission are exercisable are—
 (a) the preservation and enhancement of natural beauty in England, both in the areas designated under this Act as National Parks or as areas of outstanding natural beauty and elsewhere;
 (b) encouraging the provision or improvement, for persons resorting to National Parks, or facilities for the enjoyment thereof and for the enjoyment of the opportunities for open-air recreation and the study of nature afforded thereby."

(3) In section 3 (power of Minister to give directions), in subsection (1) after the word "Commission" in the first place it occurs there shall be inserted the words "or to the Council" and after that word in the second place it occurs there shall be inserted the words "or Council."

(4) Before section 5 (National Parks) there shall be inserted the following section—

 "Application of Part II of this Act in Wales

 4A.—(1) The provisions of this Part of this Act shall, subject to the next following subsection, apply to land in Wales as they apply to land in England.

 (2) Where a provision of this Part of this Act confers a function on the Countryside Commission as respects England (or areas of any description in England), the Countryside

Council for Wales shall have the corresponding function as respects Wales (or areas of a similar description in Wales)."

(5) In sections 5(2) and 6(1) the words "and Wales" shall be omitted.

(6) Before section 51 (long-distance routes) there shall be inserted the following section—
"Application of Part IV of this Act in Wales
50A.—(1) The provisions of this Part of this Act shall, subject to the next following subsection, apply to land in Wales as they apply to land in England.

(2) Where a provision of this Part of this Act confers a function on the Countryside Commission as respects England (or land of any description in England), the Countryside Council for Wales shall have the corresponding function as respects Wales (or land of a similar description in Wales)."

(7) In section 51(1) the words "or Wales" shall be omitted.

(8) In sections 62(1) and 64(5) (consultation requirements as to land in National Parts), after the word "Commission" there shall be inserted the words "(where the Part in England) or the Council (where the Part in Wales)."

(9) In section 65 (access orders), in subsection (5), after the word "Park" in both places in which it occurs, there shall be inserted the words "in England" and after that subsection there shall be inserted the following subsection—

"(5A) The preceding subsection shall apply in relation to National Parks in Wales, and the Council, as it applies in relation to National Parks in England, and the Commission."

(10) In section 85 (general advisory duties)—
  (a) for the words "the duties of the Commission" there shall be substituted the words "their respective duties";
  (b) after the word "Commission," in the second place in which it occurs, there shall be inserted the words "and the Council";
  (c) in paragraph (b), after the word "Commission" there shall be inserted the words ", or, as the case may be, to the Minister and the Council,"; and
  (d) in paragraph (c), after the word "Commission" there shall be inserted the words "(as respects England) or to the Council (as respects Wales)."

(11) After section 86 (information services provided by Commission regarding National Parks) there shall be inserted the following section—
"Information services to be provided by Council
86A. The provisions of section 86 of this Act shall apply to the Council in relation to National Parks and other land in Wales as they apply to the Commission in relation to National Parks and other land in England."

(12) In section 87 (designation of areas of outstanding natural beauty)—
  (a) in subsection (1), after the word "Commission" there shall be inserted the words ", or as the case may be, the Council,";
  (b) after that subsection there shall be inserted the following subsection—
    "(1A) The following provisions shall apply to the Council in relation to land in Wales as they apply to the Commission in relation to land in England."

(13) In section 88 (application of provisions of Part II to designated areas), after subsection (2) there shall be inserted the following subsection—
"(2A) The provisions of section 4A of this Act shall apply to the provisions mentioned in the preceding subsection for the purposes of their application to areas of outstanding natural beauty as the provisions of that section apply for the purposes of Part II of this Act."

(14) In section 90(4) (consultation before making certain byelaws) after the word "Commission" there shall be inserted the words "as regards land in England) or the Council (as regards land in Wales)."

(15) In section 91(1) (consultation before making certain byelaws) after the word "Commission" there shall be inserted the words "(as regards land or waterways in England) or the Council (as regards land or waterways in Wales)."

(16) In section 114 (interpretation), after the definition of "area of outstanding natural beauty" there shall be inserted the following definitions—
"the Commission" means the Commission established by section one of this Act;
"the Council" means the "Countryside Council for Wales;".

(17) In the first Schedule (procedure for certain orders), in paragraph 2(5), after the word "Commission" where it first appears there shall be inserted the words ", the Council" and after that word in the second place it appears there shall be inserted the word ", Council."

The Countryside Act 1968 (c.41)

2.—(1) The Countryside Act 1968 shall be amended as follows.

(2) In section 1 (additional general functions)—
(a) for subsection (1) there shall be inserted the following subsections—
"(1) The National Parks Commission shall in future be known as the 'Countryside Commission' and shall exercise functions in relation to England.

(1A) The functions of the Countryside Commission (in this Act referred to as 'the Commission') in England and the corresponding functions of the Countryside Council for Wales (in this Act referred to as 'the Council') in Wales shall be enlarged in accordance with this Act.";
(b) in subsection (2)—
  (i) after the word "recreation" there shall be inserted the words "and the study of nature"; and
  (ii) at the end, there shall be inserted the words "; and the purposes for which the functions of the Council in Wales are to be exercised are the corresponding purposes specified in section 130(2) of the Environmental Protection Act 1990.";
(c) in subsection (3) for the word "shall" there shall be substituted the words "and the Council shall each."

(3) In section 2 (new functions)—
(a) in subsection (1), for the word "shall" where it first appears there shall be substituted the words "and the Council shall each" and after the word "Commission" in the second and third place it appears there shall be inserted the words "or Council";
(b) in subsections (2) and (3), after the word "Commission" where it first appears there shall be inserted the words "and the Council" and after that word in the second place it appears there shall be inserted the words "or Council";
(c) in subsection (4), after the word "Commission" where it first appears there shall be inserted the words "and the Council" and after that word in the second and third place it appears there shall be inserted the words "or Council";
(d) in subsection (5), after the word "Commission" where it first appears there shall be inserted the words "or to the Council" and after that word in the second place it appears there shall be inserted the words "or, as the case may be, the Council";
(e) in subsection (5)(b), after the word "Commission" in each place it appears there shall be inserted the words "or Council";
(f) in subsection (6) after the word "Commission" there shall be inserted the words "and the Council";
(g) in subsections (7), (8) and (9), after the word "Commission" where it first appears there shall be inserted the words "and the Council" and after that word in the second place it appears there shall be inserted the words "or Council."

(4) In section 4 (experimental projects or schemes)—
(a) in subsection (1), after the word "Commission" where it first appears there shall be inserted the words "and the Council" and after that word in the second place it appears there shall be inserted the words "or Council";
(b) in subsection (3) after the word "Commission" there shall be inserted the words "or, as the case may be, the Council";
(c) in subsection (4) after the word "Commission" there shall be inserted the words "or Council";
(d) in subsection (5) after the word "Commission" where it first appears there shall be inserted the words "or by the Council" and after that word in the second place it appears there shall be inserted the words "or Council";
(e) in subsection (6), after the word "Commission" where it first appears there shall be inserted the words "or of the Council" and after that word in the second place it appears there shall be inserted the words "or Council."

(5) In section 8 (sailing, boating and fishing in country parks), in subsection (5) after the word "Commission" there shall be inserted the words "(if the works are in England) or the Council (if the works are in Wales)."

(6) In section 12 (facilities in or near National Parks)—
(a) in subsection (1) after the word "Commission" where it first appears there shall be inserted the words "or, as the case may be, the Council" and after that word in the second place it appears there shall be inserted the words "or the Council";
(b) in subsection (5) after the word "Commission" there shall be inserted the words "(if the National Park in England) or the Council (if the National Parks is in Wales)."

(7) In section 13 (control of boats etc. in National Parks) in subsection (4), after the word "Commission" there shall be inserted the words "(if the National Park is in England) or the Council (if the National Park is in Wales)."

(8) In section 13 (provision of facilities by Forestry Commissioners), in subsection (5) for the word "shall" there shall be inserted the words "and the Countryside Council for Wales shall each."

(9) In section 38 (avoidance of pollution) after the words "the Commission" there shall be inserted the words ", the Council."

(10) In section 41 (byelaws etc.)—
(a) in subsection (2), for the word "may" there shall be substituted the words "and the Council may each";
(b) in subsection (5), after the word "Commission" there shall be inserted the words "(as respects a park or area in England) or the Council (as respects a part or area in Wales)";
(c) in subsection (8), for the words "were a local authority" there shall be substituted the words "and the Council were local authorities";
(d) in subsection (9), for the words "or the Commission" there shall be substituted the words ", the Commission or the Council."

(11) In section 45 (agreements with landowners), in subsection (1) after the word "Commission" there shall be inserted the words ", the Council."

(12) In section 46 (application of general provisions of 1949 Act), in subsection (2), at the end there shall be inserted "and any reference to the Nature Conservancy Council, so far as referring to the Countryside Council for Wales for purposes connected with their nature conservation functions (within the meaning of section 131 of the Environmental Protection Act 1990) shall include a reference to that Council for purposes connected with their countryside functions (whether conferred by this Act, the Act of 1949 or otherwise)."

(13) In section 49 (interpretation), after the definition of "bridleway" there shall be inserted the following definitions—

" 'the Commission' means the Countryside Commission;
'the Council' means the Countryside Council for Wales;"

Local Government Act 1972 (c.70)

3. In Part I of Schedule 17 to the Local Government Act 1972 (discharge of planning and countryside functions in National Parks), after paragraph 21A there shall be inserted the following paragraph—

"Construction of references to the Countryside Commission

21B. In this Part of this Schedule, references to the Countryside Commission shall, in relation to a National Park in Wales, be construed as references to the Countryside Council for Wales."

Local Government Act (c.7)

4. In section 7 of the Local Government Act 1974 (supplementary grants for expenditure on National Parks), in subsection (3) after the word "Commission" there shall be inserted the words "(as respects National Parks in England) and the Countryside Council for Wales (as respects National Parks in Wales)" and in section 9 of that Act (grants and loans by the Countryside Commission)—
(a) in subsection (1), for the word "may" there shall be substituted the words "and the Countryside Council for Wales may each" and after the word "Commission" in the second place it appears there shall be inserted the words "or, as the case may be, the Council";
(b) in subsection (2), after the word "Commission" there shall be inserted the word "or the Countryside Council for Wales";
(c) in subsection (3), for the words "Countryside Commission's power" there shall be substituted the words "the power of the Countryside Commission and of the Countryside Council for Wales" and after the word "Commission" in the second place it appears there shall be inserted the words "or to the Council."

Highways Act 1980 (c.66)

5.—(1) The Highways Act 1980 shall be amended as follows.
(2) In section 105A (environmental assessment for highway projects) in subsection (6)(a), after the word "land" there shall be inserted the words "in England" and, at the end, there shall be inserted the words "or the Countryside Council for Wales, if it relates to land in Wales falling within that paragraph of that subsection."
(3) In section 120 (orders for extinguishment or diversion of public paths), in subsection (2)(c), at the end there shall be inserted the words "(if the National Park is in England) or the Countryside Council for Wales (if the National Park is in Wales)."

Wildlife and Countryside Act 1981 (c.69)

6.—(1) The Wildlife and Countryside Act 1981 shall be amended as follows.

(2) In section 34 (limestone pavement orders), in subsection (6) in the definition of "the Commission," the words "and Wales" shall be omitted.

(3) In section 43 (maps of National Parks showing certain areas of moor or heath), in subsection (1A) the words "by the Countryside Commission" shall be omitted and—
  (a) in subsection (1B) for the word "shall" there shall be substituted the words "and the Countryside Council for Wales shall each" and for the word "may" there shall be substituted "the Commission and the Council may each";
  (b) in subsection (1C), after the word "Commission" there shall be inserted the words "or, as the case may be, the Council."

(4) Section 45 (power to vary orders designating National Parks) shall be subsection (1) of that section and, in that subsection, after the word "Park" in the first place it appears there shall be inserted the word "in England"; and at the end there shall be inserted, as subsection (2) of that section, the following words—

"(2) Subsection (1) shall apply to the Countryside Council for Wales, in relation to any National Park in Wales, as it applies to the Countryside Commission in relation to any National Park in England."

(5) In section 47(2) (power of Secretary of State to give grants) after the word "Commission" there shall be inserted the words "or the Countryside Council for Wales."

(6) In section 49 (extension of power to appoint wardens), in subsection (1)(b), after the word "authority" in the second place it appears there shall be inserted the words ", the Countryside Council for Wales." and, in subsection (4), after the word "Commission" in both places it appears there shall be inserted the words "or the Countryside Council for Wales."

The Road Traffic Regulation Act 1984 (c.27)

7. In section 22 of the Road Traffic Regulation Act 1984 (traffic regulation orders in special areas), in subsection (1)(a)(iv), after the word "Commission" there shall be inserted the words "or the Countryside Council for Wales" and, in subsection (4), for the words from "or" in the first place it appears to "may," in the second place it appears, there shall be substituted ", the Countryside Council for Wales and the Countryside Commission for Scotland may each."

The Water Act 1989 (c.15)

8. In section 152 of the Water Act 1989 (restrictions on disposal of land) in subsection (5)(c)(i), after the word "Commission" there shall be inserted the words "(as respects land in England) or the Countryside Council for Wales (as respects land in Wales)"; and, in subsection (5)(d), after the word "Commission," where it first appears there shall be inserted the words "or the Countryside Council for Wales" and at the end there shall be inserted the words "or that Council."

Section 132 SCHEDULE 9

AMENDMENT OF ENACTMENTS CONFERRING NATURE CONSERVANCY FUNCTIONS

National Parks and Access to the Countryside Act 1949 (c.97)

1.—(1) The National Parks and Access to the Countryside Act 1949 shall be amended as follows.

(2) After section 15 there shall be inserted the following section—

"Meaning of 'Nature Conservancy Council'

15A. In this Part of this Act references to 'the Nature Conservancy Council' are references—
  (a) in relation to land in England, to the Nature Conservancy Council for England;
  (b) in relation to land in Scotland, to the Nature Conservancy Council for Scotland; and
  (c) in relation to land in Wales, to the Countryside Council for Wales."

(3) In section 16(5) (agreements in Scotland for establishing nature reserves), in paragraph (c) for the words "Nature Conservancy Council" there shall be substituted "Nature Conservancy Council for Scotland."

(4) In section 103 (general provisions as to acquisition of land)—
  (a) in subsection (1), after the words "the Nature Conservancy Council" there shall be inserted the words "(as defined in section 15A of this Act)"; and
  (b) in subsection (2), for the words "the Nature Conservancy Council" in both places there shall be substituted the words "the Nature Conservancy Council for Scotland."

(5) In section 106 (supplementary provisions as to bye-laws), in subsection (1), after the words "the Nature Conservancy Council" there shall be inserted the words "(as defined in section 15A of this Act)."

Deer (Scotland) Act 1959 (c.40)

2. In section 1 of the Deer (Scotland) Act 1959 (constitution of the Red Deer Commission), in subsection (4)(a) there shall be inserted at the end of the words "for Scotland."

Deer Act 1963 (c.36)

3. In section 11 of the Deer Act 1963 (power to grant licences), after subsection (2) there shall be inserted—

"(3) In this section 'the Nature Conservancy Council' means in relation to the doing of an act in Wales, the Countryside Council for Wales and in relation to the doing of an act in England, the Nature Conservancy Council for England."

Countryside Act 1968 (c.41)

4.—(1) The Countryside Act 1968 shall be amended as follows.

(2) In section 15 (areas of special scientific interest)—
(a) in subsection (2), the words "in the national interest" shall be omitted and, after the words "any such land" there shall be inserted the words "(or of any adjacent land)"; and
(b) after subsection (6) there shall be inserted the following subsection—

"(6A) In this section references to 'the Nature Conservancy Council' or 'the Council' are references to the Nature Conservancy Council for England, the Nature Conservancy Council for Scotland or the Council, according as the land in question is in England, Scotland or Wales."

(3) In section 37 (protection for interests in countryside) for the words "Nature Conservancy Council" there shall be substituted the words ", the Council, the Nature Conservancy Council for England and the Nature Conservancy Council for Scotland."

Conservation of Seals Act 1970 (c.30)

5. In section 10 of the Conservation of Seals Act 1970 (power to grant licences), after subsection (4) there shall be inserted the following subsection—

"(5) In this section a reference to 'the Nature Conservancy Council' is a reference to the Nature Conservancy Council for England, the Nature Conservancy Council for Scotland or the Countryside Council for Wales, according as the area in question is in or is in waters adjacent to England, Scotland or Wales."

Badgers Act 1973 (c.57)

6.—(1) Section 9 of the Badgers Act 1973 (power to grant licences) shall be amended as follows.

(2) In subsection (2)(a), for the words "Nature Conservancy Council" there shall be substituted the words "Nature Conservancy Council for England, the Nature Conservancy Council for Scotland or the Countryside Council for Wales (according as the area specified in the licence is in England, Scotland or Wales)."

(3) In subsection (4)—
(a) for the words from "the Nature" to "functions" there shall be substituted the words "each of the following bodies, namely, the Nature Conservancy Council for England, the Nature Conservancy Council for Scotland and the Countryside Council for Wales as to the exercise in the respective areas of those Councils of the functions of those Ministers; and
(b) after the word "Council" in the second place it appears, there shall be inserted the words "for the area specified in the licence."

Import of Live Fish (Scotland) Act 1978 (c.35)

7. In section 1 of the Import of Live Fish (Scotland) Act 1978 (power to limit imports) in subsection (2), after the word "Council" there shall be inserted the words "for Scotland."

Import of Live Fish (England and Wales) Act 1980 (c.27)

8. In section 1 of the Import of Live Fish (England and Wales) Act 1980 (power to limit imports), in subsection (2) after the word "Council" there shall be inserted the words "for England, the Countryside Councils for Wales."

Highways Act 1980 (c.66)

9. In section 105A of the Highways Act 1980 (environmental assessment of highway projects), for subsection (6)(c) there shall be substituted the following paragraph—

(c) the Nature Conservancy Council for England or the Countryside Council for Wales, if it relates to land in England or, as the case may be, in Wales, falling within paragraph (c)."

Animal Health Act 1981 (c.22)

10.—(1) The Animal Health Act 1981 shall be amended as follows.
(2) In section 21 (destruction of wildlife on infection)—
(a) in subsection (3), after the word "Council" there shall be inserted the words "for the area to which it will apply";
(b) in subsection (9), after the definition of "animals" there shall be inserted the following definition—

" 'Nature Conservancy Council' means the Nature Conservancy Council for England, the Nature Conservancy Council for Scotland or the Countryside Council for Wales."

(3) In section 22 (powers of entry for s.21), in subsection (7)(a) for the words from "the Nature Conservancy" to "1973," there shall be substituted the words "a Nature Conservancy Council under section 132 of the Environmental Protection Act 1990."

Wildlife and Countryside Act 1981 (c.69)

11.—(1) The Wildlife and Countryside Act 1981 shall be amended as follows.
(2) In section 10(5) (consultation with Council required before taking or killing a bat) after the word "Council" there shall be inserted the words "for the area in which the house is situated or, as the case may be, the act is to take place."
(3) In section 15(2) (endangered species) for the word "Council" there shall be substituted the word "Councils."
(4) In section 16 (power to grant licences)—
(a) in subsection (9)(a) and (9)(c), before the word "Nature" there shall be inserted the word "relevant";
(b) in subsection (10)(a), for the words "the Nature Conservancy Council" there shall be substituted the words "each of the Nature Conservancy Councils" and, after the word "exercise" there shall be inserted the words "in the area of that Council";
(c) in subsection (10)(b), before the word "Council" there shall be inserted the word "relevant Nature Conservancy"; and
(d) after subsection (10) there shall be inserted the following subsection—

"(11) For the purposes of this section a reference to a relevant Nature Conservancy Council is a reference to the Nature Conservancy Council for the area in which it is proposed to carry on the activity requiring a licence."

(5) In section 22(3) (power of Secretary of State to amend Schedules 5 or 8 to Act) for the words "to him by the Nature Conservancy Council" there shall be substituted the words "jointly to him by the Nature Conservancy Councils", and at the end of that subsection there shall be inserted the words—

"and the functions of the Nature Conservancy Councils under this subsection shall be special functions of the Council for the purposes of section 133 of the Environmental Protection Act 1990."

(6) In section 24 (functions of Nature Conservancy Council)—
(a) in subsection (1), for the word "Council" there shall be substituted the words "Councils, acting jointly," for the words "the passing of this Act" there shall be substituted the words "October 30, 1991" and at the end there shall be inserted the words—

"and the functions of the Nature Conservancy Councils under this subsection shall be special functions of the Councils for the purposes of section 133 of the Environmental Protection Act 1990";

(b) in subsection (2), for the words from "the Council" to the end there shall be substituted the words "to that advice being given.";
(c) for subsection (3) there shall be substituted the following subsection—

"(3) The Secretary of State shall lay before each House of Parliament a copy of any advice so given and the statements accompanying it."; and

(d) in subsection (4), for the word "Council" there shall be substituted the words "Nature Conservancy Councils."
(7) In section 27 (interpretation of Part I)—
(a) in subsection (1), in the definition of authorised person, for the words "the Nature Conservancy Council" there shall be substituted the words "any of the Nature Conservancy Councils"; and
(b) after subsection (3) there shall be inserted the following subsection—

"(3A) Any reference in this Part to the Nature Conservancy Councils is a reference to the Nature Conservancy Council for England, the Nature Conservancy Council for Scotland and the Countryside Council for Wales."

(8) In Part II (nature conservation etc.), before section 28 there shall be inserted the following section—

"Construction of references to Nature Conservancy Council

27A. In this Part references to 'the Nature Conservancy Council' are, unless the contrary intention appears, references—
- (a) in relation to land in, or land covered by waters adjacent to, England, to the Nature Conservancy Council for England;
- (b) in relation to land in, or land covered by waters adjacent to, Scotland, to the Nature Conservancy Council for Scotland; and
- (c) in relation to land in, or land covered by waters adjacent to, Wales, to the Countryside Council for Wales;

and references to 'the Council' shall be construed accordingly."

(9) In section 29 (special protection for certain area of special scientific interest), in subsection (4)(a), for the words "commencement date" there shall be substituted the words "making of the order."

(10) In section 29 (special protection for certain areas of special scientific interest), in subsection (4)(a), after the word "Council" there shall be inserted the word "written."

(11) In section 29 (protection for areas of special scientific interest), in subsection (11), for the words "paragraph 17 of Schedule 3 to the Nature Conservancy Council Act 1973" there shall be substituted the words "paragraph 20 of Schedule 6 to the Environmental Protection Act 1990."

(12) In section 33 (Ministerial guidance) in subsection (1) for the word "Council" there shall be substituted the word "Councils."

(13) In section 52 (interpretation of Part II), in subsection (1) at the end there shall be inserted the following words—

"'the Nature Conservancy Councils' means the Nature Conservancy Council for England, the Nature Conservancy Council for Scotland and the Countryside Council for Wales;

and references to 'the Nature Conservancy Council' shall be construed in accordance with section 27A."

Roads (Scotland) Acts 1984 (c.54)

12. In section 20A of the Roads (Scotland) Act 1984 (environmental assessment of roads projects), in subsection (6)(c) after the word "Council" there shall be inserted the words "for Scotland."

Agriculture Act 1986 (c.49)

13. In section 18 of the Agriculture Act 1986 (environmentally sensitive areas), in subsection (2)—
- (a) in paragraph (a) after the word "Council" there shall be inserted the words "for England";
- (b) in paragraph (b) for the words "Countryside Commission and the Nature Conservancy Council" there shall be substituted the words "Countryside Council for Wales";
- (c) in paragraph (c) after the word "Council" there shall be inserted the words "for Scotland."

Channel Tunnel Act 1987 (c.53)

14. In paragraph 5 of Schedule 2, and in paragraph 17 of Schedule 3, to the Channel Tunnel Act 1987, after the words "Nature Conservancy Council" there shall be inserted the words "for England."

Norfolk and Suffolk Broads Act 1988 (c.4)

15. The Norfolk and Suffolk Broads Act 1988, for each reference to the Nature Conservancy Council there shall be substituted a reference to the Nature Conservancy Council for England.

Electricity Act 1989 (c.29)

16. In Schedule 9 to the Electricity Act 1989 (preservation of amenity)—
- (a) in paragraph 2(2) for the words from "the Nature" to "Wales," where it first appears, there shall be substituted the words "and—
- (a) where the activities which he is authorised by his licence to carry on include activities in

England, the Nature Conservancy Council for England and the Historic Buildings and Monuments Commission for England; and
(b) where those activities include activities in Wales, the Countryside Council for Wales and"; and
(b) in paragraph 4(2), after the words "Conservancy Council" there shall be inserted the words "for Scotland."

Water Act 1989 (c.15)

17.—(1) The Water Act 1989 shall be amended as follows:
(2) In section 9 (environmental duties)—
(a) in subsection (1) after the words "Conservancy Council" there shall be inserted the words "for England or the Countryside Council for Wales" and after the word "land" where it first appears there shall be inserted the words "in England or (as the case may be) in Wales";
(b) in subsection (4), after the word "Council" there shall be inserted the words "in question".

(3) In section 10 (codes of practice), in subsection (4) after the words "Conservancy Council" there shall be inserted the words "for England, the Countryside Council for Wales."

(4) In section 152 (restriction on disposals of land), in subsection (5)(c)(i) after the word "interest" there shall be inserted the words "in England" and after the word "Council" there shall be inserted the words "for England."

Sections 135, 136 and 137 SCHEDULE 10

TRANSFER SCHEMES AND STAFF OF EXISTING COUNCILS

PART I

TRANSFER SCHEMES: NATURE CONSERVANCY COUNCIL

Making and approval of schemes

1.—(1) Before such date or dates as the Secretary of State may direct, the Nature Conservancy Council shall make, and submit to the Secretary of State for his approval, their transfer scheme or scheme under section 135 of this Act (in this Part of this Schedule referred to as a "transfer scheme").

(2) A transfer scheme shall not take effect unless approved by the Secretary of State, who may modify such a scheme before approving it.

(3) The Secretary of State may make a transfer scheme himself if—
(a) he decides not to approve a scheme which has been submitted to him before the due date (with or without modifications); or
(b) no scheme is submitted to him for approval before the due date;
but nothing in this sub-paragraph shall prevent the Secretary of State from approving any scheme which may be submitted to him after the due date.

(4) A scheme made by the Secretary of State shall be treated for all purposes as having been made by the Council and approved by him.

Modification of schemes

2.—(1) If at any time after a transfer scheme has come into force the Secretary of State considers it appropriate to do so, having consulted any of the Councils established by section 128 of this Act (in this Schedule referred to as "the new Councils") which may be affected, he may by order provide that the scheme shall for all purposes be deemed to have come into force with such modifications as may be specified in the order.

(2) An order under sub-paragraph (1) above may make, with effect from the coming into force of the scheme, such provision as could have been made by the scheme and in connection with giving effect to that provision from that time may contain such supplemental, consequential and transitional provision as the Secretary of State considers appropriate.

Provision of information to Secretary of State

3. It shall be the duty of the Nature Conservancy Council and the new Councils to provide the Secretary of State with all such information and other assistance as he may reasonably require for the purposes of or in connection with the exercise of any power conferred on him by paragraphs 1 and 2 above.

Contents of schemes

4. A transfer scheme may—
  (a) define the property, rights and liabilities to be allocated to a particular new Council by specifying or describing them or by referring to all the property, right and liabilities comprised in a specified part of the undertaking of the Nature Conservancy Council (or partly in one way and partly in the other);
  (b) create in favour of a new Council—
      (i) an interest in or right over property transferred in accordance with the scheme (or any earlier scheme) to another new Council;
      (ii) new rights and liabilities as between that Council and the others;
  (c) provide that any rights or liabilities specified or described in the scheme shall, or shall to any extent, be enforceable either by or against each of the new Councils or by or against any two of the new Councils which are so specified;
  (d) require a new Council to enter into written agreements with, or execute other instruments in favour of, another new Council;

and a scheme may make such supplemental, incidental and consequential provision as the Nature Conservancy Council considers appropriate (including provision as to the order in which transfers or transactions are to be regarded as having occurred).

5. For the avoidance of doubt property, rights and liabilities of the Nature Conservancy Council may be allocated to a new Council notwithstanding—
  (a) that they would not, or would not without the consent or concurrence of another person, otherwise be capable of being transferred or assigned;
  (b) that, in the case of foreign property, steps must be taken by the Council to secure its effective vesting under the relevant foreign law.

PART II

TRANSFER SCHEMES: THE COUNTRYSIDE COMMISSION

Making and approval of schemes

6.—(1) Before such date or dates as the Secretary of State may direct, the Countryside Commission shall make, and submit to the Secretary of State for his approval, their transfer scheme or schemes under section 136 of this Act (in this Part of this Schedule referred to as a "transfer scheme").

(2) A transfer scheme shall not take effect unless approved by the Secretary of State, who may modify such a scheme before approving it.

(3) The Secretary of State may make a transfer scheme himself if—
  (a) he decides not to approve a scheme which has been submitted to him before the due date (with or without modifications); or
  (b) no scheme is submitted to him for approval before the due date;

but nothing in this sub-paragraph shall prevent the Secretary of State from approving any scheme which may be submitted to him after the due date.

(4) A scheme made by the Secretary of State shall be treated for all purposes as having been made by the Countryside Commission and approved by him.

Modification of schemes

7.—(1) If at any time after a transfer scheme has come into force the Secretary of State considers it appropriate to do so, having consulted the Countryside Council for Wales and the Countryside Commission, he may by order provide that the scheme shall for all purposes be deemed to have come into force with such modifications as may be specified in the order.

(2) An order under sub-paragraph (1) above may make, with effect from the coming into force of scheme, such provision as could have been made by the scheme and in connection with giving effect to that provision from that time may contain such supplemental, consequential and transitional provision as the Secretary of State considers appropriate.

Provision of information to Secretary of State

8. It shall be the duty of the Countryside Council for Wales and the Countryside Commission to provide the Secretary of State with all such information and other assistance as he may reasonably require for the purposes of or in connection with the exercise of any power conferred on him by paragraphs 6 and 7 above.

Contents of scheme

9.—(1) A transfer scheme may—
(a) define the property, rights and liabilities to be allocated to the Countryside Council for Wales by specifying or describing them or by referring to all the property, rights and liabilities comprised in a specified part of the undertaking of the Countryside Commission (or partly in one way and partly in the other);
(b) create in favour of the Countryside Commission an interest in or right over property transferred in accordance with the scheme (or any earlier scheme) to the Countryside Council for Wales;
(c) require the Countryside Council for Wales to enter into written agreements with, or execute other instruments in favour of, the Countryside Commission;
and a scheme may make such supplemental, incidental and consequential provision as the Countryside Commission consider appropriate (including provision as to the order in which transfers or transactions are to be regarded as having occurred).

(2) Paragraph 5 above shall apply to transfer schemes under section 136 of this Act.

PART III

EMPLOYMENT OF STAFF OF EXISTING BODIES

Proposals for staff of Nature Conservancy Council

10. Not later than such date or dates as the Secretary of State may determine, the Nature Conservancy Council shall prepare and submit to the Secretary of State for approval proposals that would secure that an offer is made by one of the new Councils to each person who will be entitled to receive an offer under section 137 of this Act.

11.—(1) The Secretary of State may, after consultation with the new Councils—
(a) approve the proposals submitted to him under paragraph 10 above or modify the proposals before approving them;
(b) if he decides not to approve the proposals or if the Nature Conservancy Council fail to submit the proposals by the due date, make his own proposals;
and any proposals made by the Secretary of State shall be treated for all purposes as if they were made by the Council and approved by him.

(2) It shall be the duty of the Nature Conservancy Council and the new Councils to provide the Secretary of State with all such information and other assistance as he may reasonably require for the purposes of or in connection with the exercise of any power conferred on him by this paragraph.

Proposals for certain staff of the Countryside Commission

12. Not later than such date or dates as the Secretary of State may determine, the Countryside Commission shall prepare and submit to the Secretary of State for approval proposals as to which of their employees are to receive offers of employment from the Countryside Council for Wales under section 137 of this Act.

13.—(1) The Secretary of State may, after consultation with the Countryside Council for Wales—
(a) approve the proposals submitted to him under paragraph 12 above or modify the proposals before approving them;
(b) if he decides not to approve the proposals or if the Countryside Commission fail to submit the proposals by the due date, make his own proposals;
and any proposals made by the Secretary of State shall be treated for all purposes as if they were made by the Commission and approved by him.

(2) It shall be the duty of the Countryside Commission and the Countryside Council for Wales to provide the Secretary of State with all such information and other assistance as he may reasonably require for the purposes of or in connection with the exercise of any power conferred on him by this paragraph.

Offers of employment

14.—(1) Each new Council shall, before such date as the Secretary of State may direct, make offers of employment in accordance with this paragraph to those persons allocated to that Council by the proposals under paragraph 10 above as approved by the Secretary of State.

(2) The Countryside Council for Wales shall, before such date as the Secretary of State may direct, make offers of employment in accordance with this paragraph to those persons who are the subject of proposals under paragraph 12 above as approved by the Secretary of State.

(3) The terms of employment to be offered shall be such that they are, taken as a whole, not less favourable to the person to whom the offer is made than the terms on which he is employed on the date on which the offer is made.

(4) An offer under this paragraph shall not be revocable during the period of three months commencing with the date on which it is made.

Continuity of employment, redundancy etc.

15. Where a person becomes an employee of a new Council in consequence of an offer made under paragraph 14(1) or (2) above, then, for the purposes of the Employment Protection (Consolidation) Act 1978, his period of employment with the Nature Conservancy Council, or as the case may be, the Countryside Commission shall count as a period of employment by the new Council and the change of employment shall not break the continuity of the period of employment.

16. Where an offer is made to a person in pursuance of paragraph 14(1) or (2) above, none of the redundancy procedures applicable to such a person shall apply to him; and where that person ceases to be employed by the Nature Conservancy Council or, as the case may be, the Countryside Commission—
   (a) on becoming employed by a new Council, or
   (b) having unreasonably refused an offer,
Part VI of the Employment Protection (Consolidation) Act 1978 shall not apply to him and he shall not be treated for the purposes of any superannuation or other pension scheme as having been retired on redundancy.

Disputes

17.—(1) Any dispute as to whether an offer under paragraph 14(1) or (2) above complies with sub-paragraph (3) of that paragraph shall be referred to and determined by an industrial tribunal.

(2) An industrial tribunal shall not consider a complaint referred to it under sub-paragraph (1) above unless the complaint is presented to the tribunal before the end of the period of three months beginning with the date of the offer or, where the tribunal is satisfied that it was not reasonably practicable for that to be done, within such further period as the tribunal considers reasonable.

(3) Subject to sub-paragraph (4) below, there shall be no appeal from the decision of an industrial tribunal under this paragraph.

(4) An appeal to the Employment Appeal Tribunal may be made only on a point of law arising from a decision of, or in proceedings before, an industrial tribunal under this paragraph.

Section 139 SCHEDULE 11

TRANSITIONAL PROVISIONS AND SAVINGS FOR PART VII

PART I

COUNTRYSIDE FUNCTIONS

Preliminary

1. In this Part of this Schedule—
   "the appointed day" means the day appointed under section 130(4) of this Act;
   "the Commission" means the Countryside Commission;
   "the Council" means the Countryside Council for Wales;
   "relevant," in relation to anything done by or in relation to the Commission before the appointed day, means anything which, if it were to be done on or after the appointed day, would be done by or in relation to the Council or, as the case may be, by or in relation to both the Commission (so far as concerning England) and the Council (so far as concerning Wales).

Continuity of exercise of functions

2.—(1) Any relevant thing done by or in relation to the Commission before the appointed day shall, so far as is required for continuing its effect on and after that date, have effect as if done by or in relation to the Council or, as the case may be, by or in relation to both the Council and the Commission.

(2) Any relevant thing which, immediately before the appointed day, is in the process of being done by or in relation to the Commission may be continued by or in relation to the Council or, as the case may be, by or in relation to both the Council and the Commission.

Construction of references to the Countryside Commission

3.—(1) This paragraph applies to any provision of any agreement, or of any instrument or other document, subsisting immediately before the appointed day which refers (in whatever terms) to the Commission and does so (or is to be construed as doing so) in relation to, or to things being done in or in connection with, Wales.

(2) Any provision to which this paragraph applies shall, subject to sub-paragraphs (3) and (4) below, have effect on and after the appointed day with the substitution for, or the inclusion in, any reference to the Commission of a reference to the Council, according as the reference concerns Wales only or concerns both England and Wales.

(3) Any provision to which this paragraph applies which refers in general terms to members of or to persons employed by or agents of the Commission shall have effect on and after the appointed day with the substitution for, or the inclusion in, any such reference of a reference to members of or persons employed by or agents of the Council, according as the reference concerns Wales only or concerns both England and Wales.

(4) Any provision to which this paragraph applies which refers to a member or employee of the Commission shall have effect on and after the appointed day with the substitution for, or the inclusion in, any such reference of—

(a) a reference to such person as the Council may appoint, or
(b) in default of appointment, to the member or employee of the Council who corresponds as nearly as may be to the member or employee in question,

according as the reference concerns Wales only or concerns both England and Wales.

4.—(1) This paragraph applies to any provision of a local Act passed, or subordinate legislation made, before the appointed day which refers (in whatever terms) to the Commission and relates to, or to things being done in or in connection with, Wales.

(2) The Secretary of State may by order make such consequential modifications of any provision to which this paragraph applies as appear to him to be necessary or expedient.

(3) Subject to any exercise of the power conferred by sub-paragraph (2) above, any provision to which this paragraph applies shall have effect on and after the appointed day with the substitution for, or inclusion in, any reference to the Commission of a reference to the Council, according as the reference concerns Wales only or concerns both England and Wales.

Existing areas of outstanding natural beauty and long distance routes

5.—(1) This paragraph applies to—
(a) any area of land which immediately before the appointed day is an area of outstanding natural beauty designated under section 87 of the 1949 Act of which part is in England and part is in Wales (referred to as "the two parts" of such an area); and
(b) any long distance route under Part IV of that Act of which some parts are in England and other parts in Wales.

(2) On and after the appointed day the two parts of an area to which this paragraph applies shall be treated as if each were a distinct area of outstanding natural beauty; and accordingly, so far as may be necessary for the purpose of applying paragraphs 2 and 3 above, anything done by or in relation to the Commission in relation to both parts of that area shall be treated as having been done in relation to the part in Wales by or in relation to the Council.

(3) On and after the appointed day any route to which this paragraph applies shall not cease, by virtue of this Part of this Act, to be a single route for the purposes of Part IV of the 1949 Act; but any function which before that day is exercisable by or in relation to the Commission shall, on and after that day be exercisable by or in relation to the Commission (so far as concerns parts of the route in England) and by or in relation to the Council (so far as concerns parts of the route in Wales).

(4) On or after the appointed day the Commission and the Council shall each exercise any function of theirs in relation to an area or route to which this paragraph applies only after consultation with the other; and the Commission and the Council may make arrangements for discharging any of their functions in relation to such an area or route jointly.

PART II

NATURE CONSERVATION FUNCTIONS

Preliminary

6. In this Part of this Schedule—

"appointed day" means the date appointed under section 131(3) of this Act;
"appropriate new council" shall be construed in accordance with paragraph 7 below; and
"new council" means a council established by section 128(1) of this Act.

7.—(1) In this Part of this Schedule a reference to "the appropriate new council" is, in relation to or to things done in connection with property, rights or liabilities of the Nature Conservancy Council which are transferred by section 135(2) of this Act to a new council, a reference to that new council.

(2) Subject to sub-paragraph (1) above, a reference in this Part of this Schedule to "the appropriate new council" is, in relation to anything else done before the appointed day by or in relation to the Nature Conservancy Council in the exercise of or in connection with any function of theirs (other than a function corresponding to a special function of the new councils)—
  (a) a reference to the new council by whom the nature conservation function corresponding to that function is exercisable on and after that date; or
  (b) where the thing done relates to a matter affecting the area of more than one new council, a reference to each new council by whom the nature conservation function corresponding to that function is exercisable on and after that date;
and in relation to anything done in the exercise of or in connection with any function of the Nature Conservancy Council corresponding to a special function of the new councils a reference to "the appropriate new council" is a reference to the joint committee or, where directions under section 133(5) of this Act have been given, the new council by whom the corresponding special function is dischargeable (on behalf of the new councils) on and after that day.

(3) Any question arising under this paragraph as to which new council is the appropriate new council in relation to any particular function of the Nature Conservancy Council may be determined by a direction given by the Secretary of State.

Continuity of exercise of functions

8.—(1) Anything done (or deemed by any enactment to have been done) by or in relation to the Nature Conservancy Council before the appointed day shall, so far as is required for continuing its effect on and after that date, have effect as if done by or in relation to the appropriate new council.

(2) Anything which immediately before the appointed day is in the process of being done by or in relation to the Nature Conservancy Council may be continued by or in relation to the appropriate new council as if it had been done by or in relation to that council.

Construction of references to the Nature Conservancy Council

9.—(1) This paragraph applies to any agreement, any instrument and any other document subsisting immediately before the appointed day which refers (in whatever terms) to the Nature Conservancy Council, other than a scheme provided by that Council under paragraph 12 of Schedule 3 to the Nature Conservancy Council Act 1973.

(2) Any agreement, instrument or other document to which this paragraph applies shall have effect on and after the appointed day with the substitution—
  (a) for any reference to the Nature Conservancy Council of a reference to the appropriate new council;
  (b) for any reference in general terms to members of or to persons employed by or agents of the Nature Conservancy Council of a reference to members of or persons employed by or agents of the appropriate new council; and
  (c) for any reference to a member or officer of the Nature Conservancy Council of a reference to such person as the appropriate new council may appoint or, in default of appointment, to the member or employee of that council who corresponds as nearly as may be to the member or officer in question.

10.—(1) This paragraph applies to any provision of a local Act passed, or subordinate legislation made, before the appointed day which refers (in whatever terms) to the Nature Conservancy Council.

(2) The Secretary of State may by order make such consequential modifications of any provision to which this paragraph applies as appear him to be necessary or expedient.

(3) Subject to any exercise of the power conferred by sub-paragraph (2) above, any provision to which this paragraph applies shall have effect on and after the appointed day with the substitution for each reference to the Nature Conservancy Council of a reference to such one or more of the new councils as may be appropriate, according as the provision relates to, or to things being done in or in connection with, England, Scotland or Wales.

Pensions for Nature Conservancy Council staff

11.—(1) The repeal by this Act of paragraph 12 of Schedule 3 to the Nature Conservancy

Council Act 1973 shall not affect the operation on and after the appointed day of any scheme provided by the Nature Conservancy Council for the payment to or in respect of its officers of pensions, allowances or gratuities.

(2) Any such scheme shall have effect on and after the appointed day with the substitution for any reference to the Nature Conservancy Council of a reference to the Secretary of State.

Existing nature reserves and areas of special scientific interest

12.—(1) This paragraph applies to any land which, immediately before the appointed day is—
  (a) a nature reserve (within the meaning of Part III of the 1949 Act) which is managed by, or under an agreement entered into with, the Nature Conservancy Council or which is the subject of a declaration under section 35 of the 1981 Act; or
  (b) an area of special scientific interest which has been notified by the Nature Conservancy Council under section 28(1) of the 1981 Act or is treated by section 28(13) of that Act as having been notified under section 28(1)(a) of that Act or is an area to which an order unless section 29(1) of that Act relates;

and of which part is in England and part is in Wales or, as the case may be, part is in England and part is in Scotland (referred to as "the two parts" of such a reserve or area).

(2) On and after the appointed day, the two parts of any reserve or area to which this paragraph applies shall be treated as if each were a distinct nature reserve or area of special scientific interest; and accordingly, so far as may be necessary for the purpose of applying paragraphs 8 and 9 above, anything done by or in relation to the Nature Conservancy Council affecting both parts of that reserve or area shall be treated as having been done by or in relation to each of the two parts separately.

(3) On and after the appointed day the new council exercising functions as respects either part of a reserve or area to which this paragraph applies shall exercise those functions only after consultation with the new council exercising functions as respects the other part; and those councils may make arrangements for discharging any of those functions jointly.

PART III

SUPPLEMENTARY

13. Paragraphs 3, 4, 5, 8, 9, 10 and 12 above are without prejudice to any provision made by or under this Part of this Act in relation to any particular functions, property, rights or liabilities; and, in particular, nothing in this Schedule applies in relation to contracts of employment made by the Countryside Commission or the Nature Conservancy Council.

14. The Secretary of State may, in relation to any particular functions of the Countryside Commission or the Nature Conservancy Council, by order exclude, or modify or supplement any provision of this Schedule or make such other transitional provision as he may think necessary or expedient.

15. In this Schedule "the 1949 Act" means the National Parks and Access to the Countryside Act 1949 and "the 1981 Act" means the Wildlife and Countryside Act 1981.

Sections 140 and 142   SCHEDULE 12

INJURIOUS OR HAZARDOUS SUBSTANCES: ADVISORY COMMITTEE

1. The Secretary of State shall appoint the members of the committee, and shall appoint one of those members to be chairman.

2. The committee shall include persons who appear to the Secretary of State to be representative of—
  (a) persons engaged in carrying on industrial or commercial undertakings;
  (b) persons having scientific knowledge of matters concerning pollution of the environment;
  (c) bodies concerned with the protection or improvement of the environment; and
  (d) bodies concerned with the protection of persons using substances or articles subject to regulation under section 140 or 142 of this Act.

3. The Secretary of State may make provision by regulations with respect to the terms on which members of the committee are to hold and vacate office, including the terms on which any person appointed as chairman is to hold and vacate office as chairman.

4. The Secretary of State shall provide the committee with such services and other facilities as appear to him to be necessary or expedient for the proper performance of the committee's functions.

5. The Secretary of State may pay to the members of the committee such remuneration (if any) and such allowances as may be determined by the Secretary of State with the consent of the Treasury.

Section 144   SCHEDULE 13

AMENDMENTS OF HAZARDOUS SUBSTANCES LEGISLATION

PART I

ENGLAND AND WALES

1. The Planning (Hazardous Substances) Act 1990 shall be amended as provided in this Part of this Schedule.

2.—(1) Section 2 (appropriate Minister to be hazardous substances authority for land used or to be used by statutory undertakers) shall be omitted.

(2) In section 7(3), for the words from "means" to "with" in the third place it occurs there shall be substituted the words "means consultations with the Health and Safety Executive and with."

(3) In section 10(2), for the words from the beginning to "3" there shall be substituted the words "A hazardous substances authority."

(4) In section 28(1)—

(a) in paragraph (a), for the words following the word "consent" there shall be substituted the words "made to that authority;
   (aa) to applications under section 17(1) made to that authority;"; and
(b) after paragraph (d), there shall be inserted the following words—
"; and every such register shall also contain such information as may be prescribed as to the manner in which applications for hazardous substances consent have been dealt with."

(5) In section 29, in subsection (3) and (4), for the words "appropriate body" there shall be substituted the words "Health and Safety Executive."

(6) In section 38(5) for the words "1 to 3" there shall be substituted "1, 3."

(7) In section 39(1), in the definition of "hazardous substances authority," for the word "to," in the second place it occurs, there shall be inserted the word "and."

3. In section 7(1)(a) (applications for consent), after the word "applications" there shall be inserted the words "under this Act."

4. In section 11 (deemed hazardous substances consent in transitional cases)—
(a) in subsection (2) for the words "immediately before the relevant date" there shall be substituted the words "while it was so present"; and
(b) in subsection (7), in paragraph (a), at the beginning there shall be inserted the words "to the condition that" and, for paragraphs (b) and (c), there shall be substituted the words ", and
   (b) to such other conditions (if any) as are prescribed for the purposes of this section and are applicable in the case of that consent."

5. In section 12 (deemed consent: government authorisation), at the end there shall be added the following subsection—

"(6) A government department or the Secretary of State shall, as respects any hazardous substances consent deemed to be granted by virtue of directions under this section, send to the hazardous substances authority concerned any such information as appears to be required by them for the purposes of a register under section 28."

6. In section 13 (applications for hazardous substances consent in place of subsisting consent subject to conditions), subsection (7) shall be omitted.

7. In section 22 (validity of decisions as to applications), in subsection (4), for the words "1971 Act" there shall be substituted the words "principal Act."

8. In section 25(1)(c) (provisions of principal Act capable of application to hazardous substances contravention notices), after "184," there shall be inserted "186,"

9. Before section 27 there shall be inserted the following section—

"Fees for consent applications

26A.—(1) Provision may be made by regulations for the payment of a fee of the prescribed amount to a hazardous substances authority in respect of an application for, or for the continuation of, hazardous substances consent.

(2) Regulations under this section may provide for the payment to the Secretary of State of a fee of the prescribed amount in respect of any application which is, by virtue of regulations under section 25, deemed to have been made for hazardous substances consent.

(3) Regulations under this section may provide—
 (a) for the transfer of prescribed fees received by a hazardous substances authority in respect of any application which is referred to the Secretary of State under section 20;
 (b) for the remission of refunding of a prescribed fee (in whole or in part) in prescribed circumstances or in pursuance of a direction given by the Secretary of State;
and the regulations may make different provision for different areas or for different cases or descriptions of cases."

10. In section 303(6) of the Town and Country Planning Act 1990 (meaning of "Planning Acts" for purposes of fees chargeable under that section), at the end there shall be inserted the words "or the Planning (Hazardous Substances) Act 1990.")

PART II

SCOTLAND

11.—(1) The Town and Country Planning (Scotland) Act 1972 shall be amended as provided in this paragraph.

(2) Section 56B (appropriate Minister to be planning authority in respect of hazardous substances in relation to land used or to be used by statutory undertakers) shall be omitted.

(3) In section 56D(1)(a) (applications for consent, after the word "applications" there shall be inserted the words "under this Act."

(4) In section 56D(5) for the words from "means" to "with" in the third place it occurs there shall be substituted the words "means consultations with the Health and Safety Executive and with."

(5) After section 56D there shall be inserted the following section
"Fees
 56DA.—(1) The Secretary of State may by regulations make provision for fees of the prescribed amount in respect of applications for, or for the continuation of, hazardous substances consent—
 (a) made to an urban development corporation under section 56A(2) above to be paid to the corporation;
 (b) referred to him under section 32 above as having effect by virtue of section 56F below to be paid to him;
 (c) deemed to have been made to him under section 85(7) below by virtue of regulations made under section 97B(10) below to be paid to him.
 (2) Regulations made under this section may provide for—
 (a) the transfer to the Secretary of State of any fee received by a planning authority in respect of an application referred to in paragraph (b) or (c) of subsection (1) above;
 (b) the remission of refunding of a prescribed fee (in whole or in part) in prescribed circumstances or in pursuance of a direction given by him;
and the regulations may make different provision for different areas or for different cases or descriptions of cases."

(6) In section 56E(5) for the words "a planning authority other than the appropriate Minister" there shall be substituted the word "they."

(7) In section 56G (deemed consent: government authorisation), at the end there shall be added the following subsection—
"(5) A government department or the Secretary of State shall, as respects any hazardous substances consent deemed to be granted by virtue of directions under this section, send to the planning authority concerned any such information as appears to be required by them for the purposes of a register under section 56N."

(8) In section 56H (applications for hazardous substances consent in place of subsisting consent subject to conditions) subsection (5) shall be omitted.

(9) In section 56N(1)—
 (a) in paragraph (a), for the words following the word "consent" there shall be substituted the words "made to that authority;
  (aa) to applications under section 56K(2) above made to that authority;" and
 (b) after paragraph (d), there shall be inserted the following words—
 ", and every such register shall also contain such information as may be prescribed as to the manner in which applications for hazardous substances consent have been dealt with."

(10) In section 56O, in subsections (2) and (3), for the words "appropriate body" there shall be substituted the words "Health and Safety Executive."

(11) In section 97B(10(c) (hazardous substances contravention notices), after "89A" there shall be inserted "and 166."

12.—(1) Section 38 of the Housing and Planning Act 1986 (transitional provisions) shall be amended as provided in this paragraph.

(2) In subsection (4), for the words "immediately before the commencement date" there shall be substituted the words "while it was so present."

(3) In subsection (9)—
(a) for the words "subject to the conditions that—(a)" there shall be substituted the words "subject to—
(a) the condition that";
(b) for paragraphs (b and (c) there shall be substituted—
"(b) such other conditions (if any) as are prescribed, by statutory instrument subject to annulment in pursuance of a resolution of either House of Parliament, for the purposes of this section and are applicable in the case of that consent."

13. In section 87 of the Local Government, Planning and Land Act 1980 (fees for planning applications etc.), at the end there shall be inserted the following subsection—

"(9) Without prejudice to the generality of subsection (1) above the reference in that subsection to an application for any consent includes, in relation to a planning authority in Scotland, an application under section 56K(2) of the Town and Country Planning (Scotland) Act 1972 for the continuation of hazardous substances consent."

Section 148   SCHEDULE 14

AMENDMENTS OF THE PREVENTION OF OIL POLLUTION ACT 1971

1. The prevention of Oil Pollution Act 1971 shall be amended as follows.

2. In section 19 (prosecutions), after subsection (4), there shall be inserted the following subsection—

"(4A) Any document required or authorised, by virtue of any statutory provision, to be served on a foreign company for the purposes of the institution of, or otherwise in connection with, proceedings for an offence under section 2(2A) of this Act alleged to have been committed by the company as the owner of a vessel shall be treated as duly served on that company if the document is served on the master of the vessel; and any person authorised to serve any document for the purposes of the institution of, or otherwise in connection with, proceeding for an offence under this Act (whether or not in pursuance of the foregoing provisions of this subsection) shall, for that purpose, have the right to go on board the vessel in question.

(4B) In subsection (4A) of this section a 'foreign company' means a company or body which is not one to whom any of the following provisions applies—
(a) sections 695 and 725 of the Companies Act 1985;
(b) Articles 645 and 673 of the Companies (Northern Ireland) Order 1986,
so as to authorise the service of the document in question under any of those provisions."

3. After that section there shall be inserted the following section—
"Power to detain vessels
19A.—(1) Where a harbour master has reason to believe that the master or owner of a vessel has committed an offence under section 2(2A) of this Act by the discharge from the vessel of oil, or a mixture containing oil, into the waters of the harbour, the harbour master may detain the vessel.

(2) Subsections (1) and (2) of section 692 of the Merchant Shipping Act 1894 (enforcing detention of ship) shall apply in relation to a vessel detained under subsection (1) of this section as they apply in relation to a ship detained that Act but as if—
(a) in subsection (1) (penalties where ship proceeds to sea while subject to detention)—
    (i) for the words from 'any commissioned officer' to 'and if' there were substituted the word 'and'; and
    (ii) for the reference to competent authority there were substituted a reference to the harbour authority; and
(b) in subsection (2) (penalties where a ship so proceeds to sea when any officer authorised to detain the ship is on board), for any reference to any officer authorised to detain the ship, or any surveyor or officer of the Secretary of State or any officer of Customs and Excise there were substituted a reference to the harbour master or any person acting on his behalf.

(3) Where a harbour master detains a ship other than a United Kingdom ship (within the meaning of section 21(2) of the Merchant Shipping Act 1979) under this section he shall immediately notify the Secretary of State who shall then inform the consul or diplomatic

representative of the State whose flag the ship is entitled to fly or the appropriate maritime authorities of that State.

(4) A harbour master who exercises the power conferred by subsection (1) of this section shall immediately release the vessel—
(a) if no proceedings for the offence in question are instituted within the period of seven days beginning with the day on which the vessel is detained;
(b) if such proceedings, having been instituted within that period, are concluded without the master or owner being convicted;
(c) if either—
    (i) the sum of £55,000 is paid to the harbour authority by way of security, or
    (ii) security which, in the opinion of the harbour authority, is satisfactory and is for an amount not less than £55,000 is given to the harbour authority,
by or on behalf of the master or owner; or
(d) where the master or owner is convicted of the offence, if any costs or expenses ordered to be paid by him, and any fine imposed on him, have been paid.

(5) The harbour authority shall repay any sum paid in pursuance of subsection (4)(c) of this section or release any security so given—
(a) if no proceedings for the offence in question are instituted within the period of seven days beginning with the day on which the sum is paid; or
(b) if such proceedings, having been instituted within that period, are concluded without the master or owner being convicted.

(6) Where a sum has been paid, or security has been given, by any person in pursuance of subsection (4)(c) of this section and the master or owner is convicted of the offence in question, the sum so paid or the amount made available under the security shall be applied as follows—
(a) first in payment of any costs or expenses ordered by the court to be paid by the master or owner; and
(b) next in payment of any fine imposed by the court;
and any balance shall be repaid to the first mentioned person.

(7) Any reference in this section to a harbour master or a harbour authority shall, where the harbour in question consists of or includes the whole or any part of a dockyard port within the meaning of the Dockyard Ports Regulation Act 1865, be construed as including a reference to the Queen's harbour master for the port.

(8) For the purposes of this section in its application to England and Wales and, subject to section 30(4A) of this Act, in its application to Northern Ireland—
(a) proceedings for an offence are instituted—
    (i) when a justice of the peace issues a summons or warrant under section 1 of the Magistrates' Courts Act 1980 in respect of the offence,
    (ii) when a person is charged with the offence after being taken into custody without a warrant,
    (iii) when a bill of indictment is preferred by virtue of section 2(2)(b) of the Administration of Justice (Miscellaneous Provisions) Act 1933;
and where the application of this paragraph would result in there being more than one time for the institution of proceedings, they shall be taken to have been instituted at the earliest of those times; and
(b) proceedings for an offence are concluded without the master or owner being convicted on the occurrence of one of the following events—
    (i) the discontinuance of the proceedings;
    (ii) the acquittal of the master or owner;
    (iii) the quashing of the master or owner's conviction for the offence;
    (iv) the grant of Her Majesty's pardon in respect of the master or owner's conviction for the offence.

(9) For the purposes of this section in its application to Scotland—
(a) proceedings for an offence are instituted—
    (i) on the granting by the sheriff of a warrant in respect of the offence on presentation of a petition under section 12 of the Criminal Procedure (Scotland) Act 1975;
    (ii) when, in the absence of a warrant or citation, the master or owner is first brought before a court competent to deal with the case;
    (iii) when, in a case where he is liberated upon a written undertaking in terms of section 18(2)(a), 294(2)(a) or 295(1)(a) of the Criminal Procedure (Scotland) Act 1975, the master or owner appears at the specified court at the specified time;
    (iv) when, in a case mentioned in paragraph (iii) above where the master or owner fails to appear at the specified court at the specified time, the court grants warrant for his apprehension;
    (v) when summary proceedings are commenced in terms of section 331(3) of the Criminal Procedure (Scotland) Act 1975; and

(b) proceedings for an offence are concluded without the master or owner being convicted on the occurrence of one of the following events—
  (i) the court makes a finding of not guilty or not proven against the master or owner in respect of the offence;
  (ii) the proceedings are expressly abandoned (other than *pro loco et tempore*) by the prosecutor or are deserted simpliciter;
  (iii) the conviction is quashed;
  (iv) the accused receives Her Majesty's pardon in respect of the conviction.

(10) This section shall not apply in relation to any vessel of Her Majesty's navy or to any Government ship (within the meaning of section 80 of the Merchant Shipping Act 1906)."

4. In section 20(1) (power of court to direct amount of unpaid fine to be levied by distress or poinding and sale of vessel) after the words "is not paid" there shall be inserted the words ", or any costs or expenses ordered to be paid by him are not paid,".

5. In section 24(2) (application of Act to Government ships), for the words "and subsection (4) of section 16" there shall be substituted the words ", subsection (4) of section 16 and subsection (10) of section 19A."

6. In section 25(1) (power to extend provisions of Act to Isle of Man, Channel Islands etc.), after the words "other than section 3" there shall be inserted the words "or 19A".

7. In section 30 (provisions as to Northern Ireland), after subsection (4), there shall be inserted the following subsection—

"(4A) In its application to proceedings in Northern Ireland, subsection (8)(a) of section 19A of this Act shall have effect as if—
(a) in sub-paragraph (i), for the references to section 1 of the Magistrates' Courts Act 1980 there were substituted a reference to Article 20 of the Magistrates' Courts (Northern Ireland) Order 1981; and
(b) for sub-paragraph (iii) there were substituted—
  '(iii) when an indictment is presented under section 2(2)(c), (e) or (f) of the Grand Jury (Abolition) Act (Northern Ireland) 1969;'."

Section 162 SCHEDULE 15

CONSEQUENTIAL AND MINOR AMENDMENTS OF ENACTMENTS

Statutory nuisances: Scotland

1. In section 3 of the Public Health (Scotland) Act 1897 at the end there shall be added the following paragraph—

"The word 'ratepayer' means a person who either is liable to pay any of the community charges or community water charges imposed under the Abolition of Domestic Rates Etc. (Scotland) Act 1987 (or would be so liable but for any enactment or anything provided or done under any enactment) or is a non-domestic ratepayer."

Exclusion of Alkali Works Act for prescribed processes

2. In the Alkali, &c. Works Regulation Act 1906 there shall be inserted, after section 2, the following section—
"Relation to Environmental Protection Act 1990, Part I
2A.—(1) The preceding provisions of this Part of this Act shall not apply to any process which is a prescribed process as from the date which is the determination date for that process.
(2) The 'determination date' for a prescribed process is—
  (a) in the case of a process for which an authorisation is granted, the date on which the enforcing authority grants it, whether in pursuance of the application or, on an appeal, of a direction to grant it;
  (b) in the case of a process for which an authorisation is refused, the date of the refusal or, on an appeal, of the affirmation of the refusal.
(3) In this section 'authorisation', 'enforcing authority' and 'prescribed process' have the meaning given in section 1 of the Environmental Protection Act 1990 and the reference to an appeal is a reference to an appeal under section 15 of that Act.".

and, immediately before section 25, as section 24A, a section in the same terms as the section 2A inserted after section 2.

Stray dogs

3.—(1) The following provisions of the Dogs Act 1906 shall be amended as follows.

(2) The amendments made to section 3 by section 39(2) of the Local Government Act 1988 and section 128(1)(a) of the Civic Government (Scotland) Act 1982 shall cease to have effect.

(3) In section 4—
(a) subsection (1) shall be omitted;
(b) in subsection (2), for the words "so taken to a police station" there shall be substituted the words "taken to a police station in pursuance of section 150(1) of the Environmental Protection Act 1990";
(c) in subsection (2)(a), for the words from "his name and address' to "other" there shall be substituted the words "this fact and shall furnish his name and address and the police officer shall, having complied with the procedure (if any) prescribed under subsection (5) below, allow the finder to remove the dog";
(d) in subsection (3), for the words from "fails" to "section" there shall be substituted the words "removes the dog but fails to keep it for at least one month,"; and
(e) after subsection (3) or, as respects Scotland, subsection (4) there shall be inserted as subsection (4) or subsection (5) the following subsection—

"( ) The Secretary of State may, by regulations made by statutory instrument, prescribe the procedure to be followed under subsection (2)(a) above and any instrument containing regulations under this subsection shall be subject to annulment in pursuance of a resolution of either House of Parliament."

Statutory nuisances

4.—(1) The following provisions of the Public Health Act 1936 (matters deemed statutory nuisances) shall be amended as follows.

(2) In section 141, for the words "Part III of this Act" there shall be substituted the words "Part III of the Environmental Protection Act 1990".

(3) In section 259(1), for the words "Part III of this Act" there shall be substituted the words "Part III of the Environmental Protection Act 1990."

(4) In section 268—
(a) in subsection (1), for the words "Part III" there shall be substituted the words "Part III of the Environmental Protection Act 1990 and Parts";
(b) in subsection (2), for the words "the said Part III" there shall be substituted the words "Part III of the Environmental Protection Act 1990"; and
(c) in subsection (3), for the words "Part III of this Act" there shall be substituted the words "Part III of the Environmental Protection Act 1990."

5.—(1) Section 151 of the Mines and Quarries Act 1954 (matters deemed statutory nuisances) shall be amended as follows.

(2) In subsection (2), for the words "Part III of the Public Health Act 1936" there shall be substituted the words "Part III of the Environmental Protection Act 1990."

(3) In subsection (3), for the words "Part III of the Public Health Act 1936" there shall be substituted the words "Part III of the Environmental Protection Act 1990."

(4) In subsection (5), for the words "Part III of the Public Health Act 1936" there shall be substituted the words "Part III of the Environmental Protection Act 1990."

Exclusion of Clean Air Act 1956 for prescribed processes

6. In the Clean Air Act 1956 there shall be inserted, immediately before section 17, the following section—

"Relation to Environmental Protection Act 1990, Part I
16A.—(1) The preceding provisions of this Act shall not apply to any process which is a prescribed process as from the date which is the determination date for that process.

(2) The 'determination date' for a prescribed process is—
(a) in the case of a process for which an authorisation is granted, the date on which the enforcing authority grants it, whether in pursuance of the application or, on an appeal, of a direction to grant it;
(b) in the case of a process for which an authorisation is refused, the date of the refusal or, on an appeal, of the affirmation of the refusal.

(3) In this section 'authorisation', 'enforcing authority' and 'prescribed process' have the meaning given in section 1 of the Environmental Protection Act 1990 and the reference to an appeal is a reference to an appeal under section 15 of that Act."

Statutory nuisances

7.—(1) The following provisions of the Clean Air Act 1956 (references to statutory nuisances) shall be amended as follows.

(2) In section 18(2) and (5) for the words "section ninety-two of the Public Health Act 1936" there shall be substituted the words "the provisions of Part III of the Environmental Protection Act 1990."

(3) In section 21(1)—
 (a) for the words "or the Clean Air Act 1968" there shall be substituted the words ", the Clean Air Act 1968 or the Environmental Protection Act 1990"; and
 (b) in paragraph (a), at the end, there shall be inserted the words "and Part III of the Environmental Protection Act 1990,".

8. The Radioactive Substances Act 1960 shall be amended by the insertion in Part I of Schedule 1 (exclusion of other controls) at the end, of the following paragraph—

"9. Part III of the Environmental Protection Act 1990."

9. In section 1(1)(g) of the Hovercraft Act 1968 (power to exclude noise nuisance proceedings), after the word "1974" there shall be inserted the words "or Part III of the Environmental Protection Act 1990."

Goods vehicle operators' licences: pollution offences

10.—(1) The following provisions of the Transport Act 1968 shall be amended as follows.
(2) In section 69 (revocation, suspension etc. of goods vehicle operators' licence on grounds of convictions, etc.)—
 (a) in subsection (1)(b)(i), for the words "paragraphs (a) to (fff)" there shall be substituted the words "paragraphs (a) to (ffff)", and
 (b) in subsection (4), after paragraph (fff) there shall be inserted the following paragraph—

"(ffff) a conviction of the holder of the licence or a servant or agent of his under—
  (i) section 3 of the Control of Pollution Act 1974;
  (ii) section 2 of the Refuse Disposal (Amenity) Act 1978;
  (iii) section 1 of the Control of Pollution (Amendment) Act 1989; and
  (iv) section 33 of the Environmental Protection Act 1990."

(3) In section 108(1) (statutory nuisance proceedings in relation to waterways), for the words "said Act of 1936" there shall be substituted the words "Environmental Protection Act 1990."

National Park Wardens

11. In section 42 of the Countryside Act 1968 (National Park Wardens), in subsection (4)(a), for the words "section 1 of the Litter Act 1983" there shall be substituted the words "section 87 of the Environmental Protection Act 1990."

Exclusion of Clean Air Act 1968 for prescribed processes

12. In the Clean Air Act 1968 there shall be inserted, after section 11, the following section—

"Relation to Environmental Protection Act 1990, Part I
11A.—(1) The preceding provisions of this Act shall not apply to any process which is a prescribed process as from the date which is the determination date for that process.
(2) The 'determination date' for a prescribed process is—
 (a) in the case of a process for which an authorisation is granted, the date on which the enforcing authority grants it, whether in pursuance of the application or, on an appeal, of a direction to grant it;
 (b) in the case of a process for which an authorisation is refused the date of the refusal or, on an appeal, of the affirmation of the refusal.
(3) In this section 'authorisation', 'enforcing authority' and 'prescribed process' have the meaning given in section 1 of the Environmental Protection Act 1990 and the reference to an appeal is a reference to an appeal under section 15 of that Act."

Sale of electricity: Scotland

13. In section 170A(3) of the Local Government (Scotland) Act 1973 (restriction on sale of electricity by local authority) after the word "prescribed," there shall be inserted the words "or in cases where it is produced from waste,".

Workplace emissions into the air

14. Section 5 of the Health and Safety at Work etc. Act 1974 (general duty in relation to harmful emissions into the air from prescribed premises) shall be amended by the insertion—
 (a) in subsection (1), at the beginning, of the words "Subject to subsection (5) below,"; and

(b) after subsection (4), of the following subsections—

"(5) The foregoing provisions of this section shall not apply in relation to any process which is a prescribed process as from the date which is the determination date for that process.

(6) For the purposes of subsection (5) above, the 'determination date' for a prescribed process is—
(a) in the case of a process for which an authorisation is granted, the date on which the enforcing authority grants it, whether in pursuance of the application or, on an appeal, of a direction to grant it;
(b) in the case of a process for which an authorisation is refused, the date of the refusal or, on an appeal, of the affirmation of the refusal.

(7) In subsections (5) and (6) above 'authorisation', 'enforcing authority' and 'prescribed process' have the meaning given in section 1 of the Environmental Protection Act 1990 and the reference to an appeal is a reference to an appeal under section 15 of that Act."

Water, noise and atmospheric pollution

15.—(1) The following provisions of the Control of Pollution Act 1974 shall be amended as follows.

(2) In section 30D, after the words "and 1965" there shall be inserted the words "and of the Environmental Protection Act 1990."

(3) In section 61(9), at the end, there shall be inserted the words "(in relation to Scotland) or section 82 of the Environmental Protection Act 1990 (in relation to England and Wales)."

(4) In section 65(8), at the end, there shall be inserted the words "(in relation to Scotland) or section 82 of the Environmental Protection Act 1990 (in relation to England and Wales)."

(5) In section 74(2), after paragraph (b), there shall be inserted the following:
"; or
(c) under section 80(4) of the Environmental Protection Act 1990,".

(6) In section 76(4)(a), after the words "part of a" there shall be inserted the words "process subject to Part I of the Environmental Protection Act 1990 or."

(7) In section 78(1), after the words "unless the" there shall be inserted the words "burning is part of a process subject to Part I of the Environmental Protection Act 1990 or the."

(8) In section 79(4), after the words "emissions from any" there shall be inserted the words "process subject to Part I of the Environmental Protection Act 1990 or."

(9) In section 80(3), after the words "relates to a" there shall be inserted the words "process subject to Part I of the Environmental Protection Act 1990 or a."

16.—(1) The Control of Pollution Act 1974 shall be further amended as follows.

(2) In section 31 (control of pollution of rivers etc.) in subsection (2)(b) at the end there shall be inserted—

"(v) an authorisation granted under Part I of the Environmental Protection Act 1990 for a prescribed process designated for central control; or
(vi) a waste management licence granted under Part II of the Environmental Protection Act 1990; or"

(3) In section 32 (control of discharges into rivers etc.) in subsection (4) after paragraph (b) there shall be inserted "or
(c) is authorised by an authorisation granted under Part I of the Environmental Protection Act 1990 for a prescribed process designated for central control,".

Exclusion of Part II of Control of Pollution Act 1974 for radioactive substances: Scotland

17. For subsection (6) of section 56 of the Control of Pollution Act 1974 (interpretation of Part II) there shall be substituted the following subsection—

"(6) Except as provided by regulations made under this subsection, nothing in this Part of this Act applies to radioactive waste within the meaning of the Radioactive Substances Act 1960; but regulations may—
(a) provide for prescribed provisions of this Part of this Act to have effect with such modifications as the Secretary of State considers appropriate for the purposes of dealing with such radioactive waste;
(b) make such modifications of the Radioactive Substances Act 1960 and any other Act as the Secretary of State considers appropriate in connection with regulations made under paragraph (a) above."

Statutory nuisances

18. In Section 33(2) of the Land Drainage Act 1976 (restriction on deposit of spoil), for the

words "Part III of the Public Health Act 1936" there shall be substituted the words "Part III of the Environmental Protection Act 1990."

Refuse Disposal: Scotland

19.—(1) Section 1 of the Refuse Disposal (Amenity) Act 1978 (provision by waste disposal authorities of places etc. for disposal of refuse) shall be amended in relation to Scotland as follows.

(2) In subsection (1) at the end there shall be inserted the words "and to dispose of refuse so deposited."

(3) In subsection (6) for the words from "mandamus" to the end of the subsection there shall be substituted the words "by proceedings under section 45 of the Court of Session Act 1988."

(4) In subsection (7) the definition of "local authority" and the word "and" which follows it shall be omitted.

Street cleansing: Scotland

20. In section 25 of the Local Government and Planning (Scotland) Act 1982, for subsection (3) there shall be substituted—

"(3) In subsection (2) above 'cleansing' means such cleansing as appears to the islands or as the case may be district council to be necessary in the interests of public health or safety or of the amenities of their area but does not include operations for the removal of snow or ice and 'relevant land' means any land, in the open air, to which members of the public have access and which is not comprehended in a public road within the meaning of the Roads (Scotland) Act 1984."

Byelaws relating to straw or stubble burning

21. Section 43 of the Criminal Justice Act 1982 (creation by byelaws of offences relating to burning of straw or stubble) shall cease to have effect.

Functions assignable to London port health authority

22. In section 7(4) of the Public Health (Control of Disease) Act 1984 (enactments functions under which are assignable to London port health authority), after the paragraph (k) inserted by paragraph 23 of Schedule 6 to the Building Act 1984, there shall be inserted the following paragraphs—

"(l) Part I of the Environmental Protection Act 1990;
(m) Part III of the Environmental Protection Act 1990;".

Street cleaning, etc.: restriction of traffic

23. Section 14 of the Road Traffic Regulation Act 1984 (temporary prohibition or restriction of traffic) shall be amended as follows.

(2) In section 14, after subsection (3) there shall be inserted the following subsection—

"(3A) Subject to the following provisions of this section and to sections 15 and 16 of this Act, a highway or roads authority may also make an order under subsection (1) or issue a notice under subsection (3) above where the authority is satisfied (or as the case may be) where it appears to the authority that traffic on the highway or road should be restricted or prohibited for the purpose of enabling the duty imposed by subsection (1)(a) or (2) of section 89 of the Environmental Protection Act 1990 (litter clearing and cleaning) to be discharged."

Statutory nuisance

24. In section 76(1)(b) and (4)(a) of the Building Act 1984, for the words "sections 93 to 96 of the Public Health Act 1936" there shall be substituted the words "section 80 of the Environmental Protection Act 1990."

Registers of deposits etc. at sea: Northern Ireland Assembly control of regulations

25. In section 25(3) of the Food and Environment Protection Act 1985, after paragraph (a)(ii) there shall be inserted the following sub-paragraph—

"(iii) in section 14(8), for the words from 'and any such power' onwards there shall be substituted the words 'and any such regulations shall be subject to negative resolution within the meaning of section 41(6) of the Interpretation Act (Northern Ireland) 1954; and'."

Constitution of authorities for waste disposal

26. In section 10 of the Local Government Act 1985 (joint arrangements for waste disposal functions), in subsection (4), for the words "Part I of the Control of Pollution Act 1974" there shall be substituted the words "Part II of the Environmental Protection Act 1990."

Meaning of household waste: competition

27. In Schedule 1 to the Local Government Act 1988 (competition: collection of household waste), paragraph 1 shall be amended as follows—
   (a) in sub-paragraph (1), the words "In the application of this Part to England and Wales," shall be omitted;
   (b) in sub-paragraph (2)(a), for the words "section 12 of the Control of Pollution Act 1974" there shall be substituted the words "section 45 of the Environmental Protection Act 1990";
   (c) in sub-paragraph (3), for the words "section 30(4) of the Control of Pollution Act 1974" there shall be substituted the words "section 75(8) of the Environmental Protection Act 1990"; and
   (d) sub-paragraph (4) shall be omitted.

Exclusion of Water Act 1989 controls of exercise of trade effluent function in case of prescribed processes

28.—(1) Section 74 of the Water Act 1989 (control by Secretary of State of exercise of trade effluent functions in certain cases) shall be amended as follows.
   (2) In subsection (1), after the word "shall" there shall be inserted the words "subject to subsection (3) below."
   (3) After subsection (2), there shall be inserted the following subsections—
   "(3) The provisions of Schedule 9 shall not apply in relation to any trade effluent produced or to be produced in any process which is a prescribed process designated for central control as from the date which is the determination date for that process.
   (4) The 'determination date' for a prescribed process is—
      (a) in the case of a process for which an authorisation is granted, the date on which the enforcing authority grants it, whether in pursuance of the application or, on an appeal, of a direction to grant it;
      (b) in the case of a process for which an authorisation is refused, the date of the refusal or, on an appeal, of the affirmation of the refusal.
   (5) In this section, 'authorisation', 'enforcing authority' and 'prescribed process' have the meaning given in section 1 of the Environmental Protection Act 1990 and the references to designation for central control and an appeal are references respectively to designation under section 4 and an appeal under section 15 of that Act."

Exclusion of Part III of Water Act 1989 for discharges from prescribed processes

29.—(1) Section 108 of the Water Act 1989 (no pollution offence where discharge authorised) shall be amended as follows.
   (2) In subsection (1)—
   (a) after paragraph (a), there shall be inserted the following paragraph—
      "(aa) an authorisation for a prescribed process designated for central control granted under Part I of the Environmental Protection Act 1990;";
   (b) in paragraph (b), at the beginning, there shall be inserted the words "a waste management licence or."
   (3) In subsection (9) the word "and" shall be omitted and at the end, there shall be inserted the words "; 'waste management licence' means such a licence granted under Part II of the Environmental Protection Act 1990."

Contents of registers of National Rivers Authority

30. In section 117(1) of the Water Act 1989 (registers for purposes of pollution control) at the end, there shall be inserted the following paragraph—
   "(f) any matter about which particulars are required to be kept in any register under section 20 of the Environmental Protection Act 1990 (particulars about authorisations for prescribed processes, etc.) by the chief inspector under Part I of that Act."

Carriers of controlled waste

31.—(1) The Control of Pollution (Amendment) Act 1989 shall be amended as follows.

(2) In the following provisions, for the words "disposal authority" and "disposal authorities" there shall be substituted the words "regulation authority" and "regulation authorities" respectively, that is to say, in sections 1(4)(a), 2(1), (2)(b) and (e), (3)(a) and (e) and (4)(a), (b) and (c), 3(1), (2) and (6), 4(1), (3), (4), (5) and (8)(b) and (c), 5(1) and (4)(a), 6(1), (2), (3), (5), (6), (7)(a) and (c), (8) and (9) and 7(1), (2), (3)(a) and (8).

(3) In section 6(1) (offences justifying seizure of vehicles), in paragraph (a)(i)—
(a) after "1974" there shall be inserted the words "or section 33 of the Environmental Protection Act 1990"; and
(b) after the word "unlicensed" there shall be inserted the words "deposit, treatment or."

(4) In section 7 (enforcement)—
(a) in subsection (1), for the words from "91" to "information)" there shall be substituted the words "68(3), (4) and (5), 69, 70 and 71 of the Environmental Protection Act 1990 (powers of entry, of dealing with imminent pollution and to obtain information)";
(b) in subsection (2), paragraph (b) shall be omitted; and
(c) in subsection (8), for the words "97 of the Control of Pollution Act 1974" there shall be substituted the words "72 of the Environmental Protection Act 1990."

(5) In section 9(1)—
(a) in the definition of "controlled waste"—
    (i) for the words ", subject to subsection (2) below," there shall be substituted the words ", at any time,"; and
    (ii) for the words "in Part I of the Control of Pollution Act 1974" there shall be substituted the words "for the purposes of Part II of the Environmental Protection Act 1990";
(b) the definition of "disposal authority" shall be omitted; and
(c) after the definition of "prescribed" there shall be inserted the following definition—
    " 'regulation authority' means a waste regulation authority for the purposes of Part II of the Environmental Protection Act 1990;"

Section 9(2) shall be omitted.

Section 162

SCHEDULE 16

REPEALS

PART I

ENACTMENTS RELATING TO PROCESSES

Chapter	Short title	Extent of repeal
1906 c. 14.	Alkali, &c. Works Regulation Act 1906.	The whole Act so far as unrepealed.
1956 c. 52.	Clean Air Act 1956.	Section 17(4).
		In section 29(1), in the proviso, paragraph (a).
		In section 31(1), the words from "(other" to "1906)".
		Schedule 2.
1968 c. 62.	Clean Air Act 1968.	Section 11.
1972 c. 70.	Local Government Act 1972.	In section 180(3), paragraph (b).
1973 c. 65.	Local Government (Scotland) Act 1973.	In section 142(2), paragraph (b).
1974 c. 37.	Health and Safety at Work etc. Act 1974.	Section 1(1)(d) and the word "and" preceding it.
		Section 5.
1974 c. 40.	Control of Pollution Act 1974.	In section 76(4), the words "or work subject to the Alkali Act".
		In section 78(1), the words "or work subject to the Alkali Act".

Chapter	Short title	Extent of repeal
	In section 79(4), the words "or work subject to the Alkali Act". In section 80(3), the words "or work subject to the Alkali Act". In section 84(1), the definition of "a work subject to the Alkali Act". In section 103(1)(a), the words "Alkali Act or the". In section 105(1), the definition of "the Alkali Act".	
1990 c. 43.	Environmental Protection Act 1990.	In section 79(10), the words following "Part I".

Note: The repeal of the Alkali, &c. Works Regulation Act 1906 does not extend to Northern Ireland.

PART II

ENACTMENTS RELATING TO WASTE ON LAND

Chapter	Short title	Extent of repeal
1974 c. 40.	Control of Pollution Act 1974.	Sections 1 to 21. Sections 27 to 30.
1978 c. 3.	Refuse Disposal (Amenity) Act 1978.	Section 1.
1982 c. 45.	Civic Government (Scotland) Act 1982.	Sections 124 and 125 and in section 126, subsections (1) and (3).
1988 c. 9.	Local Government Act 1988.	In Schedule 1, in paragraph 1, in sub-paragraph (1) the words "in the application of this Part to England and Wales," and sub-paragraph (4).
1989 c. 14.	Control of Pollution (Amendment) Act 1989.	In section 7(2), paragraph (b) and the word "and" preceding it. In section 9, in subsection (1), the definition of "disposal authority" and subsection (2).
1989 c. 15.	Water Act 1989.	In Schedule 25, in paragraph 48, sub-paragraphs (1) to (6).
1989 c. 29.	Electricity Act 1989.	In Schedule 16, paragraph 18.
1990 c. 43.	Environmental Protection Act 1990.	In section 34(3)(b), the words following "below". Section 36(8).

Note: The repeal in the Refuse Disposal (Amenity) Act 1978 does not extend to Scotland.

PART III

ENACTMENTS RELATING TO STATUTORY NUISANCES

Chapter	Short title	Extent of repeal
1936 c. 49.	Public Health Act 1936.	Sections 91 to 100. Sections 107 and 108. Sections 109 and 110. In section 267(4), "III".
1956 c. 52.	Clean Air Act 1956.	Section 16. In section 30(1), the words from "or a nuisance" to "existed".

Chapter	Short title	Extent of repeal
1960 c. 34.	Radioactive Substances Act 1960.	In Schedule 1— (a) In paragraph 3, the words "and ninety-two"; (b) in paragraph 3, the words "subsection (2) of section one hundred and eight"; and (c) in paragraph 8, the words "and sixteen".
1961 c. 64.	Public Health Act 1961.	Section 72.
1963 c. 33.	London Government Act 1963.	In Schedule 11, in Part I, paragraph 20.
1963 c. 41.	Offices, Shops and Railway Premises Act 1963.	Section 76(3).
1969 c. 25.	Public Health (Recurring Nuisances) Act 1969.	The whole Act.
1972 c. 70.	Local Government Act 1972.	In section 180(3), paragraph (j). In Schedule 14— (a) in paragraph 4, the words "107(1) and (2), 108"; (b) paragraph 11; and (c) paragraph 12.
1974 c. 40.	Control of Pollution Act 1974.	In section 57, paragraph (a). Sections 58 and 59. In section 69, in subsection (1), paragraph (a) and, in paragraph (c), the words "section 59(2) or", and in subsection (3) the words "section 59(6) or" and paragraph (i). In Schedule 2, paragraphs 11 and 12.
1982 c. 30.	Local Government (Miscellaneous Provisions) Act 1982.	Section 26(1) and (2).
1989 c. 17.	Control of Smoke Pollution Act 1989.	Section 1.
1990 c. 8.	Town and Country Planning Act 1990.	In Schedule 17, paragraph 1.

Note: The repeals in the Clean Air Act 1956, the Control of Pollution Act 1974 and the Control of Smoke Pollution Act 1989 do not extend to Scotland.

PART IV

ENACTMENTS RELATING TO LITTER

Chapter	Short title	Extent of repeal
1974 c. 40.	Control of Pollution Act 1974.	Section 22(1) and (2).
1982 c. 43.	Local Government and Planning (Scotland) Act 1982.	Section 25(1).
1983 c. 35.	Litter Act 1983.	Sections 1 and 2. Section 12(1).
1986 c. ii.	Berkshire Act 1986.	Section 13.
1987 c. xi.	Exeter City Council Act 1987.	Section 24.
1988 c. viii.	City of Westminster Act 1988.	The whole Act.
1990 c. vii.	London Local Authorities Act 1990.	Section 43.

PART V

ENACTMENTS RELATING TO RADIOACTIVE SUBSTANCES

Chapter	Short title	Extent of repeal
1960 c. 34.	Radioactive Substances Act 1960.	Section 2(1). In section 4, subsection (1) and in subsection (2) the word "further". Section 7(3)(a). Section 8(1)(a). In section 12, subsection (1), in subsection (2)(b) the words "of waste" and, at the end "and", and in subsection (3)(b) the words "subsection (1) or". In section 19(1) the definition of "the Minister". Section 21(4). In Schedule 1, paragraphs 9 and 11.

PART VI

ENACTMENTS RELATING TO NATURE CONSERVATION AND COUNTRYSIDE MATTERS

Chapter	Short title	Extent of repeal
1968 c. 41.	Countryside Act 1968.	In section 15(2), the words "in the national interest". Section 19. In section 46(2), the words "and (2)".
1973 c. 54.	Nature Conservancy Council Act 1973.	In section 1, subsections (1), (2) and (4) to (8). Sections 2 and 4. In Schedule 1, paragraphs 6, 10 and 12. In Schedule 3, Parts I and II.
1981 c. 69.	Wildlife and Countryside Act 1981.	In section 34(6) the words "and Wales". Section 38. In section 43(1A) the words "by the Countryside Commission". In Schedule 13, paragraph 5.

PART VII

ENACTMENTS RELATING TO DEPOSITS AT SEA

Chapter	Short title	Extent of repeal
1972 c. 52.	Town and Country Planning (Scotland) Act 1972.	In section 56A(1), the words "and to section 56B below". Section 56B. In section 56E(2)(e) and 56K(5)(b), the words "or Health and Safety Commission". In section 56F(1), the words "and (3)". Section 56F(3). Section 56H(5). In section 56J(5), the words from "other" to "applies". In section 56M(3), the words "Subject to subsection (4) below,". Section 56M(4).

Chapter	Short title	Extent of repeal
		In section 56N, in subsection (1)(b), the words from "or" to "would be" and subsection (2).
		In section 56O, the definition of "the appropriate body" and the word "and" immediately following.
1986 c. 63.	Housing and Planning Act 1986.	In Part II of Schedule 7, in paragraph 8 the word "56B,".
1989 c. 29.	Electricity Act 1989.	In Schedule 17, paragraph 37(1)(b).
1990 c. 10.	Planning (Hazardous Substances) Act 1990.	In section 1, the words "2 or".
		Section 2.
		Section 3(6).
		In section 9(2)(e) and 18(2)(b), the words "or Health and Safety Commission".
		In section 11(7), the words "to the conditions that".
		Section 13(7).
		In section 15(1), the words from "other" to applies)".
		Section 20(6).
		Section 21(7).
		Section 27(4).
		In section 28(1), the words "authority who are a" and the words "by virtue of section 1 or 3".
		In section 28(1)(b), the words "or but for section 2 would be".
		Section 28(2).
		In section 29(6), the definition of "the appropriate body" and the word "and" immediately following that definition.
		In section 30(1), the words "by virtue of section 1 or 3".
		Section 33.
		In section 38(2), the words "(being a local planning authority)".
		In section 39(2), the entries for "the 1971 Act", "the appropriate Minister" and "operational land".
		In section 39(4), the words "2," and "and his undertaking a statutory undertaking".
		In section 39(5), the word "2,", in the first place it occurs and the words following "undertaker" in the second place it occurs.
		In section 39(6), the words "and their undertakings statutory undertakings".
		Section 39(7) and (8).
1990 c. 11.	Planning (Consequential Provisions) Act 1990.	In Schedule 2, paragraph 82(2).

PART VIII

ENACTMENTS RELATING TO DEPOSITS AT SEA

Chapter	Short title	Extent of repeal
1985 c. 48.	Food and Environment Protection Act 1985.	Section 5(c), (d) and (e)(iii). Section 6(1)(a)(iii). Schedule 4.

PART IX

MISCELLANEOUS ENACTMENTS

Chapter	Short title	Extent of repeal
1906 c. 32.	Dogs Act 1906.	Section 4(1).
1974 c. 40.	Control of Pollution Act 1974.	Section 100.
1982 c. 45.	Civic Government (Scotland) Act 1982.	Section 128(1).
1982 c. 48.	Criminal Justice Act 1982.	Section 43.
1988 c. 9.	Local Government Act 1988.	Section 39(2) and (4).
1988 c. 33.	Criminal Justice Act 1988.	Section 58.

APPENDICES

Appendix 1:	The Environmental Protection (Prescribed Processes and Substances) Regulations 1991 (S.I. 1991 No. 472) (as amended by S.I. 1991 No. 836).
Appendix 2:	The Environmental Protection (Applications, Appeals and Registers) Regulations 1991 (S.I. 1991 No. 507).
Appendix 3:	Integrated Pollution Control: A Practical Guide (DOE/WO Guidance 1993).
Appendix 4:	The Environmental Protection (Duty of Care) Regulations 1991 (S.I. 1991 No. 2839).
Appendix 5:	Waste Management: The Duty of Care (DOE/SO/WO Code of Practice, December 1991).
Appendix 6:	The Statutory Nuisance (Appeals) Regulations 1990 (S.I. 1990 No. 2276).
Appendix 7:	Code of Practice on Litter and Refuse under section 89 of the Environmental Protection Act 1990 (November 1990).
Appendix 8:	The Genetically Modified Organisms (Contained Use) Regulations 1992 (S.I. 1992 No. 3217).
Appendix 9:	The Genetically Modified Organisms (Deliberate Release) Regulations 1992 (S.I. 1992 No. 3280).

APPENDIX 1

ENVIRONMENTAL PROTECTION

ENVIRONMENTAL PROTECTION (PRESCRIBED PROCESSES AND SUBSTANCES) REGULATIONS 1991

(S.I. 1991 No. 472)

In force from:

April 1, 1991 (England and Wales) and April 1, 1992 (Scotland)

Enabling power:

Environmental Protection Act 1990, s.2.

Background:

Part I of the Environmental Protection Act 1990 provided for integrated pollution control as well as for the control of air pollution by local authorities. Section 2 provides that the Secretary of State may, by regulations, prescribe processes and substances for control. Prescribed processes may not be carried on or prescribed substances released into any environmental medium without prior authorisation after a date which the Secretary of State may prescribe.

These regulations:
 (a) prescribe processes and substances for control; and
 (b) designate the prescribed process either for central control by Her Majesty's Inspectorate of Pollution in England and Wales or by Her Majesty's Industrial Pollution Inspectorate or river purification authorities in Scotland or for local authority air pollution control.

Schedule 1 contains the descriptions processes prescribed for control and Scheds. 4–6 prescribe the substances. Rules for interpreting Sched. 1 are to be found in Sched. 2. Schedule 3 prescribes the date from which authorisation is required for the carrying on of the prescribed processes or the release of the prescribed substances.

These regulations have been amended by the Environmental Protection (Amendment of Regulations) Regulations 1991 (S.I. 1991 No. 836). The Amendment Regulations deal with the prescribed date for existing processes and provide that:
 (a) in the case of a process for which an authorisation is granted, the prescribed date is the date on which the enforcing authority grants it, whether as a result of the application, or following a successful appeal;
 (b) in the case of a process for which authorisation is refused, the prescribed date is the date of the refusal or the affirmation of refusal following an unsuccessful appeal.

Processes come under control on a rolling timetable which extends to 1996. Further minor amendments which are essentially clarification in nature have been made by the Environmental Protection (Prescribed Processes and Substances) (Amendment) Regulations 1992 (S.I. 1992 No. 614).

However, S.I. 1992 No. 614 introduced one substantive amendment; Sched. 1, para. 6 deleted the previous requirement that combustion processes were controlled only where gases were emitted through a common stack, where the emissions arose from two or more boilers or furnaces.

In March 1993 the DoE issued a Consultation Paper proposing amendments to S.I. 1991 No. 472. The amendments may result in replacement regulations.

43/App. 1   *Environmental Protection Act 1990*

Statutory reference:

Environmental Protection Act 1991, s.2.

Amendments:

S.I. 1991 No. 836 amended Sched. 3. S.I. 1992 No. 614 amended reg. 4, Scheds. 1 and 2.

Note to Sched. 2, Pt. I:

The Environmental Protection (Prescribed Processes and Substances) (Amendment) Regulations 1992 (S.I. 1992 No. 614) amended the Prescribed Processes and Substances Regulations 1991 (S.I. 1991 No. 472) by, among other amendments, those to Sched. 1, s.1.3 (dealing with combustion processes). These amendments brought under control certain existing processes which the previous definition left out of control. The newly affected processes were accordingly required to submit an application for authorisation by July 1, 1992, over a year later than similar processes which were brought under control by the 1991 Regulations. S.I. 1992 No. 614, Sched. 2 therefore amends Pt. I of Sched. 3 to the 1991 Regulations to ensure that the newly affected processes can continue to be carried on if an application for authorisation is made before July 1, 1992. In relation to the newly affected processes therefore, paras. (2)–(7) of this Part (S.I. 1991 No. 472, Sched. 3, Pt. I) must be read as amended by S.I. 1992 No. 614, Sched. 2 as follows:

1. Part I of Schedule 3 to the 1991 Regulations shall apply to a process which by virtue of these Regulations becomes a process to which paragraph (a) of Part A of Section 1.3 of Schedule 1 to the 1991 Regulations applies as if—

   (a) in paragraph 2, for "1st April 1991" there were substituted "1st April 1992";
   (b) in paragraph 3(1)(ii), for the words from "the day after" to the end of the sub-paragraph there were substituted "1st July 1992";
   (c) in paragraph 3(2), for "1 April 1991" there were substituted "1st April 1992";
   (d) paragraph 4 were omitted;
   (e) in paragraph 5, for the words "within the appropiate period specified in paragraph 4" there were substituted "by not later than 30th June 1992";
   (f) in paragraph 6, for "1st April 1991" there were substituted "1st April 1992"; and
   (g) in paragraph 7, for the words from "1st April 1990" to "of that process" there were substituted "1st April 1991 and 30th June 1992".

Note to Sched. 2, Pt. II:

The Environmental Protection (Prescribed Processes and Substances) (Amendment) Regulations 1992 (S.I. 1992 No. 614) amended the Prescribed Processes and Substances Regulations 1991 (S.I. 1991 No. 472) by, among other amendments, those relating to Sched. 1, s.1.3, Pt. B (dealing with combustion processes), Sched. 1, s.2.2 (dealing with non-ferrous metals) and Sched. 1, s.5.1 (dealing with incineration). These amendments brought under control certain existing processes which the previous definition left out of control. The newly affected processes were accordingly required to submit an application for authorisation by July 1, 1992, over a year later than similar processes which were brought under control by the 1991 Regulations. S.I. 1992 No. 614, Sched. 2 therefore amends Pt. II of Sched. 3 to the 1991 Regulations to ensure that the newly affected processes can continue to be carried on if an application for an authorisation is made before July 1, 1992. In relation to the newly affected processes therefore, paras. (10)–(14) of this Part (S.I. 1992 No. 472, Sched. 3, Pt. II) must be read as amended by S.I. 1992 No. 614, Sched. 2, as follows:

2. Part II of Schedule 3 to the 1991 Regulations shall apply to a process which by virtue of these Regulations becomes a process to which Part B of Section 1.3, 2.2 or 5.1 of Schedule 1 to the 1991 Regulations applies as if—
  (a) in paragraph 10, for the words from "the date specified" to the end of the paragraph there were substituted "1st April 1992";
  (b) in paragraph 11(1)(ii), for the words from "the day after" to the end of the sub-paragraph there were substituted "1st July 1992";
  (c) in paragraph 11(2), for the words from "in the period" to "(when changed)" there were substituted "on or after 1st April 1992 and before 1st July 1992";
  (d) paragraph 12 were omitted;
  (e) in paragraph 14(i), for the words from "the earlier date" to "falls" there were substituted "1st April 1992"; and
  (f) in paragraph 14(ii), for "that earlier date" there were substituted "1st April 1992".

Citation, application and commencement

1.—(1) These regulations may be cited as the Environmental Protection (Prescribed Processes and Substances) Regulations 1991.

(2) These regulations shall come into force in England and Wales on April 1, 1991 and in Scotland on April 1, 1992.

Interpretation

2. In these regulations—
  "the Act" means the Environmental Protection Act 1990;
  "background concentration" has the meaning given to that term in Regulation 4(7);
  "Part A process" means a process falling within a description set out in Schedule 1 hereto under the heading "Part A" and "Part B process" means a process falling within a description so set out under the heading "Part B"; and
  "particulate matter" means grit, dust or fumes.

Prescribed Provisions

3.—(1) Subject to the following provisions of these Regulations, the descriptions of processes set out in Schedule 1 hereto are hereby prescribed pursuant to section 2(1) of the Act as processes for the carrying on of which after the prescribed date an authorisation is required under section 6.

(2) Schedule 2 has effect for the interpretation of Schedule 1.

(3) In paragraph (1), the prescribed date means the appropriate date set out or determined in accordance with Schedule 3.

Exceptions

4.—(1) Subject to paragraph (6), a process shall not be taken to be a Part A process if it has the following characteristics, namely—
  (i) that it cannot result in the release into the air of any substance prescribed by Regulation 6(1) or there is no likelihood that it will result in the release into the air of any such substance except in a quantity which is so trivial that it is incapable of causing harm or its capacity to cause harm is insignificant; and
  (ii) that it cannot result in the release into water of any substance prescribed by Regulation 6(2) except in a concentration which is not greater than the background concentration; and

(iii) that it cannot result in the release into land of any substance prescribed by Regulation 6(3) or there is no likelihood that it will result in the release into land of any such substance except in a quantity which is so trivial that it is incapable of causing harm or its capacity to cause harm is insignificant.

(2) Subject to paragraph (6), a process shall not be taken to be a Part B process unless it will, or there is a likelihood that it will, result in the release into the air of one or more substances prescribed by Regulation 6(1) in a quantity greater than that mentioned in paragraph (1)(i) above.

(3) A process shall not be taken to fall within a description in Schedule 1 if it is carried on in a working museum to demonstrate an industrial process of historic interest or if it is carried on for educational purposes in a school as defined in section 114 of the Education Act 1944 or, in Scotland, section 135(1) of the Education (Scotland) Act 1980.

(4) The running on or within an aircraft, hovercraft, mechanically propelled road vehicle, railway locomotive or ship or other vessel of an engine which propels it shall not be taken to fall within a description in Schedule 1.

[(4A) The running of an engine which is designed to propel an aircraft, hovercraft, mechanically propelled road vehicle, railway locomotive or ship or other vessel in order to test it before installation or in the course of its development shall not be taken to fall within a description in Schedule 1.]

(5) A process shall not be taken to fall within a description in Schedule 1 if it is carried on as a domestic activity in connection with a private dwelling.

[(5A) A process which would otherwise fall within section 6.4 of Schedule 1 shall not be taken to fall within that or any other section of that Schedule if it is carried on at an installation in respect of which a nuclear site licence under section 1 of the Nuclear Installations Act 1965 is for the time being in force.]

(6) Paragraphs (1) and (2) do not exempt any process described in Schedule 1 from the requirement for authorisation if the process may give rise to an offensive smell noticeable outside the premises where the process is carried on.

(7) In these regulations, "background concentration" means any concentration of the relevant substance which would be present in the release irrespective of any effect the process may have had on the composition of the release and, without prejudice to the generality of the foregoing, includes such concentration of the substance as is present in:—

(a) water supplied to the premises where the process is carried on;
(b) water abstracted for use in the process; and
(c) precipitation onto the premises on which the process is carried on.

Enforcement

5.—(1) The descriptions of processes set out in Schedule 1 under the heading "Part A" are designated pursuant to section 2(4) of the Act for central control.

(2) The description of processes set out in Schedule 1 under the heading "Part B" are so designated for local control.

Prescribed substances: release into the air, water or land

6.—(1) The description of substances set out in Schedule 4 are prescribed pursuant to section 2(5) of the Act as substances the release of which into the air is subject to control under sections 6 and 7 of the Act.

(2) The descriptions of substances set out in Schedule 5 are so prescribed as substances the release of which into water is subject to control under those sections.

(3) The descriptions of substances set out in Schedule 6 are so prescribed as substances the release of which into land is subject to control under those sections.

SCHEDULE 1   Regulation 3(1)

DESCRIPTIONS OF PROCESSES

Chapter 1: The Production of Fuel and Power and Associated Processes

1.1 Gasification and associated processes

Part A

(a) Reforming or refining natural gas.
(b) Odorising natural gas or liquified petroleum gas.
(c) Producing gas from coal, lignite, oil or other carbonaceous material or from mixtures thereof other than from sewage or the biological degradation of waste.
(d) Purifying or refining any product of any of the processes described in paragraphs (a), (b) or (c) or converting it into a different product.

In this section, "carbonaceous material" includes such materials as charcoal, coke, peat and rubber.

Part B

Nil

1.2 Carbonisation and associated processes

Part A

(a) The pyrolysis, carbonisation, distillation, liquefaction, partial oxidation or other heat treatment of coal, lignite, oil, other carbonaceous material (as defined in Section 1.1.) or mixtures thereof otherwise than with a view to gasification or making of charcoal.
(b) The purification or refining of any of the products of a process mentioned in paragraph (a) or its conversion into a different product.

Nothing in paragraph (a) or (b) refers to the use of any substance as a fuel or its incineration as a waste or to any process for the treatment of sewage.

[In paragraph (a), the heat treatment of oil does not include heat treatment of waste oil or waste emulsions containing oil in order to recover the oil.]

Part B

Nil

1.3 Combustion processes

Part A

(a) burning any fuel in a boiler or furnace with a net rated thermal input of 50 megawatts or more or, when the process is carried on by the same person at the same location, burning any fuel in any of two or more boilers or furnaces with an aggregate net rated thermal input of 50 megawatts or more, [(disregarding any boiler or furnace with a net rated thermal input of less than 3 megawatts).]
(b) burning any fuel in a gas turbine or compression ignition engine with a net rated thermal input of 50 megawatts or more or [when the process is carried on by the same person at the same location, burning any fuel in] any of two or more such turbines or engines with an aggregate net rated thermal input of 50 megawatts or more [(disregarding any such turbine or engine with a net rated thermal input of less than 3 megawatts);
(c) burning any of the following in an appliance with a net rated thermal input of three megawatts or more otherwise than as a process which is related to a Part B process—
  (i) waste oil;
  (ii) recovered oil;
  (iii) any fuel manufactured from, or comprising, any other waste.

Part B

The following processes unless carried on in relation to any Part A process—
(a) burning any fuel in a boiler or furnace with a net rated thermal input of not less than 20 megawatts (but less than 50 megawatts);
(b) burning any fuel in a gas turbine or compression ignition engine with a net rated thermal input of not less than 20 megawatts (but less than 50 megawatts);
(c) burning as fuel, in an appliance with a net rated thermal input of less than three megawatts, waste oil or recovered oil;
(d) burning in an appliance with a net rated thermal input of less than three megawatts solid fuel which has been manufactured from waste by a process involving the application of heat;
(e) burning, in any appliance, fuel manufactured from, or including, waste (other than waste oil or recovered oil or such fuel as is mentioned in paragraph (d)) if the appliance has a net rated thermal input of less than three megawatts but at least 0.4 megawatts or is located with other appliances which each have a net rated thermal input of less than three megawatts [and the aggregate net rated thermal input of all the appliances is] at least 0.4 megawatts.

In paragraph (c) of Part A and paragraph (e) of Part B, "fuel" does not include gas produced by biological degradation of waste; and for the purposes of this section—
"net rated thermal input" is the rate at which fuel can be burned at the maximum continuous rating of the appliance multiplied by the net calorific value of the fuel and expressed as megawatts thermal; and
"waste oil" means any mineral based lubricating or industrial oil which has become unfit for the use for which it was intended and, in particular, used combustion engine oil, gearbox oil, mineral lubricating oil, oil for turbines and hydraulic oil; and
"recovered oil" means waste oil which has been processed before being used.

1.4 Petroleum processes

Part A

(a) The loading, unloading or other handling of, the storage of, or the physical, chemical or thermal treatment of—
  (i) crude oil;
  (ii) stabilised crude petroleum;
  (iii) crude shale oil;
  (iv) any associated gas.
(b) The loading, unloading or other handling of, the storage of, or the physical chemical or thermal treatment of, condensate in conjunction with the carrying on of any process described in paragraph (a) above.
(c) Any process not falling within any other description in this Schedule by which the product of any process described in paragraph (a) or (b) above is subject to further refining or conversion or is used (otherwise than as a fuel or solvent) in the manufacture of a chemical.

Part B

Nil

Chapter 2: Metal Production and Processing

2.1 Iron and steel

Part A

(a) Loading, unloading or otherwise handling or storing iron ore except in the course of mining operations.
(b) Loading, unloading or otherwise handling or storing burnt pyrites.
(c) Crushing, grading, grinding, screening, washing or drying iron ore or any mixture of iron ore and other materials.
(d) Blending or mechanically mixing grades of iron ore or iron ore with other materials.
(e) Pelletising, calcining or sintering iron ore (except as part of a smelting process).
(f) Making, melting or refining iron, steel or any ferro-alloy in any furnace other than a furnace described in Part B in this section.

(g) Any process for the refining or making of iron, steel or any ferro-alloy in which air or oxygen or both are used unless related to a process described in Part B of this section.
(h) The desulphurisation of iron, steel or any ferro-alloy made by a process described in this Part of this section.
(i) Heating iron, steel or any ferro-alloy (whether in a furnace or other appliance) to remove grease, oil or any other non-metallic contaminant (including such operations as the removal by heat of plastic or rubber covering from scrap cable), if related to another process described in this Part of this section.
(j) Any foundry process (including ancillary foundry operations such as the manufacture and recovery of moulds, the reclamation of sand, fettling, grinding and shot-blasting) if related to another process described in this Part of this section.
(k) Any process otherwise falling within a description in Part B of this section, if the process involves the use of a furnace with a designed melting capacity of 25 tonnes or more per hour and the carrying on of the process by the person concerned at the location in question is likely to produce 4,000 tonnes or more of special waste in any 12 month period.
(l) Handling slag in conjunction with a process described in paragraph (f) or (g).

Nothing in paragraph (a) or (b) of this Part of this section applies to the handling or storing of other minerals in association with the handling or storing of iron ore or burnt pyrites.

Part B

(a) Making, melting or refining iron, steel or any ferro-alloy in—
  (i) an electric arc furnace with a designed holding capacity of less than seven tonnes; or
  (ii) a cupola, rotary furnace, induction furnace or resistance furnace.
(b) Refining iron or making iron, steel or any ferro-alloy where air or oxygen or both are used, if related to another process described in paragraph (a) above.
(c) The desulphurisation of iron, steel or any ferro-alloy, if the process does not fall within paragraph (h) of Part A of this section.
(d) Any such process as is described in paragraph (i) of Part A above, if not falling within that paragraph.
(e) Any foundry process (including ancillary foundry operations such as the manufacture and recovery of moulds, the reclamation of sand, fettling, grinding and shot-blasting) if related to another process described in this Part of this section.

Any description of a process in this section includes, where the process produces slag, the crushing, screening or grading or other treatment of the slag if that process is related to the process in question.

2.2 Non-ferrous metals

Part A

(a) The extraction or recovery from any material—
  (i) by chemical means or the use of heat of any non-ferrous metal or alloy of non-ferrous metal or any compound of a non-ferrous metal; or
  (ii) by electrolytic means, of aluminium,
if the process may result in the release into the air of particulate matter or any metal, metalloid or any metal or metalloid compound or in the release into water of a substance described in Schedule 5 or does not fall within paragraph (b) of Part B of this section. In this paragraph 'material' includes ores, scrap and other waste.
(b) The mining of zinc or tin where the process may result in the release into water of cadmium or any compound of cadmium.
(c) The refining of any non-ferrous metal or non-ferrous metal alloy except where the process is related to a process falling within a description in paragraphs (a), (c) or (d) of Part B of this section.
(d) Any process other than a process described in paragraphs (b), (c) or (d) of Part B of this section for making or melting any non-ferrous metal or non-ferrous metal alloy in a furnace, bath or other holding vessel if the furnace, bath or vessel employed has a designed holding capacity of five tonnes or more.
(e) Any process for producing, melting or recovering by chemical means or by the use of heat any of the elements listed below or any alloy whatsoever, if the percentage by weight of any of those elements which the alloy, in molten form, contains exceeds the relevant percentage specified below, and the process may result in the release into the air of particulate matter or smoke which contains any of those elements—

antimony	1%
arsenic	1%
beryllium	0.1%
chromium	2%
[lead 23% when present in an alloy containing copper and 2% when present in any other alloy]	
magnesium	10%
[manganese 15% when present in an alloy containing copper and 4% when present in any other alloy]	
phosphorus	1%
platinum	1%
selenium	0.5%

(f) Any process for producing, melting or recovering (whether by chemical means or by electrolysis or by the use of heat) cadmium or mercury or any alloy containing more than 0.05 per cent by weight of either of those metals in aggregate.

(g) Any manufacturing or repairing process involving the use of beryllium or selenium or an alloy of one or both of those metals if the process may occasion the release into the air of any substance described in Schedule 4.

(h) The heating in a furnace or other appliance of any non-ferrous metal or non-ferrous metal alloy for the purpose of removing grease, oil or any other non-metallic contaminant (including such operations as the removal by heat of plastic or rubber covering from cable), if related to another process described in this Part of this Section.

(i) Any foundry process (including ancillary foundry operations such as the manufacture and recovery of moulds, the reclamation of sand, fettling, grinding and shot-blasting) if related to another process described in this Part of this section.

(j) Any process otherwise falling within a description in paragraphs (a), (b), (d), (e) or (f) of Part B of this section if the carrying on the process by the person concerned at the location in question is likely to produce 1,000 tonnes or more of special waste in any 12 month period.

Part B

(a) The making or melting of any non-ferrous metal or non-ferrous metal alloy in any furnace, bath or other holding vessel with a designed holding capacity of less than five tonnes (together with any incidental refining).

(b) The extraction or recovery of copper, aluminium or zinc from mixed scrap by the use of heat.

(c) Melting zinc or a zinc alloy in conjunction with a galvanising process.

(d) Melting zinc or aluminium or an alloy of one or both of these metals in conjunction with a die-casting process.

(e) Any such process as is described in paragraph (h) of Part A above, if not related to another process described in that Part.

(f) Any foundry process (including ancillary foundry operations such as the manufacture and recovery of moulds, the reclamation of sand, fettling, grinding and shot-blasting) if related to another process described in this Part of this section.

2.3 Smelting processes

Part A

Smelting or calcining sulphides or sulphide ores, including regulus or mattes.

Part B

Nil

Chapter 3: Mineral Industries

3.1 Cement and lime manufacture and associated processes

Part A

(a) Making cement clinker.
(b) Grinding cement clinker.
(c) Any of the following processes, where the process is related to a process described in

paragraphs (a) or (b), namely, blending cement; putting cement into silos for bulk storage; removing cement from silos in which it has been stored in bulk; and any process involving the use of cement in bulk, including the bagging of cement and cement mixtures, the batching of ready-mixed concrete and the manufacture of concrete blocks and other cement products.
- (d) The heating of calcium carbonate or calcium magnesium carbonate for the purpose of making lime.
- (e) The slaking of lime for the purpose of making calcium hydroxide or calcium magnesium hydroxide where the process is related to a process described in paragraph (d) above.

Part B

- (a) Any of the following processes, if not related to a process falling within a description in Part A of this Section—
  - (i) storing, loading or unloading cement or cement clinker in bulk prior to further transportation in bulk;
  - (ii) blending cement in bulk or using cement in bulk other than at a construction site, including the bagging of cement and cement mixtures, the batching of ready-mixed concrete and the manufacture of concrete blocks and other cement products.
- (b) The slaking of lime for the purpose of making calcium hydroxide or calcium magnesium hydroxide unless related to a process falling within another description in this Schedule.

3.2 Processes involving asbestos

Part A

- (a) Producing raw asbestos by extraction from the ore except where the process is directly associated with the mining of the ore.
- (b) The manufacture and, where related to the manufacture, the industrial finishing of the following products where the use of asbestos is involved—
  asbestos cement
  asbestos cement products
  asbestos fillers
  asbestos filters
  asbestos floor coverings
  asbestos friction products
  asbestos insulating board
  asbestos jointing, packaging and reinforcement material
  asbestos packing
  asbestos paper or card
  asbestos textiles.
- (c) The stripping of asbestos railway vehicles except—
  - (i) in the course of the repair or maintenance of the vehicle;
  - (ii) in the course of recovery operations following an accident; or
  - (iii) where the asbestos is permanently bonded in plastic, rubber or a resin.
- (d) The destruction by burning of a railway vehicle if asbestos has been incorporated in, or sprayed on to, its structure.

Part B

The industrial finishing of any product mentioned in paragraph (b) of Part A of this section if the process does not fall within that paragraph.
In this section, "asbestos" means any of the following fibrous silicates—
actinolite, amosite, anthophyllite, chrysotile, crocidolite and tremolite.

3.3 Other mineral fibres

Part A

Manufacturing—
   (i) glass fibre;
   (ii) any fibre from any mineral other than asbestos.

Part B

Nil

3.4 Other mineral processes

Part A

Nil

Part B

(a) The crushing, grinding or other size reduction or the grading, screening or heating of any designated mineral or mineral product except where—
    (i) the process falls within a description in another section of this Schedule;
    (ii) the process is related to another process falling within such a description; or
    (iii) the operation of the process is unlikely to result in the release into the air of particulate matter.
(b) Any of the following processes unless carried on at an exempt location or as part of a process falling within another description in this Schedule—
    (i) crushing, grinding or otherwise breaking up coal or coke or any other coal product;
    (ii) screening, grading or mixing coal, or coke or any other coal product;
    (iii) loading or unloading coal, coke or any other coal product except unloading on retail sale.
(c) The crushing, grinding or other size reduction, with machinery designed for that purpose, of bricks, tiles or concrete.
(d) Screening the product of any such process as is described in paragraph (c).
(e) Coating roadstone with tar or bitumen.

In this section—
    "coal" includes lignite;
    "designated mineral or mineral product" means—
        (i) clay, sand and any other naturally occurring mineral other than coal or lignite;
        (ii) metallurgical slag;
        (iii) boiler or furnace ash produced from the burning of coal, coke or any other coal product;
        (iv) gypsum which is a by-product of any process; and
    "exempt location" means—
        (i) any premises used for the sale of coal, coke or any coal product by retail where at least 90 per cent on aggregate of the coal, coke and coal products which are removed from those premises are supplied to persons purchasing in quantities of 10 tonnes or less; or
        (ii) any premises to which coal, coke or any coal product is supplied only for use there.
Nothing in this section applies to any process carried on underground.

3.5 Glass manufacture and production

Part A

The manufacture of glass frit or enamel frit and its use in any process where that process is related to its manufacture.

Part B

(a) The manufacture of glass at any location where the person concerned has the capacity to make 5,000 tonnes or more of glass in any 12 month period, and any process involving the use of glass which is carried on at any such location in conjunction with its manufacture.
(b) The manufacture of glass where the use of lead or any lead compound is involved.
(c) The making of any glass product where lead or any lead compound has been used in the manufacture of the glass except—
    (i) the making of products from lead glass blanks;
    (ii) the melting, or mixing with another substance, of glass manufactured elsewhere to produce articles such as ornaments or road paint;
(d) Polishing or etching glass or glass products in the course of any manufacturing process if—

(i) hydrofluoric acid is used; or
(ii) hydrogen fluoride may be released into the air.

3.6 Ceramic production

Part A

(a) Firing heavy clay goods or refractory goods in a kiln where a reducing atmosphere is used for a purpose other than coloration.
(b) Vapour glazing earthenware or clay with salts.

Part B

Firing heavy clay goods or refractory goods in a kiln where the process does not fall within a description in Part A of this Section.
In this section, "clay" includes a blend of clay with ash, sand or other materials.

Chapter 4: The Chemical Industry

(See paragraph 4 of Schedule 2 as to cases where processes described in this chapter of the Schedule fall within two or more descriptions.)

4.1 Petrochemical processes

Part A

(a) Any process for the manufacture of olefins.
(b) Any process for the manufacture of any chemical which involves the use of a product of a process described in paragraph (a).
(c) Any process for the manufacture of any chemical which involves the use of a product of a process described in paragraph (b) otherwise than as a fuel or solvent.
(d) Any process for the polymerisation of an olefin or of a product of a process mentioned in paragraphs (b) or (c).

Part B

Nil

4.2 The manufacture and use of organic chemicals

Part A

Any of the following processes unless falling within a description set out in Section 6.8—
(a) the manufacture or recovery or polymerisation of styrene or vinyl chloride;
(b) any process of manufacture involving the use of vinyl chloride;
(c) the manufacture of acetylene, any aldehyde, amine, isocyanate, nitrile, organic acid or its anhydride, any organic sulphur compound or any phenol, if the process may result in the release of any of those substances into the air;
(d) any process for the manufacture of a chemical involving the use of, or which may result in the release into the air of, any substance mentioned in paragraph (c);
(e) the manufacture or recovery of carbon disulphide;
(f) any manufacturing process which may result in the release of carbon disulphide into the air;
(g) the manufacture or recovery of any pyridine, methyl pyridine or di-methyl pyridine;
(h) the manufacture of any organo-metallic compound;
(i) the manufacture, purification or recovery of any acrylate;
(j) any process for the manufacture of a chemical involving the use of any acrylate.

Part B

Nil

4.3 Acid processes

Part A

(a) Any process for the manufacture, recovery, concentration or distillation of sulphuric acid or oleum.

(b) Any process for the manufacture of any oxide of sulphur but excluding any combustion or incineration process other than the burning of sulphur.
(c) Any process for the manufacture of a chemical which uses, or may result in the release into the air of, any oxide of sulphur but excluding any combustion or incineration process other than the burning of sulphur.
(d) Any process for the manufacture or recovery of nitric acid.
(e) Any process for the manufacture of any acid-forming oxide of nitrogen.
(f) Any other process (except the combustion or incineration of carbonaceous material as defined in Section 1.1 of this Schedule) which is likely to result in the release into the air of any acid-forming oxide of nitrogen.
(g) Any process for the manufacture of phosphoric acid.

Part B

Nil

4.4 Processes involving halogens

Part A

The following processes if not falling within a description in any other section of this Schedule—
(a) any process for the manufacture of fluorine, chlorine, bromine or iodine or of any compound comprising only—
   (i) two or more of those halogens; or
   (ii) any one or more of those halogens and oxygen;
(b) any process of manufacture which involves the use of, or which is likely to result in the release into the air or into water of, any of those four halogens or any of the compounds mentioned in paragraph (a) other than the use of any of them as a pesticide (as defined in Schedule 6) in water;
(c) any process for the manufacture of hydrogen fluoride, hydrogen chloride, hydrogen bromide or hydrogen iodide or any of their acids;
(d) any process for the manufacture of chemicals which may result in the release into the air of any of the four compounds mentioned in paragraph (c);
(e) any process of manufacture (other than the manufacture of chemicals) involving the use of any of the four compounds mentioned in paragraph (c) which may result in the release of any of those compounds into the air, other than the coating, plating or pickling of metal.

Part B

Nil

4.5 Inorganic chemical processes

Part A

(a) The manufacture of hydrogen cyanide or hydrogen sulphide other than in the course of fumigation.
(b) Any manufacturing process involving the use of hydrogen cyanide or hydrogen sulphide.
(c) Any process for the manufacture of a chemical which may result in the release into the air of hydrogen cyanide or hydrogen sulphide.
(d) The production of any of the following or of any compound containing any of them—
   antimony
   arsenic
   beryllium
   gallium
   indium
   lead
   palladium
   platinum
   selenium
   tellurium
   thallium,
where the process may result in the release into the air of any of those elements or compounds or the release into water of any substance described in Schedule 5.

(e) The recovery of any element or compound referred to in paragraph (d) where the process may result in any such release as is mentioned in that paragraph.
(f) The use in any process of manufacture, other than the application of a glaze or vitreous enamel, of any element or compound referred to in paragraph (d) where the process may result in such a release as is mentioned in that paragraph.
(g) The production or recovery of cadmium or mercury or of any of their compounds.
(h) Any process of manufacture which involves the use of cadmium or mercury or of any compound of either of those elements or which may result in the release into the air of either of those elements or any of their compounds.
(i) The production of any compound of—
chromium
magnesium
manganese
nickel
zinc.
(j) The manufacture of any metal carbonyl.
(k) Any process for the manufacture of—
  (i) a metal;
  (ii) a chemical,
involving the use of a metal carbonyl.
(l) The manufacture or recovery of ammonia.
(m) Any process for the manufacture of a chemical which involves the use of ammonia or may result in the release of ammonia into the air other than a process in which ammonia is used only as a refrigerant.
(n) The production of phosphorus or of any oxide, hydride or halide of phosphorus.
(o) Any process for the manufacture of a chemical which involves the use of phosphorus or any oxide, hydride or halide of phosphorus or which may result in the release into the air of phosphorus or of any such oxide, hydride or halide.

Part B

Nil

4.6 Chemical Fertiliser Production

Part A

(a) The manufacture of chemical fertilisers.
(b) The conversion of chemical fertilisers into granules.

In this section, "chemical fertilisers" means any inorganic chemical to be applied to the soil to promote plant growth; and "inorganic chemical" includes urea.

Part B

Nil

4.7 Pesticide production

Part A

The manufacture or the formulation of chemical pesticides if the process—
  (i) may result in the release into water of any substance described in Schedule 5; or
  (ii) if the carrying on of the process by the person concerned at the location in question is likely to produce 500 tonnes or more of special waste in any 12 month period.

Part B

Nil

In this section "pesticide" has the same meaning as in Schedule 6.

4.8 Pharmaceutical production

Part A

The manufacture or the formulation of a medicinal product if the process—

(i) may result in the release into water of any substance described in Schedule 5; or
(ii) if the carrying on of the process by the person concerned at the location in question is likely to produce 1,000 tonnes or more of special waste in any 12 month period.

Part B

Nil

In this Section, "medicinal product" means any substance or article (not being an instrument, apparatus or appliance) manufactured for use in one of the ways specified in section 130(1) of the Medicines Act 1968.

4.9 The storage of chemicals in bulk

Part A

The storage, other than as part of another Part A process and other than in a tank for the time being forming part of a powered vehicle, of any of the substances listed below except where the total capacity of the tanks installed at the location in question in which the relevant substance may be stored is less than the figure specified below in relation to that substance;

any one or more acrylates	20 tonnes
acrylonitrile	20 tonnes
anhydrous ammonia	100 tonnes
anhydrous hydrogen fluoride	1 tonne
toluene di-isocyanate	20 tonnes
vinyl chloride monomer	20 tonnes

Part B

Nil

Chapter 5: Waste Disposal and Recycling

5.1 Incineration

Part A

(a) The destruction by burning in an incinerator of any waste chemicals or waste plastic arising from the manufacture of a chemical or the manufacture of a plastic.
(b) The destruction by burning in an incinerator, other than incidentally in the course of burning other waste, of any waste chemicals being, or comprising in elemental or compound form, any of the following—
bromine
cadmium
chlorine
fluorine
iodine
lead
mercury
nitrogen
phosphorus
sulphur
zinc.
(c) The destruction by burning of any other waste, including animal remains, otherwise than by a process related to a Part B process, on premises where there is plant designed to incinerate such waste at a rate of one tonne or more per hour.
(d) The cleaning for reuse of metal containers used for the transport or storage of a chemical by burning out their residual content.

Part B

(a) The destruction by burning in an incinerator other than an exempt incinerator of any waste, including animal remains, except where related to a Part A process.
(b) The cremation of human remains.
In this section—

"exempt incinerator" means any incinerator on premises where there is plant designed to incinerate waste, including animal remains, at a rate of not more than 50 kgs per hour, not being an incinerator employed to incinerate clinical waste, sewage sludge, sewage screenings or municipal waste (as defined in Article 1 of EC Directive 89/369/EEC; and for the purposes of this section, the weight of waste shall be determined by reference to its weight as fed into the incinerator;

"waste" means solid, liquid or gaseous wastes [(other than gas produced by biological degradation of waste)]; and

"clinical waste" means waste ... which falls within the descriptions in paragraph (a) or (b) of the definition of such waste in the Collection and Disposal of Waste Regulations 1988 (or would fall in one of those paragraphs but for Regulation 2(3) of those regulations).

5.2 **Recovery processes**

Part A

The recovery by distillation of any oil or any organic solvent or the cleaning or regeneration of carbon, charcoal or ion exchange resins by removing matter which is, or includes, any substance described in Schedules 4, 5 or 6 except where the process is carried on in relation to any other process which involves the production or use of the same substance as the substance which is recovered, cleaned or regenerated.

Part B

Nil

5.3 **The production of fuel from waste**

Part A

Making solid fuel from waste by any process involving the use of heat other than making charcoal.

Part B

Nil

Chapter 6: Other Industries

6.1 **Paper and pulp manufacturing processes**

Part A

(a) The making of paper pulp by a chemical method if the person concerned has the capacity at the location in question to produce more than 25,000 tonnes of paper pulp in any 12 month period.
(b) Any process related to making paper pulp or paper (including processes connected with the recycling of paper such as de-inking) if the process may result in the release into water of any substance described in Schedule 5.

In this paragraph, "paper pulp" includes pulp made from wood, grass, straw and similar materials and references to the making of paper are to the making of any product using paper pulp.

Part B

Nil

6.2. **Di-isocyanate processes**

PART A

(a) Any process for the manufacture of any di-isocyanate or a partly polymerised di-isocyanate.
(b) Any manufacturing process involving the use of toluene di-isocyanate or partly polymerised toluene di-isocyanate which may result in a release into the air which contains toluene di-isocyanate.

(c) Any process for the manufacture of foams or elastomers involving the use of toluene di-isocyanate or partly polymerised toluene di-isocyanate.
(d) The hot-wire cutting, thermal debonding or flame bonding of polyurethane foams or polyurethane elastomers.

PART B

Any process not falling within any other description in this Schedule where the carrying on of the process by the person concerned at the location in question is likely to involve the use of five tonnes or more of di-isocyanates or partly polymerised di-isocyanates (or in aggregate of both) in any 12 month period.

6.3 Tar and bitumen processes

Part A

Any process not falling within any other description in this Schedule involving the distillation or heating of tar or bitumen in connection with any process of manufacture where the carrying on of the process by the person concerned at the location in question is likely to involve the use of five tonnes or more of bitumen or of tar or, in aggregate, of both in any 12 month period.

Part B

NIL

6.4 Processes involving uranium

Part A

The following processes ...
(a) the treatment of any ore, concentrate or material containing uranium, its compounds or alloys in order to produce uranium, its compounds or alloys; or
(b) the manufacture of, and any process involving the use of uranium hexafluoride or of any other volatile compound or uranium; or
(c) the mechanical processing or casting of uranium, its compounds or alloys.

Part B

Nil

6.5 Coating Processes and Printing

Part A

(a) The application or removal of a coating material containing one or more tributyltin compounds of triphenyltin compounds, if carried out at a shipyard or boatyard where vessels of a length of 25 metres or more can be built or maintained or repaired.
(b) The treatment of textiles if the process may result in the release into water of any substance described in Schedule 5.
(c) The application to a substrate of, or the drying or curing after such application of, printing ink or paint or any other coating as, or in the course of, a manufacturing process where the carrying on of the process by the person concerned at the location in question is likely to produce 1,000 tonnes or more of special waste in any 12 month period.

Part B

(a) Any process described in paragraph (c) of Part A (other than the respraying of vehicles) where—
  (i) the process does not fall within that paragraph by reason of the qualification relating to special waste;
  (ii) the process may result in the release into the air of particulate matter or of any volatile organic compound; and
  (iii) the carrying on of the process by the person concerned at the location in question is likely to involve the use in any 12 month period of—
    (aa) 20 tonnes or more of any printing ink, paint or other coating material which is applied in solid form; or

(bb) 20 tonnes or more of any metal coatings which are sprayed on in molten form; or
(cc) five tonnes or more of organic solvents.
(b) Any process for the respraying of road vehicles not falling within paragraph (c) of Part A above if the process may result in the release into the air of particulate matter or of any volatile organic compound and the carrying on of the process by the person concerned at the location in question is likely to involve the use of two tonnes or more of organic solvents in any 12 month period.
In this section—
"coating material" includes paint, varnish, lacquer, dye, any metal oxide coating, any adhesive coating, any elastomer coating and any metal or plastic coating; and
in calculating for the purposes of Part B the amount of organic solvents used in a process, account shall be taken both of solvents contained in coatings and solvents used for cleaning or other purposes.

6.6 The manufacture of dyestuffs, printing ink and coating materials

Part A

Any process not falling within a description in any other section of this Schedule—
(a) for the manufacture of dyestuffs if the process involves the use of hexachlorobenzene;
(b) for the manufacture or formulation of a printing ink or coating material where the carrying on of the process by the person concerned at the location in question is likely to produce 1,000 tonnes or more of special waste in any 12 month period.

Part B

Any process not falling within a description in any other section of this Schedule—
(a) for the manufacture or formulation of printing ink or any other coating material containing, or involving the use of, an organic solvent, where the carrying on of the process by the person concerned at the location in question is likely to involve the use of 100 tonnes or more of organic solvents in any 12 month period;
(b) for the manufacture of any powder for use as a coating where there is the capacity to produce 200 tonnes or more of such powder in any 12 month period.
In this section, "coating material" has the same meaning as in Section 6.5.

6.7 Timber processes

Part A

(a) The curing or chemical treatment as part of a manufacturing process of timber or of products wholly or mainly made of wood if any substance described in Schedule 5 is used.
(b) The use of wood preservatives where the carrying on of the process by the person concerned at the location in question is likely to produce 500 tonnes or more of special waste in any 12 month period.

Part B

The manufacture of products wholly or mainly of wood at any works if the process involves the sawing, drilling, sanding, shaping, turning, planing, curing or chemical treatment of wood ("relevant processes") and the throughput of the works in any 12 month period—
(i) where wood is sawed but is not subjected to any other relevant processes at the works, is likely to exceed 10,000 cubic metres; or
(ii) in any other case, is likely to exceed 500 cubic metres.
For the purposes of this paragraph—
"throughput" shall be calculated by reference to the amount of wood which is subjected to any of the relevant processes but where, at the same works, wood is subject to two or more relevant processes no account shall be taken of the second or any subsequent process; and
"works" includes a sawmill or any other premises on which relevant processes are carried out on wood.

6.8 Processes involving rubber

Part A

Nil

Part B

(a) The mixing, milling or blending of—
   (i) natural rubber; or
   (ii) synthetic elastomers,
   if carbon black is used.
(b) Any process which converts the product of a process falling within paragraph (a) into a finished product if related to a process falling within that paragraph.

6.9 The treatment and processing of animal or vegetable matter

Part A

Any of the following processes, unless falling within a description in another section of the Schedule or an exempt process, namely, the processing in any way whatsoever, storing or drying by the application of heat of any dead animal (or part thereof) or any vegetable matter where the process may result in the release into water of a substance described in Schedule 5: but excluding any process for the treatment of effluent so as to permit its discharge into controlled waters or into a sewer unless the treatment process involves the drying of any material with a view to its use as an animal feedstuff.

Part B

(a) Any process mentioned in Part A of this section unless an exempt process—
   (i) where the process may not result in the release into water of any substance described in Schedule 5; but
   (ii) may release into the air a substance described in Schedule 4 or any offensive smell noticeable outside the premises on which the process is carried on.
(b) Breeding maggots in any case where five kg or more of animal or of vegetable matter or, in aggregate, of both are introduced into the process in any week.

In this Section—
   "animal" includes a bird or a fish; and
   "exempt process" means—
      (i) any process carried on on a farm or agricultural holding other than the manufacture of goods for sale;
      (ii) the manufacture or preparation of food or drink for human consumption but excluding—
(a) the extraction, distillation or purification of animal or vegetable oil or fat otherwise than as a process incidental to the cooking of food for human consumption;
(b) any process involving the use of green offal or the boiling of blood except the cooking of food (other than tripe) for human consumption;
(c) the cooking of tripe for human consumption elsewhere than on premises on which it is to be consumed; and
   "green offal" means the stomach and intestines of any animal, other than poultry or fish, and their contents.

SCHEDULE 2 — Regulation 3(2)

Rules for the Interpretation of Schedule 1

1. These rules apply for the interpretation of Schedule 1 subject to any specific provision to the contrary in that Schedule.

2. Any description of a process includes any other process carried on at the same location by the same person as part of that process: but this rule does not apply in relation to any two or more processes described in different sections of Schedule 1 which, accordingly, require distinct authorisation.

3. Where a person carries on a process which includes two or more processes mentioned in the same section of Schedule 1 those processes shall be treated as requiring authorisation as a single process; and if the processes involved are described in both Part A and Part B of the same section, they shall all be regarded as part of a Part A process and so subject to central control.

4. Where a process falls within two or more descriptions in Schedule 1, that process shall be regarded as falling only within that description which fits it most aptly: but where two or more descriptions are equally apt and a process falls within descriptions in different sections of Chapter 4, it shall be taken to fall within the description in whichever relevant section is first mentioned in the sequence, 4.5; 4.2; 4.1; 4.4; 4.3; 4.6; 4.7; 4.8; 4.9.

5. Notwithstanding the rules set out in paragraphs 2 and 3—
   (a) the processes described in Part B of section 1.3 do not include the incidental storage, handling or shredding of tyres which are to be burned;
   (b) the process described in paragraph (b) of Part B of section 2.2 does not include the incidental storage or handling of scrap which is to be heated other than its loading into a furnace;
   (c) the process described in paragraph (a) in Part B of section 5.1 does not involve the incidental storage or handling of wastes and residues other than animal remains intended for burning in an incinerator used wholly or mainly for the incineration of such remains or residues from the burning of such remains in such an incinerator;
   (d) the process described in Part B of section 6.5 does not include the cleaning of used storage drums prior to painting and their incidental handling in connection with such cleaning.

6. The unloading of coal, lignite, coke or any other coal product or iron ore or burnt pyrites for use in a prescribed process by a person other than the person carrying on the process at the place where the process is carried on shall be treated as part of the process.

7.—(1) Where by reason of the use at different times of different fuels or different materials or the disposal at different times of different wastes, processes of different descriptions are carried out with the same plant or machinery and those processes include one or more Part A processes and one or more other processes, the other processes shall be regarded as within the descriptions of the Part A processes.

(2) Where by reason of such use or disposal as is mentioned in paragraph (1), processes of different descriptions are carried out with the same plant or machinery and those processes include one or more Part B processes and one or more other processes (but no Part A processes), all those processes shall be regarded as within the descriptions of the Part B processes.

[(7A) The reference to "any other process" in paragraph 2 and the references to "other processes" in paragraph 7 do not include references to a process (other than one described in Schedule 1) of loading or unloading any ship or other vessel.]

8. Where in the course of any prescribed process not falling within a description in Chapter 5 in Schedule 1, waste is used, whether as fuel or otherwise, the description of that process includes the disposal or treatment of that waste in the course of that process, whether the waste was produced by the person carrying on the process or acquired by him for such disposal or treatment.

9. References in Schedule 1 and this Schedule to related processes are references to separate processes carried on by the same person at the same location.

10. "Special waste" means waste which is for the time being the subject of regulations under section 17 of the Control of Pollution Act 1974 or Section 62 of the Act.

11. References to a process involving the release of a substance falling within a description in Schedule 4 or 5 hereto do not affect the application of paragraphs (1) and (2) of Regulation 4.

SCHEDULE 3   Regulation 3(1) and (3)

Date From Which Authorisation is Required Under Section 6 of the Act

Part I

1. This Part of this Schedule applies in the case of a Part A process carried on in England or Wales.

2. The prescribed date in the case of a Part A process is, except in the case of an existing process, April 1, 1991.

3.—(1) In the case of an existing process, the prescribed date is—
   (i) in a case falling within paragraph (2), the date at which the change mentioned in that paragraph is made unless later than the date applicable in accordance with sub-paragraph (ii);
   (ii) where sub-paragraph (i) does not apply and subject to paragraph 5, the day after that on

which the period for applying for authorisation in accordance with the Table in paragraph 4 expires.

(2) A case falls within this paragraph if the person carrying on the process makes a substantial change in the process on or after April 1, 1991 and that change—
  (i) has not occasioned construction work which is in progress on that date; or
  (ii) is not the subject of a contract for construction work entered into before that date.

4. Application for authorisation to carry on an existing process shall be made in the relevant period specified in the following Table—

Any process falling within a description set out in—	Application to be made	
	Not earlier than	Not later than
Paragraph (a) of Section 1.3	1st April 1991	30th April 1991
Any other paragraph of Chapter 1	1st April 1992	30th June 1992
Section 2.1 or 2.3	1st January 1995	31st March 1995
Section 2.2	1st May 1995	31st July 1995
Chapter 3	1st December 1992	28th February 1993
Section 4.1, 4.2, 4.7 or 4.8	1st May 1993	31st July 1993
Section 4.3, 4.4, 4.6 or 4.9	1st November 1993	31st January 1994
Section 4.5	1st May 1994	31st July 1994
Chapter 5	1st August 1992	31st October 1992
Chapter 6	1st November 1995	31st January 1996

5. Where paragraph 3(1)(ii) would otherwise apply and application is duly made in accordance with section 6 of the Act within the appropriate period specified in paragraph 4 for authorisation to carry on a process, the prescribed date as respects the carrying on by the applicant (or other person in his place) of the process to which the application relates is the determination date for that process.

6. Subject to paragraph 7 below, references in this Part to an existing process are to a process—
  (i) which was being carried on at some time in the 12 months immediately preceding April 1, 1991; or
  (ii) which is to be carried on at a works, plant or factory or by means of mobile plant which was under construction or in course of manufacture or in the course of commission at that date, or the construction or supply of which was the subject of a contract entered into before that date.

7. A process shall cease to be an existing process for the purposes of this Part if at any time between April 1, 1990 and the last day by which an application is otherwise required to be made for authorisation for the carrying on of that process, the process ceases to be carried on and is not carried on again at the same location (or with the same mobile plant) within the following 12 months.

[8. In this Part and subsequent provisions of the Schedule—
"the determination date" for a prescribed process is—
  (a) in the case of a process for which an authorisation is granted, the date on which the enforcing authority grants it, whether in pursuance of the application or, on an appeal, of a direction to grant it;
  (b) in the case of a process for which an authorisation is refused, the date of the refusal or, on an appeal, of the affirmation of the refusal;
"substantial change" has the same meaning as in section 10 of the Act.]

Part II

9. This Part of this Schedule applies in the case of a Part B process carried on in England or Wales.

10. The prescribed date in the case of a Part B process is, except in the case of an existing process, the date specified in paragraph 12 below as the date from which application may be made for authorisation to carry on an existing process of the same description.

11.—(1) In the case of an existing process, the prescribed date is, subject to paragraph 13,—
  (i) in a case falling within paragraph (2), the date at which the change mentioned in that paragraph is made;
  (ii) where sub-paragraph (i) does not apply, the day after that on which the period for applying for authorisation in accordance with the Table in paragraph 12 expires.
(2) A case falls within this paragraph if the person carrying on the process makes a substantial change in the process in the period specified in paragraph 12 in relation to the description of processes which comprise that process (when changed) and that change—
  (i) has not occasioned construction work which is in progress at the beginning of that period; or
  (ii) is not the subject of a contract for construction work entered into before the beginning of that period.
12. Application for authorisation for an existing process shall be made in the relevant period determined in accordance with the following Table—

	Application to be made	
Any process falling within a description set out in—	Not earlier than	Not later than
Paragraph (a), (b), (c) or (e) of Section 1.3, Section 3.5, 3.6, 5.1 or 6.7 or paragraph (b) of Section 6.9	1st April 1991	30th September 1991
Section 2.1, 2.2, 3.1, 3.2 or 3.4	1st October 1991	31st March 1992
Paragraph (d) of Section 1.3, Section 6.2, 6.5, 6.6 or 6,8 or paragraph (a) of Section 6.9	1st April 1992	30th September 1992

13. Where application is duly made in accordance with section 6 of the Act for authorisation for the carrying on of an existing Part B process, the prescribed date as respects the carrying on by the applicant (or another person in his place) of the process to which the application relates is the determination date for that process.

14. References in this Part to an existing process are to a process—
  (i) which was being carried on at some time in the 12 months immediately preceding the earlier date mentioned in paragraph 12 in relation to the description of processes within which the process falls; or
  (ii) which is to be carried on at a works, plant or factory or by means of mobile plant which was under construction or in course of manufacture or in the course of commission at that earlier date, or the construction or supply of which was the subject of a contract entered into before that date.

Part III

15. This Part of this Schedule applies in the case of a Part A process carried on in Scotland.

16. The prescribed date in the case of a Part A process is, except in the case of an existing process, April 1, 1992.

17.—(1) In the case of an existing process, the prescribed date is—
  (i) in a case falling within paragraph (2), the date at which the change mentioned in that paragraph is made unless later than the date applicable in accordance with sub-paragraph (ii);
  (ii) where sub-paragraph (i) does not apply and subject to paragraph 19, the day after that on which the period for applying for authorisation in accordance with the Table in paragraph 18 expires.
(2) A case falls within this paragraph if the person carrying on the process makes a substantial change in the process on or after April 1, 1992 and that change—
  (i) has not occasioned construction work which is in progress on that date; or
  (ii) is not the subject of a contract for construction work entered into before that date.

18. Application for authorisation to carry on an existing process shall be made in the relevant period specified in the following Table—

	Application to be made	
Any process falling within a description set out in—	Not earlier than	Not later than
Chapter 1	1st April 1992	30th June 1992
Section 2.1 or 2.3	1st January 1995	31st March 1995
Section 2.2	1st May 1995	31st July 1995
Chapter 3	1st December 1992	28th February 1993
Section 4.1, 4.2, 4.7 or 4.8	1st May 1993	31st July 1993
Section 4.3, 4.4, 4.6 or 4.9	1st November 1993	31st January 1994
Section 4.5	1st May 1994	31st July 1994
Chapter 5	1st August 1992	31st October 1992
Chapter 6	1st November 1995	31st January 1996

19. Where paragraph 17(1)(ii) would otherwise apply and application is duly made in accordance with Section 6 of the Act within the period specified in paragraph 18 for authorisation to carry on a process, the prescribed date as respects the carrying on by the applicant (or another person in his place) of the process to which the application relates is the determination date for that process.

20. Subject to paragraph 21 below, references in this Part to an existing process are to a process—
   (i) which was being carried on at some time in the 12 months immediately preceding April 1, 1992; or
   (ii) which is to be carried on at a works, plant or factory or by means of mobile plant which was under construction or in course of manufacture or in the course of commission at that date, or, where construction or manufacture had not been begun before that date, the construction or supply of which was the subject of a contract entered into before that date.

21. A process shall cease to be an existing process for the purposes of this Part if at any time between April 1, 1992 and the last date by which an application is otherwise required to be made for authorisation for the carrying on of that process, the process ceases to be carried on and is not carried on again at the same location (or with the same mobile plant) within the following 12 months.

Part IV

22. This Part of this Schedule applies in the case of a Part B process carried on in Scotland.

23. The prescribed date in the case of a Part B process is, except in the case of an existing process, the date specified in paragraph 25 below as the date from which application may be made for authorisation to carry on an existing process of the same description.

24.—(1) In the case of an existng process the prescribed date is, subject to paragraph 26,—
   (i) in a case falling within paragraph (2), the date at which the change mentioned in that paragraph is made;
   (ii) where sub-paragraph (i) does not apply, the day after that on which the period for applying for authorisation in accordance with the Table in paragraph 25 expires.

(2) A case falls within this paragraph if the person carrying on the process makes a substantial change in the process in the period specified in paragraph 25 in relation to the description of processes which comprise that process (when changed) and that change—
   (i) has not occasioned construction work which is in progress at the beginning of that period; or
   (ii) is not the subject of a contract for construction work entered into before the beginning of that period.

25. Application for authorisation for an existing process shall be made in the relevant period specified in the following Table—

	Application to be made	
Any process falling within a description set out in—	*Not earlier than*	*Not later than*
Paragraph (a), (b), (d) or (e) of Section 1.3, Section 3.2, 3.5, 3.6, 5.1 or 6.7 or paragraph (b) of Section 6.9	1st April 1992	31st July 1992
Paragraph (c) of Section 1.3	1st April 1992	30th September 1992
Section 2.1, 2.2, 3.1 or 3.4	1st August 1992	30th November 1992
Section 6.2, 6.5, 6.6 or 6.8 or paragraph (a) of Section 6.9	1st December 1992	31st March 1993

26. Where application is duly made in accordance with section 6 of the Act for authorisation for the carrying on of an existing Part B process, the prescribed date as respects the carrying on by the applicant (or another person in his place) of the process to which the application relates is the determination date for that process.

27. References in this Part to an existing process are to a process—
   (i) which was being carried on at some time in the 12 months immediately preceding the earlier date mentioned in paragraph 25 in relation to the description of processes within which the process falls; or
   (ii) which is to be carried on at a works, plant or factory or by means of mobile plant which was under construction or in course of manufacture or in the course of commission at that earlier date, or the construction or supply of which was the subject of a contract entered into before that date.

SCHEDULE 4   Regulation 6(1)

Release Into The Air: Prescribed Substances

Oxides of sulphur and other sulphur compounds
Oxides of nitrogen and other nitrogen compounds
Oxides of carbon
Organic compounds and partial oxidation products
Metals, metalloids and their compounds
Asbestos (suspended particulate matter and fibres), glass fibres and mineral fibres
Halogens and their compounds
Phosphorus and its compounds
Particulate matter.

SCHEDULE 5   Regulation 6(2)

Release Into Water: Prescribed Substances

Mercury and its compounds
Cadmium and its compounds
All isomers of hexachlorocylohexane
All isomers of DDT
Pentachlorophenol and its compounds
Hexachlorobenzene
Hexachlorobutadiene
Aldrin
Dieldrin
Endrin
Polychlorinated Biphenyls
Dichlorvos
1,2-Dichloroethane
All isomers of trichlorobenzene
Atrazine
Simazine
Tributyltin compounds
Triphenyltin compounds
Trifluralin

Fenitrothion
Azinphos-methyl
Malathion
Endosulfan.

SCHEDULE 6 Regulation 6(3)

Release Into Land: Prescribed Substances

Organic solvents
Azides
Halogens and their covalent compounds
Metal carbonyls
Organo-metallic compounds
Oxidizing agents
Polychlorinated dibenzofuran and any congener thereof
Polychlorinated dibenzo-p-dioxin and any congener thereof
Polyhalogenated biphenyls, terphenyls and naphthalenes
Phosphorus
Pesticides, that is to say, any chemical substance or preparation prepared or used for destroying any pest, including those used for protecting plants or wood or other plant products from harmful organisms; regulating the growth of plants; giving protection against harmful creatures; rendering such creatures harmless; controlling organisms with harmful or unwanted effects on water systems, buildings or other structures, or on manufactured products; or protecting animals against ectoparasites.
Alkali metals and their oxides and alkaline earth metals and their oxides.

APPENDIX 2

ENVIRONMENTAL PROTECTION

The Environmental Protection (Applications, Appeals and Registers) Regulations 1991

(S.I. 1991 No. 507)

In force from:

April 1, 1991 (England and Wales) and April 1, 1992 (Scotland)

Enabling power:

Environmental Protection Act 1990, ss.10(8), 11(1), (3)–(7), 15(10), 10(1)–(3), (10) and 22(6) and Sched. 1, paras. 1–3, 6 and 7.

Background:

Part I of the Environmental Protection Act 1990 makes provision for Integrated Pollution Control as well as the system of local authority air pollution control. Section 6 provides that no person shall carry on a prescribed process after the date prescribed or determined for that description of process unless he has applied for and been granted authorisation by the enforcing authority.

These Regulations set out the procedures to be followed and the information to be submitted on an application for authorisation, as well as on an application for a variation of conditions of an authorisation. The regulations provide exemptions from the requirements for reasons of national security and commercial confidentiality. The regulations also set out the procedures and time limits for appeals to the Secretary of State. Finally they prescribe the matters to be included in registers of public information which the enforcing authorities are required to maintain.

Statutory reference:

Environmental Protection Act 1990, ss.6, 15, 20 and 22.

Amendments:

S.I. 1991 No. 836 amended regs. 3 and 5.

Citation, commencement and interpretation

1.—(1) These Regulations may be cited as the Environmental Protection (Applications, Appeals and Registers) Regulations 1991 and shall come into force in England and Wales on 1st April 1991 and in Scotland on 1st April 1992.

(2) In these Regulations, "the 1990 Act" means the Environmental Protection Act 1990.

Applications for an authorisation

2.—(1) An application to an enforcing authority for an authorisation under section 6 of the 1990 Act shall be in writing and, subject to paragraphs (2) and (3) below, shall contain the following information—
  (a) the name of the applicant, his telephone number and address and, if different, any address to which correspondence relating to the application should be sent and, if the applicant is a body corporate, the address of its registered or principal office;

(b) in a case where the prescribed process will not be carried on by means of mobile plant—
  (i) the name of any local authority in whose area the prescribed process will be carried on;
  (ii) the address of the premises where the prescribed process will be carried on;
  (iii) a map or plan showing the location of those premises; and
  (iv) if only part of those premises will be used for carrying on the process, a plan or other means of identifying that part;
(c) in a case where the prescribed process will be carried on by means of mobile plant—
  (i) the name of the local authority in whose area the applicant has his principal place of business; and
  (ii) the address of that place of business;
(d) a description of the prescribed process;
(e) a list of prescribed substances (and any other substances which might cause harm if released into any environmental medium) which will be used in connection with, or which will result from, the carrying on of that process;
(f) a description of the techniques to be used for preventing the release into any environmental medium of such substances, for reducing the release of such substances to a minimum and for rendering harmless any such substances which are released;
(g) details of any proposed release of such substances into any environmental medium and an assessment of the environmental consequences;
(h) proposals for monitoring any release of such substances, the environmental consequences of any such release and the use of any techniques described in accordance with sub-paragraph (f) above;
(i) the matters on which the applicant relies to establish that the objectives mentioned in section 7(2) of the 1990 Act (including the objective referred to in section 7(7)) will be achieved and that he will be able to comply with the general condition implied by section 7(4);
(j) any additional information which he wishes the enforcing authority to take into account in considering his application.

(2) Paragraph (1) above shall apply in relation to an application to a local enforcing authority for an authorisation in respect of a prescribed process designated for local control (other than that mentioned in paragraph (3) below) as if the words in brackets in sub-paragraph (i) were omitted and references to the release of substances into any environmental medium were references to the release of substances into the air.

(3) Paragraph (1) above shall apply in relation to an application to a local enforcing authority for an authorisation to carry on any prescribed process involving only the burning of waste oil in an appliance with a net rated thermal input of less than 0.4 megawatts as if the following sub-paragraphs were substituted for sub-paragraphs (d) to (i)—

"(d) the name and number of the appliance (if any) and the name of its manufacturer;
(e) the net rated thermal input of the appliance and whether or not it is constructed or adapted so as to comply with the specification for fixed, flued fan-assisted heaters in Part 2 of the specification for oil-burning air heaters published by the British Standards Institution and numbered BS 4256 1972;
(f) details of the type of fuel to be used and its source;
(g) details of the height and location of any chimney through which waste gases produced by the appliance would be carried away;
(h) details of the efflux velocity of the waste gases leaving such a chimney produced by the appliance in normal operation;

(i) details of the location of the fuel storage tanks of the appliance;".

(4) In this regulation—

"net rated thermal input" is the rate at which fuel can be burned at the maximum continuous rating of the appliance multiplied by the net calorific value of the fuel and expressed as megawatts thermal;

"waste oil" means any mineral based lubricating or industrial oil which—

 (a) has become unfit for the use for which it was intended and, in particular, used combustion engine oil, gearbox oil, mineral lubricating oil, oil for turbines and hydraulic oil; and
 (b) is generated only as a result of activities carried out by the applicant on the premises where the process is to be carried on.

Variation of conditions of an authorisation

3.—(1) Any notice given to an enforcing authority under section 11(1)(a) of the 1990 Act of a proposed relevant change in a prescribed process shall be in writing.

(2) An application to an enforcing authority under any provision of section 11 of the 1990 Act for the variation of the conditions of an authorisation shall be in writing.

(3) A person making—

 (a) a request to an enforcing authority under section 11(1)(b) of the 1990 Act for a determination of the matters mentioned in section 11(2); or
 (b) an application to such an authority under any provision of section 11 for the variation of the conditions of an authorisation,

shall furnish the authority with his name, address and telephone number and shall also furnish the authority—

 (i) in a case where the prescribed process will not be carried on by means of mobile plant, with the address of the premises where the prescribed process will be carried on;
 (ii) in a case where the process will be carried on by means of mobile plant, with the address of his principal place of business;
 (iii) in all cases, with a statement of any changes as respects any information supplied under regulation 2(1)(a) to (c) above.

(4) Subject to paragraph (5) below, a person making—

 (a) a request to an enforcing authority under section 11(1)(b) of the 1990 Act for a determination of the matters mentioned in section 11(2); or
 (b) an application to such an authority under section 11(5) for the variation of the conditions of an authorisation,

shall also furnish the authority with—

 (i) a description of any proposed change in the manner in which the prescribed process will be carried on;
 (ii) a statement of any changes as respects the matters dealt with in regulation 2(1)(e) to (i) above which would result if any proposed change in the manner of carrying on the prescribed process were made;
 (iii) any additional information which he wishes the authority to take into account in considering his application; and
 (iv) in the case of an application under section 11(5) of the 1990 Act, an indication of the variations which he wishes the authority to make.

(5) Paragraph (4) above shall apply in relation to a process mentioned in regulation 2(3) above as if sub-paragraph (ii) were omitted.

(6) A person making an application to an enforcing authority under section 11(3)(b) or (4)(b) of the 1990 Act ... for the variation of the conditions of an authorisation shall also furnish the authority with—

 (a) an indication of the variations which he wishes the authority to make;

(b) a statement of any changes in any information supplied to the authority under paragraph (3) above; and
(c) any additional information which he wishes the authority to take into account in considering his application.

(7) A person making an application to an enforcing authority for the variation of the conditions of an authorisation under section 11(6) of the 1990 Act shall also furnish the authority with—
(a) an indication of the variations which he wishes the authority to make; and
(b) any additional information which he wishes the authority to take into account in considering his application.

Consultation

4.—(1) Subject to regulations 6 and 7(2) below, the persons to be consulted under paragraph 2, 6 or 7 of Schedule 1 to the 1990 Act are—
(a) the Health and Safety Executive, in all cases;
(b) the Minister of Agriculture, Fisheries and Food, in the case of all prescribed processes designated for central control which will be carried on in England;
(c) the Secretary of State for Wales, in the case of all prescribed processes designated for central control which will be carried on in Wales;
(d) the Secretary of State for Scotland, in the case of all prescribed processes designated for central control which will be carried on in Scotland;
(e) the National Rivers Authority, in the case of all prescribed processes designated for central control which will be carried on in England and Wales and which may result in the release of any substance into waters which are controlled waters for the purposes of Chapter I of Part III of the Water Act 1989 (c. 15);
(f) the sewerage undertaker or, in relation to Scotland, the regional or islands council, in the case of all prescribed processes designated for central control which may involve the release of any substance into a sewer vested in the undertaker or the council;
(g) the Nature Conservancy Council for England, the Nature Conservancy Council for Scotland or the Countryside Council for Wales—
　(i) in the case of all prescribed processes designated for central control which may involve a release of any substance;
　(ii) in the case of all prescribed processes designated for local control which may involve a release of any substance into the air,
which may affect a site of special scientific interest within the Council's area;
(h) the harbour authority, in the case of all prescribed processes designated for central control which may involve a release of any substance into a harbour managed by the harbour authority.

(2) Subject to regulation 7(5)(a) below, the period for notification under paragraph 2(1), 6(2) or 7(2) of Schedule 1 to the 1990 Act shall be the period of 14 days beginning with—
(a) in the case of a notification under paragraph 2(1), the day on which the enforcing authority receives the application for an authorisation;
(b) in the case of a notification under paragraph 6(2), the day on which the authority notifies the holder of an authorisation in accordance with section 10(5) of that Act; and
(c) in the case of a notification under paragraph 7(2), the day on which the authority receives the application for a variation of an authorisation.

(3) In paragraph (1)(h) above and regulation 7(3)(c) below, "harbour authority" has the same meaning as in section 57(1) of the Harbours Act 1964 (c. 40).

Advertisements

5.—(1) Subject to paragraph (4) and regulation 6 below, an advertisement—
   (a) by an applicant under paragraph 1(2) of Schedule 1 to the 1990 Act; or
   (b) by the holder of an authorisation under paragraph 6(2) or 7(2) of that Schedule,
shall be published in one or more newspapers circulating in the locality in which the prescribed process will be carried on.

(2) Subject to regulation 7(5)(b) below, any such advertisement as is mentioned in paragraph (1) above shall be published within a period of 28 days beginning 14 days after—
   (a) in the case of an advertisement under paragraph 1(2) of Schedule 1 to the 1990 Act, the day on which the application for an authorisation is made;
   (b) in the case of an advertisement under paragraph 6(2) of that Schedule, the day on which the holder of the authorisation is notified in accordance with section 10(5) of that Act;
   (c) in the case of an advertisement under paragraph 7(2) of that Schedule, the day on which the application for a variation is made.

(3) Subject to regulation 7(4) below, any such advertisement as is mentioned in paragraph (1) above shall—
   (a) state the name of the applicant or, as the case may be, of the holder of the authorisation;
   (b) give the address of the premises on which the prescribed process will be carried on;
   (c) describe briefly the prescribed process;
   (d) state where any register which contains particulars of the application or of the action to be taken may be inspected and that it may be inspected free of charge; and
   (e) explain that any person may make representations in writing to the enforcing authority within the period of 28 days beginning with the date of the advertisement and give the authority's address.

(4) The preceding provisions of this [regulation] do not apply in relation to any prescribed process which will be carried on by means of mobile plant.

Exemption for waste oil burners

6.—(1) The requirements of paragraph 1(2), 2, 6 or 7 of Schedule 1 to the 1990 Act shall not apply in relation to any process involving only the burning of waste oil in an appliance with a net rated thermal input of less than 0.4 megawatts.

(2) In this regulation—
"net rated thermal input" has the same meaning as in regulation 2(4) above; and
"waste oil" means any mineral based lubricating or industrial oil which has become unfit for the use for which it was intended and, in particular, used combustion engine oil, gearbox oil, mineral lubricating oil, oil for turbines and hydraulic oil.

National security and confidential information

7.—(1) This regulation applies where in relation to an application or an authorisation—
   (a) a direction given by the Secretary of State under section 21(2) of the 1990 Act applies;

(b) notice is given to the Secretary of State under section 21(4) of that Act;
(c) an application is made to an enforcing authority under section 22(2) of that Act; or
(d) an objection is made to such an authority under section 22(4) of that Act.

(2) Subject to paragraph (3) below, the requirements of paragraph 2(1), 6(2) or 7(2) of Schedule 1 to the 1990 Act shall not apply in so far as they would require a person mentioned in regulation 4(1)(f), (g), or (h) above to be consulted on information which is not to be included in the register by virtue of section 21 or 22 of that Act.

(3) Information which is not to be included in the register by virtue of section 22 of the 1990 Act shall not be excluded by paragraph (2) above if—
   (a) in the case of any person mentioned in regulation 4(1)(f) above, it is information about the release of any substance into a sewer vested in that person;
   (b) in the case of any person mentioned in regulation 4(1)(g) above, it is information about the release of any substance—
      (i) designated for central control;
      (ii) designated for local control which may involve a release of any substance into the air,
      which may affect a site of special scientific interest in that person's area; or
   (c) in the case of any person mentioned in regulation 4(1)(h) above, it is information about the release of any substance into a harbour managed by a harbour authority.

(4) The requirements of paragraph 1(2), 6(2) or 7(2) of Schedule 1 to the 1990 Act shall not apply in so far as they would require the advertisement of information mentioned in regulation 5(3) above which is not to be included in the register by virtue of section 21 or 22 of that Act.

(5) Where a matter falls to be determined under section 21 or 22 of the 1990 Act—
   (a) the period for notification under paragraph 2(1), 6(2) or 7(2) of Schedule 1 to that Act shall be the period of 14 days beginning 14 days after the day on which the matters to be determined under section 21 or 22 of that Act are finally disposed of;
   (b) the period within which an advertisement is to be published in the manner specified in regulation 5(1) above shall be the period of 28 days beginning 14 days after the day on which the matters to be determined under section 21 or 22 of the 1990 Act are finally disposed of.

(6) For the purposes of paragraph (5) above, the matters to be determined under section 21 or 22 of the 1990 Act are finally disposed of—
   (a) on the date on which the Secretary of State determines under section 21 of that Act whether or not information is to be included in the register;
   (b) on the date on which the enforcing authority is treated under section 22(3) of that Act as having made a determination;
   (c) in a case where the enforcing authority determines under section 22(2) or (4) of that Act that the information in question is commercially confidential, on the date of the authority's determination;
   (d) in a case where the enforcing authority determines under section 22(2) or (4) of that Act that the information in question is not commercially confidential, on the date on which the period for bringing an appeal expires without an appeal being brought or, if such an appeal is brought within that period, on the date of the Secretary of State's final determination of the appeal or, as the case may be, the date on which the appellant withdraws his appeal.

Transmitted applications

8. Where an application for an authorisation is transmitted under paragraph 3(1) of Schedule 1 to the 1990 Act to the Secretary of State for determination, a request by the applicant or the enforcing authority concerned that the Secretary of State exercise one of the powers under paragraph 3(3) of that Schedule shall be made to him in writing within the period of 21 days beginning with the day on which the applicant is informed that the application is being transmitted to the Secretary of State.

Notice of appeal

9.—(1) A person who wishes to appeal to the Secretary of State under section 15 or 22(5) of the 1990 Act shall give to the Secretary of State written notice of the appeal together with the documents specified in paragraph (2) below and shall at the same time send to the enforcing authority a copy of that notice together with the documents specified in paragraph (2)(a) and (f) below.

(2) The documents mentioned in paragraph (1) above are—
(a) a statement of the grounds of appeal;
(b) a copy of the relevant application;
(c) a copy of any relevant authorisation;
(d) a copy of any relevant correspondence between the appellant and the enforcing authority;
(e) a copy of any decision or notice which is the subject-matter of the appeal;
(f) a statement indicating whether the appellant wishes the appeal to be in the form of a hearing or to be disposed of on the basis of written representations.

(3) If the appellant wishes to withdraw an appeal he shall do so by notifying the Secretary of State in writing and shall send a copy of that notification to the enforcing authority.

Time limit for bringing appeal

10.—(1) Subject to paragraph (2) below, notice of appeal in accordance with regulation 9(1) above is to be given—
  (a) in the case of an appeal by a person who has been refused the grant of an authorisation under section 6 of the 1990 Act, before the expiry of the period of six months beginning with—
    (i) the date of the decision which is the subject-matter of the appeal; or
    (ii) in the case of an appeal against a deemed refusal of an application for an authorisation, the date on which the application is deemed under the provisions of paragraph 5(2) of Schedule 1 to the 1990 Act to have been refused;
  (b) in the case of an appeal by a person who is aggrieved by the conditions attached to his authorisation or who has been refused a variation of an authorisation on an application under section 11 of the 1990 Act, before the expiry of the period of six months beginning with the date of the decision which is the subject-matter of the appeal;
  (c) in the case of an appeal in respect of a decision of an enforcing authority to revoke an authorisation, before the date on which the revocation of the authorisation takes effect;
  (d) in the case of an appeal by a person on whom a variation notice, an enforcement notice or a prohibition notice is served, before the expiry of the period of two months beginning with the date of the notice which is the subject-matter of the appeal;
  (e) in the case of an appeal in respect of a decision of an enforcing authority that information is not commercially confidential, before

the expiry of the period of 21 days beginning with the date of the notice of determination.

(2) The Secretary of State may in a particular case allow notice of appeal to be given after the expiry of the periods mentioned in paragraph (1)(a), (b) or (d) above.

Action upon receipt of notice of appeal

11.—(1) Subject to paragraph (4) below, the enforcing authority shall, within 14 days of receipt of the copy of the notice of appeal in accordance with regulation 9(1) above—
  (a) in the case of an appeal by a person in respect of a decision of an enforcing authority to revoke an authorisation or on whom a variation notice, an enforcement notice or a prohibition notice is served, give written notice of it to any person who appears to the enforcing authority likely to have a particular interest in the subject-matter of the appeal; and
  (b) in any other case give written notice of it—
    (i) to any person who made representations to the authority with respect to the grant or variation of the authorisation; and
    (ii) to any person who was required to be consulted on the application under paragraph 2, 6 or 7 of Schedule 1 to the 1990 Act pursuant to regulation 4(1) above.
(2) A notice under paragraph (1) above shall—
  (a) state that an appeal has been lodged;
  (b) give the name of the appellant and—
    (i) where the prescribed process will not be carried on by means of mobile plant, the address of the premises where the prescribed process will be carried on;
    (ii) where the prescribed process will be carried on by means of mobile plant, the address of this principal place of business;
  (c) describe the application or authorisation to which the appeal relates;
  (d) state that a copy of any representations made to the enforcing authority by any person mentioned in paragraph (1)(b) above will be sent to the Secretary of State and the appellant and will be considered by the Secretary of State when determining the appeal unless, within 21 days of the date of the notice, the person who made the representations requests the Secretary of State to disregard them;
  (e) state that representations with respect to the appeal may be made to the Secretary of State in writing by any recipient of the notice within a period of 21 days beginning with the date of the notice; and
  (f) state that if a hearing is to be held wholly or partly in public, a person mentioned in paragraph (1)(a) or (b)(i) above who makes representations with respect to the appeal and any person mentioned in paragraph (1)(b)(ii) above will be notified of the date of the hearing.
(3) The enforcing authority shall, within 14 days of sending a notice under paragraph (1) above, send to the Secretary of State a copy of any representations made to that authority by any person mentioned in paragraph (1)(b) above and shall notify the Secretary of State of the persons to whom and the date on which the notice was sent.

(4) The preceding provisions of this regulation do not apply in the case of an appeal brought under section 22(5) of the 1990 Act.

Written representations

12.—(1) Where the appellant informs the Secretary of State that he wishes the appeal to be disposed of on the basis of written representations, the enforcing authority shall submit any written representations to the Secretary of State not later than 28 days after receiving a copy of the documents mentioned in regulation 9(2)(a) and (f) above.

(2) The appellant shall make any further representations by way of reply to any representations from the enforcing authority not later than 17 days after the date of submission of those representations by the enforcing authority.

(3) Any representations made by the appellant or the enforcing authority shall be dated and submitted to the Secretary of State on the date they bear.

(4) When the enforcing authority or the appellant submits any representations to the Secretary of State they shall at the same time send a copy of them to the other party.

(5) The Secretary of State shall send to the appellant and the enforcing authority a copy of any representations made to him by the persons mentioned in regulation 11(1) above and shall allow the appellant and the enforcing authority a period of not less than 14 days in which to make representations thereon.

(6) The Secretary of State may in a particular case—
 (a) set later time limits than those mentioned in this regulation;
 (b) require exchanges of representations between the parties in addition to those mentioned in paragraphs (1) and (2) above.

Hearings

13.—(1) The Secretary of State shall give the appellant and the enforcing authority at least 28 days written notice (or such shorter period of notice as they may agree) of the date, time and place fixed for the holding of any hearing in respect of an appeal under section 15 or 22(5) of the 1990 Act.

(2) Subject to paragraph (4) and (5) below, in the case of a hearing which is to be held wholly or partly in public, the Secretary of State shall, at least 21 days before the date fixed for the holding of the hearing, publish a copy of the notice mentioned in paragraph (1) above—
 (a) in a case where the prescribed process will not be carried on by means of mobile plant, in a newspaper circulating in the locality in which the prescribed process which is the subject of the appeal will be carried on; and
 (b) in a case where the appeal is in respect of a decision of an enforcement authority to revoke an authorisation or against a variation notice, an enforcement notice or a prohibition notice in respect of a prescribed process carried on by means of mobile plant, in a newspaper circulating in the locality in which the prescribed process was carried on at the time when the notice of revocation, variation notice, enforcement notice or prohibition notice was served,
and shall serve a copy of the notice mentioned in paragraph (1) above on every person mentioned in regulation 11(1)(a) and (b)(i) above who has made representations in writing to the Secretary of State and on any person who was required under regulation 11(1)(b)(ii) above to be notified of the appeal.

(3) The Secretary of State may vary the date fixed for the holding of any hearing and paragraphs (1) and (2) above shall apply to the variation of a date as they applied to the date originally fixed.

(4) The Secretary of State may also vary the time or place for the holding of a hearing but shall give such notice of any such variation as appears to him to be reasonable.

(5) Paragraph (2) above shall not apply in the case of a hearing in respect of an appeal brought under section 22(5) of the 1990 Act.

(6) The persons entitled to be heard at a hearing are—
 (a) the appellant;
 (b) the enforcing authority; and

(c) any person required under regulation 11(1)(b)(ii) above to be notified of the appeal.

(7) Nothing in paragraph (6) above shall prevent the person appointed to conduct the hearing of the appeal from permitting any other person to be heard at the hearing and such permission shall not be unreasonably withheld.

(8) After the conclusion of a hearing, the person appointed to conduct the hearing shall make a report in writing to the Secretary of State which shall include his conclusions and his recommendations or his reasons for not making any recommendations.

Notification of determination

14.—(1) The Secretary of State shall notify the appellant in writing of his determination of the appeal and shall provide him with a copy of any report mentioned in regulation 13(8) above.

(2) The Secretary of State shall at the same time send—
(a) a copy of the documents mentioned in paragraph (1) above to the enforcing authority and to any persons required under regulation 11(1)(b)(ii) above to be notified of the appeal; and
(b) a copy of his determination of the appeal to a person mentioned in regulation 11(1)(a) and (b)(i) above who made representations to the Secretary of State and, if a hearing was held, to any other person who made representations in relation to the appeal at the hearing.

Registers

15. Subject to sections 21 and 22 of the 1990 Act, a register maintained by an enforcing authority under section 20 of that Act shall contain—
(a) all particulars of any application for an authorisation made to the Authority;
(b) all particulars of any notice to the applicant by the authority under paragraph 1(3) of Schedule 1 to that Act and of any information furnished in response to such a notice;
(c) all particulars of any representations made by any person required to be consulted under paragraph 2, 6 or 7 of Schedule 1 to the 1990 Act pursuant to regulation 4(1) above;
(d) all particulars of any authorisation granted by the authority;
(e) all particulars of any variation notice, enforcement notice or prohibition notice issued by the authority;
(f) all particulars of any notice issued by the authority withdrawing a prohibition notice;
(g) all particulars of any notification given to the holder of an authorisation by the authority under section 10(5) of that Act;
(h) all particulars of any application for the variation of the conditions of an authorisation under section 11(4)(b) of that Act;
(i) all particulars of any revocation of an authorisation effected by the authority;
(j) all particulars of any notice of appeal under section 15 of that Act against a decision by the authority, the documents relating to the appeal mentioned in regulation 9(2)(a), (d) and (e) above, any written notification of the Secretary of State's determination of such an appeal and any report accompanying any such written notification;
(k) details of any conviction of any person for any offence under section 23(1) of that Act which relates to the carrying on of a prescribed process under an authorisation granted by the authority, including the name of the offender, the date of conviction, the penalty imposed and the name of the Court;
(l) all particulars of any monitoring information relating to the carrying

on of a prescribed process under an authorisation granted by the authority obtained by the authority as a result of its own monitoring or furnished to the authority in writing by virtue of a condition of the authorisation or section 19(2) of that Act;
(m) in a case where any such monitoring information is omitted from the register by virtue of section 22 of that Act, a statement by the authority, based on the monitoring information from time to time obtained by or furnished to them, indicating whether or not there has been compliance with any relevant condition of the authorisation;
(n) all particulars of any report published by an enforcing authority relating to an assessment of the environmental consequences of the carrying on of a prescribed process in the locality of premises where the prescribed process is carried on under an authorisation granted by the authority; and
(o) all particulars of any direction (other than a direction under section 21(2) of the 1990 Act) given to the authority by the Secretary of State under any provision of Part I of that Act.

16.—(1) A register maintained by a local enforcing authority which is not a port health authority shall (in addition to the particulars required by regulation 15 above) contain all particulars of such information contained in any register maintained by the chief inspector or river purification authority as relates to the carrying on in the area of the local enforcing authority of prescribed processes in relation to which the chief inspector or river purification authority has functions under Part I of the 1990 Act.
(2) In Scotland, a register maintained by—
(a) the chief inspector shall (in addition to the particulars required by regulation 15 above) contain all particulars of such information contained in any register maintained by a river purification authority as relates to the carrying on in the area of the authority of prescribed processes in relation to which the authority has functions under Part I of the 1990 Act;
(b) each river purification authority shall (in addition to the particulars required by regulation 15 above) contain all particulars of such information contained in any register maintained by the chief inspector as relates to the carrying on in the area of the authority of prescribed processes in relation to which the chief inspector has functions under Part I of that Act.

17. Nothing in regulation 15 or 16 above shall require an enforcing authority, to keep in a register maintained by them—
(a) monitoring information four years after that information was entered in the register; or
(b) information which has been superseded by later information four years after that later information was entered in the register.

6th March 1991

Michael Heseltine
Secretary of State for the Environment

6th March 1991

David Hunt
Secretary of State for Wales

6th March 1991

James Douglas-Hamilton
Parliamentary Under Secretary of State,
Scottish Office

APPENDIX 3

INTEGRATED POLLUTION CONTROL: A PRACTICAL GUIDE (DOE/WO 1993)

1. INTRODUCTION

1.1 This document provides guidance on the operation of Integrated Pollution Control (IPC) under Part I of the Environmental Protection Act 1990 ("the Act") and lists more detailed guidance which is available from various sources. It replaces "Integrated Pollution Control: A Practical Guide", first issued in February 1991. IPC applies to the most potentially polluting or technologically complex industrial processes throughout England and Wales. The enforcing (and authorising) authority is Her Majesty's Inspectorate of Pollution (HMIP). IPC is being introduced progressively between 1 April 1991 and 1 November 1995.

1.2 A similar but separate system of IPC, also introduced by Part I of the Act, came into operation in Scotland from 1 April 1992, and will also be introduced in Northern Ireland.

1.3 Part I further provides the basis for a system for controlling emissions to air alone from generally less polluting processes. For such processes local authorities (districts and London and metropolitan boroughs, and in some cases port health authorities) are the enforcing authorities. Separate guidance relating to the local authority air pollution control system is available from the Department of the Environment (contact: 071.276.8322).

1.4 This Practical Guide, produced jointly by the Department of the Environment and the Welsh Office, explains the Act and the relevant Regulations made under it as they apply to IPC in England and Wales. All the guidance in this document is informal; it should not be taken as an authoritative interpretation of the Act nor of any subordinate legislation referred to in the document. It does **not** constitute guidance to the Chief Inspector pursuant to section 7(11) of the Act, although appropriate parts of it may be reflected in any such guidance.

1.5 Relevant information and guidance is also contained in:
  (a) **The Environmental Protection Act 1990** itself (ISBN 0 10 544390 5, £14.45);
  (b) **The Environmental Protection (Prescribed Processes and Substances) Regulations 1991** (S.I. 1991 No. 472, ISBN 0 11 013472 9, £3.85), prescribing the processes and substances which come under HMIP and local authority control respectively and specifying the implementation timetable;
  (c) **The Environmental Protection (Applications, Appeals and Registers) Regulations 1991** (S.I. 1991 No. 507, ISBN 0 11 013507 5, £2.55), setting down the detailed procedures for the making and handling of applications and appeals and itemising the information which must be included in public registers;
  (d) **The Disposal of Controlled Waste (Exceptions) Regulations 1991** (S.I. 1991 No. 508, ISBN 0 11 013508 3, £1.00), providing for the interface between the controls under Part I of the Act and those under Part I of the Control of Pollution Act 1974;
  (e) **The Environmental Protection (Authorisation of Processes) (Determination Periods) Order 1991** (S.I. 1991 No. 513, ISBN 0 11 013513 X, £1.00), extending the standard four-month decision period in certain cases;
  (f) **The Environmental Protection (Amendment of Regulations) Regulations 1991** (S.I. 1991 No. 836, ISBN 0 11 013836 8, £0.60), rectifying an inconsistency between S.I. 1991 No. 472 and Schedule 15 to the Act, and correcting two minor errors in S.I. 1991 No. 507;
  (g) **The Environmental Protection (Prescribed Processes and Substances)**

(**Amendment**) **Regulations 1991** (S.I. 1992 No. 614, ISBN 0 11 023614 9, £1.05), clarifying one or two areas of uncertainty and correcting errors in S.I. 1991 No. 472; and

(h) the **Chief Inspector's Guidance Notes** on specific processes, providing details of the processes covered in each Note, abatement equipment, the standards to be achieved and compliance requirements.

These items can all be obtained through HMSO. In addition, HMIP has produced the following documents which are available free of charge to applicants from HMIP offices:

(i) "**Application Form for an Authorisation under IPC and Guidance to Applicants for Authorisation**"—comprising a form for operators to use in seeking an authorisation and describing the sort of information HMIP needs to determine an application; and

(j) the **HMIP Integrated Pollution Control Fees and Charges Scheme (England and Wales) 1992**.

1.6 IPC is being applied to existing processes according to a rolling programme. It applied from 1 April 1991 for new processes of all descriptions and existing processes which are substantially varied, in addition to large combustion plant. **Annex A** shows the timetable set out in the Regulations (S.I. 1991 No. 472) for bringing existing process categories within IPC. The process-specific guidance notes which the Chief Inspector is issuing to his Inspectors are being produced in advance of the dates on which the various descriptions of existing process come under the control of the system. Once published, these guidance notes will be available from HMSO.

2. ORIGINS AND OBJECTIVES OF IPC

2.1 Releases of polluting substances from industrial processes to the three environmental media of air, water and land were subject traditionally to separate control regimes. However, the Fifth Report of the Royal Commission on Environmental Pollution (1976—Cmnd. 6371) proposed that polluting releases should be directed to the environmental medium where the least environmental damage would be done. This proposal was accompanied by the recommendation that a body be created with responsibility for ensuring that wastes were disposed so as to minimise effects in all three environmental media, thus achieving the optimum environmental solution overall. This is the basis of the term **Best Practicable Environmental Option (BPEO)** which is a key element of IPC.

2.2 These recommendations were reinforced in a scrutiny report on pollution control by the Cabinet Office Efficiency Unit in 1986. This reported that for as long as the three environmental media were treated separately there was a danger that the allocation of resources would not reflect an overall view of where the problems were most severe; and that the end result would be a haphazard disposal of pollutants unrelated to an overall assessment of the optimum solution for the environment as a whole. Accordingly, as a first step towards a new system of integrated pollution control in England and Wales, HMIP was established in April 1987. A consultation paper was issued in 1988, setting out the Government's proposals for a new system of integrated pollution control.

2.3 The main objectives of IPC are:
(a) to prevent or minimise the release of prescribed substances and to render harmless any such substances which are released; and
(b) to develop an approach to pollution control that considers releases from industrial processes to all media in the context of the effect on the environment as a whole.

It has the following additional aims:

(c) to improve the efficiency and effectiveness of pollution controls on industry;
(d) to streamline and strengthen the regulatory system, clarify the roles and responsibilities of HMIP, other regulatory authorities, and the firms they regulate;
(e) to contain the burden on industry, particularly by providing for a "one stop shop" on pollution control for the potentially most seriously polluting processes;
(f) to provide the appropriate framework to encourage cleaner technologies and the minimisation of waste;
(g) to maintain public confidence in the regulatory system through a clear and transparent system that is accessible and easy to understand and is clear and simple in operation;
(h) to provide a flexible framework that is capable of responding both to changing pollution abatement technology and to new knowledge on the effects of pollutants; and
(i) to provide a means to fulfil certain international obligations relating to environmental protection.

3. PRESCRIBED PROCESSES AND SUBSTANCES

Prescribed Processes

3.1 IPC applies to all processes in England and Wales falling within any description of process prescribed for the purpose by the Secretary of State in regulations. **The Environmental Protection (Prescribed Processes and Substances) Regulations 1991** (S.I. 1991 No. 472, as amended by S.I. 1991 No. 836 and S.I. 1992 No. 614) list in Schedule 1 the descriptions of process to which the controls apply. The Schedule is divided into "Part A" and "Part B": "Part A" processes are those prescribed for IPC; "Part B" processes are those for local authority air pollution control. IPC regulates those processes with the greatest potential for serious pollution to the three environmental media; processes regulated under the local authority air pollution control system are those with less serious potential to pollute.

3.2 Regulation 4 excludes certain processes from control, even though they are listed in the Schedule. For example, exclusions may be appropriate if: prescribed substances are only released to air and land in quantities that are so trivial that the release cannot do any harm; processes are undertaken in a working museum; or the process involves the running of an engine to propel an aircraft or railway locomotive.

3.3 Schedule 2 clarifies what should be taken to form part of a prescribed process for the purpose of interpreting Schedule 1. Thus, in broad terms, once a process is defined in Schedule 1, all the related parts of the process come under control, provided that they are at the same location and carried on by the same person, and that they do not warrant authorisation in their own right.

3.4 The Regulations also contain the implementation timetable set out at **Annex A**. Schedule 3 to the Regulations sets out the transitional arrangements for existing processes, including the dates by which applications must be made.

Prescribed Substances

3.5 IPC is concerned with the control of releases to all three environmental media—air, water and land (as defined in section 1 of the Act). The Regulations list the substances which are most harmful or potentially polluting when released into the environment; these substances are subject to special requirements to ensure the use of the Best Available Techniques Not Entailing Excessive Cost (BATNEEC) to prevent their release to specified environmental media or (if that is not practicable) to minimise and render harmless such releases. All other substances which might cause harm if released into any medium are subject additionally to the use of BATNEEC to render them harmless.

3.6 There are three separate lists of prescribed substances according to whether the substance is to be controlled in relation to air, water or land releases. The lists of prescribed substances are in Schedules 4 (air), 5 (water) and 6 (land) to the Regulations; and are reproduced in **Annex B** to this guidance.

4. APPLICATION PROCEDURES

The Application

4.1 **The Environmental Protection (Applications, Appeals and Registers) Regulations 1991** (S.I. 1991 No. 507, as amended by S.I. 1991 No. 836 and S.I. 1992 No. 614) establish the detailed procedure for applications for IPC authorisations. The application must be made in writing and must contain the information specified in the Regulations. The details include: the name and address of the applicant; the address where the prescribed process will be carried on, with outline map or plan; a description of the prescribed process; a list of prescribed substances used in connection with or resulting from the process; a description of the techniques to be used to prevent or minimise releases; details of any proposed release of prescribed substances and an assessment of the environmental consequences; and proposals for monitoring releases.

4.2 The application also should point out clearly any information which the applicant wishes to be withheld from public registers on the grounds of national security or commercial confidentiality, as provided for in sections 21 and 22 of the Act.

4.3 Application forms together with further guidance on completion (see 1.5(i) above) are available from HMIP offices.

Timing of Applications

4.4 For *existing* processes—which form the vast majority of processes to come within IPC—applications should be made at the due time in the overall IPC implementation programme or when the process is to be changed substantially. For *new* processes with normal characteristics, and for which Chief Inspector's guidance exists, it will generally be appropriate for applications to be made when full designs have been drawn up, but prior to construction commencing.

4.5 For such processes which are not excessively complex or novel, it is likely that the operator will be in a position at the design stage to submit an application which provides all the information—including proposals covering management of the plant and training of operating staff—to enable HMIP to place it in the public register, carry out the required consultations and make a determination within the normal four-month period. If, in the course of construction or commissioning, changes have to be made which would lead to the need for the authorisation to be varied, it would be open to the applicant to apply in the due way, or to HMIP to institute the appropriate variation procedures.

Staged Applications

4.6 For some novel and complex new processes, with long lead times for design and construction, it will not be possible for HMIP to determine an application at the design stage. It may be desirable in such cases for applicants to seek HMIP involvement at the earlier stage of process design, so that for example options relating to the best practicable environmental option are not closed off prematurely. In cases of this kind, the applicant should seek HMIP's agreement to the use of a staged application procedure, under which HMIP and the applicant agree a plan for the application and supporting information to be submitted in a number of tranches, as the process plans are developed progressively.

4.7 Once the use of the procedure has been argued, it will be open to the operator to submit an application either at the point at which he is selecting the primary process, or—perhaps more commonly—when the outline of the process design is completed. He should provide as much information as he reasonably can at that time. The application will, subject to the normal rules on commercial confidentiality, be placed in the public register. It will need to be advertised by the operator and be subject to consultation in the usual way. However, by agreement between HMIP and the operator (under paragraph 5 of Schedule 1 to the Act), the application will not be determined within the usual four-month period. Instead, under the phased plan, the operator will agree to provide HMIP with the additional information required to determine the application as it becomes available during the design, construction and commissioning stages. Each tranche of this additional information will, subject to the normal rules on commercial confidentiality, be placed in the public register and be subject to consultation in the usual way. At an appropriate point, usually at commissioning, the application will be finally determined. As the application will be open to public scrutiny and statutory consultation at each stage, possible objections to the proposal will be more likely to emerge at an early stage and the risks of significant abortive expenditure by the operator will be reduced correspondingly. Charges will be calculated for staged applications on the basis of time and resources required, rather than the usual application fee.

4.8 Even when the portfolio of Chief Inspector's guidance notes is complete, circumstances may arise exceptionally where an operator with a major and innovative new process or product in mind finds that no Chief Inspector's guidance exists, or the extant guidance is not directly relevant to the particular approach he wishes to adopt. It is for the operator himself to assemble the necessary expertise and information about available techniques to deliver the process or product, and HMIP will not provide free consultancy advice. However, in line with the transitional arrangements relating to the Chief Inspector's notes, HMIP Headquarters staff will be ready to consider with applicants the standards that are likely to be required. Approaches in such cases should be made to the Chief Inspector in the first instance. When the idea has been developed sufficiently, the operator should submit an application which may be handled through a phased authorisation procedure, as described above. At that time, HMIP may, if it considers it appropriate, place in the public register a record of any prior discussions that have taken place.

Additional Information

4.9 Paragraph 1(3) of Schedule 1 to the Act also gives HMIP the power to require the applicant to furnish any further information necessary to enable an application to be determined. However, there may be cases where it is necessary for HMIP to obtain information from other sources. Where it does so, the content of such information should be disclosed to the applicant and other interested parties and they should be given an opportunity to comment on it before the application is determined.

Time Limit for Considering an Application

4.10 Paragraphs 5(1) and (3) of Schedule 1 to the Act provide that the enforcing authority will have a set period in which to determine applications for authorisations. Where the application does not contain commercially confidential information or information affecting national security this will be four months from the date the enforcing authority receives the application. However, a separate Order under the Act—the **Environmental Protection (Authorisation of Processes) (Determination Periods) Order 1991** (S.I. 1991 No. 513)—provides that where an applicant claims that the application contains details affecting commercial confidentiality or national security, the period will be four months from the day on which that claim is finally determined.

4.11 By agreement with the applicant, under paragraph 5 of Schedule 1 to the Act, HMIP may in appropriate cases take longer than four months to determine an application. This may be appropriate for design stage applications in particular.

4.12 **Figure I** shows the main steps and timetable for dealing with applications; **Figure II** sets out the procedures in more detail.

Refusal of an Application

4.13 HMIP must refuse to grant an authorisation unless it considers that the applicant will be able to carry on the process in compliance with the conditions to be included in the authorisation. Those conditions can only be

Figure I: Application—main steps and timetable

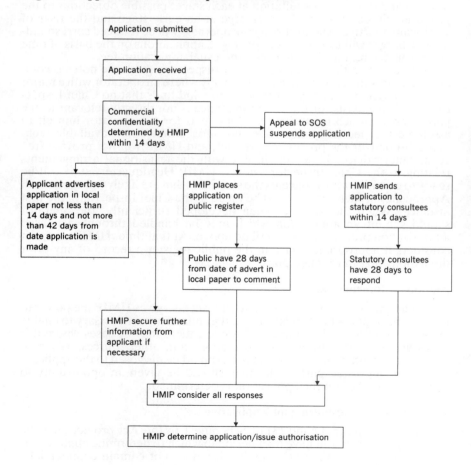

Figure II: Applications—detailed procedures

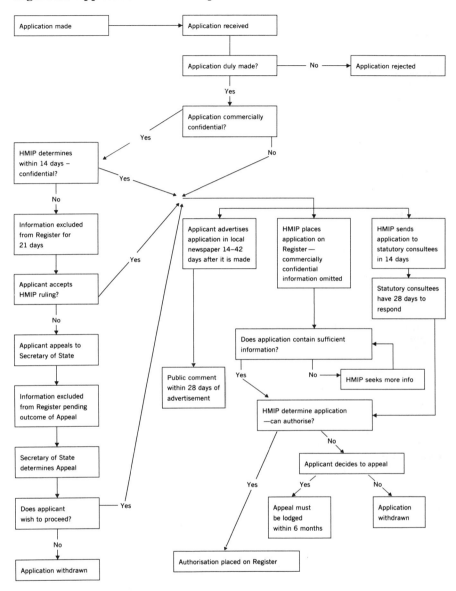

set if HMIP has the information it needs. It is vital, therefore, that the application is a comprehensive document. If information is not provided in enough detail, HMIP will notify the applicant in writing of the additional information it requires and the time within which it should be provided. If this information is not forthcoming, HMIP then has the right under Schedule 1 to refuse to proceed with the application. The application must also be accompanied by the correct fee, otherwise the application will not be duly made and HMIP may refuse to consider it. Separate guidance which explains the fees and charges scheme under IPC is available from HMIP (see 1.5(j) above).

5. CONSULTATION PROCEDURES

5.1 Statutory consultees are identified in Regulation 4 of the **Environmental Protection (Applications, Appeals and Registers) Regulations 1991** (as amended), and include, for example, the Health and Safety Executive and National Rivers Authority. HMIP must notify them of an application for an authorisation, or a variation of an authorisation involving substantial change, within 14 days of receipt. The Act provides that statutory consultees will then have 28 days in which to respond. Where an operator has applied for information to be excluded on the grounds of commercial confidentiality or national security, Regulation 7 provides that this notification takes place not less than 14 days and not more than 28 days after the final determination of the application for exclusion.

Public Participation and Registers

5.2 The IPC system was designed to encourage a significant degree of public involvement in the decision-making process. In addition to an application being referred to specific statutory consultees, Regulation 5 provides that the public must also be afforded the opportunity to comment in respect of applications for authorisations, and variations of authorisations involving substantial change. The Regulation places a duty on the applicant to advertise in a local newspaper details of the prescribed process and its location, together with a statement that public representations may be made, and to whom.

5.3 The advertisement must be made not less than 14 days and not more than 42 days after the day on which an application for an authorisation (or variation) is made, or the day on which the holder of an authorisation is notified in accordance with section 10(5) of the Act. Regulation 7 again provides for slightly different arrangements for applications which contain commercially confidential or national security information.

5.4 HMIP must consider any representations it receives when determining the application. Before making representations, the public can examine the application, which must be placed in a register as soon as possible after it is received by HMIP.

5.5 In line with the Government's commitment to public access to environmental information, the Act provides for a system of public registers containing details of IPC applications and authorisations, of any variation or enforcement procedures, of monitoring information and of other relevant documents.

5.6 Registers of information on IPC processes are available for inspection free of charge at HMIP Regional Headquarters offices in Leeds, Bristol and Bedford and at local authority offices. Copies of entries may be obtained on payment of a charge. The registers at these offices hold information relating to IPC processes within their respective areas. In addition, an index to the entire register, but not the register itself, is available at HMIP Headquarters in London. Sections 20–22 of the Act deal with registers of information, and the exclusion from them of information on grounds of commercial confidentiality and national security information. Regulation 15 of the **Environmental Protection (Applications, Appeals and Registers) Regulations 1991** (as amended) provides more detail on the information that is contained in the register. A leaflet explaining the public's right of access to information under Part I of the Act—**"The Environmental Protection Act 1990, Part I AND YOU"**—is available free of charge from HMIP Regional Headquarters and from local authorities.

Exclusion on Grounds of Commercial Confidentiality

5.7 Section 22 of the Act allows for information to be withheld from the public register for reasons of commercial confidentiality, in circumstances where the disclosure of information would prejudice a person's commercial interests to an unreasonable degree. An applicant who seeks to have information kept or removed from the public register for reasons of commercial confidentiality should demonstrate that disclosure of the information would negate or diminish a commercial advantage, or produce or increase a commercial disadvantage which is unreasonable given the nature of the information and the financial effect of disclosure.

Exclusion on Grounds of National Security

5.8 Section 21 of the Act provides for information to be withheld from the public register when, in the opinion of the Secretary of State, its disclosure would prejudice national security. This provision is used only rarely, and may be initiated by either the operator or by the Secretary of State.

6. AUTHORISATIONS

6.1 The Act (section 6) provides that no prescribed process may be operated after the date specified in the regulations for that description of process without an authorisation from HMIP.

6.2 HMIP is required to grant an authorisation, subject to any conditions which the Act requires or empowers it to impose, or to refuse it. HMIP must refuse it unless it considers that the applicant will be able to carry on the process in compliance with the conditions to be included in the authorisation. The Secretary of State has reserve powers to direct HMIP whether or not to grant an authorisation, and to make directions as to the conditions which are, or are not, to be included in an authorisation.

6.3 In setting the conditions within an authorisation, section 7 of the Environmental Protection Act 1990 places HMIP under a duty to ensure that certain objectives are met. The conditions should ensure that:
- the best available techniques not entailing excessive cost ("BATNEEC") are used to prevent or, if that is not practicable, to minimise the release of prescribed substances into the medium for which they are prescribed; and to render harmless both any prescribed substances which are released and any other substances which might cause harm if released into any environmental medium;
- releases do not cause, or contribute to, the breach of any direction given by the Secretary of State to implement European Community or international obligations relating to environmental protection, or any statutory environmental quality standards or objectives, or other statutory limits or requirements; and
- when a process is likely to involve releases into more than one medium (which will probably be the case in most processes prescribed for IPC), the best practicable environmental option ("BPEO") is achieved (*i.e.* the releases from the process are controlled through the use of BATNEEC so as to have the least effect on the environment as a whole).

6.4 The conditions in the authorisation must ensure that *all* these various objectives are met. If two separate objectives implied different standards (for example if one implied a tighter limit on a particular release than another) the tighter standard would prevail. In practice this means that HMIP must as a minimum ensure that BATNEEC is achieved, but may in some circumstances need to set more stringent conditions to achieve other section 7 objectives. An authorisation issued by HMIP will contain specific conditions to ensure that it fulfils the objectives contained in section 7 of the Act. Conditions may, among other matters, relate to the method of operation, the training of staff, abatement techniques used to reduce the release of substances etc. Releases will be regulated by conditions in authorisations limiting explicitly the substances that can be released to the various environmental media, and may be both in terms of their concentration and the amount of the substances released.

6.5 HMIP also has power to include any other conditions which appear to it to be appropriate. However, it would not be possible for HMIP to cover every eventuality in an authorisation. In addition, therefore, to the specific conditions required to be spelt out by HMIP in the authorisation, there is an implied condition in every authorisation that operators will use BATNEEC to prevent or, if that is not practicable, to minimise the release of prescribed substances into the medium for which they are prescribed, and to render harmless both any releases of prescribed substances which do occur, and any other releases. This implied condition complements the duty on HMIP to require the use of BATNEEC, and applies to all aspects of the process other than those regulated by a specific condition set by HMIP.

6.6 The implied condition is designed to cover the most detailed level of plant design and operation, where only the operator can reasonably be expected to know and understand what the demands of pollution control require in practice. For this reason, the Act provides that in any proceedings for an offence or failure to comply with the implied condition, the onus of proving that the operator was in fact using BATNEEC (and thus complying with the implied condition) falls on the operator himself.

Transfers of Authorisations

6.7 An authorisation for carrying on a prescribed process may be transferred by the holder to any other person. The Act requires the person to whom it is transferred to notify HMIP of that fact within twenty-one days of the transfer. Upon transfer the authorisation will continue to have effect as before subject to the same conditions. It is an offence to fail to notify HMIP of a transfer of an authorisation.

7. REQUIRED STANDARDS AND BEST AVAILABLE TECHNIQUES NOT ENTAILING EXCESSIVE COST (BATNEEC)

The Meaning of BATNEEC

7.1 All IPC processes under Part I of the Act are subject to the BATNEEC requirements. In general terms, what is BATNEEC for one process is likely to be BATNEEC for a comparable process. But in each case it is in practice for HMIP (subject to appeal to the Secretary of State) to decide what is BATNEEC for the individual process and the inspector concerned will take into account variable factors such as configuration, size, other individual characteristics of the process and local environment factors in doing so. Guidance on what constitutes BATNEEC for each description of prescribed process is provided in the Chief Inspector's Guidance Notes to assist both inspectors and operators.

7.2 It should always be borne in mind that BATNEEC is one of a number of objectives set out in section 7 of the Act, which must be achieved and in respect of which conditions will be included in an authorisation.

"BAT"

7.3 It is helpful to consider the words "best available techniques" separately and together.

7.4 "Best" must be taken to mean most effective in preventing, minimising or rendering harmless polluting releases. There may be more than one set of techniques that achieves comparable effectiveness—that is, there may be more than one set of "best" techniques.

7.5 "Available" should be taken to mean procurable by the operator of the process in question. It does not imply that the technique has to be in general use, but it does require general accessibility. It includes a technique which has been developed (or proven) at pilot scale, provided this allows its implementation in the relevant industrial context with the necessary business confidence. It does not imply that sources outside the UK are "unavailable". Nor does it imply a competitive supply market. If there is a monopoly supplier the technique counts as being available provided that the operator can procure it.

7.6 "Techniques" is defined in section 7(10) of the Act. The term embraces both the plant in which the process is carried on and how the process is operated. It should be taken to mean the components of which it is made up and the manner in which they are connected together to make the whole. It also includes matters such as numbers and qualifications of staff, working methods, training and supervision and also the design, construction, lay-out and maintenance of buildings, and will affect the concept and design of the process.

"NEEC"

7.7 "Not entailing excessive cost" (NEEC) needs to be taken in two contexts, depending on whether it is applied to new processes or existing processes. Nevertheless, in all cases BAT can properly be modified by economic considerations where the costs of applying best available techniques would be excessive in relation to the nature of the industry and to the environmental protection to be achieved.

New Processes

7.8 In many cases, for new processes it is expected that BAT and BAT-NEEC will be synonymous. However, the following principles should apply:
- the cost of the best available techniques must be weighed against the environmental damage from the process; the greater the environmental damage, the greater the costs of BAT that can be required before costs are considered excessive;
- the objective is to prevent damaging releases or to reduce such releases so far as this can be done without imposing excessive costs; if after applying BATNEEC serious harm would still result, the application can be refused; and
- as objective an approach as possible to the consideration of what is BATNEEC is required. The concern is with what costs in general are excessive; the lack of profitability of a particular business should not affect the determination.

Existing Processes

7.9 In relation to existing processes, the Chief Inspector is concerned additionally with establishing timescales over which old processes will be upgraded to new standards, or as near to new standards as possible, or ultimately closed down.

7.10 Even though it relates to a single medium, the Secretary of State considers that the approach adopted in the EC Air Framework Directive is helpful in relation to the operation of IPC across all three media. Article 12 of the Directive, for example, which applies to all plants requiring an authorisation under the Directive, requires, where necessary, the imposition of appropriate conditions in authorisations, on the basis of developments as regards BAT and the environmental situation and also on the basis of the desirability of avoiding excessive costs for the plants in question, having regard to the economic circumstances of the industrial sector concerned.

7.11 Article 13, which applies only to processes existing prior to July 1987, requires certain factors to be taken into account:

"In the light of an examination of developments as regards best available technology and the environmental situation, the Member States shall implement policies and strategies, including appropriate measures, for the gradual adaption of [specified] existing plants to the best available technology, taking into account in particular:
- the plant's technical characteristics,
- its rate of utilization and length of its remaining life,
- the nature and volume of polluting emissions from it,
- the desirability of not entailing excessive costs for the plant concerned, having regard in particular to the economic situation of undertakings belonging to the category in question."

Release Limits

7.12 Clearly BATNEEC may be expressed in technological terms, *i.e.* a requirement to employ specified hardware. It may also be expressed in terms of release standards. Having identified the best techniques and the releases they are capable of producing, it is possible to express BATNEEC as a performance standard: that is, a technique which produces release levels of X or better where X are the values yielded by the identified BATNEEC. HMIP will normally express BATNEEC in these terms so as not to constrain the development of cleaner techniques nor to restrict unduly operators' choice of means to achieve a given standard.

The Promulgation of BATNEEC

7.13 The inspector determining the case must decide what is BATNEEC in relation to each application, and translate that decision into conditions to be included in the authorisation. There must, however, be broad consistency in these decisions, especially between processes of the same kind. It is important for process operators and the public that BATNEEC is determined and applied in a transparent, rational and consistent way. In part this will be achieved by the application of the general guidance in the paragraphs above. A further important ingredient will be the guidance notes on each class of process which the Chief Inspector will issue to his inspectors.

The Role of the Chief Inspector's Guidance Notes

7.14 Process-specific guidance notes are being published in advance of the processes coming within IPC. These will be reviewed and updated if necessary at intervals of not more than four years.

7.15 These notes all have a similar structure. They:
- have an introduction which includes a definition of the process covered by the note;
- set out the general requirements for new and existing plant, including those of any plan or direction made by the Secretary of State; and
- set out the release limits to air, water and land which HMIP believes can be achieved by the application of BATNEEC and BPEO to the process.

Annexes then cover:
- a description of the process and the plant used;
- a list of the prescribed substances most likely to be present in releases to the environment;
- the techniques for pollution abatement which represent BATNEEC for the process;
- the monitoring necessary to demonstrate compliance with release limits; and
- additional requirements such as training and contingency planning.

7.16 In the case of new processes, it is expected that plant will be designed to achieve the standards in the appropriate guidance note. For existing processes, the guidance note will indicate the timescale on which it will generally be appropriate to upgrade to new plant standards. Inspectors will use these general standards as a backcloth in determining what is appropriate in each individual case, having regard also to variable factors, the sort of consideration listed in the Air Framework Directive and the need to achieve BPEO where there are releases to more than one environmental medium.

7.17 The standards included in the Chief Inspector's guidance notes are the subject of thorough review and consultation. Industry and other interested bodies have the opportunity to comment. The key stages in the process are as follows:
 (a) review by HMIP or its consultants of best available techniques around the world. Techniques are identified which are used in or can be translated into a UK industrial context and which are or can be demonstrated to be commercially viable;
 (b) before the first draft of a process guidance note is prepared, HMIP assembles an agenda of the key issues likely to be addressed in the note. This is circulated to those with a direct interest in the industry sector affected by the note, who thus have an early opportunity to comment on the proposed coverage and, if they wish, to suggest techniques and standards that should be considered;
 (c) when a substantive draft has been prepared, HMIP circulates it for comment within Government and to the representatives of the industries and other bodies affected. The Chief Inspector takes the comments into account in preparing a further draft for wider, final consultation. If major questions about standards emerge, there may need to be fuller discussion;
 (d) the guidance note is issued for final consultation within Government, with industry and with other interested parties; and
 (e) following any changes arising from the comments received, the guidance note issues.

7.18 In this way, the Chief Inspector canvasses a broad spectrum of views in arriving at what he considers appropriate standards for each process. The Chief Inspector remains the final arbiter of what the notes contain, subject to any directions or statutory guidance from the Secretary of State.

7.19 Production of guidance notes to the timetable or implementing IPC requires that firm deadlines be set for each of the above stages.

Transitional Guidance for New Processes and Processes undergoing Substantial Change

7.20 Once a full portfolio of guidance notes has been established, there should be a clear and detailed framework within which operators can prepare applications. Some operators will, however, wish to submit applications in respect of new processes, or substantially changed existing processes, before the programme of developing guidance notes for processes is complete, or for processes which are so novel that published guidance for the process is not directly relevant.

7.21 In these cases, HMIP is ready to consider with potential applicants the standards that are likely to feature in future guidance, so that they can frame applications accordingly. Preliminary discussion of such standards is handled by HMIP Headquarters staff rather than by the local inspector, and correspondence should in the first instance be addressed to the Chief Inspector. This ensures consistency in areas where formal written guidance does not yet exist. The Chief Inspector may decide that it would be advisable to bring forward production of the appropriate guidance note.

Status of the Guidance Notes

7.22 The Chief Inspector's Guidance Notes have no statutory force. They do, however, represent the view of HMIP on appropriate techniques for particular processes and are therefore a material consideration to be taken into account in every case. HMIP must be prepared to give reasons for departing from the guidance in any particular case.

7.23 Where a guidance note exists, or guidance on standards is supplied for a particular case or purpose (as per paragraph 7.21), that guidance will not prejudice the final decision on a particular application, which will be taken following consideration of the applicant's case and of any representations from the public and the statutory consultees.

8. VARIATION PROCEDURES

8.1 The Act enables either HMIP or an operator to initiate variation of an authorisation when a change to a process is proposed. Different procedures apply, depending on whether the change is "substantial" or "relevant".

8.2 HMIP's power, under section 10 of the Act, to vary an authorisation relates to an important aspect of the concept of BATNEEC: as pollution control techniques and technology improve or if the understanding of environmental risk changes, so the environmental standards required of industry should be changed. Section 4(9) places a duty on the Chief Inspector to keep abreast of developments in pollution abatement techniques and technology. HMIP has power to vary the conditions in an authorisation at any time, and it is under a duty to do so if at any time the conditions it then judges appropriate are different from those which the authorisation contains currently. The Act requires that the conditions in each authorisation shall, in any case, be reviewed at least every four years.

8.3 Section 11 of the Act provides for authorisations to be varied at the instigation of the operator. **The Environmental Protection (Applications, Appeals and Registers) Regulations 1991** (as amended) set out the procedure to be followed in this instance. The provisions are designed to cover a wide range of circumstances such as the upgrading and replacement of plant, the introduction of additional plant, the updating of control practices, changes in feedstocks, products, production levels or capacity, and so on.

8.4 Alternative procedures are provided to give the flexibility to cover the range of circumstances in which industry may need to seek variations. In the general case, where an operator wishes to carry out an alteration in the process, he can notify HMIP of the proposed relevant change, and ask it to determine whether the change would entail a variation in the conditions of the authorisation. If it would, HMIP must determine whether it would in fact consider making a variation, and if so what. The operator is free to consider in the light of that whether he wishes to continue with his planned change. A simplified procedure is also allowed for where it is clear from the outset either that what the operator wishes is a variation to the conditions themselves, as opposed to a change in the process which might entail such a variation, or that the operator is clear about the variation to the conditions which will be needed as a result of the proposed change.

8.5 It is not intended that IPC should handicap industry by imposing unnecessary delays or restrictions. Processes involving frequent changes in inputs, throughput and outputs, such as occur in the speciality chemicals industry, need to be able to operate within a regime that provides full environmental control but which allows the changes inherent in the process to take place without unnecessary delay. Under IPC it is possible in appropriate cases to define an "envelope" of release limits for the process in question, within which the operator is able to make adjustments without the prior approval of HMIP. The onus is on the operator to propose and justify such an "envelope" in his application.

Relevant Change

8.6 A "relevant change" in a prescribed process is defined in section 11(11) of the Act as "a change in the manner of carrying on the process which is capable of altering the substances released from the process or of affecting the amount or any other characteristic of any substance so released". In practice, this is likely to embrace all but the most minor adjustments to the process and could include, for example, changes in the method of storing or possibly even the amount of feedstock stored on site.

Substantial Change

8.7 There are arrangements for consultation and public participation if a proposed alteration is a substantial change. "Substantial change" is defined in section 10(7) of the Act as a "substantial change in the substances released from the process or in the amount of any other characteristic of any substance so released".

8.8 Guidance on what constitutes a substantial change for a particular class of process will be included in the relevant Chief Inspector's Guidance Note. Until a note covering a particular class of process is produced, a change will generally be regarded as substantial if it results in an increase in the rate, concentration or absolute quantity of a prescribed substance released, unless HMIP can be satisfied that no significant environmental harm will result. Where operators believe that a proposed change may lead to an increase in releases, they should consult HMIP Regional Headquarters in writing, who will determine whether or not the change is substantial.

8.9 **Figure III** of this guidance seeks to explain the key variation procedures diagrammatically.

9. CHARGING

9.1 The 1990 Act (section 8) provides for the Secretary of State to introduce charges to recover the costs incurred by HMIP in operating IPC. The charging scheme has now been set up, and covers the costs of considering and issuing authorisations, compliance monitoring, enforcement, sampling and analysis of releases, maintaining the public register, and associated administrative costs, but does not cover wider policy work.

9.2 The scheme operates on the basis of three categories of charges, as follows:
- an *application fee*, to cover the costs of considering each IPC application;
- a *subsistence charge*, payable annually, for the holding of each IPC authorisation, to cover the ongoing costs of inspection, monitoring and enforcement;
- a *substantial variation fee*, to cover the costs of considering an application for subsequent substantial variation of an authorisation.

9.3 In order to relate the size of IPC fees and charges to the amount of regulatory effort involved, payments due on a particular process will, in most cases, be linked to the number of defined "components" which the process contains, with the fees and charges under the scheme taking the form of flat-rate per-component sums.

9.4 Full details of the charging scheme are set out in the explanatory booklet which accompanies the IPC scheme (see 1.5(j) above). This lists the levels of charges for the three categories, and explains the circumstances in which each becomes payable, and any exceptions to the general rules governing charging. The method of payment is also explained, as are the consequences of non-payment.

10. FUNCTIONS OF HMIP

10.1 The Act sets out the various functions of HMIP with regard to IPC.

Figure III: Variations

The Secretary of State can also direct that HMIP should exercise the enforcement functions of a local authority specified in the direction as regards processes designated for local authority control. These transferred functions would relate, as do those of the local authorities, to the control of air pollution only. There has been little need to exercise this power to date.

10.2 Formally, most of the powers and duties referred to in this note as HMIP's are conferred on the Chief Inspector, who is appointed by the

Secretary of State. The Chief Inspector has power to delegate any of his functions to other inspectors appointed by the Secretary of State for the purposes of IPC. The Act also confers a number of specific powers on inspectors—to enter premises, take samples, obtain information etc.—to enable them to carry out their functions.

10.3 A list of addresses of all the HMIP offices is at **Annex C**, and a map of the areas covered by each is at **Annex D**.

11. ENFORCEMENT

11.1 HMIP has a number of powers in the Act to enforce the conditions of an authorisation. If HMIP believes that an operator is contravening any of the conditions (or is likely to) it may serve an "enforcement notice" on him (under section 13). This will specify the matters constituting (or likely to constitute) the contravention and require specified steps to be taken, in a specified period, to remedy the situation.

11.2 Where HMIP considers that there is an imminent risk of serious pollution—whether or not there has been breach of the authorisation—it is under a duty to serve a "prohibition notice" (section 14). The notice would specify the risk, the steps which must be taken to remove it and the time by which they must be taken. It would also suspend the authorisation for whatever aspects of the operation were causing the risk; and could in addition impose conditions relating to any part of the process for which the authorisation was not suspended.

11.3 HMIP also has power (under section 12) to revoke an authorisation by written notice. In particular, it may do so where it has reason to believe that the process for which the authorisation is in force has not been carried on for a period of twelve months. The Act does not, however, circumscribe the power: the Chief Inspector may decide, for example, to revoke an authorisation in cases where there has been persistent failure to comply with conditions.

11.4 In all these cases, the Secretary of State has a reserve power of direction over the Chief Inspector.

Offences and Remedies

11.5 The Act provides (section 23) that it is an offence, amongst other things, to operate a prescribed process without an authorisation, or in contravention of the conditions within an authorisation; to fail to give notice of a transfer of authorisation; to fail to comply with an enforcement or prohibition notice; to fail (without reasonable excuse) to comply with a requirement imposed by an inspector under his powers of entry, or intentionally to obstruct him in exercising those powers; to fail (without reasonable excuse) to comply with a requirement to provide information, or knowingly or recklessly to make a false or misleading statement; and intentionally to make a false entry in any record required to be kept as a condition of authorisation.

11.6 As an alternative to prosecution in the Magistrates' Court for alleged failure to comply with an enforcement or prohibition notice, HMIP may, in order to secure compliance with the notice, take proceedings against the operator in the High Court (section 24).

11.7 A court may, by virtue of section 26, instead of or as well as imposing a penalty for breaching an authorisation or prohibition or enforcement notice, order the person convicted of the offence to take specified steps that are within his power to remedy the matters that were the subject of the offence. The order may also specify the time within which the steps must be taken. In addition, the Chief Inspector, with the approval of the Secretary of State, is empowered to arrange for reasonable steps to be taken to remedy any harm caused as the result of such an offence. The operator may be required to pay the full costs of such clean-up action (section 27).

11.8 General provisions of the Act provide that, where an offence committed by a body corporate is proved to have been committed with the consent or connivance of or because of the neglect of any director, manager or similar officer of the body, that officer is liable as well as the body corporate itself.

Crown Immunity

11.9 Under the Act, IPC processes operated by the Crown are subject to control by HMIP in the normal way. HMIP is able to set conditions in authorisations and to issue other notices. Information on IPC processes operated by the Crown are, subject to any exclusion for reasons of national security or commercial confidentiality, placed in the public register. If breaches of authorisations occur in Crown run premises, it is not possible for HMIP to institute criminal proceedings; but HMIP is able, under section 159 of the Act, to apply to the High Court for a declaration that such a breach is unlawful.

12. APPEALS

12.1 The Act gives operators a right of appeal to the Secretary of State against:
- the refusal to grant or vary an authorisation; the revocation of an authorisation; the conditions attached to an authorisation; variation, enforcement and prohibition notices (section 15 of the Act); or
- a determination that information is not commercially confidential, and must as a consequence be included in the public register (section 22(5) of the Act).

12.2 An appeal against revocation has the effect of suspending that revocation, but appeals against other notices do not have this effect. An appeal against a determination that information is not commercially confidential has the effect of preventing the entry of the information in the register pending the final determination or withdrawal of the appeal.

12.3 The appeals system is given effect by the **Environmental Protection (Applications, Appeals and Registers) Regulations 1991** (as amended). Regulation 9 requires that any appeal must be made in writing to the Secretary of State, and must be accompanied by the documents specified in the Regulations. Appeals should be addressed to the Secretary of State, and sent to the Department of the Environment, IPC Appeals Branch, Room AGO1, Romney House, 43 Marsham Street, London SW1P 3PY (for sites in England); or to the Welsh Office, IPC Appeals, Environment Division 3, Cathays Park, Cardiff CF1 3NQ (for sites in Wales). In section 15 cases, HMIP will place the notice of appeal in the public register.

12.4 The Regulations also specify in Regulation 10 the time limits for bringing an appeal: for section 15 appeals (except for appeals against revocation) these deadlines may be extended by the Secretary of State, but he would consider doing so only in the most compelling circumstances. If the appeal is out of time, and no extension is allowed, the appeal will not be considered.

12.5 The appellant must state, when making the appeal, whether written representations or a hearing is the desired method of proceeding. A hearing will be held if either party asks for it, or if, exceptionally, the Secretary of State determines that a hearing is the more appropriate course.

12.6 A notice specifying the date, time and place for the holding of a hearing of a section 15 appeal must normally be published in the locality of the process, and will be sent to persons who have made representations about the appeal. The procedure at a hearing is left to the appeal inspector, but he will be concerned to ensure that interested parties who wish to give evidence have a fair opportunity to do so.

12.7 The written representations procedure is explained diagrammatically in **Figure IV**. The procedures adopted by the Department on receipt of an appeal, whether dealt with by written representations or following a hear-

Figure IV: Appeals—Written procedure

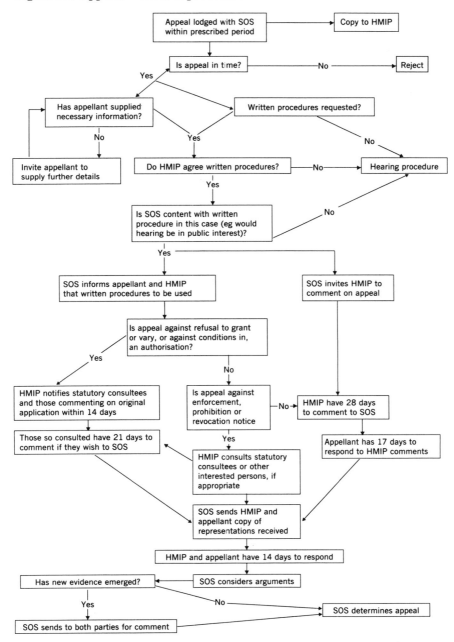

ing, are specified in the Regulations. More detailed guidance will be available from the Department in due course.

13. INTERFACE WITH OTHER LEGISLATION

13.1 The essential feature of IPC is that releases to all three environmental media are controlled by a single authority at one and the same time and BATNEEC is applied to the process which produces them in order to minimise the total environmental impact. As well as the environmental benefits of this approach, there are important practical benefits to all parties, not least that of "one stop shopping" for operators, who need deal as a result with only one enforcing authority for the process.

13.2 In recognition of its role in ensuring quality standards for controlled waters, the **National Rivers Authority (NRA)** is controlled by HMIP about all applications relating to processes which involve releases into such waters. The NRA has the power to require HMIP to set conditions within its authorisation relating to discharges to controlled waters (although HMIP may set additional or tighter conditions over releases to water, if for example higher standards are available under BATNEEC than those required by the NRA to safeguard water quality objectives). If the NRA certifies that in its opinion a release will lead to a failure to achieve a water quality objective, the authorisation cannot be granted. The NRA has powers to require HMIP to vary the conditions of an authorisation at any time. Its monitoring functions as regards the water environment and its powers to take proceedings are unaffected by these arrangements. A Memorandum of Understanding sets out the agreement between HMIP and the NRA on their respective roles and the working relationship between them. Copies are available from HMIP's London Headquarters.

13.3 HMIP is empowered to set conditions relating to the *generation and management* of wastes, whether intended for recycling, incineration, landfill or any other treatment or disposal. But IPC does not cover the final disposal of wastes in or on land. Such operations remain subject to separate control by the **Waste Regulation Authority (WRA)**, and no conditions in the IPC authorisation will regulate it. HMIP is obliged to inform the WRA when waste generated from a process will require landfill disposal.

13.4 IPC is not designed to cover the keeping, use or disposal of radioactive substances, which are the subject of the **Radioactive Substances Act 1960 (RSA 60)**. Because of the very distinct nature of these substances, an IPC process involving the keeping, use or disposal of radioactive substances will continue to require registration or authorisation under that Act. If conflicting terms were placed on an operator by HMIP under section 7 of the Act and by a regulation or authorisation under the RSA 60, then the "IPC conditions" would not apply.

13.5 The objective of the authorisations issued under Part I of the Act is to achieve environmental, not worker, protection (see section 7(1) of the Act). Full co-operation between the **Health and Safety Executive (HSE)** and their agents on the one hand and HMIP inspectors on the other is important to ensure that the controls that each place on scheduled processes are effective and compatible. Neither set of controls should affect adversely the protection of the environment or of workers. Where environmental protection demands tighter standards of control than are required to safeguard persons at work, these tighter standards should apply provided that they have no adverse effects on worker protection. HSE are consulted in advance on the guidance notes that are produced specifying the appropriate controls for particular industrial sectors before issue, and any general conflicts that can be anticipated are resolved. They are also statutory consultees on individual applications. Copies of the Memorandum of Understanding between HMIP and HSE are available from HMIP's London Headquarters.

ANNEX A

Timetable for implementing integrated pollution control

EPA Sched. 1 Ref	Process	Comes within IPC	Apply Between
	Fuel & Power Industry		
1.3	Combustion (>50MWth) Boilers and Furnaces	1.4.91	[1.4.91] & 30.4.91
1.1	Gasification	1.4.92	1.4.92 & 30.6.92
1.2	Carbonisation	1.4.92	1.4.92 & 30.6.92
1.3	Combustion (remainder)	1.4.92	1.4.92 & 30.6.92
1.4	Petroleum	1.4.92	1.4.92 & 30.6.92
	Waste Disposal Industry		
5.1	Incineration	1.8.92	1.8.92 & 31.10.92
5.2	Chemical Recovery	1.8.92	1.8.92 & 31.10.92
5.3	Waste Derived Fuel	1.8.92	1.8.92 & 31.10.92
	Mineral Industry		
3.1	Cement	1.12.92	1.12.92 & 28.2.93
3.2	Asbestos	1.12.92	1.12.92 & 28.2.93
3.3	Fibre	1.12.92	1.12.92 & 28.2.93
3.5	Glass	1.12.92	1.12.92 & 28.2.93
3.6	Ceramic	1.12.92	1.12.92 & 28.2.93

EPA Sched. 1 Ref	Process	Comes within IPC	Apply Between	Chief Inspector's Note Issues
	Chemical Industry			
4.1	Petrochemical	1.5.93	1.5.93 & 31.7.93	1.11.92
4.2	Organic	1.5.93	1.5.93 & 31.7.93	1.11.92
4.7	Chemical Pesticide	1.5.93	1.5.93 & 31.7.93	1.11.92
4.8	Pharmaceutical	1.5.93	1.5.93 & 31.7.93	1.11.92
4.3	Acid Manufacturing	1.11.93	1.11.93 & 31.1.94	1.5.93
4.4	Halogen	1.11.93	1.11.93 & 31.1.94	1.5.93
4.6	Chemical Fertiliser	1.11.93	1.11.93 & 31.1.94	1.5.93
4.9	Bulk Chemical Storage	1.11.93	1.11.93 & 31.1.94	1.5.93
4.5	Inorganic Chemical	1.5.94	1.5.94 & 31.7.94	1.11.93

ANNEX A—*cont.*

Timetable for implementing integrated pollution control

EPA Sched. 1 Ref	Process	Comes within IPC	Apply Between	Chief Inspector's Note Issues
	Metal Industry			
2.1	Iron and Steel	1.1.95	1.1.95 & 31.3.95	1.7.94
2.3	Smelting	1.1.95	1.1.95 & 31.3.95	1.7.94
2.2	Non-ferrous	1.5.95	1.5.95 & 31.7.95	1.11.94
	Other Industry			
6.1	Paper Manufacturing	1.11.95	1.11.95 & 31.1.96	1.5.95
6.2	Di-isocyanate	1.11.95	1.11.95 & 31.1.96	1.5.95
6.3	Tar and Bitumen	1.11.95	1.11.95 & 31.1.96	1.5.95
6.4	Uranium	1.11.95	1.11.95 & 31.1.96	1.5.95
6.5	Coating	1.11.95	1.11.95 & 31.1.96	1.5.95
6.6	Coating Manufacturing	1.11.95	1.11.95 & 31.1.96	1.5.95
6.7	Timber	1.11.95	1.11.95 & 31.1.96	1.5.95
6.9	Animal and Plant Treatment	1.11.95	1.11.95 & 31.1.96	1.5.95

ANNEX B

Prescribed Substances

Release to air:
Prescribed substances
Oxides of sulphur and other sulphur compounds
Oxides of nitrogen and other nitrogen compounds
Oxides of carbon
Organic compounds and partial oxidation products
Metals, metalloids and their compounds
Asbestos (suspended particulate matter and fibres), glass fibres and mineral fibres
Halogens and their compounds
Phosphorus and its compounds
Particulate matter.

Release to water:
Prescribed substances
Mercury and its compounds
Cadmium and its compounds
All isomers of hexachlorocyclohexane
All isomers of DDT
Pentachlorophenol and its compounds
Hexachlorobenzene
Hexachlorobutadiene
Aldrin
Dieldrin
Endrin
Polychlorinated Biphenyls
Dichlorvos
1,2-Dichloroethane
All isomers of Trichlorobenzene
Atrazine
Simazine
Tributyltin compounds
Triphenyltin compounds
Trifluralin
Fenitrothion
Azinphos-methyl
Malathion
Endosulfan.

Release to land:
Prescribed substances

Organic solvents
Azides
Halogens and their covalent compounds
Metal carbonyls
Organo-metalllic compounds
Oxidising agents
Polychlorinated dibenzofuran and any cogener thereof
Polychlorinated dibenzo-p-dioxin and any other congener thereof
Polyhalogenated biphenyls, terphenyls and naphthalenes
Phosphorus
Pesticides, that is to say, any chemical substance or preparation prepared or used for destroying any pest, including those used for protecting plants or wood or other plant products from harmful organisms; regulating the growth of plants; giving protection against harmful creatures; rendering such creatures harmless; controlling organisms with harmful or unwanted effects on water systems, buildings or other structures, or on manufactured products; or protecting animals against ectoparasites.
Alkali metals and their oxides and alkaline earth metals and their oxides.

ANNEX C

HMIP offices and addresses

HMIP HEADQUARTERS

Romney House
43 Marsham Street
LONDON SW1P 3PY
Tel: 071-276 8061
Fax: 071-276 8605

HMIP NORTH DIVISION

Divisional Headquarters	**North East Region**	**North West Region**
Stockdale House (1st Floor) Headingley Business Park 8 Victoria Road Headingley LEEDS LS6 1PF Tel: 0532 786636 Fax: 0532 740464	Stockdale House LEEDS Vincent House 2 Woodland Road DARLINGTON DL3 7PJ Tel: 0325 380635 Fax: 0325 467996 Don House Pennine Centre 20-22 Hawley Street SHEFFIELD S1 1HD Tel: 0742 700459 Fax: 0742 762398	Mitre House Church Street LANCASTER LA1 1BG Tel: 0524 382100 Fax: 0524 382642 Unit 2 Kings Court Manor Park RUNCORN WA7 1HR Tel: 0928 579522 Fax: 0928 579327

HMIP EAST DIVISION

Divisional Headquarters
Howard House
40-64 St John's Street
BEDFORD MK42 0DL
Tel: 0234 272112
Fax: 0234 218355

South Region
2 Marsham Street
LONDON SW1P 3EB
Tel: 071-276 5594
Fax: 071-276 6544

3 East Grinstead House
London Road
EAST GRINSTEAD
West Sussex RH10 1RR
Tel: 0342 312016
Fax; 0342 311565

Anglia Region
Howard House
BEDFORD

Mill House (4th Floor)
Brayford Side North
LINCOLN LN1 1YW
Tel: 0522 512566
Fax: 0522 546544

Carter House (4th Floor)
49-50 High Street
CHELMSFORD CM1 1DE
Tel: 0245 490473
Fax: 0245 495872

HMIP WEST DIVISION

Divisional Headquarters
Highwood Pavilions
Jupiter Road
Patchway
BRISTOL BS12 5SN
Tel: 0272 792653
Fax: 0272 794650

Middle Region
McLaren Buildings
Room 1317
2 Masshouse Circus
Queensway
BIRMINGHAM B4 7NR
Tel: 021-236 7674
Fax: 021-236 1533

The Marches House
Midway
NEWCASTLE-UNDER-LYME
Staffordshire ST5 1DT
Tel: 0782 711113

South West Region
High Pavilions

Wales Region
Brunel House (11th Floor)
2 Fitzalan Road
CARDIFF CF2 1TT
Tel: 0222 49558
Fax: 0222 499924

ANNEX D

APPENDIX 4

ENVIRONMENTAL PROTECTION

ENVIRONMENTAL PROTECTION (DUTY OF CARE) REGULATIONS 1991

(S.I. 1991 No. 2839)

In force from:
April 1, 1992

Enabling power:
Environmental Protection Act 1990, s.34(5).

Background:

Section 34 of the EPA 1990 imposes a duty of care on anyone who deals with controlled waste in any way, or who, as a broker, has control of such waste. Such persons are required under that duty to ensure that there is no unauthorized or harmful deposit, treatment or disposal of the waste, to prevent escape of waste whether that waste is in their control or that of another, and to ensure that any transfer of the waste is to an authorized person, and that a written description of the waste is also transferred.

These regulations impose requirements for documentation on the transfer of controlled waste. The transferor and transferee are obliged to complete and sign a transfer note at the same time as the written description of the waste is transferred. The transfer note must identify the waste to be transferred, its quantity, how it is stored, the time and place of transfer, and provide details of the transferor and transferee. The transferor and transferee are required to keep the written description of the waste and the transfer note (or copies) for two years from the date of transfer, and to supply a copy of that documentation to a waste regulation authority if required. The duty of care will not apply to household waste. Breach of the duty of care or the Regulation is a criminal offence.

Statutory reference:

See also the General Note to s.34 of the EPA 1990.

Citation, commencement and interpretation

1.—(1) These regulations may be cited as the Environmental Protection (Duty of Care) Regulations 1991 and shall come into force on April 1, 1992.

(2) In these regulations—

"the 1990 Act" means the Environmental Protection Act 1990;

"transferor" and "transferee" mean respectively, in relation to a transfer of controlled waste by a person who is subject to the duty imposed by section 34(1) of the 1990 Act, the person who in compliance with that section transfers a written description of the waste and the person who receives that description.

Transfer notes

2.—(1) The transferor and the transferee shall, at the same time as the written description of the waste is transferred, ensure that such a document as is described in paragraph (2) ("a transfer note") is completed and signed on their behalf.

(2) A transfer note shall—

(a) identify the waste to which it relates and state—

(i) its quantity and whether on transfer it is loose or in a container;
(ii) if in a container, the kind of container; and
(iii) the time and place of transfer;
(b) give the name and address of the transferor and the transferee;
(c) state whether or not the transferor is the producer or importer of the waste and, if so, which;
(d) if the transfer is to a person for authorized transport purposes, specify which of those purposes; and
(e) state as respects the transferor and the transferee which, if any, of the categories of person shown in column 1 of the following Table describes him and provide any relevant additional information specified in column 2 of the Table.

Category of person	Additional information
An authority which is a waste collection authority for the purposes of Part II of the 1990 Act.	
A person who is the holder of a waste management licence under section 35 of the 1990 Act or of a disposal licence under section 5 of the Control of Pollution Act 1974(a).	If the waste is to be kept, treated or disposed of by that person, the relevant licence number and the name of the licensing authority.
A person to whom section 33(1) of the 1990 Act does not apply by virtue of regulations under subsection (3) of that section.	
A person registered as a carrier of controlled waste under section 2 of the Control of Pollution (Amendment) Act 1989(b).	The name of the waste regulation authority with whom he is registered and his registration number.
A person who is not required to be so registered by virtue of regualtions under section 1(3) of that Act.	
A waste disposal authority in Scotland.	

Duty to keep copies of written descriptions of waste and transfer notes

3. The transferor and the transferee shall each keep the written description of the waste and the transfer note or copies thereof for a period of two years from the transfer of the controlled waste.

Duty to furnish documents

4. A person who has been served by a waste regulation authority with a notice in writing specifying or describing any document and requiring its production shall, if the document is one which at that time he is under a duty to keep under Regulation 3, furnish the authority with a copy of it at the authority's office specified in the notice and within the period (not being less than seven days) so specified.

APPENDIX 5

WASTE MANAGEMENT: THE DUTY OF CARE (DOE/SO/WO CODE OF PRACTICE, DECEMBER 1991)

STEP BY STEP ADVICE

1. IDENTIFY AND DESCRIBE THE WASTE

1.1. Anyone subject to the duty of care who has some "controlled waste" should establish what that waste is.

Is it "controlled waste"?

1.2. First, **is it waste at all?** The term "waste" has a wide meaning, and it is not possible simply to list what is or is not waste, as this can only be determined on the facts of each case. When the question has come before them, the courts have consistently taken the line that waste is defined from the point of view of the person producing or discarding it. With this in mind, where there is any doubt about whether or not something is waste, it may be helpful to ask the following questions *as if from the point of view of the person producing or discarding it*:
  (a) is it what would ordinarily be described as waste?
  (b) is it a scrap material?
  (c) is it an effluent or other unwanted surplus substance?
  (d) does it require to be disposed of as broken, worn out, contaminated or otherwise spoiled?
  (e) is it being discarded or dealt with as if it were waste?

1.3. If the answer to *any* of these questions is "yes", the substance, material or article in question should be considered to be waste. Moreover, anything which is discarded or dealt with as if it were a waste must be presumed to be waste unless it is proved not to be.

1.4. **Is it "controlled waste"?** Waste from households,[1] commerce or industry is "controlled waste". The main exceptions that are *not* "controlled waste" are waste from agricultural premises, waste from mines and quarries, explosives and most radioactive waste.

What are the problems of the waste?

1.5. Waste cannot be simply divided between the safe and the hazardous. There are safe ways of dealing with any waste, but equally any waste can be hazardous to human health or the environment if it is wrongly managed. Whether waste poses a problem depends on knowing what will happen to it as much as what it is made of. For most waste it is not necessary to know more than what it is in very general terms. But subsequent holders must be provided with a description of the waste that is full enough to enable them to manage the waste properly. Even everyday items may cause problems in handling or treatment.

1.6. In looking for waste problems it may help to ask such questions as:
  (a) does the waste need a special container to prevent its escape or to keep it from the air? what type of container suits it and what material can the container be made of?
  (b) can it safely be mixed with any other waste? with what should it not be mixed?
  (c) can it safely be crushed and transferred from one vehicle to another?
  (d) can it safely be incinerated? are there special requirements for its incineration such as minimum temperature and combustion time?
  (e) can it safely be buried in a landfill site with other waste?

---

[1] Householders are exempt from the duty of care for their own household waste (Annex A, A7).

1.7. Anything unusual in waste can pose a problem. So can anything out of proportion. Ordinary household waste, and waste from shops or offices, often contains small amounts of potentially hazardous substances. This may not matter if they are mixed in a large quantity of other waste. What are worth identifying as potential problems are significant quantities of an unexpected substance, or unusual amounts of an expected substance, in waste.

1.8. Note that certain especially dangerous or difficult wastes, "special wastes", are subject to strict legal controls quite apart from and additional to the requirements of the duty of care (Annex Diii).

What goes in a description?

1.9. A transfer note must be completed, signed and kept by the parties to the transfer if waste is transferred; this is a requirement of the Environmental Protection (Duty of Care) Regulations 1991, and any breach of those regulations is an offence (Annex C Regulations on Keeping Records). This note must state the quantity of waste transferred and how it is packed—whether loose or in a container and, if in a container, the kind of container. There must also be a description of the waste, either separately or combined as a single document with the transfer note. It is good practice to label drums or similar closed containers with a description of the waste. Under the regulations the parties must keep the transfer note and the description for two years. The description should always mention any **special problems**, requirements or knowledge. In addition it should include some combination of:
   (a) the type of premises or business from which the waste comes;
   (b) the name of the substance or substances;
   (c) the process that produced the waste; and
   (d) a chemical and physical analysis.

1.10. The description must provide enough information to enable subsequent holders to avoid mismanaging the waste. When writing a description it is open to the holder to ask the manager who will handle the waste what he needs to know. For most wastes, those that need only a simple description, either (a) or (b) will do. Wastes presenting more difficulty will need a fuller description including some or all of (a) to (d). Each element of the description is dealt with in 1.12 to 1.18 below.

Special problems

1.11. The description should always contain any information which might affect the handling of the waste. This should include:
   (a) special problems identified under paragraphs 1.5 to 1.7 above;
   (b) any information, advice or instructions about the handling or disposal of the waste given to the holder from a waste regulation authority[2] or the suppliers of material or equipment;
   (c) details of problems previously encountered with the waste;
   (d) changes to the description since a previous load.

(A) Source of the waste: type of premises or business

1.12. It may sometimes be enough to describe the source of the waste by referring either to the use of the premises where the waste is produced or to the occupation of the waste producer.

---

[2] In the case of processes regulated under Integrated Pollution Control in England and Wales, HM Inspectorate of Pollution may give advice to the producer of waste that is relevant to its subsequent management prior to its final disposal or treatment. In Scotland the Integrated Pollution Control authority will be either the chief inspector of HM Industrial Pollution Inspectorate or the River Purification Authority. This advice should also be included in the description.

1.13. Such a "source of waste" description is recommended as the common sense simple description where businesses produce a mixture of wastes none of which has special handling or disposal requirements or where there are no special handling or disposal requirements which cannot be identified from such a simple description. Such a description must make it clear what type of wastes are produced and the contents of the wastes and their proportions must be only such as might be expected.

(B) Name of the substance

1.14. The waste may be described by saying what it is made of. This may be in physical and chemical terms or by the common name of the waste where this is equally helpful. Such a description by name is recommended for waste composed of a single simple material.

(C) Process producing the waste

1.15. The waste may be described by saying how it was produced. Such a description would include details of materials used or processed, the equipment used and the treatment and changes that produced the waste. If necessary this would include information obtained from the supplier of the materials and equipment.

1.16. This should form part of the description for most industrial wastes and some commercial wastes.

(D) Chemical and physical analysis

1.17. A description based on process producing the waste (C) will not go far enough where the holder does not know enough about the source of the waste. It will often not be adequate where:
  (a) wastes, especially industrial wastes, from different activities or processes are mixed; or
  (b) the activity or process alters the properties or composition of the materials put in.

1.18. For such wastes an analysis will usually be needed; in cases of doubt, the holder may find it helpful to consult the intended waste manager as to whether he needs an analysis to manage the waste properly. Where it is necessary the holder should detail the physical and chemical composition of the waste itself including, where different substances are mixed, their dilutions or proportions. The holder might either provide this information himself or obtain a physical or chemical analysis from a laboratory or from a waste management contractor.

2. KEEP THE WASTE SAFELY

The problem

2.1. All waste holders must act to keep waste safe against:
  (a) corrosion or wear of waste containers;
  (b) accidental spilling or leaking;
  (c) accident or weather breaking contained waste open and allowing it to escape;
  (d) waste blowing away or falling while stored or transported;
  (e) scavenging of waste by vandals, thieves, children, trespassers or animals.

2.2. Holders should protect waste against these while they have it themselves. They should also protect it for its future handling requirements. Waste should reach not only its next holder but a licensed facility or other final destination without escape. Where waste is to be mixed immediately, for example in a transfer station, a civic amenity site or a municipal collection vehicle, it only needs to be packed well enough to reach that immediate destination; preventing its escape after that stage would be up to the next holder. However, there are wastes that may need to reach a disposal or treatment site in their original containers, for example drummed waste. In such cases holders will need to know through how many subsequent hands, under what conditions, for how long and to what ultimate treatment their waste will go in order to satisfy themselves that it is packed securely enough to reach its final destination intact. If an intermediate holder alters waste in any way, by mixing, treating or repacking it, then he will be responsible for observing all this advice on keeping waste safe.

Storing waste securely

2.3. Security precautions at sites where waste is stored should prevent theft, vandalism or scavenging of waste. Holders should take particular care to secure waste material attractive to scavengers, for example building and demolition materials.

2.4. Segregation of different categories of waste where they are produced may be necessary to prevent the mixing of incompatible wastes, for example avoiding reactions in mixtures, and may assist the marketing or disposal of waste to specialist outlets. Where segregation is practised on sites, the waste holder should ensure that his employees and anyone else handling waste there are aware of the locations and uses of each segregated waste container.

Containers

2.5. Waste handed over to another person should be in some sort of container, which might include a skip. The only reasonable exception would be loose material loaded into a vehicle and then covered sufficiently to prevent escape before being moved. Waste containers should suit the material put in them.

2.6. It is good practice to label drums or similar closed containers with a note of the contents when stored or handed over; this could be a copy of the waste description.

Waste left for collection

2.7. Waste left for collection outside premises should be in containers that are strong and secure enough to resist not only wind and rain but also animal disturbance, especially for food waste. All containers left outside for collection will therefore need to be secured or sealed (for example drums with lids, bags tied up, skips covered). To minimise the risks, waste should not be left outside for collection longer than necessary.

3. TRANSFER TO THE RIGHT PERSON

3.1. Waste may only be handed on to authorised persons or to persons for authorised transport purposes. Full lists of these are in subsections (3) and (4) of section 34 of the Act, a copy of which is in Annex A. This section of the code advises on who these persons are and what checks to carry out *before* making an arrangement or contract for transferring waste.

Public waste collection

3.2. Local authorities collect waste from households and from some commercial premises. They do this either with their own labour or using private contractors who will be registered carriers (Annex Dii). Private persons are exempt from the duty in connection with their own household waste produced on their premises (Annex A, A7). If there is any doubt about whether or not a particular waste can go in the normal collection, the producer should ask the local authority (the borough, district or islands council).

Using a waste carrier

3.3. A waste holder may transfer waste to someone who transports it—a waste carrier—who may or may not also be a waste manager (Annex Dii). Subject to certain exemptions, anyone carrying waste in the course of their business, or in any other way for profit, must be registered with a waste regulation authority. Each authority's register of carriers is open to public inspection. Holders may therefore for the purpose of the duty of care use these registers as a reference list of carriers who are authorised to transport waste. However, inclusion on an authority's register is *not* a recommendation or guarantee of a carrier's suitability to accept any particular type of waste. The holder should remain alert to any sign that the waste may not be legally dealt with by a carrier.

3.4. Anyone intending to transfer waste to a carrier will need to check that the carrier is registered or is exempt from registration. A registered carrier's authority for transporting waste is either his certificate of registration or a copy of his certificate of registration *if it was provided by the waste regulation authority*. The certificate or copy certificate will show the date on which the carrier's registration expires. All copy certificates must be numbered and marked to show that they are copies and have been provided by the waste regulation authority. Photocopies are not valid and **do not** provide evidence of the carrier's registration.

3.5. In all cases other than those involving repeated transfers of waste, the holder should ask to see, and should check the details of, the carrier's certificate or copy certificate of registration. In addition, before using any carrier for the first time, the holder should check with the waste regulation authority with which the carrier is registered that his registration is still valid, even if his certificate appears to be current. The waste regulation authority with whom a carrier is registered is the authority where the carrier has his principal place of business; the authority's name and other details are shown on the certificate. The holder should provide the authority with the carrier's name and registration number as shown on the certificate.

3.6. In practice, the only exempt carriers who might take waste from a holder are:
— charities and voluntary organisations;
— waste collection authorities (local authorities) collecting any waste themselves (though an authority's contractors are not exempt);
— British Rail when carrying waste by rail; and
— ship operators where waste is to be disposed of under licence at sea.

For a transitional period, a carrier may be exempt where he applied for registration before 1 April 1992 and a decision on his application has not been made. In all cases other than those involving repeated transfers of waste, the holder should ask the carrier to confirm the type of exemption under which he transports waste. In addition, before using for the first time a carrier who claims to be exempt, the holder should ask the carrier to provide evidence that the exemption which he claims is valid.

Sending waste for disposal or treatment

3.7. A "waste manager" is anyone who stores waste or who processes it in some intermediate way short of final disposal or who reclaims waste or who disposes of it. All these activities are licensed, by waste disposal authorities, who issue "disposal licences"; from 1993 these will be called "waste regulation authorities" and "waste management licences". (In this code the term "waste management licence" is used to cover either licence.) The licence includes conditions which usually limit the type and quantity of waste that the operator may deal with and the way in which the waste is managed. The conditions will also govern such matters as operating hours and pollution control on site.

3.8. *Before* choosing a waste manager as the next person to take some waste a holder will need to:
   (a) check that the manager does have a licence; and
   (b) establish that the licence permits the manager to take the type and quantity of waste involved.

3.9. A waste holder should check this not merely by asking the waste manager but by examining his licence. The holder in turn should show the manager the description of the waste involved. If the holder doubts whether the licence does cover his particular waste he can ask the waste manager or, if he is still not satisfied, the authority who issued the licence.

3.10. Some forms of treatment or disposal of waste do not require licences because they have been exempted by regulations, for example baling up waste paper. If a selected waste manager is not licensed because what he is doing is exempt then he should say so and state which type of exemption he comes under. It is not taking enough care for a holder to consign waste to a contractor who states that he is exempt but does not give the grounds. The holder delivering waste to an exempt waste manager should check that the waste is within the scope of the exemption. The exemptions are limited to specific circumstances and types of waste. If in doubt about the exemption of a particular activity the holder may seek advice from the waste regulation authority for the area where the activity takes place. (For more explanation of licensing and exemptions see Annex Di.)

3.11. A holder of waste should make these same checks on licences and exemptions wherever he delivers waste even if he is not the producer. A carrier should always check that the next holder he delivers to is an authorised person and that the description of the waste he carries is within the licence or exemption of any waste manager to whom he delivers, unless he is only providing the transport to a contract directly between the producer and the waste manager. In that case the producer should make all the checks on the waste manager.

3.12. In Scotland only, local authorities may operate their own disposal sites for publicly collected waste. Such sites in some cases also take waste directly from commerce or industry. Such sites are not licensed but are instead subject to terms and conditions in resolutions passed by the authorities which are broadly similar to those in waste management licences. It is necessary to:
   (a) check that such sites are operated by the local waste disposal authority; and
   (b) establish that the resolution permits the authority to take the type and quantity of waste involved.

In England and Wales, waste disposal sites are being taken out of direct local authority operation; once this is complete both public and private disposal sites will be equally subject to licensing.

Checks on repeated transfers

3.13. Full checks on carriers and waste managers do not need to be repeated if transfers of waste are repetitive—the same type of waste from the same origin to the same destination. The obvious example is waste collection from commercial premises.

3.14. For a series of identical loads making up one transaction there is no need to see the licence of a waste manager or, in Scotland, the local authority's resolution, or the registration certificate of a waste carrier every time a load is handed over. However, licences, registration or evidence of exemption *should* be examined afresh in the following cases:
   (a) whenever a new transaction is involved, that is if the description or destination of the waste has changed;
   (b) where several different carriers or disposers are collecting waste at

one place and there might be a danger of an unauthorised carrier collecting a load—for example, a construction or demolition site from which several hauliers are taking waste away;
(c) as a minimum precaution, the licence, resolution, registration or evidence of exemption should be seen and checked at least once a year even if nothing has changed in a series of repeated transfers;
(d) where there has been a change in the licence conditions of the destination.

4. RECEIVING WASTE

4.1. The previous three sections of this code look at transfers from the point of view of the person transferring the waste to someone else. This section offers advice to persons receiving waste, whether at its ultimate destination or as an intermediate holder.

Checking on the source of waste

4.2. Checking is not only in one direction. No-one should accept waste from a source that seems to be in breach of the duty of care. Waste may only come *either* from the person who first produces or imports it *or* from someone who has received it, who must therefore be one of the persons entitled to receive waste (section 3). On the handover of waste, the previous holder and the recipient will complete a transfer note in which the previous holder will declare which category of person entitled to hold waste he is. The recipient should ensure that this is properly completed before accepting waste. Checking back in this way need not be as thorough as checking forward. Recipients should not need to see any waste management licence of the previous holder. However, the first time a carrier delivers waste, it would be reasonable to see either the registration certificate or official copy certificate, or to request confirmation of the type of exemption under which the carrier is transporting the waste.

4.3. Before receiving any waste, a holder should establish that it is contained in a manner suitable for its subsequent handling, and final disposal or reclamation. Where the recipient provides containers he should advise what waste may be placed in them.

4.4. The recipient should also look at the description and seek more information from the previous holder if this is necessary to manage the waste.

Co-operation with the previous holder

4.5. Anyone receiving waste should co-operate with the previous holder in any steps they are taking to comply with the duty. That means in particular supplying correct and adequate information that the previous holder may need.

4.6. The previous holder needs to know enough about the later handling of his waste—how it is likely to be carried, stored and treated—to pack and describe it properly. The recipient should give such information.

4.7. Under the regulations on keeping records (Annex C) anyone receiving waste must receive a description and complete a transfer note. The recipient must declare on the transfer note which category of authorised person he is, with details. Before making any arrangement to receive waste a waste manager should show to the previous holder his waste management licence or a statement of the type of exemption from licensing under which he is operating; and a carrier should show his certificate of registration, an official copy of his certificate of registration or evidence of the type of exemption from registration under which he transports waste. It would be sensible for every waste management site office to hold a copy of the waste management licence or a statement of the type of exemption; and for every vehicle used by a carrier to carry an official copy of the carrier's certificate of registration or evidence of the type of exemption under which he transports waste.

5. CHECKING UP

5.1. The previous sections describe normal procedures for transferring waste from the producer to its final destination. Most of the checking that is reasonable is already built into these procedures and the transfer note system (Annex C). This section gives advice on what further checks are advisable and the action to take when checks show that something is wrong.

Checks after transfer

5.2. Most waste transfers require no further action from the person transferring waste after the waste has been transferred. A producer is under no specific duty to audit his waste's final destination, however undertaking such an audit and periodic site visits thereafter would be a prudent means of protecting his position by being able to demonstrate the steps he had taken to prevent subsequent illegal treatment of his waste.

5.3. One exception is where a holder makes arrangements with more than one party, for example a producer arranges two contracts, one for disposal and another for transport to the disposal site. In that case the holder should establish that he not only handed the waste to the carrier but that it reached the disposer.

Checks after receipt

5.4. Any waste holder, but especially a waste manager receiving waste, has a strong practical interest in the description being correct and containing adequate information. A waste management licence will control the quantities and types of waste that may be accepted and how they may be managed. It is within his capacity as a waste manager to ensure that descriptions of waste received are indeed correct. Anyone receiving waste should make at least a quick visual check that it appears to match the description. For a waste manager it would be good practice to go beyond this by fully checking the composition of samples of waste received.

Causes for concern

5.5. Every waste holder should be alert for any evidence that suggests that the duty of care is not being observed or that illegal waste handling is taking place. Obvious causes for concern that any holder should notice when he accepts or transfers waste include:
  (a) waste that is wrongly or inadequately described being delivered at a waste management site;
  (b) waste being delivered or taken away without proper packing so that it is likely to escape;
  (c) failure of the person delivering or taking waste to complete a transfer note properly, or an apparent falsehood on the transfer note;
  (d) an unsupported claim of exemption from licensing or registration; and
  (e) failure of waste consigned via a carrier to arrive at a destination with whom the transferring holder has an arrangement.

5.6. Other causes of concern may come to light. Waste holders do not *have* to check up after waste is handed on, but they may become aware of where it is going, and should act on such information if it suggests illegal or careless waste management.

Action to take with other holders

5.7. A holder who only suspects that his waste is not being dealt with properly should first of all check his facts, in the first place with the next (or sometimes the previous) holder. This may involve asking that further details should be added to a waste description, for more information about the exact status of the holder for the purposes of waste management licensing or carrier registration, why they may be entitled to an exemption, or simply where waste went to or came from.

5.8. If a holder is not satisfied with the information or is certain that waste he handles is being wrongly managed by another person then his first action should normally be to refuse to transfer or accept further consignments of the waste in question to or from the person acting wrongly, unless and until the problem is remedied. Such a stop may not be practicable in all cases, for example to avoid breach of a contract to deliver or accept waste or because there is no other outlet immediately available for the waste. Steps should be taken to minimise such inflexibility. One possible measure would be for new waste contracts to provide for termination if a breach of the duty occurs and is not rectified.

5.9. If an arrangement that has proved wrong in some respect does have to continue temporarily for these reasons then the holder should take stringent precautions. For example where waste has been misdescribed he should analyse further consignments, where waste has been collected or delivered without being properly packed he should inspect each further load and where it has not reached a legitimate destination he should check that each load does arrive in future.

Reporting to waste regulation authorities

5.10. Waste regulation authorities are responsible for the registration of waste carriers and the licensing of waste management. As such they have a major interest in breaches of the duty of care which might contribute to illegal waste management. They are also equipped with the powers and expertise to prevent or pursue offences and to advise on the legal and environmentally sound management of waste.

5.11. Holders should tell their waste regulation authority where they know or suspect that:
   (a) there is a breach of the duty of care; or
   (b) waste is carried by an unregistered carrier not entitled to exemption; or
   (c) waste is treated, stored or disposed of without a licence or in a way not permitted by the licence or, in Scotland, by the terms and conditions of an authority's resolution.

6. EXPERT HELP AND ADVICE

6.1. A waste holder may not always have the knowledge or expertise to discharge his duty of care. He should then seek expert help and advice. The holder is still the person responsible for discharging his own duty of care, a responsibility that cannot be transferred to an expert adviser.

Help with analysing, describing and handling waste

6.2. Waste consultants and waste managers offer services to examine waste problems, identify wastes and recommend storage and handling methods. A waste holder may also use an analytical laboratory to establish the nature of unknown waste that he needs to describe. A consultant or laboratory acting only in this way can only advise, and cannot take over the duty of care from the holder. However reliable the expert, the holder himself needs to ask the right questions. Where he is faced with an unknown substance or a known waste but no disposal outlet, he needs to establish not only what it is but what special needs it has for storage, transport or treatment, and what the possible outlets for it may be, whether disposal or reclamation.

Help with choosing a destination

6.3. A consultant may put a waste holder in touch with a legitimate outlet for his waste. Alternatively waste managers or carriers themselves may offer expert advice on a destination for a waste. A large waste management organisation with a variety of disposal or reclamation methods under its control may be able to provide all the waste management services a holder needs. Otherwise it may be necessary to shop around several firms for advice on whether or not they would accept a waste. If a consultant arranges a waste transfer to such an extent that he controls what happens to the waste, he is a broker, and shares responsibility with the two holders directly involved for the proper transfer of the waste.

6.4. If the next holder is himself a source of advice he may sometimes undertake the analysis and write the waste description on behalf of the previous holder; what he may not do is undertake the checks or complete a transfer note for which the previous holder is responsible.

Help from local authorities

6.5. A *waste collection authority* will be able to tell a waste holder whether a particular waste may or will be collected as part of their normal public waste collection.

6.6. *Waste regulation authorities* have expertise in the management of all types of controlled waste but are *not* in a position to offer advice to every waste holder on how he should deal with his waste. Information that **is** held by waste regulation authorities and is available for any enquirer to examine on request is:
   (a) the register of waste carriers maintained by each authority; the register is a list of carriers currently registered with that authority; registered carriers are authorised for the purpose of the duty of care to transport controlled waste; and
   (b) the public register of waste management licences and, in Scotland only, of resolutions made by authorities, which includes a full copy of each licence issued in the area of the authority, from which a waste holder can check on the waste that a site is entitled to take.

Waste management papers

6.7. Detailed advice on good practice is given in the series of Waste Management Papers issued by the Department of the Environment and published by HMSO. These cover subjects including the handling, treatment and disposal of particular wastes and waste management licensing.

SUMMARY CHECKLIST

This section draws together in one place a simple checklist of the main steps that are normally necessary to meet the duty of care. As with the code as a whole, *this does not mean that completing the steps listed here is all that needs to be done under the duty of care*. The checklist cross-refers to key sections of the code for fuller advice.

refer to paragraphs

(a) Is what you have waste? if yes, — 1.2–1.3
(b) is it controlled waste? if yes, — 1.4
(c) while you have it, protect and store it properly, — 2.1–2.4
(d) write a proper description of the waste, covering: — 1.9–1.10
  — any problems it poses; — 1.5–1.7
  and, *as necessary to others who might deal with it later*, one or more of:
  — the type of premises the waste comes from; — 1.12–1.13
  — what the waste is called; — 1.14
  — the process that produced the waste; and — 1.15–1.16
  — a full analysis; — 1.17–1.18
(e) select someone else to take the waste; they must be one or more of the following and must *prove* that they are:
  — a registered waste carrier; — 3.3–3.5
  — exempt from registration; — 3.6
  — a waste manager licensed to accept the waste; — 3.7–3.9
  — exempt from waste licensing; — 3.10
  — a waste collection authority; or — 3.2
  — a waste disposal authority operating within the terms of a resolution (Scotland only); — 3.12
(f) pack the waste safely when transferring it; — 2.5–2.7
(g) check the next person's credentials when transferring waste to them; — 3.4–3.6 & 3.8–3.14
(h) complete and sign a transfer note; — Annex C, C3–C4
(i) hand over the description and complete a transfer note when transferring the waste; — 1.9–1.10 & Annex C, C3–C4
(j) keep a copy of the transfer note signed by the person the waste was given to, and a copy of the description, for two years; — Annex C, C5
(k) when *receiving* waste, check that the person who hands it over is one of those listed in (e), or the producer of the waste, obtain a description from them, complete a transfer note and keep the documents for two years. — 4.2–4.7 & 5.4
(l) Whether transferring *or* receiving waste, be alert for any evidence or suspicion that the waste you handle is being dealt with illegally at any stage, in case of doubt question the person involved and if not satisfied, alert the waste regulation authority. — 5.5–5.11

ANNEX A

The Law on the Duty of Care

What the duty requires

A.1. The duty of care is set out in section 34 of the Act (a copy is printed at the end of this Annex). Those subject to the duty must try to achieve the following four things:
  (a) to prevent any other person committing the offences of disposing of "controlled waste" (see Glossary) or treating it, or storing it
    — without a waste management licence; or
    — breaking the conditions of a licence; or
    — in a manner likely to cause pollution or harm to health;

(b) to prevent the escape of waste, that is, to contain it;
(c) to ensure that, if the waste is transferred, it goes only to an "authorised person" or to a person for "authorised transport purposes"—these are listed in subsections (3) and (4) of section 34 of the Act (a copy is printed at the end of this Annex);
(d) when waste is transferred, to make sure that there is also transferred a written description of the waste, a description good enough to enable each person receiving it
— to avoid committing any of the offences under (a) above; and
— to comply with the duty at (b) to prevent the escape of waste.

A.2. Those subject to the duty must also comply with regulations which require them to keep records and make them available to authorities. These regulations are additional to the code of practice, and they are summarised at Annex C.

A.3. **Failing to observe the duty or the regulations is a criminal offence.**

Who is under the duty?

A.4. The duty and therefore this code apply to any
— importer, producer or carrier of controlled waste;
— person who keeps, treats or disposes of controlled waste (a "waste manager");
— broker who has control of controlled waste.

In the code and these Annexes all these persons who are subject to the duty are referred to as "holders" of waste.

A.5. There is no definition of "*broker*" in the Act. A broker is a person who arranges the transfer of waste which he does not himself hold to such an extent that he controls what happens to it.

A.6. Employers are responsible for the acts and omissions of their employees. They therefore should provide adequate equipment, training and supervision to ensure that their employees observe the duty of care.

Exemption for householders

A.7. The only exception to the duty is for occupiers of domestic property for "household waste" (see Glossary) from the property. Note that this does *not* exempt:
(a) a householder disposing of waste that is not from his property (for example waste from his workplace; or waste from his neighbour's property); or
(b) someone who is not the occupier of the property (for example a builder carrying out works to a house he does not occupy is subject to the duty for the waste he produces).

What each waste holder has to do

A.8. A waste holder is not absolutely responsible for ensuring that all the aims of the duty of care (listed in A.1.) are fulfilled. A holder is only expected to take measures that are
(a) reasonable in the circumstances, *and*
(b) applicable to him in his capacity.

A.9. The *circumstances* that affect what is reasonable will include:
(a) what the waste is;
(b) the dangers it presents in handling and treatment;
(c) how it is dealt with; and
(d) what the holder might reasonably be expected to know or foresee.

A.10. The *capacity* of the holder is who he is, how much control he has over what happens to the waste and in particular what his connection with the waste is; is he the importer, producer, carrier, keeper, treater, disposer or broker? Different measures will be reasonable for each.

A.11. Waste holders can be responsible only for waste which is at some time under their control; it is not a breach of the duty to fail to take steps to prevent someone else from mishandling any other waste. However, a holder's responsibility for waste which he at any stage controls extends to what happens to it at other times, insofar as he knows or might reasonably foresee. Further guidance on the reasonable limits of responsibilities is in Annex B.

Offences and penalties

A.12. Breach of the duty of care is a criminal offence. It is an offence irrespective of whether or not there has been any other breach of the law or any consequent harm or pollution. The offence is punishable by a fine of up to £2,000 on summary conviction or an unlimited fine on conviction on indictment.

The code of practice

A.13. This code of practice has statutory standing. The Secretary of State is obliged by the Act to issue practical guidance on how to discharge the duty; this code forms that guidance. The code is admissible as evidence in court. The court shall then take the code into account in determining any question to which it appears relevant. The code may therefore be used by a court in deciding whether or not an accused has complied with his duty of care.

Environmental Protection Act 1990

Duty of care etc. as respects waste

Duty of care etc. as respects waste

34.—(1) Subject to subsection (2) below, it shall be the duty of any person who imports, produces, carries, keeps, treats or disposes of controlled waste or, as a broker, has control of such waste, to take all such measures applicable to him in that capacity as are reasonable in the circumstances—
  (a) to prevent any contravention by any other person of section 33 above;
  (b) to prevent the escape of waste from his control or that of any other person; and
  (c) on the transfer of the waste to secure—
    (i) that the transfer is only to an authorised person or to a person for authorised transport purposes; and
    (ii) that there is transferred such a written description of the waste as will enable other persons to avoid a contravention of that section and to comply with the duty under this subsection as respects the escape of waste.

(2) The duty imposed by subsection (1) above does not apply to an occupier of domestic property as respects the household waste produced on the property.

(3) The following are authorised persons for the purpose of subsection (1)(c) above—
  (a) any authority which is a waste collection authority for the purposes of this Part;
  (b) any person who is the holder of a waste management licence under section 35 below or of a disposal licence under section 5 of the Control of Pollution Act 1974;
  (c) any person to whom section 33(1) above does not apply by virtue of regulations under subsection (3) of that section;
  (d) any person registered as a carrier of controlled waste under section 2 of the Control of Pollution (Amendment) Act 1989;
  (e) any person who is not required to be so registered by virtue of regulations under section 1(3) of that Act; and
  (f) a waste disposal authority in Scotland.

(4) The following are authorised transport purposes for the purposes of subsection (1)(c) above—
  (a) the transport of controlled waste within the same premises between different places in those premises;
  (b) the transport to a place in Great Britain of controlled waste which has been brought from a country or territory outside Great Britain not having been landed in Great Britain until it arrives at that place; and
  (c) the transport by air or sea of controlled waste from a place in Great Britain to a place outside Great Britain;

and "transport" has the same meaning in this subsection as in the Control of Pollution (Amendment) Act 1989.

(5) The Secretary of State may, by regulations, make provision imposing requirements on any person who is subject to the duty imposed by subsection (1) above as respects the making and retention of documents and the furnishing of documents or copies of documents.

(6) Any person who fails to comply with the duty imposed by subsection (1) above or with any requirement imposed under subsection (5) above shall be liable—
  (a) on summary conviction, to a fine not exceeding the statutory maximum; and
  (b) on conviction on indictment, to a fine.

(7) The Secretary of State shall, after consultation with such persons or bodies as appear to him representative of the interests concerned, prepare and issue a code of practice for the purpose of providing to persons practical guidance on how to discharge the duty imposed on them by subsection (1) above.

(8) The Secretary of State may from time to time revise a code of practice issued under subsection (7) above by revoking, amending or adding to the provisions of the code.

(9) The code of practice prepared in pursuance of subsection (7) above shall be laid before both Houses of Parliament.

(10) A code of practice issued under subsection (7) above shall be admissible in evidence and if any provision of such a code appears to the court to be relevant to any question arising in the proceedings it shall be taken into account in determining that question.

(11) Different codes of practice may be prepared and issued under subsection (7) above for different areas.

ANNEX B

Responsibilities Under the Duty of Care

B.1. The main sections of the code address all waste holders who are subject to the duty of care. In law all the responsibilities for a waste under the duty are spread among all those who hold that waste at any stage, but responsibilities are not spread evenly. Some holders will have greater or less responsibility for some aspects of the duty, according to their connection with the waste (Annex A9–A11 above). This Annex offers advice for each category of waste holder on their particular responsibilities. This Annex is neither comprehensive nor self-contained guidance for particular categories of waste holder. It only draws out questions of the allocation of responsibility. All waste holders should follow the main advice in the code of practice.

Waste producers

B.2. The duty of care applies to a person who "produces" waste. No definition of "produces" is offered in the Act. The starting point for deciding who is a producer of any waste is deciding how it has become waste. There is a definition of "waste" in section 75 of the Act, continuing the effect of the definition in the Control of Pollution Act 1974, and this can be interpreted with the help of past court judgments. Something may become waste either by being changed in some way (for example by being contaminated or broken) or, if there is no such change, by a decision or change of attitude on the part of the holder of the object or substance (deciding that it is surplus or unwanted). Where an action is involved the waste producer will be the person committing the action. Where no action is involved the waste producer will be the person holding the object or substance who takes the decision that it is waste. In most cases this should be quite unambiguous, but the circumstances of contracting, and especially the construction and demolition industries, have given rise to conflicting views of who is a waste producer and who is subject to the duty of care.

B.3. In such cases the producer of construction or demolition waste may be regarded as the person undertaking the works which give rise to that waste, not the person who issues instructions or lets contracts which give rise to waste. The client for works, although he may take decisions as a result of which waste is created, is not himself producing the waste created by the works. Where there are several contractors and sub-contractors on site, the producer of a particular waste is the particular contractor or sub-contractor who (or whose employees) takes an action which creates waste, or, who begins to treat something as if it were waste (by discarding it). Where a client or contractor makes arrangements for the carriage or disposal of waste, for example by letting a disposal sub-contract to a haulier for waste produced on site by a demolition sub-contractor, then that client or contractor will be acting as a broker in respect of the transfer between the two sub-contractors; in such a case all three parties will be under the duty. In practice it is likely that every contractor involved on a site will either be producing or carrying away some waste and will be subject to the duty as producer or carrier and therefore liable to account for the measures they have taken to comply with the duty in respect of that waste. It would also be prudent for the client to take reasonable steps to ensure that all the contractors he employs or supervises comply with the duty of care.

B.4. Waste producers are solely responsible for the care of their waste while they hold it. Waste producers are normally best placed to know what their waste is and to choose the disposal or treatment method, if necessary with expert help and advice. They bear the main responsibility for the description of waste which leaves them being correct and containing all the information necessary for handling, treatment or disposal. If they also select a final treatment or disposal destination then they share with the waste manager of that destination responsibility for ensuring that the waste falls within the terms of any licence or exemption.

B.5. Producers bear the main responsibility for packing waste to prevent its escape in transit. Waste leaving producers should be packed in a way that subsequent holders could rely on.

B.6. Using a registered or exempt carrier does not necessarily let a producer out of all responsibility for checking the later stages of the disposal of his waste. The producer and the disposer may sometimes make all the arrangements for the disposal of waste, and then contract with a carrier simply to convey the waste from one to the other. Such a case is very little different in practice from that where there is no intermediate carrier involved. If a producer arranges disposal then he should undertake the same care in selecting the disposer as if he were delivering the waste himself, however many other parties there are between.

B.7. It is not possible to draw a line at the gate of producers' premises and say that their responsibility for waste ends there. A producer is responsible according to what he knows or should have foreseen. So if he hands waste to a carrier not only should it be properly packed when transferred, but the producer should take account of anything he sees or learns about the way in which the carrier is subsequently handling it. The producer would not be expected to follow the carrier but he should be able to see whether the waste is loaded securely for transport when it leaves, and he may come to learn or suspect that it is not ending up at a legitimate destination. A producer may notice a carrier's lorries returning empty for further loads in a shorter time than they could possibly have taken to reach and return from the nearest lawful disposal site; or a producer may notice his carrier apparently engaged in the unlawful dumping of someone else's waste. These would be grounds for suspecting illegal disposal of his own waste. The same reasoning applies when a producer makes arrangements with a waste manager for the treatment or disposal of waste. The producer shares the blame for illegal treatment of his waste if he ignores evidence of mistreatment; a producer should act on knowledge to stop the illegal handling of waste (paragraphs 5.5 to 5.11).

Waste importers

B.8. Waste importers should act in most respects as if they were the producers of the waste they import. Regulations governing the transfrontier shipment of hazardous waste ensure that the final destination of the waste is already established. The importer bears the main responsibility for ensuring the adequacy of the accompanying description, the packaging of the waste on entry to Great Britain and the fitness of the destination to deal with the waste.

Waste carriers

B.9. A waste carrier is responsible for the adequacy of packaging while waste is under his control, he should not rely totally on how it is packed or handed over by the previous holder. For any waste he should at least look at how it is contained to ensure that it is not obviously about to escape. His own handling in transferring and transporting waste should take account of how it is packed, or if necessary he may need to repack it or have it repacked to withstand handling.

B.10. A waste carrier would not normally be expected to take particular measures to provide a new description of the waste he carried unless he altered it in some way. The description would normally be provided by the waste producer, unless the producer is a householder not subject to the duty, in which case the person first taking waste from the householder would have to ensure that a description was furnished to the next holder. When accepting any waste a carrier should make at least a quick visual inspection to see that it appears to match the description, but he need not analyse the waste unless there is reason to suspect an anomaly or the waste is to be treated in some way not foreseen by the producer.

B.11. If a carrier or any other intermediate holder does alter waste in any way, by mixing, treating or repacking it, he will need to consider whether a new description is necessary. The description received may continue to serve for waste that is merely compacted or mixed with similar waste, but if it has deteriorated or decomposed or been altered in any way that matters for handling and disposal then a new description should be written.

B.12. Where there is a contract between the producer and the waste manager and a carrier is contracted solely to provide transport, he may rely on the producer checking the scope of the licence or exemption of the waste manager to whom the waste is delivered. In other cases the carrier should check this himself.

Waste brokers

B.13. A waste broker arranging the transfer of waste between a producer and a waste manager, to such an extent that he controls what happens to the waste, is taking responsibility for the legality of the arrangement. He should ensure that he is as well informed about the nature of the waste as if he were discharging the responsibilities of both producer and waste manager. He is as responsible as either for ensuring that a correct and adequate description is transferred, that the waste is within the scope of any waste licence or exemption, that it is carried only by a registered or exempt carrier and that documentation is properly completed. If he does not directly handle the waste then he cannot be held responsible for its packaging, but he should undertake the same level of checks after transfer and the same action on any cause for suspicion as any other waste holder.

Waste managers

B.14. Waste managers, like waste carriers, should normally be able to rely on the description of waste supplied to them. However in treating or disposing of waste they are in a stronger position to notice discrepancies between the description and the waste and therefore bear a greater responsibility for checking descriptions of waste they receive. Sample checks on the composition of waste received would be good practice.

B.15. Waste managers are also in a good position to notice evidence that waste has been wrongly dealt with or falsely documented before it reaches them. For example a waste manager may receive waste which is documented as coming directly from one producer but which shows signs of having been mixed or treated at some intermediate stage. A manager is to some extent responsible for following up evidence of previous misconduct just as he is for subsequent mismanagement of waste, that is to the extent that he knew or should have foreseen it and to the extent that he can control what happens.

ANNEX C

Regulations on Keeping Records

C.1. The Environmental Protection (Duty of Care) Regulations 1991 (made under section 34(5) of the Act) require all those subject to the duty to make records of waste they receive and consign, keep the records and make them available to waste regulation authorities.

C.2. The regulations require each party to any transfer to keep a copy of the description which is transferred. An individual holder might transfer onward the description of the waste that he received unchanged in which case it would be advisable for the same of clarity to endorse the description for onward transfer to the effect that the waste was sent onwards as received. If a different description of waste is transferred onwards, whether or not this reflects any change in the nature or composition of the waste, then copies of both descriptions must be made. The holder making the copy need not be the author of the description, which will often be written only by the producer and reused unchanged by each subsequent holder.

C.3. The regulations also require the parties to complete, sign and keep a transfer note. The transfer note contains information about the waste and about the parties to the transfer.

C.4. While transfers of waste must be documented, nothing in the regulations requires *each* individual transfer to be separately documented. In the case of, for example, weekly or daily collections of waste from outside shops or commercial premises, or the removal of a large heap of waste by multiple lorry trips this would be unrealistic because of the number of individual loads and the absence of any necessary contact between the parties to the transfer. It would be reasonable for a single transfer note to cover multiple consignments of waste transferred at the same time or over a period (not exceeding a year) provided that the description and all the other details on the transfer note (who and what the parties are) are the same for all consignments covered by the note. A single transfer note could not cover a series of transfers between different holders nor transfers of wastes of different descriptions.

C.5. The regulations require these records (both the descriptions and the transfer notes) to be kept for at least two years. Holders must provide copies of these records if requested by any waste regulation authority.

C.6. One purpose of documentation is to create an information source of use to other holders. It is open to holders to ask each other for details from records, especially to check what happened to waste after it was consigned. A holder might draw conclusions and alert the waste regulation authority to any suspected breach of the duty if such a request were refused.

C.7. There is no compulsory form for keeping these records. It is recognised that a number of holders already keep records of waste in a manner that meets the requirements of the regulations with little or no further adaptation. A suggested standard form for voluntary use is included in this Annex.

C.8. **Breach of any provision of the regulations is an offence.**

Duty of Care: Controlled Waste Transfer Note

Section A—Description of Waste

1. Please describe the waste being transferred:

2. How is the waste contained?

   Loose ☐ *Sacks* ☐ *Skip* ☐ *Drum* ☐ *Other* ☐ → *please describe*:

3. What is the quantity of waste (number of sacks, weight etc.):

Section B—Current holder of the waste

1. Full Name (BLOCK CAPITALS):
2. Name and address of Company:
3. Which of the following are you? (Please ✓ one or more boxes)

   producer of the waste ☐

   importer of the waste ☐

   waste collection authority ☐

   waste disposal authority (Scotland only) ☐

   holder of waste disposal or waste management licence ☐ → *Licence number: Issued by:*

   exempt from requirement to have a waste disposal or waste management licence ☐ → *Give reason:*

   registered waste carrier ☐ → *Registration number: Issued by:*

   exempt from requirement to register ☐ → *Give reason:*

43/App. 5   *Environmental Protection Act* 1990

Section C—Person collecting the waste

1. Full Name (BLOCK CAPITALS):
2. Name and address of Company:
3. Which of the following are you? (Please ✓ one or more boxes)

   ☐ holder of waste disposal or waste management licence → Licence number:
   Issued by:

   ☐ exempt from requirement to have a waste disposal or waste management licence → Give reason:

   waste collection authority

   waste disposal authority (Scotland only)

   ☐ registered waste carrier → Registration number:
   Issued by:

   exporter

   ☐ exempt from requirement to register → Give reason:

Section D

1. Address of place of transfer/collection point:
2. Date of transfer:
3. Time(s) of transfer (for multiple consignments, give 'between' dates):
4. Name and address of broker who arranged this waste transfer (if applicable):
5. Signed: Signed:

   Full name: Full Name:
   (BLOCK CAPITALS)   (BLOCK CAPITALS)
   Representing: Representing:

FED 0443 (10/91 OSD2)

ANNEX D

Other Legal Controls

D.1. This code offers guidance on the discharge of a waste holder's duty of care under section 34 of the Act. Holders are also subject to other statutory requirements, some of the most important of which are set out here.

i. Waste disposal and waste management licensing

Current Controls

D.2. In *England and Wales* under the Control of Pollution Act 1974, *waste disposal licences* are required to authorise the:
   (a) **deposit** of controlled waste on land;
   (b) **disposal** of controlled waste by means of plant or equipment; and
   (c) **use of plant or equipment** to deal with controlled waste in one of the ways prescribed in Schedule 5 of the Collection and Disposal of Waste Regulations 1988 (S.I. 1988 No. 819, published by HMSO). Briefly, treating waste by baling, compacting, incinerating, pulverising, sorting, storing, processing, shredding, or composting may require a licence.

D.3. In *England and Wales, exemptions* from the requirement to have a waste disposal licence for any of the activities listed above are to be found in:
   (a) Schedule 6 of the Collection and Disposal of Waste Regulations 1988;
   (b) Regulation 4 of the Control of Pollution (Landed Ships' Waste) Regulations 1987 (S.I. 1987 No. 402, published by HMSO), with the amendments made by the Control of Pollution (Landed Ships' Waste) (Amendment) Regulations 1989 (S.I. 1989 No. 65, published by HMSO); and
   (c) the Disposal of Controlled Waste (Exceptions) Regulations 1991 (S.I. 1991 No. 508, published by HMSO).

D.4. In *Scotland* the position is broadly similar but licensing requirements and exceptions are set out in the Control of Pollution (Licensing of Waste Disposal) (Scotland) Regulations 1977 (S.I. 2006 (S.153), published by HMSO).

Future Controls

D.5. From April 1993, the new system of *waste management licences* under the Environmental Protection Act 1990 will be introduced. Under the Act, licences will be required to authorise the:
   (a) deposit of controlled waste on land;
   (b) treatment, keeping or disposal of controlled waste on land;
   (c) treatment, keeping or disposal of controlled waste by means of mobile plant; and
   (d) treatment, keeping or disposal of controlled waste in a manner likely to cause pollution of the environment or harm to human health.

D.6. *Exemptions* from these requirements will be prescribed in new regulations under section 33(3) of the Act which will replace those, currently in force in England and Wales, in the Collection and Disposal of Waste Regulations 1988.

ii. The registration of waste carriers

D.7. Subject to certain provisions, section 1(1) of the Control of Pollution (Amendment) Act 1989 ("the 1989 Act") makes it an offence to transport controlled waste without being registered. The requirement to register applies to any person who transports controlled waste to or from any place in Great Britain in the course of any business of his or otherwise with a view to profit. For this purpose, "transport" includes the transport of waste by road, rail, air, sea or inland waterway. The Controlled Waste (Registration of Carriers and Seizure of Vehicles) Regulations 1991 (S.I. 1991 No. 1624, published by HMSO) require each waste regulation authority to establish and maintain a register of waste carriers; and set out the basis on which the registration system operates. Guidance on registration is provided in DOE Circular 11/91, Welsh Office Circular 34/91 and Scottish Office Environment Department Circular 18/91.

D.8. Anyone subject to the duty of care must ensure that, if waste is transferred, it is transferred only to an authorised person or to a person for authorised transport purposes. Among those who are "authorised persons" are:
  (a) any person registered with a waste regulation authority as a carrier of controlled waste; and
  (b) any person who is exempt from registration by virtue of regulations made under section 1(3) of the 1989 Act. The exemptions at present in force are set out in regulation 2 of the Controlled Waste (Registration of Carriers and Seizure of Vehicles) Regulations 1991.

D.9. It is not an offence under section 1(1) of the 1989 Act to transport controlled waste without being registered in the circumstances set out in (a)–(c) below. The following are also "authorised transport purposes" for the duty of care:
  (a) the transport of controlled waste between different places within the same premises;
  (b) the transport to a place in Great Britain of controlled waste which has been brought from a country or territory outside Great Britain and is not landed in Great Britain until it arrives at that place. This means that the requirement to register as a carrier applies only from the point at which imported waste is landed in Great Britain; and
  (c) the transport by air or sea of controlled waste being exported from Great Britain.

iii. Special waste

D.10. Certain difficult or dangerous wastes ("special wastes") are subject to additional requirements in the Control of Pollution (Special Waste) Regulations 1980 (S.I. 1980 No. 1709, published by HMSO) made under section 17 of the Control of Pollution Act 1974. (These will eventually be superseded by regulations under section 62 of the Environmental Protection Act 1990.)

D.11. Special waste is subject to the duty of care, including the advice in the code of practice and the requirements of the Environmental Protection (Duty of Care) Regulations 1991, in the same way as any other controlled waste. Compliance with the duty of care does not in any way discharge the need also to comply with the special waste regulations.

D.12. It should be noted that the completion of special waste consignment note procedures, or of the similar procedures for landed ships' waste,[3] go some way towards meeting the purposes of the duty of care regulations. The information in these consignment notes will include almost all the information required in a duty of care transfer note, except some of the details relating to authorised persons. These could be added so that no separate note need be made. A copy of a consignment note would be furnished on request to an authority in place of a transfer note.

iv. Road transport of dangerous substances

D.13. Waste holders have obligations in respect of the regulations and associated codes of practice concerned with the transport of dangerous substances. For national transport the relevant regulations are:
  (a) the Dangerous Substances (Conveyance by Road in Road Tankers and Tank Containers) Regulations 1981 (S.I. 1981 No. 1059, published by HMSO);
  (b) the Classification, Packaging and Labelling of Dangerous Substances Regulations 1984 (S.I. 1984 No. 1244, published by HMSO);
  (c) the Road Traffic (Carriage of Dangerous Substances in Packages etc.) Regulations 1986 (S.I. 1986 No. 1951, published by HMSO), and (Amendment) Regulations of 1989 (S.I. 1989 No. 105, published by HMSO); and
  (d) the Dangerous Substances in Harbour Areas Regulations 1987 (S.I. 1987 No. 37, published by HMSO).

v. International waste transfers

D.14. Holders have obligations in respect of the import or export of waste. At present these obligations are set in the Transfrontier Shipment of Hazardous Waste Regulations 1988 (S.I. 1988 No. 1562, published by HMSO). Completion of the consignment note used in connection with these regulations would include almost all the information required on a transfer note, and may be used in a similar manner to a special waste consignment note (D.12 above).

---

[3] The Control of Pollution (Landed Ships' Waste) Regulations 1987 (S.I. 1987 No. 402, published by HMSO).

vi. Health and safety

D.15. Waste holders also have a duty to ensure, so far as is reasonably practicable, the health and safety of their employees and other persons who may be affected by their actions in connection with the use, handling, storage or transport of waste, by virtue of sections 2 and 3 of the Health and Safety at Work etc. Act 1974.

D.16. Holders also have a duty to comply with the Control of Substances Hazardous to Health Regulations 1988 (S.I. 1988 No. 1657, published by HMSO) (and in particular the requirement to carry out an assessment of the risks of their activities).

ANNEX E

Glossary of Terms Used in this Code of Practice

The Act: the Environmental Protection Act 1990.

The 1989 Act: the Control of Pollution (Amendment) Act 1989.

Carrier: a person who transports controlled waste, within Great Britain, including journeys into and out of Great Britain.

A **registered carrier** is registered with a waste regulation authority under the 1989 Act.

An **exempt carrier** is a waste carrier who is not required to register under the 1989 Act because:
  (a) he is exempt from registration by virtue of regulation 2 of the Controlled Waste (Registration of Carriers and Seizure of Vehicles Regulations 1991; or
  (b) he is transporting waste in the circumstances set out in section 1(2) of the 1989 Act. These circumstances are also "authorised transport purposes" as defined in section 34(4) of the 1990 Act.

Controlled waste: as defined in section 75 of the Act, that is, household, commercial and industrial waste, as modified by the Collection and Disposal of Waste Regulations 1988.

Holder: a person who imports, produces, carries, keeps, treats, or disposes of controlled waste or, as a broker, has control of such waste.

A **licensed waste manager** is one in possession of a licence under section 35 of the Act *or*, for a transitional period, under section 5 of the Control of Pollution Act 1974. Note that not all persons licensed under section 35 are disposers or reclaimers; licences are also issued for the treatment or keeping of waste by intermediate holders.

An **exempt waste manager** is one exempted from licensing by regulations under section 33(3) of the Act.

Producer: a person whose actions give rise to controlled waste including deciding to discard an article, material or substance.

Waste collection authority: local authority responsible for collecting waste; as defined in section 30(3) of the Act.

Waste disposal authority: as defined in section 30(2) of the Act, that is a local authority responsible for arranging the disposal of publicly collected waste. **In Scotland**, a waste disposal authority may itself act as a waste manager.

Waste regulation authority: as defined in section 30(1) of the Act; the authority charged with the issue of waste management licences under section 35 of the Act (or, for a transitional period until section 35 of the Act comes into force, the authority charged with issuing waste disposal licences under section 5 of the Control of Pollution Act 1974).

APPENDIX 6

ENVIRONMENTAL PROTECTION

STATUTORY NUISANCE (APPEALS) REGULATIONS 1990

(S.I. 1990 No. 2276)

In force from:

January 1, 1991

Enabling power:

Environmental Protection Act 1990, Sched. 3, para. 1(4) and the Control of Pollution Act 1974, ss.70(2) and 104(1).

Background:

Part III of the Environmental Protection Act 1990 provides for the abatement of statutory nuisances. Section 80 provides that where a local authority is satisfied that a statutory nuisance exists, or is likely to occur or recur, in its area it shall serve an abatement notice on either the person responsible for the nuisance or on the owner or occupier of the premises as the case may be. Section 80(3) provides that the person served with the abatement notice may appeal against it to a magistrate's court within 21 days of the service. These regulations set out the grounds on which such appeals may be made; the procedure to be followed where the appellant claims that the notice should have been served on another; the action the court may take to give effect to its decision on appeal; the cases in which an abatement notice is to be suspended; and the revocation of a provision of the Control of Noise (Appeals) Regulations 1975. The regulations were amended (S.I. 1990 No. 2483) to correct a minor defect.

Statutory reference:

Environmental Protection Act 1990, s.80.

Citation, commencement and interpretation

1.—(1) These regulations may be cited as the Statutory Nuisance (Appeals) Regulations 1990 and shall come into force on January 1, 1991.
 (2) In these regulations—
 "the 1974 Act" means the Control of Pollution Act 1974; and
 "the 1990 Act" means the Environmental Protection Act 1990.

Appeals under section 80(3) of the 1990 Act

2.—(1) The provisions of this Regulation apply in relation to an appeal brought by any person under section 80(3) of the 1990 Act against an abatement notice served upon him by a local authority.
 (2) The grounds on which a person served with such a notice may appeal under section 80(3) are any one or more of the following grounds that are appropriate in the circumstances of the particular case—
　(a) that the abatement notice is not justified by section 80(3) of the 1990 Act;
　(b) that there has been some informality, defect or error in, or in connection with, the abatement notice;
　(c) that the authority have refused unreasonably to accept compliance

with alternative requirements, or that the requirements of the abatement notice are otherwise unreasonable in character or extent, or are unnecessary;
(d) that the time, or, where more than one time is specified, any of the times, within which the requirements of the abatement notice are to be complied with is not reasonably sufficient for the purpose;
(e) where the nuisance to which the notice relates—
   (i) is a nuisance falling within section 79(1)(a), (d), (e), (f) or (g) of the 1990 Act and arises on industrial, trade or business premises, or
   (ii) is a nuisance falling within section 79(1)(b) of the 1990 Act and the smoke is emitted from a chimney,
that the best practicable means were used to prevent, or to counteract the effects of, the nuisance;
(f) that, in the case of a nuisance under section 79(1)(g) of the 1990 Act, the requirements imposed by the abatement notice by virtue of section 80(1)(a) of that Act are more onerous than the requirements for the time being in force, in relation to the noise to which the notice relates, of—
   (i) any notice served under section 60 or 66 of the 1974 Act, or
   (ii) any consent given under section 61 or 65 of the 1974 Act, or
   (iii) any determination made under section 67 of the 1974 Act;
(g) that the abatement notice should have been served on some person instead of the appellant, being—
   (i) the person responsible for the nuisance, or
   (ii) in the case of a nuisance arising from any defect of a structural character, the owner of the premises, or
   (iii) in the case where the person responsible for the nuisance cannot be found or the nuisance has not yet occurred, the owner or occupier of the premises;
(h) that the abatement notice might lawfully have been served on some person instead of the appellant being—
   (i) in the case where the appellant is the owner of the premises, the occupier of the premises, or
   (ii) in the case where the appellant is the occupier of the premises, the owner of the premises,
and that it would have been equitable for it to have been so served;
(i) that the abatement notice might lawfully have been served on some person in addition to the appellant, being—
   (i) a person also responsible for the nuisance,
   (ii) a person who is also an owner of the premises, or
   (iii) a person who is also an occupier of the premises,
and that it would have been equitable for it to have been so served.

(3) If and so far as an appeal is based on the ground of some informality, defect or error in, or in connection with, the abatement notice, the court shall dismiss the appeal if it is satisfied that the informality, defect or error was not a material one.

(4) Where the grounds upon which an appeal is brought include a ground specified in paragraph (2)(h) or (i) above, the appellant shall serve a copy of his notice of appeal on any other person referred to, and in the case of any appeal to which this Regulation applies he may serve a copy of his notice of appeal on any other person having an estate or interest in the premises in question.

(5) On the hearing of the appeal the court may—
(a) quash the abatement notice to which the appeal relates, or
(b) vary the abatement notice in favour of the appellant in such manner as it thinks fit, or
(c) dismiss the appeal;

and an abatement notice that is varied under sub-paragraph (b) above shall be final and shall otherwise have effect, as so varied, as if it had been so made by the local authority.

(6) Subject to paragraph (7) below, on the hearing of an appeal the court may make such order as it thinks fit—
- (a) with respect to the person by whom any work is to be executed and the contribution to be made by any person towards the cost of the work, or
- (b) as to the proportions in which any expenses which may become recoverable by the authority under Part III of the 1990 Act are to be borne by the appellant and by any other person.

(7) In exercising its powers under paragraph (6) above, the court—
- (a) shall have regard, as between an owner and an occupier, to the terms and conditions, whether contractual or statutory, of any relevant tenancy and to the nature of the works required, and
- (b) shall be satisfied before it imposes any requirement thereunder on any person other than the appellant, that that person has received a copy of the notice of appeal in pursuance of paragraph (4) above.

Suspension of notices

3.—(1) Where—
- (a) an appeal is brought against an abatement notice served under section 80 of the 1990 Act, and—
- (b) either—
  - (i) compliance with the abatement notice would involve any person in expenditure on the carrying out of works before the hearing of the appeal, or
  - (ii) in the case of a nuisance under section 79(1)(g) of the 1990 Act, the noise to which the abatement notice relates is noise caused in the course of the performance of some duty imposed by law on the appellant, and
- (c) either paragraph (2) does not apply, or it does apply but the requirements of paragraph (3) have not been met,

the abatement notice shall be suspended until the appeal has been abandoned or decided by the court.

(2) This paragraph applies where—
- (a) the nuisance to which the abatement notice relates—
  - (i) is injurious to health, or
  - (ii) is likely to be of a limited duration such that suspension of the notice would render it of no practical effect, or
- (b) the expenditure which would be incurred by any person in the carrying out of works in compliance with the abatement notice before any appeal has been decided would not be disproportionate to the public benefit to be expected in that period from such compliance.

(3) Where paragraph (2) applies the abatement notice—
- (a) shall include a statement that paragraph (2) applies, and that as a consequence it shall have effect notwithstanding any appeal to a magistrates' court which has not been decided by the court, and
- (b) shall include a statement as to which of the grounds set out in paragraph (2) apply.

Revocations

4.—(1) Regulation 4 of the Control of Noise (Appeals) Regulations 1975 is hereby revoked.

(2) In Regulation 10(1) of those regulations the word "58," shall be omitted.

APPENDIX 7

CODE OF PRACTICE ON LITTER AND REFUSE UNDER SECTION 89 OF THE ENVIRONMENTAL PROTECTION ACT (NOVEMBER 1990)

Issued under section 89 of the Environmental Protection Act 1990

INTRODUCTION

Litter has been the subject of much legislation in recent years, brought forward by successive governments. The Control of Pollution Act 1974 (COPA), the Refuse Disposal (Amenity) Act 1978 and the Litter Act 1983, have all sought to bring about a cleaner, tidier local environment.

The 1983 Litter Act provided for a maximum penalty of £400 (now increased to £1,000) for anyone convicted of dropping and leaving litter. Section 22 of COPA apportioned responsibility for cleaning roads in England and Wales between different tiers of local authority. Section 25 of the Local Government and Planning (Scotland) Act 1982 had the same effect in Scotland. Yet, there has until now been no clear and unambiguous requirement for local authorities (or other owners of land to which the public has access, or which is in full view of the public) to keep their land clear of litter and refuse. Part IV of the Environmental Protection Act 1990 ("the Act") makes good this deficiency.

However, the Government recognises that the eradication of litter from our streets and other open spaces will never be achieved simply by attacking the symptoms. Only when there is a universal realisation that dropping litter is fundamentally anti-social and unacceptable will we see an end to a littered local environment.

In order to secure the change in attitude required of many people, the Government has provided grant-in-aid under the Litter Act 1983 to the Tidy Britain Group (which engages in various educational and promotional programmes). Funding has also been provided for the Groundwork Trust and for local environment improvement schemes under the Urban Programme. The work of these bodies continues.

But, despite these measures, it is inevitable that some will continue to be dropped and, recognising that litter begets more litter, the Government considers it important to ensure that any litter which is dropped is swiftly and efficiently cleared away. So the Act places a new duty on the Crown, local authorities, designated statutory undertakers and the owners of some other land to keep land to which the public has access clear of litter and refuse, as far as is practicable. (In the case of designated statutory undertakers, the duty may apply additionally to land to which the public does not have access.) The duty also applies to the land of designated educational institutions. The Act requires the Secretary of State, under section 89(7), to issue a Code of Practice to which those under the duty are required to have regard.

Objective

The objective of this Code of Practice is
"to provide guidance on the discharge of the duties under section 89 by establishing reasonable and generally acceptable standards of cleanliness which those under the duty should be capable of meeting."
It will immediately be apparent that this Code, in its approach to litter clearance, is innovative in at least two ways. Firstly, it attempts, by defining standards of cleanliness which are achievable in different types of location and under differing circumstances, to ensure uniformity of standards across Great Britain.

Secondly, the Code is concerned with *output standards* rather than *input standards*—that is to say, it is concerned with *how clean* land is, rather than *how often it is swept*. Indeed, this Code does not suggest cleaning frequencies at all—it simply defines certain standards which are achievable in different situations. This may mean that an area which all but escapes littering will seldom need to be swept whereas a litter blackspot may need frequent attention. It will be seen, then, that the Code offers considerable scope for local authorities and others to target their resources to areas most in need of them, rather than simply sweeping a street because of the dictates of an arbitrary rota. Expressed in its simplest terms: "If it isn't dirty, don't clean it".

Further guidance

The appendix, which is not part of the Code of Practice issued under section 89(7), provides advice on "best practice" methods which might be adopted to help achieve the described standards (although different practices which achieved the same ends would be perfectly acceptable). Steps which bodies under the duty might take to strengthen public commitment to cleanliness are also suggested in this section.

The Duty

Section 89(1) of the Act places on the Crown and (in England and Wales) county, district and London borough councils, the Common Council of the City of London, and the Council of the Isles of Scilly and (in Scotland) regional councils, district or islands councils, joint boards (collectively known as 'principal litter authorities') a duty to ensure that all land in their direct control which is open to the air and to which the public has access is kept clear of litter and refuse, so far as is practicable. In addition, where the duty extends to roads, they must also be kept clean—again, as far as practicable. (For definitions of the land to which the duty applies see section 86.)

Section 86(9) transfers the responsibility for cleaning all roads except motorways (which remain with the Secretary of State) from the highways authorities to the district and borough councils. As regards Scotland, section 86(10) assigns the responsibility for cleaning all roads except motorways (which remains with the relevant roads authority) to the district and islands councils. (For simplicity, the word "road" is used freely throughout the Code and should, where appropriate, be read as "highway or, in Scotland, road". For definitions of the terms "relevant highway" and "relevant road" see sections 86(9) and (10), and 98(5) of the Environmental Protection Act 1990.)

A similar duty is placed on designated statutory undertakers. (Section 98(6) defines "statutory undertaker" as, broadly speaking, bodies authorised by an Act of Parliament to carry on transport-related undertakings. British Rail, London Regional Transport and BAA are just three examples of such a statutory undertaker.) One difference between the duty as it applies to statutory undertakers and the duty applying to principal litter authorities is that the duty on the statutory undertakers might cover some land in the direct control of a statutory undertaker *to which the public has no right of access* (such as railway embankments).

The duty also applies to land in the open air and which is in the direct control of the governing body or local education authority of designated educational institutions (see section 98(2) and (3)).

Similar duties may be imposed by principal litter authorities (other than county councils, regional councils or joint boards) on owners of other land by designating their land as a 'litter control area'. The types of land which may be so designated will be described by the Secretary of State in orders.

An important criterion for inclusion in the list of land which might be designated is that it should be land to which the public [is] entitled or permitted to have access with or without payment. (Examples of the type of land which might be designated are supermarket car parks and privately-owned shopping malls.)

Persons under the duty are required by subsection 89(10) to have regard to the Code of Practice in discharging their duty.

The Act allows the Secretary of State to specify descriptions of animal faeces to be included within the definition of refuse. He may also, by regulation, prescribe particular kinds of things which, if on a road, are to be treated as litter or refuse.

Practicability

The *caveat* in the summary of the duty concerning practicability is very important. It is inevitable that on some occasions circumstances may render it impracticable (if not totally impossible) for the body under the duty to discharge it. It will be for the courts to decide, in all cases brought before them, whether or not it was impracticable for a person under the duty to discharge it, but certain circumstances are foreseeable in which the discharge of the duty may be considered by the courts to be impracticable.

For instance, to clear litter or refuse from a railway embankment, or a motorway or other busy road, may entail a restriction of traffic (in the interests of safety both for cleaners and travellers, and to ensure the minimum disruption for road and rail users).

Such restrictions often require detailed planning weeks or even months beforehand, as a consequence of which it may be that litter will have to remain for longer than might otherwise be tolerable. There may be cases where litter or refuse is left as a result of an unforeseeable circumstance or special event. In the first few months after the legislation comes into force, some areas may be affected by the accumulations of many years. Both these circumstances may present particular cleaning difficulties. Similarly, bad weather may make it impossible to clean an area. Moreover, if the weather conditions are exceptionally severe, it may be that resources would have to be diverted to emergency work, making sweeping and cleaning an impracticability. Considerations of safety might also suggest that to clear a very heavily used pedestrian area during peak hours *without risking injury* would be impracticable.

There is also the consideration of what it is reasonable to expect a body under the duty to achieve. For example, whilst the standards in the Code would normally apply throughout the year, it may not be reasonable, or indeed practicable, to expect them to be met on Christmas or New Year's Day.

Enforcement

In the great majority of cases those under the duty will wish to achieve the highest possible standards of cleanliness. However, the Act makes provision for the occasion when a body under the duty may not discharge it adequately. Under section 91 a citizen aggrieved by the presence of litter or refuse on land to which the duty applies may, after giving five days' written notice, apply to the magistrates' court (or, in Scotland, the Sheriff) for a 'litter abatement order' requiring the person under the duty to clear away the litter or refuse from the area which is the subject of the complaint. Failure to comply with a litter abatement order may result in a fine (with additional fines accruing for each day the area remains littered). Any person contemplating enforcement action should not just consider the presence of litter but is advised to consider whether the body in question is complying with the standards in the Code before notifying them, since, under section

91(11) the Code is admissible in evidence in any court proceedings brought under that section.

It may be thought that the requirement on the part of the aggrieved citizen to give the duty body five days' notice before bringing an action, together with the inevitable delay between summons and hearing, will in practice allow a body far longer—maybe several months—to deal with accumulations of litter than the period of hours contemplated (for the most part) by this Code (see below). This is not so. Firstly, the courts are specifically empowered (under section 91(12)) to award costs to a complainant where the court is satisfied that *at the time the complaint was made to it* the land was defaced by litter or refuse—even if the land is clean at the time the case comes to court. Secondly, a citizen aggrieved by the persistent failure or wilful refusal of a duty body to discharge its duty would be entitled to apply to the High Court or, in Scotland, to the Court of Session, for Judicial Review of that body's actions.

Similarly, local authorities can act against any other local body under the duty which appears to them to be failing to clear land of litter and refuse. Under section 92, if a local authority is satisfied that any land covered by the duty is defaced by litter or refuse, or that defacement is likely to recur, they can serve a 'litter abatement notice' on the person under the duty to keep that land litter-free. The notice may require that the litter or refuse be removed within a specified time and/or that the land must not be allowed to become defaced by litter or refuse again. Non-compliance with a litter abatement notice may result in a fine (with additional fines accruing for each day the area remains littered).

In either case it will be a defence for the person under the duty to show that he has complied with the duty. The Code of Practice is admissible as evidence in court proceedings and if any of its provisions appear relevant to the court in determining any question before it, (*e.g.* whether or not the duty has been discharged) the court shall take account of them.

Cleanliness Standards

This Code of Practice is based on the concept of four standards of cleanliness:
- no litter or refuse, known as grade A;
- predominantly free of litter and refuse apart from small items, known as grade B;
- widespread distribution of litter and refuse with minor accumulations, known as grade C;
- heavily littered with significant accumulations, known as grade D.

Animal faeces, as prescribed by the Secretary of State in regulations, will not necessarily imply an area has fallen to a specific standard. They may be present where the cleanliness of the area has fallen to grade B, C or D, and must be considered alongside other litter refuse.

(Photographs showing examples of various cleanliness standards in a variety of locations appear at the end of the Code.)

Whilst it is obvious that the first standard of cleanliness (grade A) is the ideal, it is not reasonable to expect that standard to be maintained at all times in all places; technical difficulties may make it impossible to achieve in some circumstances, and it is unlikely to be maintained for long periods in heavily trafficked areas. Grade A should be seen as the standard which a thorough conventional sweeping/litter-picking should achieve in most circumstances—although it is accepted that it may not last for very long. A few items of litter dropped onto a grade A surface will not necessarily be sufficient to degrade that area to grade B.

It will be a matter for the courts to decide how large an area should be considered for the purposes of assessing defacement by litter and refuse, where relevant comparing photographic evidence with the photographic examples in the Code. That will depend on circumstances—whether, for example, a single mound of litter in an otherwise clear street means that the street as a whole has fallen to grade C or D, and therefore the body concerned has failed to discharge its duty.

Zones

The Code has two key principles:
- areas which are habitually more heavily trafficked should have accumulations of litter cleared away more quickly than less heavily trafficked areas; and
- larger accumulations of litter and refuse should be cleared more quickly than smaller accumulations.

The Code therefore divides land types into 11 broad categories of zones according to land usage and volume of traffic. Within the broad descriptions of zones set out below it will be for the local authority or other body under the duty to allocate geographical areas to particular zones (including, where applicable, breaches for the purposes of Category 5 Zone, roads for Category 6 and 7 Zones, educational land for Category 8 Zone, railway embankments for Category 9 and 10 Zones and canal land for Category 11). It is clear that this allocation must be given due publicity, not least to avoid unjustified complaints, although how it chooses to do so will be a matter for the individual body under the duty. Annotated maps in town halls, libraries and other central offices might be appropriate.

Section 95 requires certain local authorities to keep a register on which are recorded details of land which has been designated a 'litter control area' and where street litter control notices [have been] issued. Bodies under the duty could use a similar arrangement to publicise their zonings.

In allocating geographical areas to the various zones the duty body will need to use its best judgment, possibly after a period of consultation. It is recognised that there is a level of detail below which it would not be practicable to allocate land to different zones. The duty body will want to avoid, for example, dividing a particular street into 3 different zones simply because it displays characteristics of each of those zones.

Categories

The concepts of standards of cleanliness, practicability and zonings are brought together in this part of the Code which identifies, for different situations, practicable and achievable response times during which the duty body should restore the land in question to a particular condition.

It is stressed that the time periods given below are response times for cleaning an area which has become littered. They do not represent intervals between sweeps, which in many cases could be much longer. Again, 'if it isn't dirty, don't clean it'.

a. General zones

In categories 1 to 4 below, the period from 8pm to 6am is to be discounted for the purpose of assessing compliance with the standards, subject to the proviso in Category 1 Zone below.

It is recognised that on grassed areas, grade A is now always achievable.

Category 1 Zone

So far as is practicable, in town centres, shopping centres, shopping streets, major transport centres (including railway and bus stations and airports), central car parks and other public places where large numbers of people congregate, grade A should be achieved after cleaning. If this falls to grade B, it should be restored to grade A within six hours. If it falls to grade C it should be restored to grade A within three hours and grade D should be restored to grade A within one hour.

If the standard should fall to grade B or below during the period from 8pm to 6am, it should be restored to grade A by 8am.

Category 2 Zone

So far as is practicable, in high density residential areas (containing, for example, terraced houses and flats), land laid out as recreational areas where large numbers of people congregate, and suburban car parks and transport centres, grade A should be achieved after cleaning. If this falls to grade B, it should be restored to grade A within twelve hours. If it falls to grade C [it] should be restored to grade A within six hours, and grade D within three hours.

Category 3 Zone

So far as is practicable, in low density residential areas (containing, for example, detached and semi-detached houses), other public parks, other transport centres and areas of industrial estates grade A should be achieved after cleaning. If this falls to grade C, it should be restored to grade A within twelve hours, and if it falls to grade D it should be restored to grade A within six hours.

Category 4 Zone

So far as is practicable, in all other areas grade A should be achieved within one week of the standard falling to grade C, and 60 hours of the standard falling to grade D.

b. Beaches

In establishing a cleansing standard for beaches careful consideration has been given to the practical difficulties encountered in collecting and removing litter, and the damage to sensitive habitats which may result from such operations.

The duty on any body to clean beaches extends only to the land above (in England and Wales) Mean High Water or (in Scotland) Mean High Water Springs.

Category 5 Zone

Local authorities should identify those beaches in their ownership or control which might reasonably be described as 'amenity beaches'. Any assessment should take into account the level of use of the beach for recreational purposes.

As a *minimum* standard, all beaches identified by the local authority as amenity beaches should be generally clear of all types of litter and refuse between May and September inclusive. This applies to items or materials originating from discharges directly to the marine environment as well as discards from beach users. The same standard should apply to inland beaches where substantial numbers of bathers or other beach users may congregate.

c. Roads

Zoning of roads will depend upon their importance within the road network and their environment. For the purpose of this Code, the following hierarchy of roads is adopted:
   i. Motorways
   ii. Strategic routes (all-purpose trunk roads and principal local roads which carry more than 15,000 or 10,000 vehicles per day in urban and rural areas respectively (*i.e.* annual average daily traffic two-way over 24 hour period)).
   iii. All other roads not included in ii.

Each category can exist within an urban or rural environment. In urban areas category (iii) roads which form an obvious part of the local environment should be subject to the same standards of cleanliness as defined in Zones 1 to 4 above. Urban roads in categories (i) and (ii) which, by their nature, are free from pedestrian use (or largely so for non-motorway strategic routes), are clearly used largely to get traffic *through* an area (rather than to service the local area) and are subject to heavy traffic flows, should fall within Zone 6 below. Category (iii) roads not included in Zones 1 to 4, should fall within Zone 7 below.

Although in all cases standards and times relating to clearance of litter or refuse from the roads and related hard-shoulder and verge should be adhered to, as far as is practicable, it is recognised that for reasons of road safety (applying both to those doing the litter clearance and road users generally), and for reasons of avoiding traffic congestion, it will not always be possible to adhere to them. Where this is not possible, the first practicable opportunity should be taken in connection with other maintenance work which takes place to carry out a litter clearance in association with it. These considerations arise particularly in relation to motorways and strategic routes which are subject to continuously heavy traffic flows and where traffic management measures reduce capacity, which may result in severe congestion and delay for users.

In developing a cleansing regime to deal with litter and refuse the duty authority should not forget that it has a duty under section 89 of the Act to keep roads clean. This may include such activities as street sweeping and washing. Care should always be taken to ensure that leaves, debris or litter do not block gulleys, causing flooding.

Category 6 Zone—Motorways and Strategic Routes

On motorways and strategic routes (which may be the responsibility either of the Secretary of State or the local authority), and on associated lay-bys, grade A should be achieved after cleaning of paved areas, and grade B should be achieved after cleaning of verges. If the standard falls to grade C, the area should be restored to grade A (paved areas) or grade B (verges) within four weeks. If the standard falls to grade D, the area should be restored to grade A (paved areas) or grade B (verges) within one week.

In the case of central reservations these time limits shall not apply, but it might be practicable to restore them to grade A and grade B respectively when other work is carried out either on the central reservation itself or in a part of the carriageway immediately adjacent.

Category 7 Zone—Local Roads

For local roads not falling within Zones 1 to 4, and on associated lay-bys, grade A should be achieved after cleaning of paved areas and grade B after cleaning of verges. If the standard falls to grade C, the area should be restored to grade A (paved areas) or grade B (verges) within two weeks. If the standard falls to grade D, the area should be restored to grade A (paved areas) or B (verges) within five days.

d. Educational institutions

Category 8 Zone—Educational Institutions

The aim when cleaning relevant land of designated educational institutions should be to remove all litter and refuse (grade A).

As a minimum standard during school, college or university terms, grade B should be achieved after cleaning on all relevant land of designated educational institutions. If the standard falls to grade C it should be restored to at least grade B within 24 hours (excluding weekends and half term holidays).

During other periods, if the land in question is used for a purpose authorised by the governing body or managers of the institution, it shall be restored to grade B within one week of its having fallen to grade C.

Out of term time, where the land in question has fallen to grade C, the governing body or managers will ensure that it is returned to grade B as soon as is practicable.

e. Railway embankments

In this section, the references to railway embankments should also be taken to include cuttings, levels and sidings.

In establishing realistic response times and cleansing standards for railway embankments, account has to be taken of access problems, safety of those undertaking clearance work and of rail users and need to avoid disruption to rail services. Due regard should be taken to avoid damage to sensitive habitats.

In areas where the origin of litter or refuse is external to railway activities, clearance arrangements should be on a partnership basis involving the railway undertaking, local authorities and amenity groups, to eliminate blackspots.

Although clearance standards and response times should be adhered to so far as practicable, it is recognised that access, safety and traffic movement may sometimes preclude full adherence. In order to recover the position, the first practicable opportunity should be taken to undertake litter clearance in conjunction with track maintenance work.

The references in Categories 9 and 10 to railway undertakings should be taken to include light railway undertakings.

Category 9 Zone—Railway embankments within 100 metres of station platform ends

Grade B should be attained after clearance. If the standard falls to grade C, the area should be restored to grade B within 2 weeks. If the standard falls to grade D, the area should be restored to grade B within 5 days.

Category 10 Zone—Railway embankments within urban areas (other than defined in Category 9 Zone)

This category comes into effect from April 1, 1992.

Grade B should be attained after clearance. If the standard falls to grade C, the area should be restored to grade B within 6 months. If the standard falls to grade D, the area should be restored to grade B within 3 months.

f. Canal towpaths and embankments

In areas where the origin of litter or refuse is external to the activities of the canal or inland navigation undertaking, clearance arrangements should be on a partnership basis involving the undertaking, local authorities and amenity groups, to eliminate blackspots.

Although clearance standards and response times should be adhered to so far as practicable, it is recognised that access to canal embankments may sometimes preclude full adherence to these areas. (This should not affect adherence to the standards for towpaths.) In order to recover the position, the first practicable opportunity should be taken to undertake litter clearance.

Category 11 Zone—Canal towpaths, to which the public has right of access, in urban areas

On paved areas, Grade A should be achieved after clearance. If the standard falls to grade C, the area should be restored to grade A within 2 weeks. If the standard falls to grade D, the area should be restored to grade A within 5 days.

On grassed or non-paved areas, Grade B should be achieved after clearance. If the standard falls to grade C, the area should be restored to grade B within 4 weeks. If the standard falls to grade D, the area should be restored to grade B within 1 week.

APPENDIX 8

HEALTH AND SAFETY

The Genetically Modified Organisms (Contained Use) Regulations 1992

(S.I. 1992 No. 3217)

Made .... *15th December 1992*
Laid before Parliament .... *23rd December 1992*
Coming into force .... *1st February 1993*

ARRANGEMENT OF REGULATIONS

PART I

INTERPRETATION AND GENERAL

1. Citation and commencement.
2. Interpretation.
3. Application.
4. Meaning of "work" and "at work".
5. Modification of section 3(2) of the Health and Safety at Work etc. Act 1974.

PART II

NOTIFICATION OF AND CONSENT FOR ACTIVITIES INVOLVING GENETIC MODIFICATION

6. Prohibition of certain work with genetically modified organisms outside containment.
7. Risk assessment.
8. Notification of the intention to use premises for activities involving genetic modification for the first time.
9. Notification of individual activities involving genetic modification.
10. Additional provisions relating to notifications and consents.
11. Establishment of a genetic modification safety committee.

PART III

CONDUCT OF ACTIVITIES INVOLVING GENETIC MODIFICATION

12. Standards of occupational and environmental safety and containment.
13. Emergency plans.
14. Notification of accidents.

PART IV

DISCLOSURE OF INFORMATION NOTIFIED AND PUBLICITY

15. Disclosure of information notified.
16. Register of notifications.

PART V

ADDITIONAL DUTIES PLACED ON THE EXECUTIVE

17. Duties on receiving notifications.
18. Information to be sent to the Secretary of State.
19. Reports to the European Commission.

Part VI

MISCELLANEOUS AND GENERAL

20. Exemption certificates.
21. Enforcement and civil liability.
22. Fees for notifications.
23. Transitional provisions.
24. Extension outside Great Britain.
25. Revocation.

THE SCHEDULES

Schedule 1. Definition of genetic modification.
Schedule 2. Criteria for the classification of organisms.
Schedule 3. Parameters to be taken into account in risk assessments, as far as they are relevant, under regulation 7.
Schedule 4. Information required for a notification under regulation 8(1).
Schedule 5. Information required for a notification under regulation 9.
Schedule 6. Containment measures for micro-organisms of Group II.

The Secretary of State, being the designated (S.I. 1991 No. 775) Minister for the purpose of section 2(2) of the European Communities Act 1972 (c.68) in relation to the control and regulation of genetically modified organisms, in the exercise of the powers conferred on her by the said section 2 and sections 15(1), (2), (3)(b) and (c), (4)(a), (5)(b) and (9), 43(2), (4), (5) and (6), 52(2) and (3) and 82(3)(a) of, and paragraphs 1(1)(b) and (c) and (5), 4(1), 6(1), 14, 15(1), 16 and 20 of Schedule 3 to, the Health and Safety at Work etc. Act 1974 (c.37, ss.15, 43, 50 and 52 were amended by Sched. 15 to the Employment Protection Act 1975 (c.71) paras. 6, 12, 16 and 17 respectively) ("the 1974 Act") and of all other powers enabling her in that behalf and for the purpose of giving effect without modifications to proposals submitted to her by the Health and Safety Commission under section 11(2)(d) of the 1974 Act after the carrying out by the said Commission of consultations in accordance with section 50(3) of that Act, hereby makes the following Regulations:—

Part I

INTERPRETATION AND GENERAL

Citation and commencement

1. These Regulations may be cited as the Genetically Modified Organisms (Contained Use) Regulations 1992 and shall come into force on 1st February 1993.

Interpretation

2.—(1) In these Regulations, unless the context otherwise requires—
"the 1989 Regulations" means the Genetic Manipulation Regulations 1989 (S.I. 1989 No. 1810);
"accident" means any incident involving a significant and unintended release of genetically modified organisms in the course of an activity involving genetic modification which presents an immediate or delayed hazard to human health or to the environment;

"approved" means approved in writing for the time being by the Executive;

"activity involving genetic modification" means any operation involving the contained use of a genetically modified organism;

"contained use" means any operation in which organisms are genetically modified or in which such genetically modified organisms are cultured, stored, used, transported, destroyed or disposed of and for which physical barriers or a combination of physical barriers with chemical or biological barriers or both, are used to limit their contact with the general population and the environment;

"the contained use Directive" means Council Directive No. 90/219/EEC (O.J. No. L117, May 8, 1990) on the contained use of genetically modified micro-organisms;

"the Executive" means the Health and Safety Executive;

"genetic modification" in relation to an organism means the altering of the genetic material in that organism by a way that does not occur naturally by mating or natural recombination or both and within the terms of this definition—
   (a) genetic modification occurs at least through the use of the techniques listed in Part I of Schedule 1; and
   (b) the techniques listed in Part II of that Schedule are not considered to result in genetic modification,
and "genetically modified" shall be construed accordingly;

"genetic modification safety committee" means the committee established in accordance with regulation 11;

"micro-organism" means a microbiological entity, cellular or non-cellular, capable of replication or of transferring genetic material including animal or plant cell cultures;

"organism" means a biological entity capable of replication or of transferring genetic material and includes a micro-organism;

"self-cloning" means the removal of nucleic acid from a cell or organism, followed by the re-insertion of all or part of that nucleic acid—with or without further enzymic, chemical or mechanical steps—into the same cell type (or cell-line) or into a phylogenetically closely related species which can naturally exchange genetic material with the donor species;

"Type A operation" means any activity involving genetically modified micro-organisms for the purposes of teaching, research, development, or for non-industrial or non-commercial purposes on a scale at which the practices and conditions of the operations relative to the culture, volume and numbers of organisms involved is such that—
   (a) the system used to keep the organisms under containment reflects good microbiological practice and good occupational safety and hygiene; and
   (b) it is possible easily to render the organisms inactive by standard laboratory decontamination techniques;

"Type B operation" means any activity involving the genetic modification of micro-organisms other than a Type A operation.

(2) Genetically modified organisms shall be classified—
(a) in the case of micro-organisms—
   (i) as Group I micro-organisms if they comply with such of the criteria set out in Part I of Schedule 2 as are applicable to the particular case, determined in accordance with the guidelines set out in Part II of that Schedule which gives effect to Commission Decision 91/448/EEC (O.J. No. L239, August 12, 1991), or
   (ii) as Group II micro-organisms if they do not comply with the said criteria; or

(b) in the case of genetically modified organisms other than micro-organisms, in accordance with the criteria set out in Part III of Schedule 2.

(3) In these Regulations, unless the context otherwise requires—

(a) a reference to a numbered Part, regulation or Schedule is a reference to the Part, regulation or Schedule in these Regulations so numbered; and

(b) a reference to a numbered paragraph is a reference to the paragraph so numbered in the regulation or Schedule in which that reference occurs.

Application

3.—(1) These Regulations shall have effect with a view to protecting persons against risks to their health, whether immediate or delayed, and for the protection of the environment, arising from activities involving genetically modified organisms.

(2) Regulations 8 to 12 shall not apply to the transport of genetically modified organisms by road, rail, inland waterway, sea or air.

(3) These Regulations shall not apply to the genetic modification of organisms solely by any of the techniques referred to in Part III of Schedule 1 or to any organisms so modified.

(4) Insofar as these Regulations relate to the protection of the environment, they shall only apply to genetically modified micro-organisms.

(5) Nothing in these Regulations shall prejudice any requirement imposed by or under any enactment which relates to public health or the protection of the environment.

(6) These Regulations shall not extend to Northern Ireland.

Meaning of "work" "at work"

4. For the purpose of these Regulations and Part I of the Health and Safety at Work etc. Act 1974 (c.37) the meaning of "work" shall be extended to include any activity involving genetic modification and the meaning of "at work" shall be extended accordingly.

Modification of section 3(2) of the Health and Safety at Work etc. Act 1974

5. Section 3(2) of the Health and Safety at Work etc. Act 1974 shall be modified in relation to an activity involving genetic modification so as to have effect as if the reference to a self-employed person therein is a reference to any person who is not an employer or an employee and the reference in it to his undertaking includes a reference to such an activity.

PART II

NOTIFICATION OF AND CONSENT FOR ACTIVITIES INVOLVING GENETIC MODIFICATION

Prohibition of certain work with genetically modified organisms outside containment

6.—(1) Subject to paragraph (2), any operation in which organisms are genetically modified or in which such genetically modified organisms are cultured, stored, used, transported, destroyed or disposed of is prohibited unless it is undertaken in conditions of contained use in accordance with these Regulations.

(2) Paragraph (1) shall not apply to any operation in which—

(a) genetically modified organisms are cultured, stored, used, trans-

ported, destroyed or disposed of, where such organisms are or are contained in a product marketed in pursuance of—
   (i) a consent granted by the Secretary of State under section 111(1) of the Environmental Protection Act 1990 (c.43), or
   (ii) a written consent given by another competent authority of a member State in accordance with Article 13(4) of Council Directive 90/220/EEC (O.J. No. L117, May 8, 1990) on the deliberate release into the environment of genetically modified organisms, and
in either case, the operation is conducted in accordance with any conditions or limitations attached to that consent,
   (b) genetically modified organisms are released or marketed in circumstances in which the consent of the Secretary of State is required under section 111(1) of the Environmental Protection Act 1990.
(3) In this regulation, "product" means a product consisting of or containing a genetically modified organism or a combination of genetically modified organisms.

Risk assessment

7.—(1) A person shall not—
   (a) use any premises for activities involving genetic modification for the first time; or
   (b) undertake any activity involving genetic modification,
unless he has ensured that, before commencing that use or activity, as the case may be, a suitable and sufficient assessment of the risks created thereby to human health and the environment has been made.
(2) Without prejudice to the generality of paragraph (1), the purposes of the assessment undertaken under that paragraph shall include—
   (a) classifying any genetically modified organisms involved in the activity in accordance with the provisions of Schedule 2; and
   (b) where appropriate, making decisions about the levels of containment required for the activity concerned.
(3) In making the assessment required by paragraph (1) the person undertaking that assessment shall—
   (a) in particular, take due account of the parameters set out in Schedule 3 in as far as they are relevant; and
   (b) in a case in which the Executive has approved a method in relation to the activity involving genetic modification concerned or in relation to a particular element of that assessment, undertake the assessment in accordance with that method.
(4) The assessment shall be reviewed forthwith if—
   (a) there is reason to suspect that the assessment is no longer valid; or
   (b) there has been a significant change in the activity to which the assessment relates.
(5) The person making the assessment shall make a record of it and of any subsequent review and shall keep that record for at least 10 years from the date on which use of the premises or the activity, as the case may be, to which the assessment related, ceased.

Notification of the intention to use premises for activities involving genetic modification for the first time

8.—(1) Subject to the following paragraphs of this regulation and regulation 10, no person shall undertake any activity involving genetic modification at any premises for the first time, unless he has notified the Executive of his intention to do so at least 90 days in advance or before such shorter time as the Executive may approve and with that notification has furnished the particulars specified in Schedule 4.

(2) In the case of activities involving the genetic modification of micro-organisms, separate notifications shall be made of an intention to use the premises for activities involving genetically modified micro-organisms of Group I or Group II.

(3) In the case of activities involving genetically modified micro-organisms of Group II, the premises shall only be used for those activities after the Executive has given its consent.

(4) In any other case, the use of the premises for the activity may be commenced at or after the end of the period of 90 days, or such shorter period as the Executive may have approved in pursuance of paragraph (1), unless the Executive objects in writing before the end of the relevant period.

(5) In any case in which a consent is required under paragraph (3), the Executive shall communicate its decision on the application in writing within 90 days after the application was received.

(6) Nothing in this regulation shall prevent a person from notifying under regulation 9 an individual activity which he intends to undertake in the premises at the same time as making a notification under this regulation; in such a case he shall not commence the activity except in accordance with the time periods specified in this regulation.

Notification of individual activities involving genetic modification

9.—(1) Subject to the following paragraphs of this regulation and regulation 10, no person shall undertake any activity involving genetic modification unless he has notified the Executive of his intention to do so at least 60 days in advance or before such shorter time as the Executive may approve and has furnished the particulars specified in the following paragraphs of this regulation and, except in the case of an activity to which paragraph (5) applies, the activity may be commenced after the expiry of the relevant period if by then the Executive has not objected in writing.

(2) In the case of an activity which is—
(a) a Type A operation involving only micro-organisms classified as Group I; or
(b) an activity involving genetically modified organisms other than micro-organisms and which satisfy the criteria set out in Part III of Schedule 2,

it shall be a sufficient compliance with paragraph (1) if the person undertaking the activity keeps a record of such activities and forthwith after the end of each calendar year notifies the Executive—
    (i) of the total number of risk assessments under regulation 7 undertaken during that year;
    (ii) where appropriate, that he is intending to continue to undertake such activities; and
    (iii) that the information notified to the Executive in accordance with regulation 8 remains correct.

(3) In the case of an activity which is a Type B operation involving only micro-organisms classified as Group I, the specified particulars for the purposes of paragraph (1) shall be those specified in Part I of Schedule 5.

(4) In the case of an activity which is—
(a) a Type A operation involving genetically modified micro-organisms classified as Group II; or
(b) an activity involving genetically modified organisms other than micro-organisms and which do not satisfy the criteria set out in Part III of Schedule 2,

the specified particulars for the purposes of paragraph (1) shall be those specified in Parts I and II of Schedule 5.

(5) In the case of an activity which is a Type B operation involving genetically modified micro-organisms classified as Group II, the specified

particulars for the purposes of paragraph (1) shall be those specified in Parts I, II and III of Schedule 5 and the activity shall only be commenced with the consent of the Executive.

(6) In any case in which a consent is required under paragraph (5), the Executive shall communicate its decision on the application in writing within 90 days after the application was received.

(7) The Executive may accept as a single notification a connected programme of work covering more than one activity involving genetic modification at one site, or a single activity carried on by the same person at more than one site.

Additional provisions relating to notification and consents

10.—(1) Where necessary for the purpose of evaluating a notification made under regulation 8 or 9, the Executive may require in writing the person making the notification to give such additional information relating to the proposal as it may specify and, in such a case, the person making the notification shall not proceed with the activity involving genetic modification, until the Executive gives its approval, and the period between the time when the Executive requires the information and the notifier responds to the satisfaction of the Executive shall not be taken into account in calculating the periods of days referred to in the provisions concerned.

(2) Any consent granted by the Executive under regulation 8 or 9 may be granted subject to conditions or to a limit of time and may be revoked or varied at any time and in such a case the person undertaking the activity shall comply with those conditions.

(3) In so far as they relate to the protection of the environment, the Executive shall not grant, vary or revoke a consent under regulation 8 or 9, or give its approval under paragraph (1), without the agreement of the Secretary of State.

(4) Where a person making a notification in pursuance of regulation 8 or 9 subsequently makes a significant change in any premises or activity to which the notification relates or becomes aware of any new information which would affect the particulars previously notified, he shall forthwith notify the Executive thereof.

(5) If information subsequently becomes available to the Executive which could have significant consequences for the risks to health or the environment created by an activity involving genetic modification which has been notified to it, it may require the notifier to modify the conditions under which the activity is carried out, or to suspend or terminate the activity.

(6) Notifications made in pursuance of regulations 8 and 9 shall be in a form approved by the Executive.

Establishment of a genetic modification safety committee

11. A person who undertakes an assessment made for the purposes of regulation 7(1) shall establish a genetic modification safety committee to advise him in relation to that assessment.

Part III

Conduct of Activities Involving Genetic Modification

Standards of occupational and environmental safety and containment

12.—(1) For any activity involving genetically modified micro-organisms of Group I, the principles of good microbiological practice and the following principles of good occupational safety and hygiene shall apply—

(a) to keep workplace and environmental exposure to any physical, chemical and biological agent adequately controlled;
(b) to exercise engineering control methods at source and to supplement these with appropriate personal protective clothing and equipment where necessary;
(c) to test and maintain control measures and equipment;
(d) to test, when necessary, for the presence of viable process organisms outside the primary physical containment;
(e) to provide training of personnel; and
(f) to formulate and implement local rules for the safety of personnel.

(2) For the purpose of paragraph (1) "adequate" in relation to the control of an agent means adequate having regard only to the nature of the agent and the nature and degree of exposure to such an agent and "adequately" shall be construed accordingly.

(3) For any activities involving genetically modified micro-organisms of Group II in Type A operations, in addition to the principles set out in paragraph (1) the containment measures shall be determined by a method approved by the Executive.

(4) For any activities involving genetically modified micro-organisms of Group II in Type B operations, in addition to the principles set out in paragraph (1) the containment measures set out in Schedule 6 shall be applied at an appropriate level so as to ensure a high level of health and safety and environmental protection.

(5) For any activities involving genetically modified organisms other than micro-organisms, the principles set out in paragraph (1) shall be applied in as far as they are appropriate.

Emergency plans

13.—(1) Where the assessment made in accordance with regulation 7(1) shows that as a result of any reasonably foreseeable accident the health or safety of persons outside the premises in which an activity involving genetic modification is carried on is liable to be affected or there is a risk of damage to the environment, the person undertaking the activity shall ensure that a suitable emergency plan is prepared with a view to securing the health and safety of those persons and the protection of the environment.

(2) The person preparing the plan shall consult such persons, bodies and authorities as are appropriate and shall inform the emergency services in writing of the plan and of the hazards to which the plan relates.

(3) The person undertaking the activity involving genetic modification which is the subject of the emergency plan shall take appropriate measures to inform persons who are liable to be affected by an accident of the safety measures and the correct behaviour to adopt in the event of an accident.

(4) The information required to be given in pursuance of paragraph (3) shall be repeated and brought up to date at appropriate intervals and shall be made publicly available.

Notification of accidents

14.—(1) Where an accident occurs, the person undertaking the activity involving genetically modified organisms shall forthwith notify the Executive of it and shall provide the following information—
(a) the circumstances of the accident;
(b) the identity and quantity of genetically modified organisms released;
(c) any information necessary to assess the effects of the accident on the health of the general population and on the environment; and
(d) the emergency measures taken.

(2) Where the Executive receives a notification in pursuance of paragraph (1), the Executive shall—

(a) ensure that any emergency, medium and long term measures are taken;
(b) immediately inform any other member State that could be affected by the accident;
(c) collect, where possible, the information necessary for a full analysis of the accident and, where appropriate, make recommendations to avoid similar accidents in the future and to limit their effects; and
(d) send to the European Commission the information provided for under paragraph (1), together with an analysis of the accident and details of any recommendations made to avoid similar accidents in the future and to limit their effects.

PART IV

DISCLOSURE OF INFORMATION NOTIFIED AND PUBLICITY

Disclosure of information notified

15.—(1) The information notified in pursuance of regulations 8 to 10 shall not be treated as relevant information for the purposes of section 28 of the Health and Safety at Work etc. Act 1974.

(2) Where a person making a notification in pursuance of regulations 8 to 10 indicates that it contains certain information the disclosure of which might harm his competitive position and should be kept confidential, full justification for that indication shall be given and in such a case after consulting the notifier the Executive shall decide which information shall be kept confidential and shall inform the notifier of its decision.

(3) Nothing in paragraph (2) shall apply to the following information which shall not be kept confidential—
(a) the name and address of the notifier and the location of the activity involving genetic modification;
(b) the purpose of the activity;
(c) the description of the genetically modified organism involved;
(d) methods and plans for monitoring the genetically modified organism and for emergency response; and
(e) the evaluation of foreseeable effects and in particular pathogenic effects and ecologically disruptive effects.

(4) Notwithstanding paragraph (3), where the Executive is satisfied on the basis of detailed evidence submitted to it by the notifier and where appropriate, after consultation with the notifier, that it is necessary to withhold, for the time being, certain of the information specified in paragraph (3) in order to protect his intellectual property rights, the Executive shall withhold that information to the extent and for so long as it is necessary to protect those rights.

(5) Information which is kept confidential in accordance with paragraph (2) or withheld in accordance with paragraph (4) shall be disclosed only—
(a) to the Secretary of State;
(b) to the European Commission or the competent authority for Northern Ireland or another member State;
(c) for the purpose of any legal proceedings;
(d) with the consent of the notifier; or
(e) to the extent necessary to evaluate the notification.

(6) A person who receives information in accordance with sub-paragraph (e) of paragraph (5) shall not use that information except for a purpose of the Executive or the Secretary of State.

(7) Where the notifier has requested that certain information in the notification shall be kept confidential in accordance with paragraph (2) or withheld in accordance with paragraph (4), the Executive shall not disclose any of that information (except in accordance with paragraph (5)) until at least 14 days after it has reached a decision under the relevant paragraph.

(8) After consulting the notifier, the Executive may review any decision made under paragraph (2) or (4) and shall inform the notifier of the result of that review.

(9) Where, for whatever reason, the notifier withdraws the notification, the Executive shall not thereafter disclose any of the information supplied.

Register of notifications

16.—(1) The Executive shall maintain a register of notifications to which regulation 8(3) or 9(5) relate (for which the consent of the Executive is required) and that register shall be open to inspection by members of the public at any reasonable time.

(2) The register referred to in paragraph (1) shall contain in relation to each such notification—
  (a) such of the information referred to in regulation 15(3) as has not been withheld in accordance with paragraph (4) of that regulation; and
  (b) a statement as to whether or not the consent of the Executive has been granted.

(3) The information referred to in sub-paragraph (a) of paragraph (2) shall be entered in the register within 14 days of its receipt by the Executive and the information referred to in sub-paragraph (b) of that paragraph within 14 days of the decision whether to grant the consent or not having been made, except that where the notifier has requested that certain information specified in regulation 15(3) be withheld in accordance with regulation 15(4), that information shall only be entered in the register not less than 14 days but not more than 28 days after the Executive has made a decision not to withhold that information.

(4) Copies of the register shall be maintained at—
  (a) the area office of the Executive in whose area the notifier is situated; and
  (b) Baynards House, 1, Chepstow Place, Westbourne Grove, London W2 4TF, and
  (c) Magdalen House, Stanley Precinct, Merseyside, L20 3QZ.

PART V

ADDITIONAL DUTIES PLACED ON THE EXECUTIVE

Duties on receiving notifications

17. The Executive shall examine a notification under regulation 8 or 9 for—
  (a) the conformity with the requirements of these Regulations;
  (b) the accuracy and completeness of the information given;
  (c) the correctness of the classification of the organisms to which the notification relates in accordance with Schedule 2; and
  (d) where appropriate, the adequacy of the waste management, safety and emergency response measures.

Information to be sent to the Secretary of State

18. Forthwith after receipt, the Executive shall send to the Secretary of State a copy in each case of—

(a) any notification received under regulation 8 or 9;
(b) any requirement for further information under regulation 10(1) and the response thereto; and
(c) any notification relating to an accident under regulation 14,

and if requested to do so by the Secretary of State shall require additional information under regulation 10(1).

Reports to the European Commission

19. The Executive shall send to the European Commission reports of notifications for which a consent is required under regulation 9(5) and summary reports of the application of these Regulations in accordance with Article 18 of the contained use Directive.

Part VI

Miscellaneous and General

Exemption certificates

20.—(1) Subject to paragraph (2) and to any provisions imposed by the Communities in respect of the control and regulation of genetically modified organisms, the Executive may, with the agreement of the Secretary of State in so far as the exemption relates to the environment, by a certificate in writing, exempt any person or class of persons, genetically modified organism or class of genetically modified organisms from all or any of the requirements or prohibitions imposed by these Regulations and any such exemption may be granted subject to conditions and to a limit of time and may be revoked by a certificate in writing at any time.

(2) The Executive shall not grant any such exemption unless, having regard to the circumstances of the case and in particular to—
(a) the conditions, if any, that it proposes to attach to the exemption; and
(b) any requirements imposed by or under any enactments which apply to the case, it is satisfied that the health and safety of persons who are likely to be affected by the exemption or the protection of the environment will not be prejudiced in consequence of it.

Enforcement and civil liability

21.—(1) Insofar as any provision of regulations 6 to 14 is made under section 2 of the European Communities Act 1972 (c.68)—
(a) the provisions of the Health and Safety at Work etc. Act 1974 relating to enforcement and offences shall apply to that provision as if that provision had been made under section 15 of that Act; and
(b) in the event of a breach of duty imposed by that provision, it shall confer a right of action in civil proceedings if that breach of duty causes damage.

(2) Notwithstanding regulation 3 of the Health and Safety (Enforcing Authority) Regulations 1989 (S.I. 1989 No. 1903), the enforcing authority for these Regulations shall be the Executive.

Fees for notifications

22.—(1) Fees shall be payable in accordance with paragraph (2) by a notifier to the Executive in relation to any matter referred to in that paragraph.

(2) The fees referred to in paragraph (1) shall be—

(a) subject to sub-paragraph (b), on each notification of the intention to use premises for activities involving genetic modification for the first time under regulation 8, £100;
(b) on each notification of the intention to use premises for activities involving genetic modification for the first time, where a consent is required under regulation 8(3), £130;
(c) subject to sub-paragraph (d), on each notification of individual activities involving genetic modification under regulation 9, £180;
(d) on each notification of individual activities involving genetic modification for which a consent is required under regulation 9(5), £270.

(3) This regulation shall not apply to any notification made for the purposes of regulation 23(1) or (3) (which relates to transitional provisions).

Transitional provisions

23.—(1) Where before 1st February 1993 a person had notified the Executive of his intention to undertake activities involving genetic modification which complied with regulation 5(1) and (2)(a) of the 1989 Regulations as then in force, that notification shall be treated as satisfying the requirements of regulation 8 except that regulation 8(3) shall apply to that activity on or after 1st February 1994.

(2) Before 2nd May 1993 it shall be a sufficient compliance with regulation 8 if the notifier commences the activity having notified his intention to do so 30 days in advance or such shorter time in advance as the Executive may approve and regulation 8(3) shall not apply to activities commenced before 2nd May 1993 until 1st February 1994.

(3) Where before 1st February 1993 a person had notified the Executive of his intention to undertake activities involving genetic modification which complied with regulation 5(1) and (2)(b) of the 1989 Regulations as then in force, that notification shall be treated as satisfying the requirements of regulation 9 except that regulation 9(5) shall apply to that activity on or after 1st February 1994.

(4) Before 2nd April 1993 it shall be a sufficient compliance with regulation 9 if the notifier of an activity involving genetic modification had notified it in accordance with that regulation 30 days in advance or such shorter time in advance as the Executive may approve and regulation 9(5) shall not apply to activities commenced before 2nd April 1993 until 1st February 1994.

(5) Regulation 10 shall apply to any notification made on or after 1st February 1993.

Extension outside Great Britain

24. These Regulations shall apply in relation to premises and activities outside Great Britain to which sections 1 to 59 and 80 to 82 of the Health and Safety at Work etc. Act 1974 apply by virtue of the Health and Safety at Work etc. Act 1974 (Application Outside Great Britain) Order 1989 (S.I. 1989 No. 840) as they apply to premises and activities within Great Britain.

Revocation

25. The 1989 Regulations are revoked.

Signed by order of the Secretary of State.

15th December 1992

Patrick McLoughlin
Parliamentary Under Secretary of State,
Department of Employment.

SCHEDULE 1

Regulations 2(1) and 3(3)

DEFINITION OF GENETIC MODIFICATION

PART I

Examples of techniques constituting genetic modification

1. Examples of the techniques which constitute genetic modification which are referred to in sub-paragraph (a) of the definition of genetic modification in regulation 2(1) are—
   (a) recombinant DNA techniques consisting of the formation of new combinations of genetic material by the insertion of nucleic acid molecules, produced by whatever means outside the cell, into any virus, bacterial plasmid or other vector system so as to allow their incorporation into a host organism in which they do not occur naturally but in which they are capable of continued propagation;
   (b) techniques involving the direct introduction into an organism of heritable material prepared outside the organism including micro-injection, macro-injection and micro-encapsulation; and
   (c) cell fusion (including protoplast fusion) or hybridisation techniques where live cells with new combinations of heritable genetic material are formed through the fusion of two or more cells by means of methods that do not occur naturally.

PART II

Techniques which are not considered to result in genetic modification

2. The following techniques are not considered to result in genetic modification if they do not involve the use of recombinant-DNA molecules or genetically modified organisms—
   (a) in vitro fertilisation;
   (b) conjugation, transduction, transformation or any other natural process; and
   (c) polyploidy induction.

PART III

Techniques to which these Regulations do not apply

3. These Regulations shall not apply to the following techniques of genetic modification if they do not involve the use of genetically modified organisms as recipient or parental organisms—
   (a) mutagenesis;
   (b) the construction and use of somatic hybridoma cells (for example for the production of monoclonal antibodies);
   (c) cell fusion (including protoplast fusion) of plant cells where the resulting organisms can also be produced by traditional breeding methods;
   (d) self-cloning of non-pathogenic naturally occurring micro-organisms which fulfil the criteria of Group I for recipient micro-organisms; and
   (e) self-cloning of non-pathogenic naturally occurring organisms other than micro-organisms which fulfil the criteria of Part III of Schedule 2.

SCHEDULE 2

Regulation 2(2)

CRITERIA FOR THE CLASSIFICATION OF ORGANISMS

PART I

Criteria as applicable for classification of micro-organisms in Group I

1. Recipient or parental organism
   (a) non-pathogenic;
   (b) no adventitious agents;

(c) proven and extended history of safe use or built-in biological barriers, which, without interfering with optimal growth in the reactor or fermenter, confer limited survivability and replicability, without adverse consequences in the environment.

2. Vectors/Insert
(a) well characterised and free from known harmful sequences;
(b) limited in size as much as possible to the genetic sequences required to perform the intended function;
(c) should not increase the stability of the construct in the environment (unless that is a requirement of intended function);
(d) should be poorly mobilisable;
(e) should not transfer any resistance markers to micro-organisms not known to acquire them naturally (if such acquisition could compromise use of drugs to control disease agents).

3. Genetically modified micro-organisms
(a) non-pathogenic;
(b) as safe in the reactor or fermenter as recipient or parental organism, but with limited survivability and/or replicability without adverse consequences in the environment.

4. Other genetically modified micro-organisms that could be included in Group I if they meet the conditions in paragraph 3
(a) those constructed entirely from a single prokaryotic recipient (including its indigenous plasmids and viruses) or from a single eukaryotic recipient (including its chloroplasts, mitochondria, plasmids, but excluding viruses);
(b) those that consist entirely of genetic sequences from different species that exchange these sequences by known physiological processes.

PART II

Guidelines as applicable for classification of micro-organisms in Group I

For classification into Group I the following guidelines should be used to further interpret Part I of this Schedule.

5. Characteristics of the recipient or parental organism(s)
(1) Non-pathogenic
The recipient or parental organisms can be classified as non-pathogenic if they satisfy the conditions of one of the following sub-paragraphs—
(a) the recipient or parental strain should have an established record of safety in the laboratory and/or industry, with no adverse effects on human health and the environment;
(b) the recipient or parental strain does not meet the conditions of sub-paragraph (a) above but it belongs to a species for which there is a long record of biological work including safety in the laboratory and/or industry, showing no adverse effects on human health and the environment;
(c) if the recipient or parental strain does not satisfy the conditions of sub-paragraph (a) above and belongs to a species for which there is no record of biological work including safe use in the laboratory and/or industry, appropriate testing (including, if necessary, animals) must be carried out, in order to establish non-pathogenicity and safety in the environment;
(d) if a non-virulent strain of an acknowledged pathogenic species is used, the strain should be as deficient as possible in genetic material that determines virulence so as to ensure no reversion to pathogenicity. In the case of bacteria, special attention should be given to plasmid or phage-borne virulence determinants.
(2) No adventitious agents
The recipient or parental strain/cell line should be free of known biological contaminating agents (symbionts, mycoplasms, viruses, viroids, etc.), which are potentially harmful.
(3) The recipient or parental strain/cell line should have proven and extended history of safe use or built-in biological barriers, which, without interfering with optimal growth in the

reactor or fermenter, confer limited survivability and replicability, without adverse consequences in the environment (applicable only for Type B operations).

6. Characteristics of the vector
(1) The vector should be well characterised
   For this purpose the following characteristics should be taken into account.
   (a) Information on composition and construction
      (i) the type of the vector should be defined (virus, plasmid, cosmid, phasmid, transposable element, minichromosome, etc.);
      (ii) the following information on the constituent fragments of the vector should be available—
         (aa) the origin of each fragment (progenitor genetic element, strain of organism in which the progenitor genetic element naturally occurred),
         (bb) if some fragments are synthetic, their functions should be known;
      (iii) the methods used for construction should be known.
   (b) Information on vector structure
      (i) the size of the vector should be known and expressed in basepairs or D;
      (ii) the function and relative positions of the following should be known—
         (aa) structural genes,
         (bb) marker genes for selection (antibiotic resistance, heavy metal resistance, phage immunity, genes coding for degradation of xenobiotics, etc.),
         (cc) regulatory elements,
         (dd) target sites (nic-sites, restriction endonuclease sites, linkers, etc.),
         (ee) transposable elements (including provirus sequences),
         (ff) genes related to transfer and mobilisation function (*e.g.* with respect to conjugation, transduction or chromosomal integration),
         (gg) replicon(s).
(2) The vector should be free from harmful sequences
   The vector should not contain genes coding for potentially harmful or pathogenic traits (*e.g.* virulence determinants, toxins, etc.) unless for Type A operations, such genes constitute an essential feature of the vector without, under any conditions or circumstances, resulting in a harmful or pathogenic phenotype of the genetically modified micro-organism.
(3) The vector should be limited in size as much as possible to the genetic sequences required to perform the intended function.
(4) The vector should not increase the stability of the genetically modified micro-organism in the environment (unless that is a requirement of the intended function).
(5) The vector should be poorly mobilisable
   (a) If the vector is a plasmid—
      (i) it should have a restricted host-range;
      (ii) it should be defective in transfer-mobilisation factors *e.g.* Tra^-, Mob^+, for Type A operations or Tra^-, Mob^+, for Type B operations.
   (b) If the vector is a virus, cosmid or phasmid—
      (i) it should have a restricted host-range;
      (ii) it should be rendered non-lysogenic when used as a cloning vector (*e.g.* defective in the cI-lambda repressor).
(6) It should not transfer any resistance markers to micro-organisms not known to acquire them naturally (if such acquisition could compromise use of drugs to control disease agents).

7. Required characteristics of the insert
(1) The insert should be well characterised
   For this purpose, the following characteristics should be taken into account.
   (a) The origin of the insert should be known (genus, species, strain).
   (b) The following information on the library from which the insert originated, should be known—
      (i) the source and method for obtaining the nucleic acid of interest (cDNA, chromosomal, mitochondrial, etc.);
      (ii) the vector in which the library was constructed (*e.g.* lambda gt 11, pBR322, etc.) and the site in which the DNA was inserted;
      (iii) the method used for identification (colony, hybridisation, immuno-blot, etc.);
      (iv) the strain used for library construction.

(c) If the insert is synthetic, its intended function should be identified.
(d) The following information on the structure of the insert is required—
    (i) information on structural genes, regulatory elements;
    (ii) size of the insert;
    (iii) restriction endonuclease sites flanking the insert;
    (iv) information on transposable elements and provirus sequences.
(2) the insert should be free from harmful sequences—
    (a) the function of each genetic unit in the insert should be defined (not applicable for Type A operations);
    (b) the insert should not contain genes coding for potentially harmful or pathogenic traits (*e.g.* virulence determinants, toxins, etc.), (unless for Type A operations, such genes constitute an essential part of the insert without, under any circumstances, resulting in a harmful or pathogenic phenotype of the genetically modified micro-organism).
(3) The insert should be limited in size as much as possible to the genetic sequences required to perform the intended function.
(4) The insert should not increase the stability of the construct in the environment (unless that is a requirement of intended function).
(5) The insert should be poorly mobilisable.
For instance, it should not contain transposing or transferable provirus sequences and other functional transposing sequences.

8. Required characteristics of the genetically modified micro-organism
(1) The genetically modified micro-organism should be non-pathogenic.
This requirement is reasonably assured by compliance with all the requirements above.
(2) (a) The genetically modified micro-organism should be as safe (to man and the environment) as the recipient or parental strains (applicable only for Type A operations);
    (b) the genetically modified micro-organisms should be as safe in the reactor or fermentor as the recipient or parental strains, but with limited survivability and/or replicability outside the reactor or fermenter without adverse consequences in the environment (applicable only for Type B operations).

9. Other genetically modified micro-organisms that could be included in Group I if they meet the conditions in paragraph 8 above
(1) Those constructed entirely from a single prokaryotic recipient (including its indigenous plasmids and viruses) or from a single eukaryotic recipient (including its chloroplasts, mitochondria, plasmids, but excluding viruses).
(2) Those that consist entirely of genetic sequences from different species that exchange these sequences by known physiological processes.

PART III

Criteria for the classification of organisms other than micro-organisms

10. An organism which satisfies the criteria of this Part is a genetically modified organism—
    (a) which is not a genetically modified micro-organism; and
    (b) which is as safe in the containment facility as any recipient or parental organism.

SCHEDULE 3   Regulation 7(3)

PARAMETERS TO BE TAKEN INTO ACCOUNT IN RISK ASSESSMENTS, AS FAR AS THEY ARE RELEVANT, UNDER REGULATION 7

Characteristics of the donor, recipient or (where appropriate) parental organism

1. The following matters shall be investigated and assessed in relation to any organism which is or will be a donor, recipient or parental organism—
    (a) the name, species, subspecies and strain of the organism;
    (b) the degree of relatedness between the donor, recipient (and where appropriate the parental) organism in relation to which the assessment is being carried out;

(c) the sources of the organism;
(d) the reproductive cycle of the organism;
(e) history of prior genetic modifications to the organism;
(f) the stability of the genetic traits of the organism;
(g) the nature of the pathogenicity, virulence, infectivity, toxicity, and vectors of disease transmission of the organism;
(h) the base sequence, frequency of mobilisation and specificity of the organism's indigenous vectors;
(i) the presence in the organism of genes which confer resistance;
(j) the host range of an organism which is a parasite or pathogen;
(k) the organism's other potentially significant physiological traits, and the stability of those traits;
(l) the organism's natural habitat and geographic distribution;
(m) the climatic characteristics of the organism's natural habitat;
(n) the significant involvement of the organism in environmental processes, including nitrogen fixation and pH regulation;
(o) the interaction of the organism with other organisms in the environment and its effect on those organisms, including its likely competitive or symbiotic properties;
(p) the ability of the organism to form survival structures, including seeds, spores or sclerotia.

Characteristics of the modified organism

2. The following matters shall be investigated and assessed in relation to an organism in relation to which a risk assessment under regulation 7 is carried out—
   (a) the description of the modification, including the technique used or proposed to be used to introduce a vector or insert into the organism;
   (b) the nature and source of the vector introduced into the organism;
   (c) the function of the genetic modification and/or of the new nucleic acid;
   (d) the structure and amount of any vector or donor nucleic acid remaining in the final construction of the modified organism;
   (e) the stability of the genetic traits introduced into the organism;
   (f) the frequency of mobilisation of inserted vector or genetic transfer capability;
   (g) the rate and level of expression of the new genetic material in the organism, and the method and sensitivity of measurement of that rate and level;
   (h) the activity of the expressed protein.

Health considerations

3. The following matters shall be investigated and assessed in relation to an organism in relation to which a risk assessment under regulation 7 is carried out—
   (a) toxic or allergenic effects of non-viable organisms and/or their metabolic products;
   (b) product hazards;
   (c) comparison of the modified micro-organism to the donor, recipient or (where appropriate) parental organism regarding pathogenicity;
   (d) capacity of colonisation;
   (e) if the organism is pathogenic to humans who are immunocompetent—
       (i) diseases caused and mechanism of pathogenicity including invasiveness and virulence,
       (ii) communicability,
       (iii) infective dose,
       (iv) host range, possibility of alteration,
       (v) possibility of survival outside of human host,
       (vi) presence of vectors or means of dissemination,
       (vii) biological stability,
       (viii) antibiotic-resistance patterns,
       (ix) allergenicity,
       (x) availability of appropriate therapies.

Environmental considerations

4. The following matters shall also be investigated and assessed in relation to an organism in relation to which a risk assessment under regulation 7 is carried out—
   (a) the factors affecting survival, multiplication and dissemination of the modified organism in the environment;

(b) the available techniques for detection, identification, and monitoring of the modified organism in the environment;
(c) the available techniques for detecting transfer of the new genetic material to other organisms;
(d) the known and predicted habitats of the modified organism;
(e) the ecosystems to which the modified organism could be disseminated as a result of an escape;
(f) the anticipated mechanism and result of interaction between the modified organism and the organisms which might be exposed in case of the escape of the organism;
(g) the known or predicted effects of the organism on plants and animals, including pathogenicity, infectivity, toxicity, virulence, vector or pathogen allegenicity, colonisation, predation, parasitism, symbiosis and competition;
(h) the known or predicted involvement of the organism in biogeochemical processes, including nitrogen fixation and pH regulation;
(i) the availability of methods for decontamination of the area in case of release to the environment.

SCHEDULE 4 Regulation 8(1)

INFORMATION REQUIRED FOR A NOTIFICATION UNDER REGULATION 8(1)

A notification required for the purpose of regulation 8(1) shall include the following information—
(a) the name and address of the person responsible for carrying out the activity and the names of persons responsible for supervision, monitoring and safety together with details of their training and qualifications;
(b) address of the premises where the activity is to be carried on and its grid reference and, where appropriate, a description of the sections of the installation;
(c) a description of the nature of the activity to be undertaken, the likely scale of the operation and in particular, in the case of micro-organisms, their classification (whether in Group I or Group II);
(d) a summary of the risk assessment undertaken in accordance with regulation 7;
(e) the names and capacities of the members of the genetic modification safety committee;
(f) comments made by the genetic modification safety committee on the local arrangements for risk assessment;
(g) the names of the biological and deputy biological safety officers concerned with the intended activities (if any);
(h) the name of the supervisory medical officer (if any);
(i) the arrangements for health surveillance (if any); and
(j) any other information the Executive needs for the purpose of maintaining the register referred to in regulation 16.

SCHEDULE 5 Regulation 9

INFORMATION REQUIRED FOR A NOTIFICATION UNDER REGULATION 9

PART I

Information required under regulation 9(3)

1. A notification required for the purposes of regulation 9(3) shall include the following information—
(a) the name and address of the person responsible for carrying out the activity;
(b) address of the premises where the activity is to be carried out;
(c) the date of the notification referred to in regulation 8(1);
(d) the parental organism used, or where applicable the host-vector system used;
(e) the source and the intended function of the genetic material involved in the modification;
(f) the identity and characteristics of the genetically modified organism;
(g) the purpose of the activity including the expected results;
(h) where appropriate the culture volumes to be used or the scale of the activity;

(i) details of waste treatment including levels of live genetically modified micro-organisms in the waste; and
(j) a summary of the risk assessment required in accordance with regulation 7 and of the comments of the genetic modification safety committee on it.

PART II

Additional information required under regulation 9(4)

2. In addition to the information required under Part I a notification made for the purposes of regulation 9(4) shall contain the following information—
   (a) a description of the sections of the installation involved and the methods for handling the organisms;
   (b) a description of the predominant meteorological conditions and the potential sources of danger arising from the location of the installation;
   (c) a description of the protective and supervisory methods to be applied throughout the duration of the activity; and
   (d) in the case of micro-organisms, the containment level to which the micro-organism has been allocated in accordance with the risk assessment made in accordance with regulation 7(1) and in any case the safety precautions to be observed.

PART III

Additional information required under regulation 9(5)

3. In addition to the information required under Parts I and II a notification made for the purposes of regulation 9(5) shall contain the information specified in paragraph 5.

4. If it is not technically possible, or if it does not appear necessary to give the information specified in paragraph 5, the reason shall be stated. The level of detail required in response to each subset of considerations is likely to vary according to the nature and scale of the proposed activity. In the case of information already submitted to the Executive by the notifier under these Regulations (or the 1989 Regulations) reference can be made to that information by him.

5. The additional information required is—
   (a) information about the genetically modified micro-organisms—
       (i) the identity and characteristics of the genetically modified micro-organisms,
       (ii) the purpose of the contained use or the nature of the product,
       (iii) the host-vector system to be used where applicable,
       (iv) the culture volume to be used,
       (v) behaviour and characteristics of the micro-organisms in the case of changes in the conditions of containment or release into the environment,
       (vi) overview of the potential hazards associated with the release of the micro-organisms into the environment, and
       (vii) substances which are or may be produced in the course of use of the micro-organisms other than the intended product;
   (b) information about personnel—
       (i) the maximum number of persons working in the installation; and
       (ii) the number of persons who will work directly with the micro-organisms;
   (c) information about the installation—
       (i) the activity in which the micro-organisms are to be used,
       (ii) the technological processes used,
       (iii) a description of the sections of the installation involved, and
       (iv) the predominant meteorological conditions and specific hazards arising from the location of the installation;
   (d) information about waste management—
       (i) types, quantities and potential hazards arising from the use of the micro-organisms,
       (ii) waste management techniques used including recovery of liquid or solid wastes and the inactivation techniques used, and
       (iii) ultimate form and destination of inactivated wastes;

(e) information about accident prevention and emergency response plans—
    (i) the sources of hazards and conditions under which accidents might occur,
    (ii) the preventive measures applied such as safety equipment, alarm systems, containment methods and procedures and available resources,
    (iii) a description of information given to workers, and
    (iv) the information necessary for the Executive to evaluate any emergency plan prepared in accordance with regulation 13;
(f) the full risk assessment referred to in regulation 7; and
(g) any other information the Executive needs for the purpose of maintaining the register referred to in regulation 16.

SCHEDULE 6   **Regulation 12(4)**

CONTAINMENT MEASURES FOR MICRO-ORGANISMS OF GROUP II

1. The containment measures for Type B operations using micro-organisms from Group II shall be chosen by the user from the levels in the Table below as appropriate to the micro-organism and the operation in question in order to ensure the protection of health of the general population and the environment.

2. Type B operations shall be considered in terms of their unit operations. The characteristics of each operation will dictate the physical containment to be used at that stage. This will allow the selection and design of process, plant and operating procedures best fitted to ensure adequate and safe containment. Two important factors to be considered when selecting the equipment needed to implement the containment are the risk of, and the effects consequent on, equipment failure. Engineering practice may require increasingly stringent standards to reduce the risks of failure as the consequence of that failure becomes less tolerable.

	Containment Levels		
SPECIFICATIONS	B2	B3	B4
1. Viable micro-organisms should be contained in a system which physically separates the process from the environment (closed system)	Yes	Yes	Yes
2. Exhaust gases from the closed system should be treated so as to:	Minimise release	Prevent release	Prevent release
3. Sample collection, addition of materials to a closed system and transfer of viable micro-organisms to another closed system, should be performed so as to:	Minimise release	Prevent release	Prevent release
4. Bulk culture fluids should not be removed from the closed system unless the viable micro-organisms have been:	Inactivated by validated means	Inactivated by validated chemical or physical means	Inactivated by validated chemical or physical means
5. Seals should be designed so as to:	Minimise release	Prevent release	Prevent release
6. Closed systems should be located within a controlled area	Optional	Optional	Yes, and purpose-built
(a) Biohazard signs should be posted	Optional	Yes	Yes

		Containment Levels	
SPECIFICATIONS	B2	B3	B4
(b) Access should be restricted to nominated personnel only	Optional	Yes	Yes, via airlock
(c) Personnel should wear protective clothing	Yes, work clothing	Yes	Yes, A complete change
(d) Decontamination and washing facilities should be provided for personnel	Yes	Yes	Yes
(e) Personnel should shower before leaving the controlled area	No	Optional	Yes
(f) Effluent from sinks and showers should be collected and inactivated before release	No	Optional	Yes
(g) The controlled area should be adequately ventilated to minimise air contamination	Optional	Optional	Yes
(h) The controlled areas should be maintained at an air pressure negative to atmosphere	No	Optional	Yes
(i) Input air and extract air to the controlled area should be HEPA filtered	No	Optional	Yes
(j) The controlled area should be designed to contain spillage of the entire contents of the closed system	Optional	Yes	Yes
(k) The controlled area should be sealable to permit fumigation	No	Optional	Yes
7. Effluent treatment before final discharge	Inactivated by validated means	Inactivated by validated chemical or physical means	Inactivated by validated physical means

APPENDIX 9

ENVIRONMENTAL PROTECTION

GENETICALLY MODIFIED ORGANISMS (DELIBERATE RELEASE) REGULATIONS 1992

(S.I. 1992 No. 3280)

In force from:

February 1, 1993

Enabling powers:

European Communities Act 1972, s.2(2) and Environmental Protection Act 1990, ss.106(4) and (5), 107(8), 111(1), (4), (5), (7) and (11), 122(1) and (4) and 126(1).

Background:

Directive 90/220/EEC on deliberate release into the environment of genetically modified organisms aims to harmonize the laws of Member States on the deliberate release of genetically modified organisms. The Directive requires Member States to put in place prior consenting procedures for the deliberate release of genetically modified organisms.

These regulations implement in the United Kingdom the requirements of Directive 90/220/EEC and require that consents be obtained before the release and/or marketing of genetically modified organisms.

The Regulations were amended by the Genetically Modified Organisms (Deliberate Release) Regulations 1993, S.I. 1993 No. 152. The 1993 Regulations correct a defect in the 1992 Regulations to provide that the advice of the Committee appointed under s.124 of the Environmental Protection Act 1990 as to applications for consents must be placed on the public register of information kept under s.122 of the Act within 14 days of its being received by the Secretary of State.

Statutory reference:

Environmental Protection Act 1990, s.111.

PART I

Citation and commencement

1. These regulations may be cited as the Genetically Modified Organisms (Deliberate Release) Regulations 1992 and shall come into force on February 1, 1993.

Interpretation

2. In these regulations—
  "the Act" means the Environmental Protection Act 1990;
  "the Commission" means the Commission of the Communities;
  "the Deliberate Release Directive" means Council Directive 90/220/EEC on the deliberate release into the environment of genetically modified organisms;
  "genetically modified organisms" means genetically modified organisms or a combination of genetically modified organisms;
  "heritable genetic material" means genes or other genetic material, in any form, whether in cellular or sub-cellular entities, which are capable of being replicated or transferred by any means;
  "local authority" means—

(a) in Greater London, a London borough council, the Common Council of the City of London and the Sub-Treasurer of the Inner Temple and the Under-Treasurer of the Middle Temple,
(b) outside Greater London, a district council and the Council of the Isles of Scilly, and
(c) in Scotland, an islands or district council;

"product" means a product consisting of or including genetically modified organisms, and "approved product" means a product marketed in pursuance of and in accordance with a consent granted by the Secretary of State under section 111(1) of the Act or a written consent given by another competent authority of a member State in accordance with Article 13(4) of the Deliberate Release Directive.

Artificial techniques of genetic modification

3. The following techniques are prescribed as artificial techniques for the purposes of section 106(4) of the Act:
(a) the insertion by any method into a virus, bacterial plasmid or other vector system of a nucleic acid molecule, which has been produced by any method outside that virus, bacterial plasmid or other vector system, so as to produce a new combination of genetic material which is capable of being inserted into an organism in which that combination does not occur naturally and within which it will be heritable genetic material;
(b) the insertion into an organism, by micro-injection, macro-injection, micro-encapsulation or other direct means, of heritable genetic material prepared outside that organism;
(c) the fusion (including protoplast fusion) or hybridization, by any method that does not occur naturally, of two or more cells to form cells which have new combinations of heritable genetic material and which (if derived solely from plant cells) cannot be produced by traditional breeding methods;
(d) where they involve the use of recombinant DNA molecules—
  (i) *in vitro* fertilization,
  (ii) conjugation, transduction, transformation or any other natural process,
  (iii) polyploidy induction.

Capacity of organisms for causing harm

4.—(1) For the purposes of sections 110(1), 112(5) and (7)(a) and 117(1) of the Act there shall be disregarded—
(a) the capacity of genetically modified organisms of the description specified in paragraph (2) for causing harm of the description specified in paragraph (3), and
(b) harm, caused by genetically modified organisms of the description specified in paragraph (2), which is of the description specified in paragraph (3).

(2) The genetically modified organisms specified in this paragraph are genetically modified organisms which control—
(a) the number or activity (or both) of any organisms, or
(b) toxic wastes.

(3) The harm specified in this paragraph is harm caused to any organisms by genetically modified organisms which have been released or marketed in pursuance of and in accordance with—
(a) a consent granted by the Secretary of State under section 111(1) of the Act, or

(b) a written consent given by another competent authority of a member State in accordance with Article 13(4) of the Deliberate Release Directive.

PART II

RELEASING ORGANISMS

Consent to release organisms

5.—(1) Subject to paragraphs (3) and (4), the cases and circumstances prescribed under section 111(1)(a) of the Act in relation to the release of any genetically modified organisms are any cases and circumstances other than the release of an approved product in accordance with the conditions and limitations to which the use of the product is subject.

(2) An application for a consent to release genetically modified organisms must be made in writing to the Secretary of State, and must be made either—
  (a) for one or more releases of one or more descriptions of genetically modified organisms on the same site for the same purpose within a limited period, or
  (b) for one or more releases of one description of genetically modified organisms on one or more sites for the same purpose within a limited period.

(3) Paragraph (1) shall not apply to a person who—
  (a) has notified the Health and Safety Executive, under Regulation 5(1)(a) of the Genetic Manipulation Regulations 1989, of his intention to carry out an activity involving an intentional introduction into the environment, and
  (b) carries out the activity in accordance with that notification before May 2, 1993.

(4) Paragraph (1) shall not apply to a person who releases a product which was marketed in the United Kingdom before February 1, 1993 and is not an approved product.

Information to be contained in application for consent to release

6.—(1) Subject to Regulation 7 (Exemptions from Regulation 6), the following is the information which an application for a consent to release genetically modified organisms must contain:—
  (a) the information prescribed in Schedule 1 to these regulations, to the extent that such information is appropriate to the proposed release,
  (b) information on data or results from any previous release of the organisms, or of organisms of the same description, which has been carried out by the applicant, and information from any previous application for the release of the organisms, or of organisms of the same description, which the applicant has made to the Secretary of State in accordance with the Act and these regulations or to another competent authority of a Member State in accordance with Article 5 of the Deliberate Release Directive,
  (c) a statement evaluating the impacts and risks posed to human health and the environment by the release of the organisms,
  (d) a statement whether the detailed description of the organisms and the details of the purpose for which the organisms will be released have been published, and the bibliographic reference for any information so published.
  (e) a summary, in the format established by the Commission under Article 9(1) of the Deliberate Release Directive, of the information contained in the application.

(2) The information prescribed in Schedule 1 shall be included in the application at the level of detail which is appropriate to the nature and scale of the proposed release.

(3) Where the applicant considers, on the basis that it is not technically possible or it does not appear to the applicant to be necessary, that it is not appropriate for the application to contain the information prescribed in one or more of the paragraphs of Schedule 1, the application shall contain a statement of the reasons why the inclusion of the information is not appropriate.

(4) The application must contain the description of the methods used to obtain the information contained in the application in accordance with paragraph (1) and a bibliographic reference, or, where standardized or internationally recognized methods are used, a reference to which method was used to obtain the information and its bibliographic references, together with the name of the body or bodies responsible for carrying out the studies.

(5) The application may in addition contain data or results from an application for consent to release genetically modified organisms previously made by some other person, provided that a copy of that person's agreement in writing is contained in the application.

Exemptions from Regulation 6

7. An application for a consent to release genetically modified organisms need not contain the information prescribed in Regulation 6(1)(a) and (b) if—
- (a) the information was contained either—
  - (i) in an application which was made by the same person in relation to a previous release of those organisms or of the same description of organisms, or
  - (ii) in an application which was made by some other person in relation to a previous release of those organisms or of the same description of organisms,
- (b) the application refers to the previous application in which the information was contained, and
- (c) where paragraph (a)(ii) applies, the application contains the agreement in writing of the person who made the previous application to a reference to that application being made.

Advertisement of application for consent to release

8.—(1) Subject to paragraph (2), a person who makes an application for a consent to release genetically modified organisms shall, not less than 14 days and not more than 28 days after acknowledgement of receipt of that application is sent to him by the Secretary of State, cause to be published in a newspaper or newspapers circulating in the areas likely to be affected by the proposed release a notice containing the following information—
- (a) the name and address of the applicant,
- (b) the general description of the organisms to be released,
- (c) the location and general purpose of the release, and
- (d) the foreseen dates of the release.

(2) Where the information on the location of the release which has been placed on the register kept by the Secretary of State under section 122 of the Act differs in its level of detail from that contained in the application for consent, the notice shall contain the level of detail regarding the location of the release which appears on the register.

(3) A person who makes an application for a consent to release genetically modified organisms shall, not less than 14 days and not more than 28 days after acknowledgement of receipt of that application is sent to him by the Secretary of State, give to the following persons notice that he has made the application and the information prescribed in paragraph (1)(a) to (d)—
- (a) the owner or owners of the site of the proposed release, if a person other than the applicant,

(b) the local authority for the area of the proposed release,
(c) the Nature Conservancy Council for England, Scottish Natural Heritage or the Countryside Council for Wales, as appropriate, according to whether the release will be in England, Scotland or Wales,
(d) the Countryside Commission, if the release will be in England,
(e) the Forestry Commission,
(f) the National Rivers Authority or, if the release will be in Scotland, the river purification board or islands council for the area of the proposed release,
(g) the water undertaker for the area of the proposed release or, if the release will be in Scotland, the regional or islands council for the area of the proposed release,
(h) each member of the genetic modification safety committee established by the applicant under Regulation 11 of the Genetically Modified Organisms (Contained Use) Regulations 1992.

General condition on consents to release organisms

9. In section 112 of the Act (Consents: limitations and conditions) there shall be substituted for paragraph (b) of subsection (5) the following paragraph—
"(b) notify the Secretary of State of—
  (i) any new information which becomes available with regard to any risks there are of damage to the environment being so caused, and
  (ii) the effects of any releases by him for the assessment of any risks there are of damage to the environment being so caused by such organisms being released or marketed;".

PART III

MARKETING ORGANISMS

Consent to market products

10.—(1) The cases and circumstances prescribed under section 111(1)(a) of the Act in relation to the marketing of any genetically modified organisms are any cases and circumstances other than the marketing of a product in accordance with a written consent given by another competent authority of a Member State in accordance with Article 13(4) of the Deliberate Release Directive.

(2) An application for a consent to market genetically modified organisms must be made in writing to the Secretary of State, and must be made either—
(a) where the product has not previously been marketed in pursuance of and in accordance with a consent granted by the Secretary of State under section 111(1) of the Act or a written consent given by another competent authority of a Member State in accordance with Article 13(4) of the Deliberate Release Directive, or
(b) where the product is intended for a use for which it has not previously been marketed in pursuance of and in accordance with a consent granted by the Secretary of State under section 111(1) of the Act or a written consent given by another competent authority of a Member State in accordance with Article 13(4) of the Deliberate Release Directive.

Information to be contained in application for consent to market

11.—(1) The following is the information which an application for a consent to market genetically modified organisms must contain:—

(a) the information prescribed in Schedule 1 to these regulations, to the extent that such information is appropriate to the nature and scale of the release which may result from the marketing,
(b) information on data or results from any previous release of the organisms, or of organisms of the same description, which have been carried out by the applicant, and information from any previous application for consent to release the organisms, or organisms of the same description, which the applicant has made to the Secretary of State in accordance with the Act and these regulations or to another competent authority of a member State in accordance with Article 5 of the Deliberate Release Directive,
(c) subject to paragraph (5), the information prescribed in Schedule 2 to these regulations,
(d) a summary, in the format established by the Commission under Article 12(3) of the Deliberate Release Directive, of the information contained in the application.

(2) The information prescribed in Schedule 1 shall be included in the application at the level of detail which is appropriate to the nature and scale of the release which may result from the marketing, and shall take into account the diversity of sites of use of the product, including—
(a) information on data and results obtained from research and developmental releases concerning the ecosystems which could be affected by the use of the product, and
(b) an assessment of any risks for human health or the environment related to the genetically modified organisms contained in the product, including information obtained from the research and development stage on the impact of the release on the environment.

(3) Where the applicant considers, on the basis that it is not technically possible or it does not appear to the applicant to be necessary, that it is not appropriate for the application to contain the information prescribed in one or more of the paragraphs of Schedule 1, the application shall contain a statement of the reasons why the inclusion of the information is not appropriate.

(4) The application must contain the description of the methods used to obtain the information prescribed in Schedule 1 and a bibliographic reference or, where standardised or internationally recognized methods are used, a reference to which method was used to obtain the information and its bibliographic references, together with the name of the body or bodies responsible for carrying out the studies.

(5) Where the applicant considers, on the basis of the results of any release in pursuance of and in accordance with a consent granted by the Secretary of State under section 111(1) of the Act or a written consent given by another competent authority of a Member State in accordance with Article 13(4) of the Deliberate Release Directive, or on substantive, reasoned scientific grounds, that the placing on the market and use of the product do not pose a risk to human health or the environment, he may propose not to supply the information prescribed in Part II of Schedule 2.

(6) The application may in addition contain data or results from an application for consent to market genetically modified organisms previously made by some other person, provided that a copy of that person's agreement in writing is contained in the application.

Transitional provision for marketing

12. Regulation 10(1) shall not apply to a person who markets a product which—

(a) was marketed by him in the United Kingdom before February 1, 1993, and
(b) is not an approved product,
until February 1, 1995.

PART IV

DUTIES AFTER THE MAKING OF APPLICATIONS

Duty of the applicant after applying for consent

13.—(1) In section 111 of the Act (Consents required by certain persons), after subsection (6) there shall be inserted the following subsection—
"(6A) Where an applicant for consent for releasing or marketing genetically modified organisms becomes aware, before his application is either granted or rejected, of any new information with regard to any risks there are of damage to the environment being caused as a result of the organisms being released or marketed, he shall notify the Secretary of State of that new information forthwith."
(2) In section 118(1)(e) of the Act (Offences), after the words "section 108(5) or (6)" there shall be inserted the words "or section 111(6A)".

Duties of the Secretary of State on receiving applications for consent to release

14.—(1) The Secretary of State shall within 30 days of receiving an application for a consent to release genetically modified organisms forward to the Commission a summary of that application in the format established by the Commission under Article 9(1) of the Deliberate Release Directive.
(2) The Secretary of State shall—
(a) examine an application for a consent to release genetically modified organisms for its conformity with the requirements of the Act and of these regulations,
(b) evaluate the risks posed by the proposed release,
(c) if necessary, carry out such tests or inspections as may be necessary for control purposes,
(d) where appropriate, take into account any comments made by the competent authority or authorities of Member States following the circulation to them by the Commission of the summary referred to in paragraph (1) above, and
(e) record his conclusions in writing.

Decisions by the Secretary of State on applications for consent to release

15.—(1) The Secretary of State shall not grant a consent to release genetically modified organisms as it relates to the protection of human health without the agreement of the Health and Safety Executive.
(2) The Secretary of State shall communicate his decision on an application for a consent to release genetically modified organisms to the applicant before the end of a period of 90 days beginning with the day on which the application was received.
(3) The period prescribed in paragraph (2) shall not include any period beginning with the day on which the Secretary of State gives notice in writing under section 111(6) of the Act that further information in respect of the application is required and ending with the day on which that information is received by the Secretary of State.
(4) The Secretary of State shall inform the competent authority or authorities of each Member State and the Commission of his decision on each application for consent to release genetically modified organisms.
(5) The Secretary of State shall not revoke or vary a consent to release

genetically modified organisms as it relates to the protection of human health without the agreement of the Health and Safety Executive.

Duties of the Secretary of State in relation to applications for consent to market

16.—(1) The Secretary of State shall examine an application for consent to market genetically modified organisms for its conformity with the requirements of the Act and of these regulations, giving particular attention to the environmental risk assessment and the recommended precautions related to the safe use of the product.

(2) Before the end of a period of 90 days beginning with the day on which he receives an application for consent to market genetically modified organisms the Secretary of State shall either—
  (a) forward to the Commission—
    (i) the application,
    (ii) a summary of the application in the format established by the Commission under Article 12(3) of the Deliberate Release Directive,
    (iii) a statement of the conditions under which he proposes to consent to the marketing of the product,
    (iv) where acceded to by the Secretary of State, details of any proposal by the applicant under Regulation 11(5) not to comply with any of the requirements of Regulation 11(1)(c), and
    (v) his favourable opinion on the application, or
  (b) inform the applicant that the proposal does not fulfil the requirements of the Act and of these regulations and is rejected.

(3) The Secretary of State shall not forward his favourable opinion on the application as it relates to the protection of human health where the Health and Safety Executive has informed him that it does not fulfil the requirements of the Act and of these regulations.

(4) The period prescribed in paragraph (2) shall not include any period beginning with the day on which the Secretary of State gave notice in writing under section 111(6) of the Act that further information in respect of the application is required and ending with the day on which that information is received by the Secretary of State.

(5) The Secretary of State shall immediately inform the competent authority or authorities of each Member State and the Commission of any other information he receives from the applicant before or after the granting of the consent.

(6) Where no objection has been raised by a competent authority of a Member State the Secretary of State shall, within a period of 60 days beginning with the day on which the documents referred to in paragraph (2)(a) were forwarded to the competent authority or authorities of the Member States by the Commission, grant consent to market the genetically modified organisms and inform the competent authority or authorities of the Member States and the Commission that he has done so.

(7) Where an objection has been raised by a competent authority of a Member State and the Commission has taken a favourable decision under Article 13(3) of the Deliberate Release Directive, the Secretary of State shall grant consent to market the genetically modified organisms and inform the competent authority or authorities of the Member States and the Commission that he has done so.

(8) The Secretary of State shall not revoke or vary a consent to market genetically modified organisms as it relates to the protection of human health without the agreement of the Health and Safety Executive, and shall immediately inform the competent authority or authorities of each Member State and the Commission of any decision to revoke or vary a consent.

Part V

Register of Information

Information to be included in register

17.—(1) The register kept by the Secretary of State under section 122 of the Act shall contain the particulars set out in paragraphs (2) to (7).

(2) In relation to a prohibition notice served under section 110 of the Act—
  (a) the name and address of the person on whom the notice is served,
  (b) the description of the genetically modified organisms in relation to which the notice is served,
  (c) the location at which the genetically modified organisms are proposed to be released,
  (d) the purpose for which the genetically modified organisms are proposed to be released or marketed,
  (e) the reason for the service of the notice,
  (f) any date specified in the notice as the date on which the prohibition is to take effect.

(3) Subject to paragraph (4), in relation to an application for a consent under section 111(1) of the Act—
  (a) the name and address of the applicant,
  (b) the general description of the genetically modified organisms in relation to which the application is being made,
  (c) the location at which the genetically modified organisms are proposed to be released,
  (d) the general purpose for which the genetically modified organisms are proposed to be released or marketed,
  (e) the foreseen dates of the release,
  (f) the methods and plans for monitoring the genetically modified organisms and for emergency response,
  (g) the evaluation of the environmental impact of the genetically modified organisms, in particular any pathogenic and/or ecologically disruptive effects, and
  (h) either—
    (i) the conditions or limitations in accordance with which the committee appointed by the Secretary of State under section 124 of the Act has advised that the consent should be granted, or
    (ii) a summary of the reasons why that committee has advised that the consent should not be granted.

(4) Where—
  (a) the application is for a consent to market genetically modified organisms,
  (b) an application for a consent to release genetically modified organisms contains a statement that a detailed description of the organisms and the details of the purpose for which the organisms will be released have been published, or
  (c) the Secretary of State is notified, under the conditions of a consent to release genetically modified organisms which he granted in relation to an application, that a detailed description of the organisms and the details of the purpose for which the organisms will be released have been published,

the information prescribed under paragraph (3)(b) shall be the detailed description of the organisms in relation to which the application is made and the information prescribed under paragraph (3)(d) shall be the details of the purpose for which the organisms will be released.

(5) In relation to consents granted under section 111(1) of the Act—

(a) the fact that the consent has been granted, and a reference to the application in respect of which it was granted,
(b) any conditions or limitations to which the consent is subject,
(c) any information supplied to the Secretary of State in accordance with those conditions or limitations,
(d) the fact that the consent has been revoked or varied, and the contents of the notice by which the consent was revoked or varied.

(6) In relation to information furnished under section 111(6A) or 112(5)(b)(i) of the Act, any new information which becomes available with regard to any risks there are of damage to the environment, and in relation to information furnished under section 112(5)(b)(ii) of the Act, the effects of any releases for the assessment of any risks there are of damage to the environment.

(7) In relation to convictions for any offence under section 118 of the Act—
(a) the name and address of the person convicted,
(b) the description of any genetically modified organisms in relation to which the conviction was obtained,
(c) the offence which was committed,
(d) the penalty imposed and any order made by the court under section 120 of the Act.

Keeping of the register

18.—(1) The information prescribed in Regulation 17(2) shall be placed on the register within 14 days of the prohibition notice being served.

(2) Subject to paragraph (3), the information prescribed in Regulation 17(3) shall be placed on the register within 14 days of the receipt by the Secretary of State of the application for consent to release or market.

(3) Where Regulation 17(4)(c) applies, the information prescribed in regulation 17(3)(b) and (d) shall be placed on the register within 28 days of the Secretary of State being notified, under the conditions of a consent to release genetically modified organisms which he granted in relation to an application, that a detailed description of the organisms and the details of the purpose for which those organisms will be released have been published.

(4) The information prescribed in Regulation 17(5)(a), (b) and (d) shall be placed on the register within 14 days of the consent being granted, revoked or varied, as appropriate.

(5) The information prescribed in Regulation 17(5)(c), (6) and (7) shall be placed on the register within 14 days of its receipt by the Secretary of State.

SCHEDULE 1 Regulations 6 and 11

Consent to Release or Market

Part I

General Information

1. The name and address of the applicant, and the name, qualifications and training of the responsible scientist and of every other person who will be responsible for planning and carrying out the release of the organisms, for carrying out the release and for the supervision, monitoring and safety of the release.

Part II

Information Relating to the Organisms

Characteristics of donor, parental and recipient organisms
2. Scientific name and taxonomy.

3. Usual strain, cultivar or other name.
4. Phenotypic and genetic markers.
5. The degree of relatedness between the donor and recipient organisms or between the parental organisms.
6. The description of identification and detection techniques.
7. The sensitivity, reliability (in quantitative terms) and specificity of detection and identification techniques.
8. The description of the geographic distribution and of the natural habitat of the organisms including information on natural predators, prey, parasites, competitors, symbionts and hosts.
9. The potential of the organisms for genetic transfer and exchange with other organisms.
10. Verification of the genetic stability of the organisms and factors affecting that stability.
11. The following pathological, ecological and physiological traits:
(a) the classification of hazard according to existing Communities rules concerning the protection of human health and the environment;
(b) the generation time in natural ecosystems, and sexual and asexual reproductive cycle;
(c) survivability, including seasonability and the ability to form survival structures, including seeds, spores and sclerotia;
(d) pathogenicity, including infectivity, toxigenicity, virulence, allergenicity, carrier (vector) of pathogen, possible vectors, host range including non-target organisms and possible activation of latent viruses (proviruses), and ability to colonize other organisms;
(e) antibiotic resistance, and potential use of these antibiotics in humans and domestic organisms for prophylaxis and therapy;
(f) involvement in environmental processes, including primary production, nutrient turnover, decomposition of organic matter and respiration.
12. The sequence, frequency of mobilization and specificity of indigenous vectors, and the presence in those vectors of genes which confer resistance to environmental stresses.
13. The history of genetic modification and of any application of additional techniques to the organism.

Characteristics of the vector
14. The nature and source of the vector.
15. The sequence of transposons, vectors and other non-coding genetic segments used to construct the genetically modified organisms and to make the introduced vector and insert function in those organisms.
16. The frequency of mobilization, genetic transfer capabilities and/or methods of determination of the inserted vector.
17. The degree to which the vector is limited to the DNA required to perform the intended function.

Characteristics of the modified organisms
18. The methods used for the modification.
19. The methods used—
(a) to construct inserts and to introduce them into the recipient organism;
(b) to delete a sequence.
20. The description of any insert and/or vector construction.
21. The purity of the insert from any unknown sequence and information on the degree to which the inserted sequence is limited to the DNA required to perform the intended function.
22. The sequence, functional identity and location of the altered, inserted or deleted nucleic acid segments in question, and in particular any known harmful sequence.

Characteristics of the genetically modified organisms
23. The description of the genetic traits or phenotypic characteristics and in particular any new traits and characteristics which may be expressed or no longer expressed.
24. The structure and amount of any vector or donor nucleic acid remaining in the final construction of the modified organisms.
25. The stability of the organisms in terms of genetic traits.
26. The rate and level of expression of the new genetic material in the organisms, and the method and sensitivity of measurement of that rate and level.
27. The activity of the gene product.
28. The description of identification and detection techniques, including techniques for the identification and detection of the inserted sequence and vector.
29. The sensitivity, reliability (in quantitative terms), and specificity of detection and identification techniques.
30. The history of previous releases or uses of the organisms.

31. In relation to human health—
(a) the toxic or allergenic effects of the non-viable organisms and/or their metabolic products,
(b) the product hazards,
(c) the comparison of the organisms to the donor, recipient or (where appropriate) parental organisms regarding pathogenicity,
(d) the capacity of the organisms for colonization, and
(e) if the organisms are pathogenic to humans who are immunocompetent—
     (i) diseases caused and mechanisms of pathogenicity including invasiveness and virulence,
     (ii) communicability,
     (iii) infective dose,
     (iv) host range and possibility of alteration,
     (v) possibility of survival outside of human host,
     (vi) presence of vectors or means of dissemination,
     (vii) biological stability,
     (viii) antibiotic-resistance patterns,
     (ix) allergenicity, and
     (x) availability of appropriate therapies.

PART III

CONDITIONS OF RELEASE

The release
32. The description of the proposed deliberate release, including the purpose or purposes of the release and the foreseen products of the release.
33. The foreseen dates of the release and time planning of the experiment including frequency and duration of releases.
34. The preparation of the site before the release.
35. The size of the site.
36. The methods to be used for the release.
37. The quantity of organisms to be released.
38. The disturbance of the site, including the type and method of cultivation, and mining, irrigation, or other activities.
39. The worker protection measures taken during the release.
40. The post-release treatment of the site.
41. The techniques foreseen for elimination or inactivation of the organisms at the end of the experiment or other purpose of the release.
42. Information on results of previous releases of those organisms, or of organisms of the same type as those which are to be released, and in particular releases on a different scale or into different ecosystems.

The environment (both on the site and in the wider environment)
43. The geographical location and national grid reference of the site onto which the release will be made, or the foreseen areas of use of the product.
44. The physical or biological proximity of the site of the organisms to humans and other significant biota.
45. The proximity to significant biotopes or protected areas.
46. The size of the local human population.
47. The local economic activities which are based on the natural resources of the area.
48. The distance to the nearest drinking water supply zone and/or areas protected for environmental purposes.
49. The climatic characteristics of the region or regions likely to be affected.
50. The geographical, geological and pedological characteristics.
51. The flora and fauna, including crops, livestock and migratory species.
52. The description of the target and non-target ecosystems likely to be affected.
53. The comparison of the natural habitat of the recipient organisms with the proposed site or sites of release.
54. Any known planned developments or changes in land use in the region which could influence the environmental impact of the release.

Part IV

The Organisms and the Environment

Characteristics affecting survival etc
55. The biological features which affect survival, multiplication and dispersal.
56. The known or predicted environmental conditions which may affect survival, multiplication and dissemination, including wind, water, soil, temperature and pH.
57. The sensitivity to specific agents.

Interactions with the environment
58. The predicted habitat of the organisms.
59. The studies on the behaviour and characteristics of the organisms and their ecological impact carried out in simulated natural environments, such as microcosms, growth rooms and greenhouses.
60. The capability of post-release transfer of genetic material—
    (a) from the genetically modified organisms into organisms in affected ecosystems,
    (b) from indigenous organisms to the genetically modified organisms.
61. The likelihood of post-release selection leading to the expression of unexpected or undesirable traits in the genetically modified organisms.
62. The measures employed to ensure and to verify genetic stability, the description of genetic traits which may prevent or minimize dispersal of genetic material, and methods to verify genetic stability.
63. The routes of biological dispersal, known or potential modes of interaction with the disseminating agent, including inhalation, ingestion, surface contact and burrowing.
64. The description of ecosystems to which the organisms could be disseminated.

Potential environmental impact
65. The potential for excessive population increase of the organisms in the environment.
66. The competitive advantage of the organisms in relation to the unmodified recipient or parental organisms.
67. The identification and description of the target organisms.
68. The anticipated mechanism and result of interaction between the released organisms and the target organisms.
69. The identification and description of non-target organisms which may be affected.
70. The likelihood of post release shifts in biological interactions or in the host range.
71. The known or predicted effects on plants and animals and non-target organisms in the environment, impact on population levels of competitors, prey, hosts, symbionts, predators, parasites and pathogens.
72. The known or predicted involvement of the organisms in biogeochemical processes.
73. Any other potentially significant interactions of the organisms with the environment.

Part V

Monitoring, Control, Waste Treatment and Emergency Plans

Monitoring techniques
74. Methods for tracing the organisms, and for monitoring their effects.
75. Specificity (to identify the organisms, and to distinguish them from the donor, recipient or the parental organisms), sensitivity and reliability of the monitoring techniques.
76. Techniques for detecting transfer of the donated genetic material to other organisms.
77. Duration and frequency of the monitoring.

Control of the release
78. Methods and procedures to avoid and/or minimize the spread of the organisms beyond the site of release or the designated area for use.
79. Methods and procedures to protect the site from intrusion by unauthorized individuals.
80. Methods and procedures to prevent other organisms from entering the site.

Waste treatment
81. Type of waste generated.
82. Expected amount of waste.
83. Possible risks.
84. Description of treatment envisaged.

Emergency response plans

85. Methods and procedures for controlling the organisms in case of unexpected spread.

86. Methods, such as eradication of the organisms, for decontamination of the areas affected.

87. Methods for disposal or sanitation of plants, animals, soils, and any other thing exposed during or after the spread.

88. Methods for the isolation of the area affected by the spread.

89. Plans for protecting human health and the environment in case of the occurrence of an undesirable effect.

SCHEDULE 2   Regulation 11

Consent to Market

PART I

GENERAL INFORMATION

1. The name of the product and the name of the genetically modified organisms in the product.

2. The name and address in the Community of the manufacturer or distributor of the product.

3. The specificity of the product and the exact conditions of use including, where appropriate, the type of environment and/or the geographical areas within the Community for which the product is suited.

4. The type of expected use of the product and the description of the persons who are expected to use the product.

PART II

ADDITIONAL RELEVANT INFORMATION

5. The measures to be taken in the event of the escape of the organisms in the product or misuse of the product.

6. Specific instructions or recommendations for storage and handling of the product.

7. The estimated level and amount of production of the product within the Community and the estimated level and amount of imports of the product into the Community.

8. Information regarding the proposed packaging for the product and its appropriateness so as to avoid the escape of genetically modified organisms during storage or at a later stage.

9. Information regarding proposed labelling including the proposals for stating, in full or summarized form, the information prescribed in paragraphs 1 to 3, 5 and 6 above.

INDEX

References are to section and Schedule number

ACTIVITIES,
   meaning, s.1
AIR POLLUTION,
   local authorities, control by, Pt. I Intro
ANNUAL REPORT,
   waste regulation authority, of, s.67
ARMED FORCES,
   premises occupied by, non-application of statutory nuisance provisions, s.79

BEST AVAILABLE TECHNIQUES NOT ENTAILING EXCESSIVE COST,
   concept of, s.7N
   genetically modified organisms, in relation to, s.109N
BEST PRACTICABLE ENVIRONMENTAL OPTION,
   concept of, s.7N
BODY CORPORATE,
   offences by, s.157

CHIEF INSPECTOR. *See also* INSPECTORS (POLLUTION)
   appointment of, s.16
   functions of, s.4
   harm, remedying, s.27
   liability, s.16
   payments to, s.8
   pollution, prevention or reduction techniques, s.4
   powers of, s.17
CLEAN AIR,
   complaints procedure, Pt. III Intro
CONTAMINATED LAND,
   consultation process, s.143N
   register of, s.143
CONTROLLED WASTE. *See* WASTE
CONTROLLED WATERS,
   release of substances into, s.28
COUNTRYSIDE,
   amendment of enactments, Sch. 8
   transitional provisions and savings, Sch. 11
COUNTRYSIDE COUNCIL FOR WALES,
   countryside functions, s.130
   establishment and membership, s.129, Sch. 6
   staff, Sch. 6
   staff of existing bodies, employment of, s.137, Sch. 10
   transfer schemes, s.136, Sch. 10
CROWN,
   application of provisions to, s.159
CROWN LAND,
   meaning, s.86

DOGS,
   collars and tags, enforcement of orders, s.151
   control of, s.149
   stray, delivery to police of local authority officer, s.150

ENFORCEMENT NOTICE,
   appeals, s.15
   power to serve, s.13
ENFORCING AUTHORITY,
   authorisations. *See* PROCESS
   enforcement notice,
      appeals, s.15
      power to serve, s.13
   High Court proceedings by, s.24
   information, furnishing, s.19
   meaning, s.1
   prohibition notice,
      appeals, s.15
      power to serve, s.14
   register,
      confidential information, exclusion of, s.22
      information affecting national security, exclusion of, s.21
      prescribed information, of, s.20
ENVIRONMENT,
   duty of care, App. 4
   genetically modified organisms in, s.107
   meaning, ss.1, 29, 107, 140, 142
   pollution of. *See* POLLUTION OF THE ENVIRONMENT
   release of substance into, meaning, s.1
ENVIRONMENT AGENCY,
   role of, Pt. II Intro
ENVIRONMENTAL PURPOSES,
   financial assistance for, s.153
EUROPEAN COMMUNITY,
   genetically modified organisms, Directives on, Pt. VI Intro
   obligations, giving effect to, s.156
   requirements, implementation of, Intro
   waste, Directives on, Pt. II Intro

FACTORY,
   definition, s.75N
FEES AND CHARGES,
   authorisations, for, s.8
   integrated pollution control, for, s.8N
   licences, for, s.41

INDEX

GAS,
   Clean Air Act provisions, application of, s.85
   meaning, ss.79, 85
GENETICALLY MODIFIED ORGANISMS, App. 8, App. 9
   acquisition, meaning, s.127
   advisory committee, s.124
   contained use, App. 8
   consultation papers, Pt. VI Intro
   delegation of functions, s.125
   deliberate release, App. 9
   descendant, meaning, s.127
   environment,
      damage to, s.107
      meaning, s.107
      present in, s.107
   functions, joint exercise of, s.126
   import, meaning, s.127
   importation, acquisition, keeping, release or marketing,
      consents required, s.111
         fees and charges, s.113
         limitations and conditions, s.112
      general duties, s.109
      prohibition notices, s.110
   information, obtaining, s.116
   inspectors,
      appointment of, s.114
      entry and inspection, rights of, s.115
      imminent danger of damage to the environment, power to deal with, s.117
   marketing, s.107
   meaning, s.106
   notification requirements, s.108
   offences, s.118
      cause, power of court to order remedy, s.120
      harm, Secretary of State remedying, s.121
      onus of proof, s.119
   organism, meaning, s.106
   premises, meaning, s.127
   prohibition notices, s.110
   purpose of provisions, s.106
   register of information, s.122
      excluded information, s.123
   release of, s.107
   risk assessment, s.108
   Royal Commission Report, Pt. VI Intro
   territorial sea, application of provisions to, s.127
GREAT BRITAIN,
   meaning, s.1
GROUND WATERS,
   meaning, s.1
GROUNDWORK FOUNDATION,
   superannuation provisions, s.154

HARM,
   chief inspector remedying, s.27
   meaning, ss.1, 29, 107, 141
HAZARDOUS SUBSTANCES,
   advisory committee, Sch. 12
   amendment of enactments, Sch. 13

HEALTH AND SAFETY EXECUTIVE,
   occupation of land by waste disposal authority, notification of, s.54
   proposed issue of licence, reference to, s.36
HIGH COURT,
   enforcement by, s.24
   statutory nuisance, provisions as to, s.81

INJURIOUS SUBSTANCES,
   advisory committee, Sch. 12
   amendment of enactments, Sch. 13
   importation etc., power to prohibit or restrict, s.140
INLAND WATERWAYS AMENITY ADVISORY COUNCIL,
   chairman, remuneration, s.155
INSPECTORS, (GENETICALLY MODIFIED ORGANISMS),
   appointment of, s.114
   entry and inspection, rights of, s.115
   imminent danger of damage to the environment, power to deal with, s.117
INSPECTORS, (POLLUTION),
   appointment of, s.16
   functions of, s.4
   guidance to, Pt. I Intro
   imminent danger of serious harm, dealing with, s.18
   liability, s.16
   powers of, s.17
INSPECTORS, (WASTE),
   appointment of, s.69
   imminent danger of serious pollution, dealing with, s.70
   obstruction of, s.70
   powers of, s.69
   powers of entry, s.69
INTERNATIONAL OBLIGATIONS,
   genetically modified organisms, on, Pt. VI Intro
   giving effect to, s.156
   implementation of, Pt. I Intro
   waste, on, Pt. II Intro
ISLES OF SCILLY,
   waste provisions, application of, s.76

JOINT NATURE CONSERVATION COMMITTEE,
   advice and information from, s.133
   constitution, Sch. 7
   establishment of, s.128

LAND,
   contaminated, register of, s.143
   litter. *See* LITTER
   meaning, s.29
   waste on. *See* WASTE
LITTER,
   abatement notice, s.92
   authorities, s.88
      summary proceedings by, s.92
   code of practice, s.89, App. 7
   control areas, s.90

INDEX

LITTER—*cont.*
  land and highways kept free of, s.89
  leaving, offence of, s.87
  fixed penalty notice, s.88
  person aggrieved, summary proceedings by, s.91
  principal authorities,
    bodies being, s.86
    duties of, s.89
  registers, duty to maintain, s.95
  relevant land, s.86
  shopping and luggage trolleys, abandoned, s.99, Sch. 4
  street,
    control notices, ss.93, 94
    regulations, s.94
  summary proceedings,
    litter authorities, by, s.92
    person aggrieved, by, s.91
  transitional provisions, s.97
  waste provisions, application of, s.96
LOCAL AUTHORITIES,
  air pollution control by, Pt. I Intro
LUGGAGE TROLLEYS,
  abandoned, s.99, Sch. 4

MOBILE PLANT,
  escape of pollution from, s.29
  licence, *see also* WASTE MANAGEMENT LICENCE
    meaning, s.36
  meaning, ss.1, 29
  prescribed process carried out by, control of, s.4

NATIONAL RIVERS AUTHORITY,
  fees and charges for licences, s.41
  proposed issue of licence, reference to, s.36
NATURE CONSERVANCY,
  amendment of enactment, Sch. 9
  transitional provisions and savings, Sch. 11
NATURE CONSERVANCY COUNCILS,
  constitution of, Sch. 6
  establishment of, s.128
  former, dissolution of, s.138
  functions of,
    general, s.132
    nature conservation, s.131
    special, s.133
  grants and loans by, s.134
  grants to, s.129
  membership, s.128, Sch. 6
  staff, Sch. 6
  staff of existing bodies, employment of, s.137, Sch. 10
  transfer schemes, ss.135, 136, Sch. 10
NATURE CONSERVATION BODY,
  occupation of land by waste disposal authority, notification of, s.54
  proposed issue of licence, reference to, s.36
NOTICES,
  service of, s.160

NUISANCE,
  statutory. *See* STATUTORY NUISANCE

OFFENCES,
  body corporate, by, s.157
  false statements in relation to licences, s.44
  fault of others, due to, s.158
  genetically modified organisms, as to, s.118
    cause, remedying, ss.120, 121
    onus of proof, s.119
  High Court enforcement,
    pollution, s.24
    statutory nuisance, s.81
  litter, leaving, s.87. *See also* LITTER
  onus of proof, ss.25, 120
  pollution control, as to, s.23
  remedy, power to order, ss.26, 120
  statutory nuisance. *See* STATUTORY NUISANCE
  waste,
    management licence, contravention of, s.33
    non-controlled, s.63
    sites and receptacles, interference with, s.60
    unlawful deposit of, s.59
OFFENSIVE TRADES,
  controls over, s.84
OIL POLLUTION,
  Act, amendment of, Sch. 14
  ships, from, s.148

POLLUTION CONTROL,
  integrated, Pt. I Intro, App. 3
POLLUTION OF THE ENVIRONMENT,
  controlled waste, dealing with, s.33
  meaning, ss.1, 29
  techniques for preventing or reducing, duties as to, s.4
PORT HEALTH AUTHORITY,
  functions of, s.4
PROCESS,
  authorisation for,
    appeals, s.15
    application for, s.6, Sch. 1
    conditions of, s.7
      variation of, s.11
    fees and charges for, s.8
    grant or refusal of, s.6
  meaning, s.1
  prescribed processes carried out under, s.6
  relevant change, notification of, s.11
  relevant expenditure attributable to, s.8
  review of, s.6
  revocation of, s.12
    failure to pay charge, on, s.8
  Secretary of State, directions of, s.6
  substantial changes, procedure for, s.11N
  transfer of, s.9
  variation by enforcing authority, s.10, Sch. 1
    appeals, s.15

INDEX

PROCESS—*cont.*
  central or local control, designation for, s.2
  enforcement notice,
    power to serve, s.13
  meaning, s.1
  prescribed,
    authorisations. *See* authorisations, *above*
    controlled waters, release into, s.28
    emissions, limits and quality objectives, s.3
    functions, discharge and scope of, ss.4, 5
    regulations, s.2, App. 1
    relevant change, notification of, s.11
    substantial change in, s.10
  prohibition notice,
    appeals, s.15
    power to serve, s.14
PROHIBITION NOTICE,
  appeals, s.15
  genetically modified organisms, at to, s.110
  power to serve, s.13

RADIOACTIVE WASTE,
  provisions not applying to, s.78
REGISTER,
  confidential information, exclusion of, ss.22, 66
  applications for, s.22N
  contaminated land, of, s.143
  deposits and incineration at sea, as to, s.147
  genetically modified organisms,
    information as to, s.122
    excluded information, s.123
  information affecting national security, exclusion of, ss.21, 65
  litter, as to, s.95
  prescribed information, of, s.20
  provision for, Pt. I Intro
  waste, as to, s.64
    confidential information, exclusion of, s.66
    information affecting national security, exclusion of, s.65
RIVER PURIFICATION AUTHORITY,
  fees and charges for licences, s.41
  inspectors, *see* INSPECTORS
  meaning, s.30
  occupation of land by waste disposal authority, notification of, s.54
  payments to, s.8
  pollution, prevention or reduction techniques, s.4
  proposed issue of licence, reference to, s.36

SCOTLAND,
  accepting, treatment, disposal or delivery of waste, power to require, s.57
  enforcing authority, s.5N
  Nature Conservancy Council. *See* NATURE CONSERVANCY COUNCILS
  principal litter authorities, s.96
  river purification authority. *See* RIVER PURIFICATION AUTHORITY

SCOTLAND—*cont.*
  Secretary of State, exercise of functions of, s.5
  statutory nuisances, s.83
  waste disposal authorities,
    duties of, s.53
    land occupied by, s.54
  waste recycling powers, s.56
SEA, POLLUTION AT,
  deposits and incineration, registers of, s.147
  Food and Environment Protection Act, amendment of, ss.146, 147
SECRETARY OF STATE,
  accepting, treatment, disposal or delivery of waste, power to require, ss.57, 58
  authorisations,
    directions as to, s.6
    fees and charges, scheme for, s.8
  codes of practice,
    litter, as to, s.89
    waste, as to, s.34
  financial assistance for environmental purposes, s.153
  general and specific directions, s.4
  genetically modified organisms,
    advisory committee, s.124
    delegation of functions, s.125
    remedying of harm, s.121
  information, obtaining,
    genetically modified organisms, as to, s.116
    pollution, in respect of, s.19
    potentially hazardous substances, about, s.142
    waste, in respect of, s.71
  injurious substances, power to prohibit or restrict, s.140
  litter,
    code of practice, s.89
    control areas, s.90
    street, provisions as to, s.94
  Nature Conservancy Councils, grants to, s.129
  processes and substances,
    functions, discharge and scope of, ss.4, 5
    prescription of, s.2
    standards, objectives or requirements, regulations on, s.3
  regulations and orders, s.161
  waste,
    code of practice, s.34
    default powers, s.72
    functions as to, s.68
    importation or exportation, power to prohibit or restrict, s.141
SHOPPING TROLLEYS,
  abandoned, s.99, Sch. 4
SHIPS,
  oil pollution from, s.148
SITE LICENCE. *See also* WASTE MANAGEMENT LICENCE
  application for, s.34
  meaning, s.35
  surrender of, s.39

INDEX

STATUTORY NUISANCE,
  abatement notice, s.80
    appeals, ss.80, 81N, App. 6
    failure to comply with, s.81
  appeals, Sch. 3, App. 6
  application of provisions, s.79
  complaints procedure, Pt. III Intro
  definitions, s.79
  default powers, Sch. 3
  High Court proceedings, s.81
  local authority,
    act or default outside area of, s.81
    expenses incurred by, s.81
    High Court proceedings, s.81
    powers, s.79
    summary proceedings, s.81
  matters constituting, s.79
  offensive trades, controls over, s.84
  person responsible, s.79
    more than one, s.81
  powers of entry, Sch. 3
  Public Health Act controls, termination of, s.84
  Scotland, in, s.83
  summary proceedings,
    local authority, by, s.80
    persons aggrieved, by, s.82

STRAW AND STUBBLE BURNING,
  regulations, s.152

SUBSTANCE,
  meaning, ss.1, 29, 140, 142, 143
  hazardous or injurious,
    advisory committee, Sch. 12
    amendment of enactments, Sch. 13
    power to prohibit or restrict importation etc., s.140
  potentially hazardous, information about, s.142
  prescribed,
    emissions, limits and quality objectives, s.3
    functions, discharge and scope of, ss.4, 5
    meaning, s.2
    regulations, s.2, App. 2

VISITING FORCE,
  premises occupied by non-application of statutory nuisance provisions, s.79

WASTE,
  accepting, treatment, disposal or delivery, power to require, ss.57, 58
  appeals, s.73
  authorised transport purposes, s.34
  brokers, s.34
  code of practice, s.34
  collection authorities. See WASTE COLLECTION AUTHORITY
  collection of, s.45
  commercial,
    meaning, s.75
    receptacles for, s.47
  Control of Pollution Act 1974, transfer of provisions, s.77

WASTE—cont.
  controlled, meaning, s.75
  dangerous, provision for, s.62
  default powers, s.72
  disposal of,
    authorities. See WASTE DISPOSAL AUTHORITY
    contractor, s.30
    final, s.28
    household, s.33
    meaning, s.29
    motor vehicle, from, s.33
    payment for, s.52
    plans, s.50
    unauthorised or harmful, prohibition of, s.33
  duty of care, s.34
    regulations, App. 5
  household,
    disposal of, s.33
    duty of care, s.34
    meaning, s.75
    no charge for collection of, s.45
    receptacles for, s.46
  importation or exportation, power to prohibit or restrict, s.141
  industrial,
    collection of, s.45
    meaning, s.75
    receptacles for, s.47
  inspectors,
    appointment of, s.69
    imminent danger of serious pollution, dealing with, s.70
    obstruction of, s.70
    powers of, s.69
    powers of entry, s.69
  intractable, provision for, s.62
  Isles of Scilly, application of provisions, s.76
  management licence. See WASTE MANAGEMENT LICENCE
  management publications, Pt. II Intro
  meaning, s.75
  non-controlled, s.63
  organisation of functions, Pt. II Intro
  radioactive, provisions not applying to, s.78
  receptacles,
    commercial and industrial waste, for, s.47
    household waste, for, s.46
    interference with, s.60
  recycling,
    payment for, s.52
    plans, s.49
    powers for, ss.55, 56
  reforms, Pt. II Intro
  regulation authorities. See WASTE REGULATION AUTHORITY
  sites, interference with, s.60
  special, treatment of, s.62
  treatment of, s.29
  unlawfully deposited, removal of, s.59

INDEX

WASTE COLLECTION AUTHORITY,
  authorities being, s.30
  controlled waste, collection of, s.45
  costs, contribution to, s.45
  disposal, duties as to, s.47
  privy or cesspool, emptying, s.45
  recycling,
    plans, s.49
    powers for, ss.55, 56
  registers, s.64
    confidential information, exclusion of, s.66
    information affecting national security, exclusion of, s.65
WASTE DISPOSAL AUTHORITY,
  authorities being, s.30
  companies, transition to, s.32, Sch. 2
  disposal, duties as to, s.53
  existing, s.32
  existing disposal licence, transfer of provisions, s.77
  functions of, s.51
  land occupied by, s.54
  provisions regulating, Sch. 2
  recycling, powers for, ss.55, 56
  regulation authority, also being, s.30
WASTE DISPOSAL COMPANY,
  formation of, s.32N
  transition to, s.32, Sch. 2
WASTE MANAGEMENT,
  duty of care, App. 5
WASTE MANAGEMENT LICENCE,
  appeals, s.43
  application for, s.36
  conditions, s.35
    modifications of, s.37
  contravention of, s.33
  false statements, s.44
  fees and charges for, s.41
  fit and proper person holding, s.74
  Health and Safety Executive, reference of proposal to, s.36
  meaning, s.35
  National Rivers Authority, reference of proposal to, s.36
  nature conservation body, reference of proposal to, s.36
  persons to whom granted, s.35
  planning permission required, where, s.36
  requirement to have, s.33
  requirements, failure to comply with, s.38
  revocation of, s.38
  river purification authority, reference of proposal to, s.36
  supervision of activities, s.42
  surrender of, s.39
  suspension of, s.38
  terms of, s.35
  transfer of, s.40
  variation of, s.37
WASTE REGULATION AUTHORITY,
  annual report, s.67
  authorities being, s.30
  closed landfills, duties as to, s.61
  disposal authority, also being, s.30
  disposal plans, s.50

WASTE REGULATION AUTHORITY—cont.
  functions, review by Secretary of State, s.68
  information, furnishing, s.71
  licence. See WASTE MANAGEMENT LICENCE
  regional, s.31
  registers, s.64
    confidential information, exclusion of, s.66
    information affecting national security, exclusion of, s.65
  supervision of licensed activities, s.42
WATER,
  release of substance into, ss.1, 28
WORDS AND PHRASES,
  abatement notice,
    litter, s.92
    statutory nuisance, s.80
  acquire, s.127
  activities, s.1
  agricultural land, s.152
  agriculture, s.152
  authorisation, s.1
  authorised officer, s.88
  best practicable means, s.79
  brokers, s.34
  biological matter, s.106
  cesspool, s.45
  chief finance officer, s.88
  chimney, s.79
  commercial waste, s.75
  company, s.30
  consent, s.127
  contaminated land, s.143
  control, s.32
  controlled waste, s.75
  crop residue, s.152
  Crown land, s.86
  damage, s.73
  damage to the environment, s.107
  descendant, s.127
  disposal of waste, s.29
  dust, s.79
  educational bodies, s.97
  educational institution, s.98
  enforcement notice, s.13
  enforcing authority, s.1
  environment, ss.1, 29, 107, 140–142
  existing disposal authority, s.32
  existing disposal licence, s.77
  factory, s.75n
  fault, s.73
  fit and proper person, s.74
  fumes, s.79
  gas, ss.79, 85
  general direction, s.4
  genetically modified, s.106
  Great Britain, s.1
  ground waters, s.1
  harm, ss.1, 29, 107, 141
  highway, s.98
  household waste, s.75
  import, s.127
  industrial, trade or business premises, s.79
  industrial waste, s.75
  joint board, s.98

[6]

INDEX

WORDS AND PHRASES—*cont.*
  land, s.29
  land subject to contamination, s.143
  local authority, ss.4, 79, 143, 149
  mobile plant, ss.1, 29
  mobile plant licence, s.35
  National Park Committee, s.88
  noise, s.79
  offensive trade, s.84
  organism, s.106
  Park Board, s.88
  pollution of the environment, ss.1, 29
  prejudicial to health, s.79
  premises, ss.69, 79, 127
  prescribed substance, s.2
  private dwelling, s.79
  privy, s.45
  process, s.1
  prohibition notice, s.14
  proper officer, s.88
  public place, s.149
  regional authority, s.31

WORDS AND PHRASES—*cont.*
  release, s.1
  relevant expenditure attributable to authorisations, s.8
  relevant land, s.86
  reproduction, s.106
  river purification authoriity, s.30
  site licence, s.35
  smoke, s.79
  special waste, s.62
  specific direction, s.4
  statutory undertaker, s.98
  street litter control notice, s.93
  substance, ss.1, 29, 140, 142, 143
  substantial change, s.10
  trade, s.84
  treatment of waste, s.29
  variation notice, s.10
  visiting force, s.79
  waste, s.75
  waste disposal contractor, s.30
  waste management licence, s.35